OUTLINE CONTENTS

Todd & Wilson's
Textbook on Trusts

Todd & Wilson's

Textbook on

Trusts

··

Eighth edition

Sarah Wilson
LLB, MA, PhD

OXFORD
UNIVERSITY PRESS

OXFORD
UNIVERSITY PRESS

Great Clarendon Street, Oxford OX2 6DP

Oxford University Press is a department of the University of Oxford.
It furthers the University's objective of excellence in research, scholarship,
and education by publishing worldwide in

Oxford New York

Auckland Cape Town Dar es Salaam Hong Kong Karachi
Kuala Lumpur Madrid Melbourne Mexico City Nairobi
New Delhi Shanghai Taipei Toronto

With offices in

Argentina Austria Brazil Chile Czech Republic France Greece
Guatemala Hungary Italy Japan Poland Portugal Singapore
South Korea Switzerland Thailand Turkey Ukraine Vietnam

Oxford is a registered trade mark of Oxford University Press
in the UK and in certain other countries

Published in the United States
by Oxford University Press Inc., New York

British Library Cataloguing in Publication Data

Data available

Library of Congress Cataloging in Publication Data

Data available

Typeset by Newgen Imaging Systems (P) Ltd., Chennai, India
Printed in Great Britain
on acid-free paper by
Ashford Colour Press Ltd, Gosport, Hampshire

ISBN 978–0–19–920326–0

1 3 5 7 9 10 8 6 4 2

DETAILED CONTENTS

4   The three certainties and the significance of the 'beneficiary principle'   98

5   Formalities and other requirements for validity   123

6   Perpetuities   139

7 Introduction to resulting and constructive trusts 154

8 Resulting trusts, gifts to non-charitable unincorporated associations and pension funds 171

9 Beneficial interests in the family home: a case study 189

14 Cy près 322

15 The office of trustee: commencement and termination 335

16 Powers, discretions and duties of trustees 367

19 Remedies   436

PREFACE

This book continues the tradition begun by Paul Todd in being aimed primarily at law students in their second or third year of undergraduate study at university. It is an introductory text, and therefore it is shorter than many traditional textbooks on trusts available today. This edition, like its predecessors, aims to state the law as briefly and as clearly as possible without sacrificing clarity in the more complex areas. In terms of scope, I have prioritised areas commonly taught on trusts courses rather than attempting to encompass everything about equity and trusts, thus giving less coverage to those aspects of equity and trusts usually covered elsewhere in undergraduate law programmes (notably land law, contract, and English legal system). In this spirit, I have always been mindful to concentrate on principle rather than detail. This edition continues this emphasis, but it is also an important point of departure in another respect. This is because I am also starting to develop an approach whereby the law relating to trusts is more closely integrated with the scholarship which has grown up around it. An important development in this regard for this text has been the launch of its Online Resource Centre, which includes an emphasis on wider reading. The website will continue to be used in this manner, because while the study of trusts can be enriched greatly by reference to the work of academics, the extent to which this is possible in the text itself is limited by constraints of space. Thus, I will continue to develop the website to emphasise the importance of engaging with writings on the subject in the process of learning and understanding. In this vein, I will be suggesting that it is not only the academic writings which relate to English trusts law which can enhance understanding and appreciation of it. It will become very quickly apparent that trusts arise across social and economic life, and domestic and commercial environs, and this text's emphasis will thus embrace a number of ways in which trusts and their operation can be understood and appreciated. Gradually, I will be introducing into the study of trusts academic studies of related but distinct spheres of economy and society, regulation, sociology and critical approaches to professional practise and cultures.

In terms of the actual *content* of this current edition, greatest coverage continues to be given to areas most squarely within the ambit of equity and trusts, and which students are unlikely to know much about prior to undertaking the study of equity and trusts. This includes proprietary remedies, and in chapter 19 on remedies I try to show not only how the law is very complex, but how it is also highly dynamic on account of the prominence of principles of proprietary entitlement and restitution. Considerable space therefore continues to be devoted to discussion of the principles which are guiding proprietary tracing claims, constructive trusteeship, and restitutionary actions, with continuing emphasis of *BCCI Ltd* v *Akindele* [2001] Ch 437 and *Foskett* v *McKeown* [2000]. The 2005 edition drew attention to the highly significant House of Lords' decision in *Twinsectra Ltd* v *Yardley* [2002] 2 All ER 377, but now *Twinsectra*'s observations on dishonesty and accessory liability themselves need to be revisited in light of the recent decision of the Privy Council in *Barlow Clowes International Ltd (in liquidation)* v *Eurotrust International Ltd* [2006] 1 All ER 333.

In the early parts of the text, the introduction given to the nature of trusts and the uses to which they can be put has been completely overhauled to give greater accommodation of the way in which business and commercial dimensions of trusts are increasingly capturing students' interest alongside better developed analytical directions provided by succession, the family home, and charity. This is potentially another dynamic point of reference, and it is envisaged that the coverage of 'commercial dimensions' of trusts given in this text might well increase over time. This is also likely to be the case with trusts law and pension funds, which, like family trusts, *are* concerned with asset management, while being indicative of very different social and economic conditions from times when family settlements dominated—and indeed were responsible for shaping—trusts law. At the other end of the spectrum is the not very dynamic area of perpetuity rules, and I recognise that declining popularity of perpetuities on university teaching syllabi means that few trusts courses will cover this at all. Notwithstanding, I have chosen to retain the much abbreviated chapter which was new for the 2005 edition for the sake of completeness at least. However, although perpetuities are increasingly not taught in their own right, private trusts remain subject to perpetuity requirements, and students need to have some appreciation that they exist and what purpose they might serve. It is also the case that perpetuity rules interface with understanding the features of charitable trusts, and also the existence and operation of private *purpose* trusts.

It is also the case that this edition builds on a chapter which was completely new in the 2005 edition. This was an introduction to constructive and resulting trusts. It was noted at the time that this represented an important first step that this text was taking towards greater 'conceptual treatment' of constructive and resulting trusts, which is currently the fashion among scholars, including those who write academic texts for students. This trend for 'conceptual' treatment does of course relate to the way in which increasingly materials are structured and analysed on the basis of the *type* of trust involved, giving this primacy of place, rather than the *context* in which the trust has arisen, or the *use* to which it has been put. The 2005 edition's new 'Introduction to' chapter—which involved introducing the basic features and operation of constructive and resulting trusts, focusing on fundamental features of 'type'—has been expanded slightly in this edition in light of case law developments. Alongside this, the spirit of this chapter remains very definitely intact: it is essentially a prelude to a number of 'case studies' on constructive and resulting trusts which follow immediately thereafter. While I do think that this book will benefit from some conceptual treatment of constructive and resulting trusts in this manner, I am not a 'conceptual purist'. Thus, I continue to believe that the best way of acknowledging the conceptual qualities of constructive and resulting trusts is through this introductory chapter, but at the same time the distinct 'case study' chapters give appropriate regard to the vast array of actual uses and applications, which are also highly diverse, to which the basic trust model can be put in twenty-first century society and economy. I feel very strongly that this may well be undersold in a single chapter entitled 'constructive trusts' and another for 'resulting trusts'. Thus, the introductory chapter serves as an important acknowledgement of the growing conceptual treatment of constructive and resulting trusts across the work of many academics, while providing foundational understanding for a more complex application of these devices, where their diversity is duly acknowledged.

The previous edition of this text published in 2005 made reference to an observation made in the 1999 edition to the way in which 'an apparently large number of people . . . think that the law of trusts does not change very much'. On the contrary, this edition has engaged in considerable 'monitoring' of highly dynamic areas, such as remedies, and it has also sought to take stock of another fast-changing area in the sphere of trusts arising from shared homes. In this vein, the 'case study' chapter on the family home has been substantially re-written to take account of a number of things. First, it has noted the implications of the Civil Partnership Act 2004 for determining property interests where same-sex couples elect to 'register' their civil partnership. It has also sought to offer a commentary upon the growing influence of proprietary estoppel in resolving disputed home ownership which is now supported by a sizeable and coherent body of Court of Appeal authorities. The previous edition did note the decisions in *Gillet v Holt* [2001] Ch 210 and *Yaxley v Gotts* [2000] Ch 162, and this edition brings them together with *Campbell v Griffin* [2001] WTLR 981; *Jennings v Rice* [2003] 1 P & C R 8; and *Ottey v Grundy* [2003] WTLR 1253 to point to the emergence of a distinct trend in this direction. This does of course include *Oxley v Hiscock* [2004] 3 All ER 703, which not only supports the above observation, but which also now appears to be the leading authority on the quantification of beneficial interests in a family home.

The changes to the case study of the family home also include a discussion of the progress of the Law Commission's Cohabitation Project announced in 2005. Thus, this edition has been able to note the publication of Consultation Paper No. 179 *Cohabitation: The Financial Consequences of Relationship Breakdown*. Reference is made to the Law Commission's insistence that this is not a comprehensive review of the law relating to cohabiting couples, and is concerned with financial hardships which can fall on those whose relationships break down, or upon the death of their partner. Nevertheless, the chapter explains that underpinning this project are many of the difficulties which befell the ill-fated *Sharing Homes* Discussion Paper, published in 2002. This edition thus aims to provide a brief but comprehensive overview of the Consultation as it stands, in terms of what the Law Commission is seeking to achieve in relation to property entitlements, and how it is seeking to effect changes which it feels are needed to reflect better the nature of cohabitation across a range of 'intimate' relationships. It is anticipated that more extensive coverage will be made of this in the next edition, in light of the responses which the Law Commission is bound to receive regarding this Consultation, and on account that the Law Commission anticipates the publication of a report in summer 2007.

This edition also touches base with areas of Law Commission activity elsewhere in trusts law. It makes very brief reference to the Law Commission's proposals published in Consultation Paper No. 175 on *Capital and Income in Trusts: Classification and Apportionment*. This is a very important project for this text's coverage of trustees' powers and duties relating to investment *generally*, and the project itself relates *specifically* to reforming current rules governing classifications of income and capital, and their apportionment in order to maintain a fair balance between different beneficiaries. Notwithstanding, the coverage which is given to it in this edition is brief because, following the Consultation Paper's publication, the Law Commission has stressed that work on this project has currently been suspended until 2007, to allow the completion of the Cohabitation Project to take place. Elsewhere in the broad sphere of trustees' duties and related questions of liability, the coverage which was given to the Law Commission's Consultation Paper on trustee exemption clauses in 2005 has now been updated to include the conclusions drawn in *Report on Trustee Exemption Clauses* (Law Com. 301) published in July

2006. Coverage is quite detailed and extensive given the implications which this text considers might flow from the Law Commission's decision to achieve reform through a 'rule of practice' system; and this is one area where it is suggested that appreciating the implications of future directions can be enhanced by making reference to literatures relating to professional practise and its regulation.

Although it is far from easy—given the amount of Law Commission activity in the broad sphere of trusts law—to ensure this text provides an up-to-date account of current trends in law *reform*, as well as the law *making* which is occurring in the courts, it is also the case that at the time this text was written, a number of Bills remained under Parliamentary consideration, and under huge time pressures created by the opening of the November 2006 Parliamentary session. The most important one relating to trusts law was of course the Charities Bill, originally presented in Parliament in 2004. A number of changes were made to the text's coverage of the law relating to charities in the 2005 edition, in contemplation of its enactment, but in the intervening time the Bill was actually 'timed out' of Parliamentary consideration in 2005 on account of the General Election. It was quickly reintroduced into Parliament thereafter, and during 2006 it progressed with some speed through Parliament. The Charities Act 2006 received Royal Assent at a point beyond which it has been possible to make major changes to this text, but as the chapter explains, it is appropriate to have retained its existing structure and direction for several reasons. The outline of the original Bill given in the 2005 edition—as it pertained to the legal definition of charity—has been fleshed out to include more coverage on the key constituents within this; namely, the statutory list of charitable purposes and the new approach to public benefit. The initial discussion of the new Act includes excerpts from the Parliamentary consideration given to it during 2006.

This edition also makes fleeting reference to the Companies Act 2006, which was also before Parliament when this new edition was prepared. Although this does not relate to this text's approaches to trusts law to any great extent, enactment of new companies legislation will influence coverage of fiduciary relationships and liability in equity flowing from 'fiduciary office' in subsequent editions. This is particularly so in relation to use made by a fiduciary of a principal's property, opportunities, and information, because in the corporate context, such matters will also need to be analysed in light of the partial codification of directors' duties and new approaches to corporate opportunities. In this present edition, reference made to the Companies Act 2006 has actually arisen in the context of another new Act which is not squarely one of 'trusts law' but does have huge potential application in relation to fiduciary conduct. The Fraud Act 2006 (also before Parliament at the time this edition was written) is set to revolutionise criminal responses to fraud generally, and has considerable potential implications for trustees more specifically. So in this edition, the chapter relating to breach of trust contains a much expanded account of the criminal liability which can be incurred by trustees, in addition to the chapter's main focal point of liability in equity. The extent of this coverage on the new criminal law might be reduced in future editions as the Fraud Act 2006 becomes more inculcated into legal culture, but at this stage it is very important that its potential applications in respect of trustees is explained fully. This is not simply because this signals a whole new approach to the *criminal* liability which can be incurred by trustees, but because fundamentally it may well alter perceptions of the implications of trusteeship *itself*, from the perspective of trustees and beneficiaries alike.

When commencing your study of trusts it is worth appreciating that concepts in trusts law are very difficult, and this is not helped by the way in which many appear to be 'abstract' rather than tangible, and the way in which the accompanying terminology can on occasion be very confusing. In recognition of this, every effort has been made to make the materials as accessible as possible, while trying to explain the concepts as fully as possible. And it is also worth remembering that although you will find things difficult at times, trusts is a really fascinating subject which is *definitely* worth the effort which it will take trying to get to grips with. This was my impression as a student, and it certainly remains so now that I am a teacher myself. It is also the case that my own experiences as a student as well as a teacher strongly suggest that the best law students are not those who necessarily do the most work, but those who think hardest about the subject. I encourage my own students to email me, and each other, since this is a good way of discussing things. It also gives insight into areas of difficulty, and often encourages me to consider things I might have missed.

I would like to thank Anna Lawson for the inspiration she provided as a supportive colleague at the University of Leeds, and which she continues to provide in relation to 'trusts matters'. It is also the case that special thanks are due to my husband and colleague Gary Wilson for all the support he provides, all the time, and especially for his thoughtful and extremely valuable insights into trusts law. And lastly (but certainly not least), I would also like to thank the editorial and production staff at OUP for all their hard work in helping to prepare this edition, and for their support and expertise, from which as an author I continue to benefit considerably.

It remains only for me to encourage you to enjoy your study of trusts.

The law is, as far as possible, stated as it stood 31 January 2007.

Sarah Wilson
s.j.wilson@law.keele.ac.uk

TABLE OF CASES

Note: In citations 'ST' indicates a settlement trust and 'WT' a will trust.

TABLE OF STATUTES

STATUTORY INSTRUMENTS

1

Law and equity and an introduction to the trust

1.1 English law and two types of ownership

The purpose of this textbook is not to provide any detailed discussion of the concept of ownership in English law, as readers will have some familiarity with the nature of ownership, in terms of its rootings in 'property', its nature of entitlements and rights, and how it might differ for example from possession. Nevertheless, it is also the case that the essence of understanding the trust, its essential features and its operation lies in appreciation of ownership, and the way in which in English law distinction is drawn between ownership at law and that which subsists in equity. It will very shortly become apparent that these types of ownership as they operate in English law are very different, but that nevertheless they are capable of simultaneous existence, and will often arise simultaneously in respect of property. Indeed, this book is all about the consequences of the simultaneous occurrence of these two types of ownership.

1.1.1 Equitable and legal title: *Westdeutsche Landesbank Girozentrale* v *Islington LBC*

The starting point for considering the simultaneous existence of two types of ownership is of course property. And, it is very clear and apparent in the course of everyday encounters that most personal property (i.e., goods, or property which is not land) is owned by one person absolutely. In this typical scenario of ownership, ownership of the item is not split up in any way, and the property concerned is the property of its 'owner'. The position is different in situations where a person (or persons) holds property on trust for another (or others).

Unlike in the case of absolute ownership, in the simplest variety of trust, there will be two people simultaneously owning the property in question. However, the relationship each person will have to the property will be quite different from that of the other. In this situation, where property is held on trust, there is a legal owner, who is called a trustee. He has essentially a management role, and is subject to duties in respect of the property and the administration of the trust. There is also an equitable owner, who is called a *cestui que trust*, or beneficiary. It is the beneficiary who is entitled to enjoy the property, and whose position is therefore closest to being what a layman might consider to be an owner. It is to the beneficiary that the trustee's duties are owed, and he can enforce them against the trustee.

	Before	After
Legal title—burdensome (managerial in nature)	Settlor	Trustee
Equitable title (beneficial: provides enjoyment)	None	Beneficiary or *cestui que trust* Note: either trustee or beneficiary may also be settlor

Figure 1.1 The creation of a trust

Trust fundamentals: separation of property into two distinct 'estates'

As the diagrammatic representation in figure 1.1 illustrates, it is the separation of ownership into equitable and legal estates which is fundamental to the law of trusts. It is this which provides the key to the whole thing, and the foundation for the remainder of this book on the law of trusts. In this book devoted to the law of trusts, the importance of equitable ownership will be emphasised throughout. This is unsurprising at one level, given the subject matter of the book, but this is itself premised on the way in which understanding equitable ownership is very important. It will become clear just how valuable equitable rights are, both in terms of the benefits which equitable ownership confers upon those who are so entitled, but also in terms of the ways in which it defines concomitant responsibilities and duties for those who are trustees of the property.

Before any substantive consideration of equitable ownership can be made, some attention must be given to the way in which the trust, and distinct legal and equitable titles, actually arise. There are important introductory considerations to be made of how these very valuable and formidable rights are created, and how the law knows when such an arrangement has come into being. The starting point for understanding how the trust, and the distinct forms of ownership which characterise it, come into being is the decision in *Westdeutsche Landesbank Girozentrale* v *Islington London Borough Council* [1996] AC 669, and particularly the now very famous passage from the judgment of Lord Browne-Wilkinson. That judgment insisted, probably as part of the *ratio* of the case, that the owner of any property is vested with legal title alone. It is only when separation of title is sought that distinct equitable ownership will arise. Indeed, it is clear in light of *Westdeutsche* that distinct equitable title is not recognised as being vested with separate existence unless and until title is separated into legal and equitable estates:

A person solely entitled to the full beneficial ownership of money or property, both at law and in equity, does not enjoy an equitable interest in that property. The legal title carries with it all rights. Unless and until there is a separation of the legal and equitable estates, there is no separate equitable title.

This analysis suggests that, in absence of a trust, equitable ownership would appear to have no intrinsic value. This does of course require some thought given that it is equitable title which is more readily equated with 'value' through its associations with entitlement, benefit and enjoyment, while legal title more readily connotes responsibility and burden. Moreover, bare legal title is usually regarded as having no value (see, e.g., some of the cases considered in chapter 5), but it is also the case that in absence of a trust, people who are legal owners of property believe, entirely correctly, that their ownership gives them valuable rights. The obvious way to explain this apparent paradox is to observe that, in the absence of a trust, owners at law hold equitable title as well. Indeed, it is the equitable, rather than the legal title which carries with it the valuable rights of ownership, and while the duties of legal ownership are not any different in character, they cease to be burdensome when owed by one person to himself.

Title to property: legal and equitable interests
In earlier editions of this book, depictions of figure 1.1 had shown the settlor, as the original owner, as being vested with legal and equitable title 'before' a trust came into existence. However, the true position, as set out by Lord Browne-Wilkinson above, is that all rights are subsumed within the legal title; that is, in the absence of a trust it is legal title itself which is valuable. Since one cannot argue with House of Lords' *rationes*, the analysis in the previous editions has had to be changed. For present purposes it probably does not matter a great deal—the difference is no more than semantic. Lord Browne-Wilkinson's approach does however significantly affect resulting trusts (which are considered in chapter 7) and tracing in equity (chapter 19), where arguments based on the idea that settlors might simply be able to keep the equitable title they have always had, parting only with their legal title, have had to be abandoned.

Separation of title into distinct ownership: the trust and requirement
of 'something more'
There is also one further crucial point of understanding which arises from this. Just as it is so that it is the appearance of distinct equitable title upon separation of ownership which is of essence to, and actually forms the basis of the law of trusts, it is also vital to understand that a trust will not automatically arise upon separation of ownership. This is considered in more depth in chapters 7 and 19, and also in chapter 3, but for the moment, further explanation can be gleaned from the case of *Westdeutsche*. Again, Lord Browne-Wilkinson insisted that it is not separation of ownership into distinct equitable and legal titles which gives rise to a trust, and something more is required. This 'something more' is that the basis of all trusts is *conscience*. What this reasoning proposes is that a trust actually arises by virtue of, and precisely because the conscience of the legal owner is affected, and this requires him to hold property as owner at law on behalf of the equitable owner. Usually, the conscience of the legal owner is 'affected' in this way from his undertaking of trusteeship (and its attendant duties) which is voluntary in nature (although as chapter 3 reveals, there can be some difficulty with this in circumstances where the settlor is found to have declared himself trustee). However, it is also the case that actual imposition upon the conscience of an individual can arise where legal title, and thus (initially in absence of a trust) ownership property has been acquired through inequitable conduct on his part (greater explanation is given of this latter type of situation in chapters 7, 9 and 11).

The relationship between trustee and beneficiary is one which the law recognises as being fiduciary, and trustees will accordingly owe fiduciary duties to beneficiaries. The nature of such duties will be considered more fully in chapter 15, but for now it is sufficient to clarify that legal ownership arising in the context of the trust can be particularly onerous.

Westdeutsche Landesbank Girozentrale v *Islington London Borough Council* is a very important case, which will be discussed on many occasions throughout this book.

1.1.2 Ownership and land: conceptual peculiarities and difficulties over terminology

The purpose of this paragraph is simply to clarify terms which are used later on. All the above applies to land, as well as goods, money, shares, etc. However, for technical reasons, which for the most part do not affect the law of trusts (or at least in so far as they do they are summarised below) it is actually not possible to own land. This may also come as a surprise to students who are unfamiliar with land law. The technical position is that one can have title to an estate in land. The term 'title', for the purposes of this book, can be taken to mean the same as ownership—the differences between title and ownership are irrelevant to the law of trusts. The title is not to the land itself, however, but to an estate in land. Title to an estate can be divided, by means of a trust, into separate legal and equitable elements.

Title, interest and estates in land
An estate in land can be regarded as a right to possess land for a period of time. Leasehold estates, for example, are often for a fixed number of weeks, months or years. The period of time can be infinite, as with the usual freehold estate, which is called the fee simple absolute in possession—this is the estate most people buy when purchasing freehold property. But there are also lesser freehold estates. For example, a settlement of land, intended to keep the land in the family, may be in the form of a life estate to the surviving widow, followed by a fee simple in favour of the eldest son. Both the widow and eldest son have estates immediately, even though the son has no right to possess the land yet. All settlements must inevitably contain an estate which does not give an immediate right to possession. It is also possible to have entailed estates, which pass automatically on death, usually to a male heir, and which cannot therefore be left by will.

Subject to the provisions of the 1925 property legislation, which is beyond the scope of this book, it is possible for estates in land to be held in trust, thereby splitting legal and equitable title. The real point of this next section, however, is to explain the terms that will be used when talking about trusts involving land, and why reference shall not be made to ownership of land, except on occasions as a convenient shorthand.

1.2 Early history of equity

1.2.1 Why a dual system of ownership: common law and equity?

A comprehensive legal history of modern equity is beyond the scope of this book, but a brief account of its development, beginning with feudalism and culminating with the Judicature Acts 1873–5, is essential for understanding the dual ownership which underpins the law of trusts. Indeed, this is a journey tracing the reason why the English legal system divides into common law and equity; why there are two different systems and until recently two separate jurisdictions, and how and why it is that equity is able to confer property rights at all. Equity and trusts are found exclusively in England and other non-Roman legal systems, and neither has any place, for example, on the Continent. That a legal system should develop two different concepts of ownership, both of which can apply simultaneously to the same property, and effectively create two separate legal systems, is by no means self-evident. The reason lies in historical differences between England and Continental countries, dating from the feudal era, and in particular the Norman Conquest.

1.2.2 Feudalism and the Norman Conquest

Although equity is English in origin, it developed as an incidental result of feudalism. In pre-feudal times land was owned absolutely. The essence of the feudal system was that, in relatively lawless times, landowners collectively and for their mutual protection, bound themselves to an overlord, who was often a military expert, offering service (often of a military nature) or produce to the overlord in exchange for protection. Eventually the land became held on condition that services or produce were provided, and tenure of land became the exclusive bond between overlord and tenant.

Although feudalism became universal, it was not centralised; each great estate or manor had its own overlord and its own law and customs. It is true that the Crown in Europe granted some of its own land to lords in exchange for money or military services, so the Crown became supreme lord of some, but not all, of the land. But the system was essentially *ad hoc*, and indeed came into being *because* of the lawlessness resulting from the lack of a strong central government.

The peculiarity of English feudalism after 1066 came about because the chief landowners forcibly resisted the attempt of William I to assert supremacy over them. William therefore confiscated all land following his successful conquest, and subsequently allowed it to be held (or often redeemed) only from the Crown (directly by overlords), in exchange for money or services. So *all* land came to be held from the Crown, in exchange for money or services. It is still technically so held, though the services have usually not been collected for so long that they are barred by limitation (time-barred). Thus in England alone feudal land tenure became centralised, and was imposed from above with the Crown as supreme landlord.

The large landowners or overlords, holding title directly (or immediately) from the Crown, allowed others to hold from them, also as tenants in exchange for personal services. These tenants thus held *immediately* from their lords, and *mediately* from the Crown. They allowed yet others to hold some of their land from them on similar bases, and so on, so large tenurial chains developed.

Eventually the system became so complex that it created problems for the overlords in collecting their feudal dues, and subinfeudation was therefore abolished (except for the Crown) by the statute *Quia Emptores* 1290. This statute is still in force, having survived an attempt to repeal it in 1967, and is often regarded as being a pillar of the law of real property. The result is that today nearly all land is held directly from the Crown.

The original services were personal in nature; tenure was therefore for life only, and was inalienable. It soon became clear, however, that it was more efficient to allow families to remain in possession of land over successive generations if they so wished, or if they did not, to allow them to alienate (e.g., sell) the land, and to convert the services into money payments. Unfortunately (for the lords at any rate), as soon as services became converted into money payments, their value was quickly lost through inflation. However, this also meant that lords increasingly kept and managed their own demense lands and hired labour to work them, and demense land itself was able to become a valuable economic asset. Further, this also provided important opportunities for the rising professional classes, as stewards, administrators and lawyers became central through their employ for a fee under a contract and not by vassalage and land. This development of contractual relationships, while not strictly central, is important for our study of the emergence of modern equity through its enablement of continued domination of the landed elite within feudal social hierarchy.

Devaluation of dues and the demise of feudalism
The devaluation of dues meant that many fell obsolete and remained uncollected when they eventually became statute-barred. Many which remained were abolished after the Civil War in 1660 by the Tenures Abolition Act. The Crown was the main beneficiary by then, as supreme landlord, of the remaining feudal incidents; they were abolished because they effectively constituted extra-Parliamentary revenue for the Crown, and military tenures promoted the creation of private armies.

The legal historian McFarlane has noted that in the fourteenth and fifteenth centuries the relationship between lord and man was no longer tenurial but became focused instead on cash payments for services. Pluknett has developed this and refined it by connecting the decline of tenurial relationships and the refocus on money payments to the abolition of subinfeudination for fees under *Quia Emptores* in 1290. More interestingly still, Waugh actually places this development earlier than *Quia Emptores*.

Emergence of a more recognisable pattern of land ownership and system of interests
Nevertheless, though the value of the services themselves diminished, important feudal incidents remained long after 1150. For example, the lord was entitled to payment on succession of land to an heir, and to the right of escheat if a tenant died without an heir, which meant that the land reverted to him. He was also entitled to various rights when the land was held by a minor. As long as any feudal dues remained valuable the lords desired to protect them, and rules about title to land at common law were developed to aid this process. Many of the rights arose on the death of a tenant, especially if there was no heir or the heir was a minor, and could have been avoided by conveying the land to younger adult members of the family, or leaving the land by will. For this reason taxes were imposed on conveyances, and until 1540 freehold estates could not be left by will. It was also important to be able to ascertain who held the land, so until at least 1535 transfers of land at common law had to be open and notorious, whereas many people preferred secret transfers. For similar reasons it was necessary for all conveyances to take immediate effect, so future interests (and therefore settlements) could not be created at common law until 1540.

Earliest recognition of modern equitable jurisdiction
Equity's flexibility and its orientation towards achieving justice will become evermore apparent in reading this text. What will also become very plain is its capacity to evolve and develop to meet new perceived inflexibilities and new needs.

Important foundations for this were laid by the medieval Chancellor's work in relation to the rigidity of the common law of the time. The Chancellor of the King's Court was usually an ecclesiastic who had the power to issue royal writs. This function became discretionary, and came to be based on notions of conscience and justice, while his powers to act against individuals were enforceable by him with the use of imprisonment. It was upon these foundations that the Chancellor's office started to take on many of the features of a court and eventually, probably during the fifteenth century, the Court of Chancery was born.

However, although this is a simple and uncomplicated way of looking at equity and its origins, again it has to be said that equity is far from straightforward. Indeed, the very idea that equity was not originally a substantive system to be contrasted with the law must be taken alongside the fact that equity only truly started to exist as such from the sixteenth century, *and also the state of the common law at this time.* According to legal historian Milsom 'There was no common law, no body of substantive rules from which equity could be different. And the idea that the law could be unjust, if comprehensible at all, would have been abhorrent. Failures were mechanical.' But it is nevertheless true that forms of action had ceased to be flexible by the mid-fourteenth century. Milsom suggests that it was during the sixteenth century that the common law started to become liberated from medieval procedural constraints and begins to be viewed as a substantive set of rules. In contrast, equity remains highly individual and is based on individual decisions, so much so that in 1670 Vaughan CJ maintained that 'Equity is a universal truth and there can be no precedent in it'.

Equity, the common law and originality in approach
Thus, there is undoubtedly more to equity's original development than the avoidance of restrictions placed on transfers by the common law and avoidance of feudal dues, but nevertheless equity retains its original character in this regard. It will become apparent how equitable doctrines still develop where doctrines at common law are regarded as inflexible: for example, illustrations can be found in the development of the doctrine of promissory estoppel and the ways in which the trust has traditionally sought to mitigate harshness of the privity doctrine. There is also the estoppel licence and possibly a new variety of the constructive trust. Equity's early role in seeking to avoid feudal dues is also illustrative of the trust's long-standing function as a tax avoidance device. Moreover, it should be becoming clear that surrounding the emergence of the common law as a set of cogent rules, and certainly prior to it, equity's role appeared to be seen as remedying failures of process. Chancellors would see themselves as perfecting the human defects of process which could arise at common law, by focusing on a person's conscience to achieve an outcome which was just. Here, equity's focus on the conscience of an individual ensured that there was no need for the formalism and technicality characteristic of the common law; it was also responsive to individual circumstances and, moreover, a chancery decree would bind only parties to the suit.

Although the thrust of the Chancellor's power could in principle be exercised without altering the substance of the common law in question, the practical result of his jurisdiction was that the exercise of common law rights was affected significantly. Indeed, it may be that in light of the Chancellor's ability to refuse to issue a writ to a claimant at common law, or to compel conveyance of property by its owner to someone else, conflict between the two systems was inevitable. Indeed, conflict did arise, but not until much later. As has already been suggested, at this early stage the common law was not terribly clearly defined, and the conflict which did occur much later was not altogether apparent from the King's (through his Chancellor) exercise of residual discretion.

1.2.3 The chancellor, discretion and the 'Use'

The Use was a device which emerged from about 1230. However in this text we shall be looking at its Use from around 1400. Here, it actually represents the ancestor of the modern trust. The Use's origins can be traced to the appearance of general Uses as devices for holding land on behalf of another, arising from the way in which feudal tenure had ensured that title passed by succession automatically to the eldest son. This made provision for younger children difficult to achieve, and it was on succession that feudal dues (known as incidents) became payable to the lord. The Use sought to avoid these consequences, and also to respond to the common law's refusal to allow any separation between ownership and enjoyment of land.

At its simplest, the mechanics of the Use ensured that a conveyance would be made to one party, usually a lawyer or cleric, but subject to instructions relating to the use of land for the benefit of the *cestui que use*. The real problem was that legal title would not be vested in the party intended to enjoy the property: the party intended to benefit had, according to an anonymous writing from 1502, no protection and 'no more to do with the land than the greatest stranger in the world'. From around 1400 the Chancellor ensured that land for this type of benefit was directed in this way by acting on the conscience of the legal owner. Because he still retained legal title, the common law was theoretically unaffected by this, while the *cestui que use* came to be regarded as the equitable owner.

However, this was not the 'triumph' of the trust, and Henry VII passed anti-avoidance (of feudal dues) legislation in 1490 and 1504. The Use and its ability to create estates and interests in land was able to help avoid payment of dues upon death, because legal estates needed only rarely to be transferred. Nevertheless, when the Chancellor created the Use it was necessary to decide which equitable estates would be protected. One meaning of the maxim 'equity follows the law' is that equity recognises all the estates (and other interests in land) recognised by the common law. In fact, for a greater part of equity's history, and today, equity has also recognised estates and interests which are not recognised at common law; today, however, this is mainly because limits have been placed on the number of possible legal estates in land by the 1925 property legislation.

The Statute of Uses: the death of the Use?
Given that one of the most important functions of the Use was the avoidance of feudal dues, and that soon a great proportion of land was held to Uses, the combination of legal and equitable title was achieved through execution of the Use by conveying the legal estate to the *cestui que use*. The Crown as supreme landlord was affected significantly by its growth, and Henry VIII enacted the Statute of Uses in 1535 to check its creativity, and to try to liberalise duties due. But instead of curbing its application, the Statute actually fostered greater creativity through the invention of the 'Use upon a Use': it was this which eventually became called a trust by 1700.

1.3 **An outline of modern equitable principles**

In its early days, equitable jurisdiction was exercised on an *ad hoc* basis, and its transformation into a modern system did not come about until after around 1700, by which time Chancellors tended to be lawyers rather than ecclesiasts and a system of precedent was beginning to develop. Yet many features of the early use remain in the modern trust. Indeed it was necessary for equity to retain many of its early features to avoid conflict with the common law. It should be noted, however, that today's trust applies to goods as well as land.

It may be that the development of principles some 200 years ago, followed by increased rigidity in the law more recently, has had undesirable consequences. The eighteenth century was, after all, before modern banking practices and limited liability companies (as presently constituted) existed. Most trusts tended to be of the family settlement variety. Yet the principles that were well-suited to such settlements also apply in essence today. We shall see in chapter 4 how assumptions based on family-type trusts impeded until very recently the development of the law relating to certainties, and it may also be that trustees' duties are too onerous for similar reasons. The heart of these difficulties lies in the way in which family trusts are not in their nature intended as risky ventures, and a significant difficulty is in guarding against fraud of the trustees. To apply similar principles to professional trustees, who may well be expected to take business risks, is arguably inappropriate.

1.3.1 **The equitable maxims**

As equity became more formalised a framework emerged within which its development could become shaped. These principles became embodied in the form of equitable maxims. The maxims are not rules to be construed like statutes, but rather a general basis around which much of the law of equity has formed. They frequently appear as part of the reasoning in judgments. All have relevance to the law of trusts—the first was a rationalisation of the basis of the jurisdiction exercised originally by the medieval Chancellor, and the second we have already come across. Many of the rest will appear in later sections and chapters, so for convenience all of the 12 usually quoted are listed below, though their full explanations come at appropriate parts of the book.

   (1) Equity will not suffer a wrong without a remedy.

   (2) Equity follows the law.

   (3) Where there is equal equity, the law shall prevail.

   (4) Where the equities are equal, the first in time shall prevail.

   (5) He who seeks equity must do equity.

   (6) He who comes to equity must come with clean hands.

   (7) Delay defeats equities.

   (8) Equality is equity.

   (9) Equity looks to the intent rather than the form.

 (10) Equity looks on that as done which ought to be done.

(11) Equity imputes an intention to fulfil an obligation.

(12) Equity acts *in personam*.

Though only the above 12 are usually regarded as the definitive equitable maxims, equity has developed additional principles which may be treated to all intents and purposes as if they were among the maxims. The following may not be an exhaustive list, but all these principles will appear again in the book.

(i) The principle that **'equity will not assist a volunteer'** is fundamental to the discussion in chapter 3 which relates to the constitution of trusts and the effecting of gifts.

(ii) Also at the heart of chapter 3 is the mantra that **'equity will not perfect an imperfect gift'**.

(iii) The way in which **'equity will not construe a valid power out of an invalid trust'** has very strong references to materials in chapters 2 and 4 which reveal the nature of the trust, and also the conditions which must be satisfied in order for a valid trust to exist.

(iv) That **'equity will not permit the provisions of a statute intended to prevent fraud to be used as an instrument for fraud'** will be explained in materials relating to formality requirements for trusts, in chapters 5 and 11, and accommodating the need for a trust to operate in certain situations where this might be difficult to achieve, as illustrated in chapters 9 and 10.

(v) The way in which **'equity will not permit a trust to fail for want of a trustee'** is a theme which runs throughout this text in some form or another!

The exact language of these maxims and principles appears to vary slightly between different authorities.

1.3.2 Equity interests and action *in personam*

One feature of equitable jurisdiction has always been that it is exercised against specific persons—equity acts *in personam*. This is also an important maxim of equity. In the case of the use the remedy was personal against the feoffee to uses, who held the legal estate in the land. Also in a modern trust the action is against the owner of the legal estate in land, or the legal owner of money or goods. Consequently it does not matter, for example, if the land, money or goods are themselves situated abroad, so long as the legal owner or trustee can be found.

Nevertheless, as equity developed it acted not only against the original legal owner of the property, but also against subsequent owners in certain circumstances, and will be explained shortly. As a result of this it is reasonable to describe certain equitable rights as property rights, and to talk about equitable title to land, and equitable ownership of goods. It is also the case that various statutory provisions, and in particular the 1925 property legislation (largely beyond the scope of this text) and some taxation legislation (considered in chapter 5) treat equitable interests as property interests. So although it is still accurate to say that equity acts *in personam*, some equitable rights also have the characteristics of rights *in rem*. As will appear from the following sections, however, there are significant differences between legal and equitable title or ownership.

1.3.3 Nature of legal and equitable ownership

The description of the use shows that it was the equitable ownership which was enjoyed; the feoffee to uses merely managed the property on behalf of the *cestui que use*. The same position obtains with the modern trust. Legal ownership, or trustee-ship, is a management function. So far from being desirable, a trustee undertakes onerous duties (on which, see chapters 15 and 16, and also 18), and is often paid for undertaking trusteeship (e.g., banks, solicitors—for conditions attaching to payment). The equitable owner, or beneficiary, on the other hand, is entitled to enjoy the property. Of course, where no trust is imposed, legal ownership is itself desirable (most owners of goods would be surprised if it were otherwise); the reasons for this have already been examined at the outset of this chapter.

Equitable ownership shares with its legal counterpart one of the most important features of any property right, that it can be disposed of. Property is a transferable commodity. Formality requirements for dispositions of equitable titles and interests are considered in chapter 5.

1.3.4 Other equitable interests

The equitable principles discussed in this section do not apply only to full equitable ownership of chattels or estates in land arising out of the types of transactions already considered. Equity also recognises other interests in property which are less than full ownership, and some of the following cases and examples are about equitable interests, rather than full equitable ownership.

For example, suppose A has freehold legal title to land, and contracts to lease the land to B for seven years. Under the contract, B is entitled to possession and enjoy-ment of the land for that period. The contract is enforceable at common law, just like any other contract, and if a lease is not executed, or B is denied possession or enjoyment of the land, he can claim damages. The common law does not recognise B as actually being lessee, however, until the lease is executed in the prescribed formal manner. But unlike many contracts, this arrangement is also enforceable in equity, allowing B to claim the equitable remedies of specific performance, which forces A to execute the lease, and injunction, which stops A acting in a manner inconsistent with the grant of the lease. Furthermore, 'equity looks on that as done which ought to be done', and B is treated as if he were *already* a lessee in equity, even if no formal lease has yet been executed (*Walsh* v *Lonsdale* (1882) 20 Ch D 9). So a contract for a lease can create an immediate equitable interest in land, called an estate contract (a lease being an estate in land), to which the equitable principles discussed below apply.

The same applies to contracts for lesser legal rights in land. A contract to create a legal easement (e.g., a right of way—a right much less extensive than legal owner-ship) can give rise to an equitable easement, which is another equitable interest less than full ownership. Additionally, there are some interests in land which exist only in equity, for example, restrictive covenants, which are a narrowly defined specialist type of contract between landowners. The principles discussed in this section apply to these interests also.

Terminologically, so far as land is concerned, an *estate*, whether legal or equitable, connotes an interest akin to ownership; an *interest in land* can include an estate, but also includes rights that are much less extensive than ownership.

1.3.5 **Equitable remedies**

Some specific applications of equitable remedies are discussed in chapter 19, but it is necessary even at this stage to introduce the equitable remedies, and consider the general principles applicable to them.

Originally equity developed its own remedies, which were not available to the common law. Nor did equity administer common law remedies. This position was to some extent altered by the Common Law Procedure Act 1854, which gave the common law courts some jurisdiction to give equitable remedies, and the Chancery Amendment Act 1858, which allowed the Court of Chancery to award the common law derived remedy of damages, but only in addition to, or in substitution for an equitable remedy.

As will be explained shortly, in 1873–5 the courts were fused, but the principles governing the grant of equitable remedies were not changed by that legislation, and are still applicable to actions to protect equitable interests or estates, and other rights having an equitable origin. Thus, it is still necessary to consider the equitable remedies separately from the common law remedies.

The main equitable remedies are the injunction and specific performance. For breach of fiduciary duty (see chapter 15) there is also the remedy of account, and sometimes equity imposes a constructive trust (see chapters 7, 9, 10, 11 and 19). Damages could not originally be awarded, and can be now only on the basis of the 1858 Act. In any event the quantum of equitable damages may differ from that appropriate in a common law action.

Equitable remedies are available for breaches of equitable obligations, such as those considered in chapters 11 and 15, but in addition injunctions can be used to prevent the commissions of torts. For some torts, such as negligence claims arising out of road accident cases, the remedy is obviously inappropriate, but it can be useful for continuing torts, such as trespass or nuisance. As will be seen in chapter 15, injunctions can also be used to prevent abuses of confidential information.

1.3.5.1 *Equitable remedies discretionary*

A major difference between the two systems is that whereas common law remedies are available as of right, equitable remedies retain the discretionary nature of early equitable jurisdiction. Although for the creation of wholly new equitable rights and principles the onset over the last two centuries or so of defined systems of precedent and law reporting has curtailed the early discretion somewhat, the remedies are nevertheless still discretionary, even though that discretion is now exercised according to fairly clear and even rigid principles. The discretionary nature of the remedies can lead to dire consequences. If an equitable estate or interest depends on the award of an equitable remedy, a refusal to grant the remedy destroys the interest.

1.3.5.2 *Exercise of the discretion*

A common ground for refusal of a remedy is the behaviour of the party claiming the equitable remedy. This is because 'he who comes into equity must come with clean hands'. For example, in *Coatsworth* v *Johnson* (1886) 54 LT 520, CA the claimant was in possession of land under a contract for a lease, where no lease that would be recognised at common law had been executed. The landlord in fact turned the claimant out, and the claimant sued for trespass. He would have won the action had he been regarded as a lessee, either at common law or in equity. As we saw above, equity in principle enforces contracts for leases, and would normally regard the claimant as being an equitable lessee. In the particular case he was in breach of various covenants under the agreement, however. In these circumstances, the Court of Appeal held the equitable remedy would have been refused, and the claimant *therefore lost his interest*. Thus he was thrown back on his common law rights, and of course he had no lease at common law. So he lost. Not only is this case a good example of the discretionary nature of equitable remedies, but also emphasises the need to treat common law and equitable rights and remedies separately. Also, the entire interest was lost because the remedy was refused.

Equity, discretion and the importance of conduct

The behaviour of the party claiming the remedy is not the only factor. Innocent claimants can also lose their remedies. For example, a remedy might also be refused if to grant it would put the other party in breach of a contract with a third party (*Warmington* v *Miller* [1973] QB 877). Other grounds for refusing the remedy are that severe hardship might be caused to the defendant, or in a contract action where the contract has been forced on the defendant through unfair pressure (even in the absence of undue influence or duress).

The existence of a discretion does not, however, imply that it is unlimited. In *Mountford* v *Scott* [1975] Ch 258, an argument was advanced that equity ought not to enforce an option, granted for £1, to purchase a house for £10,000. The argument was based on the undoubted rule that equity will not specifically enforce a promise at the instance of a volunteer, although the promise, if under seal, may found an action for damages at common law (see further chapter 3). It was argued by the defendant that this rule should be extended to this situation, where the consideration for the grant of the option was a token payment, and that the claimants should therefore have been left to their remedy in damages. Brightman J summed up the issue thus:

As the plaintiffs had made no more than a token payment for the defendant's promise, are the plaintiffs, so far as the equitable remedy of specific performance is concerned, in the position of volunteers who ought to be left to their remedy in damages?

The argument was rejected by Brightman J, whose decision was upheld in the Court of Appeal.

1.3.6 **Equitable rights and third parties**

So far we have considered only remedies against the trustee or, where the interest arises out of a contract, the other contracting party. For equitable rights to be regarded in any sense as property rights, however, it is necessary also to consider the extent to which they can bind third parties.

Legal title: 'good against the world'

The position of legal rights arising from title at law is that they are enforceable against anyone, and they are said to 'bind the world'. Equitable rights on the other hand do not do so, and they might in this respect be perceived as lesser rights on account of the impact they can have on third parties. Illustration of this position and the issues it raises can be made through the very simple example provided by a trustee who tries to sell property to which he has ostensible ownership: he has legal title, and he is attempting to dispose of the property on the basis that ownership is unencumbered. He does not declare that he holds the property on trust for the benefit of another. The maxim that legal title is good against the world is coupled by the somewhat weaker sounding position that 'equitable title binds all except for the *bona fide* purchaser of the legal estate for value, without notice of the equitable title or interest'.

This position ensures that parties will only be bound by equitable interests where their consciences have been affected, and according to the position above, the conscience of such a person will be affected where he is not a good faith purchaser for value without notice of the equitable interest. In this situation, where property is passed to a third party, he will take it subject to any equitable entitlement to it. A person who *is* such a *bona fide* purchaser for value and without notice, is known as 'equity's darling' and will take a legal estate free from any equitable rights. The rationale for this is that 'equity's darling' will be, like an equitable owner himself, an innocent victim of a breach of trust, and 'where there is equal equity, the law shall prevail'. This is the basis of the equitable notice doctrine.

Equity and law: Cave v Cave

In *Cave* v *Cave* (1880) 15 Ch D 639, Charles Cave, as sole trustee and family solicitor, stole trust money and purchased a house with it. As a result of this transaction, the moneys in the trust fund were converted into land, so that the beneficiaries of the fund became beneficiaries of the land. The fraudulent trustee/solicitor then raised money by way of legal mortgage at a time when a legal mortgage took effect by way of a conveyance of the entire freehold estate to the mortgagee, with a covenant to re-convey the property to the mortgagor if the money loaned, plus interest and administration charges, was repaid to the mortgagee on a fixed date. When these conditions were met, equity enforced this covenant and also allowed the mortgagor to demand a later re-conveyance, subject to repayment of the capital loaned, plus interest and administration charges. Here, the mortgagee obtained legal title, and he also provided value, in the form of the money advanced. Accordingly, Fry J held that he had no notice of the beneficiaries' interest. There was no suggestion that the mortgagee was acting in bad faith, and he was therefore a *bona fide* purchaser of the legal estate for value without notice of the beneficiaries' equitable interests, so legal title passed to the mortgagee free of encumbrance.

1.3.6.1 *Conditions attached to the doctrine of notice*

Equity and the 'purchaser for value'

For a third party to take free of an equitable interest in property, the purchase must be one for value. Value includes not only consideration recognised at common law, but also equitable consideration. Thus, for example, as well as value in terms of money or money's worth (recognised as consideration by both systems), equity also recognises a future marriage as consideration, and so it constitutes value for the purposes of the *bona fide* purchaser rule. On the other hand, the common law allows contracts under seal to be enforced even in the absence of consideration; equity does not take the same view, and such contracts do not provide value for the purposes of this rule (nor incidentally can such contracts be enforced using equitable remedies). Where the value is money, the purchaser must pay all the money before receiving notice of the equitable interest.

Purchaser for value 'without notice'
Notice itself includes not only actual, but also constructive notice. For dealings in land this has traditionally meant that the purchaser must inquire about equitable interests with no less diligence than he would inquire of legal interests, and these standards are determined by ordinary conveyancing practice. Thus a careless purchaser is not protected; nor is one who could have discovered the existence of an interest by inspecting the land. Additionally, knowledge of an agent (e.g., solicitor) is imputed, so that the purchaser is treated as having any knowledge that his agent acquires. In *Cave* v *Cave*, however, Charles Cave acted as solicitor for both the mortgagor and the mortgagee, and obviously he knew the truth, but Fry J held that his notice would not be imputed to the mortgagee since he was party to a fraud. Fry J said (at p. 644):

. . . the act done by the agent [Charles Cave] is such as cannot be said to be done by him in his character of agent, but is done by him in the character of a party to an independent fraud on his principal [mortgagee], and that is not to be imputed to the principal as an act done by his agent.

The details of precisely what constitutes notice is covered in land law textbooks and is beyond the scope of this book, but it is worth observing that the notice doctrine developed from land transactions, which are characterised by their thoroughness and lack of haste. For this reason, the notice doctrine works strictly against purchasers. The courts have shown a marked reluctance to apply quite so rigorous a doctrine in ordinary commercial transactions, which are characterised by their informality and speed (see further chapter 19).

Equitable interests, third party rights and the doctrine of notice
It is clear that equity further recognises a category of entitlements described as 'equities' or 'mere equities'. This terminology is intended to distinguish them from full equitable proprietary interests. These have been determined to include the deserted wife's equity (as in *National Provincial Bank Ltd* v *Ainsworth* [1965] AC 1175), and the right to have a transaction set aside on grounds of fraud or undue influence (e.g., in *Barclays Bank* v *O'Brien* considered below). Where these mere equities relate to property (as in both the cases above, but for different reasons) they have a limited ability to affect third parties who acquire ownership of it, but it must be appreciated that they are not true interests in property itself. And, the notice doctrine applies not only to full equitable ownership or title but also to these lesser forms of equitable interest in property.

Equities' unconscionable bargains and the doctrine of undue influence
There has been a hub of activity in the area of undue influence in recent years. The doctrine of undue influence has developed in relation to the law of contract, and it has done so to allow a contract to be set aside where the circumstances are such that a person benefiting from the transaction was aware of circumstances in which the

other party may have been acting under the influence of another. As the law has developed it has become apparent that a strong contextual setting for such situations has arisen in respect of financial guarantee transactions, as in the paradigm case of *Barclays Bank* v *O'Brien* [1994] 1 AC 80. In *O'Brien* the House of Lords held that the wife had signed mortgage documentation under the undue influence of her husband, and, that because the mortgagee (the bank) had not taken reasonable steps to ensure that the transaction had been entered into freely, it had constructive notice of the undue influence. As a result, the wife was able to have the transaction set aside.

Undue influence, relationships, notice and enquiries: the new law
In *O'Brien* the undue influence was relationship based, and arose on account of the relationship between the wife and the influencing party, her spouse. Following *O'Brien* and another case decided at the same time, *CIBC Mortgages Plc* v *Pitt* [1994] 1 AC 200, the House of Lords in *Royal Bank of Scotland* v *Etridge (No. 2)* [2001] 4 All ER 449 widened the types of relationship which would put creditors on enquiry. Lord Nicholls argued that there was no reason to single out sexual relationships for special protection, referring in his judgment to the decision of the Court of Appeal in *Credit Lyonnais Bank Nederland* v *Burch* [1997] 1 All ER 144 as an example of a case where the relationship between guarantor and debtor had been that of employee and employer in which the *O'Brien* principles were relevant and had been appropriately applied. The types of relationship attracting protection under *O'Brien*, he considered, should not be narrowly prescribed and should not require creditors to assess the degree of trust and confidence existing in any particular relationship. On this basis, protection should extend to all cases where the relationship between guarantor and debtor was non-commercial.

In *Etridge*, the House of Lords confirmed the distinction made in *O'Brien* and *Pitt* between surety and joint loan cases. Lord Nicholls went on to suggest that cases in which a spouse was agreeing to guarantee the debts of their spouse's company should be treated in the same way as surety cases. This should be so even if the guarantor spouse was him/herself a shareholder, a secretary or director in that company as the holding of any of these positions did not necessarily reflect ability to control the company's affairs. Lord Nicholls declared that creditors were not required to ensure that the surety's consent was free from undue influence nor were they required to instruct solicitors to do this. He affirmed the general *O'Brien* approach and stated that:

The furthest a bank can be expected to go is to take reasonable steps to satisfy itself that the wife has had brought home to her, in a meaningful way, the practical implications of the proposed transaction. This does not wholly eliminate the risk of undue influence or misrepresentation. But it does mean that a wife enters into a transaction with her eyes open so far as the basic elements of the transaction are concerned.

Priorities between successive equitable interests
The equitable maxim 'Where there is equal equity, the law shall prevail', applies only where the purchase made is in respect of a legal estate or title. A purchaser of an *equitable* estate or interest will not generally, therefore, take priority over a prior equitable interest. Another maxim applies: 'Where the equities are equal, the first in time shall prevail'. In other words, priorities of equitable interests generally rank according to the order of time in which they have been created (there are a limited

number of exceptions concerning mortgages, which are outside the scope of this book).

In *Cave v Cave*, the value of the property was greater than the amount raised on the first mortgage, so Charles Cave raised further money on a second mortgage. The second mortgagee, like the first, had no notice of the beneficiaries' interests. However, he could not obtain a legal estate, since that had already been conveyed to the first mortgagee (the usual position prior to the 1925 legislation), and so this second mortgage took effect as a mortgage in equity only. Even though he had acted *bona fide*, therefore, had given value and had no notice of the prior equitable interests of the beneficiaries, he was not a *bona fide* purchaser of the *legal* estate for value without notice. He therefore took subject to the claimants' prior equitable interest, Fry J observing (at p. 648) 'As between persons having only equitable interests, if their equities are in all other respects equal, priority of time gives the better equity, or, "*Qui prior est tempore potior' est jure*".'

1.3.6.2 *Application to property other than land*

The notice doctrine originally developed from land transactions, but has been extended to all other forms of property. Indeed, today it is far more important in relation to other forms of property than it is to land. This is because in addition to the way in which previous editions of this book have reported that 'the importance of the doctrine in relation to land has been much reduced by the 1925 property legislation', the impact of the Land Registration Act 2002 must also be considered (see below).

In relation to personal property (that which is not land) the same fundamental distinction between legal and equitable ownership applies. In the case of goods, common law ownership can be enforced against anyone at all (subject, in the case of sale of goods, to the exceptions contained in the Factors Act 1889, ss. 2, 8 and 9, and the Sale of Goods Act 1979, ss. 21–26, which are discussed in detail in works on sale of goods). Equitable ownership, by contrast, can be lost to a *bona fide* purchaser for value who does not know of the equitable ownership. The different wording is deliberate on account that it seems that many of the detailed workings of the notice doctrine (e.g., constructive and imputed notice considered above) may well apply only to land. The position with personal property is similar, but probably not identical, since this will involve transactions which are less lengthy and quicker, and not subject to the same level of enquiry and process.

Notice

Purchasers of property other than land Although the doctrine theoretically applies to goods as well as land, in practice buyers of goods are rarely bound by equitable interests in them, as they generally have no reason to suspect that the seller, if he has legal title, does not also have equitable title. In the first place, the vast majority of goods are not held in trust. Also, transfers of goods do not normally involve the degree of investigation and documentation that would be appropriate in the case of land, so an assumption of absolute ownership is normally reasonable.

If the seller does not have legal title, such title can nevertheless pass to the buyer in certain circumstances (under the Factors Act and Sale of Goods Act sections mentioned above), but these circumstances are drawn up in such a way that it is almost inconceivable that a buyer who acquires title in this way would be acting in bad faith, or have any notice of an equitable interest. On the other hand, if the seller has no title, and the buyer also acquires no title, because the Factors Act, etc. provisions do not apply in his favour, he will necessarily be bound by any prior equitable interests. This will be so whether or not he acts in good faith, and whether or not he has notice, because he does not acquire any legal title.

It is possible to conclude in the case of goods, that in practice the determining factor will be whether the buyer acquires legal title to the goods, rather than the presence or absence of good faith or notice.

Currency The position is quite different, however, where money is concerned, at least where it is being used as currency and there has been quite a spate of recent litigation on this (see further chapter 19). Where money is stolen, or a cheque forged by altering the name of the payee, the thief can pass legal title in the money, even though he has no title to it himself, because of an exception to the common law principle that a man cannot pass a title that he does not have (*nemo dat quod non habet*). Money stolen in this way may (for example) be laundered through bank accounts, given to friends, spent at gambling clubs or used to purchase tangible property. The legal title will be passed on by the thief, and in general, the thief will disappear or not be worth suing. The victim of the theft may in certain circumstances be able to assert equitable title in the money against the recipients, however, and the precise circumstances where this can be done are considered in chapter 19, where again the distinction between legal and equitable ownership is of fundamental importance. One of the main issues considered there is the state of knowledge required to bind the recipient, which probably differs in some respects from the way the notice doctrine has traditionally applied to land.

1.3.6.3 *Equitable rights as rights in rem*

To conclude this discussion, equity began by acting *in personam*, without affecting common law title or ownership. This is similar to the situation today, where let us say, the owner of a ship charters it for a period to a time charterer. The charterer can assert contractual rights against the owner, but these are simply personal rights against the owner, and although the charterer is entitled to use the vessel, the ownership of the vessel remains entirely unaffected by the charterparty. Furthermore, the charterer cannot enforce his charterparty against a purchaser of the vessel—not at any rate directly.

It may well be that equitable rights began like present-day contractual rights, enforceable only against the original feoffee to uses. Equity developed, however, as contract has not, to allow wide-ranging enforcement against subsequent legal owners. It is therefore not a full description of equitable rights to say that they are merely rights *in personam*. Some (classified as mere equities) undoubtedly are merely rights *in personam*, but others have many of the properties of rights *in rem*, and it is not unreasonable to describe these as additionally giving rights of ownership.

Equitable rights as proprietary rights
So it is reasonable to describe certain equitable rights as property rights, and to talk about equitable title to land, and equitable ownership of goods. It is also the case that various statutory provisions, and, in particular, the 1925 property legislation and some taxation legislation, treat equitable interests as property interests. Thus,

s. 53(1)(c) of the Law of Property Act 1925 (considered in depth in chapter 5) provides:

[A] disposition of an equitable interest or trust subsisting at the time of the disposition must be in writing signed by the person disposing of the same, or by his agent thereunto lawfully authorised by writing or by will.

This clearly suggests the existence of equitable interests, which are presumably property interests, and which therefore have the characteristics of rights *in rem*.

The courts have also accepted that at any rate some equitable rights can have the characteristics of rights *in rem*. In *Baker* v *Archer-Shee* [1927] AC 844, a beneficiary was considered to be the owner of dividends for tax purposes. In *National Provincial Bank Ltd* v *Ainsworth* [1965] AC 1175, the House of Lords distinguished between equitable interests in land, which were full property rights capable of binding third parties as overriding interests under s. 70(1)(g) of the Land Registration Act 1925, and 'mere equities', which were not capable of binding third parties at all.

Rights in law, equity and illegality: the case of Tinsley v Milligan
In *Tinsley* v *Milligan* [1994] 1 AC 340, Stella Tinsley and Kathleen Milligan jointly purchased a home which was registered in Tinsley's name alone. On the principles set out in chapters 7 and 9, the beneficial interest would have been shared between Tinsley and Milligan in equal shares; but to both Tinsley's and Milligan's knowledge, the home was registered in Tinsley's name alone to enable Milligan to make false claims to the Department of Social Security for benefits. After a quarrel Tinsley moved out, and claimed possession from Milligan. Milligan counterclaimed, seeking a declaration that the house was held by Tinsley on trust for both of them in equal shares. Tinsley argued that Milligan's claim was barred by the common law doctrine *ex turpi causa non oritur actio* and by the principle that 'he who comes to equity must come with clean hands'.

The House of Lords held (Lord Keith and Lord Goff dissenting) that because the presumption of resulting trust applied (see chapter 7), Milligan could establish her equitable interest without relying on the illegal transaction, and was therefore entitled to succeed. The case supports the argument, it is suggested, that Milligan's resulting trust interest was a property interest in its own right, which had an existence that was independent of the precise arrangement between the couple. Had it been no more than merely a collection of personal rights against Tinsley, Milligan would surely have failed, since she would have been unable to assert those rights without disclosing the fraud. Lord Browne-Wilkinson went so far as to say:

More than 100 years have elapsed since the fusion of the administration of law and equity. The reality of the matter is that, in 1993, English law has one single law of property made up of legal and equitable interests. Although for historical reasons legal estates and equitable estates have differing incidents, the person owning either type of estate has a right of property, a right *in rem* not merely a right *in personam*. If the law is that a party is entitled to enforce a property right acquired under an illegal transaction, in my judgment the same rule ought to apply to any property right so acquired, whether such right is legal or equitable.

Even if (as the authors would suggest) this statement goes too far, it is clear at the very least that some equitable rights also have the characteristics of rights *in rem*.

Similar principles were applied by the Court of Appeal in *Rowan* v *Dann* (1992) P & CR 202. Rowan was a farmer in financial difficulties, who entered into sham leases of his land with somebody with whom he intended to go into a joint business venture (cattle-embryo transplanting). His sole intention in granting the leases was to keep the land out of the hands of creditors, and no rent was ever paid, but no creditors were in the event actually defrauded. When the joint venture failed to get off the ground, the farmer successfully claimed his land back on a resulting trust. The resulting trust arose in Rowan's favour by reason of the failure of the joint venture project, and, as in *Tinsley* v *Milligan*, it was unnecessary for Rowan to rely on the illegal purpose.

Like *Tinsley* v *Milligan*, *Rowan* v *Dann* supports the view that Rowan's interest was not merely a personal right against Dann, but an independent property interest. Legal title will not be lost merely because it has been obtained as part of a fraudulent transaction, and these cases suggest that the same is true for equitable titles.

Equitable rights as rights in personam
It is also still true to say, however, that equitable rights have some of the characteristics of rights *in personam*. Indeed, some equitable rights, such as the 'mere equities' considered by the House of Lords in *National Provincial Bank Ltd* v *Ainsworth* (above), do not have the characteristics of rights *in rem* at all.

In *Richard West and Partners (Inverness) Ltd* v *Dick* [1969] 2 Ch 424, the Court of Appeal held that the English courts had jurisdiction to grant a decree of specific performance of a contract for the sale of land abroad (in Scotland). The defendant was within the jurisdiction, and Harman LJ observed:

> . . . that the Court of Chancery, acting as it does *in personam*, is well able to grant specific performance of a contract to buy or sell foreign land, provided the defendant is domiciled within its jurisdiction.

Reasoning along similar lines was adopted by the Court of Appeal in *Lightning* v *Lightning Electrical Contractors Ltd*, CA, 23 April 1998, where English law was applied to determine that land in Scotland was held on resulting trust, even though there would have been no resulting trust under Scots law (see further chapter 7).

Equity, property and ability of equity to act in personam
The ability of equity to act *in personam* can be useful in any case where the property is situated abroad. The worldwide *Mareva* injunction (see chapter 19) depends on equity acting *in personam*, as does equity's ability to trace property through civil law jurisdictions (see chapter 19). In these cases, however, the personal rights are presumably additional to any real rights created. If the land or other property were in England, beneficial interests in it would surely not be defeated merely because the trustee was abroad.

However, there may be situations where the beneficiary's rights are limited by the personal nature of the action. It is also often the trustee, not the beneficiary, who takes action against a third party in respect of the trust property. For example, where property is leased it is the trustee who sues for rent: *Shalit* v *Joseph Nadler Ltd* [1933] 2 KB 79. Of course, the trustee is accountable to the beneficiary, and can be required by the beneficiary to sue, but the beneficiary cannot sue the third party directly. This really is a case where the trustee's rights are rights *in rem*, whereas those of the beneficiary are limited to a personal action against the trustee.

Equitable ownership and negligence suits
Generally speaking, only the owner of property at the time that it is damaged can sue in negligence. It is probable that an equitable owner does not count for these

purposes, and that only the legal owner can sue. Again, of course, the equitable owner can require the legal owner to sue. In *Leigh & Sillivan Ltd v Aliakmon Shipping Co. Ltd, The Aliakmon* [1986] AC 785, buyers of a quantity of steel coils failed in a negligence action against the shipowners who had badly stowed the cargo aboard *The Aliakmon*, as a result of which it suffered damage, because property in the cargo had not passed to them by the time the damage occurred. The buyers alternatively claimed that they were equitable owners of the cargo (on the grounds that equity treats as done that which ought to be done, and that property ought to pass to them). However, Lord Brandon thought that even if they were equitable owners, that would not give them the right to sue in negligence:

My Lords, under this head Mr Clarke [for the buyers] put forward two propositions of law. The first proposition was that a person who has the equitable ownership of goods is entitled to sue in tort for negligence anyone who by want of care causes them to be lost or damaged without joining the legal owner as a party to the action. . . .

In my view, the first proposition cannot be supported. . . . If . . . the person is the equitable owner of the goods and no more, then he must join the legal owner as a party to the action, either as co-plaintiff if he is willing or as co-defendant if he is not. This had always been the law in the field of equitable ownership of land and I see no reason why it should not also be so in the field of equitable ownership of goods.

He also held that the buyers in fact had no equitable ownership (following *Re Wait* [1927] 1 Ch 606; considered in a different context in chapter 4), so that these remarks are technically *obiter dicta*, but they were expressly adopted by the Court of Appeal in *MCC Proceeds Inc. v Lehman Brothers International (Europe), The Independent*, 19 January 1998, and applied to a conversion action. Mummery LJ observed that if the beneficiary could sue directly, the defendant would be subject to actions from both legal and equitable owners, and that there would be a problem of multiplicity of actions. Although if the claimant had had actual possession, or an immediate right to possession of goods, a conversion claim would have lain for interference with that possessory right, beneficial title on its own will not found a claim in conversion.

Equity negligence and some exceptional circumstances
These cases should be contrasted with *White v Jones* [1995] 2 AC 207, upholding *Ross v Caunters* [1980] Ch 297. Here, an intended beneficiary under a will successfully sued the solicitors for drawing up a will in such a way as to exclude him, although obviously he did not (because of the solicitor's negligence) obtain even equitable title to the disputed property. These cases should be regarded as exceptional, in that there was nobody apart from the intended beneficiary who was in any position to bring an action. The general position is as stated in the previous paragraph.

We would suggest, therefore, that although for many purposes equitable rights have the characteristics of rights *in rem*, vestiges of their personal origins still remain.

Purely personal rights
The case of *National Provincial Bank Ltd v Ainsworth* [1965] AC 1175 in the House of Lords distinguished between equitable interests in land, which were full property rights capable of binding third parties as overriding interests under s. 70(1)(g) of the Land Registration Act 1925, and 'mere equities', which were not capable of binding third parties at all. The right at issue in *Ainsworth* was the so-called 'deserted wives'

equity', or the right, enforceable as against her husband, to occupy the matrimonial home. Although equitable remedies were available to enforce the right, the reasoning was that no equitable interest in land had been created. Therefore, the right was not enforceable against a mortgagee where the husband had defaulted on the mortgage. (Note that the actual decision in *Ainsworth* has since been affected by statute, currently the Matrimonial Homes Act 1983.) Another situation where equity may not have gone down the *Walsh* v *Lonsdale* route, reasoned from the existence of an equitable remedy to the existence of an interest in land, is where there is a contractual or estoppel licence; there appears to be no clear-cut authority that these can be interests in land (and indeed, most of what Paul Todd wrote in [1981] Conv 347 still stands). However, exactly when equity will recognise that it has established a property interest is still unclear; in *Walsh* v *Lonsdale* itself, the contract was to create a legal estate in land, but the restrictive covenant, which is recognised as a property right only in equity, shows that equitable property rights are not limited to that situation. What is clear is that there is a category of equitable rights which is purely personal, although it is not clear what rights fall into that category.

1.4 The Judicature Acts 1873–1875

One of the main defects of the English system of justice up until the mid-19th century was that common law and equity were administered in separate courts. The Court of Chancery had no power to grant common law remedies, nor did the common law courts have power to grant equitable remedies. This meant that litigants might have to commence two separate actions in order to obtain justice.

Some slight improvement was introduced by the Common Law Procedure Act 1854, which gave the common law courts the power to award certain equitable remedies. The most useful of these was an order for specific delivery. Up to 1854, a common law court had no power to order a defendant to hand over property which did not belong to him. The court could only compel the defendant to pay a sum of money as damages for wrongful detention of the property. The 1854 Act allowed the court to compel the defendant to hand over the property itself.

On the Chancery side, the major defect was the inability of the Court of Chancery to award a sum of money as damages in lieu of granting an equitable remedy. The Chancery Amendment Act 1858 (Lord Cairns' Act) gave the Court of Chancery a discretion to award 'equitable' damages where no other remedy was appropriate.

The effect of these two Acts was to make it easier for a claimant to bring actions to a satisfactory conclusion in a single court. However, this did nothing to improve a second major defect. The main complaint about the courts was that they were agonisingly inefficient. The Court of Chancery in particular had a terrible reputation for delay and needless technicality (see, for example, the satirical picture painted in Charles Dickens' *Bleak House*).

Early alleviation and the enactment of the Judicature Acts 1873–1875
In spite of the 1854 and 1858 enactments, until 1873 common law and equity continued to be administered in different courts, equity being administered only in the

Court of Chancery. The legislation of 1873–5 provided that subsequently the High Court, though divided for convenience into divisions, would administer both systems. Section 25 of the 1873 Act, now replaced by the Supreme Court Act 1981, s. 49, provided that in a case of conflict the rules of equity were to prevail: this was effectively also the position before 1873.

The 1873–5 Acts were almost certainly intended to be procedural only, and that was probably their only effect—the generally held view is that they did not alter the substantive law.

There are those who argue, however, that as a result of the procedural fusion of the two systems, equity's freedom to develop has been fettered by virtue of its closer association with the common law. It is probably true that its original flexibility and rapid development have been largely curtailed, and that it is now almost as rigid and rule-bound as the common law. Of course it still continues to develop: see, for example, chapters 7 *et seq*. for developments in the application of resulting and constructive trusts to new situations. The doctrine of promissory estoppel has already been mentioned, and a great deal of attention is paid to its growing signifi- cance in the context of family homes in chapter 9. The pace of equitable develop- ment today, however, is little (if any) faster than that of the common law.

Equity, freedom, autonomy and the implications of fusion
At least three observations can be made about equity's continuing evolution and its relationship with law. First, it is probable that legislation, whose role and extent have increased greatly since 1875, today takes on many of the functions once taken on by equity; where the law appears rigid and unjust, legislation is now a possible and realistic answer. It may well be better suited to modern democratic conditions than the exercise of discretionary power by a court. Megaw LJ, for example, expressed this view in *Western Fish Products Ltd* v *Penwith District Council* [1981] 2 All ER 204, 218. Additionally, the nature of case law makes it inevitably uncertain as a method of law reform.

The second observation is that the curtailment of equitable discretion is explic- able as a simple consequence of the development of effective law reporting inevitably leading to precedents coming to be regarded as binding. Probably it has little to do with the 1873–5 legislation.

The third observation is that unfettered judicial discretion may nowadays be a bad thing; it is arguably better in a society in which expectations are relied upon to promote certainty, rather than discretion. Not only is the latter quality inherently unpredictable, but if administered by a court it is also retroactive. Its exercise can therefore cause considerable injustices, especially where commercial and property transactions are concerned.

Distinctiveness beyond fusion: equity and the forging of a separate identity
It has been suggested by Lord Diplock in *United Scientific Holdings Ltd* v *Burnley Borough Council* [1978] AC 904, that since 1875 law and equity should themselves be considered as being fused, and that it is no longer meaningful to speak as though rules of equity still retain a separate identity. Whether or not this is correct (and it is difficult to see it as being more than a semantic argument), there are practical reasons for continuing to treat the two systems separately. Rights which owe their derivation to equitable principles differ, as we saw in 1.4, from those which derive from the common law. Both types of right can exist simultaneously in a given

situation, and it is without doubt more convenient to continue to subject them to a separate analysis.

In *Walsh* v *Lonsdale* (1882) 20 Ch D 9, for example, the tenant had a periodic tenancy at common law, and a 17-year equitable lease. If the landlord had sold the land to a third party, the common law tenancy, as a right *in rem*, would certainly have bound the purchaser, whereas the equitable lease would only have done so on the basis of the notice doctrine discussed above. The conclusion that we would draw is that it is still sensible to consider common law and equity separately, even after both doctrines have been administered in the same court for 120 years.

1.5 The 1925 property legislation

The 1925 property legislation comprised the Law of Property Act, Settled Land Act, Land Charges Act and Land Registration Act. The Land Charges Act was amended and re-enacted in 1972. They are mainly of interest to land law students, but their effect on trusts and equitable doctrines has also been quite considerable.

The main purpose of the 1925 property legislation was to make it easier for people to sell or otherwise alienate land. The ability to alienate land easily had become increasingly necessary following the social upheavals brought about by the First World War, and much of the legislation was directed towards improving the conveyancing process.

Effect on equity and trusts
The main effect on equity and trusts of this legislation was twofold. In the first place, as a result of the 1925 legislation, many estates in land could exist only in equity. The key consequence of this was of course that they are no longer recognised at common law, and therefore no longer bind everyone in the world. Secondly, the notice doctrine, applying as it did to equitable titles and interests, was severely curtailed. The basic idea was to allow equitable estates in land to be overreached, in which case the purchaser did not need to be concerned with them. Lesser equitable interests were to be made subject to a registration requirement, with registration replacing notice, but with purchasers taking title free of unregistered interests. Conveyancers would clearly have liked to have seen the notice doctrine disappear entirely from land transactions following thereafter, but the policymakers of the time provided a system of transition in the form of the Land Charges Act 1925. Nevertheless, more recently, the Land Registration Act 2002 has proffered the aim of universal registration still further. In reality, however, even prior to 2002, the notice doctrine survived only to a relatively small extent.

1.5.1 Legal estates and notice of equitable estates and interests

The Law of Property Act 1925, s. 1, reduced the number of possible legal estates in land to two: those that are now commonly known as freehold (fee simple absolute in possession), which must take immediate effect; and leasehold (term of years absolute). Future freehold interests and life interests, as are commonly found in settlements, can exist only in equity, and concurrent interests in land take effect only behind what is now known as a trust of land (i.e., in equity). In this respect, the 1925 legislation increased the contribution of equity to the law of real property.

Broadly speaking, the 1925 legislation distinguishes between equitable estates in land (i.e., those akin to full ownership), and interests less than ownership. For most equitable interests, but not estates, the 1925 legislation replaced the notice doctrine with registration provisions; such interests today generally can be and have to be registered for protection against purchasers. The idea is that if the interest is regis- tered the purchaser has notice; if it is not registered, the purchaser is not bound whether or not he has notice in fact.

The details of the registration systems, provided for by the Land Charges and Land Registration Acts, are dealt with in land law textbooks and are beyond the scope of this book. Trusts lawyers need to be aware of them in as much as they reduce the importance of the notice doctrine.

1.5.2 The Land Registration Act 1925: making sense of the Law of Property Act 1925

Accompanying the reduction of legal estates possible in land, and the apparent increase in equitable ownership which would result inevitably from this, the long- term aim was for all titles and interests to be registered under the provisions of the Land Registration Act 1925. As far as interests are concerned, some are made over- riding interests under s. 70, in which case they bind purchasers irrespective of registration. Some were what is known as overreachable, but all others are regis- trable as minor interests. If they are not so registered, then by virtue of s. 20(1), they will not bind a transferee for valuable consideration. Since there are no other types of interest, there is no room under these provisions for the application of the notice doctrine, there being no requirement under s. 20(1) for either good faith or lack of notice.

It was not possible to register all titles immediately, however, and a transitional system was set up, the provisions of which are now to be found in the Land Charges Act 1972, which still applies to unregistered titles. Under these provisions, land charges on a list (in s. 2 of the Act) have to be registered for protection, registration constituting actual notice (under the Law of Property Act 1925, s. 198) and the effect of non-registration depending on the class of charge concerned: Land Charges Act 1972, s. 4. Estate contracts, for example (Class C(iv)), are void if not reg- istered against any purchaser, for money or money's worth, whether or not the pur- chaser has notice or even acts in good faith. An illustration of this can be seen in the very famous land law case of *Midland Bank Trust Co. Ltd* v *Green* [1981] AC 513, which involved a sham sale between husband and wife, intended specifically to defeat their son's valuable option to purchase a farm.

Unregistered land: notice doctrine lives on
The notice doctrine has not in fact been completely abolished for dealings involv- ing unregistered land. The courts have been unhappy with the logic of *Midland Bank Trust Co. Ltd* v *Green*, and have tended to interpret the Land Charges Act narrowly, thereby allowing the notice doctrine to survive, at least on the margins. For example, not all equitable interests are expressly covered by the Land Charges Act, for land to which the regime of that Act still applies. For those that are omitted

the old notice doctrine continues to apply, the courts having decisively rejected the argument that the Act should be interpreted widely, if possible, so as to cover all equitable interests that are not overreachable (see, e.g., *E.R. Ives Investments Ltd* v *High* [1967] 2 QB 379, and in particular, *Shiloh Spinners Ltd* v *Harding* [1973] AC 691, where Lord Wilberforce addressed this argument specifically). Equity has also developed new interests since 1925, such as that in *Binions* v *Evans* [1972] 1 Ch 359 (see 10.3), which are obviously not covered by the legislation.

Previous editions of this text have engaged in lengthy discussion about the 'gaps' left by the 1925 legislation and the continuing import of the notice doctrine on account of this. Appreciation of this can still be gleaned from consulting key texts in land law, but in terms of interactions of land transactions, this edition's interest is very much focused on the significance of such dealings with property for what they reveal about equity and its nature and operation. This must now be seen in light of the provisions of the Land Registration Act 2002. Again, the direction of this is not an analysis of the legislation as such, but a reflection on the impact it will have for the operation of equity.

1.5.3 The Land Registration Act 2002

A significant amount of the material originally located in this chapter has been cut in this edition on account of the Land Registration Act 2002. The chapter has retained some account of the origins of equity and its close ancestral roots with land ownership and title to land. It has also tried to explain that notwithstanding the system of land registration as envisioned by the 1925 property legislation, the doctrine of notice has remained active to some degree in land transactions. This was envisaged, and even intended in some respects by the protagonists of the 1925 reforms as a mechanism for transition. However, it is also the case that the doctrine of notice has also remained alive on account of matters which were not foreseen, let alone actually intended. Here unintended and unforeseen 'gaps' in the legislation have contributed to this, and on account of equity's own creativity, new interests and rights not even recognised in the early twentieth century have evolved over time.

The regime of the 2002 Act is to eliminate unregistered land, and at one level the system envisaged in its place, whereby the availability of as much information as possible through a system of registration, has long been within land lawyers' aspirational memory. At this level, it is not surprising that the new legislation has sought to clarify different interests in the land concerned, and make their prioritisation against one another more readily apparent, and thus to protect the positions of different parties (and especially third parties). In this respect, a *bona fide* purchaser for valuable consideration will concretise his position through a registered disposition, and as Oakley (*Parker and Mellows' The Modern Law of Trusts*) notes with some amusement this will ensure he is 'the Registrar's darling'. What is truly remarkable about the new scheme is the way in which registration does not simply report interests and entitlements, putting others on notice of them: the new regime actually creates these interests and entitlements.

Towards a scheme of universal registration: policy origins of the
Land Registration Act 2002
The origins of the Land Registration Act 2002 lie in the 1998 Law Commission Consultation Paper entitled 'Land Registration for the Twenty-First Century' (Law

Com. 254, Cmnd 4027), and the subsequent Report entitled 'Land Registration for the Twenty-First Century: A Conveyancing Revolution' (Law Com. 271, July 2001). This contained a draft Bill which became law in 2002.

In many key respects, the original spirit of the 1925 legislation remains unaltered, as reflected in the need to ensure (Law Com. 2001, para. 1.5) the integrity of the Register as 'a complete and accurate reflection of the state of the title of the land at any given time, so that it is possible to investigate title to land online', and one 'with the absolute minimum of additional enquiries and inspections'. At the heart of this cardinal principle lay the 'conveyancing revolution' with the intention that this could be achieved online. This would itself be achieved through creation of a system of electronic, paperless conveyancing.

Achieving 'complete and accurate reflection of the state of the title of the land at any given time'

The Law Commission was keen to ensure that in the proposed new system of conveyancing the role of overriding interests should be as restricted as possible: these should exist only where it would be unreasonable to expect registration, and many more interests should actually be capable of registration. It would also be the case that these interests would only actually be created upon, and actually *by* registration. Indeed, complimenting this, the introduction of electronic conveyancing would, according to the Law Commission, itself reduce the number of overriding interests as it will not be possible for many interests to exist at all unless they are registered. In focusing this attention on registerability not only as a record of entitlement, but actually as the means of achieving it, The Law Commission Report identified a number of interests which would be overriding (in para. 2.27 of the Report, including interests arising from actual occupation by virtue of beneficial interests under a trust or other informally arising estoppel etc.; easements and profits; local land charges and customary and public rights etc.)

Under the new scheme, four elements of registration would seek to achieve this 'complete and accurate reflection of the state of land at any given time'. The **Property Register** is a register of the property itself, containing descriptions of the land concerned (verbal descriptions and maps), as well as rights which its estate owners enjoy over other land; e.g., easements and covenants. The **Proprietorship Register** documents the name and address of the current registered proprietor, and also grades his or her title. This is classified in degrees of title: title which is absolute, arises in respect of freehold and leasehold; good leasehold in respect of leaseholds subject to any estate, right or interest 'affecting . . . the title of the lessor to grant the lease'; the title of possessory (awarded when applicants in possession of land cannot prove their right to possess any estate, interest or right through documentation) and 'qualified' title recorded where it appears to the Registrar that the title can be established only for a limited period or subject to certain reservations. There is also the **Charges Register**, which records the disadvantageous features of legal ownership of the estate concerned, and includes for example charges and notices of leases, restrictive covenants, easements and matrimonial home rights. Finally there is the **Land Certificate** which must be issued on first registration, and contains all the information recorded in the register. It may be issued to the proprietor or retained at the Land Registry, unless the land is mortgaged, in which case it *must* be lodged at the Registry, until the mortgage is cancelled. The land certificate must be updated 'on every registered transmission'. The way in which the land certificate provides the proprietor with a ready means of proving title means that its role is similar to that of old title deeds, and it is 'admissible' as evidence of the matters contained in it.

The rationale behind new land registration rules and their operation is clear, and the primacy of clarification, ready and reliable schemata for prioritisation of different interests, and particularly the protection of parties, is more than apparent. The mechanics behind this scheme of universal registration are less easy to identify, and happily for this course, they are less important, their significance being much more pertinent for a course in land law. It is the rationale and what it will achieve that is more significant for this consideration of equity and its role in dealings in land. Nevertheless, the mechanics and the rules' scope for success (as well as their feared limitations) are very interesting, especially in light of the envisioned role of electronic conveyancing in the pursuit of universal registration.

There is an excellent account of the new Act by Lizzie Cooke in [2002] 66 Conv 11–34, and the true value of this article for students of equity lies in the analysis given of the 'basics of registration', and then 'protection and priority'. But the healthy scepticism which is expressed about the technological dimensions of the much vaunted e-conveyancing, and the potential for 'gaps' in integrity apparently inherent in a world of paper-less transactions, also make very interesting reading.

 online resource centre

FURTHER READING

Todd [1981] Conv 347.

Glover and Todd [1995] 5 Web JCLI.

Todd [1996] 4 Web JCLI.

Jones and Palmer [1997] 1 Web JCLI.

Cooke [2002] 66 Conv 11–34.

Thompson [2002] Conv 174.

2

The nature of the trust: its operation and applications in society and economy

It will become apparent shortly that the trust is put to a variety of uses in English law. This is on account of its special feature of dividing ownership of property into distinct legal and equitable title. Just by way of reiteration of the key point made in chapter 1, a trust involves a division of the ownership of property. The settlor is the original owner of property and creates a trust by conveying legal title to it to one or more trustees, manifesting an intention that it is to be held on trust for one or more beneficiaries. The trustees of property become its owners at common law, and are given control of the property, but also responsibility for it.

What will become clear in due course is that this is the scenario which arises in what is known as an express trust. This is a trust which is expressly created by the settlor. It is important to understand this at this stage because trusts which are not expressly created by a settlor in this way can nevertheless still arise, and indeed they do. This is explained by reference to trusts which are constructive and ones which are resulting (and which are often associated with trusts which are 'implied' or arise from operation of law).

It is also important to understand that no trust is created unless legal title is actually vested in (i.e., given to) the trustee (as explained in chapter 3). This is so regardless of even very clear intentions of a settler to create a trust. Vesting legal title in the trustee is known as 'constituting' the trust, and there upon trustees come under equitable obligations enforceable by the beneficiaries.

2.1 An introduction to the basic nature of the trust and some key features

Through this basic model of an express trust, and by reference to the process of constituting the trust, it is possible to glean the essence of a trust. This will become even more apparent in the text below, in which the trust is compared with the features and operation of other civil law concepts arising from contract. For present purposes, it is sufficient to note that:

- It is not necessary for settlors, trustees and beneficiaries to be different people.

A settlor can validly constitute a trust by declaring *himself* trustee of his own property, on behalf of one or more beneficiaries. This is discussed in detail in chapter 3. The settlor may be a beneficiary, and will always be in the case of a resulting trust (see chapter 7). A trustee may be the beneficiary, or one of a number of beneficiaries. Settlors can even be trustees *and* beneficiaries, as illustrated in the case study of the family home.

- The property subject to, and thus settled *on trust* can include an equitable interest.

In other words a beneficiary under a trust may constitute a further trust of his equitable interest, thereby creating a sub-trust. Sub-trusts are common in tax-avoiding settlements. The beneficiary under the sub-trust can himself repeat the process, creating a further sub-trust, and there is no limit to the number of times this process may be repeated.

- The application of the trust to purposes which are charitable.

The illustrations and points which have been made up to now in this chapter relate to trusts which are known as 'private' trusts. This means that they are privately created trusts, the defining term for which is trusts which are 'non-charitable'. It will become apparent that charitable trusts are created alongside private trusts, but they have different features and are subject to different rules. A brief reference will be made to this below in this chapter, but the substantive law relating to charitable trusts is examined once this text's coverage of the essential features and operation of **non-charitable private** trusts is completed. Prior to the consideration given to charitable trusts (which is located in chapters 12–14), it is sufficient to say that in a charitable trust there may be no true beneficiaries at all. Instead, these arrangements are enforced by the Attorney-General, and their validity *as* charitable trusts is determined by special rules which apply only to charitable trusts (all of which will be explained in chapters 12–14).

- The creation of private trusts for purposes rather than beneficiaries.

The example of the private trust provided up to this point, where property is settled on trust for a beneficiary, assumes that the beneficiary has a full equitable interest in the property concerned and there are no restrictions on the use to which can be made of this property. However, it will become clear in chapter 4 that it may be possible to create what are known as private (i.e., non-charitable) *purpose* trusts, benefiting a defined group of people. Arguably, these people are not true beneficiaries, because they are constrained to use the property for a particular purpose. An example might be a conveyance of land to A and B, in trust to be used as a football pitch for the employees of X Ltd. The employees are arguably not true beneficiaries, because they cannot use the land in any way they wish. Nevertheless, the trust is probably valid, because in spite of this they have sufficient interest in the property to be able to enforce the equitable obligations owed by the trustees. In this broad 'alternative' non-charitable trust scenario there may also be an anomalous category of unenforceable trusts, which do, nevertheless, share other characteristics of ordinary trusts. These arrangements, which are also considered in chapter 4, seem to be limited to trusts for the benefit of animals and the maintenance of tombs, and should be regarded as exceptional.

Before proceeding with the substantive analysis of the law relating to trusts—both non-charitable and also charitable—there is now the opportunity to check understanding of these core ideas by taking a closer look at *why* trusts are created and *who* creates them.

2.2 Introducing different types of trust: express, implied, resulting, and constructive trusts explained

It was suggested above that many of the trusts which will be encountered in this text will be express trusts. This type of arrangement—where a trust arises from the express wishes of a settlor to settle property on trust—is easiest to understand, and it is used as a starting point to explain and illustrate the creation and operation of trusts more generally. The 'express trust' scenario is where the settlor has expressed an intention to set up a trust, but reference was also made to the way in which there are other types of trust which need explaining and illuminating. In one respect this is key to understanding the vast number of different uses to which the trust is being put in current times, and to which it could also be potentially applied, because this does require appreciation of trusts which are resulting and constructive. It is also the case that, as it will become apparent in chapter 5, more technically, these latter types of trust are not subject to the same formality requirements which express trusts must meet in order to be valid. In other words, it is important to understand that there are different types of trust to consider. Thus, in addition to the way in which a trust can be created expressly by a settlor, note must be made of the way in which private (i.e., non-charitable trusts) can also be:

(i) *Constructive*. A *constructive trust* will arise in a number of different factual situations which will often appear to be diverse. However, all constructive trusts have in common that they will arise where a trust is imposed by the courts irrespective of the intention of the owner (of what becomes the 'trust property'), and in this respect they can be said to arise from the operation of law.

(ii) *Resulting trusts* are also found in a diverse variety of factual situations, but are more difficult to pin down than constructive trusts which are essentially (with limited exception) impositions of trusteeship in unconscionable situations. In seeking to understand resulting trusts, it is helpful to remember that all resulting trusts do have one element in common. Although legal title is vested in a trustee, the settlor and the beneficiary are actually the same person. In understanding how this transpires, it will do so for two reasons: for present purposes, this is explained in a very simple manner, in anticipation of fuller consideration given in chapters 7 *et seq*. Broadly (and with emphasis on simplicity at this introductory stage), this will occur because the settlor has tried to create a trust in favour of a third-party beneficiary, and although legal title has been transferred from him, he has failed to divest himself of equitable interest in the property. Here, equitable title never leaves him. Alternatively, a resulting trust will arise where property has been divested from him, but it is for some reason later returned back to him.

Both constructive and resulting trusts require far more consideration than this very basic introduction is intended to give. Chapter 7 offers an introduction to constructive and resulting trusts by way of introducing these less 'formal' (in terms of creation) trusts, and thereafter their essential characteristics and operational features. Thereafter, through chapters 8, 9, 10 and 11, the workings of resulting and constructive trusts will be explored through discussions of: the ways in which associations without legal personality can hold property; pension funds; trusts arising from cohabitation; secret trusts, and equitable fraud. Thereafter, the materials in chapters 15, 18 and 19 include discussions of the application of constructive trusts to liabilities which arise both for fiduciaries, and also strangers to a trust for unauthorised profits which are made from trust property, or the receipt of trust property which has been applied in breach of trust.

2.2.1 Other terminology used in explaining classifications of trusts

It will also become apparent from examining sources of trusts law itself and especially academic writings, that a vast array of terminology can be used to help in the classification of trusts.

- References made to EXPRESS trusts as being EXECUTED or EXECUTORY.

Following on from the way in which, much as it sounds, an express trust arises where a settlor expressly settles property on trust for a beneficiary or beneficiaries, in some cases and commentaries of academics reference will be made to trusts which are 'executed' and ones which are 'executory'. This book does not attach any significance to this terminology beyond initially explaining it at this introductory point. Essentially the difference between these terms is that while in an executed trust the settlor has made clear the interests which are to be taken by the beneficiaries, in an executory trust scenario, defining the beneficial interests under the trust does not become clear until a further document is executed. In this latter situation, a valid trust is created, but it remains executory until the further 'instructions' are executed. This distinction does not really impact on this text's analysis at all, and it remains only to note that stricter rules of construction apply to executed trusts than to ones which are executory: this is because in the latter scenario the courts are concerned with more 'open' questions relating to ascertaining a settlor's true intentions, in absence of specific directions on the application of property to beneficiaries.

- References to trusts which are IMPLIED trusts.

Reference is made by a number of writers to *implied* trusts to explain the arrangement which arises where the settlor's intention to create a trust is not expressed as such but can instead be inferred either from his words, or even conduct. Opinion is divided on whether this categorisation serves useful purpose. At one level it is a convenient and accurate term for trusts which are not created with express words, but equally it will become apparent that words (which do not actually say 'I declare that') are capable of amounting to an express trust on account that this is what settlers intended to do. In this manner, reference to an 'implied trust' might be seen as more appropriate where express words are not used, but it is not obvious that this serves a purpose which could not be achieved by using the terminology of resulting or constructive trust.

- References made to trusts which are 'BARE trusts'.

Bare or 'simple' trusts are said to arise when property is held by a trustee, in trust for an adult beneficiary with an interest in property which is described as *absolute*. This pertains to situations where, essentially, the beneficiary may at any time request that legal title is conveyed to him, and in which upon having this request the trustee must comply with it. In circumstances where a trustee must convey legal title to the beneficiary upon his request, it is perhaps not surprising that the trustee of a 'bare' trust is not subjected to the duties relating to trusteeship which pertain to other 'special' trusts. A common illustration of this scenario is where a solicitor acts on behalf of a client. In a number of transactions, most commonly the purchase of a domestic dwelling house, a solicitor will hold money on behalf of a client in anticipation of completion; and upon completion, the client will instruct the solicitor to pay over moneys falling due, and the solicitor must do so. In this scenario, a bare trust arises *ab initio* on account that property is given to a trustee to hold on behalf of its original owner. It can also arise when at sometime after its creation, a trust *becomes* a bare one. This can be illustrated by a trust which confers a life interest in property to A, and upon A's death, passes to B absolutely: upon A's death, B becomes entitled to the property *absolutely*, and the trustee must convey legal title to B upon his request.

2.3 Circumstances in which trusts are created

Trusts arise in many everyday situations, which cover widely differing circumstances. What will become clear is that the basic nature of the trust is thus widely adaptable to a number of different social and economic scenarios. Although principles which apply to each variety of trust are similar rather than identical, in many respects it is remarkable just how much variety can be derived from the same basic concept.

2.3.1 Trusts relating to family arrangements

2.3.1.1 *Family settlement arrangements*

The purpose of many express trusts (i.e., those which are deliberately created by a settlor) is the retention of wealth by the wealthy. This is what will be seen to underpin many of the private trusts which are encountered in this text which arise today, and it was ever thus. The modern trust and the concomitant entitlements of beneficiaries and duties of trustees, have grown up around family settlements which have over centuries sought to tie up wealth within a family, and were drafted to minimise both free disposal within the family itself and also to minimise exposure to taxation. These arrangements can be made by will, but it can be advantageous from a taxation viewpoint for them to be constituted during the life of the settlor (i.e., *inter vivos*). Although they were more important historically than they are today, family settlements are still common, and frequently give rise to litigation. It is not, of course, the function of this book to comment on the desirability or otherwise of these schemes. This is a political question, on which views may validly differ. Only the legal consequences are appropriate for discussion here.

Administration of family trusts

The trustees may be members of the family, and in the early days of such settlements often were. They may be solicitors who are familiar with the family business. Neither of these appointments is considered by the courts to be very desirable, however, because of the likelihood of conflicts of interest where the trustee is too closely connected to, or involved with, the beneficiaries. There is even a possibility of fraud, especially where family members are constituted trustees. So in the rare cases where the court has to appoint trustees (say, where the existing trustees fail to carry out their duties—see further chapters 4 and 15), family members or solicitors are unlikely candidates. It was probably because the modern law of trusts largely developed at a time when this sort of trust was exceedingly common, and when the trustees were normally family members, that the nature of trustees' duties (on which, see chapters 15, 16 and 18) is so stringent.

Family trusts may also be administered by the trustee and executor departments of banks. Proper professional administration can be of the greatest importance if tax benefits are to be maximised. Banks charge quite heavily for taking on these duties, by way of a charging clause that they insist on putting into the trust instrument. The charges are therefore usually fixed at the outset, and do not depend on how the trust is administered. This, as we shall see, will be very important when we come to consider conflicts of interest in chapter 15.

The terminology relating to settlements will arise again throughout the book. All settlements involve the creation of successions of interests, and the simplest form would be where A leaves property to B for life and thereafter for C. B is the *life tenant*, and is usually entitled to the immediate income from the property. He is sometimes referred to as an income beneficiary. C is entitled in remainder. He is the *remainder-man*, sometimes referred to as a capital beneficiary.

In this case the extent of C's interest is known at the outset, and so it is a *vested* interest. Suppose, on the other hand, the gift is to B for life and then to the first of C, D and E to marry. It is unknown yet which will marry first, and the interests of C, D and E are said to be contingent. More is made of this distinction in chapter 6.

In citations of cases 'ST' indicates a settlement trust and 'WT' a will trust.

2.3.1.2 *Trusts arising from marriage or cohabitation*

Also located within the broad setting of 'family property' are trusts arising from marriage, or from cohabitation of a family home. However, these arrangements are perhaps less overtly concerned with wealth and more with determining issues of ownership of a family home, either because the relationship between the parties has broken down, or a third party acquires an interest in the property (e.g., the position of a financial lender who has a charge over the property). It is also the case that the nature of the trust arrangement itself in these scenarios can be quite different from the express creation of a trust as illuminated above. While some trusts relating to family homes will be expressly created, trusts which are resulting and constructive trusts will often arise in these (often) informal family arrangements. A common example of such a situation, and the operation of a trust within it is where a wife or female cohabitee (X) provides money towards the purchase of a home, which, though intended to be jointly occupied, is conveyed into the name of the man alone (Y). Y holds X's interest in the home on resulting trust, so that both parties share equitable title. Or in circumstances where property is legally vested in Y alone, but Y makes a representation to X that the home is 'both of theirs', then Y can be deemed to hold legal title as a constructive trustee on trust for both himself and X. The 'workings' of such an arrangement are explored fully in chapter 9's consideration of the family home. This will also explain the growing significance of proprietary estoppel in disputes relating to shared homes.

2.3.1.3 *Trusts and succession*

Closely related to maintaining familial wealth, and determinations of the ownership of a family home are questions relating to succession. Trusts do have a limited role to play in succession, but the main function of this section is to explain terms which will be used later in various parts of the book.

When a person dies, the legal and beneficial entitlement to all his property passes to his 'personal representatives'. If he made a will in which he appointed specific persons to be his personal representatives, they are known as his 'executors', and their first task is to obtain probate of the will (i.e., have the will registered by the registrar). Thereafter, their duty is to meet the debts and funeral expenses of the deceased out of his property, and then to distribute the rest in accordance with the instructions given in the will.

Trusts, succession and intestacy
When a person dies intestate (i.e., without making a will), a statutory scheme provided by the Administration of Estates Act 1925 comes into play. This attempts to give effect to what most people are assumed to intend to happen to their property after their deaths, by providing first for any widow or widower, then for children and so on, so that the closest relations obtain the benefits which the deceased would probably have wished for them. The scheme extends outwards, so that if the deceased has no close relatives, his more distant relations will benefit. If he has no relations at all, the property passes to the Crown.

Since there is no will, his personal representatives will not be executors, but 'administrators' (i.e., the persons who have obtained a grant entitling them to administer the estate). These will usually be the persons who are entitled to the property. If the deceased left a widow, she is entitled to a grant of administration, permitting her to distribute the property; if there is no widow, the right passes to the children, and so on.

The distinction between executors and administrators was material to the discussion in *Re Gonin* [1979] Ch 16 (see chapter 3).

Trustees, executors and personal representatives
Whether the personal representatives are executors of a will or administrators on intestacy, their duties are the same, and many of the rules which apply to trustees (see chapters 14–16) apply also to them. They hold their office for life, but the active duties are usually completed within one or two years. They must collect in all the deceased's assets, pay all debts and expenses, and then distribute the property either in accordance with the terms of the will or the statutory scheme, as the case may be.

Gifts, property and the 'residuary legatee'
Wills commonly provide for specific gifts to relatives or friends. A gift of land is called a 'devise', and its recipient a 'devisee'; a gift of personal property, including money, is a 'legacy', and its recipient a 'legatee'. Property which is not specifically

disposed of by will is called 'the residue', and the entitled person(s) the 'residuary legatee(s)'. If a specific gift fails for any reason (possible reasons appear in chapter 4), it is added to the residue. In practice, this often comprises the bulk of the property, as it is usual to provide small specific gifts to selected friends and relatives, and simply leave the rest to the person whom one most desires to benefit.

Trusts arising on death
Trusts may arise on a death, either because the will specifies that some property is to be held on trust, or because the intended recipient is under age 18, so that the legal title must be held for her until she reaches that age. Where trusts are deliberately created, it is usual to name the persons who are to act as trustees, and when the executors have completed their administration, they must transfer that property to the trustees. Often, the same persons will be named as both executors and trustees, and will continue to hold the legal title in their new capacity.

Death, the administration of property and the role of executors
It is important to appreciate that the legatees, devisees, and beneficiaries under any trust created by the will have no beneficial interest in that property until such time as the executors appropriate (i.e., earmark) property to meet the gifts or trusts created by the will. What they have is merely a right to demand the proper administration of the estate by the executors. Similarly, persons entitled on an intestacy have no beneficial interest in the property until the administrators have paid off all the liabilities affecting the deceased's property and prepared their accounts, showing what is available for those persons. For the sake of convenience, the persons entitled under an intestacy are referred to as the 'next-of-kin' rather than legatees, etc.

It is possible for a partial intestacy to occur, for example, where the deceased failed to specify in his will who the residuary legatee is to be, or where the residuary gift fails. In such a case, the property will pass to the next-of-kin, as provided by the statutory scheme.

2.3.2 Trusts arising in personal asset maintenance and management

There are also a number of other trusts which are associated with personal asset *maintenance* but which signal their application outside the context of family wealth and even the family home. These include:

- Trusts relating to share holdings.

Shares are often owned out-and-out by the shareholder, but they may also be held by nominees. This practice is most common in holdings of shares in public, rather than private companies, and in this scenario, the nominee is often a bank. In that case the legal estate is held by the nominee in trust for the shareholder. One reason for this might be if it is intended that the trustee should manage the portfolio, as would be the case, for example, with a unit trust.

- Trusts arising from pensions provision.

The rise of pension funds and the need to create a workable legal framework for the operation and safe-guarding of pension assets has brought the trust into prominence in respect of one of the biggest socio-economic issues of current times. The attractiveness of the trust arrangement was crucially recognised in the Report of

Sir Roy Goode's *Pension Law Review Committee* (1993, Cmnd 2342). The Committee's recommendations resulted in the passage of the Pensions Act 1995. The 1995 Act sought to reflect the importance of rigorous regulation and supervision of pension schemes, and one of its principal tenets was its accommodation of the reality that the beneficiaries under a pension scheme differed from under the normal trust arrangement; indeed, the entitlement of beneficiaries under a pension scheme could be seen to arise from contractual origins (provided by their contracts of employment). This aside, the trust was deemed best able to promote the expedient and safe use of such schemes, subject to some modification of its 'normal' operations from specific pensions legislation.

The issue of pensions and their operation in contemporary society is one of the most important socio-economic issues of today. With the combination of declining birth-rate, longer life expectancy and a broader global context signalling the dismantling of the welfare state, the focus on privately-funded pensions outside state provision have come increasingly to the fore. Today's issues arise very strongly from the need to plan for tomorrow, and private pension schemes (occupational and otherwise) are very much concerned with planned long-term personal asset management. In this respect, while the trust's traditional associations are strongly with wealth and its preservation, it is nevertheless significant that it is these age-old principles which are envisioned as the blueprint for this personal asset management into the twenty-first century. This is a testament to the trust's versatility, adaptability, and also to its endurance. This is so notwithstanding that demonstrating how pension funds are modelled on the trust instrument will reveal some crucial departures from 'ordinary' trust principles, as it will become clear in chapter 8.

- Trusts arising from personal insolvency.

The protective trust is a special type of trust that was developed as a method of protecting family property against the consequences of the family falling into debt. Generally speaking, any property owned by a debtor can be taken to satisfy his creditors, and in the extreme event of bankruptcy, all of the debtor's property becomes vested in his trustee in bankruptcy, including of course any interest under a family settlement.

Trusts for protection, bankruptcy and the significance of the nineteenth century
In the nineteenth century, when family settlements were commoner than today, such an interest would usually be a life interest, and where improvidence was feared, this interest might be made determinable upon the bankruptcy or attempted alienation of the interest on the part of its owner. At first, the practice was to provide for a gift over to some other member of the family if the life interest was thus brought to an end, but by the latter part of the nineteenth century a more satisfactory solution was discovered, and today a protective trust consists of a determinable life interest, the determination of which brings into play a discretionary trust in favour of the former life tenant, his spouse and children (if any), and ultimately his next-of-kin who would inherit in the event of his death.

The protective trust and its operation in bankruptcy
The obvious advantages are that on the bankruptcy or alienation of the debtor's property the interest in the trust property simply ceases to exist, and cannot be claimed by creditors or the trustees in bankruptcy. The property itself remains in the hands of

the trustees who can distribute the income as they see fit in the circumstances. If the reason for the determination is the actual indebtedness of the former life tenant, it would clearly be pointless to make payments to him, as the creditors could then seize the money, but the lifestyle of the family can be maintained by paying the income instead to the wife, or directly to those who supply his needs, since they can apply it for the 'use and benefit' of the former life tenant without placing money directly into his hands. It is not even necessary to set out in express terms the nature of the trusts, since s. 33 of the Trustee Act 1925 provides a model form which can be invoked simply by directing that the property shall be held on 'protective trusts' for the benefit of the person who is to be the life tenant (called 'the principal beneficiary' in the section).

Limitations of the protective trust

There are two main limitations. First, it is not possible to settle property upon oneself via such trusts, and protective trusts would usually be created by the parent of the principal beneficiary on his behalf. Second, the life interest must be made *determinable* upon the relevant event—that is, so defined that it ends naturally on the happening of the event. If, on the other hand, it is made subject to a *condition subsequent*, that condition may be void as a device to defeat one's creditors. The difference is purely one of language, and is devoid of moral principle.

Bankruptcy and the assets available to creditors: the significance of the family home

The references made to the family home in this context do of course relate to the strong possibility that in the event of bankruptcy, a trustee in bankruptcy is likely to want to seek the sale of the family home in order to satisfy the claims of creditors. And in this light, traditionally it was the position that if a trustee in bankruptcy wishes to pursue this, it is only in exceptional circumstances (see, for example, *Re Solomon* [1967] Ch 573 *and Re Lowrie* [1981] 3 All ER 353) that he will not be able to do so. It is of course possible to analyse this contentious position of the family home as a reflection of deeply entrenched retributionist ideas which have associated bankruptcy with misconduct, or at the very least irresponsibility and improvidence, rather than *misfortune*, since Victorian times. It might instead be seen more simply as part of the 'economic reality' of creditor entitlement to be paid for the money he has advanced to the debtor.

In some respects, the Insolvency Act 1986—where the law relating to personal insolvency is largely located, alongside that of corporate insolvency—entrenched further associations of indebtedness with irresponsibility, through contending that for some bankruptcy might represent 'an easy solution for those who can bear with equanimity the stigma of their own failure' (Sir Kenneth Cork, see below). However, the provisions of s. 335A state that where an application for sale of a home is made, the court shall make an order which it considers just and reasonable, having regard to a number of factors relating to the family home's 'own claim to protection', as alluded to in the judgment of Megarry V-C in *Re Bailey* [1977] 1 WLR 278.

Predictably, the provisions focus on the interests of the bankrupt's creditors, who are identified in s. 335A(a). In addition, where the proposed sale includes a dwelling house which 'is or has been the home of the bankrupt or the bankrupt's spouse or former spouse', the provisions of s. 335A(b) determine that the court's calculus of just and reasonable involves it having regard to a number of factors. These factors located in s. 335A(b) relate to (i) the **conduct** of the spouse or former spouse, so far as contributing to the bankruptcy; (ii) the **needs and financial resources** of the spouse or former spouse; and (iii) the **needs of any children**. In these circumstances, the court will also have regard to (c) all the circumstances of the case **other than the needs of the bankrupt**.

This is hardly a protection charter, though, because where an application for sale is made after one year following the vesting of a bankrupt's property in the trustee in bankruptcy, the assumption will be made that the interests of creditors do outweigh all other 'competing' considerations, apart from those which reflect 'exceptional circumstances' (which itself appears to reflect the position prior to the 1986 Act). Thus this is a mechanism for *delay* rather than *protection* in many respects, but greater *delay* (and arguably also even *protection*) of a bankrupt's property does appear to flow from the Enterprise Act 2002. In spirit and intendment, this enactment signalled a strongly changed emphasis across bankruptcy law, by seeking to align the consequences of bankruptcy (essentially, disqualification as a bankrupt and attendant impotencies) and prospects for rehabilitation to degrees to which a bankrupt could be deemed to have contributed to his bankruptcy (see G. Wilson and S. Wilson (2001) *JCLS*, 211–33). In relation to a bankrupt's family home, the Enterprise Act (which amends the Insolvency Act 1986) provides that where the trustee in bankruptcy has not sold the property or applied for an order of possession within three years of the date of the bankruptcy, the property reverts to the bankrupt, and is thus not part of the estate which can be applied to creditors' claims.

2.3.3 **Trusts arising in commercial arrangements**

In one respect, the growing significance of trusts law outside its traditional roots in family arrangements, and its increasing applications in commerce and business activity and practice is alluded to later in this chapter, by looking at trusts and loan arrangements which derive from the law of contract. On another level, the way in which entrepreneurial activity is politically at centre-stage is evident from the attention paid to the new Companies Act 2006, whilst it was before Parliament. Along with changes in law which have already been made to e-commerce and corporate insolvency, and the emphasis given to business fraud within the genesis of the Fraud Act 2006, the reforms in company law point to the New Labour Government's political economy being strongly oriented towards promoting— in the words of Gordon Brown MP, Chancellor of the Exchequer, in 1999—a 'pro-enterprise and pro-opportunity Britain'.

The current discourses on company law, along with those underpinning the Enterprise Act's new provisions for personal and corporate insolvency, is that entrepreneurial activity is itself defined by taking risks. Risk-taking is at the heart of a healthy wealth-creating economy, but even legitimate and appropriate risk-taking may not 'pay off', and in these circumstances business failure is a possibility. In the event of a corporate insolvency (the legal term given to an incorporated business's inability to pay its debts) all business assets will become available for satisfying the claims of its creditors. In a context where there is likely to be a disparity between assets which are available and claims made in respect of them, the priority of claims will be determined by statute. Indeed, in 1982 the Report of Sir Kenneth Cork's *Committee on Insolvency Law and Practice* (Cmnd 8558) proposed that one of the core aims of modern insolvency law must be to ensure a 'workable system of clear priorities and ranking amongst creditors'. Accordingly, this system is now found in the Insolvency Act 1986 as amended by the Enterprise Act 2002, and all assets of a business will become subject to this statutory system of priorities.

Loans, security and the ordinary consequences of corporate insolvency
This position of business assets and business creditors in the event of an insolvency illustrates one very clear importation of trust principles into commercial dealings. The discussion on *Quistclose* trusts which occurs shortly, shows how by this mechanism money is advanced by a creditor to a borrower, but is so subject to a trust. This means that the property never becomes part of a business's assets, and thus it will not form part of what becomes available for creditors *generally* in the event of insolvency. Thus, this is a mechanism by which a *particular* creditor can protect his own position viz. what would otherwise be competing claims.

Thus, the protection of credit advanced, which can be achieved through making it subject to a trust, might in many respects be regarded as a most suitable response to the inevitable exigencies of business: businesses do fail, even where practices are sound and responsible, and in these circumstances ordinary unsecured creditors (i.e., those who make advances without taking security) will often lose out. This general attractiveness of a trust arrangement might increase still further in light of changes which have been made to the position of certain creditors in the Enterprise Act 2002, and especially that of a *secured* creditor known as a 'floating charge' holder.

Loans, trusts and insolvency: the significance of the Enterprise Act 2002
In the operation of such a charge, a creditor will take as security for his loan what is known as a 'floating charge' over a company's more 'fluid' assets, such as 'stock-in-trade'. This can be a very attractive arrangement for companies because it allows them to deal freely with their 'fluid' assets, until they become fixed by 'crystallisation', which will be triggered by a number of possible events, including actual or imminent insolvency. Upon crystallisation, the holder of such a charge would then commonly appoint an administrative receiver for the purposes of realising his security. However, the Enterprise Act's provisions have now made the traditional position of a floating charge holder less attractive in two distinct ways. This is on account of the Act's primary 'twin' objectives: first, to try to promote the rescue of struggling companies where this is possible, and second, to improve the position of unsecured creditors where this is not.

The Act now prevents the holder of a floating charge from appointing an administrative receiver, whom (by way of recap) he would engage in order to realise his own security. This is so as to enhance a failing company's prospects of being rescued; either through a voluntary arrangement (with creditors) or administration (in which an appointed administrator puts together a 'rescue package' to try to save the company from insolvent liquidation). It is also the case that the floating charge holder's traditional position in the statutory ranking of creditors upon insolvency (as determined in the Insolvency Act 1986) has changed on account of the 2002 Act. While holders of floating charges still rank above 'general creditors of the company', it is also the case that prior to being paid under the new statutory scheme, a 'prescribed proportion' is now taken from them, and applied to helping to meet the claims of unsecured creditors. According to s. 176A of the Insolvency Act 1986 (inserted by the Enterprise Act) floating charge holders will only be paid the amount which 'exceeds the amount required for the satisfaction of unsecured creditors', which is effectively the amount remaining after the 'prescribed proportion' has been removed.

The trust as the new security in commercial transactions?
From the documentation which accompanied the Enterprise Act, this is actually quite a complex calculation process, and certainly beyond the scope of this text. But it is worth noting that the *Enterprise Act Evaluation Planning Paper* (published in 2003 by the Insolvency Service) does suggest that the amount set aside for unsecured creditors in this manner can be up to £600,000. This measure operates unless it is felt that 'the cost of making a distribution to unsecured creditors would be disproportionate to the benefits', which is recognition that notwithstanding the *spirit* of these reforms, pursuing this method of redistribution in favour of unsecured creditors may be uneconomic in some circumstances. However, the *Evaluation's* invitation for consultation on the proposed operation of these 'prescribed part' provisions does intimate recognition of inherent difficulties, and especially ones relating to potential scope of operation. Although it does not express this quite so directly, the *Evaluation* is concerned to determine whether these provisions may be going too far, and may operate beyond helping to protect unsecured creditors.

It is not difficult to see these provisions as ones which are helping to convert unsecured creditors into secured creditors at the expense of those who *do* seek to protect themselves by security for their loans. The outcomes of this 'evaluation' remain to be seen, but it is not difficult to imagine that floating charges might well become far less attractive for lenders. In one respect this might well diminish what is an important 'life-line' for struggling businesses, but from the perspective of lenders *themselves*, they are likely to be looking at other possibilities for securing their advances. In these conditions, it may be that creditors will increasingly look towards the trust as a mechanism which provides security through its protection of assets from the consequences of a debtor's insolvency.

Commercial trusts and ordinary trust principles?
It is clear at one level that trusts which protect loans made to businesses do so on account of the features which underpin the operation of all trusts; these are, of course, the division of title to property into legal and beneficial ownership, coupled with the intention of the owner of property that it should be subject to the trust. And even prior to the changes introduced by the Enterprise Act 2002 which, it is suggested, might well heighten the trust's attractiveness in commercial transactions, a number of academic commentators have observed the growing 'commercial applications of trusts'. It is also the case that the Law Commission has commented on the growing use of trusts in the sphere of commercial dealings, in its recent *Report on Trustee Exemption Clauses* (considered in chapter 18; for this point, see especially para. 6.80). However, in making this observation, the Law Commission also highlighted some important features which distinguish so-called 'commercial trusts' from those arrangements otherwise made outside the domain of commercial dealings. The Law Commission remarked that settlors in such arrangements tend to be market equals of trustees, and are thus well versed in the needs of business and the risks which pertain to commercial transactions, and the technical operation of trusts (para. 6.81). It was also observed (in para. 6.82) that

where the settlor acts in the course of a business (which would cover the majority of corporate settlors and some individuals) it will only be in very unusual circumstances that the transaction being entered into is of a type with which his is not familiar.

2.3.4 **Charities, trade unions and unincorporated associations**

Trusts can also be used to enable property to be held for the benefit of people who for some reason cannot hold it themselves. Interestingly, some of the earliest uses made of the trust instrument were for Franciscan friars for this very purpose. Incorporated bodies, such as companies, which are incorporated under the Companies Acts, and universities, which are incorporated by charter, have legal personality, and can therefore hold property themselves. So there is no need, for example, for treasurers or directors to hold the property on their behalf as trustees, and normally they do not. As we shall see, however, they may owe fiduciary duties, which are akin to those of trustees.

Charities (on which see chapters 12, 13, and 14) can also be incorporated, in which case they too may hold property in their own right. If they do so, the courts are undecided whether they hold absolutely, subject to the articles of association under the Companies Acts, or whether they are held on trust for charitable purposes. We will come upon purpose trusts again in chapter 4, and we shall see that they are rather unusual in that there are no true beneficiaries.

Not all charities are incorporated, however. Unincorporated bodies have no legal personality, and cannot hold property themselves. In the case of unincorporated charities, the property is held by trustees, who are often individuals, for the purposes of the charity. Donations to charity therefore commonly give rise to trusts.

2.3.4.1 *Trusts and non-charitable associations*

A trust can also, in theory, be a method of enabling property to be held by Members' clubs, which are also unincorporated. Nominated trustees (who would usually be officers of the club) could hold the property on trust for the members. This gives rise to no difficulties as long as the membership is fixed, or the club is of short duration (e.g., a club which is geared to a specific, one-off event). Most clubs have a fluctuating membership, however, and in this case, as we shall see, the trust solution can give rise to perpetuity problems, because the interests of future members may not vest until outside the perpetuity period (on which, see further chapter 6). This is not a problem that arises in the case of charities, because they are exempt from the perpetuity rules.

Unincorporated societies: the significance of the trust (and the contract)
The usual analysis for Members' clubs is not based on the trust, therefore. The usual analysis is that the present members hold the club property absolutely, subject to their *contractual* rights and duties arising from membership. These may, for example, prevent them taking their share of the club property for themselves on resignation, or at any other time. They may allow the officers to decide how the property is to be used. If property is held by officers, they will hold it as agents of the members, not as trustees.

Trade unions are in a peculiar (and unique) position, being regarded as unincorporated for most purposes, though sharing some of the features of corporate bodies.

Section 10 of the Trade Union and Labour Relations (Consolidation) Act 1992 (re-enacting earlier legislation) prevents them from being corporate entities, but also provides that the trustees of a union hold on trust *for the union itself*, not for the members. So a union, unlike other unincorporated bodies, can be an equitable owner, though not a legal owner of property. Another feature of unions is that the trustees are nominal owners of the property only, and have no significant discretion, because rule books nearly always provide that they act under the directions of the executive.

2.4 **Trusts distinguished from similar common law concepts**

Working from the peculiarities of two different types of ownership, we can see quite clearly that the trust, where ownership is separated into ownership at law and that which subsists in equity, interfaces the twin systems (and until recently jurisdictions) of equity and law. However, this is a long way from being able to point to exactly what a trust is and indeed what it does. It is true that the trust will give a non-legal owner enforceable rights in respect of the trust property, but while its function is clear enough and perhaps easy to understand, a trust isn't always easy to define. Part of the reason for this is that the trust is an extremely flexible instrument, as the examples in figure 2.1 (on p. 46) illustrate.

This is, of course, connected directly to the attention which has already been drawn to the use which is made of trusts, across widely differing social and economic situations, of which the examples given above are *illustrative* but by no means exhaustive. It is of course the case that understanding *what* a trust *is* is in many ways a prelude to understanding how it is used, and in many respects it would be appropriate to have considered this more fully before looking at common uses made of the trust. However, it is also the case that appreciating how trusts are used might help us to understand more about what, fundamentally, a trust *is*. The trust is not easy to 'pin down' in many respects, and this is complicated further by the way in which other wholly different legal devices are applied to similar situations to those where trusts are to be found. For example, we have already seen that Members' clubs are normally based on contract not trust, but that the property of charities which are unincorporated is held by trustees. It is also the case that while banks may be trustees if they are specifically constituted as such, ordinary accounts create only a debtor–creditor relationship. In the commercial–corporate sphere, company directors are not usually trustees, but it will become apparent (in chapter 15) that they share many trustees' duties.

In light of these difficulties this book has traditionally looked at concepts found within the common law to try to explain what a trust *is* by looking at what it *is not*. Indeed, by looking at what is special about a trust (and what is not a characteristic of a number of common law concepts), this approach can help foster appreciation of *what* a trust is, and *why* it is able to do the things it can. In this edition, exploring what a trust can do that other legal devices cannot has been pursued through considering the common law contract arrangement itself, and also the loan which is based on principles of ordinary contract law.

2.4.1 **The trust in light of the contract**

A private trust, then, is created either by a declaration of trust by the settlor, in which case he becomes trustee himself, or by his arranging for someone else to act as trustee. The beneficiary (or if a purpose trust, the person who can enforce it) need not be a party to the arrangement at all. Yet it is the *beneficiary*, and not the settlor, who can enforce the trust, because the settlor retains no interest in the property (in his capacity *as* settlor—he can of course be a beneficiary). This is so whether or not the beneficiary has given any consideration, because he is in effect the recipient of a gift. So it is only the third party to the arrangement who can enforce it.

Trusts, contracts, enforceability and the doctrine of privity
Earlier editions of this book have explained that while a third party (i.e., not one of the original contracting parties) can benefit from a contract, they cannot generally enforce it themselves by legal action, by virtue of the privity of contract doctrine. This is the essence of ways in which the trust has interfaced with the law of contract historically. Here, the trust was able to provide a means by which enforceable legal rights could be made in favour of a third party without having to use the law of contract, and thus without falling foul of the doctrine of privity. Indeed, the creation of a trust in favour of a recipient is very similar to making him a gift: he need do nothing in return, the gift gives him enforceable rights and, once made, the gift cannot be revoked. Traditionally, this was in contrast with the position of the contract, which was always revocable by the parties to it, but this must now be reviewed in light of reforms to the law of contract brought about by the Contracts (Rights of Third Parties) Act 1999.

Contract law and criticism of the doctrine of privity
The privity of contract doctrine has long attracted criticism, especially in relation to contracts which were clearly intended to provide a third party with a benefit, and the very famous case of *Beswick* v *Beswick* [1968] AC 58 (considered below) is an illustration of its capability to produce some very harsh results. Indeed, Mrs Beswick's fortune turned solely on her ability to enforce the contract as administratrix of her husband's estate. In 1998 the Law Commission published its recommendations for reform of this branch of contract law in *Privity of Contract: Contracts for the Benefit of Third Parties* (Law Com. 242), and this was followed by the 1999 Act. It is now possible for a person who is not party to a contract to enforce it where, according to s. 1, his right to enforce a term of the contract has been expressly provided for by the contract or (subject to s. 1(2) where this will not apply where on proper construction of the contract it appears that the parties did not intend the term to be enforceable by the third party) the term purports to confer a benefit for him.

1999 Act and contracting out
Greater consideration of this Act is given in chapter 3, but some very brief consideration must be given to the suggestion that as a result of it, a contract is no longer revocable by the contracting parties. This proposition must, even at this stage, be seen in light of the way in which the Act itself allows the parties to 'contract out' of the general position (i.e., giving the third party enforceable rights, and thus effectively making the arrangement revocable) by virtue of s. 1(2). Recommendations of the Law Commission were also mindful of the need to give careful consideration to

the rights of the contracting parties to vary or cancel, and that this should be lost once the third party (X) had relied on it and accepted it; while the Law Commission's recommendation that the contracting parties may expressly reserve the right to vary or cancel the third party's reliance or acceptance is provided for by s. 2.

Contract and the trust: complementarity and historical association
While the traditional position of a contract was that (outside the narrow and well-established exceptions to the privity doctrine) it could not be enforced by anyone who was not a party to it, trusts are enforceable by beneficiaries who need not be party to the arrangement. Furthermore, the contract and trust have traditionally operated in actual reverse of one another in this respect, in that it is the beneficiary and no one else who can enforce the trust—and this includes the settlor, who while always being part of the arrangement is unable to enforce it. Moreover, concepts of irrevocability and permanence also marked the trust as something quite distinct from the trust. In examining these related concepts of enforceability and revocability, it thus follows that the main distinction between the trust and the contract has now ceased to exist, and that in the law of contract itself we now find the facility for both types of transaction.

Of course traditionally, if the trustee was acting by virtue of a contract with the settlor, for example, if he was acting as his solicitor or banker, then the settlor could enforce the contract. It may also be that a settlement of property by A on B, subject to a condition that B holds it for the benefit of X, always leads to the implication of a contract between A and B. A's remedies are in contract, however, and these are quite different from those available to a beneficiary for breach of trust.

However, in spite of recent reforms, it would be a mistake not still to consider the significance of the trust alongside contract law. To fail to explore just why the trust has been such a useful device in light of the rules of contract in English law on account of relatively recent changes would be grossly to undersell its role in modern society hitherto.

2.4.1.1 *A traditional contract example*
Suppose, for example, A contracts with B that, in consideration of a payment by A to B of a sum of money, B pays X an annuity for his (X's) life. No trust is constituted, however. Assume also that X does not provide consideration for this benefit, and is not party to the arrangement. X is therefore unable to enforce the contract in his own right. This is shown diagrammatically in figure 2.1.

A can enforce the contract, but often such arrangements are made in favour of wives, sons or daughters, in which case A may well predecease them. In that event, after A's death A's personal representatives will be able to enforce the contract on A's behalf. As a third party, X cannot force them to do so, however, and cannot sue B directly. Of course, if X is A's personal representative, X can sue in that capacity, but not as a third party.

The leading authority is the House of Lords' decision in *Beswick v Beswick* [1968] AC 58. A coal merchant (Peter Beswick), who was over 70 years old, transferred his business to his nephew, who in return agreed, among other things, that he would, after Peter Beswick's death, pay £5 a week to his widow. (This may not sound like a great deal of money, but the agreement was made almost 30 years ago. It would be the equivalent of some £50–£60 a week today, or enough to make a substantial

By contract with B, A agrees to confer a benefit on X

```
┌─────────────┐   Contract between A and    ┌─────────────┐
│             │   B—A can enforce, but       │             │
│      A      │───    X cannot—A and B    ───│      B      │
│             │   can revoke or vary at      │             │
└─────────────┘       any time               └─────────────┘
                                                     │││
                                          X has no enforceable
                                                 action
                                                     │││
                                            ┌─────────────┐
                                            │      X      │
                                            │ (intended to│
                                            │  benefit)   │
                                            └─────────────┘
```

A settles property on trust for X

```
┌─────────────┐   A has no further          ┌─────────────┐
│      A      │   interest or action        │      B      │
│  (Settlor)  │───   —arrangement        ───│  (Trustee)  │
│             │     irrevocable             │             │
└─────────────┘                             └─────────────┘
                                                     │││
                                              Only X can
                                                enforce
                                                     │││
                                            ┌─────────────┐
                                            │      X      │
                                            │(Beneficiary)│
                                            └─────────────┘
```

Figure 2.1 Trust and contract

difference to Mrs Beswick's lifestyle.) Peter Beswick died about 18 months later, and his widow took out letters of administration to his estate (i.e., she became his administratrix: see further below).

Beswick v Beswick
The traditional contract approach Mrs Beswick sued to enforce the contract against the nephew. The House of Lords held that she was not able to sue in her own right (i.e., she could not sue as X), but that she could sue as administratrix of her late husband's estate (i.e., as A, one of the contracting parties). Here, she was literally stepping into the shoes of her late husband. She was also able to obtain specific performance of payment of the annuity to herself (in her personal capacity).

2.4.1.2 *Enforcement of the contract by the other contracting party (A)*

Here, Mrs Beswick was suing as a party to the contract, and the reforms introduced by the Contracts (Rights of Third Parties) Act 1999 Act do not affect remedies available to the promisee. Although this was considered by the Law Commission, no changes to the law were recommended, and it is clear that if X is capable of enforcing directly, this is actually now far less important than it used to be. Where specific performance is available to A (or his personal representatives), he can ensure that the third party X can obtain the benefit of the contract, as it was envisaged by the parties at the time of its making. Indeed, here, A can ensure that X obtains the benefit he has bargained for.

The contract's limitations However, the case of *Beswick* is itself illustrative of the difficulties which can be characteristic of the operation of specific performance, and its availability in the case itself depended upon, among other things, the fact that B, the Beswicks' nephew, had received all the consideration (the transfer to him of the goodwill in Mr Beswick senior's business). Moreover, the availability of specific performance generally depends on mutuality of enforcement. This will be considered in some detail in chapter 19, but in essence this means that it will be available as a remedy only where the contract would also be specifically enforceable in the other direction (here, by B against A). This was the case in *Beswick* itself because Mr Beswick senior (A) had promised to transfer the goodwill of a business, but it will by no means always be the case that this requirement will be met. Indeed, while the more modern approach to specific performance focuses on the most appropriate remedy (see further chapter 19), it is also the case that it is unlikely to be ordered where consideration moving from A to B is money alone.

'Compensatory' nature of contractual damages In situations where A or his personal representatives cannot obtain specific performance, but where B does not perform the bargain at all, A can get his property back on grounds of total failure of consideration. This may be of no benefit to X of course, unless A chooses to make another similar arrangement for his benefit. Where B has partially performed the bargain, the return of property on the grounds of total failure of consideration will not be available to A, who is now forced to rely on contractual damages.

The problem here lies in the fact that contractual damages are compensatory, and where the contract is intended to provide a benefit for a third party, it is easy to see that A has actually suffered no loss himself. Thus, in most cases, A will be limited to the recovery of nominal damages. While there is limited authority that A can recover all that X could have recovered had he been a contracting party himself—particularly in the *dicta* of Lush LJ in *Lloyd's* v *Harper* (1880) 16 Ch D 290, and of Lord Denning MR in *Jackson* v *Horizon Holidays Ltd* [1975] 1 WLR 1468, it is almost certain that these views are wrong. In *Beswick* v *Beswick* itself, all Their Lordships apart from Lord Pearce thought that, had specific performance not been available, the administratrix would have been entitled to nominal damages only, as Mr Beswick's estate had suffered no loss. A similar view was taken by all members of the House of Lords in *Woodar Investment Developments Ltd* v *Wimpey Contractors (UK) Ltd* [1980] 1 WLR 277, where the *dicta* referred to above in *Lloyd's* v *Harper* and *Jackson* v *Horizon Holidays Ltd* were disapproved.

Thus, *Woodar Investment Developments Ltd* v *Wimpey Contractors (UK) Ltd* stands as authority for the proposition that where specific performance is not available, in most other cases damages recoverable by A will be nominal. The view was also expressed in *Woodar* (particularly by Lords Salmon, Keith and Scarman) that the law was very unsatisfactory, but could only be altered by statute. Any such attestation would now seem unlikely in light of the Law Commission's recommendation and resulting legislation, but there are however exceptions to the *Woodar* principle, including the one which can be found in *Lloyd's* v *Harper*, where one party contracts as trustee for another. Here, where A contracts as X's trustee, the contracting party's damages will be calculated on the beneficiary's loss. However, the beneficiary will not be able to sue directly, but he must require the trustee to sue on his behalf.

2.4.1.3 *A trust example*

Traditionally, this was very different in a trust example, where instead of B being a contracting party, he was instead constituted trustee for X. Not only was X capable of suing B in his own right, but once constituted, the trust represented a permanent and irrevocable arrangement whereby A and B were no longer free to vary the arrangement to X's detriment, on the basis that this would be akin to making a gift to X, and then taking it back again. It was for this reason that the creation of a trust was able to avoid the privity of contract rules. This is perfectly in order of course so long as this is what A and B intend. Now the Contracts (Rights of Third Parties) Act 1999 removes this crucial distinction between the contract and the trust.

2.4.2 **Trusts and loans**

When you lend money to a friend or business partner, or deposit money in a bank account, your friend, business partner or bank becomes a debtor, not a trustee, and you become a creditor, not a beneficiary. It should be clear from the above that a debtor will be in a very different position from a trustee. A debtor's liability to repay a loan is contractual, and therefore strict, subject to the terms of the loan. In other words, it does not require proof of negligence or bad faith. It is not avoided, for example, by the theft by a third person either of the money loaned, or of any property purchased with the money, however innocent the debtor may be. On the other hand, the property the creditor has loaned passes to the debtor, so if the debtor goes bankrupt, the creditor takes his place as one among many unsecured creditors, and is unlikely to see the return of any or all his money.

Beneficiary's position contrasted with debtor's
A trustee's duties are less strict (see chapters 15, 16, and 18), but in the event of a trustee's bankruptcy, a beneficiary is in the position of a secured creditor, because he has retained equitable property, which will be protected from the claims of the general creditors. In effect, the property never becomes part of the debtor's estate.

   Both legal and equitable obligations can coexist, however, so that a loan can also constitute a trust. Thus, a creditor can also be a beneficiary, and this protects him in the event of the debtor's bankruptcy.

2.4.2.1 *Express declaration of trusteeship by debtor*

The most certain method of making a loan to a debtor which will also give rise to a trust in favour of the creditor, is to require the debtor to declare himself trustee on behalf of the creditor. A common commercial transaction where this is routinely done is the bankers' documentary credit, where the bank, on releasing to its customer shipping documents, which are its security, to enable the customer to re-sell goods (and hence obtain money to repay the bank), protects itself against the bankruptcy of its customer by taking a trust receipt, under which the customer (typically) declares himself trustee for the bank of the goods until they are sold, and trustee of the proceeds of sale once the goods are sold. Thus the bank becomes both creditor and beneficiary under the trust, and hence retains equitable title in the goods and (if sold) the proceeds of sale. Since the customer obtains the goods only as trustee, if he goes bankrupt, whether before or after the goods are sold, the bank will be able to claim the goods or the proceeds of sale (so long as they are traceable under the equitable rules described in chapter 19) in preference to the general creditors.

Other examples of the use of trusts to protect against bankruptcy are considered in chapter 3.

2.4.2.2 No express declaration of trusteeship by debtor

Even where words of trust are not expressly used, the courts have held, in a line of authorities going back at least 150 years, that where A advances to B an identifiable sum of money for a particular purpose, the obligations of trusteeship are imposed upon B.

The leading authority is the House of Lords decision in *Barclays Bank Ltd* v *Quistclose Investments Ltd* [1970] AC 567. The case revolved around Rolls Razor Ltd, who were in serious financial difficulties and had an overdraft with Barclays Bank of some £484,000, against a permitted limit of £250,000. If Rolls Razor were to stay in business, it was essential for them to obtain a loan of around £210,000 in order to pay dividends which they had declared on their ordinary shares, and which in the absence of such a loan they were unable to pay. They succeeded in obtaining the loan from Quistclose Investments Ltd, who agreed to make the loan on the condition 'that it is used to pay the forthcoming dividend due on July 24, next'. The sum was paid into a special account with Barclays Bank, on the condition (agreed with the bank) that the account would 'only be used to meet the dividend due on July 24, 1964'.

The House of Lords judgment and the finding of a trust

Rolls Razor went into voluntary liquidation on 27 August, without having paid the dividend. Barclays wanted to count the money in the special account against Rolls Razor's overdraft, but the House of Lords held that Barclays held the money on trust for Quistclose, so that Quistclose was able to claim back the entire sum. Lord Wilberforce stated (at p. 580):

> The mutual intention of the respondents [Quistclose] and of Rolls Razor Ltd, and the essence of the bargain, was that the sum advanced should not become part of the assets of Rolls Razor Ltd, but should be used exclusively for payment of a particular class of creditors, namely, those entitled to the dividend. A necessary consequence from this, by process simply of interpretation, must be that if, for any reason, the dividend could not be paid, the money was to be returned to the respondents: the word 'only' or 'exclusively' can have no other meaning or effect.
>
> That arrangements of this character for the payment of a person's creditors by a third person give rise to a relationship of a fiduciary character or trust, in favour, as a primary trust, of the creditors, and secondarily, if the primary trust fails, of the third person, has been recognised in a series of cases over some 150 years.

Quistclose

The effect of the decision, of course, was that the money loaned by Quistclose was secured from the consequences of Rolls Razor's bankruptcy, since it never became part of Rolls Razor's general assets.

Note that it was Barclays, who as bankers had legal title to the money, who were held to be trustees. This raised the issue of the bank's notice of the trust since, on the principles in chapter 1, they would have taken free of Quistclose's interest in the absence of notice. Lord Wilberforce commented (at p. 582):

It is common ground, and I think right, that a mere request to put the money into a separate account is not sufficient to constitute notice. But [in this case] . . . there is no doubt that the bank was told that the money had been provided on loan by a third person and was to be used only for the purpose of paying the dividend. This was sufficient to give them notice that it was trust money and not assets of Rolls Razor Ltd: the fact, if it be so, that they were unaware of the lender's identity (though the respondent's name as drawer was on the cheque) is of no significance.

He went on to say that the bank was also aware that Rolls Razor could not itself, without a loan from an outside source, provide the money to pay the dividend, and that the bank never contemplated that the money so provided could be used to reduce the existing overdraft.

2.4.2.3 *Money must be for a specific purpose*

The decision in *Quistclose* seems to depend on the fact that the money was to be used for a specific purpose, that that purpose was known to the recipient, and that the money was paid into a special account, which could be used for no other purpose. The last requirement, for a special account, may not be absolutely rigid, but at the very least the money must be earmarked for the particular purpose *and no other*, in order to negative the inference that the payments are to be included in the general assets of the company. In the absence of such a requirement, a prospective purchaser through a car import company, for example, who pays a deposit of £1,000 for the purpose of importing a car, would be able to reclaim that £1,000 in the event of the car import company going into liquidation before the car is obtained. The payment, after all, is made for a particular purpose, which is known to the recipient (the company), but except in the unlikely event that the company can use that money for *no purpose other* than obtaining the car, the prospective purchaser is not protected on *Quistclose* principles. The position is somewhat similar to cases where money has been paid to a company for the purpose of obtaining an allotment of shares, but no trust has been held to have been created. Commenting on those cases, Lord Wilberforce said (at p. 581):

I do not think it necessary to examine these cases in detail, nor to comment on them, for I am satisfied that they do not affect the principle on which this appeal should be decided. They are merely examples which show that, in the absence of some special arrangement creating a trust . . . , payments of this kind are made upon the basis that they are to be included in the company's assets. They do not negative the proposition that a trust may exist where the mutual intention is that they should not.

The significance of the separate account

The setting up of a special fund negates the inference that the payments are to be included in the company's assets, but so long as that inference is negated, it may be that a special fund is not absolutely necessary. In *Re EVTR* [1987] BCLC 646, for example, the appellant, Barber, who had just won £240,000 on premium bonds, agreed to assist a company for whom he had worked in purchasing new equipment. He accordingly deposited £60,000 with the solicitors to the company, and authorised them to release it 'for the sole purpose of buying new equipment'. The money was not paid into a special fund, but was paid out by the company in pursuit of the purpose. Before the new equipment was delivered EVTR went into receivership. The Court of Appeal held that Barber was entitled to recover his money (or at any rate, the balance of £48,536, after agreed deductions) on *Quistclose* principles. Dillon LJ also thought (at p. 649):

> . . . in the light of *Quistclose*, that if the company had gone into liquidation, or the receivers had been appointed, and the scheme had become abortive before the £60,000 had been disbursed by the company, the appellant would have been entitled to recover his full £60,000, as between himself and the company, on the footing that it was impliedly held by the company on a resulting trust for him as the particular purpose of the loan had failed.

Something less than a separate account

At this stage, however, the money would not have been held in a special account, but the inference that it was intended to be included as part of the general assets would have been negated by other factors. The existence of a special account does not appear, then, to be absolutely essential, so long as the inference that the payments are to be included in the company's assets is negated.

A *Quistclose* argument failed in *Anglo Corporation* v *Peacock AG*, CA (unreported), 12 February 1997, where the recipient clearly did not take the money on the understanding that it was to be separated from his general assets and used for a specific purpose. Referring to the House of Lords decision in *Westdeutsche* v *Islington BC* [1996] AC 669 (see chapters 7 and 19), the Court of Appeal placed greater emphasis on the state of mind of the recipient, whereas previous cases had tended to concentrate on the state of mind of the lender. The decision was that the *Quistclose* claim failed because the recipient of the money (AG) 'did not believe it had reached any agreement about the basis on which it would accept the money, and unlike *Quistclose* and *Re Kayford* [below] there was no identifiable trust property, such as money in a special account, on which the trust could be imposed'. This appears at first sight to suggest the necessity for a special account, but is equally consistent with the absence of a special account being a factor, but not necessarily a conclusive factor, against the existence of an agreement; by contrast, obviously the existence of a special account is strong evidence in favour of an agreement.

Quistclose trusts and commercial reality

The reality is, however, that *Quistclose* trusts are often used when the trustee is in liquidation. Merely to have a personal action against the trustee is therefore useless; it is essential for the lender to be able to point to a fund of money held by the trustee and say 'that money is my property'. To be able to do this it is necessary to be able to identify the money, and this is clearly easiest where the money has been paid into a special account. It is not essential, however, so long as the money can be traced on the principles discussed in chapter 19. In *Re Kayford Ltd* [1975] 1 WLR 279 (chapter 3), where it was held that a trust fund had been set up for customers of an insolvent company, Megarry J did not think it fatal that the money had been mixed with small amounts of other money. The case was not decided on *Quistclose* principles, but it was essential to be able to establish that the money belonged in equity to the customers; a personal action against the company would have availed them nothing. The money in *Kayford* was clearly traceable, however, so there was no problem even though there were other small sums in the account.

2.4.2.4 *Money already owed to trustee*

For the purposes of *Quistclose* type trusts, it does not seem to matter where the money comes from. In *Quistclose* itself it was a loan made voluntarily by a third party. *EVTR* also involved a voluntary disposition. In *Carreras Rothmans Ltd v Freeman Mathews Treasure Ltd* [1985] Ch 207, on the other hand, the money paid into the special account was money that Carreras Rothmans (CR) were contractually obliged to pay to Freeman Mathews Treasure (FMT) in any event. Applying *Quistclose*, however, Peter Gibson J held that the money in the special account was held on trust.

The plaintiff (cigarette manufacturers) engaged the defendant advertising agency. The defendant contracted as principal with production agencies and advertising media. The arrangement was that CR paid a monthly fee to FMT, which was used:

(a) as payment in arrears for FMT's services, and

(b) to enable FMT to pay debts incurred to agency and media creditors.

The defendant (FMT) got into financial difficulties, but needed funds to pay its production agencies and advertising media if it was to carry on acting for the claimant.

Carreras Rothmans also knew that if FMT went into liquidation still owing money to media creditors, the media creditors would have sufficient commercial power to compel CR to pay, and therefore (although they were not legally obliged to do so) they would in practice have to pay twice over. An agreement was therefore made between CR and FMT whereby the claimants would pay a monthly sum into a special account at the defendant's bank, the money to be used:

only for the purposes of meeting the accounts of the media and production fees of third parties directly attributable to CR's involvement with the agency.

Payments, action and timing of liquidation

The first payment (of just under £600,000) was made at the end of July, covering debts incurred in June. Unlike the position in the cases discussed above, however, this was money which CR owed to FMT in any event.

The defendant went into liquidation before the debts were cleared. CR immediately found another advertising agency, and to avoid jeopardising its advertising campaign, paid the debts of the media creditors, taking assignments of those debts. Of the money in the special account, Peter Gibson J held that it was held by FMT (and hence by the liquidator) on trust, since it had been paid for a specific purpose, and he made an order requiring the liquidator to carry out that purpose (i.e., payment to the third parties). He did not think it relevant (at pp. 221–2) that CR was under a contractual obligation to pay the money to FMT in any event, noting (at p. 222C–E) that:

if the common intention is that property is transferred for a specific purpose and not so as to become the property of the transferee, the transferee cannot keep the property if for any reason that purpose cannot be fulfilled. I am left in no doubt that the provider of the moneys in the present case was the plaintiff. True it is that its own witnesses said that if the defendant had not agreed to the terms of the contract letter, the plaintiff would not have broken its contract but would have paid its debt to the defendant, but the fact remains that the plaintiff made its payment on the terms of that letter and the defendant received the moneys only for the stipulated purpose. That purpose was expressed to relate only to the moneys in the account. In my judgment therefore the plaintiff can be equated with the lender in *Quistclose* as having an enforceable right to compel the carrying out of the primary trust.

2.4.2.5 *Enforcement of Quistclose trusts*

Lord Wilberforce's view (at p. 580) was that there was a primary trust in favour of the creditors, who in *Quistclose* were the shareholders, and then on the failure of the primary trust a secondary trust in favour of 'the third person', who is earlier identified as the provider of the money. Since the provider of the money was able to claim it back, it must be assumed that in Lord Wilberforce's view, the primary trust had failed. Similarly, in *EVTR*, the provider of the money was able to claim it back, the primary purpose of the trust having failed. In both cases the secondary trust was enforced, and since the settlor was also beneficiary, these must have been resulting trusts (see further chapter 7).

In *Carreras Rothmans* the primary trust, to pay the media advertisers, could still be carried out, and the order made was to that effect. Peter Gibson J even thought (at p. 223) that the third-party creditors might themselves have had enforceable rights, although the order was applied for by CR. Since enforceable rights are given only to beneficiaries under trusts, the clear implication is that whereas the beneficiary is the provider of the money once the primary trust has failed, the beneficiary under the primary trust is the person to whom payment is to be made.

Difficulties with Carreras Rothmans

There are, however, a number of difficulties with this view, as P.J. Millett QC (as he then was), counsel for CR, pointed out in his article based on the case at (1985) 101 LQR 269. First, it is by no means obvious why the primary trust had failed in *Quistclose* itself, since payment of the dividends could still be carried out. Only Harman LJ in the Court of Appeal ([1968] 1 Ch 540) really addressed this issue, commenting (at p. 548) that:

> . . . The money was deposited with the respondent bank, and accepted on the footing that it should only be used for payment of the dividend. That purpose was, however, frustrated by the liquidation of Rolls Razor on the following August 27 before the dividend had been paid, thus making its payment illegal.

It is illegal for a company which is in liquidation to pay dividends to its shareholders, at any rate using its own money, but as Millett pointed out, the money did not belong beneficially to Rolls Razor. Indeed, there was no theoretical reason why Rolls Razor needed to be involved at all; the identity of the trustee was immaterial. Since the money was not theirs, and there was no reason why anybody *apart from Rolls Razor* could not pay the amount of the dividends, it is difficult to see why the payment became illegal on the liquidation of Rolls Razor.

A resolution—or the creation of additional difficulties?

A possible answer to this is that in determining whether the primary purpose has failed, you look not at whether it has become impossible to achieve, but at whether the settlor's motive has been frustrated. Clearly, it had been in *Quistclose*, since the whole point was to keep Rolls going, and although payment to the shareholders could still theoretically be made, there would obviously be no point in doing this, at any rate from Quistclose's viewpoint.

Although this might appear to be the obvious explanation, there are a number of difficulties with it. First, there were no words of trust in *Quistclose*, and the only reason for inferring a trust was that the money had been lent for a specific purpose. Had it been lent 'to keep Rolls Razor afloat', there would have been no trust. It seems strange, therefore, in deciding whether the trust has failed, to ignore the specific purpose, which can still be carried out, in favour of the purpose of keeping Rolls Razor afloat, which cannot. Second, as Millett observed, nowhere else in the law does a trust fail because it no longer accords with the settlor's wishes; it fails only when performance becomes impossible or illegal, and that had not happened here.

Implied trusts and no expression

Nevertheless, we feel that this is the correct explanation of *Quistclose*. There were no words of trust, and it was therefore necessary to imply a trust. In determining the terms of an implied trust, all relevant factors are taken into account, including, but not necessarily limited to, the words that were used. In other words, there is no reason why the terms of the trust should necessarily correspond with the specific purpose. An implied trust, even of land, does not require writing (see chapters 5 and 10), and it is interesting that in *Rowan v Dann* (1992) P & CR 202 (discussed in chapter 1), the Court of Appeal enforced what was effectively an oral *Quistclose* trust of land; it is true that they enforced the secondary trust, which as a resulting trust would not have required writing either, but no doubt was cast on the validity of the primary trust, which had failed.

Options in Carreras Rothmans

Millett was constrained in *Carreras Rothmans* to arrive at a different analysis, however. On the above view, it might have been possible to argue that the primary trust had failed (although that would depend on CR's motive being to keep FMT afloat, whereas arguably CR was concerned only with its own advertising campaign, and had no interest in FMT), but then CR would have obtained the £600,000 back. Since, however, it was contractually bound to pay the £600,000, Millett presumably thought that FMT's liquidators would simply have been able to sue in contract if this were the result, as indeed they did regarding the next month's payment (of £780,000) which had not, by the time of FMT's liquidation, even been paid into the special account. So an argument based on the failure of the primary trust (even assuming it was possible on the facts) would not have appealed to Millett.

So it was assumed that the primary trust had not failed in *Carreras Rothmans*, and on Lord Wilberforce's analysis, and as indeed Peter Gibson J thought in *Carreras Rothmans*, the media advertisers were therefore the beneficiaries. But the media advertisers did not sue; Carreras Rothmans did. Millett got the result that he wanted in *Carreras Rothmans*, an order to pay the money to the media advertisers not to CR (to avoid the potential contractual liability discussed in the previous paragraph), but an order obtained not by the media advertisers but by CR.

Implications if Carreras Rothmans is correct

Assuming that *Carreras Rothmans* is correct, therefore (by no means a certainty given that it is a first instance decision which has not been followed) where (as will become clear) the decision appears inconsistent with the reasoning in the judgment, the question is, on what basis could CR enforce the trust? It is not sufficient that CR had taken assignments of the media advertiser's rights, partly because for tactical reasons CR expressly disclaimed reliance on assignment and partly because that would have led to payment back to CR and not to the media advertisers. It is also unclear from the report exactly what assignments they had taken; debt actions against a company which is in liquidation are valueless, and (at least as far as it is possible to tell from the report), CR had not taken assignments of any other rights the third party creditors might have.

Millett's explanation was that the reason CR could enforce the trust was that they were the beneficiaries all along, under both the primary and the secondary trusts. (In passing, it is worth observing that both primary and secondary trusts therefore become resulting trusts, which also allows for an oral *Quistclose* trust of land.) It is possible to find support for the view that the provider of the money can enforce the trust from *Quistclose* itself, where Lord Wilberforce observes (at p. 581) that:

the lender acquires an equitable right to see that [the money advanced] is applied for the primary designated purpose . . . if the primary purpose cannot be carried out, the question arises if a secondary purpose (i.e., repayment to the lender) has been agreed, expressly or by implication: if it has, the remedies of equity may be invoked to give effect to it . . .

Merits of Millett's views

We would suggest, however, that this passage is not very convincing, since all it appears to support is the view that if the primary trust is not carried out, the lender acquires an equitable right to enforce the *secondary* trust.

Millett then had to argue that, even though CR were beneficiaries, the order should be to pay the media advertisers, not CR themselves (for the reasons already set out). He therefore argued that they had a power to direct the trustees to carry out the stated purpose. The problem with this argument is that directions to trustees are in principle revocable, and on this view, therefore, the lender can revoke any directions and claim the money back at any time, as beneficiary.

Quistclose would not have to wait for Rolls Razor to go into liquidation, should they choose to claim the money back earlier. Millett's general position on revocation is not, in the author's view, the most convincing part of his article, but in cases such as *Quistclose* and *Carreras Rothmans*, it is certainly possible to imply a contractual term between settlor and trustee (who are clearly in a contractual relationship with each other), that the settlor will not revoke his directions unless the purpose of the *directions* is frustrated. The purpose of the directions had clearly been frustrated in *Quistclose*, but arguably not in *Carreras Rothmans*, if CR's main concern was merely to ensure the continuation of their advertising campaign.

To conclude, Lord Wilberforce's analysis in *Quistclose* can probably be justified in spite of difficulties over why the primary trust had failed. However, if *Quistclose* is correct, the decision in *Carreras Rothmans* is not, since CR should have had no right to enforce the order. Millett's analysis is inconsistent with Lord Wilberforce's, and lacks the beauty of simplicity, but (unsurprisingly in the circumstances) is consistent with the *decision* in all the cases, including *Carreras Rothmans*. It also avoids the problems of failure of primary purpose in *Quistclose*.

Another possible view is that the primary trust in *Quistclose* cases is a pure purpose trust without true beneficiaries at all. This view was taken by Megarry J in *Re Northern Developments (Holdings) Ltd* (unreported) 6 October 1978, but considered in *Carreras Rothmans* and discussed by P.J. Millett QC in the article referred to above.

Quistclose trusts and the significance of Twinsectra v Yardley
The most significant consideration which has been given to *Quistclose* trusts in recent times is that of the House of Lords, in the very important decision in *Twinsectra* v *Yardley* [2002] 2 All ER 377. The case is a very important decision on the liability which can be incurred by a third party to a trust where there has been a breach of that trust committed by a trustee to it. In the parlance of equity and trusts, the issues raised by 'assisting' a breach of trust, or being an 'accessory' in the breach of a trust will be considered later in chapter 19. This decision is also an important point of reference for this chapter's consideration of the nature of the trust, and its central features, at this point, through discussion of the *Quistclose* trust.

Twinsectra: the Quistclose trust explored through its facts
In a case involving two solicitors, *Twinsectra* arose initially through the involvement of one (Leach) with the purchase of land for a client. To complete the purchase the client needed to borrow £1 million. A lender, Twinsectra, was found but was only willing to make the loan if repayment was secured by a solicitor's personal undertaking. The first solicitor was unwilling to give such an undertaking so the client approached the second solicitor (Sims) who represented himself as acting for the client. The second solicitor then received the loan money after his firm gave an undertaking to the lender *inter alia* that the loan moneys were to be retained until such time as they are applied to the client's purchase; that the loan moneys would be utilised solely for the acquisition of property on behalf of the client and for no other purposes; and that the loan would be repaid together with interest.

The second solicitor sought assurances from the client that the money would be used in the acquisition of property and received them through the first solicitor. The money was then released to the first solicitor as instructed by the client. The first solicitor considered the money as held on account for the client and paid it out on the client's instructions, and took no steps to ensure that the money was only applied in the acquisition of property. In the event, the client used a substantial part of it for other purposes. The second solicitor became bankrupt and the loan was not repaid. The lender commenced proceedings against the borrower and both solicitors. The action against the first solicitor, Leach, alleged that he had dishonestly assisted in the second solicitor's breach of trust. The matters of concern here hinged on whether a trust did exist in respect of the loan: this would form the basis for establishing that there had been a breach of trust in the (second) solicitor's conduct. This in turn would affect the liability of the other solicitor. It would also allow for the recovery of the sums which had not been applied in accordance with the lender's instructions.

A Quistclose trust arising through a loan for specific purposes?
The crucial consequence of the loan found to be subject to a trust would be that property subject to a trust remains distinctive from other assets which might be the subject of competing claims. On *Quistclose* this can be achieved on there being a resulting trust in favour of the provider of the property. The ability to determine that the loan was held by Sims subject to a trust in favour of Twinsectra was crucial to being able to establish a breach of trust had arisen where the loan had been applied in contravention with the undertaking to apply it to the purchase of property for which it had been advanced. Problems in establishing this arose in the way in which it was argued that there was no intention to create a trust, and that there

was an absence of obvious 'specific purpose' on account of the way in which the money was to be applied to an unspecified purchase of property.

The House of Lords held that intention to create a trust (of the property held by Sims) could be found on the construction of the undertaking that the money was to be used for the acquisition of property and for no other purpose. This gave rise to an obligation on Sims' part to release the money to Leach only for the acquisition of property—an obligation which was fiduciary rather than contractual in nature. At first instance no trust had been found on account of lack of certainty of objects, because the proposed acquisition related to property which was unspecified, the Court of Appeal concluding there was a trust in which beneficial interest was either in suspense or held by the borrower (subject to the lender's contractual right to determine the application of the property).

In the House of Lords, Lord Millett, who provided the analysis of the *Quistclose* trust for his Brethren considered the most appropriate location of beneficial interests underlying a trust invoked by advancing money for a specific purpose. His conclusion ultimately was that beneficial interest in advancements of this nature, in these circumstances, is held on resulting trust for the lender. But other possibilities were considered; for example, that the trust is in favour of those (people or purposes) intended to benefit from the trust; that beneficial interest is held by the borrower, and that it is held in 'suspense'.

What is interesting about this case is the way in which it gives lengthy and extensive consideration to the other views considered and advanced, and ultimately to why the resulting trust in favour of the lender was the one ultimately to be preferred. The conclusion that a resulting trust arose in favour of the lender, and that this operated subject to the mandate of the borrower to apply the sums advanced to the specified purposes, ensured that Sims did hold the money on (resulting) trust for Twinsectra. At that point, it did not matter that the money was advanced to be applied to a purpose rather than to benefit an identifiable individual.

2.5 Trusts and restitution: beyond *quasi*-contract?

Restitution leads on from the discussions above on account of its conceptual location alongside the law of contract. Often classified as '*quasi*-contract', there is a basic consensus that restitution is concerned with reversing an unjust enrichment which one has received at the expense of another. Writers on the law of obligations point to the significance of features of contract and also tort which have shaped restitution's unique nature, while also noting that it is actually a ubiquitous doctrine which is found almost universally across different systems of law, in some form.

The crucial question here is how restitution might apply in the context of this study of equity and the law of trusts, given that its strongest traditional associations are to be found in *quasi*-contract. It will become clear that questions of restitution are currently never far away from what is at the heart of this text: this is the determination of rights and interests relating to property within the trust arrangement, on account of the way in which ownership is vested in one party for the benefit of another. Where trust property falls into the hands of those who are not entitled to it, it is clear that there should be a remedy of some sort, but on what basis should this arise? These issues are ones which arise in chapter 19. It will become clear within chapter 19 that in the context of remedies pertaining to misapplied trust property, the principles which govern remedies based on proprietary entitlement, and which involve 'tracing' trust property into the hands of another, are not entirely clear in respect of their availability or operation and effect. But equally there is concern that despite the enthusiasm for restitution among judges and particularly academic commentators, there is also concern that, in the words of Lord Woolf in *Westdeutsche* v *London Islington Borough Council* [1996] AC 669:

[t]hose concerned with developing the law of restitution are anxious to ensure that, in certain circumstances, the plaintiff should have the right to recover property which he has unjustly lost . . . in my view such development is not based on sound principle and in the name of unjust enrichment is capable of producing most unjust results [and even that] [t]he search for a perceived need to strengthen the remedies of a plaintiff claiming in restitution involves, to my mind, a distortion of trust principles.

That having been said, since *Westdeutsche*, more recent cases like *Foskett* v *McKowen* [2000] 2 WLR 1299 and *BCCI* v *Akindele* [2001] Ch 437 are suggesting a move away from restitution. Thus, it may well be the case that this is signalling that a more coherent approach to remedies based on proprietary entitlement will in due course transpire.

2.6 Trusts and powers

2.6.1 Fixed and discretionary trusts

So far the assumption has been made that the extent of the beneficial interests under a trust has been known at the outset, and indeed many trusts are of this nature. An example might be property divided equally among the sons of the settlor. Each son has an interest which is fixed and ascertainable from the outset. Trusts arising from undivided shares in land, for example, are normally fixed trusts because each co-owner will have a defined share from the start.

This situation is by no means universal, however. With many trusts, the trustees are given a discretion as to how the property is to be distributed, usually within a defined class of possible beneficiary. This type of trust is usually termed a discretionary trust, although the term 'trust power' is also sometimes used. Obviously, nobody within the class of possible beneficiaries (such people are referred to as 'objects', as we shall see in chapter 4), can claim a defined interest, or indeed any interest at all, unless and until the trustees' discretion is exercised in their favour. Yet though the trustees have a discretion as to how the property is distributed, that discretion does not extend to a refusal to distribute it at all. The trustees *must* administer the trust. They *must* appoint (i.e., decide who from within the class will benefit, and also the size of each beneficial interest). But whom they appoint, and in what proportions, is up to them.

Family trusts used often to be of this nature for tax reasons. There were a number of advantages in giving discretion to the trustees. One was to enable them to alter the beneficial interests to take advantage of changing tax circumstances. Another was that tax liability attached in some circumstances only where rights were created, and none of the beneficiaries has any right to the property at all unless and until the discretion is exercised in their favour. Discretionary trusts have been hard hit by recent tax legislation, however, and are probably less common today.

As we shall see in chapter 4, the distinction between fixed and discretionary trusts is important, as the orthodox view is that different requirements of certainty of object apply.

2.6.2 **Nature of powers**

A power (sometimes called a 'mere power') differs from a discretionary trust in the following respects. First, the legal title is given, not to trustees, but to donees of the power. They have a discretion not only as to *how* to distribute the property, but also as to *whether* to distribute it. They are under no obligation to appoint at all. In other words, whereas a trust is imperative, because the trustees must appoint, a power is discretionary, because the donees of a power need not appoint at all—the choice is theirs.

There may be limited exceptions to this position. In *Klug* v *Klug* [1918] 2 Ch 67, a mother who disapproved of her daughter's marriage without her consent capriciously refused to exercise a power in her favour. On application by the public trustee, the court ordered that the power should be exercised. This case was relied on in *Mettoy Pension Trustees* v *Evans* [1991] 2 All ER 513, noted at [1991] Conv 364, where Warner J held that the court could enforce a fiduciary power in the same manner as a discretionary trust. The case is unusual, however, in that there was nobody else who was capable of exercising the power. Assuming that these cases are correct, they create limited exceptions where non-exercise of a power is capricious, and where there is nobody available to exercise a power. The cases do not affect the general principle that where donees of a power make a *bona fide* decision not to exercise it, the courts will not compel them to do so.

What happens where a power is not exercised?
If the donees of a power do not appoint, a gift or trust over may have been provided for in default of appointment. A gift or trust over is a gift or trust which takes effect where the property has not otherwise been fully disposed of. It must be provided for in the original trust instrument, and if it has, it will take effect. If not, the property goes on resulting trust to the settlor (see further chapter 7).

A special power of appointment
A power to distribute property to a limited class of persons (either specified persons, or specified groups or 'classes' of people called the 'objects' of the power) is called a 'special power of appointment'. If no particular instructions are given to the donee of a power, or restrictions as to whom property might be given, the power conferred is known as a 'general power of appointment'. There is also a category of intermediate, or hybrid powers, where a donee is given power to appoint to anyone except those within a particular class. In each case a donee may also be an object of the power. Obviously, a donee under a general power of appointment is in a position akin to that of an absolute owner. The distinction between general and special powers of appointment is of importance when considering perpetuities (chapter 6).

Understanding the purpose of powers: a hangover from the past

The purpose of mere powers is not immediately apparent. Probably they are a hangover from days when testators did not trust wives and eldest sons to administer family property in the manner that they regarded as sensible. So, although the settlor in general terms wished to benefit his wife or eldest son, he did not wish to give them enforceable rights. Therefore the property was settled on somebody else, who had the power to appoint to the wife or eldest son, but need not do so if such appointment appeared unwise.

In recent years the practice has arisen of creating powers with discretionary trusts over, in default of appointment, where the donees under the power are the same people as the trustees under the discretionary trust. In most respects this has an identical effect to a discretionary trust. For example, if A is given power to appoint to B, C or D, with a trust over in default in favour of E and F, A cannot avoid appointing altogether, and this is no different from a discretionary trust in favour of B, C, D, E and F. The only exception might be where A refuses to carry out his duties at all, and the court is required ultimately to distribute the property. In the case of a power with trust over, B, C and D would have no claim. If the instrument was in the form of a single trust, they would. But it is unlikely that settlors have frequent regard to this extreme and pathological situation.

Trust/power distinction and a modern significance

So why use a power and trust over in default? As we shall see in chapter 4, between 1955 and 1971 the certainty of object test for powers was thought to be less stringent than that for discretionary trusts. In other words, an instrument which was valid as a power might be invalid as a discretionary trust, if there was a wide range of objects. It therefore became common practice to draft powers with a wide range of objects, which were valid, while confining the trust over to a narrow range of objects. Such an instrument could be valid, whereas if drafted as a trust alone it would fall foul of the certainty of object requirements. If this is indeed the explanation for such instruments, one might expect that they will become less common now that, since 1971 the certainty tests for trusts and powers have been regarded as being practically the same.

As with discretionary trusts, the objects of the power have no definable interest in the property unless that power is exercised in their favour. The objects can come to court to enforce the power, however, to the very limited extent that the court will restrain disposal of the property otherwise than in accordance with the terms of the power.

2.6.3 The extent of the discretion and the nature of enforcement

For mere powers, the donee's discretion seems to be unfettered except to the extent that he must not dispose of the property otherwise than in accordance with the terms of the power.

So far as discretionary trusts are concerned, though members of the class of possible beneficiaries have no defined interest in the property unless and until the trustees' discretion is exercised in their favour, nevertheless, they have sufficient *locus standi* to come to court to enforce the trust. Clearly the degree to which enforcement is possible is limited by the discretionary nature of the arrangement, but the courts will restrain the trustees from acting contrary to the terms of the trust instrument. And if they refuse to distribute at all, a court can remove them and appoint new trustees, or in the final analysis distribute the property itself. Furthermore, unlike donees of mere powers, the trustees' discretion is not absolute. In considering its exercise, they must make a survey of the entire field of objects, and consider each individual case responsibly, on its merits: *per* Lord Wilberforce in *Re Baden's Deed Trusts, McPhail* v *Doulton* [1971] AC 424. The requirement that discretion must be properly exercised is not merely academic. In *Turner* v *Turner* [1984] Ch 100, the trustees (who were relatives of the settlor, without any previous experience or understanding of trusts) simply acted on the instructions of the settlor (i.e., did not exercise their own discretion at all, but effectively delegated it to him). Mervyn Davies J held that the appointments they made were invalid.

Trusts and powers: explaining the duties of trustees and donees of a power
Where a power with discretionary trust over is created, where the donees of the power and the trustees are the same people, we saw above that this is very like a discretionary trust. On principle, therefore, the exercise of the power should be controlled in the same way as that of a discretionary trust, rather than a mere power. Sir Robert Megarry V-C provides some support for this view in *Re Hay's ST* [1982] 1 WLR 1202, holding that the extent of the duty to consider both whether or not a power should be exercised, and how it should be exercised, is stronger when the power is given to someone who is also a trustee, than when a mere power is exercised. For example, it is not sufficient simply to appoint property to the objects who happen to be at hand, whereas the donee of a mere power can do this. It seems that it is necessary periodically to consider whether or not to exercise the power, and at least to appreciate the width of the field of objects, even if it is not possible to compile a list of all the objects or ascertain accurately their number. Also, individual appointments need to be considered on their merits. It is not clear whether Sir Robert Megarry V-C regarded this duty as the same as in the case of discretionary trusts, or a lesser duty, though still more stringent than in the case of a mere power.

The extent of the duty is important, at least on the orthodox view, when considering certainty of objects, and we shall return to it in chapter 4.

2.6.4 Distinguishing between trusts and powers

The distinction between discretionary trusts and powers is often extremely fine. It is a matter of construing the settlor's intention, and therefore no precise criteria can be laid down. The courts have no particular presumption one way or the other, and in the days when certainty requirements used to be much stricter for discretionary trusts than powers, the courts refused to spell valid powers out of invalid trusts (see the equitable maxims referred to in chapter 1).

If the settlor provides for a gift over or trust over in default of appointment, or has otherwise provided for this contingency, a power must be intended. This is because a trustee *must* appoint. The converse statement does not follow, however, and the courts will by no means presume a trust because there is no gift over in default. If in this case a power is construed, a failure to appoint leads to a resulting trust in favour of the settlor.

Reasons to distinguish from a power

There are a number of reasons why it is necessary to distinguish between trusts and powers:

(a) The duties of donees and trustees and method of enforcement are different (see above).

(b) The certainty of object rules used to be different, and may still be in detailed respects (see chapter 4).

(c) Suppose an appointment has become impossible, perhaps because the donee or trustee has died. In default of appointment under a power, either the instrument will provide for a gift over, or there will be a resulting trust back to the settlor. The objects have no claim. In the case of a discretionary trust, however, the property will ultimately be distributed among the objects. If the discretion is given to one person in particular, say a particular member of a family, and he dies without exercising that discretion, the court itself must do so, and in *Burrough* v *Philcox* (1840) 5 My & Cr 72, Lord Cottenham held that the property should be divided equally among the objects. This solution will not always be sensible except in family-type trusts, however, and where it is not the courts will not adopt it (*Re Baden's Deed Trusts, McPhail* v *Doulton* [1971] AC 424, see chapter 4).

online
resource
centre

FURTHER READING

Bridge (1992) OJLS 333.

Millett (1985) 101 LQR 269.

Thompson [2002] 66 Conv 387.

Wilson and Wilson (2001) 1 *Journal of Corporate Law Studies* 211.

3

Constitution of trusts and covenants to settle

One of the major themes of the law of trusts (which has already been touched on in chapter 2) lies in a comparison between contracts and trusts. A beneficiary under a fully constituted trust (let us call him A) is in a very different position from someone (B) who is entitled to benefit as a party to a contract but who is not a beneficiary under a trust. Somebody (C) who merely expects to receive a benefit as a third party to a contract between two other people is in a different position again. This chapter is essentially concerned with an analysis of those differences.

Section 3.1 details the requirements necessary for someone (let us call her X) to be in the position of A. If these requirements are not met, in other words if there is not a fully constituted trust, X may still be in the position of B or C. A likely possibility is that there is a contract to create a trust in X's favour, and if so X's rights and remedies (if any) are covered in 3.2. X may have either legal or equitable rights and remedies, or both, and they will differ. Both therefore have to be distinguished and considered.

Yet another possibility is that there is a fully constituted trust, not of tangible property, but of contractual rights themselves. This possibility is considered, along with its implications, below.

3.1 Constitution of trusts

In general, the legal title to trust property must be transferred to trustees for a valid trust to be constituted. The trustees must have control of the property. If formalities are required for this transfer, for example, in the case of land or shares, then they must be complied with. In the case of land in an area of compulsory registration of title, the relevant registration of title must be carried out.

3.1.1 Effect of constitution of trust

The effect of constituting a trust is:

(a) The arrangement becomes irreversible by the settlor; a gift once given cannot be revoked (unless the settlor has, by the terms of the trust, specifically granted himself or someone else a power to revoke the settlement).

(b) It confers to the beneficiaries enforceable rights in relation to the property (assuming a private non-purpose trust), whether or not they have provided any consideration: *Paul v Paul* (1882) 20 Ch D 742. Indeed, it is only the beneficiaries, and not the settlor, who can enforce the trust, because the settlor retains no interest in the property (assuming he is not also a trustee or beneficiary).

(c) It confers to the beneficiaries an equitable interest in the property which forms the subject matter of the trust.

3.1.2 Vesting of property in trustees

In order for a valid private trust to come into existence, these two elements are both necessary and sufficient:

(a) There must be a manifest intention on the part of the settlor to create a trust (and not to effect some other kind of transaction, such as making an outright gift or loan). The intention must be expressed in a way which complies with the certainty requirements (see chapter 4).

(b) The trust property must be properly vested in trustees who hold it in that capacity on behalf of the beneficiaries. A trust involves a division of the ownership of property. The trustees become owners at common law, and are given control of the property. The beneficiaries become owners in equity, and in effect it is they who may enjoy the property.

Constituting a trust: can be constituted 'by accident'
It is not necessary that the property be transferred in the manner that the settlor intended. If it is conveyed to trustees in any manner, even accidentally, this is sufficient to constitute the trust: *Re Ralli's WT* [1964] Ch 288 and also *Strong v Bird* (1874) LR 18 Eq 315, both considered below.

Usually, the property will be transferred to third parties as trustees, although the settlor may alternatively constitute himself trustee.

3.1.3 Equity will not perfect an imperfect gift

Conversely, if the trust property is not properly vested in trustees, then there is no trust: equity will not perfect an imperfect gift. *Milroy v Lord* (1862) 4 De GF & J 264 is the leading authority.

The settlor had executed a voluntary deed, purporting to transfer shares to a trustee on trust for the claimants. The voluntary deed was incapable of transferring legal title, however, since that could only be achieved by registering the name of the transferee in the books of the bank.

The Court of Appeal in Chancery held that no trust had been constituted, Turner LJ stating that there is no equity to perfect an imperfect gift:

... in order to render a voluntary settlement valid and effectual, the settlor must have done everything which, according to the nature of the property comprised in the settlement, was necessary to be done in order to transfer the property and render the settlement binding upon him. He may of course do this by actually transferring the property to the persons for whom he intends to provide, and the provision will then be effectual, and it will be equally effectual if he transfers the property to a trustee for the purposes of the settlement, or declares that he himself holds it on trust for those purposes; ... but, in order to render the settlement binding, one or other of these modes must ... be resorted to, for there is no equity in this Court to perfect an imperfect gift. The cases I think go further to this extent, that if the settlement is intended to be effectuated by one of the modes to which I have referred, the Court will not give effect to it by applying another of those modes. If it is intended to take effect by transfer, the Court will not hold the intended transfer to operate as a declaration of trust, for then every imperfect instrument would be made effectual by being converted into a perfect trust.

The last act of the settlor and the 'rule in Re Rose'

Where the settlor does not constitute himself trustee (on which, see 3.1.4), generally speaking, the legal title has actually to be transferred to the trustees, but Turner LJ (in *Milroy* v *Lord*, above) requires only that the settlor must have done everything which was necessary to be done in order to transfer the property. It is possible, therefore, for a trust to be constituted where the settlor has done all that is within his power to constitute the trust by transferring the property to a trustee, but has been thwarted by formalities which are outside his control. Equity regards the trust as constituted by the last act of the settlor.

Equity 'perfection' and the 'last act [of the settlor]'

This principle was applied in *Re Rose* [1952] Ch 499, CA, where the settlor intended to transfer shares, but where the directors of the company had an effective veto over any transfer. Rose executed transfers in shares in the required form in March 1943, but they could not take effect (at any rate at common law) until the directors of the company had registered them. They did this in June 1943. Rose died more than five years after executing the transfers, but less than five years after they were registered. If the effective date of the transfer was June 1943 then estate duty was payable, whereas if the transfer took effect in March it was not.

The Court of Appeal held that the date of constitution of the trust was when the settlor had done all he could, rather than when the directors consented to, and registered the transfer. Equity regarded the property as transferred by Rose's last act. Evershed MR said (at pp. 511–12) that he adopted in full the words of Jenkins J in *Re Rose* [1949] 1 Ch 78:

I was referred on that to the well known case of *Milroy* v *Lord*, and also to the recent case of *In re Fry* [see below]. Those cases, as I understand them, turn on the fact that the deceased donor had not done all in his power, according to the nature of the property given, to vest the legal interest in the property in the donee. In such circumstances it is, of course, well settled that there is no equity to complete the imperfect gift. . . . In *Milroy* v *Lord* the . . . document was not the appropriate document to pass any interest in the property at all. In this case, as I understand it, the testator had done everything in his power to divest himself of the shares in question . . .

The 'rule in Re Rose' and the significance of Re Fry

In *Re Fry* [1946] 1 Ch 312, by contrast, more may have been required from the testator effectively to transfer legal title to the shares. The reason in this case that the shares could not be registered was because Treasury consent had not been obtained, as required by the Defence (Finance) Regulations 1939, under which shares could not be registered until Treasury consent was obtained. Although all the requisite forms had been filled in by the donor, the required Treasury consent had not been obtained before he died.

This may appear, at first sight, to be similar to *Rose*, but as Romer J explained (at pp. 317–18):

Now I should have thought it was difficult to say that the testator had done everything that was required to be done by him at the time of his death, for it was necessary for him to obtain permission from the Treasury for the assignment and he had not obtained it. Moreover, the

Treasury might in any case have required further information of the kind referred to in the questionnaire submitted to him, or answers supplemental to those which he had given in reply to it; and, if so approached, he might have refused to concern himself with the matter further, in which case I do not know how anyone else could have compelled him to do so.

In this case, therefore, the testator may not have done all that was required, so the principles later elaborated in *Re Rose* could not apply.

It is not entirely clear what mechanism is operating in *Re Rose*, and the case is not without its difficulties. We have explored at least some of them in 'Re Rose: Revisited' [1998] CLJ 57, pp. 46–54.

In search of guiding principles

One possibility is that once the settlor has done all that he needs to do to constitute the trust (or effect an out-and-out transfer) he is treated as if he has declared himself trustee of the property until legal title is actually transferred to the trustees (or, in the case of an out-and-out transfer, to the transferee). This is problematic however, as it would appear to conflict with the principles discussed below. This section reveals a long line of authorities which are testament to the courts' reluctance to infer declaration of trusteeship by the settlor in absence of clear intention on his part to become a trustee. On the contrary, Rose clearly intended to make a gift of the shares to his wife, and not to become trustee of them, which is itself very difficult to square with a declaration of trust analysis.

The 'last act' and the imposition of a trust

Another possibility is that equity imposes a constructive trust over the intervening period. It will not normally matter which of these approaches is correct, but arguably declarations of trust of land must be in writing unless they can be categorised as implied, resulting or constructive trusts (see chapters 5, 7 and 9). In *Mascall v Mascall* (1984) 50 P & CR 119, the Court of Appeal applied *Re Rose* to registered land, but since the requisite writing was present the categorisation argument was not further advanced. The transferor had executed a transfer and sent it to the Inland Revenue, and also handed the land certificate to the transferee. At this stage, before the transfer and land certificate had been sent to the Land Registry for registration of the transferee as proprietor, the transferor changed his mind, after a quarrel with the transferee. The Court of Appeal held the transfer effective, since it was for the transferee to apply to the Land Registry for registration as proprietor, and the transferor had done everything he had to do to complete the transfer.

Re Rose and entrenchment of Mascall v Mascall

Although *Mascall v Mascall* is silent on whether the trust in *Re Rose* is express or constructive, it is difficult to see what resemblance, in any way the testator in *Rose* bears, to those whose conduct has become the basis of the cases considered in chapter 11 (or in chapters 10 or 19). Indeed in 'Revisited' we suggested that far from there being reasons why equity would wish to impose a constructive trust on Rose and people like him, there were sound reasons of policy why equity would wish to look kindly on those who wished to dispose of their property in favour of others. Moreover, the alternative solution, that the donor is taken to have declared himself trustee for the intervening period also looks wrong in principle given that he had intended a gift, and equity will not normally infer a declaration of trusteeship from an incomplete gift (see next section). Furthermore, on closer examination, *Re Rose* is very difficult to distinguish from *Re Fry* since the directors in *Rose* were not under any obligation to register the transfer (although they may well have routinely done so in practice), and so could presumably, had they felt so inclined, have refused to do so, or have required further particulars from the donor. It is here that both cases (*Fry* and *Rose* alike) contrast with the position in *Mascall* where the Land Registry was under a statutory duty to register the title.

'Hard case' and 'right result'
While it is the case that *Re Rose* has the feel of a 'right result' for the family in relation to liability for estates duty, the article draws attention to the fact that any analysis which is based on trusteeship would also entail Rose being liable as trustee, and thus charged with the obligation of looking after the shares on the beneficiary's behalf, and also open to attendant liability. Happily, this was for a short time only, and the directors (of whom the testator was one) were unlikely not to effect the transfer in favour of his wife (also a director). Nevertheless, it is not difficult to envisage that on different facts, the outcome might not have been so positive. However, much as *Re Rose* might appear to be wrong in principle, it must be regarded as good authority, not only because it was applied in *Mascall* v *Mascall* (not withstanding express argument that *Rose* was wrong), but also because it was approved by the House of Lords in *Vandervell* v *IRC* [1967] 2 AC 691 (see chapter 5).

While the CLJ article considers in some detail the difficulties raised by *Re Rose*, it does also suggest that in light of *Westdeutsche Landesbank Girozentrale* v *Islington London Borough Council* [1966] AC 669 (see chapter 19) we now have the opportunity to explain the case in such a way which avoids the difficulties of articulating it around a trust analysis.

3.1.4 Declaration of self as trustee

In *Milroy* v *Lord*, Turner LJ also allows for the settlor to declare himself trustee, in which case no transfer of the legal title is necessary. The courts are not keen, however, except in the clearest cases, to infer on the part of a settlor an intention to declare himself trustee, because of the onerous nature of trusteeship. An intention must be shown to create a trust, rather than to effect some other transaction (e.g., an outright gift). By contrast, an intention to make an outright gift will more easily be inferred.

Thus, in *Jones* v *Lock* (1865) LR 1 Ch App 25, the father of a baby boy handed a cheque to his nine-month old son, uttering words which made it clear that he meant the child to have the sum represented by the cheque, although he immediately removed the cheque from the baby for safe-keeping. He died some days later, without having endorsed (signed) the cheque, which would have been necessary to pass title in it to the child. The court refused to construe his actions as amounting to a declaration of trust, with himself as trustee, in favour of the child.

Need for irrevocable intention
Lord Cranworth LC did not think that an irrevocable intention to part with the property had been manifested. There was an intention to make an outright gift, but no gift had actually been made. It was not, therefore, a declaration of trust.

A similar result obtained in *Richards* v *Delbridge* (1874) LR Eq 11. Delbridge wished to give his infant grandson, Richards, the lease he had on his place of business as a bone manure merchant. He endorsed on the lease: 'This deed and all thereto belonging I give to Edward Benetto Richards from this time forth, with all the stock-in-trade'. He gave the lease to Richards' mother to hold for Richards, but died before the lease was actually delivered to Richards himself. It was held that there had been no transfer of the lease to Richards, nor a declaration of trust in his favour. Sir George Jessel MR refused to infer a declaration of trust from the failed gift:

> The principle is a very simple one. A man may transfer his property . . . in one of two ways: he may do such acts as amount in law to a conveyance or assignment of the property, and thus completely divest himself of the legal ownership, in which case the person who by those acts acquires the property takes it beneficially, or on trust, as the case may be; or the legal owner of the property may, by one or other of the modes recognised as amounting to a valid declaration of trust, constitute himself a trustee, and, without an actual transfer of the legal title, may so deal with the property as to deprive himself of its beneficial ownership, and declare that he will hold it from that time forward on trust for the other person. It is true that he need not use the words, 'I declare myself a trustee', but he must do something which is equivalent to it, and use expressions which have that meaning . . . for a man to make himself trustee there must be an expression of intention to become a trustee, whereas words of present gift shew an intention to give over property to another, and not to retain it in the donor's own hands for any purpose, fiduciary or otherwise.

Donors 'intentions; distinguishing gifts and trusts
The above passage emphasises the difference between gift and trust: so that the donor of a gift retains no interest after the property has been transferred; whereas a trustee's fiduciary obligations continue. It is no surprise, therefore, that the courts will not infer a declaration of trusteeship from a failed gift.

In the above passage, however, Jessel MR observed that the settlor need not use the words, 'I declare myself a trustee', but he must do something which is equivalent to it. It is possible to infer declaration of trusteeship from conduct, or from words which can be construed as equivalent to a declaration of trusteeship, or from a mixture of the two. In *Paul v Constance* [1977] 1 WLR 527, Constance was injured at work, and obtained £950 in damages, which he put into a bank account in his name alone. The evidence suggested, however, that the money was intended for himself and Mrs Paul, with whom he was living, but he was not married to Mrs Paul, and the reason for not opening a joint account was to avoid embarrassment for her (this was apparently on the instigation of the bank manager).

Subsequent additions were made to the account, in particular from bingo winnings which Constance and Paul played as a joint venture. One withdrawal of £150 was also made, which was divided equally between them.

Constance died, and the question at issue was whether Mrs Paul could claim any share of the fund. If the money in the account had belonged solely to Constance, then his wife, Mrs Constance, from whom he had parted, would be entitled to it on his death.

Paul v Constance
Declaration of trust The Court of Appeal held that Constance held the money on trust for Mrs Paul. No words of trust were used, but regard was had to the unsophisticated character of Constance, and the nature of his relationship with Mrs Paul. Scarman LJ said:

> . . . there must be clear evidence from what is said or done of an intention to create a trust . . . 'an intention to dispose of property or a fund so that somebody else to the exclusion of the disponent acquires a beneficial interest in it.' . . .

When one looks at the detailed evidence to see whether it goes as far as that—and I think that the evidence does go as far as that—one finds that from the time that the deceased received his damages right up to his death he was saying, on occasions, that the money was as much the plaintiff's as his. When they discussed the damages, how to invest them or what to do with them and when they discussed the bank account, he would say to her: 'The money is as much yours as mine'. . . .

It might, however, be thought that this was a borderline case, since it is not easy to pinpoint a specific moment of declaration . . .

Declarations, requirements and a 'borderline' case
There are two further points to make regarding *Paul v Constance*. First, in addition to Constance's conduct, there are his words: 'The money is as much yours as mine.' These may not obviously seem equivalent to a declaration of trusteeship, but surely what he is really saying is that although (because the bank manager advised it) legal title to the money would be vested in Constance, the money in fact belonged to both of them. Since Constance had legal title, it could only be the equitable title that was shared, so, in fact, these words are exactly appropriate for a declaration of trusteeship. We discuss similar informal words of declaration in chapter 9.

The second point is that Scarman LJ thought it difficult to pinpoint a specific moment of declaration. If it had been impossible to do so, we would suggest that there ought to have been no trust. Trusts are, in principle, irrevocable, and there must be a moment at which the irrevocable commitment is made. Before that moment, Constance could have changed his mind. Afterwards, he could not. That is essential to the nature of a trust, although in the case itself it was difficult to pinpoint exactly which moment this was.

Declarations of trust and financial distress
There are also a number of cases where companies in financial trouble have been held to have declared themselves trustee of various moneys for their customers, or others with whom they deal. The result has been that the beneficiaries have taken in preference to the general creditors. In *Re Kayford Ltd* [1975] 1 WLR 279, a mail order company was in financial difficulties. In order to protect customers in the event of insolvency, the company considered setting up a separate bank account, called the 'Customers' Trust Deposit Account' to hold the customers' deposits and payments until their goods were delivered, the intention of the company being that this money should be kept separate from the company's general funds. But the company took the advice of the bank, and instead of opening a new account, used a dormant account (with a small credit balance) in the company's name. On the winding up of the company Megarry J held that the money in the account (apart from a small credit balance) was held on trust for the customers.

Hence, the customers were not mere creditors of the company but beneficial owners of the moneys which they had paid until such time as their goods were delivered. Megarry J observed that:

it is well settled that a trust can be created without using the words 'trust' or 'confidence' or the like: the question is whether a sufficient intention to create a trust has been manifested.

Nor did he consider it fatal that the money had not been put into a separate account, but mixed with other moneys:

In *Re Nanwa Gold Mines Ltd* [1955] 1 WLR 1080 the money was sent on the faith of a promise to keep it in a separate account, but there is nothing in that case or in any other authority that

I know of to suggest that this is essential. I feel no doubt that here a trust was created. From the outset the advice (which was accepted) was to establish a trust account at the bank. The whole purpose of what was done was to ensure that the moneys remained in the beneficial owner-ship of those who sent them, and a trust is the obvious means of achieving this. No doubt the general rule is that if you send money to a company for goods which are not yet delivered, you are merely a creditor of the company unless a trust is created. The sender may create a trust by using appropriate words when he sends the money (though I wonder how many do this, even if they are equity lawyers), or the company may do it by taking suitable steps on or before receiving the money. If either is done, the obligations in respect of the money are transformed from contract to property, from debt to trust. Payment into a separate bank account is a useful (though by no means conclusive) indication of an intention to create a trust, but of course there is nothing to prevent the company from binding itself by a trust even if there are no effective banking arrangements . . . I should, however, add one thing. Different consider-ations may perhaps arise in relation to trade creditors; but here I am concerned only with members of the public, some of whom can ill afford to exchange their money for a claim to a dividend in the liquidation, and all of whom are likely to be anxious to avoid this.

However, the context of *Kayford* does now seem dated in light of modern con-sumer protection legislation, and Megarry J's judgment on the requirements of declarations of trust must, on one level, be read in light of this. Nevertheless, the commentary about the circumstances which can give rise to declarations of trust is still of utmost importance for trusts lawyers, who must be able to appreciate and understand a number of fundamental values, and how they have developed: there will always be a need to consider how these values might be applied in novel situ-ations. *Re Nanwa Gold Mines Ltd* was an early *Quistclose*-type trust (for the require-ments of which see chapter 2). As in the *Quistclose* situation, however, it is essential to be able to establish that the money belongs in equity to the customers; a personal action by them against the company after it had been wound up would clearly have availed them nothing. Therefore the money must be traceable on the principles in chapter 19. It was in *Kayford*, since the amount in the account never dropped below the amount of the small initial deposit, so that the excess could be clearly identified as trust property. Obviously, where the money is kept entirely separate, in a separate account, no difficulties of identification arise.

Re Kayford was applied by the Court of Appeal in *Re Chelsea Cloisters Ltd* (1980) 41 P & CR 98, where a 'tenants' deposit account' was set up to hold deposits against damage and breakages. Even in the absence of words of trust, however, there has to be evidence of an intention to create a trust, which is an irrevocable step, depriving the company of all beneficial interest in the money. It is not enough merely to put the money into a separate account. The requisite intention was not present in *Re Multi Guarantee Co. Ltd* [1987] BCLC 257, where the Court of Appeal distinguished the two previous cases. It had not been finally decided what to do with the money in the account, so an irrevocable intention was not established.

These cases have been criticised by Professor Michael Bridge (1992) 12 OJLS 333, at pp. 355–7, and one must wonder whether they actually take us any nearer to understanding what the courts will regard as being equivalent to the words 'I declare myself trustee'.

3.1.5 **Constitution of trusts and perfection of gifts by equity: recent developments**

Three recent decisions are relevant to this discussion of incomplete gifts and the constitution of trusts. These are: *Choitram (T) International SA* v *Pagarani* [2001] 2 All ER 492; *Pehrsson* v *von Greyerz* (unreported); and especially *Pennington* v *Waine* [2002] 1 WLR 2075. While these cases are important in this context (and shall be discussed in chronological order), they also touch on many issues which we proposed in respect of the *Re Rose, Rose* v *IRC* litigation.

Milroy v *Lord and the constitution of trusts: the significance of Choitram* v *Pagarani*
Dealing first with *Choitram* v *Pagarani* (before considering how the cases can be seen to interface), the starting point for considering its significance is the criteria for the constitution of a trust as laid out in *Milroy* v *Lord. Choitram* v *Pagarani's* significance lies in the manner in which its facts presented the courts with circumstances which did not demonstrate direct fit with the two methods for the creation of a fully constituted trust as laid down by the authority provided by *Milroy* v *Lord. Choitram* v *Pagarani* involved a wealthy Indian businessman who wished for a charitable foundation to be set up to receive a large portion of his wealth after his death. The source of the charitable foundation's benefit was to come from the shares and deposit and credit balances in companies which the businessman owned. To this end, and knowing he was in his last illness in 1992, a trust deed establishing the charitable foundation was drafted and signed by the donor, with the deed stating that he was the settlor, and appointing seven trustees of whom he was one. Upon his death shortly afterwards, no share transfers had been executed in favour of the foundation, and nor had a formal declaration of trust been executed. The decision at first instance found that there was no trust in favour of the foundation because there was no effective transfer of property, and neither had there been an effective declaration of trust. This was upheld on appeal to the Court of Appeal of the British Virgin Islands. In the Privy Council the appeal was allowed on grounds that it was found that the settlor had constituted the trust, and that the language and articulation of 'gift' by the donor in the context of the charitable foundation could only be interpreted as intending the creation of a trust. In this manner, according to Lord Browne-Wilkinson, the case was consistent with, and did not breach the requirements of *Milroy* v *Lord*. As his Lordship explained:

Although the words used by [the donor] are normally appropriate to an outright gift— 'I give to X'—in the present context there is no breach of the principle in *Milroy* v *Lord* if the words of [the] gift (to the foundation) are given their only possible meaning in this context. The foundation has no legal existence apart from the trust declared by the foundation trust deed. Therefore the words 'I give to the foundation' can only mean 'I give to the Trustees of the Foundation trust deed to be held by them on trusts of the Foundation trust deed'. Although the words are apparently words of outright gift they are essentially words of gift on trust.

Re Rose, questions of constitution and Pehrsson v *von Greyerz*
The case of *the Trustees of the Property of Pehrsson* v *von Greyerz* (unreported) (Privy Council, 16 June 1999) was another case involving shares as trust property and in considering whether the purported arrangement had become constituted as a valid

trust, the Privy Council had to consider whether the status and the significance of the appointment of trustees of shares alone had the effect of constituting the trust. This question arose in light of a purported transfer by Pehrsson to von Greyerz of shares in a company, and the execution of documentation which was not appropriate for doing this. Presiding Lord Hoffman found that there was no evidence that a transfer of the beneficial interest in the shares to the respondent, and all the dealings which the appellant had with her were concerned only with procuring the registration of shares in the former's name. On this basis it was impossible to construe a gift as having taken place before the transfer had been registered, a gift which if this had been the case, would have concerned a gift and transfer of the shares' beneficial interest. It was held in the Privy Council that the intended recipient (von Greyerz) could not rely on the rule in *Re Rose* until transfers for the shares had been executed in her favour by the nominee shareholders, and the latter had either delivered the transfers to her or constituted themselves as agents for her. Until one of these courses of action had taken place, the nominee shareholders remained nominees for the appellant, Mr Pehrsson. The transfers were in fact not executed until the same day as registration, and up until the time of delivery or constitution of agency, it remained open for the donor to countermand the gift.

The third and very important decision is the decision in *Pennington* v *Waine* [2002] 1 WLR 2075. This is in essence a consideration of the *Rose* v *IRC* litigation, and particularly the principle of the donor having done everything in his power to effect the transfer which it embodies. The Court of Appeal judgment in *Pennington* v *Waine* suggests that it is now possible for mere completion of the relevant documents of transfer to give rise to an assignment in equity of the property concerned to the intended recipient, in circumstances where the donor cannot be said to have done everything in his power to effect the transfer of the property. The principle of 'everything in his power' is, of course, a development of the rule in *Milroy* v *Lord*, and has become known as the 'rule in *Re Rose*'.

Equity, incomplete gifts and the 'rule in Re Rose': Pennington v Waine
The case of *Pennington* v *Waine* raises some very interesting issues about the 'rule in *Re Rose*', and provides an updated context for us to reiterate a number of the concerns about it which were discussed in [1998] CLJ 46, and in the previous edition of this textbook. Despite our misgivings, *Rose* was approved in *Mascall* v *Mascall*, and it actually appears now even to have been extended. *Pennington* v *Waine* does suggest that the 'rule in *Re Rose*' might have been extended to situations where a transfer can fall considerably short of the donor having done everything in his power, but where it would be unconscionable for the gift not to be 'completed' in favour of the intended recipient. As with *Re Rose* and a number of these cases, the disputation concerned the gift of company shares, the formalities of transfer requiring the registration of the new owner on the company's register of shareholders under the Companies Act 1985, s. 182. This ensures that the possession of share certificates provides evidence of share ownership but does not constitute it, and thus mere delivery will not alone constitute transfer of ownership.

The facts of *Pennington* v *Waine* are briefly as follows. In 1998 the donor, Ada Crampton, executed a form for the transfer of 400 shares held in a family company in favour of her nephew Harold Crampton. The transfer had been drawn up by the company's auditors, and in due course it was signed by her and returned to the auditors and placed on the company's file. Ada's wish was also that her nephew should become a director of the company. Thus, the auditor wrote to Harold informing him of Ada's instructions in respect of the transfer of the shares, stating in respect of this, that no action on Harold's part was required. However, Harold's consent to act as a director was required, and he was asked to complete a prescribed form for this purpose. The auditor took no further action to transfer the shares and Ada died in November of that year without the transfer having been sent to the company for Harolds' registration as the shares' new owner. It was held in the Court of Appeal that the gift of the shares to Harold was effective in equity notwithstanding that Ada had not done everything in her power to effect the transfer. Clarke LJ regarded the execution of the share transfer form as constituting the transfer in equity of the shares. This in turn generated a bare trust upon Ada, under which she could have been compelled to procure the process of registration of the shares into Harold's name, thus completing the transfer at law.

What is particularly interesting about this judgment is the view of Arden and Schiemann LJJ of the role of conscionability in the determination of equitable assignment in circumstances where the donor had not done everything in his power to effect the transfer. This approach suggests that the test originating in *Milroy* v *Lord* of the last act of the settlor might be replaced by a different test based not on the donor's actions but on his hypothetical state of mind. This alternative test is constructed around the conscionability or otherwise of a donor's (often hypothetical) ability to revoke an incomplete gift in certain circumstances. *When* such an alternative test (to the donor's actions) would be invoked is not very clear, but the essence of the conscionability test was to be a matter for the courts to determine having regard to all the circumstances of the case. And, although there could not be any comprehensive list of factors which define and constitute unconscionability, according to Arden LJ, on the facts of the case actually before the court the relevant factors could be ascertained as:

Ada made the gift of her own free will: there is no finding that she was not competent to do this. She not only told Harold about the gift and signed a form of transfer which she delivered to Mr Pennington for him to secure registration; her agent also told Harold that he need take no action. In addition, Harold agreed to become a director of the Company without limit of time, which he could not do without shares being transferred to him. If Ada had changed her mind on (say) 10 November 1998, in my judgment the court could properly have concluded that it was too late for her to do this as by that date Harold signed the form 288A (his consent to becoming a director).

The last act of the settlor: is there really a point at which donors can do no more?
In considering why it might be that the Court's attention became focused on the donor's conscience rather than his actions in this case, it is interesting to note Clarke LJ's commentary on the requirement (of *Re Rose*) that the donor must have done everything in his power for a transfer of interest to be regarded as having taken place in equity. This discussion followed from submission by counsel on behalf of the appellant that the principle that equity will only intervene (to 'complete' the transfer) where the donor has done all in his power to perfect the gift cannot literally be true 'because there is almost always something more which the donor could have done'. Clarke LJ accepted that there was 'some force' in the argument, and indeed later appeared to accept that it must be true. It was accepted that

equity could not be regarded as intervening only where the donor has done all that he can because there are seldom situations in which the donor could not possibly do anything further.

It would thus appear at some levels that Clarke LJ addressed some of the concerns we expressed in '*Re Rose* Revisited' in 1998, in respect of circumstances whereby after the purported transfer in equity there was actually still room for discretion in decision-making in regard to it, and situations whereby what remained outstanding could not be confined to formality requirements regarding the transfer in law. However, this advancement by Clarke LJ of the 'fallacy' of the last act of the settlor does not appear remotely to be concerned with arguments which counsel caution in its application. It appears instead to have been advanced as an endorsement of and even as justification for actually extending the circumstances in which equity is prepared to regard a gift as one which is perfect or easily perfected, and as such it is an approach which invites concern on the part of the authors of '*Re Rose* Revisited'.

'Re Rose Revisited' Revisited: donors, giving, certainty and conscionability
While *Choitram* v *Pagarani* makes it clear that while equity will not come to aid a volunteer 'it will not strive officiously to defeat a gift', *Pennington* v *Waine* suggests that far too much accommodation might be being given to the position of would-be donees. It is difficult to see the very premise of a gift as not being inextricably connected with the intention of the donor, and the rules surrounding equity's strictness in not perfecting those gifts which are not perfectly made reflects this, and allows for the donor to revoke the gift before the point at which it is irrevocably made. It appears from the facts of the case, and the convincing representation of them in the passage from Arden LJ's judgment above, that the gift to Harold was intended. And, in this respect *Pennington* v *Waine* appears to be directly analogous with *Rose* v *IRC*, inasmuch as both point to situations whereby on their facts, each donor was extremely unlikely to have changed his mind. Although we do not dispute that this was the intention both in *Rose* v *IRC* and *Pennington* v *Waine*, it is easy to envisage situations where the issues surrounding intention are more equivocal and far less clear cut. The Court of Appeal has demonstrated a cavalier attitude towards the principle of *Milroy* v *Lord* which is founded upon the interests of certainty when ascertaining the wishes of the donor, and which is a cornerstone of the rules surrounding making gifts: a gift will be construed as such if a gift is intended. It appears to be putting in its place a test which subjects donors, their actions and their intentions to a test of conscionability.

Milroy v *Lord* and the case law which followed it (notably *Jones* v *Lock* and *Richards* v *Delbridge*) might be seen to have produced some harsh results, and indeed the rule against imperfectly constituted gifts has led to harsh and seemingly paradoxical results. At one point Arden LJ made clear her views that an alternative test based in conscionability provides a less paternalistic framework for the consideration of gifts and giving, and one which leads to a 'benevolent construction' of gifts which gives effects to the clear wishes of the donor.

There is much which is intelligent and considered in this alternative construction of gifts, and it is of course the case that Arden LJ positioned paternalism alongside its ideological opposite; i.e., autonomy and respect for individuals. Thus, she framed her alternative test as a mechanism for ensuring that respect is given to the original intentions of the donor, asserting that approaches which (often hypothetically) permit donors to change their minds could be regarded as paternalistic. Although there is strength in this argument, we would counsel caution in its use because one central objective which *must* inform the courts' approach to the status of imperfect gifts and the position of the parties involved is present in the very next sentence of Arden LJ's judgment. This is, of course, the need to safeguard the position of the donor. At this point, perhaps it is worth remembering that the donor is central to the process of giving, and must necessarily remain so. *Pennington* v *Waine* suggests that there is a danger that the balance may be becoming tipped in a direction which might actually work against the donor's interests (albeit mainly hypothetically), and could operate to position the potential donee at his expense.

Gifts and the creation of trusts: Pennington v *Waine, donors and their wishes*
Although both *Rose* and, more recently, *Pennington* concerned transfers which were intended as outright gifts, and property not intended to become subject to a trust, the difficulties raised by this *Pennington case* do have important application in situations where the donor at the outset at least does intend to divest himself of all interest in the property, but this time in favour of a third party who is intended to hold the property on trust for an intended beneficiary. *Pennington* v *Waine* does suggest (despite Arden LJ's insistence to the contrary) that rather serious inroads might also be made into the closely related principle that equity will not infer perfect trust from an imperfect gift. Trusts law is constructed around the essence of the trust as an arrangement which is irrevocable, and this quite rightly attaches considerable import to the intention of the donor (although it was remarked in the case itself that perhaps too little attention was paid to this by the courts when ascertaining declarations of trust by settlors). While it is the case that once the trust is in place, its enforcement is at the hands of the beneficiary to the exclusion of the donor (unless he is a party to the trust), this position arises once and *only* once the trust is fully constituted.

The traditional approach, as enumerated in *Richards* v *Delbridge* (1874) LR 11 Eq, has propounded that the finding of a trust should only be made subject to a very high standard of proof. It is thus suggested that, instead of focusing on the certainty of intention and the irrevocability of the trust arrangement which is consistent with the strict nature of the trust, the doctrine of conscionability in conception might undermine the strict nature of trust and the principle that beneficiaries until they are fully constituted as such are, and *should be* at the behest of the donor. Given that Clarke LJ was himself moved to remark in *Pennington* v *Waine* that hard cases make bad law, it is a great pity that the Court of Appeal seems to have taken an approach which appears to be less interested in the wishes of the donor than it should be, and instead of favouring certainty (even if this produces harsh results) appears to be making a move towards the much more vague notion of subjecting the donor, his actions and his intentions, to far more nebulous notions of conscionability and even paternalism.

3.1.6 Sub-trusts

A further point to note is that the property settled can include an equitable interest. In other words, a beneficiary under a trust may constitute a further trust of his equitable interest, thereby creating a sub-trust. Sub-trusts are common in tax avoiding settlements. The beneficiary under the sub-trust can himself repeat the process, creating a further sub-trust, and there is no limit to the number of times this process may be repeated.

3.2 Contracts to settle

3.2.1 Common law and equitable remedies

Even if there is no fully constituted trust, that may not be the end of the matter. Sometimes would-be settlors make contracts, either with would-be trustees or would-be beneficiaries—or both, to settle property. Assume for the moment that the contract has not yet been carried out. Though some books, and indeed cases, refer to settlors, trustees and beneficiaries in this context, this is confusing where no trust is yet in existence. If the parties had actually become trustees and beneficiaries the position would be fundamentally different. We will therefore, for clarity, preface the terms with 'would-be' to indicate that no trust has yet been constituted. Clumsy English seems a reasonable price to pay for clarity of analysis, especially in an area where lack of clarity causes most of the difficulties.

Contracts to settle are especially common if the property has yet to be acquired by the would-be settlor, for example an expected inheritance yet to be received, or expected royalties on a book, because to make a contract is the best that the would-be settlor can do. She has no existing property with which to constitute the trust, and the courts have held, e.g., in *Re Ellenborough* [1903] 1 Ch 697, that future property, or expectancies, cannot form the subject matter of a trust (see also *Re Brooks* [1939] Ch 933, considered below). Additionally, however, such contracts are sometimes made to settle existing property, which is already owned by the settlor, especially where the deal is that it will be settled by will, on the death of the would-be settlor.

In principle, such contracts to settle ought to be enforceable by whoever is party to them. However, it may be that would-be trustees cannot enforce them, and even if they can, they may not always have a worthwhile remedy.

Covenants, contract and enforceability
As any student of the English law of contract knows, a contract is enforceable if it is made by deed, and also if it is supported by consideration, but a gratuitous promise (not made by deed or under seal) cannot be enforced. Most contracts (or covenants) to settle property are made either by deed or where the parties are 'within the marriage consideration' (on which, see below). There is no reason why they should not be made for conventional (i.e., common law) consideration in money or money's worth, but in practice this is uncommon. This is important in relation to the availability of remedies.

It should be noted that whereas contracts under seal (or covenants by deed) are recognised as valid by the common law, even where no consideration moves from the promisee, they are not recognised as valid in equity. The result is that whereas the common law remedy of damages can be obtained for breach of such covenants by the would-be settlor, the equitable remedy of specific performance, which would require her actually to constitute the trust, is not. Further, as we shall see, a damages remedy is not always useful, especially at the suit of the would-be trustee.

Equity, consideration and enforceability: contrasting common law contract
Equity, on the other hand, recognises marriage consideration as valid, whereas the common law does not. Thus, even if they do not provide consideration in the conventional common law sense (e.g., money or money's worth), the husband, wife or issue of a marriage can sue in equity on a contract agreed to be made before, and in consideration of, the marriage. In such cases specific performance can be obtained to force the would-be settlor to constitute the trust, or damages in lieu of it under the Chancery Amendment Act 1858. Marriage consideration is considered in greater detail in the next section.

Of course, if the contract is for ordinary common law consideration (i.e., money or money's worth), conventional contractual principles apply, except for a possible exception in the case of would-be trustees. In this area, contracts for conventional common law consideration are uncommon, but an example of such a contract is *Re Cook's ST* [1965] 1 Ch 902 (see below).

3.2.2 Factual situations

Nearly all the cases are of essentially the same type, and it is worth briefly examining the factual nature of the situation in order to explain the issues which have arisen.

The cases have typically involved marriage settlements. The agreements to settle are usually therefore made in consideration of marriage. The parties may also enter into a deed of covenant, to which trustees, or intended trustees, may also be party. A typical arrangement might be where the husband-to-be agrees to settle not only the property he owns now, but also *property yet to be acquired* (e.g., an expected inheritance yet to be received), on the terms of the settlement. Under the terms of the settlement, the beneficiaries will usually include the issue of the marriage, and in default of such issue, the next-of-kin of the wife.

The first point to note is that the settlement usually covers not only existing, but also after-acquired property. As observed in the previous section, future property, or expectancies, cannot form the subject matter of a trust, because there is insufficient certainty of subject matter. There will usually, therefore, be no failure by the settlor properly to constitute the trust: the trust *cannot* be properly constituted, since the trust property does not yet exist.

'Marriage consideration'
Covenants The second point to note is that the agreement is made, not in consideration of money or money's worth, as with most contracts, but in consideration of marriage. The relevance of marriage consideration is that not only the parties to the contract, but also any issue of that marriage (who are said to be 'within the marriage consideration') can sue on the contract. This is, in effect, an exception to the privity of contract doctrine, and is usually regarded today as a narrow and anomalous exception to the rule that equity will not assist a volunteer. Historically, it appears to have been a device to impose on the conscience of the husband (forcing him to settle the property he had agreed to settle) at a time (before the Married Women's Property Act 1882) when the wife herself had no economic independence

(and could not sue in her own right). For example, Lee argues that ((1969) 85 LQR p. 227):

[the] doctrine of marriage consideration survives as a fossil of the long era of the wife's economic subjugation to her husband. The Married Women's Property Act and the Inheritance (Family Provision) Act sounded the death knell of that era; and so the reasons of public policy which accounted for the courts' ambivalent attitude to the covenant to settle after-acquired property belong to a closed chapter of legal history.

Nevertheless, the doctrine still survives, although it is unlikely, we would suggest, that the courts are ever likely to extend it beyond its present narrow boundaries.

'Issue' First, the marriage must actually constitute the consideration for the contract, and must therefore be a future marriage. It also seems probable that only the issue of the marriage can sue, although there are (rather inconclusive) authorities to the contrary, suggesting, for example, that step-children are within the marriage consideration. Certainly, however, the next-of-kin of the wife, who will typically be the intended beneficiaries in the event of failure of issue, are not within the marriage consideration (see *Re Plumptre's Marriage Settlement* [1910] 1 Ch 609, below). The clearest recent statement of the law can be found in Buckley J's judgment in *Re Cook's ST* [1965] 1 Ch 902:

It is an elementary general rule of law that a contract affects only the parties to it and their successors in title and that no one but a party or the successor in title to a party can sue or be sued upon it. There are, however, exceptions to this rule, some legal, some equitable and some statutory. . . .

It has long since been recognised that if marriage articles or a marriage settlement contain an executory agreement to settle property, equity will assist an intended beneficiary who is issue of the marriage to enforce the agreement. Such a beneficiary is described as being within the marriage consideration. . . . On the other hand, an intended beneficiary who is not issue of the marriage is not within the marriage consideration, is not treated as though any consideration moved from him, and will not be assisted to enforce a contract to make a settlement. Thus the next-of-kin of the covenantor who are intended to take the property which is to be brought into settlement in the event of a failure of issue cannot enforce a covenant to settle . . . nor can the children by a previous marriage of one of the parties . . . nor can the children of the marriage, if the settlement is a post-nuptial one, for in such a case, though there may be consideration as between the husband and the wife, that consideration would not be their marriage but consideration of some other kind to which their children would be strangers. . . .

Policy and limitation Furthermore, the policy behind marriage consideration would probably not go beyond providing an action against the husband. There is no authority on whether the issue of the marriage, who though parties to the marriage consideration are otherwise volunteers, can sue anyone *apart* from the husband.

The third point to note is that the parties may also have entered into a deed of covenant, to which indeed the intended trustees may also be party. At common law, parties to a deed can sue on it even in the absence of consideration, but they are limited to common law remedies (i.e., damages), and cannot obtain specific performance of the covenant. It is in any case very unlikely that the intended *beneficiaries* will be party to the covenant, at any rate if they are the issue of the marriage, since at the time of the covenant they will not have been born. For an unusual example, where a beneficiary *was* party, see *Cannon v Hartley* [1949] Ch 213 (below).

Finally, although the cases usually arise because a trust has not been constituted, the intended trustees under the settlement are often actually trustees of other family property. Another possibility is that trusts of the settlement *have* been constituted, but not of the particular property in dispute. It is likely that although no trusts had been constituted of the property in dispute, the decisions in *Kay* and *Pryce* (below) may well have been influenced by the fact that the intended trustees of the settlement were actually trustees of other property.

3.2.3 Would-be beneficiary party to the contract

If the would-be beneficiary is himself party to a covenant to settle, no problems arise and he can enforce the contract, in the same way as he could enforce any other contract. If he is party to a covenant by deed, he can obtain substantial damages at law if the would-be settlor fails fully to constitute the trust.

As has already been explained, it would be unusual under the conventional form of marriage settlement for the intended beneficiaries to be party to the deed, but an unusual case, where an intended beneficiary was a party, was *Cannon v Hartley* [1949] Ch 213, where, on the breakdown of a marriage, a father (would-be settlor) covenanted to make provision for a daughter (would-be beneficiary) by settling on her property expected later to be acquired under the will of his parents. When he received the property he refused to settle it on the agreed terms. The daughter was not of course within the marriage consideration, as the covenant itself was not made prior to or in consideration of marriage. But as a party to the deed, she could enforce the contract at common law, and obtain substantial damages. Romer J observed (at p. 223):

In the present case the plaintiff, although a volunteer, is not only a party to the deed of separation but is also a direct covenantee under the very covenant upon which she is suing. She does not require the assistance of the court to enforce the covenant for she has a legal right herself to enforce it. She is not asking for equitable relief but for damages at common law for breach of covenant.

Equity, marriage consideration and the availability of remedies
The second complication is that marriage consideration is recognised only by equity, and where the beneficiary relies on this form of consideration, she must seek an equitable remedy: specific performance or damages in lieu. As stated in chapter 1, these remedies are discretionary, although this causes no difficulty in a straightforward case.

Thus, in *Pullan v Koe* [1913] 1 Ch 9 the children of the would-be settlor, being within the marriage consideration, could obtain specific performance of a covenant in consideration of marriage that the husband and wife would settle the wife's after-acquired property of the value of £100 or upwards. More remote kin, however, not being within the consideration, would be volunteers in the eyes of equity unless they had provided other consideration of value.

If, on the other hand, the would-be beneficiary is neither party to a deed nor within the marriage consideration, and has not provided any other consideration, he will be without remedy: 'equity will not assist a volunteer' (see the equitable maxims in 1.4.1). Authority for this proposition can be found in *Re Plumptre's Marriage Settlement* [1910] 1 Ch 609, the facts of which were similar to those in *Pullan v Koe*, except that the would-be beneficiaries were the next-of-kin of the wife, and hence not within the marriage consideration.

Re Plumptre's Marriage Settlement [1910]

This case concerned a marriage settlement made in 1878, covering presently owned and after-acquired property. The settlement was of the conventional type, so that, there having been a failure of issue, the intended beneficiaries were the next-of-kin of the wife. In 1884, the husband made a gift of stock to his wife. On the death of the wife, intestate, in 1909, the intended beneficiaries attempted to enforce the covenant. Eve J held that the gift of stock should have been settled on the terms of the settlement, so that the husband was in breach of covenant by making an outright gift in favour of his wife. He also held, however, that the next-of-kin could not enforce the covenant in equity because they were volunteers.

It was also noted, in passing, that the would-be trustees, who were party to the deed of covenant, would be unable to sue at common law, because they were time-barred. The breach had occurred in 1884, when the husband had used money which should have been caught by the settlement, to make an outright gift to his wife. The case was not brought until after the wife's death in 1909. It is obvious that in cases of this type there is often a long delay between the breach and the case being brought, and that limitation is therefore often a problem in this type of case (the intended trustees' action would also have been time-barred in *Pullan v Koe*).

The result was that the stock represented by the original gift (the original stock having been sold and the money reinvested) went to the husband on the intestacy of his wife, and the next-of-kin could not enforce the covenant.

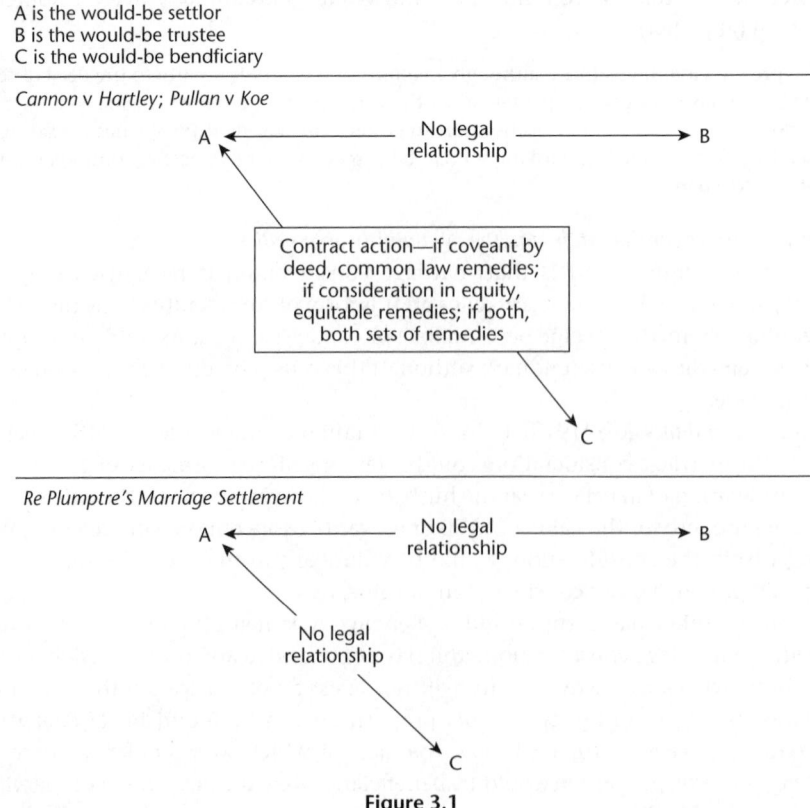

A is the would-be settlor
B is the would-be trustee
C is the would-be bendficiary

Cannon v Hartley; Pullan v Koe

A ← No legal relationship → B

Contract action—if coveant by deed, common law remedies; if consideration in equity, equitable remedies; if both, both sets of remedies

C

Re Plumptre's Marriage Settlement

A ← No legal relationship → B

No legal relationship

C

Figure 3.1

The only way in which would-be beneficiaries in a *Plumptre* situation could benefit from the covenant would be if there were other beneficiaries who were not volunteers (as in *Pullan v Koe*), such as the children of the marriage, who could enforce the covenant on behalf of the would-be beneficiaries as well as on their own behalf, or the would-be beneficiaries were themselves parties to the covenant.

These cases are illustrated in figure 3.1.

3.2.4 Would-be trustee party to the contract

The problem discussed in this section is illustrated in figure 3.2.

It might be thought that the same position should apply and that the would-be trustee should be able to sue. Of course, the initiative would lie with him; the would-be beneficiary could not force him to sue (assuming he has no action in his own right, on the principles outlined above). There are *dicta*, however, pointing to the likelihood that he will not be allowed to bring the action. In *Re Kay's Settlement* [1939] Ch 329, the would-be trustees (though they were actually trustees of other property) were party to a covenant under seal with the would-be settlor to settle after-acquired property. No consideration moved from them, however. The would-be beneficiaries were not party to the covenant, nor were they within the marriage consideration, so were therefore volunteers. The would-be trustees requested directions as to whether or not they ought to take steps to enforce the covenant or to recover damages. The court directed them not to do so. At the end of his judgment, Simonds J, following Eve J in *Re Pryce* [1917] 1 Ch 234, said:

> . . . it appears to me that . . . I must direct the trustees not to take any steps either to compel performance of the covenant or to recover damages through [the settlor's] failure to implement it.

Re Pryce and the approach in Re Cook
This *dictum* was followed by Buckley J in *Re Cook's ST* [1965] 1 Ch 902, an unusual case in which, as part of a resettlement of family capital, Sir Francis Cook covenanted with his father, Sir Herbert Cook, and with would-be trustees (who were also actual trustees of property under another settlement), that if Sir Francis sold any of the valuable pictures specified in a schedule to the agreement, during his lifetime, the proceeds would be held on the terms of the settlement. The beneficiaries under the settlement were various members of Sir Francis's family (but Sir Herbert was not himself one of the beneficiaries).

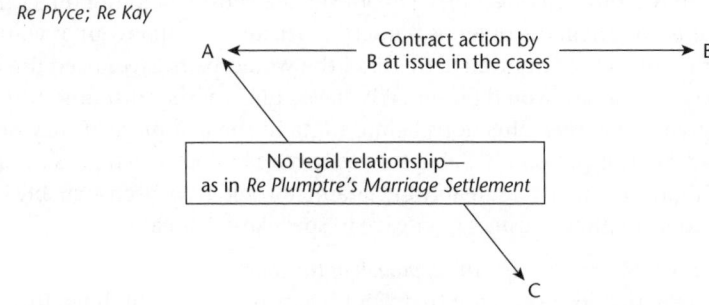

Re Pryce; Re Kay

Figure 3.2

There was no consideration for Sir Francis' covenant moving from the would-be trustees; nor, of course, was there any consideration moving from Sir Francis' children (who were beneficiaries). Buckley J found that there *was* consideration moving from Sir Herbert.

Sir Francis married several times, and gave (or purported to give) one of the pictures to one of his subsequent wives. The subsequent wife, after her divorce from him, wanted to sell it, and the trustees of the settlement sought directions from the court. The issue was whether the would-be trustees were obliged to take steps to enforce the covenant against Sir Francis. Buckley J thought not, which on the facts is perhaps not surprising, on the basis that the *Re Pryce/Re Kay's ST* line of authority was a bar to an action by the would-be trustees. In the judgment, he did not say that the trustees had no remedy, or that they should not themselves enforce the covenant, but only that they could not be compelled to do so by the would-be beneficiaries. However, the actual order was in similar terms to that in *Re Pryce/Re Kay's ST*.

Third parties, remedies and the (apparent) effect of Re Pryce, Kay and Cook
It should be appreciated that though Simonds J in the above passage talks of 'trustees', the claimants never in fact became trustees, at any rate of the property which formed the subject matter of the dispute. What happened in *Pryce*, *Kay* and *Cook* was that a would-be settlor refused to add, to an already constituted trust, further property which was yet to be acquired. The *would-be* trustees of this new property were therefore *already* trustees of a perfect trust (of other property), and the question seems to have been treated as one in which they were contemplating taking steps (as is of course perfectly proper) to get in property which is owed to a trust. The court appeared to regard them as acting on behalf of the trust (which however was of *other property*), thereby obscuring the fact that as parties to the covenant they were acting in a purely personal capacity.

The apparent effect of *Pryce*, *Kay* and *Cook* is to deprive a claimant of an otherwise perfectly valid common law contract action. It is one thing for equity to refuse to assist a volunteer, but surely quite another for it to deprive others (not the volunteers) of actions which they would otherwise have? We would suggest that we need first to consider whether the cases really do have this effect. If they do, it is necessary further to consider whether this can possibly be justified. If it cannot, then it seems perfectly plausible to argue that what are after all first instance *dicta* are wrong. Let us consider first whether the cases really do have the effect described here.

It is important to note that in none of the cases did the courts decide what the outcome would have been if the trustees had actually sued. The trustees did not do so, but merely requested directions. Obviously, the court would not direct them to sue, and force on them the onerous burdens of trusteeship, in favour of volunteers. A further point to bear in mind is that had the would-be trustees been directed to sue, the cost of the suit would presumably have fallen on the trust fund (this is one reason why trustees seek directions before suing in the first place: if they obey the court, they are not personally liable for costs in an action which goes against the trust). With the outcome presumably uncertain, it would have been arguably inapposite for a court to direct trustees to engage in speculative litigation.

Would-be trustees, remedies and the approach of the courts
Perhaps, then, the position is not that would-be trustees are prohibited from bringing an action, but only that the court would not direct them to sue, and force on them the onerous burdens of trusteeship, in favour of volunteers. Professor Elliott

has argued that the would-be trustees should have been directed that they need not sue, not that they ought not to sue: (1960) 76 LQR 100. It would indeed be perfectly proper for the court to leave the decision as to whether to exercise one's rights to the private individual, just as in any other case where a person has a right of action. On the other hand, they had requested directions, and arguably these ought to be mandatory in form.

Common law action and trustee prerogative
Let us now suppose that this is wrong, and that would-be trustees would be prevented from bringing their common law action. Can this be justified? It can be argued that to allow them to sue gives them a discretion as to whether or not to enforce the trust, and that this is inconsistent with the very nature of a trust. Since the court will not force the trustees to act in favour of a volunteer, the only possibility is to deprive them of action. The problem with this view is that they are *not yet* trustees, at any rate of the disputed property, so objections based on giving trustees discretion cannot apply. The choice given to *would-be* trustees is not whether to carry out their duties under a trust—there is no trust yet—but whether or not to become a trustee at all. This is a perfectly proper choice which anyone faced with a request to become a trustee is entitled to make.

If the would-be trustees choose to sue, and obtain specific performance (not a remedy available in any of the cases, since in none had the would-be trustees provided consideration), then they become trustees. But at that point they no longer have a discretion; once they have taken this step, they have to carry out the trust. In other words, to allow them to sue does not give trustees a discretion as to whether or not they enforce the trust. The choice is given to people who are not trustees, as to whether or not they undertake the onerous duties of trusteeship. That choice is always given to would-be trustees, and is perfectly proper.

A different view; sound(er) in policy?
Another argument is that, at any rate where the covenant is voluntary, it is for the settlor voluntarily to constitute the trust. There may be good policy reasons for taking this approach, especially when it is remembered that the covenants are usually entered into when the would-be settlor is young and the property covered often includes much of what he will acquire over an entire lifetime. Where the contract is for consideration, then arguably different considerations apply.

One problem with this view is that there is little if any authority for the proposition that it is for the settlor voluntarily to constitute the trust. There is, however, contrary authority in *Re Ralli's WT* [1964] Ch 288 (below). Another problem is that a different position ought to obtain where the contract is for consideration, but the cases do not seem to distinguish. Certainly, *Re Kay* concerns what appears to be a genuine voluntary settlement by a spinster, who only married much later. There was no marriage consideration, and hence the children of the marriage were volunteer beneficiaries. The covenant in *Re Pryce* also appears at first sight to have been voluntary, but closer examination shows that it actually formed part of a marriage settlement, with consideration moving from both husband and wife (but admittedly none from the trustees). There was no issue and the beneficiaries in default of issue were volunteers. There was consideration in *Re Cook*, but again none moving from the trustees. It does not seem that the cases distinguish between voluntary covenants and covenants for consideration, although whether consideration moving from the trustees themselves would make any difference has not been tested.

Equity and its (non-)interference in common law actions
It is also pertinent to point out that equity does not generally interfere with common law contract actions, even when they are only covenants by deed, and regardless of the age of the covenantor. If it interferes here, special considerations would have to apply.

Let us now suppose, for the sake of argument, that the cases do not have the effect of preventing the would-be trustees from suing. Suppose also that they do sue. What remedy do they get? Let us first suppose that specific performance is, in principle, available. The action for specific performance would have the effect of constituting the trust. Arguably, the equitable remedy would be being used to assist the volunteers, and that could be an argument for equity refusing to grant the remedy. It would not be an argument for interfering with the common law remedy for damages.

Where the covenant is voluntary, damages are in this case the only available remedy. Damages compensate for loss suffered and since it is the would-be beneficiary who is intended to receive the benefit, arguably the would-be trustee personally suffers no loss, if the trust is not constituted. Indeed, if the duties under the putative trust are of an onerous nature, as they will often be, the would-be trustee may actually be seen as gaining from the settlor's breach (by virtue of being relieved of an onerous obligation). On this argument the damages will be nominal.

Common law actions and how damages are held
However, Goddard argues ([1988] Conv 19) that this situation is not comparable with *Beswick* v *Beswick* [1968] AC 58 or *Woodar Investment Developments Ltd* v *Wimpey Construction (UK) Ltd* [1980] 1 WLR 277 (see 2.3.2.1), since here the would-be settlor has covenanted to transfer property to the would-be trustee, whereas in *Beswick* v *Beswick* the contract was to transfer money directly to the third party, without any intermediate transmission to the other contracting party. Arguably, therefore, the breach has deprived the would-be trustee of property to which he is entitled, and damages should compensate for that. No doubt, the would-be trustee is not intended to obtain the benefit of that property, but rather to hold it on trust, rendering the would-be trustee's loss nugatory, but this is irrelevant as far as the common law is concerned. Goddard notes that there are pre-Judicature Act authorities that the common law would grant substantial damages, and ignore equitable obligations.

If this analysis is correct, the next question is whether the would-be trustee holds the damages as trustee. If equity requires him to hold them on the trusts of the covenant, equity will be assisting a volunteer, so this seems an unlikely solution. But the would-be trustee was never intended to keep the damages beneficially. The only possible solution would be to require him to hold them on resulting trust for the settlor.

The conclusion that we would draw is that whatever *Pryce, Kay* and *Cook* decide, it is unlikely that a would-be trustee would have a useful remedy even were he allowed to sue.

3.3 Contracts (Rights of Third Parties Act) 1999: enforcement of a covenant by beneficiaries

Following the discussion of the principles above, the would-be beneficiaries *themselves* may in addition be able to bring an action at law to enforce the covenant against the settlor by virtue of the Contracts (Rights of Third Parties) Act 1999. By way of reminder, from the note made of the traditional relationship between trust and contract law in the previous chapter, the two have had their closest interactions around the doctrine of privity. Here, the trust has been shown as an important mechanism to circumvent contract law's traditional position of severely limiting the position of third parties to the contract. The trust is a device by which enforceable rights for third parties to an agreement can arise.

In the previous chapter it was noted that the privity of contract doctrine has long attracted criticism, especially in relation to contracts which were clearly intended to provide a third party with a benefit, with *Beswick* v *Beswick* [1968] AC 58 as paradigm illustration of this, the harshness which can result, and the way in which the trust can come to the aid of parties not in the (ultimately fortunate) position of Mrs Beswick. The 1999 Act followed the Law Commission's recommendations for reform of the privity doctrine published in *Privity of Contract: Contracts for the Benefit of Third Parties* (Law Com. 242). By the provisions of this Act, it is now possible for a person who is not party to a contract to enforce it where, according to s. 1, his right to enforce a term of the contract has been expressly provided for by the contract or the term purports to confer a benefit for him. However, note was also made of the way in which this facility operated subject to the provisions of s. 1(2), whereby this will not apply where on proper construction of the contract it appears that the parties did not intend the term to be enforceable by the third party. The question now arises how and in what ways this legislation might impact on situations raised in this discussion of a beneficiary's position in enforcing a covenant.

Covenants to settle and the in principle application of the 1999 Act
In principle, the provisions of the 1999 Act suggest that the contract is no longer revocable by the contracting parties in the traditional sense of contract law, and this might well provide a would-be beneficiary with a position enforceable at law to compel the settlor to enforce the covenant—or at least, receive compensation for her refusal so to do. Section 1 of the 1999 Act provides that a third party to a contract who is identifiable can enforce any term of it in her own right. This is provided that (either) the contract (or particular terms of the contract) purport to confer a benefit to her, and there is no apparent intention, on a proper construction of the terms, that she should not be conferred such enforceable rights. In terms of application, the Act applies automatically to all contracts coming into being on or after 11 May 2000: six months following the Act's enactment, and contracts created in the period between the enactment and the date of automatic application (i.e., the six months' intervening period) require an express provision as to the Act's application.

The 1999 Act: impact and operation
In terms of how this impacts on the position of covenants to settle (i.e., covenants to settle property on trust), the Act will thus normally apply. This will give the third

party enforceable rights at law against the settlor, and an entitlement to damages (in his own right) arising from the settlor's breach of covenant. And in terms of how this actually operates in the covenant situation considered at length in this chapter, consideration needs to be given first to how a third party becomes 'identifiable' for the purposes of the Act's provisions. This is governed by s. 1(3) of the Act, by which a third party is deemed identifiable where he is expressly defined in the contract by his name; he is (identifiable as) a member of a class; or (identifiable as) answering to a particular description but need not be in existence when the contract is entered into. In the covenant scenario, whereby what is at issue is the creation of a trust, the identification point is consistent with the requirement (that for a valid trust) there must be certainty of objects. This means that there must be identifiable beneficiaries who are intended to benefit from the trust (and who, once the trust comes into being, will be in a position to enforce it), and will be the subject matter of the next chapter.

The covenant context and available remedies

The way in which the third party for the purposes of the Act 'need not be in existence when the contract is entered into' is very significant in this context, because intended beneficiaries are quite often unborn when the covenants to settle property are entered into. And in terms of remedial value, by the provisions of s. 1(5) where the third party is exercising his right to enforce a contract intended to benefit him, the remedies which are available to him are such that would have been available to him in an action for breach of contract had he been a party to it. In recognition of this, the subsection states that the (normally applicable) rules governing damages, injunctions, specific performance and other relief accordingly apply to a claim brought in this way.

The 1999 Act and some very important limitations

However, there are important limitations to this, the most obvious of which can arise from within s. 1 itself, by virtue of s. 1(2). As noted above, this provides that the facility for third party enforceable rights will not apply in situations where, on proper construction of the contract, it appears that the parties did not intend the term(s) to be enforceable by parties other than those to the contract itself. This must be seen as a formidable obstruction to the creation of third party rights to enforce any covenant to settle property. In addition to this, there is an even stronger limit to the creation of enforceable third party rights by the provisions of s. 2 of the Act. This must be couched within the purported protection conferred by s. 1(2) whereby the contracting parties' right to vary or cancel the third party's entitlement is lost once the third party has relied on it and accepted the contract as it stands. However, superimposed on top of this is the mechanism of s. 2, which allows the parties expressly to reserve the right to vary or cancel the third party's reliance or acceptance.

'Would-be beneficiary's charter'?

This consideration of the 1999 Act reveals that whilst (through the provisions of s. 1) an intended beneficiary under a covenant will be in a stronger position *vis à vis* compelling the settlor to settle the property (or at least be entitled to receive an award for damages in his own right, rather than having to secure co-operation from trustees), there are significant limitations on declaring it as a 'would-be beneficiary's charter'. Where the settlor is in a position to ignore any potential rights at law arising in this way (because on the instrument's construction the third party was not intended to confer a benefit, or in the case of the covenant to settle, because the settlor has taken steps to rescind entitlements), the importance of the key case law considered above remains.

3.4 Trusts of promises

There is no reason in principle why a covenant made to would-be trustees to settle property should not of itself form the subject matter of a trust. The benefit of such a covenant, i.e., the right of the other party to sue on it, is itself a form of property: a chose in action. If a settlor so wishes, he can settle (i.e., create a fully constituted trust) of that chose in action in just the same way as he could settle any other property. All he has to do is to transfer that property—the benefit of the covenant—to the intended trustees. This will perfect the trust, and the beneficiaries can now enforce that trust just as if the subject matter were land or cash, even if they are not party to the covenant.

It has been shown how in *Re Kay's Settlement*, for example, no trust of the after-acquired *property* was constituted. But had it been decided that a valid trust had been constituted of the *covenant* (or promise), the result would have been very different: the beneficiaries, though volunteers, would have enforceable rights against the trustees of the covenant. Far from the trustees being directed not to sue on it, the beneficiaries could have required them to do so. A diagrammatic representation of this situation appears in figure 3.3.

We have to consider, then, on what basis will the courts construe a trust of a promise, and whether there are any limits on the doctrine.

3.4.1 When do trusts of promises arise?

The leading case, where a trust of a promise arose, was *Fletcher* v *Fletcher* (1844) 4 Hare 67. Ellis Fletcher covenanted with trustees by deed to pay £60,000 to his trustees, on trust for his illegitimate sons, who were outside the marriage consideration, and were thus volunteers. The surviving son, Jacob, was able to compel the trustees (note that the term is here correctly used) to enforce the covenant on his behalf. Though the *money* was never settled, Wigram V-C held that the *covenant* was

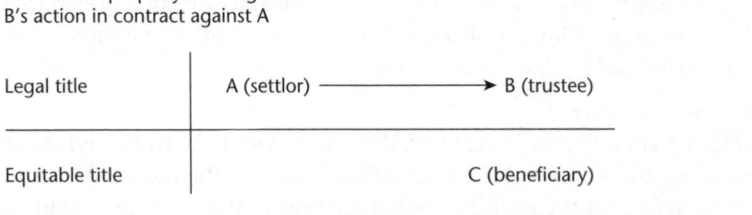

Substantive property as in Figure 3.2
B's action in contract against A

Legal title	A (settlor) ⟶ B (trustee)
Equitable title	C (beneficiary)

B holds the benefit of the contract on constituted trust for C, who can therefore force B to enforce it

Figure 3.3

held on a fully constituted trust for Jacob. Thus Jacob could enforce it in his own right, despite being a volunteer. Substantial damages were recoverable, amounting to the promised £60,000.

It seems from this case that the beneficiary can force the trustee to sue on the covenant, and that substantial damages can be recovered (at any rate where the covenant concerns the settlement of money), which will be held in trust for the beneficiary.

Principle and practice: difficulties of Fletcher v Fletcher

Although the principle of *Fletcher* v *Fletcher* is no doubt sound, there are difficulties in construing a trust of the promise on the facts. A point often made is that the trustees knew nothing of the covenant until the death of the settlor, Ellis Fletcher, and then were unwilling to enforce it. Even so, Jacob could compel the trustees to sue. However, it could be argued that the ignorance of the trustees, or their unwillingness to accept the trust, should not be a bar to a finding that Fletcher has meant to give his trustees a chose in action rather than the money itself, so creating a valid trust. The relevant intention is surely that of the settlor, not of the trustees. If a trustee is unwilling to act, 'Equity will not allow a trust to fail for want of a trustee' (see maxims, at 1.3.1), and the courts will appoint another trustee.

Ascertaining the intention of the settlor

Accepting that the relevant intention is that of the settlor, however, we still have to ask who this is. After all, this is a trust of the promise, not of the property to be settled. It is, arguably, the would-be *trustee* of the property who owns the contractual cause of action, since he can enforce it, so surely he rather than the settlor of the property is settlor of the contract? Indeed, on this view the would-be trustee of the property is both settlor and trustee of the promise, declaring himself trustee of it.

Difficulties: who owns in equity?

Now there is no doubt that the would-be trustee of the property is the *legal* owner of the contract, but who owns it in equity? Clearly not the would-be trustee, since he is not intended to take the benefit beneficially. Surely the position is that if the settlor of the property contracts with the would-be trustee as trustee of the promise, then the would-be beneficiaries of the property under the settlement are *true* beneficiaries of the promise. There is a fully constituted trust of the promise. But if the settlor of the property contracts with the would-be trustee *otherwise* than as trustee of the promise, the position is exactly as in *Pryce*, *Kay* and *Cook*. The would-be beneficiaries under the settlement are clearly not in that case beneficiaries of the promise, nor is the would-be trustee. The only possible beneficial owner of the promise is the settlor himself. In other words, in the absence of a declaration of a trust of the promise in favour of the volunteer beneficiaries, *the trustees hold the chose in action on resulting trust for the settlor.*

Settlor as beneficial owner

It would seem to follow, therefore, that although the would-be trustee is legal owner of the promise, the settlor is beneficial owner unless it (the promise) is settled in trust. It is therefore for the settlor to create the trust of the promise, and his intention is the relevant intention. Were it otherwise the would-be trustees in *Pryce*, *Kay* and *Cook* could at any time declare themselves trustees of their promise, thereby significantly improving the position of the volunteers.

Nevertheless, in cases since *Fletcher* v *Fletcher* the courts have demanded much more conclusive evidence that the settlor really did intend to settle the benefit of the covenant, before construing trusts of promises: e.g., *Re Schebsman* [1944] Ch 83 in chapter 2, and see Smith [1982] Conv 352. It is probable that were the same facts to arise today, no trust would be construed, and *Fletcher* v *Fletcher* would be considered wrongly decided in this regard.

3.4.2 **Limits to** *Fletcher* v *Fletcher*

Fletcher v *Fletcher* involved a covenant to settle money. No doubt covenants to settle other property can also form the subject matter of a trust, but there is some doubt as to whether a covenant to settle after-acquired property (i.e., mere expectations of the settlor) can be. Buckley J thought that it could not, in *Re Cook's ST* [1965] Ch 902:

Counsel for the second and third defendants have contended that on the true view of the facts there was an immediate settlement of the obligation created by the covenant, and not merely a covenant to settle something in the future . . . He relied on *Fletcher* v *Fletcher* (1844) 4 Hare 67 . . . I am not able to accept this argument. The covenant with which I am concerned did not, in my opinion, create a debt enforceable at law, that is to say, a property right, which, although to bear fruit only in the future and upon contingency, was capable of being made the subject of an immediate trust, as was held to be the case in *Fletcher* v *Fletcher*. Nor is this covenant associated with property which was the subject of an immediate trust . . . Nor did the covenant relate to property which then belonged to the covenantor . . . In contrast to all these cases, this covenant upon its true construction is, in my opinion, an executory contract to settle a particular fund or particular funds of money which at the date of the covenant did not exist and which might never come into existence. It is analogous to a covenant to settle an expectation or to settle after-acquired property. The case, in my judgment, involves the law of contract, not the law of trusts.

Subject matter of a trust and 'after-acquired' property
The view that a covenant to settle after-acquired property cannot form the subject matter of a trust has also been taken by Lee (1969) 85 LQR 213, and Barton (1975) 91 LQR 236, but this reasoning has been criticised: e.g., Meagher and Lehane (1976) 92 LQR 427. Perhaps this is the explanation for no trust of a promise being constituted in *Re Kay*, which concerned after-acquired property.

Nevertheless, it is by no means obvious why a *contract* to settle after-acquired property cannot form the subject matter of a trust, even though it is impossible to create an immediate trust of after-acquired property (see 3.2.1). The contract after all is existing not future property. The reasoning in *Re Ellenborough* [1903] 1 Ch 697 does not apply to it. There may be a remedies problem, however. We saw in chapter 2 that a party who contracts as trustee for another can claim substantial damages to hold on trust for that other, and where the contract is to settle existing property (or an existing sum of money as in *Fletcher* itself), there is no difficulty in calculating those damages. In *Re Cavendish Browne's ST* [1916] WN 341, Catherine Cavendish Browne made a voluntary settlement containing a covenant to 'convey and transfer to the trustees all the property, both real and personal, to which she was absolutely entitled by virtue of the joint operation of the wills of' two named persons. She died without having settled property to which she was so entitled in trust. Younger J, 'without delivering a final judgment, held . . . that the trustees were entitled to recover [from Catherine's administrators] substantial damages for breach of the covenant . . . and that the measure of damages was the value of the property which would have come into the hands of the trustees if the covenant had been duly performed'. Although it is not entirely clear, it appears that Catherine was *already* entitled to the property at the time that the contract was made.

After-acquired property and Re Cavendish Browne

In the above passage from *Cook*, Buckley J talks of the covenant in *Fletcher* creating a debt enforceable at law, and the same is presumably true in *Re Cavendish Browne's ST*: see also Friend [1982] Conv 280. The trust of the promise constituted the settlor as debtor of the trustees. This reasoning may not be possible where the covenant is to settle after-acquired property, however, since it will be difficult or impossible to assess damages based on the value of property which has not yet been acquired, may never be acquired, and indeed need not even yet exist. Perhaps this is the real reason for limiting the principle in *Fletcher* v *Fletcher* to covenants for existing property (but see the contrary argument by Meagher and Lehane (1976) 92 LQR 427).

3.5 Property actually transferred

Whether or not the contract to settle property is enforceable, and whether or not the trustees will be allowed to enforce it, if the settlor actually transfers the property as promised, he cannot later reclaim it, because the act of transfer will have created a perfect trust of the money. In *Re Ellenborough* [1903] 1 Ch 697 (see 3.2.1), the court would not compel Miss Emily Towry Law to pay over the legacy when it arrived, but there was no argument in favour of allowing her to reclaim earlier payments which she had made in fulfilment of the same covenant which she now declined to perform.

Nor, if *Re Ralli's WT* [1964] Ch 288 is correct, would it prevent the trust from becoming fully constituted if the property came into the trustee's hands in some other capacity than that of trustee. In *Ralli's WT* the trust was constituted by the accident that the would-be trustee was also trustee under an earlier will, and so obtained legal title by those means.

Constitution and the transfer of property

In *Ralli's WT*, Helen's father left his residue on trust for his wife for her life, thence to his two daughters, Helen and Irene. Helen, by her marriage settlement, covenanted with trustees, of whom the claimant (Irene's husband) was one, to settle all her existing and after-acquired property on Irene's children.

On Helen's death, in 1956, the claimant, who was the sole surviving trustee under the marriage settlement, was also appointed a trustee under Helen's father's will, and hence obtained title to Helen's residuary estate under her father's will, on the death of Helen's mother (in 1961). He brought an action to determine whether he held the property on the terms of Helen's will, or on the trusts of Helen's marriage settlement.

Buckley J held that the trust of the after-acquired property in the marriage settlement was completely constituted, since the claimant held the property under Helen's father's will. It was irrelevant that the claimant came by the property under Helen's father's will, rather than under Helen's marriage settlement itself:

In my judgment the circumstances that the plaintiff holds the fund because he was appointed a trustee of the will is irrelevant. He is at law the owner of the fund, and the means by which he became so have no effect upon the quality of his legal ownership . . . . It is also true that, if it were necessary to enforce performance of the covenant, equity would not assist the beneficiaries under the settlement, because they were mere volunteers; and that for the same reason the plaintiff, as trustee of the settlement, would not be bound to enforce the covenant and would not be constrained by the court to do so, and indeed, it seems, might be constrained by the court not to do so. As matters stand, however, there is no occasion to invoke the assistance of equity to enforce performance of the covenant.

How property becomes vested in trustees: is this important?
The logic of *Re Ralli's WT* extends to all cases where the trustee acquires legal title, and so long as he does so the method of acquisition is irrelevant. Thus, the principle ought still to apply if, for example, he comes by his legal title not as his executor, but as the settlor's trustee in bankruptcy, or even as a judgment creditor, or where the settlor has mortgaged his property to the would-be trustee, and the would-be trustee forecloses. However, it seems that transfer of legal title is required, and not merely physical possession.

One of the arguments considered in 3.2.4 was that it is for the settlor under a voluntary settlement voluntarily to settle the property. Yet, clearly in *Re Ralli's WT* Helen took no steps at all to settle the property, yet a fully constituted trust was held to have been created. If *Re Ralli's WT* is correct, and this is the true explanation of it, a trust can be constituted without any action at all by the settlor.

Re Ralli: what does it really mean?
So is *Re Ralli's WT* correct, and is this the true explanation of the case? Rather surprisingly, *Re Brooks* [1939] Ch 993 was not cited, Buckley J reasoning instead from *Re James* [1935] Ch 449, a *Strong v Bird* authority (see 3.5.2) which is not on all fours since that doctrine requires an intention, continuing until death, to transfer on the part of the transferor. By contrast, *Re Ralli's WT* required no intention of any kind on Helen's part. It is, however, very difficult to reconcile *Re Ralli's WT* with *Re Brooks*, which is pretty well on all fours with *Re Ralli's WT*. *Re Brooks* concerned the property of a mother and her son, and in particular a voluntary settlement of after-acquired property by the son. Lloyds Bank were the trustees under this voluntary settlement. Later, because of the exercise by his mother of a power of appointment in his favour, the son acquired property which should have been caught by the voluntary settlement. The power of appointment had been granted to his mother under her marriage settlement. But Lloyds Bank were also trustees under the marriage settlement, and hence already had legal title to this property. The issue was whether Lloyds Bank held the property for the son, or on the trusts in the son's voluntary settlement. It was held that they held the property for the son. The main issue was whether this property was existing or after-acquired property at the time the son's voluntary settlement was made. It was held that it was after-acquired property until the appointment was actually made in his favour. It could therefore not form the subject matter of a trust. *Re Ellenborough* (see 3.2.1) was followed.

The problem is that Lloyds Bank's position was exactly analogous with that of the claimant in *Re Ralli's WT*; they had acquired the property which was subject to the son's voluntary settlement otherwise than in their capacity as trustees under that settlement. Yet the opposite decision was reached to that in *Re Ralli's WT*. Both sets of reasoning cannot be correct.

Reconciling Re Ralli and Re Ellenborough

There is only one way of reconciling the cases. In *Re Ralli's WT* Helen settled a reversionary interest, which counts as existing property, even though enjoyment of it was postponed until after her mother's death. Existing property is not subject to *Re Ellenborough*, and the alternative view adopted by Buckley J was that Helen had declared herself trustee of it from the moment of her marriage settlement. If this is right there is no need to treat *Re Ralli's WT* as an authority on covenants to settle at all. It was simply an immediate declaration of trust of existing property. Trusts do have to be constituted by some act of the settlor. Of course, one would have to regard the covenants reasoning in *Re Ralli's WT* as wrong.

The only other possibility is that *Re Brooks* is wrong. With two conflicting first instance authorities, and no other clearly relevant authorities, it is impossible to reach a clear conclusion.

3.6 'Exceptions' to the principle that equity will not assist volunteers

In this section two apparent exceptions are considered to the principle that equity will not assist a volunteer. It can be argued that they are not genuine exceptions, but merely additional methods by which a trust can be fully constituted, but whether or not this is the case, they operate as if they were exceptions to the general rule.

It should also perhaps be mentioned that it would be very rare for either of the exceptions considered below to occur. No settlor would deliberately invoke them. Problems in this area, in so far as they occur at all in practice, arise *ex post facto* because of competing claims to a deceased person's property.

3.6.1 *Donatio mortis causa*

A *donatio mortis causa* (which, translated from Latin, broadly means 'gift by reason of death') is a gift made in contemplation of, and conditional upon, the death of the donor. It is different from an ordinary, immediate gift, for the donee's title does not come into existence until the death occurs: until such time, the donor may revoke. Nor is it a testamentary gift taking effect under the terms of a properly attested will. Suppose, for example, that A is terminally ill, or about to engage in a dangerous activity and, realising that death is a possibility, entrusts some of his property to B, telling him that if A should die, B may keep the property as his own. Although B has custody of the property he will not own it unless and until A dies.

If that happens, equity regards B's title as perfected, and he may claim the property in preference to anyone to whom A may have chosen to bequeath it in his will. So if A has already made a will in which all his personal property, which would otherwise include the property entrusted to B, is left to X, B has a better claim by virtue of the conditional gift.

The situations in which *donationes mortis causa* (note Latin plural) are most likely to occur are variations on something like this: A is a man and B is his mistress. A wishes to benefit B on his death, but does not wish to leave property in his will because he does not wish to disclose her existence to his 'legitimate' family. Nor, possibly for the same reason, does he wish to make an *inter vivos* transfer in her favour. The *donatio mortis causa* is the obvious device for him to use.

Equity's stringent conditions

To permit the making of a disposition which is neither an immediate perfect gift nor a formal testamentary disposition is to invite fraudulent claims intended to defeat the expectations of legatees, and it is therefore not surprising that equity hedges a *donatio mortis causa* with stringent conditions.

The necessary conditions for a *donatio mortis causa* were set out by Farwell J in *Re Craven's Estate* [1937] Ch 423:

1. The transfer must be with the intention of giving, and not simply of securing, the goods. There is no *donatio mortis causa* if A simply wants B to look after his property.

2. It must be clear that the property was handed over in contemplation of a real possibility of death, and some specific focus on the possibility of death must be shown. The donor must anticipate some hazard to life. This is usually a serious illness, but extreme hazard (such as motor racing) is also probably covered, but not normal, everyday risks, e.g., air travel.

   The gift must be conditional upon death occurring, and otherwise revocable, i.e., A must intend to keep the property himself if he survives. This requirement is superfluous where the property is a chattel which could be transferred by simple delivery, since A could obviously have made a valid immediate gift if he chose, but it is relevant where some further formal step is required to perfect the title, as e.g., in the case of land (see below).

3. The donor must have effectively parted with dominion over the subject matter of the gift. In other words, the property must have been handed over, or the means of access to it transferred, e.g., by giving B the key to the bank deposit box where the property is lodged. The test is whether the donor has put it out of his power between the dates of gift and death to alter the subject matter of gift and substitute other property for it: see also *Re Lillingston* [1952] 2 All ER 184, at p. 191. In *Woodard* v *Woodard* [1995] 3 All ER 980, the Court of Appeal inferred a *donatio mortis causa* of a car from the handing over of its keys, where the donor had also said: 'You can keep the keys, I won't be driving it any more.' It was immaterial that the car was already in the donee's possession as bailee, or that another set of keys (which the donor was in any case in no position to use) might have existed.

   It is also possible to transfer property which is not capable of physical delivery, e.g., by handing over *indicia* of title, such as a savings bank book, or (presumably) a bill of lading covering a consignment of cargo aboard a ship. The test is whether handing over the document 'amounted to a transfer', in which case possession or production of the document would entitle the possessor to the money in the account.

3.6.1.1 *Donatio mortis causa and land*

Long after most students of the law of trusts must have thought that *donatio mortis causa* cases were ancient history, a *donatio mortis causa* was successfully argued before the Court of Appeal in *Sen* v *Headley* [1991] Ch 425. It had long been thought that it was impossible to have a *donatio mortis causa* of land, because the third of Farwell J's conditions cannot be satisfied, even by delivery of the title deeds; but on the assumption that *Sen* v *Headley* is correct, this view must now be regarded as wrong.

Mr Hewett, who was, at the age of 86, on his death-bed, gave the claimant, Mrs Sen, the keys to a steel box with the title deeds to his house inside, saying to her:

The house is yours, Margaret. You have the keys. They are in your bag. The deeds are in the steel box.

It appeared that Mr Hewett and Mrs Sen had, for some 30 years, lived together as if married. Title to the house was unregistered.

After Hewett's death, the gift was challenged by his next-of-kin. There were no difficulties over Farwell J's first two criteria set out above, but at first instance ([1990] Ch 728), Mummery J thought that the third was not satisfied: Hewett had not parted with dominion over the house. He concluded, in effect, that land cannot form the subject matter of a *donatio mortis causa*.

Clearly, the transfer of title deeds could not amount to a transfer of the land itself during Hewett's lifetime, since no deed was executed, and a declaration of trust would require writing. This is because it would have to be a declaration of trust of land (see chapter 5). Here there was no documentation at all, and Margaret could at most acquire a 'mere *spes*' (hope or expectation) of obtaining the property. Mummery J's view was that the entire doctrine was anomalous, and that judicial caution should be exercised before extending it, that the policy of the law required formality for dispositions of land and interests in land, and that, accordingly, the *donatio mortis causa* doctrine would not be extended so as to allow an attempt at disposition on death which avoided the Wills Act formalities (on which, see chapter 10), or the perfection of an imperfect *inter vivos* gift.

The clear inference from Mummery J's judgment was that *donatio mortis causa* could *never* apply to land. This view, at any rate, was in line with the orthodox views that had been long held.

Mummery J was reversed in the Court of Appeal, however, on analogy with extensions of the doctrine in previous cases. In *Snellgrove* v *Bailey* (1744) 3 Atk 213, the doctrine had been applied to a gift of money secured by a bond, by delivery of the bond; in *Duffield* v *Elwes* (1827) 1 Bli (NS) 497, the House of Lords had applied the doctrine to a gift of money secured by a mortgage of land, by delivery of the mortgage deed. In each case, transfer of *indicia* of title was all that was required. (However, one problem is that, in *Duffield* v *Elwes*, Lord Eldon thought the doctrine would not apply to a gift of land by delivery of the title deeds.)

No doubt the doctrine was anomalous, but in the view of Nourse LJ, that did not justify creating anomalous exceptions to the admittedly anomalous doctrine. The only reason why, with unregistered land, transfer of the title deeds did not transfer title to the property was because of a formality statute. All *donationes mortis causa* avoid formality provisions, usually the Wills Act (on which, see further, chapter 10). There was no reason why the formality provisions relating to land should be regarded as presenting any greater obstacle than any other formality provisions, and no reason why this case should be treated differently from the cases alluded to in the previous paragraph.

It does not necessarily follow that shares in private companies, which cannot be physically transferred, can also be the subject of a *donatio mortis causa*, since registration of a new owner may be refused. They are therefore not directly analogous to land.

3.6.1.2 *Death sooner than expected*

It seems on the basis of *Wilkes* v *Allington* [1931] 2 Ch 104 that the gift is valid even if A dies sooner than expected, and even if from a different cause. The donor was suffering from an incurable disease, and made the gift knowing that he had not long to live. In fact he died even earlier than expected of pneumonia, but the gift was held to be valid. Whether the same principle would apply even if the death were completely different from A's expectation is less clear (e.g., he dies of food poisoning).

3.6.2 **The rule in** *Strong* v *Bird*

The other exception to the principle that equity will not assist a volunteer (and an example of the presumption that equitable title follows legal—see chapter 7) is the rule in *Strong* v *Bird* (1874) LR 18 Eq 315, and it could arise in some such fashion as this. A hands B his share certificates but fails to procure the transfer and registration of B as owner. He then dies, leaving a will which appoints B as his executor but makes X the legatee of all his personal property. Again, equity treats the gift as perfected, this time by the vesting of A's property in B in his capacity as executor, and the claims of the beneficiaries under the will (in this case X) are overridden.

The same principle operates if B owes A money, but A makes no effort to collect his debt and appoints B his executor: these were the facts of *Strong* v *Bird* itself. The appointment is, as it were, a conclusive release of the debt. But it must be clear that there was an intention to make the gift or release the debt, and that this intention continued until death.

Facts and central issue of law

In *Strong* v *Bird*, the defendant borrowed £1,100 from his stepmother. His stepmother lived in his house and paid rent at £212 quarterly. The money borrowed by the defendant was to be repaid by 11 deductions of £100 from quarterly rent. The stepmother made two deductions, but after that made no more, and continued to pay full £212 until her death. Verbally, she forgave the defendant the remainder of debt (but this was ineffective as a release at law). The defendant was appointed executor under her will. The residuary legatees claimed the remainder of the debt, but Jessel MR held the defendant not liable. His appointment as an executor extinguished the debt at common law since it is impossible for an executor to sue himself. It seems that equity acquiesces with the common law position, subject to the other requirements of doctrine.

In *Re Stewart* [1908] 2 Ch 251, Neville J applied the same principle to perfect imperfect *inter vivos* gift of bonds by appointment of the intended donee as executor. Equity would not interfere with the common law transfer of title. The doctrine depends on an attempt to make an immediate *inter vivos* gift of specific property, a continuing intent to make the gift until death, and the vesting of legal title in the donee.

One might argue that the logic of the rule in *Strong* v *Bird* requires that B be *voluntarily* appointed executor by A, but there is some authority that the rule operates if B becomes A's administrator, instead of his executor. This was the view of Farwell J in *Re James* [1935] Ch 449, where a housekeeper had herself appointed one of two administratrices of the testator's estate.

In *Re Gonin* [1979] Ch 16, Walton J cast doubt on *Re James*. In *Re Gonin*, the claimant alleged that, in return for her returning home after being called away during the Second World War, and going to live with and look after her parents, her parents had verbally agreed that the parental home and its contents should become hers on their deaths. The claimant's father died in 1957, leaving no estate. After the death of the claimant's mother in 1968, the claimant took out letters of administration to her estate, and began an action to determine whether she was entitled, as administratrix, to vest the freehold in the property in herself.

Executors and administrators

She claimed both land and contents (furniture) under the rule in *Strong* v *Bird*, on the basis that the claimant's mother intended to give the claimant the house on her death, and the gift was perfected by the claimant taking out letters of administration.

Walton J took the view that the appointment of an administrator was quite different to the appointment of an executor, since it is not a voluntary act of the deceased, but of the law. It was also often a matter of pure chance which of many persons entitled to a grant of letters of administration actually took them out:

Why, then, should any special tenderness be shown to a person so selected by law and not the will of the testator, and often indifferently selected among many with an equal claim? It would seem an astonishing doctrine of equity that if the person who wishes to take the benefit of the rule in *Strong* v *Bird* manages to be the person to obtain a grant then he will be able to do so, but if a person equally entitled manages to obtain a prior grant, then he will not be able to do so.

Re Gonin and questions remaining

Walton J did not need actually to decide whether the earlier authority was correct, however, since he also held that even if the rule in *Strong* v *Bird* applied to administrators, the evidence did not point to a continuing intention on the part of the claimant's mother to give the house to the claimant.

It is nevertheless possible to defend *Re James*. Kodilinye argues ([1982] Conv 14, at p. 17) that the criticisms of *Re James* by Walton J cannot stand, for a number of reasons. He argues that the crux of Jessel MR's principle is that the gift (or release in *Strong* v *Bird* itself) is perfected by the vesting of the legal title in the donee, and it is immaterial whether that vesting is brought about by the act of the donor or by the operation of law. He also points out that the need to give effect to the will of the testator is already satisfied by the requirement that the donor must have shown an intention to give *inter vivos* until his death. Therefore, there is no need for any *additional* voluntary act by the testator, such as appointing the donee executor. It must be admitted that there is some force in these arguments.

Re James was applied in *Re Ralli's WT*, but the situation there was different because no intention at all was needed on the part of the transferor. It is easier to support Farwell J's views in *Re James* than those of Buckley J in *Re Ralli's WT*.

FURTHER READING

Friend [1982] Conv 280.

Garton [2003] Conv 364.

Goddard [1988] Conv 19.

Kodiling [1982] Conv 14.

Lee (1968) 85 LQR 227.

Lowrie and Todd [1998] CLJ 46.

Rickett [2001] Conv 515.

4

The three certainties and the significance of the 'beneficiary principle'

Chapter 3 was about the vesting of property in trustees, a prerequisite to the existence of any trust. Chapters 4 to 6 are about further requirements for validity, assuming the property is so vested. This chapter deals with the requirement for certainty, and the significance of trusts law's cardinal 'beneficiary principle'.

The requirements considered in this chapter apply not only to trusts which are expressly created, but also to resulting and constructive trusts. Charitable trusts are exempt from certainty of object requirements, and they are also incidentally largely exempt from the perpetuity rules (see chapter 6). For convenience, certainty of objects requirements for powers also are included in this chapter, by way of comparison with those for discretionary trusts.

4.1 Certainty

4.1.1 Reasons for certainty requirements

There are two main reasons for certainty requirements. The first and obvious reason is to ensure that the property is correctly identified and is dealt with in accordance with the wishes of the settlor. Thus, a doubt as to those wishes leads the courts to play safe rather than risk an unauthorised disposition of a person's property. Additionally, it must be clear to the trustees themselves exactly what their duties are. The difficulty is most acute in the case of testamentary trusts, where those who have the duty of administering the estate have to rely for guidance upon whatever terms the testator may have chosen to express his desires, since obviously it is not possible to ask him.

The second reason is less obvious. Whereas today trustees usually act in a professional capacity, the typical trust of 200 years ago was very different in nature, and the rules originally developed around the older type of trust. These were often family arrangements, and one of the main concerns of the courts was that the trustees might be fraudulent and keep the trust property themselves. Equity has been criticised for making essentially the same assumptions about, e.g., banks and company directors today; the problem stems from adapting to a modern situation a set of principles which were originally developed for quite a different purpose. Certainly, a limited degree of successful adaptation has occurred, but the same basic assumption remains, namely that trustees are likely to be fraudulent.

At least until very recently, the courts have tended to over-emphasise the pathological situation, in which the trustees refuse to carry out the trust. The courts have insisted that there must exist someone with sufficient interest in the trust property to be able to come to court to compel the trustees to carry out the trust and in the final analysis the courts must be able to administer the trust themselves. This emphasis has led (at least until recently) to much more rigid certainty requirements than might otherwise have been the case.

4.1.2 The three certainties

The classification for certainty usually cited is that of Lord Langdale in *Knight* v *Knight* (1840) 3 Beav 148, 173: while the classification has been criticised, there is no doubt that it is the one adopted by the courts. The essential prerequisites of a valid private express trust are certainty as to the intention of the settlor to create a trust of property (sometimes misleadingly termed certainty of words), certainty as to the property to which the trust is to attach (also referred to as certainty of subject matter), and certainty as to the persons or 'objects' who are to benefit (certainty of object).

4.1.3 Effect of absence of certainty

If any of the certainties is absent then no valid express trust will be created, but the precise consequences will depend upon the circumstances. If the settlor attempts to declare himself trustee, the declaration will be invalid whichever certainty is not satisfied. If legal title has been transferred but there is uncertainty as to the intention to create a trust (i.e., to separate the legal and equitable titles) then the transferee will hold it free of any trust. If either of the other certainties is absent, there will be a resulting trust to the settlor (or residuary legatees, in the case of an attempt to establish a trust by will), subject to one exception: *Hancock* v *Watson* [1902] AC 14 establishes that where there is an absolute gift of property in the first instance and trusts are subsequently imposed on that property, then if the trusts fail for any reason the property is not held on a resulting trust for the settlor or his estate but will vest absolutely in the person to whom the property was given. We can see this in, e.g., *Palmer* v *Simmonds* (1854) 2 Drew 221 (below).

4.2 Certainty of intention

4.2.1 Words or intention?

Although Lord Langdale spoke of certainty in relation to the words alleged to establish the settlor's intention, this is misleading in two respects. First, it is possible to establish a trust without any writing whatever, except where the statutory formality requirements obtain (see chapter 5). A trust need not even be orally declared, as it is possible to establish an intention of a settlor to create a trust (i.e., to separate legal and equitable titles) from words or conduct; this may be inferred from the nature of the gift as a whole. No doubt *in fact* most express trusts are created by means of written documents, since they arise either by will or in a formal settlement, carefully documented to meet the settlor's tax planning needs. A modern trust precedent will be highly intricate and will attempt to provide for almost all conceivable contingencies. But in principle technical words are not necessary, since equity looks to the intention rather than the form of the transaction. It is not even necessary that the word 'trust' should have been employed, if the intention to create a trust is clear.

The second reason why Lord Langdale's statement is misleading is that even where words are present, the courts do not have regard to them alone, though they are important in construing the intention of the would-be settlor. Indeed, to rely on words alone as binding precedent would be dangerous, as the attitude of the courts has changed considerably over the last 150 years or so, especially regarding precatory words (i.e., words expressing a wish, hope or request, rather than being imperative).

4.2.2 History of precatory words

So far as testamentary gifts are concerned, up to about the middle of the 19th century the courts were disposed to find that almost any expression of desire by a testator that his property should be used in a given manner was intended to create a binding trust of that property in the hands of an executor or legatee. The reasons historically can be traced to the fact that the administration of estates lay formerly with the ecclesiastical courts, which permitted the executor to keep for himself any undisposed-of residue of property left after the specific bequests had been satisfied. When this jurisdiction was taken over by the Court of Chancery, it preferred to treat the executor as trustee of such residue for the testator's family. Almost any expression of desire or hope would be seized upon to effect this policy. Even this solution was not entirely satisfactory. Widows and eldest sons of gentry were often provided for in any event by a marriage settlement, or entail of the estate, and the courts were suspicious of their ability to manage the family property in prudent fashion (that is to say, keeping it in the family). Therefore a similar principle was applied to legatees as had formerly been applied to executors. The outcome was that precatory words like 'wish', 'hope' or even 'in confidence' that the legatee would use the gift to benefit others, were taken to create binding trusts.

Precatory words and the courts' new approach from 1830
The rationale for the lenient view taken of precatory words largely disappeared with the Executors Act of 1830, which specifically required executors to hold property in an appropriate manner. Since 1830, therefore, the courts have felt able to tighten up their attitude, the modern view being derived from the judgment of Cotton LJ in *Re Adams and the Kensington Vestry* (1884) 27 Ch D 394, 410, where it was established that beneficiaries were no longer to be made trustees unless this was the testator's clear intention, and a gift to the widow 'in full confidence that she would do what was right as to the disposal thereof between my children, either in her lifetime or by will after her decease' was treated as giving the widow an absolute interest unfettered by any trust in favour of the children. Cotton LJ thought that many of the older authorities had gone too far; he also thought that one should consider the total effect of the instrument (not only the particular words) to ascertain the testator's

intention. Other cases around the same time made it clear that the attitude of the courts towards precatory words had changed.

4.2.3 Law relating to precatory words

Since intention is all important, however, a trust may still be created by precatory words, if such intention appears from the document (or settlor's conduct) as a whole. See, for example, the cases considered in chapter 3.

Because the whole document or transaction is to be considered, it does not follow that the same precatory words will always have the same effect. Thus, in *Re Hamilton* [1895] 2 Ch 370, 373, Lindley LJ said (of a testamentary gift):

> You must take the will which you have to construe and see what it means, and if you come to the conclusion that no trust was intended, you say so, although previous judges have said the contrary on some wills more or less similar to the one you have to construe.

In *Cominsky* v *Bowring-Hanbury* [1905] AC 84, the House of Lords found a trust on the basis of words very similar to those employed in *Re Adams and the Kensington Vestry*: 'absolutely in full confidence that she [the widow] will make such use of [the property] as I would have made myself and that at her death she will devise it to such one or more of my nieces as she may think fit'.

A testator's reproduction of exact language
If on the other hand, a testator reproduces the exact language of an earlier will which has previously been held to create a trust, it may be possible to infer that he intended to use the earlier will as a precedent. If so, there is authority that the court in construing the later will should follow the earlier decision, at least unless that decision was clearly wrong (*Re Steele's WT* [1948] Ch 603). Though this case attaches great significance to the actual precatory words used, it is not really an exception to the flexible approach described above, because all the circumstances do indeed point to an intention to create a trust. It follows that draftsmen should make clear beyond doubt that precatory words are intended to indicate desire alone, unless of course a trust is indeed intended.

A further, somewhat technical, consideration is that the creation of a gift in a will, followed by the inclusion of a precatory expression in a codicil, raises a stronger inference of intention to create a trust than would be the case were both gift and precatory words to appear in the same instrument (*Re Burley* [1910] 1 Ch 215). Lastly, it should not be forgotten that the testator, while not intending to create a trust, may have subjected the property to a power of appointment (on which, see chapter 2) instead of making an outright gift to the legatee. In any case, the decision as to the testator's intention is a matter of construction of the document, and no hard and fast rule can be laid down for determining when this intention is present.

4.3 Certainty of subject matter

To satisfy the test it appears to be necessary that the trust property be defined in objective rather than subjective terms, or, in other words, so as not to be a matter on which opinions may reasonably differ. In *Palmer* v *Simmonds* (1854) 2 Drew 221, a testatrix left on trust 'the bulk' of her residuary estate, and Kindersley V-C, after consulting a dictionary, concluded that the word 'bulk' was inadequate to specify any portion of the property as trust property:

> What is the meaning then of bulk? The appropriate meaning, according to its derivation, is something which bulges out . . . Its popular meaning we all know. When a person is said to have given the bulk of his property, what is meant is not the whole but the greater part, and that is in fact consistent with its classical meaning. When, therefore, the testatrix uses that term, can I say that she has used a term expressing a definite, clear, certain part of her estate, or the whole of her estate? I am bound to say that she has not designated the subject as to which she expresses her confidence; and I am therefore of opinion that there is no trust created; that [the residuary legatee] took absolutely, and those claiming under him now take.

Since it was not possible to carve out from the residue that portion which was to be held on trust, the trust failed and the residuary legatee took the whole absolutely. This is an application of what later became the rule in *Hancock* v *Watson* [1902] AC 14.

The same result was reached in *Curtis* v *Rippon* (1820) 5 Madd 434, where not only was there uncertainty as to the property to be subject to the trust, but also as to the identity of the beneficiaries themselves. The widow received all her husband's property under his will, subject to an exhortation (using precatory words that were valid at the time) that she should use the property for the spiritual and temporal good of herself and the children, 'remembering always, according to circumstances, the Church of God and the poor'. The clause rendered uncertain even who was to benefit.

No certainty in absence of technical or objective meaning

An approach similar to that in *Palmer* v *Simmonds* was taken in *Re Kolb's WT* [1962] Ch 531, where the testator referred, in an investment clause in his will, to 'blue-chip' securities, a term generally used to designate shares in large public companies which are considered an entirely safe investment. The term has no technical or objective meaning, however, and Cross J held that its meaning in the context must depend on the standard applied by the testator, which could not be determined with sufficient certainty to enable the clause to be upheld. The case was considered in a different context in *Trustees of the British Museum* v *Attorney-General* [1984] 1 WLR 418, which is discussed in chapter 17.

Re Golay: a rogue decision or one which can be made sense of?

In *Re Golay's WT* [1965] 1 WLR 969, the testator had directed his trustees to allow 'Totty' to 'enjoy one of my flats during her lifetime and to receive a reasonable income from my other properties'. Ungoed-Thomas J felt able to uphold the gift, as the trustees could select a flat, and the income to be received by Totty could be quantified objectively by the court. If, on the other hand, Totty had been entitled to receive what the testator or a specified person considered to be reasonable, then the trust would fail, since the test would be subjective.

The judgment in *Re Golay's WT* is very short, and the case appears to be out of line with the others considered. The test cannot simply be whether the income could be objectively quantified by the court, since a court could equally well quantify 'the bulk' or 'blue-chip securities'. Can it really be supposed that a court, faced with a statutory provision which applied to 'blue-chip securities' would be unable to apply the provision? The courts can define the reasonable man. Surely they would not be defeated by 'blue-chip securities'.

We would suggest that in *Re Golay's WT*, Ungoed-Thomas J misunderstood the function of a certainty test. It is not, we would suggest, to make life easier for courts, but to ensure that the trustees can administer the trust. That is why precise object-ive definitions are required, so that the trustees know exactly which property is sub-ject to the trust, and which property is not. A 'reasonable income' would not seem sufficiently certain to satisfy that criterion, unless the view were taken that the trustees should forever be coming to court to obtain directions.

Hunter v *Moss: beautifully simple or fraught with difficulty?*

In *Hunter* v *Moss* [1994] 1 WLR 452 (followed in *Re Lewis's of Leicester Ltd* [1995] 1 BCLC 428), an oral declaration of trusteeship of 50 shares of a company's issued share capital of 1,000 shares succeeded, even though the particular shares were not ascertained or identified. However, the company was precisely identified, all the shares in that company were identical, and the quantification (50 shares) was obvi-ously precise. Moreover, as long as the trustee retained all 1,000 shares there would be no point in identifying which 50 shares were subject to the trust.

Difficulties in a case like *Hunter* v *Moss* could arise if the trustee later split up the fund, sold the shares and invested some of the proceeds in fund A and some in fund B, one of which funds would then have performed better than the other. We would suggest that this problem would not arise if the settlement had been of 5 per cent of the issued share capital, since then it would be clear that the trust owned 5 per cent of fund A and 5 per cent of fund B.

On the assumption that the case is correct, then the applicable principles ought to be those in 19.2. The trustee is mixing trust funds with his own, and the decision in *Re Hallett's Estate* (1880) 13 Ch D 696 suggests that the beneficiaries could choose which fund held their share of the proceeds. If, however, the trustee had declared other trusts of the remaining shares, the contest would be between competing beneficiaries, and there would be no reason to apply *Hallett's Estate*. *Re Diplock* [1948] Ch 465 suggests that in such circumstances, a *pari passu* distribution would be appropriate.

Hunter v *Moss criticised*

All this presupposes that the decision in *Hunter* v *Moss* is correct, but it has come under fairly heavy academic criticism, e.g., Hayton (1994) 110 LQR 335, and has been regarded as inconsistent with the Privy Council decision in *Re Goldcorp Exchange* [1995] 1 AC 74 (see also chapters 15 and 19), where an argument was unsuccessfully advanced that a seller of gold bullion (who had gone into liquidation having taken money from the purchasers) had become a trustee of an undivided share in his stocks. Peter Birks ([1995] RLR 83, 87) even went so far as to argue that from the reasoning of the Privy Council in *Re Goldcorp Exchange Ltd*: 'One inference is that the Court of Appeal's decision in *Hunter* v *Moss* [1994] 1 WLR 452 must be wrong.' In fact, neither case mentions the other, possibly because they were decided at virtually the same time, and there are quite significant differences between the two cases. In *Goldcorp*, there was no declaration of trusteeship by the vendor, so there is a certainty of intention problem; the trust property was not constant, since the vendor's gold stocks were being traded all the time; there is also much author-ity, for example in *Re Wait* [1927] 1 Ch 606, followed in *Re London Wine Co. (Shippers) Ltd* [1986] PCC 121, and *The Aliakmon* [1986] AC 785 (on which see also 1.4.6.5), for the reluctance of the courts to import notions of equitable property into commercial sales of goods, primarily for reasons connected with certainty. Any of these would have been quite convincing grounds, in my view, for distinguishing between *Hunter* and *Goldcorp*, even on the assumption that both cases are correct. A different distinction was, however, drawn by Neuberger J in *Re Harvard Securities* [1997] 2 BCLC 369; he took the view that if he was forced to choose between *Hunter* and *Goldcorp*, he was bound to follow the decision of the Court of Appeal in preference to that of the Privy Council, but also took the view that at any rate, for dealings in shares, Hunter was a correct statement of the law. The distinction between shares and other property seems difficult to justify in principle, however, and I cannot see the difficulty with *Hunter* v *Moss*, while recognising that *Goldcorp* is different, for all of the other three reasons stated above.

4.4 Certainty of objects

Certainty of objects rules serve two main functions. First, if a trustee, or donee of a power fails to carry out his duties, or exercises his discretion in an improper manner, it is important to be able to ascertain who has *locus standi* to come to court to remedy the situation. Second, a trustee, or donee of a power, has to be able to ascertain who are the objects in order to be able to exercise his discretion in a proper manner.

4.4.1 Rationale of the rules: enforcement

Once a settlement has been made, whether it creates a trust or a power, the settlor ceases to have any interest in the property. Indeed, in the common case of a settlement by will he will naturally be unable to have any further personal say. The question then arises as to what happens if the trustee, or the donee of the power, does not carry out the trust or power. Sometimes a trustee will have agreed to act for consideration (e.g., a bank acting under a remuneration clause). In that case the settlor, or his personal representatives can sue at common law in contract. It is not an altogether satisfactory action, however, as we saw in chapter 3: unless he can obtain specific performance, he will be limited to claiming damages for his own loss, which will probably be nominal only. Therefore the courts have always been very concerned that someone who benefits in equity is able to enforce the trust.

The certainty requirements to achieve this end depend on the nature of enforcement by the courts. They have taken a more realistic and less rigid view in recent years of the manner in which trusts are to be ultimately enforced. This has led to a relaxation of certainty rules, which in most respects is to be welcomed.

Generally speaking, all that is now required for this purpose is for it to be possible to tell, with certainty, whether any individual coming to court to enforce a trust or power has sufficient interest to do so: in other words whether or not he is within the class of objects. This test is called the 'individual ascertainability test'. It is not necessary to be able to draw up a list of all the objects, a much more stringent requirement called the 'class ascertainability test'. Further, in applying the individual ascertainability test, it is necessary only that definitions in the settlement be conceptually certain. The court itself can deal with evidential difficulties when an application for enforcement arises. See further, 4.4.5.2–4.4.5.4.

4.4.2 **Rationale of the rules: administering the trust**

Some writers argue (e.g., Matthews [1984] Conv 22) that this is not a proper function of certainty of objects rules at all, but the orthodox view is otherwise (see, e.g., Jill Martin in her reply in [1984] Conv 304). The certainty test required to enable trustees or donees of powers to discover all that is necessary for them to be able to carry out the trust depends on the nature of their discretion. Generally speaking, however, if a trustee or donee has to get any impression of the size or composition of the entire class in order to carry out his duties, a more stringent test is required than individual ascertainability.

4.4.3 **Operation of the rules**

The manner in which a settlement is ultimately enforced, and the nature of the discretion given to trustees or donees of powers, depend on whether a fixed trust, discretionary trust or power has been created (see chapter 2 for the distinctions). The certainty of objects requirements vary accordingly, so it is necessary to consider separately the certainty requirements for each of these categories.

4.4.4 **Powers**

The nature of mere powers has been considered in chapter 2. Donees of a power (unlike discretionary trustees) have a discretion not only as to *how* to distribute the property, but also as to *whether* to distribute it. They are under no obligation to appoint at all, subject to limited exceptions. In other words, whereas a trust is imperative, because the trustees have to appoint, a power is discretionary, because the donees of a power need not appoint at all—the choice is theirs.

If there is a gift over in default of appointment, the disposition must take effect as a power, not a trust, since the existence of the gift over is obviously inconsistent with an imperative duty to appoint. The absence of a gift over in default is not necessarily indicative of a trust, however, since the alternative construction, of a power with a resulting trust in favour of the settlor in the absence of appointment, is also possible. It will all depend on the words used in the instrument.

Certainty tests and powers of appointment
In the case of mere powers (i.e., a power not given to a fiduciary), the donee's discretion seems to be unfettered except in so far that he must not dispose of the property otherwise than in accordance with the terms of the power. The objects can come to court to enforce the power, therefore, only to the limited extent that the court will restrain disposal of the property otherwise than in accordance with the terms of the power.

This limited negative duty can be carried out and enforced so long as 'it can be said with certainty that any given individual is or is not a member of the class'. No more stringent test of certainty than the individual ascertainability test is required.

It is probably more common for powers of appointment to be given to trustees, in which case the donees of the power will not enjoy an unfettered discretion. Sir Robert Megarry V-C took the view in *Re Hay's ST* [1982] 1 WLR 1202, that the extent of the duty to consider both whether or not a power should be exercised, and how it should be exercised, is stronger when the power is given to someone who is also a trustee, than when a mere power is exercised. For example, it is not sufficient simply to appoint to the objects who happen to be at hand, whereas the donee of a mere power can do this. It seems that it is necessary periodically to consider whether or not to exercise the power, and at least to appreciate the width of the field of objects, even if it is not possible to compile a list of all the objects, or ascertain accurately their number. Also, individual appointments need to be considered on their merits:

> The trustee must not simply proceed to exercise the power in favour of such of the objects as happen to be at hand or claim his attention. He must first consider what persons or classes of persons are objects of the power within the definition in the settlement or will. In doing this, there is no need to compile a complete list of the objects, or even to make an accurate assessment of the number of them: what is needed is an appreciation of the width of the field, and thus whether a selection is to be made merely from a dozen, or, instead, from thousands or millions . . .

Tests for certainty: the significance of (distinguishing) trusts and powers
Nevertheless, if at the end of the day the donees of the power refuse to exercise it, that is a choice that they are entitled to make, and there is no reason why the courts should be required to distribute on their behalf. It is still necessary to be able to ascertain of any given individual whether or not he or she is an object of the power, since only objects of the power will have *locus standi* to enforce it, even to the limited extent of preventing the donees acting otherwise than in accordance with its terms. It is also necessary for the objects to be defined so that the donees can, as required by Sir Robert Megarry V-C above, get a feel for the width of the class.

Despite this, the duty to consider is not so stringent as to require the donees, in order to carry it out, to draw up a list of the entire class of potential beneficiaries, and there is therefore no reason in principle to apply the class ascertainability test to powers.

In *Re Gestetner's Settlement* [1953] 1 Ch 672, Harman J had to consider the validity of a power given to trustees to distribute among a very wide class, including directors and employees or former employees of a large number of companies, with a gift over in default. Since membership of the class constantly fluctuated, it was impossible to draw up a list of the entire class at any one time. He held that it was not necessary to know all the objects in order to appoint, and that it was not fatal that the entire class could not be ascertained.

In *Re Gulbenkian's Settlements* [1970] AC 508, trustees were given a power to apply income from the trust fund to maintain, among others, any person in whose house or in whose company or in whose care Gulbenkian may from time to time be residing, and there was a gift over in default of appointment. In upholding the power, the House of Lords held that the individual ascertainability test was the applicable test for powers: a power would be valid if it could be said with certainty whether any given individual was *or was not* a member of the class, and would not fail simply because it was impossible to ascertain every member of the class.

Note that the dispositions in both *Gestetner* and *Gulbenkian* must have been powers, as in each case there was a gift over in default of appointment. A gift over would be inappropriate in a discretionary trust, since the trustees are obliged to appoint.

The significance of the Gulbenkian test

There are two points specifically to note about the *Gulbenkian* test. First, the italicised words, *or was not*, are important. Second, the House of Lords expressly rejected Lord Denning MR's test in the Court of Appeal in *Gulbenkian* [1968] Ch 126, at pp. 132–4. On the basis that a power would only be held void for uncertainty if it was impossible to carry it out, he had taken the view that it should be necessary only to be able to identify one single beneficiary as being clearly within the class. The House of Lords disagreed, primarily because this test took no account of the trustees' duty to carry out the power in a fiduciary manner. The Denning test would only really be appropriate were the trustees at liberty to distribute to the first person who came to hand, and as we have seen that is not the case. The Denning test is in any case no good for enforcement purposes, where the donees of the power propose to appoint somebody who is not the object of the power. Anybody coming to court for an injunction will have to show that he or she is an object, and also that the person in whose favour it is proposed to appoint is not. That requires the ability to determine of anybody whether or not he or she is within the class. It is not sufficient to be able to say of one person alone.

The importance of these two points will become apparent later in the chapter.

4.4.5 Discretionary trusts

The nature of discretionary trusts (sometimes called 'trust powers'), and the reasons for using them, were considered in chapter 2. As with mere powers, nobody who is an object can claim a defined interest, or indeed any interest at all, unless and until the trustees' discretion is exercised in his favour. But they differ from mere powers and fixed trusts in that the trustees are under an obligation to distribute the property.

Clearly, the extent to which a discretionary trust can be enforced is limited by its discretionary nature. The courts will, however, restrain the trustees from acting contrary to the terms of the trust instrument. And if they refuse to distribute at all, a court can remove them and appoint new trustees, or in the final analysis distribute the property itself. There are also ancillary rights enjoyed by potential beneficiaries under a discretionary trust; for example, in *Re Murphy's Settlements* [1998] 3 All ER 1, an order was obtained against the settlor, to identify the trustees, to enable the potential beneficiary to assert his rights against them.

Since 1971 the test for discretionary trusts has been assimilated to that for powers (i.e., individual ascertainability). However, the test is still slightly more stringent than that for powers because the trustees must distribute, and in order to exercise their discretion must have at least some idea of the range of objects. Also, at the end of the day, if they refuse to distribute, the court must be able to distribute in their place.

4.4.5.1 *The pre-1971 approach*

Before 1971 the approach of the courts was dictated by their view of ultimate enforcement. They took the view that if the trustees refused to distribute, the court could not itself exercise any discretion on their behalf (see, e.g., the view of Jenkins LJ in *IRC* v *Broadway Cottages Trust* [1955] Ch 20). The court could remove the trustees and appoint others in their place, but in theory it could be impossible to find any other trustees prepared to execute the trust. It followed that, however unlikely this eventuality might be, at the end of the day a court had to be prepared to carry out the trust itself. Since it refused to exercise any discretion it could only divide the property equally among all the objects.

'Ultimate enforcement': a matter of logic
Although there is a logic to this conclusion, given the premises, equality of distribution will often not implement the intentions of the settlor, and indeed is quite likely to frustrate them. It seems that the equality principle originated in nineteenth-century family settlements (e.g., *Burrough* v *Philcox* (1840) 5 My & Cr 72), where it may have been the most reliable method of carrying out the settlor's intention. It is much less likely to be appropriate, however, in modern settlements, for example, dividing proceeds among employees of a company.

Nevertheless, equality of distribution was the rule, and of course it could only be done if it was possible to draw up a list of all the objects. For this reason, *Broadway* applied the class ascertainability test to discretionary trusts.

The class in *Broadway* was undoubtedly extremely wide, consisting mostly of remote issue, as well as a number of charities. Two charities (Broadway Cottages Trust and Sunnylands Trust) had received income under the settlement, and claimed an income tax exemption on it, but in order to do so they had to show that the settlement was valid. The class was never held to be unascertainable, since the charities conceded the point (perhaps unwisely, since it was conceptually certain, and only evidential difficulties prevented drawing up an entire list of objects: see further, the discussion on fixed trusts, below). The Crown for its part conceded that the individual ascertainability test was satisfied. On the basis of these concessions, the Court of Appeal held that the trust failed: *Gestetner* did not apply, since here there was no gift over, there was an obligation to distribute, and the whole range of objects had to be ascertainable.

'Ultimate enforcement', class ascertainment and the only option of the court
Jenkins LJ took the view that if the court was called upon to enforce the trust 'it could not mend the invalidity of the trust by imposing an arbitrary distribution among some only of the whole unascertainable class'. The court could only effect a distribution to all the objects equally. The irony of this is that, given that some of the objects were charities and others people, equality of distribution was probably the last thing the settlor would have wanted.

One result of this case was that the test for certainty was much more stringent for discretionary trusts than for powers (on which, see above). This had two main consequences: first, many perfectly reasonable trusts failed; second, the courts were at pains to construe doubtful dispositions as powers, rather than discretionary trusts.

4.4.5.2 *Re Baden's Deed Trusts (No. 1), McPhail* v *Doulton*

In *Re Baden's Deed Trusts (No. 1), McPhail* v *Doulton* [1971] AC 424, however, the House of Lords decisively rejected the principle of equality of distribution in a case where equal distribution would have made a nonsense of the settlor's intention. The House accepted that even in the final analysis (in other words even assuming that no trustee can be found who is prepared to execute the trust), the court could exercise the necessary discretion itself. Therefore, the reasoning in the *IRC* v *Broadway Cottages Trust* [1955] Ch 20 was inapplicable (and indeed, *Broadway Cottages* was overruled). All that is required is for it to be possible to tell, with certainty, whether any individual coming to court to enforce a trust or power has sufficient interest to do so: in other words whether or not he is within the class of objects. This requirement is of course satisfied by the individual ascertainability test.

Re Baden: a test for discretionary trusts essentially the same as for powers
The *ratio* of *Re Baden's Deed Trusts (No. 1)* is that the test for certainty for discretionary trusts is essentially the same as that for powers, the individual ascertainability test, not the class ascertainability test.

Lord Wilberforce also made the point that in applying the test the courts are concerned only with conceptual uncertainty. A trust will not fail merely because there are evidential difficulties in ascertaining whether or not someone is within the class, as the court is never defeated by evidential uncertainty, and can deal with problems of proof when an application for enforcement arises:

I desire to emphasise the distinction clearly made . . . between linguistic or semantic uncertainty which, if unresolved by the court, renders the gift void, and the difficulty of ascertaining the existence or whereabouts of members of the class, a matter with which the court can appropriately deal on an application for directions.

Thus, a trust in favour of the first 20 people who crossed Clifton suspension bridge in 1996 should be enforceable: the class is conceptually certain even though proof may be difficult. A trust in favour of 'all my friends' is different, however. It is conceptually uncertain, because 'all my friends' is not a phrase capable of precise definition. Such a trust ought therefore to fail even on the *McPhail* v *Doulton* test.

4.4.5.3 *Problems of applying the individual ascertainability test*
The outcome in *Re Baden's Deed Trusts (No. 1)* was largely consequential on the court changing its views about the ultimate enforcement of a discretionary trust. Unfortunately, the relaxation may lead to difficulties over administration. Unlike donees of mere powers, the trustees' discretion is not absolute. In considering its exercise, they must, according to Lord Wilberforce in *McPhail* v *Doulton* itself, make a survey of the entire field of objects, and consider each individual case responsibly, on its merits. This ought to require a more rigorous certainty test than individual ascertainability. For example, the Clifton suspension bridge example should fail (assuming no central record is kept of people walking over Clifton bridge), because the trustees could not possibly survey the entire field.

A new test and its impact upon trustees
Since under the new test trustees may be unable to discover the identities of all the possible beneficiaries, they will sometimes be unable to carry out their duties. Some discretionary trusts could be very difficult to administer were the trustees unable to survey the entire field of possible beneficiaries. An example might be a discretionary trust to distribute property 'according to the age and ability of the potential beneficiaries'.

Lord Wilberforce himself suggested a way out of the difficulty. He thought that even if a disposition satisfied the individual ascertainability test, it might fail if the class is so widely drawn as to be administratively unworkable. An example he gave was a gift to 'all the residents of Greater London', but the acceptable width of the class presumably depends on the exact nature of the trustees' duties, and whether they must actually survey the entire field (on which, see below).

A 'way out' for trustees: negating sensible intention
Another possible solution is that if the terms of a trust negative any sensible intention on the part of the settlor, it may fail on the grounds of capriciousness. This was suggested *obiter* by Templeman J in *Re Manisty's Settlement* [1974] Ch 17. The same applies, incidentally, to powers, and indeed *Manisty* actually concerned a valid power (see further below).

We would suggest that the real problem is the distinction, drawn by Lord Wilberforce, between, on the one hand, linguistic or semantic uncertainty which, if unresolved by the court, renders the gift void, and on the other hand, evidential difficulties of ascertaining the existence or whereabouts of members of the class (see below). We would suggest that this distinction is irrational, and loses sight of the purposes of certainty tests. As we saw in 4.3, the court (which is happy to apply the reasonable man test when required to do so) is no more defeated by linguistic or semantic uncertainty than it is by evidential difficulties. Trustees administering the trust, on the other hand, will be equally defeated by both types of uncertainty. Unfortunately, there are traces of the distinction in *Gulbenkian*, and it has been adopted by at least one of the judges in *Re Baden's Trusts (No. 2)* [1973] Ch 9 (see below), so it may well become entrenched in the law.

The new test and the doctrine of Saunders v Vautier
Another problem with the new certainty test is how, if at all, the doctrine in *Saunders* v *Vautier* (1841) 10 LJ Ch 354 applies. Under this doctrine (on which, see further, chapter 17), all the beneficiaries, collectively entitled, can (so long as they are adult and *sui juris*) terminate the trust and distribute or resettle the trust property. It is difficult to see how this doctrine can operate if the entire class of beneficiaries cannot be ascertained.

One possible answer is that *Saunders* v *Vautier* applies only to fixed trusts, on the grounds that the objects of a discretionary trust do not have full beneficial interests unless and until the trustees' discretion is exercised in their favour, but Lord Upjohn in *Gulbenkian* suggests otherwise. The other possible answer is that the courts would use a device similar to the *Benjamin* order discussed below (in relation to fixed trusts).

4.4.5.4 *Re Baden's Deed Trusts (No. 2)*

The disposition in *Re Baden's Deed Trusts* was remitted to the Chancery Division so that the House of Lords test could be applied. Eventually it came again to the Court of Appeal, where differing opinions were given: *Re Baden's Deed Trusts (No. 2)* [1973] Ch 9. By this time some 12 years had passed since Mr Baden's death, the fund was still sterilised by litigation, and a considerable proportion had been dissipated in legal costs. Sachs LJ observed that the situation 'lacks attraction'.

Baden No. 2: the Court of Appeal and the search for a workable position
The disposition was 'to or for the benefit of any of the officers and employees or ex-officers or ex-employees of the company or to any relatives or dependants of any such persons'. It was argued by John Vinelott QC, who was challenging the disposition on behalf of the executors, that it could not be shown that any person definitely is or *is not* within the class (as required by the *Gulbenkian* test). Had this ingenious argument been accepted it would have meant virtually returning to the

rejected class-ascertainability test, as Megaw LJ observed. The Court of Appeal rejected the argument, but not on identical grounds.

Sachs LJ—a focus on evidential difficulties
Sachs LJ avoided the difficulty by emphasising that the court was concerned only with conceptual certainty, so that it should not be fatal that there might be *evidential* difficulties in drawing up John Vinelott QC's list. This effectively destroys the Vinelott argument, which was addressed primarily towards *evidential* difficulties in drawing up the class. Sachs LJ also took the view that the courts would place the burden of proof, in effect, on someone claiming to be within the class. This seems acceptable if ultimate enforcement is the issue, and the test is of the *locus standi* of the claimant, but it does not help the administration of the trust.

Megaw LJ—a focus on a 'substantial number'
Megaw LJ adopted a different solution requiring that, as regards a substantial number of objects, it can be shown with certainty that they fall within the class. This is rather a vague test—clearly it is not enough to be able to show that *one* person is certainly within the class, as this test was rejected in *Gulbenkian* (see the discussion of powers, above). Presumably, the test requires evidential, as well as conceptual certainty. Maybe Megaw LJ adopted it simply because he could find no other way of rejecting Mr Vinelott's argument without returning either to the rejected *Broadway* test, or to the Denning test which had been rejected in *Gulbenkian*. Indeed, none of the judges in the Court of Appeal was able to find a satisfactory solution to this difficulty. The test may have the merit, however, of ensuring that the trustees will be able to get a feel for the width of the class, which they need to be able to exercise their discretion.

Stamp LJ—the strictest formulation of the test
Stamp LJ's test is probably the strictest of the three, and he seemed to be quite impressed by the Vinelott argument. He emphasised that it must be possible for the trustees to make a comprehensive survey of the range of objects, but he did not think it would be fatal if at the end of the survey it was impossible to draw up a list of every single beneficiary. He would have taken the view that the trust failed, had he not felt compelled to follow an early House of Lords authority, which had held that a discretionary trust for 'relations' was valid, 'relations' being defined narrowly as 'next-of-kin'.

Of the three tests, that of Sachs LJ will usually be the easiest to satisfy, but it relies heavily on an additional administrative unworkability test, the extent and application of which, as we will see in the next section, are quite unclear. We would also suggest that:

The Court of Appeal decision: what analysis can follow?

(a) The distinction drawn by Sachs LJ between conceptual and evidential uncertainty has its origin in Lord Wilberforce's speech in *McPhail v Doulton*, and indeed, there are traces of a similar distinction in *Gulbenkian*. The justification is that evidential distinctions can always be resolved by the courts, but, as we saw earlier, the courts can also resolve conceptual uncertainties. But surely, once the *Broadway* equality of distribution principle has been abandoned, the justification for certainty rules is not to assist the courts but rather the trustees in administering the trust. And trustees will be defeated just as easily by evidential as they will by conceptual difficulties.

(b) If a class is conceptually certain, then the only reason why a list of the entire class cannot be drawn up is evidential. The class ascertainability test, if it was ever meaningful at all, must have been an evidential test; if the test were simply conceptual, then there would be no difference between the individual and class ascertainability tests.

(c) We would suggest, therefore, that no good basis can be found for the conceptual/evidential distinction. Proponents of Sachs LJ's view would respond that the test of administrative workability is sufficient to ensure that the trust is workable, but in that case it is reasonable to ask why any test is needed at all apart from administrative workability. In any case, evidential issues would now need to be dealt with by the administrative workability test, and it is not obvious that that is an improvement over dealing with them as part of the individual ascertainability test itself.

(d) Megaw LJ's test is evidential and addresses the problem of making the trust workable for trustees. It is therefore (we would suggest) preferable to Sachs LJ's test.

(e) Stamp LJ's test is also evidential (indeed, entirely so, since 'next-of-kin' is not itself conceptually certain), but once the *Broadway* equality of distribution principle has been rejected, it is difficult to justify a test as strict as Stamp LJ's, since his test amounts virtually to a return to the class ascertainability test.

This, then, is an argument for preferring Megaw LJ's test, or at any rate a test similar to it.

4.4.5.5 *Administrative unworkability*

The question of administrative unworkability was considered in *Re Manisty's Settlement* [1974] Ch 17, where a power given to trustees was upheld where they were able to appoint anyone in the world apart from a small excepted class (a power where the objects are defined only by reference to an *excepted* class is called an intermediate or hybrid power). A similar decision was reached in *Re Hay's ST* [1982] 1 WLR 1202. These decisions suggest that very rarely will a power fail on grounds of administrative unworkability, simply because of the width of the class.

The courts are not concerned with questions of ultimate enforcement with a power, however, and it is arguable that the decisions in *Kay* and *Manisty* ought not to apply directly where, as here, the instrument is drafted as a trust. Indeed, in *Re Hay's ST* [1982] 1 WLR 1202 itself, Sir Robert Megarry V-C noted that: 'The words of Lord Wilberforce [about administrative unworkability] . . . are directed towards trusts, not powers.'

'Administrative (un)workability': what happens in the case of a trust?

The problem arose directly in the Divisional Court in *R v District Auditor, ex parte West Yorkshire Metropolitan County Council* [1986] RVR 24. Prior to the abolition of the Metropolitan County Councils, they were prohibited from incurring expenditure under the Local Government Act 1972, s. 137(1):

which in their opinion is in the interests of their area or any part of it or some or all of its inhabitants

after 1 April 1985.

When West Yorkshire Metropolitan County Council realised that they were going to have a large surplus on 1 April 1985, they sought to find ways of ensuring that this money could still be spent after the 1 April deadline. In their attempt to achieve this aim, they purported to set up a discretionary trust of £400,000, having a duration of 11 months, 'for the benefit of any or all or some of the inhabitants of the County of West Yorkshire'. The trust also directed the trustees to use the fund specifically:

(a) To assist economic development in the county in order to relieve unemployment and poverty.
(b) To assist bodies concerned with youth and community problems.
(c) To assist and encourage ethnic and other minority groups.
(d) To inform all interested persons of the consequences of the proposed abolition of the Council (and the other Metropolitan County Councils) and of other programs affecting local government in the county.

West Yorkshire: a case of an administratively unworkable trust?
This was held to be administratively unworkable. The inhabitants of the County of West Yorkshire numbered about two and a half million. The range of objects was held to be so hopelessly wide as to be incapable of forming anything like a class.

There are clear statements in the case that trusts may be treated differently from powers in this regard, since a court may be called upon ultimately to execute a trust, whereas it will not, of course, be required to execute a power.

The second possibility is that the terms of the trust negative any sensible intention on the part of the settlor. Indeed, in *Manisty*, Templeman J thought this was the real problem over 'residents of Greater London':

The settlor neither gives the trustees an unlimited power which they can exercise sensibly, nor a power limited to what may be described as a 'sensible' class, but a power limited to a class, membership of which is accidental and irrelevant to any settled purpose or to any method of limiting or selecting beneficiaries.

In addressing these issues the width of the class is not the only factor, since other factors may make clear what the intention of the settlor was. For example, in *Re Hay's ST* [1982] 1 WLR 1202, Sir Robert Megarry V-C said of this passage:

In *Re Manisty's Settlement* [1974] Ch 17 at 27 Templeman J appears to be suggesting that a power to benefit 'residents in Greater London' is void as being capricious 'because the terms of the power negative any sensible intention on the part of the settlor'. In saying that, I do not think that the judge had in mind a case in which the settlor was, for instance, a former chairman of the Greater London Council, as subsequent words of his on that page indicate.

Alternatively, suppose that trustees were directed to use the fund, in their discretion, to provide library facilities for the residents of Greater London. It might also be perfectly possible to infer a sensible intention on the part of the settlor. On the other hand, fairly precise guidelines were laid down in *R v District Auditor, ex parte West Yorkshire Metropolitan County Council*, but this was still insufficient to save the trust.

Suppose that even the class ascertainability test is satisfied. Then it could not be said that the disposition was administratively unworkable, because clearly the trustees could survey the entire class. Presumably, the disposition could still fail, however, if the terms were such as to negative any sensible intention on the part of the settlor.

4.4.6 Fixed trusts

It is usually argued that, since it is of the essence of a fixed trust that the property is to be divided among all the beneficiaries in fixed proportions (e.g., in equal shares), it can only be workable if the entire class of beneficiaries is known; the conventional view, therefore, is that the test of certainty is the class ascertainability test.

This was certainly the view of Jenkins LJ in *IRC* v *Broadway Cottages Trust* [1955] Ch 20, at p. 29:

There can be no division in equal shares amongst a class of persons unless all the members of the class are known.

In other words, a complete list of objects must be able to be drawn up. From the fact that in *McPhail* v *Doulton* [1971] AC 424, the House of Lords was concerned only to assimilate discretionary trusts and powers, the implication usually drawn is that the reasoning was not intended also to apply to fixed trusts.

However, there are fairly convincing contrary arguments (see, e.g., Matthews [1984] Conv 22). The orthodox view presupposes that *Broadway* still stands in so far that later cases have not directly detracted from it, but it is arguable that even when it was decided, *Broadway* was wholly out of line with other authorities, in which case there is no reason for it still to be regarded as authority for anything at all.

The central issue, we would suggest, is the basis upon which the trust property is distributed by the trustees, or if the issue becomes one of ultimate enforcement, by the courts. It is often assumed that distribution is impossible unless the entire class can be ascertained, but this need not be the case, and even if it is, application of the class ascertainability test may not necessarily resolve the difficulty.

A fixed trust: how it might work
Suppose, for example, that in 1986 Michael settled property upon trustees with directions that in 1991 the property was to be sold, and that the proceeds of sale were to be distributed equally, in favour of those of his three sons, Paul, Quentin and Richard, who are still then living. Assuming that in 1986 all three of the settlor's sons were known to be alive, it is obvious that this is a fixed trust, and that it satisfies the class ascertainability test.

Suppose now that at some time after 1986 Richard went on an Antarctic expedition, from which by 1991 he has not returned. He is thought (but not known definitely) to have perished on the expedition. The trustees sell the property, and wish to distribute it in accordance with their directions. Despite the fact that the class ascertainability test was clearly satisfied, and that the trust did not fail for want of certainty, they clearly have a problem.

If at this point the trustees asked for directions, it is likely that the court would resolve the difficulty by making a *Benjamin* order (based on *Re Benjamin* [1902] 1 Ch 723). The trustees would be directed to distribute on the basis that Richard was dead. If Richard later turned up alive, he would still have an interest in the proceeds of sale, which he would be able to claim from Paul and Quentin if it were still traceable, and assuming that his claim was not barred by limitation. The trustees personally would be protected from any action, however.

It is clear, then, that evidential difficulties, even in the distribution of fixed trusts, can be resolved by the courts. Is there any reason of logic or principle why the position should be any different if, by the time of the settlement in 1986, Richard had already embarked upon the expedition, and it was not known even then whether he was alive or dead? In those circumstances it would not after all, be possible at the date of the settlement, to draw up a list of all the objects, since it would not be possible to say with certainty whether Richard should be included or not. A strong argument can therefore be made that there is no need to apply the class ascertainability test, even to fixed trusts.

As explained earlier, in applying the individual ascertainability test, Lord Wilberforce distinguished between evidential and conceptual uncertainty, on the ground that the courts are never defeated by evidential uncertainty. Does it follow that, if the class ascertainability test does still apply to fixed trusts, the same distinction also applies? If so, it leads to some interesting consequences.

Fixed trusts and the significance of Broadway Cottages
In *Broadway* (see 4.4.5.1), although the class was very large, it was not conceptually uncertain. There was no problem over defining the class conceptually, and *it was conceded* in *Broadway*, rather than concluded from rational argument, that the class could not be ascertained. Perhaps the concession was wrongly made, and that in reality, even in *Broadway* itself, the class ascertainability test was satisfied. *Broadway* was indeed criticised in *Re Gulbenkian's Settlements* [1970] AC 508 (in particular, by Lords Reid and Upjohn), and by Lord Wilberforce in *McPhail v Doulton* (above), on the grounds that the Court of Appeal had confused conceptual and evidential uncertainty.

If, however, the distinction between conceptual and evidential uncertainty applies equally to the class as to the individual ascertainability test, it is difficult to see any difference between the two tests. If it can be said of any individual that he or she falls outside the class, then there can be no conceptual difficulty in defining the class as a whole. Indeed, there is no *conceptual* difficulty in defining the class in the above example, merely an evidential difficulty in ascertaining whether Richard is a member. In principle, however, evidential difficulties, as in *Broadway* and the example, are capable of resolution by the courts.

Fixed trusts and some concluding thoughts
We would suggest, however, that the class ascertainability test has always been an evidential test, and that the distinction between conceptual and evidential uncertainty has only ever been applied to the individual ascertainability test. Even there, I have already argued that it is inappropriate. Further, if it is accepted that a function of the certainty of object test is to ensure that the trust is administratively workable, then even if one accepts that there is no need to apply the class ascertainability test to fixed trusts, one can argue for a more rigorous test than for discretionary trusts. One way of achieving this is to apply different tests of administrative workability, since it does not follow that merely because a discretionary trust is administratively workable with a given class of objects, a trust with the same class of objects will necessarily be so if the trustees' discretion is removed. It is probably more satisfactory, however, to have a stricter certainty test for fixed trusts, albeit perhaps a test not as strict as the class ascertainability test.

Duties of trustees	Arguments for class ascertainability	Arguments for individual ascertainability
Must distribute according to instrument	*Fixed trusts* Necessary to enable trustees to distribute	Distribution on basis of *Benjamin* order
Must distribute— discretion as to how	*Discretionary trusts* Ultimate enforcement Trustees need to ascertain entire class in order to decide how to exercise their discretion	*Locus standi* Class ascertainability test leads to unjust results Administrative unworkability/ capriciousness safeguards sufficient
Need not distribute, but must consider whether to do so and if so how	*Powers* As above, except that ultimate enforcement no longer an issue	As above, except that *locus standi* only to prevent distribution inconsistent with power

Figure 4.1 Fixed trusts, discretionary trusts, and powers

4.5 The beneficiary principle and private purpose trusts

The principles relating to private (i.e., non-charitable) purpose trusts follow on naturally from the discussion on certainty of objects and particularly the primacy of the 'beneficiary principle' considered in the previous chapter.

4.5.1 Private purpose trusts

Purpose trusts may either be for a pure purpose (for example, a trust to advance a cause), where no individual directly benefits, or for the benefit of an ascertainable group of people (for example, a trust to build a school swimming pool). A private (non-charitable) purpose trust of the first type is usually struck down, because it is not enforceable by anyone. Charitable trusts (which are dealt with in chapters 12–14) are always purpose trusts, and are valid, but problems of enforcement do not arise as the Attorney-General has *locus standi* to sue.

Where an ascertainable group of people is intended to benefit, it appears that the trust is valid.

4.5.2 The beneficiary principle

We saw earlier the importance of trusts being enforceable, and in the absence of state enforcement (which occurs only for charities) this means that there must be a person with a sufficient interest to enforce the trust. As long ago as 1804, Sir William Grant MR observed, in *Morice v Bishop of Durham* (1804) 9 Ves 405, that 'There must be somebody, in whose favour the court can decree performance'. Who this person might be, and the precise nature of the enforcement, were not made clear in *Morice v Bishop of Durham*, but we suggest later that this has now been taken to mean that there has to be a beneficiary, and this case is often said to be the foundation of the 'beneficiary principle'. Leaving aside these arguments for the present, what is clear is that where the purpose is sufficiently abstract and impersonal as not directly to benefit any identifiable human being, there is nobody to enforce the trust. *Morice* v *Bishop of Durham* implies that dispositions of this nature, unless charitable, should generally therefore be void. Examples of such purposes might be the preservation of peace between nations, or the abolition of vivisection, where no individual clearly has sufficient interest to enforce the trust.

Similar sentiments to those of Sir William Grant MR were echoed by Lord Parker of Waddington in *Bowman* v *Secular Society Ltd* [1917] AC 406 at p. 441:

A trust to be valid must be for the benefit of individuals . . . or must be in that class of gifts for the benefit of the public which the courts in this country recognise as charitable . . .

(Note, however, that these views in the House of Lords are *dicta*, since the case actually concerned a valid gift to a company.)

A principle with a respectable pedigree and universal application?
Yet although the beneficiary principle has a respectable pedigree, it is only relatively recently that it has become regarded as universally applicable. Exceptions developed to it; trusts to erect or maintain tombs and monuments were upheld, as in *Pirbright* v *Salwey* [1896] WN 86 was a trust to decorate a family burial enclosure; also upheld were trusts for the maintenance of specific animals (e.g., *Re Dean* (1889) 41 Ch D 522) and (in *Re Thompson* [1934] Ch 342) a trust for the promotion and furtherance of fox hunting. It was arguable that the exceptions were of sufficient width as to negate the beneficiary principle, or at any rate to limit it to testamentary dispositions.

The modern view: Re Astor's ST
The tide turned, and the modern view can probably be said to trace its origins to *Re Astor's ST* [1952] Ch 534 (discussed in depth by L.A. Sheridan (1953) 17 LQR 46), where trustees were instructed to hold a fund upon various trusts including 'the maintenance of good relations between nations [and] . . . the preservation of the independence of newspapers'. The purposes were not charitable, but the settlement was drafted expressly (by limiting its duration) so as to be valid under the perpetuity rules (see chapter 6). The trust was held to be void, because there were no human beneficiaries capable of enforcing it. Roxburgh J held that the exceptions discussed above did not negate the general principle, or limit it to testamentary dispositions, and observed that some of the cases could be explained as trusts which were enforceable by the residuary beneficiary. This is not entirely satisfactory, however, since the residuary beneficiary has no interest in enforcing the trust, and the exception implies that wherever there is a gift over, any purpose trust that does not infringe perpetuity principles will be enforceable. It would be more satisfactory to explain these exceptional cases as incorrect, but presumably Roxburgh J felt unable to do this at first instance.

A similar case to *Astor*, where there were no clearly identifiable human beneficiaries, was *Re Shaw* [1957] 1 WLR 729, where Harman J held void on the same principle a trust to research into the development of a 40-letter alphabet. The case concerned the will of George Bernard Shaw, and although by 1950, when the will was made, Shaw was already 94 years old, Harman J noted its 'youthful exuberance'. Having also commented that the author was an indefatigable reformer, Harman J went on to note the 'marriage of incompatibles' in the will between Shaw's own work and that of a skilled equity draftsman: 'The two styles, as ever, make an unfortunate mixture.' Only copyrights and royalties were settled in the will, but these were far greater than anticipated—hence the litigation.

The purposes included the following:

(1) To institute and finance a series of inquiries to ascertain as far as possible the following statistics

    (a) the number of extant persons who speak the English language and write it by the established and official alphabet of 26 letters (hereinafter called Dr Johnson's alphabet);

    (b) how much time could be saved per individual scribe by the substitution for the said alphabet of an alphabet containing at least 40 letters (hereinafter called the proposed British alphabet) . . . ;

    (c) how many of these persons are engaged in writing or printing English at any and every moment in the world;

    (d) on these factors to estimate the time and labour wasted by our lack of at least 14 unequivocal single symbols;

    (e) to add where possible . . . estimates of the loss of income in British and American currency . . .

(2) To employ a phonetic expert to transliterate my play entitled 'Androcles and the Lion' into the proposed British alphabet assuming the pronunciation to resemble that recorded of His Majesty our late King George V, and sometimes described as Northern English . . .

The purposes having been held non-charitable (on which see further chapter 13), the settlement was struck down on the grounds that there were no identifiable beneficiaries who could enforce it.

Reasons of policy against purpose trusts
In cases of this type, the courts may have been reluctant to uphold the trusts for other reasons also. For example, Roxburgh J in *Astor* thought that it was against public policy to allow large accumulations of private capital to be dispersed with no administrative state control. These reasons cannot be decisive, however, as they could be applied to all non-charitable trusts, whether or not purpose trusts. The courts in any case disallow trusts for useless or capricious purposes (see further chapter 5).

Explaining cases which do not comply with the beneficiary principle
There remain the cases, described above, which do not comply with the beneficiary principle. We have seen that they were regarded as exceptions in *Re Astor's ST*, and similarly in *Re Endacott* [1960] Ch 232, where a gift 'to North Tawton Devon Parish Council for the purpose of providing some useful memorial to myself . . . ' was held void by the Court of Appeal. Cases such as *Re Dean* (1889) 41 Ch D 522 and *Re Thompson* [1934] Ch 342 were regarded as anomalous and not to be extended. It is a pity, however, that the Court of Appeal did not take the opportunity to overrule them, as it is very difficult to know exactly what they stand for, or on what principle they operate, or the basis upon which they are enforced.

All private trusts are subject to the rule against perpetuities (see chapter 6), and if trusts such as those in *Re Dean* and *Re Thompson* remain valid today, there are no beneficial interests capable of vesting. At common law, therefore, these were subject to the rule against inalienability, which rendered void any such trusts which were capable of lasting beyond 21 years. Moreover, with trusts of this type, neither the alternative 80-year period nor the wait and see provisions of the Perpetuities and Accumulations Act 1964 would seem to apply. It therefore follows that if such trusts remain valid at all, they must be limited to a maximum duration of 21 years.

It may also be possible to make provision for a pure purpose indirectly, using a device. One such device is considered in chapter 12. A gift is made to charity A so long as it maintains the testator's grave to the satisfaction of the testator's trustees, with a gift over to charity B. The gift over is exempt from perpetuity rules (see chapter 6), so long as B is a charity. If B is not a charity the gift over will fail for perpetuity unless the gift is appropriately limited in duration: *Re Wightwick* [1950] 1 Ch 260.

There is authority, however, that a trust to pay income to a corporation so long as the corporation maintains the testator's grave to the satisfaction of his trustees is not subject to perpetuity, at any rate at common law. In *Re Chardon* [1928] 1 Ch 464, the will provided:

I give unto my trustees the sum of two hundred pounds free of duty upon trust to invest the same upon any of the investments hereinafter authorised and pay the income thereof to the South Metropolitan Cemetery Company West Norwood during such period as they shall continue to maintain and keep the graves of my great grandfather and the said Priscilla Navone in the said Cemetery in good order and condition with flowers and plants thereon as the same have hitherto been kept by me.

Romer J held the gift valid, and the decision was followed in *Re Chambers* [1950] 1 Ch 267. It depended on the gift of the income being absolute: *Re Wightwick* [1950] 1 Ch 260.

In *Re Chardon*, if the graves were not maintained the cemetery company would have ceased to be entitled to the income; a resulting trust would have arisen and the income fallen into residue. At common law, a resulting trust probably did not attract the perpetuity rules (*Re Chardon* was decided on the common law perpetuity rule). Today, the disposition would be caught under the Perpetuities and Accumulations Act 1964, s. 12, so this device no longer works.

4.5.2.1 *Purpose trusts for benefit of identifiable objects*

Sometimes, on the other hand, identifiable people are intended directly to benefit, but the gift is nevertheless limited for a particular purpose. Here the problem is different. There are people (who must be ascertainable within the certainty of object tests discussed earlier) with an interest in enforcing the trust. It may be possible to regard these people as entitled to a full beneficial interest, subject to a condition (e.g., direction to the trustees to apply the fund only for a particular purpose), in which case these are simply ordinary private trusts.

Re Abbott: a 'right result' and a plethora of difficulties?

For example, *Re Abbott* [1900] 2 Ch 326, which concerned a trust for the maintenance of two old ladies, was upheld (see further chapter 8). There was no question of the trust being invalid, even though the fund is clearly intended to be used for a purpose, rather than simply given to the two ladies. Yet the case is probably best analysed as an ordinary trust for the two ladies, with a direction to the trustees to apply the fund only for their maintenance. In other words, this is not, in reality, treated as a purpose trust at all.

Suppose, however, that although objects can be found with an interest in enforcing the trust, none is entitled to a full beneficial interest. Although the contrary view is arguable, it is probable that only where a full beneficial interest is granted to the identifiable objects will the disposition be valid. In *Leahy v Attorney-General for New South Wales* [1959] AC 457, property was to be held on trust for 'such order of nuns of the Catholic Church or the Christian brothers as my executors and trustees shall select'. The trust was not charitable, and Viscount Simonds in the Privy Council thought that it failed as a private trust on the ground that, even though the individual members had an interest in enforcing the trust, they were not granted a full beneficial interest:

If the words 'for the general purposes of the association' were held to import a trust, the question would have to be asked, what is the trust and who are the beneficiaries? A gift can be made to persons (including a corporation) but it cannot be made to a purpose or to an object; so also, a trust may be created for the benefit of persons as *cestuis que trust*, but not for a purpose or object unless the purpose or object be charitable. For a purpose or object cannot sue, but, if it be charitable, the Attorney-General can sue to enforce it. . . . It is therefore by disregarding the words 'for the general purposes of the association' (which are assumed not to be charitable purposes) and treating the gift as an absolute gift to individuals that it can be sustained.

Leahy: a gift can be made to a person, but not to an object
A gift can therefore be made to a person, but not to an object.

Viscount Simonds's views in *Leahy* are technically *obiter dicta*, because the case is also explicable on other grounds. The gift ought also to have failed for perpetuity (although in the event it was validated by the New South Wales Conveyancing Act). Obviously, however, the reasoned views of the Judicial Committee of the Privy Council must be regarded as very strong authority, in the absence of authority to the contrary.

Somewhat inconclusive contrary authority can be found in *Re Denley's Trust Deed* [1969] 1 Ch 373, where Goff J thought that the *Astor/Endacott* principles invalidated only 'abstract or impersonal' purpose trusts:

I think there may be a purpose or object trust, the carrying out of which would benefit an individual or individuals, where that benefit is so indirect or intangible or which is otherwise so framed as not to give those persons any *locus standi* to apply to the court to enforce the trust, in which case the beneficiary principle would, as it seems to me, apply to invalidate the trust, quite apart from any question of uncertainty or perpetuity. Such cases can be considered if and when they arise. The present is not, in my judgment, of that character, and it will be seen that . . . the trust deed expressly states that, subject to any rules and regulations made by the trustees, the employees of the company shall be entitled to the use and enjoyment of the land. Apart from this possible exception, in my judgment the beneficiary principle of *Re Astor's ST* [1952] Ch 534, which was approved in *Re Endacott* [1960] Ch 232, CA—see particularly by Harman LJ—is confined to purpose or object trusts which are abstract or impersonal. The objection is not that the trust is for a purpose or object *per se*, but that there is no beneficiary or *cestui que trust*.

He went on to say that:

Where, then, the trust, though expressed as a purpose, is directly or indirectly for the benefit of an individual or individuals, it seems to me that it is in general outside the mischief of the beneficiary principle.

Re Denley: what reasoning is at work?

These quotations are unfortunately not entirely clear. One view is that the test is not whether a full beneficial interest is granted, but whether individuals who are ascertainable have *locus standi* to sue. They will have so long as the benefit is not too indirect or intangible. The trust (which was upheld by Goff J) was 'for the purpose of a recreation or sports ground primarily for the benefit of the employees of the company', with a gift over at the end of the perpetuity period to the General Hospital, Cheltenham. This view of *Denley* was adopted by Megarry J in *Re Northern Developments (Holdings) Ltd*, unreported, 6 October 1978.

Another view of *Denley*, however, is that Goff J construed it as a trust for individuals, and not as a purpose trust at all. If this view is correct then the case breaks no new ground, and all private purpose trusts remain void, apart from the anomalous exceptions discussed above. This view was taken, for example, by Vinelott J in *Re Grant's WT* [1980] 1 WLR 360 (at p. 370):

That case [*Denley*] on a proper analysis, in my judgment, falls altogether outside the categories of gifts to unincorporated association and purpose trusts. I can see no distinction in principle between a trust to permit a class defined by reference to employment to use and enjoy land in accordance with rules to be made at the discretion of trustees on the one hand, and, on the other hand, a trust to distribute income at the discretion of trustees amongst a class, defined by reference to, for example, relationship to the settlor. In both cases the benefit to be taken by any member of the class is at the discretion of the trustees, but any member of the class can apply to the court to compel the trustees to administer the trust in accordance with its terms.

A similar view can be found in (1985) 101 LQR 269, at pp. 280–2 (P.J. Millett QC).

After Re Denley: what happens now?

Given that the trust was enforceable in *Denley*, and that similar trusts will continue to be enforceable, does it matter how the case is analysed? It could certainly affect the applicable perpetuity period. Consider also the question of enforcement. If the trustees decided to use the fund to install a kidney machine for the benefit of the patients, then that can be relatively easily prevented by injunction. Suppose, however, the trustees do nothing, and no trustees can be found to build and/or maintain the sports ground. Specific performance cannot be awarded, as constant supervision would be required, and an injunction is clearly of no use.

At the end of the day, it is difficult to see what solution can be adopted, apart from distribution of the income from the fund directly to the employees of the company (not the capital, because of the gift over). That puts them into exactly the same position as a beneficiary under an ordinary fixed or discretionary trust.

The issue could also arise if the objects of the trust wanted to terminate it on the basis of *Saunders* v *Vautier* (see chapter 17, and the discussion of discretionary trusts earlier). Presumably, only beneficiaries in the conventional sense can invoke this doctrine, and if the objects of a *Denley*-style purpose have a lesser interest, they will be unable to do so.

Whatever *Denley* decides, pure purpose trusts, such as *Re Astor's ST* [1952] Ch 534 (above), are unaffected by it, and are still void. It is also clear that the individuals to whom direct or indirect benefit is given must be ascertainable within the certainty of object requirements: in *R* v *District Auditor, ex parte West Yorkshire Metropolitan County Council* [1986] RVR 24, an alternative argument that the disposition created a valid private purpose trust failed, since whatever *Denley* decided, and indeed even if there were objects with full beneficial interests, they were not ascertainable under the certainty of objects rules.

FURTHER READING

Birks [1995] RLR 83.

Hayton (1994) 110 LQR 335.

Martin [1984] Conv 304.

Matthews [1984] Conv 441.

Millett (1985) 101 LQR 269.

5

Formalities and other requirements for validity

This chapter looks further at requirements for validity not considered in chapter 4. Only express trusts (whether charitable or not) are subject to all the requirements considered in this chapter, implied, resulting and constructive trusts (see chapters 7 to 11 and 19) being expressly exempted from the statutory formality requirements of the Law of Property Act 1925, s. 53.

5.1 Introduction to the formalities requirements

There are no formality requirements for trusts, except those laid down by statute; these are now contained in the Law of Property Act 1925 s. 53. The important distinctions to bear in mind are between land and other property, and between declarations and dispositions.

Implied, resulting and constructive trusts are expressly exempted from the statutory requirements, and so, it appears, are variations of trust carried out under the Variation of Trusts Act 1958 (on which see chapter 17). As appears below, however, the distinction between implied, resulting and constructive trusts on the one hand, and express trusts on the other, may be less important than appears at first sight; it is probable that express trusts can also, in some circumstances, fall outside the operation of s. 53, even though they are not expressly exempted.

5.1.1 Reasons for the rules

Land is subject to special rules because of its value, and also because real property (i.e., land) transactions are sufficiently complex for it to be undesirable for them to be taken lightly. So far as other property is concerned, the purpose of legislation on formalities is twofold. Bear in mind that equitable interests are intangible, and that it may not be possible to trace their movement unless that movement is evidenced by written documents. The primary purpose of a writing requirement is to prevent fraud—indeed the original statute was entitled the Statute of Frauds 1677. The secondary purpose is to enable the trustees to ascertain where the equitable interests lie, to enable them to carry out the trusts.

5.1.2 The tax angle

The litigation has borne little relation to these primary and secondary purposes, however. It will become apparent that whereas declarations of trusts do not (generally) require writing, dispositions of equitable interests do. The question of what amounts to a disposition has received attention from the courts in recent years, due in part to attempts by settlors to avoid payment of *ad valorem* stamp duty (now abolished on *inter vivos* gifts). Stamp duty is imposed, not upon a transaction itself, but upon the written instrument by which property is transferred. All documents under seal, whatever their value, require a nominal 50p stamp, but more important was the additional *ad valorem* duty, whose amount was calculated as a proportion of the value of the interest being transferred. If the value of such interest was nothing, as (for example) where a bare legal estate carrying no right to beneficial enjoyment was transferred, no *ad valorem* duty was payable. It is the beneficial interest which is valuable, and if that was transferred in writing, then substantial *ad valorem* duty was payable on the written instrument. Taxpayers therefore obviously preferred to avoid transferring the valuable beneficial interest in writing if they could, arguing instead that only the legal interest had been transferred by the written instrument, the beneficial interest having been transferred orally.

With the abolition of *ad valorem* stamp duty on *inter vivos* gifts in 1985, the practical implications of much of the discussion in the first part of this chapter have disappeared. The theoretical basis remains, however, and the *Vandervell* litigation (see below shortly) still raises (albeit incidentally) live taxation issues.

5.2 Land

All the formalities which are required in the case of personalty are also needed in the case of land, but there are additional requirements also. Section 53(1)(b) of the Law of Property Act 1925 provides:

A declaration of trust respecting any land or any interest therein must be manifested and proved by some writing signed by some person who is able to declare such trust or by his will.

This provision applies to freehold and leasehold land, and also to a share in the proceeds of sale of land. The trust need not actually be declared in writing, since what is necessary is that the declaration should be evidenced in writing, and no special form of document is needed—indeed, the necessary writing may be supplied by an exchange of correspondence or the like. The writing must, however, bear the signature of the settlor and not merely his agent. Failure to comply with s. 53(1)(b) will probably not render the trust void, but only unenforceable in the absence of evidence in writing.

For further discussion of s. 53(1)(b), see chapter 9.

5.3 Declarations of trust: personalty

As far as personalty is concerned, a settlor (assuming he is *legal* owner) may create a trust merely by manifesting the intention to create it, and no special formalities are required. So, for example, the simple declaration by the owner of, e.g., a stamp collection that he holds it in trust for his nephew will be effective to create a trust of the collection. Even personalty of great value may, in theory, be settled with no greater formality than this. This is true only for *inter vivos* gifts, however. If it is desired to create a trust by will, then the will itself must comply with the provisions of s. 9 of the Wills Act 1837, as amended by the Administration of Justice Act 1982, s. 17, which will be dealt with in the chapter on secret and half-secret trusts (chapter 10).

In fact, as a matter of practice, even with *inter vivos* gifts, the intention to create a trust will usually be declared in a written document setting out in detail the terms of the trust: a major motive for the creation of settlements is tax planning, and documentary evidence for this purpose is often highly desirable.

5.4 Dispositions of equitable interests

Dispositions of equitable interests are void, whether in land or personalty, unless in writing. Section 53(1)(c) of the Law of Property Act 1925 provides:

[A] disposition of an equitable interest or trust subsisting at the time of the disposition must be in writing signed by the person disposing of the same, or by his agent thereunto lawfully authorised by writing or by will.

This provision covers both land and personalty, and even in the case of land it is much more stringent than s. 53(1)(b). The disposition must *itself* be in writing, not merely manifested and proved by writing, and failure to comply probably renders the disposition void, not merely unenforceable.

If the law were to accord with the policy discussed above, dispositions would be defined so as to include dealings with the beneficial interest which can be kept secret from the trustees, but to exclude other dealings. After all, the whole reason for treating dispositions of equitable interests differently from other dispositions is precisely because of the difficulties which would ensue were the trustees to be kept unaware of them. The precursor to this section, s. 9 of the Statute of Frauds 1677, caught 'grants and assignments', clearly reflecting this policy, but the term 'disposition' is at least theoretically wider.

Nevertheless, generally speaking the definition of 'dispositions' accords in general with the policy described. The creation of a trust, by declaration, is outside the scope of the section. So, in general, is its extinguishment (by merger with the legal interest). If the purpose of formality rules is to prevent hidden transactions which prevent trustees from ascertaining who the beneficiaries are, there is no reason ever to require them where the legal and equitable interests merge. The same ought also to apply to the extinguishment of equitable interests.

Transfers or assignments of existing equitable interests, on the other hand, normally require writing. They are within the mischief covered by the legislation if the trustees are not party to the arrangement, but not, one would have thought, if the trustees themselves are directed to transfer the interests. Nevertheless, *Grey v IRC* [1960] AC 1 suggests that writing is required even in this situation, and we would suggest that the decision is not in accord with the policy described above.

The position is not clear for a surrender of an equitable interest. A surrender cannot, of course, be kept secret from the trustees, and on the principles discussed above surrender should probably not be a disposition. The Court of Appeal held in *Re Paradise Motor Co. Ltd* [1968] 1 WLR 1125 that a disclaimer of an equitable interest is not a disposition. Danckwerts LJ commented that 'a disclaimer operates by way of avoidance and not by way of disposition'. A surrender, however, differs from a disclaimer in that surrender requires a transfer of equitable interest, whereas with a disclaimer there is never any movement of the beneficial interest at all. We would suggest that a surrender may well be a disposition, even though this does not accord with the policy described above.

5.4.1 *Grey* v *IRC*

The usual interpretation of the House of Lords case of *Grey* v *IRC* [1960] AC 1 is that a transfer of an equitable interest on its own constitutes a disposition, even if the trustees are directed to make it, and therefore must be in writing. Until recently, therefore, it would have attracted liability for *ad valorem* stamp duty.

Mr Hunter was beneficial owner of 18,000 shares of £1 each, the legal title being held by nominees. In order to transfer his beneficial interest, Mr Hunter orally directed the nominees (one of whom was Grey) to hold the shares on trust for beneficiaries under six settlements (the nominees were also the trustees under these settlements). Later the trustees/nominees executed six deeds of declaration to this effect, which were of course in writing.

In effect the whole scheme was a tax-avoidance device. If the oral direction had transferred the shares, no *ad valorem* stamp duty was payable; if the transfer had been effected by the written declaration, however, it was.

In deciding in favour of the Inland Revenue, the House of Lords held that a direction, by a beneficiary to the trustees, to transfer his interest to someone else constituted a disposition and must therefore be in writing. Lord Radcliffe did not think that s. 53(1) merely consolidated the earlier Statute of Frauds, and thought that this was a disposition, whether or not it was also within the mischief of the old s. 9. While on a literal interpretation this conclusion may well be inevitable, the transfer in *Grey* does not fall within the mischief of the legislation, as a request to trustees can hardly constitute a secret transaction.

5.4.2 **Variations on *Grey***

Suppose a beneficiary declares that he himself will hold his interest on trust for another (rather than directing the trustees to do so), so creating, in effect, a sub-trust. A commonly held view is that the issue depends on whether the equitable owner effectively gives away the totality of his interest, so that he, like the trustees who hold the legal title, becomes in turn a merely nominal owner. If so, this is in reality a case of substitution of a new beneficiary, for which on policy grounds formality ought to be required.

If, on the other hand, the equitable owner purports to assume the active role of a trustee of his equitable interest, for example, by declaring discretionary trusts, the case resembles a straightforward sub-trust, and should arguably be regarded as a declaration of trust, and not a disposition of an equitable interest at all.

Suppose that Mr Hunter had surrendered his interest, and asked the trustees immediately to declare new trusts, these not of course requiring writing. Suppose also that the trustees were happy to comply with Hunter's request. If surrenders of equitable interests do not require writing (on which, see above), this would have allowed for an easy way to achieve a *Grey* disposition without attracting stamp duty. If surrenders do require writing, however, the surrender is caught by the writing requirement, even if the declaration of new trusts is not.

5.4.3 The *Vandervell* litigation

I suggested above that, in principle, the merger of legal and equitable interests, extinguishing rather than disposing of the equitable interest, should not require writing, on the grounds that it is not a hidden transaction of the type which the law would wish to prevent. On the same principle, it should also be possible for an equitable owner orally to direct the trustees to transfer *both* their legal and his equitable interest to a single third party. In this event also, his equitable interest is extinguished, and the transaction cannot be secret from the trustees. The House of Lords came to this conclusion in *Vandervell* v *IRC* [1967] 2 AC 291.

There are two *Vandervell* cases, both arising out of a scheme which was originally intended to transfer money to endow a chair without attracting taxation, in this case surtax.

5.4.4 *Vandervell* v *IRC*

Mr Vandervell wished to make a gift of £150,000 to the Royal College of Surgeons in order to endow a chair of pharmacology. He was equitable owner of a substantial number of shares in Vandervell Products Ltd, a private limited liability company which he controlled, and which produced, among other products, the Vanwall racing car which competed in Formula 1 races from 1954–1958, and won the Manufacturers' Championship in 1958. The legal interest in Vandervell's shares was held by a bank as nominee.

In order to endow the chair, he arranged with the bank orally (presumably to avoid stamp duty) to transfer both legal and equitable interests in these shares to the Royal College of Surgeons (RCS). It was not Vandervell's intention that the college should receive the shares absolutely, with all the implications that would have had for control of Vandervell Products Ltd. The intention, rather, was that it should receive dividends on the shares large enough to provide £150,000, upon which, as a charity, it was not liable to pay tax.

Vandervell retained an option to repurchase the shares themselves for a nominal amount (£5,000), however. He did not retain it in his own name, for that would have left him liable to pay surtax on the dividends. Instead, he set up a trustee company, Vandervell Trustees Ltd, to whom the option was granted.

The RCS actually received some £266,000 by means of this device.

At this stage, therefore, the legal interest in the shares had been transferred to the RCS. Vandervell Trustees Ltd had the legal interest in the option. If the equitable interest in either remained in Vandervell himself, however, he would be liable to surtax, on the basis of s. 415 of the Income Tax Act 1952. Clearly, Vandervell had to show that he had divested himself of the entire benefit of the shares, therefore.

Although the particular income tax provision at issue in *Vandervell* has been long since replaced, the principles of using trusts, and in particular charities, as a means

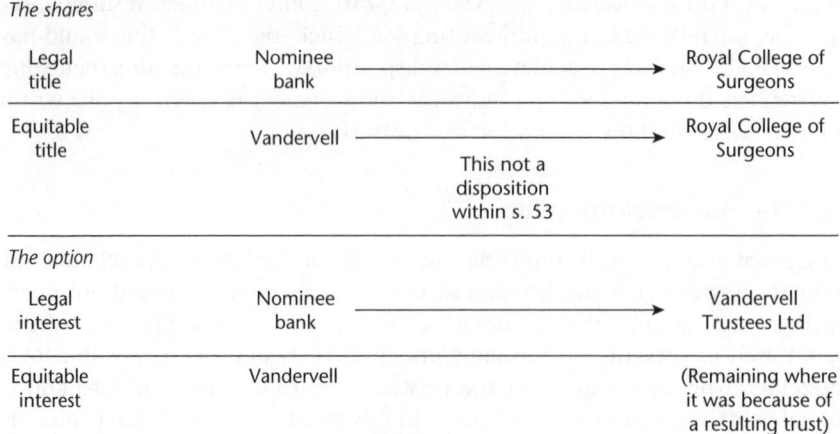

Figure 5.1 *Vandervell (No. 1)*

of avoiding taxation, still survive. The principle is essentially that liability to income tax can be minimised by ensuring that the income is received by those whose taxation liability is least. The so-called 'granny trust', where the income is paid to infant grandchildren, is a good example of this principle. Further examples of the use of the trust to avoid taxation are considered in chapter 17.

In *Vandervell* itself, as a high earner Mr Vandervell's personal liability to income tax was very high (note that surtax was being claimed, at well over the marginal rates that would have been applicable for standard-rate payers). The RCS as a charity, however, paid no income tax at all. It was important to show, therefore, that it was the charity and not Vandervell himself who was entitled to the income from the shares. The same principle applies today, where trusts are being used as a device to save income tax: the settlor must ensure that he divests himself effectively of all interest in the trust property, since even the most tenuous connection with the trust may result in the income being deemed to be that of the settlor.

That was essentially the issue in *Vandervell* itself. The shares and the option should be considered separately.

5.4.4.1 *The shares*

The Revenue initially claimed surtax from Mr Vandervell on the ground that he remained the equitable owner of the shares (although the legal title had clearly been vested in the RCS), in the absence of a separate disposition, in writing, of his equitable interest. This argument was rejected by the House of Lords, which held that s. 53(1)(c) had no application to the case where a beneficial owner, solely entitled, directs his bare trustees with regard to the legal and equitable estate. This is the most important part of the *Vandervell* litigation for formality purposes, and is in line with the policy discussed. As far as the shares themselves were concerned, therefore, both legal and equitable interests had been validly transferred despite lack of writing.

An interesting aside is that *Re Rose* [1952] Ch 449 was approved (see chapter 3): the transfer was effective as soon as Vandervell had performed his last act.

5.4.4.2 *The option*

Vandervell was liable to surtax nevertheless, because the House of Lords also held (Lords Reid and Donovan dissenting) that he had not succeeded in divesting himself of the equitable interest in the option (the legal title to which was now in the trustee company), as this was held on resulting trust for him, along with liability to pay surtax on the dividends. Vandervell was not entitled to the benefit of s. 415(1)(d) because the strict requirements of that section had not been satisfied.

This did not raise a formalities point, however, but was the result simply of Vandervell's failure to state where the equitable interest was to go. Lord Wilberforce noted that the trusts upon which the option was supposed to be held were undefined and in the air, possibly to be defined later. The trustee company itself was clearly not a beneficiary, and an equitable interest cannot remain in the air, and so the only possibility was a resulting trust in favour of the settlor. See further, chapters 2 and 7.

5.4.5 *Re Vandervell's Trusts (No. 2)*

In order to avoid further surtax liability, Vandervell in 1961 instructed the trustee company to exercise the option and repurchase the shares, and this gave rise eventually to further litigation (*Re Vandervell's Trusts (No. 2)* [1974] Ch 269) about whether Vandervell had divested himself of the option and the whereabouts of the equitable interest in the shares thereby purchased.

Clearly, the legal interest in the shares was now vested in the trustee company, Vandervell Trustees Ltd, because it had purchased them. They were also trustees under a separate trust for Vandervell's children: the £5,000 purchase money came from the children's settlement and the trustee company regarded themselves as holding the shares on trust for the children under this settlement. In other words, they regarded the equitable interest in the shares as being in the children.

Liability to surtax now depended on the whereabouts of the equitable interest in the shares during that period (although in the event the Inland Revenue was excluded as a party to the action, and the taxation point was not in fact the main issue). It was argued that, as before, it remained with Vandervell. Again, let us consider separately the option and the shares.

5.4.5.1 *The option*

The Court of Appeal held that the option was destroyed when it was exercised by the trustee company in 1961, so Vandervell's equitable interest in it (resulting from the earlier litigation) was extinguished. This was not a disposition within s. 53.

5.4.5.2 *The shares*

The Court of Appeal held that the children had the equitable interest. The shares had been placed by the trustee company on the trusts of the children's settlements, and the Court of Appeal held that Vandervell had now succeeded in divesting himself of the entire interest in these shares, there being no longer a resulting trust in his favour. This was because the later trusts were precisely defined, in favour of the children's settlements, so that it was no longer necessary for the equitable interest to remain in the settlor.

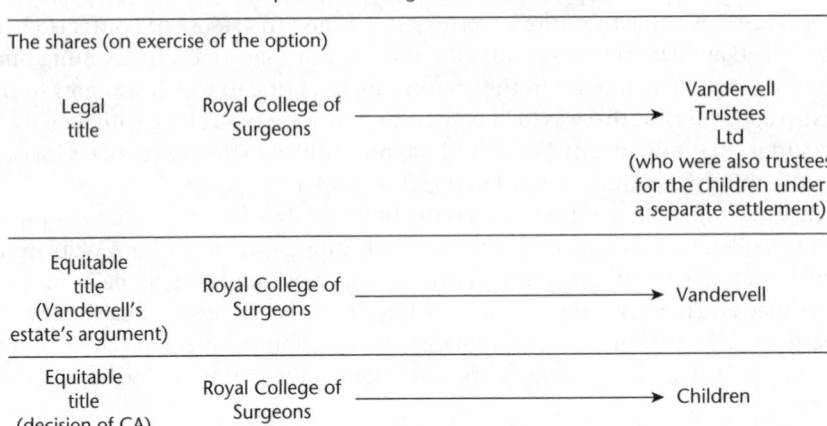

The option was extinguished when exercised

The shares (on exercise of the option)

| Legal title | Royal College of Surgeons | ⟶ | Vandervell Trustees Ltd (who were also trustees for the children under a separate settlement) |

| Equitable title (Vandervell's estate's argument) | Royal College of Surgeons | ⟶ | Vandervell |

| Equitable title (decision of CA) | Royal College of Surgeons | ⟶ | Children |

Figure 5.2 *Vandervell (No. 2)* (1961–5)

Lord Denning analysed the position as a termination of the resulting trust of the option in favour of Vandervell, and a fresh trust of the shares declared (presumably by the trustee company) in favour of the children. He thought that as to the first part, writing is not required to terminate a resulting trust, and that since the new trust was not of land no formalities were required for its creation.

So far as the formality aspects of the *Vandervell* decisions are concerned, at no stage did s. 53 operate to defeat a transaction in either case. Since none of the transactions could have been kept secret from the trustees this is in accord with the policy of the section.

In 1965 Vandervell, presumably by now justifiably fed up with his scheme, clearly relinquished by deed any interest, legal or equitable, he may still have had in the shares.

5.4.6 *Oughtred* v *IRC*

The point which arose in this third important House of Lords case is logically quite separate from that which arose in the above cases. It is virtually a pure taxation case, and it is difficult to argue either for or against the result from any general policy standpoint on formalities.

Contracts for the sale of personalty do not require writing, but in cases where the equitable remedy of specific performance is available, equity recognises that the buyer has an interest as soon as the contract is made. A possible route round s. 53 (and therefore stamp duty) might therefore be to have an oral contract for the sale of (say) shares, followed later by a formal transfer. The argument is that the oral contract, not the written transfer, conveys the equitable title; the formal transfer merely conveys the bare legal title, which is worth hardly anything for the purposes of *ad valorem* stamp duty.

This was the essence of the scheme in *Oughtred* v *IRC* [1960] AC 206. Mrs Oughtred owned 72,700 shares in William Jackson and Son Ltd absolutely. Two hundred thousand shares in the same company were held on trust for Mrs Oughtred for life, thence for her son, Peter absolutely. The parties orally agreed to exchange their interests, so that Mrs Oughtred would obtain Peter's reversionary interest (she would then have 200,000 shares outright), and in exchange Peter would obtain Mrs Oughtred's 72,700 shares. The contract was later performed.

The Revenue claimed stamp duty on the transfer of the reversionary interest in the 200,000 shares, the actual transfer of which involved writing. Oughtred's argument was that the equitable interest was transferred on the oral contract for sale, and that the later writing transferred only the bare legal title.

The argument was rejected by the House of Lords, Viscount Radcliffe and Lord Cohen dissenting. The essence of the majority view was that, although equity in appropriate circumstances can grant specific performance of a contract for the sale of shares (at any rate in a private company, where the shares are unique, but not in a public company, where equivalent shares are freely available on the stock market), and although in that case a constructive trust arises immediately in favour of the purchaser, the buyer does not have a full beneficial interest until the formal transfer. The situation was regarded as analogous to a sale of land, where the deed of conveyance is the effective instrument of transfer (and so liable to stamp duty). The minority view, on the other hand, was that the purchaser obtained a full beneficial interest immediately.

In the case of shares in a limited company, Lord Jenkins observed that:

> . . . the title secured by a purchaser by means of an actual transfer is different in kind from, and may well be far superior to, the special form of proprietary interest which equity confers on a purchaser in anticipation of such transfer . . . Under the contract, the purchaser is, no doubt, entitled in equity as between himself and the vendor to the beneficial interest in the shares, and (subject to due payment of the purchase consideration) to call for a transfer of them from the vendor as trustee for him. But it is only on the execution of the actual transfer that he becomes entitled to be registered as a member, to attend and vote at meetings, to effect transfers on the register, or to receive dividends otherwise than through the vendor as his trustee.

Transfer of legal title definitely confers additional privileges on the purchaser, therefore, and can reasonably be said to confer a superior form of proprietary interest.

In the case of land, between contract and conveyance the vendor is constructive trustee for the purchaser, but there remains a conflict of interest between the two parties (see chapter 7). This therefore differs from a normal trust (see further chapter 15), and it can reasonably be argued that at this stage the purchaser has received less than a full beneficial interest. In *Lloyds Bank plc* v *Carrick* [1996] 4 All ER 630, however, the purchaser had paid the entire purchase price and gone into occupation, so that all that remained to be done was to transfer the bare legal title. Morritt LJ expressed the view (*obiter*) that in these circumstances the vendor held on bare trust for the purchaser, so that presumably the purchaser had a full beneficial interest even prior to the conveyance.

5.5 **Equitable doctrine of part performance**

5.5.1 **Part performance and the Law of Property (Miscellaneous Provisions) Act 1989**

The equitable doctrine of part performance allows for limited avoidance of formality provisions. It developed originally from the principle that equity would not allow a statute to be used as a cloak for fraud (see further chapter 11). In recent years, however, it appeared to be developing away from a purely fraud-based doctrine into an evidential doctrine, with its own detailed rules. These rules were arguably both unsatisfactory and uncertain, and the Law Commission (Law Com. No. 164: 'Formalities for Contracts for Sale, etc. of Land') accordingly recommended the abolition of the doctrine, at any rate in relation to contracts for the sale or other disposition of land, or interests in land. Their proposals were brought into effect by the Law of Property (Miscellaneous Provisions) Act 1989, which also tightened up on formality provisions affecting land.

Formality requirements and the promotion of fraud
It seems generally to be accepted that in so far as part performance had become a rigid evidential doctrine, that has not survived the 1989 Act. But the question still arises: what if formality provisions are being relied upon to promote a fraud? It seems unlikely that the 1989 Act was ever intended to affect the fundamental principle that equity will not permit a statute to be used as a cloak for fraud. Or suppose the provisions of the 1989 Act itself are used to promote fraud? It must be presumed that the original fraud basis of the doctrine survives the 1989 Act.

It should also be noted that the 1989 Act applies only to formality provisions concerning contracts for the sale of estates and interests in land. In so far that the part performance doctrine applies to other dispositions, and declarations of trust, it has not been affected by the 1989 Act. There are also contracts, apart from those involving land, that require writing. For example, s. 90 of the Copyright, Designs and Patents Act 1988 provides that '[a]n assignment of copyright is not effective unless it is in writing signed by or on behalf of the assignor', and under the Consumer Credit Act 1974 many consumer credit agreements must be in a prescribed written form and signed. No doubt, it would be possible to apply a doctrine based on part performance if these provisions were not complied with. So, although the cases considered in this section concern land, and may therefore not survive the 1989 Act, the principles discussed still apply to other contracts. Thus, for example, an unwritten assignment of copyright may be effective, in spite of the statutory provision to the contrary, if supported by acts of part performance pointing unequivocally to the existence of such an assignment. Also, the payment of money could presumably have the same effect as described here.

Part performance and the avoidance of s. 53 of the Law of Property Act 1925
Though the doctrine can be used to avoid s. 53 of the Law of Property Act, 1925, by virtue of s. 55(d), the main cases arose from attempts to enforce a contract for a

leasehold or freehold estate in land, despite non-compliance with the formalities required by the (now repealed) Law of Property Act 1925, s. 40:

(1) No action may be brought upon any contract for the sale or other disposition of land or any interest in land, unless the agreement upon which such action is brought, or some memorandum or note thereof, is in writing, and signed by the party to be charged or by some other person thereunto by him lawfully authorised.

(2) This section applies to contracts made before or after the commencement of this Act and does not affect the law relating to part performance, or sales by the court.

Like s. 53, s. 40 replaced earlier provisions deriving from the Statute of Frauds 1677, so cases before 1925 were equally authoritative on s. 40.

There are two important points to note about s. 40. First, in the absence of the required formalities it merely prevented an action being brought upon a contract for the sale or other disposition of land or any interest in land, but did not render the contract void. Secondly, s. 40(2) expressly preserved the old equitable doctrine of part performance.

Formality and certainty: the difficulties with Steadman v Steadman
Developments in the law of part performance and in particular the House of Lords decision in *Steadman* v *Steadman* [1976] AC 576 clearly worried the Law Commission, not least because it had left the law in an extremely uncertain state. They also took the view (at page 3) that whereas the part performance doctrine was a blunt instrument for doing justice despite non-compliance with statutory formalities, equity had developed more flexible ways of dealing with the position if formalities were not observed. Accordingly, they recommended the abolition of the part performance doctrine.

The recommendations of the Commission led to the enactment of the Law of Property (Miscellaneous Provisions) Act 1989, s. 2 of which provided:

(1) A contract for the sale or other disposition of an interest in land can only be made in writing and only by incorporating all the terms which the parties have expressly agreed in one document or, where contracts are exchanged, in each . . .

(8) Section 40 of the Law of Property Act 1925 (which is superseded by this section) shall cease to have effect.

The impact of s. 40 of the Law of Property Act 1925
Apart from the tightening up of the formalities provisions in this section, it differs from its precursor in not making any provision for the part performance doctrine. However, although s. 40 was repealed and s. 40(2) not replaced, the part performance doctrine was not abolished expressly. It should also be remembered that the doctrine did not derive from s. 40(2), but from an earlier, fundamental equitable principle. Since it does not derive from statute, and since it has not been expressly abolished, is it therefore possible to argue that it still survives?

No doubt in interpreting the new statute the courts will take account of the Law Commission's recommendations, which clearly favoured the abolition of the doctrine. It is also worth noting that the section does not merely render unenforceable any contract which does not comply with its provisions, but that contracts failing to comply are void. The Commission took the view (at p. 23) that the doctrine of part performance would cease to have effect in contracts concerning land, presumably because there would be nothing for it to operate on. This was also the view taken by Professor P.H. Pettit ([1989] Conv, at p. 441):

It is an inevitable consequence of section 2 that the doctrine of part-performance no longer has a role to play in contracts concerning land. The simple fact is that under the new law if section 2 is not complied with there is no contract for either party to perform.

We would suggest that, in so far (if at all) as the doctrine had evolved from its fraud-based beginnings, the effect of the 1989 Act is to curtail those developments. Where, however, reliance on the statutory formality provisions could perpetrate a clear fraud, it is surely unlikely that equity will allow that to happen because of a new statute, which does not expressly abolish the doctrine. Nor is it a bar to the operation of the fraud doctrine that the contract is rendered void rather than merely unenforceable, since it is only rendered void by the operation of a formality statute whose provisions are being used as a cloak for fraud. The doctrine that equity will not allow a statute to be used as a cloak for fraud was applied by the Court of Appeal in *Rochefoucauld* v *Boustead* [1897] 1 Ch 196 to avoid s. 7 of the Statute of Frauds 1677 (the precursor to s. 53(1)(b) of the Law of Property Act 1925), which like s. 53(1)(b) and s. 2 of the 1989 Act, rendered non-complying dispositions void. We would suggest, therefore, that at any rate to the extent that part performance is based on the equitable fraud doctrine (see chapter 11), it is unaffected by the 1989 Act.

It is arguable, however, that equity has evolved other devices for dealing with the genuinely fraudulent case, and no longer needs to rely on the part performance doctrine. To that argument we turn in the next section.

5.5.2 **Alternatives to part performance**

5.5.2.1 *Proprietary estoppel*

In its report, the Law Commission took the view (at page 18) that if the part performance doctrine were abolished, many of the cases where injustice might be caused by an inability to plead the doctrine could be resolved by the application either of the equitable doctrine of estoppel, or various common law actions. For example, recovery of money paid by a prospective purchaser would normally be recoverable on the grounds of total failure of consideration. If work had been carried out, a *quantum meruit* claim might be made.

So far as estoppel is concerned, the effect of the doctrine (in essence) is that where one party makes a representation upon which another party relies to his detriment, the party making the representation may be estopped from later denying it. Proprietary estoppel, and its potential applications and limitations, are discussed more fully in chapter 9. There is no doubt that it is less effective for the injured party than enforcement of the unwritten contract would have been, but the Commission was of the view (at page 19) that the remedies for proprietary estoppel were sufficient to prevent injustice in most situations where previously the part performance doctrine may have operated. This may be so, in as much as the Law Commission was worried about uncertainty in its criticism of the part performance doctrine. Although it can hardly be said that the equitable estoppel doctrine is a particularly certain alternative, the discussion of shared homes in chapter 9 reveals that the courts are demonstrably showing a leaning towards estoppel-based resolutions to disputed home ownership, in preference to a constructive trust-based approach.

Estoppel reasoning and the position of third parties

There may also be difficulties with estoppel reasoning where third parties are involved. In the part performance cases there was no third party (e.g., purchaser) and the only question was whether the other party to the contract was bound. But estate contracts can also bind third parties (subject to the registration requirements of the Land Charges or Land Registration Acts, the former having been recently considered by the Court of Appeal in *Lloyds Bank plc* v *Carrick*, CA [1996] 4 All ER 630, whereas estoppels cannot be guaranteed to do so (see further chapter 9).

5.5.2.2 *Constructive trust*

Another possibility, closely related to the discussion in the previous section, is that a constructive trust might protect against any injustice that might arise from the abolition of the part performance doctrine. It seems that constructive trusts *may* arise in similar circumstances to proprietary estoppels, and there is no doubt that a full range of equitable remedies is available to protect a beneficiary under a constructive trust. Constructive trusts also give rise, unlike (probably) proprietary estoppels, to full beneficial interests, and so are capable of binding third parties also.

Constructive trusts arising from inequitable conduct are considered in chapter 7 and in detail in chapter 11, and the constructive trust may well be an alternative to part performance—like equitable estoppel, however, it is no more certain in its operation!

Alternatives to the part performance doctrine are analysed in detail by Lionel Bently and Paul Coughlan in (1990) 10 *Legal Studies*, at p. 325.

5.6 **Capacity**

As a general rule, anyone who has the capacity in law to hold a legal or equitable interest in property has also the capacity to declare a trust of it. The old rules which placed married women in a special position have long been abolished, and the repeal of the Mortmain Acts (by s. 38 of the Charities Act 1960) has removed former restrictions on trusts for corporate bodies. Two special classes of person require consideration, however: minors and persons suffering from mental abnormality.

5.6.1 **Minors**

A minor may hold the legal title to property other than land and can therefore create a trust of such property *inter vivos*. Any such settlement is, however, voidable and the minor may repudiate it during his minority or within a reasonable time of attaining his majority.

Because a minor cannot make a valid will, he cannot therefore create a trust by will. Statutory exceptions are made in the case of soldiers on military service and sailors while at sea.

Since 1925 (Law of Property Act 1925, s. 1(6)) a minor cannot hold a legal estate in land. He therefore cannot settle such an estate, but he may hold an equitable interest in land and can settle this, subject to the possibility of repudiation of the settlement.

Before the passing of the Family Law Reform Act 1969, s. 9 of which reduced the age of majority from 21 to 18 years, the High Court had the power to approve settlements of real and personal property made upon or in contemplation of marriage by males not under 20 and females not under 17 and such approval made the settlement binding. These provisions were repealed by the Family Law Reform Act 1969, s. 11, without, however, affecting anything done before that Act came into force.

5.6.2 Persons suffering from mental abnormality

A mentally abnormal person may be unable to effect a valid disposition of his property where his condition can be shown to affect his understanding of the transaction. Some transactions call for a higher degree of understanding than others. In order to make a valid will, the testator must understand not only the nature of the document itself, but be able also to evaluate the claims of all the potential donees in relation to the sum of property to be disposed of. *Inter vivos* transactions may demand a lower degree of understanding, which depends upon the size of the contemplated transfer relative to the total assets of the donor. A low degree of understanding will be sufficient if the amount of the gift is relatively trivial, but if it comprises the donor's only assets of value, so as to pre-empt the devolution of his property after his death, then the same degree of understanding is required as in the case of a will.

Capacity and mental health legislation
The Mental Health Act 1983, replacing the 1959 Act of the same title, gives the Court of Protection wide powers to manage the affairs of a person whom the judge is satisfied is incapable of managing his property and affairs by reason of mental disorder. A judge may make orders or give directions for the settlement of any property of a patient of full age. These powers may provide for the maintenance or benefit of the patient or members of his family, or for persons or purposes for which the patient might be expected to provide but for his disorder, or otherwise for the management of his affairs. Such a settlement can be varied at any time up to the death of the patient if it appears that any material fact was not disclosed when the settlement was made or that there has been some substantial change of circumstances.

In exercising these powers, the court will be guided by consideration of what the patient would be likely to do if he were not under disability. In *Re TB* [1967] Ch 247 the court approved a revocable settlement of the whole of the patient's property in favour of the patient's illegitimate son and his family, the effect of which was to prevent the property passing to collateral relatives under the rules of intestacy in the anticipated event of the patient's failure to recover testamentary capacity in his lifetime.

Since the Administration of Justice Act 1969 the court has had the power to make a will for a patient of full age whom the judge has reason to believe lacks testamentary capacity.

Applications for approval of schemes to deal with patients' property commonly have the aim of reducing tax liability, although the scheme must be for the benefit of the patient. It is not essential to provide for revocation if the patient should recover: it is sufficient that it is the sort of settlement which he would be likely to make in favour of his family if he were not subject to the abnormality.

5.7 Public policy: capricious trusts

5.7.1 Public policy; void conditions

Various trusts which would otherwise be valid are held to be void for reasons of public policy, in which case the property will be held on resulting trust for the settlor. Trusts for future-born illegitimate children fell into this category before 1970, because it was supposed that they tended to encourage immorality, and the old law still applies to pre-1970 dispositions. Since that date trusts for future-born illegitimate children have been validated, the present provisions being contained in the Family Law Reform Act 1987.

Conditions affecting dispositions may also be struck down on public policy grounds, in which case the result depends on whether the condition is construed as a condition precedent or a condition subsequent. If the former, the entire gift generally fails (although this statement must be qualified in relation to personal property) and the property results to the settlor. If the latter, the gift, but not the condition, is valid.

Capacity, public policy and illustrations of void trusts
Examples of invalid conditions are trusts tending to prevent the carrying out of parental duties, trusts in restraint of marriage and trusts which are fraudulent. Testators sometimes leave property to children subject to a condition subsequent relating to their religious upbringing. In *Blathwayt* v *Lord Cawley* [1976] AC 397, for example, a large estate (valued in 1975 at £2 million) was left in 1936 on various entailed trusts, but such that any person who became entitled was to forfeit his interest if he became a Roman Catholic (or ceased to use the name and arms of Blathwayt). It was argued that with respect to the present children, the religious condition tended to restrain the carrying out of parental duties, and was therefore void on public policy grounds, but the House of Lords held otherwise. The effect of the clause may have been to force the parents to choose between material and spiritual welfare for their offspring, but this was not necessarily contrary to public policy. In the event, however, the House of Lords held by a 3:2 majority (Lords Wilberforce and Fraser of Tullybelton dissenting) that the clause did not apply on its construction.

Void trusts, certainty and 'conditions subsequent'
Conditions subsequent can still be struck down on the grounds of uncertainty, as in *Clayton* v *Ramsden* [1943] AC 320, which concerned a forfeiture on marriage to a person 'not of Jewish parentage and of the Jewish faith'. This was held to be conceptually uncertain. But it seems that so long as a clause is not uncertain the courts will be slow to strike it down on grounds of public policy, and a somewhat similar clause to the above was upheld by the Court of Appeal in *Re Tuck's ST* [1978] Ch 49, where 'an approved wife' of Jewish blood was precisely defined, cases of dispute being dealt with by the Chief Rabbi in London. Names and arms clauses (such as the other clause in *Blathwayt*) have also been upheld (for example, *Re Neeld* [1962]

Ch 643). It may be, though, that such leniency by the courts is misplaced, because social conditions change and clauses of this nature arguably allow the dead too much freedom to interfere in the lives of the living.

5.7.2 **Capricious or useless trusts**

There is no doubt that the courts can also strike down capricious or useless trusts. An early example is *Brown* v *Burdett* (1882) 21 Ch D 667, which was an attempt to create a trust to block up windows—surprisingly, this was not an attempt to avoid window tax.

It is to be hoped that the courts tread warily where the validity of a trust is at issue, however. Public policy tests are inherently vague, and in this area in particular there is an acute shortage of judicial definition. Certainty as to the law is important in property transactions, especially for testamentary dispositions, where there is no opportunity for the settlor to correct any mistakes or failures. Public policy is always supposed to be an unruly horse and I would suggest that extensive use of such a jurisdiction would be most inappropriate in this area.

5.7.3 **Insolvency Act 1986**

The Insolvency Act 1986, replacing earlier complex provisions, empowers the court to set aside certain transactions (called 'transactions at an undervalue') whereby a debtor's property has been placed beyond reach of his creditors. Such transactions include voluntary settlements made by the debtor as well as gifts or sales made for inadequate consideration. Marriage is not regarded as adequate consideration for this purpose.

Section 339 of the Act applies only where a debtor has been adjudged bankrupt. On application by the trustee in bankruptcy, the court may set aside a 'transaction at an undervalue' made by the debtor in the two years preceding the bankruptcy, without need to show that the debtor was already insolvent (i.e., unable to meet his liabilities) at the time of the transaction. Further, a transaction made more than two but less than five years prior to the bankruptcy may be set aside on proof that the debtor was insolvent at the time.

Section 423 applies irrespective of whether the debtor has been adjudged bankrupt. Its effect is to allow any person prejudiced by a transaction at an undervalue (referred to as 'the victim'—usually a creditor) to apply to have the transaction set aside, provided he can establish that the debtor's intention was to place his assets beyond the reach of the victim or otherwise to prejudice the victim's claims against the debtor's property.

In either case, the court has a wide discretion to restore the situation to what it would have been but for the transaction in question.

online
resource
centre

FURTHER READING

Loughlin (1990) 10 *Legal Studies* 325.

Pettit [1989] Conv 441.

6

Perpetuities

This chapter follows preceding chapters which introduced the nature of the trust, and thereafter the requirements which must be met in order for a valid express trust to be created. In the former respect the trust was introduced as a highly versatile instrument which in private law operates across domestic and commercial contexts in relation to a number of interests in property. Its central feature is its ability to confer entitlements for those who are intended to benefit from the settlement, whether or not they are party to it, and to confer legal title of property *subject to the trust conferring on its holder responsibility* to manage the property concerned and safeguard the interests of the beneficiary.

Following this, extensive attention across a number of chapters has now been paid to the way in which in order to achieve a valid trust, a number of requirements must be met. The trust must be constituted (i.e., legal title must become vested in the trustee; and certainty must also be manifested in terms of intention to create a trust; the subject matter of the trust; and those who are intended to benefit from it). The previous chapter has examined legal formality requirements, and this one examines the way in which in order to be valid all private trusts must not infringe the rule against perpetuities (although the rule applies only to a much lesser extent to trusts which are charitable). In this respect, it is a logical continuation of the requirements of a valid trust. However, it is also an important point of reference for much earlier discussion on the very close relationship which the law of trusts enjoys with other aspects of property law, and increasingly the law relating to commercial transactions. The nature of the perpetuity requirements will very quickly become apparent as restricting the use made of trusts to safeguard property, and over time, a number of transactions relating to proprietary interests and entitlements have accidentally become subject to their provisions.

6.1 Introduction: permanent and irrevocable; reach of the trust

The essence of a trust is to direct that property is to be used, if not in a particular way, then applied for the benefit of a particular beneficiary. And it is in this regard that, in previous chapters we have learned that a permanent irrevocable arrangement comes into force when a settlor settles property on trust. We have had an introduction to the role of the trustee in this arrangement, and to the way in which the incumbent of such an office holds legal title to the property, and is charged with managing it in such a way to enable the beneficiary to derive benefit from it. What this chapter seeks to do is explain the trust as a permanent irrevocable arrangement in light of what is known as 'the rule against perpetuities'.

Settling property on trust: the settlor's reach
What the existence of a trust does in reality is restrict use which can be made of the property which is subject to a trust. Although the beneficiary or beneficiaries are the ones in whose favour the trust is made, the recipients of the property, and sometimes even the use they can make of it, are directed by the settlor. The trust property must be applied in accordance with the terms of the trust, and thus the settlor's wishes. At its broadest, the term 'perpetuity' applies to trust lawyers' consideration of the ability of owners of property to restrict the way in which their successors in title are able to utilise it. This is very important because it can involve looking at situations in which subsequent holders of title are not able to deal with property as freely as the person who has imposed the restrictions was once able to do. At the most extreme, this might well involve interference with free applications of property on account of the wishes of generations from beyond the recent past.

Can the dead rule the living?
The rule against perpetuities operates to place limits on the ability of the present generation to tie up property into the future. The reason for this is that property subject to a trust is property which must be applied subject to conditions, and cannot be freely used. The free use of property is prevented, and the law places limits on the way in which restrictions can limit future generations.

Trusts, wealth preservation and the 'dead hand rule'
Trusts are historically associated with the object of the preservation of wealth, and restrictions on its use will help to encourage this: settling property in such a way is advantageous from this perspective. More detailed explanation of this will follow shortly, but essentially the rule against perpetuities operates in a manner which ensures that there are limits on the time allowed for property actually to vest in its intended beneficial owner. It is from this that limits on the duration which property can be held on trust arise. This, along with the closely related rule against excessive accumulations (which fetters a settlor's ability to direct the accumulation of income generated under a trust) is a reflection of the desirability of wealth preservation and also its limits. As generations pass, the law recognises that there must be limits on the ability of one generation to dictate the preservation (or devolution) of property to generations which follow. The law central to this has evolved into two distinct rules: the rule against perpetuity and the rule against excessive accumulations. The former rule places time limits in which trust property must vest and thus be subject to a trust, and the latter places limits on how long income accumulated under a trust can be 'tied into' such settlements. However, both are premised on recognition by the law of the need to limit the way in which the living can be controlled by the wishes of their ancestors: it limits the operation of what is sometimes known as the 'dead hand rule'. As Ruth Deech has noted, in 'Lives in Being revisited' (1981) LQR, at 594:

the Rule [against perpetuities] is necessary in order to strike a balance between on the one hand the freedom of the present generation and, on the other, that of future generations to deal as they wish with the property in which they have interests. If a settlor had total liberty to dispose of his property among future beneficiaries, the recipients, being fettered by his wishes, would never enjoy that same freedom in turn.

Striking the balance: dead hand rule v present autonomy
Given that property held on trust is property which is tied, and its use restricted, the rules against perpetuities and also excessive accumulations can be seen as reflections of the tension between the preservation of wealth and the actual creation of wealth. It can furthermore even be seen as indicative of conflict between private familial wealth and a more public wider economic wellbeing, which can *itself* also cut across the preservation–creation axis. As Ruth Deech continues, in her critique of the dead hand rule (as cited above):

The liberty to make fresh rearrangements of assets is necessary . . . to be rid of irksome conditions attached by earlier donors to the enjoyment of income but also in order to be able to manoeuvre in the light of new tax laws, changes in the nature of property and in the personal circumstances of the beneficiaries, unforeseeable by the best intentioned and most perspicuous of donors.

6.2 Current law and policy focus on law reform

A more detailed consideration is now given to the rule against perpetuity and the rule against excessive accumulations in turn. The current operation of each will be considered closely alongside the proposals for their reform which are currently being considered.

6.2.1 Confusion, dissatisfaction and the Law Commission's work

Notwithstanding the rationale behind the rule against perpetuity and the rule against excessive accumulations of income in respect of property settled subject to a trust, the Law Commission's Report *The Law of Trusts. The Rules against Perpetuities and Excessive Accumulations* (Law Com. No. 251 (1998)) provides some insight into why calls for their modification, and even abolition have been made many times recently. Historically the view taken by this text has been that historical justifications for the rules, which are very much founded on family settlements and Britain's pre-industrial economy are not necessarily strong arguments for a law on perpetuities, notwithstanding the eminently sensible limiting rationale they propose. It has consistently been entreated that better ways of achieving control over settlor's desires to control are through wider powers of investment and through mechanisms for the variation of trusts.

Against this backdrop, the rules against perpetuities and excessive accumulations have twice recently been considered by the Law Commission, first in *The Law of Trusts. The Rules against Perpetuities and Excessive Accumulations*, Consultation Paper No. 133 (1993), and following responses to that paper, in the Law Commission Report of the same name, noted above. Commenting on the current regime, a twin system of common law and statutory provisions, both the Consultation and Report reflect the two central issues surrounding the rules' status in modern law. They raise the question of whether some restriction on the ability to tie up property is necessary and, thereafter, whether the current law is the best means for achieving this. The Law Commission did conclude that there was continuing need to prevent property being tied up in restricted manner, but stopped short of recommending abolition of the rule, notwithstanding extensive criticism levied at the current law. But a considerable overhaul of existing provisions was recommended.

The Law Commission's 1998 Report followed the Consultation dating from 1993, which was delayed by its own admission, and explained (at 2, 1998) on account of staff shortages, and 'the pressure to complete more urgent projects'. In this climate, although a draft Bill did follow the Report, it is difficult to predict precisely when the reforms will be given attention in Parliament, and become enacted. Even then, if (and it is more likely a question of when) the Law Commission's proposals for reform are accepted then much of the current state of the law will cease to have any relevance, at any rate prospectively. However, it is not intended that any legislation should have any automatic retroactive effect, so the common law is likely to continue to be relevant at least for one more lifetime. Nevertheless, it is also the case that the attention accorded to perpetuities in teaching undertaken by law schools has diminished in recent times, and especially from the 1990s, in light of the Law Commission's recommendations for reform. For this work too, the decision has been taken to curtail significantly coverage given to perpetuities. Thus, both the current law and also proposals for reform are considered in summary form only. They have also been examined closely alongside the Law Commission documentation (especially the 1998 Report), which is at present a permanent point of reference in this transitional phase. Making such close reference to the policy documentation will bolster understanding. And the Law Commission work does also provide, alongside the proposed direction of reforms, a fairly clear as well as comprehensive account of the current law at common law and under statute—no small thing in this very complicated and often 'clumsy' area of trusts law.

6.3 Rule against perpetuity and the structure of the law

Current law and historical background

Within the broad introduction above, we see that 'perpetuity' is a by-word for restrictions placed on future dealings with property. That desire to restrict free alienation (or use or application) of property historically has its origins in the ownership of land: historically, the desire to restrict freedom to deal freely with property has its origins in land ownership. Land ownership is in many respects still the ultimate expression of property ownership, but as the introductory chapter explained, it was with interests in land that principles of property ownership originally became carved out. As a result of the desire of landowners to preserve their rights in and enjoyment of property, those who became expert in conveyancing developed forms of 'settlements' of property designed to achieve less than unfettered entitlement to land when property passes. And it is in this context that English law has sought to restrict the extent to which these intended estrictions can operate. Just as the term 'perpetuity' is used to illustrate restrictions placed on future dealings with property, 'the rule against perpetuities' has developed to place limits on such restrictions on free dealings with property.

Rule against perpetuities: an unhelpful term?
The way the rule against perpetuities works is to operate to restrict the time within which future interests (i.e., ones which do not take effect immediately) in property created by a disposition must vest (or take effect). This is not an easy area of trusts law to comprehend, and as the Law Commission noted in its Report, even the term 'rule against perpetuities' lacks a certain intrinsic helpfulness. Notwithstanding that the term 'perpetuity' fits what has been said about the prevention of present and future generations being tied into the wishes of their ancestors, it is also the case that the rule against perpetuities is actually directly concerned with the commencement of interests, rather than with their actual duration (by restricting the time within which future interests must vest for the disposition to be valid). Although, as the Law Commission notes (at 3, 1998), restrictions on the time within which future interests can be created will almost always have the effect of limiting the life of a trust. The Law Commission, in citing Simpson (1979) 'Entails and Perpetuities' 24 Jur Rev 1, 17 also points to ambiguity in use of the term 'against', emphasising instead the permissive effect of the rule:

The rule against perpetuities, to be comprehended, must be understood as permitting them within limits, and most modern discussion of the rule . . . is distorted by a failure to appreciate that the contemporary oddity of the rule lies not in what it prevents, but in how much it allows.

6.4 Emergence of 'restrictions on restrictions': development of the common law

The common law on perpetuities developed in the sixteenth and seventeenth centuries, directed primarily at settlements of land. At that time, equity allowed the creation of future interests, whereas the common law did not. Because Uses (the early form of trust instrument, introduced in chapter 1) were executed, the *common law* was faced with the problem of dealing with future interests in land, which previously had been recognised only in equity. In summary, then, an incidental effect of the Statute of Uses was to enable successive future interests to be created at common law. One consequence of this was that land could more easily be rendered unsaleable, and in particular testators could ensure that large estates remained in the family for many generations, since by creating a succession of limited estates it was possible to ensure that nobody was in a position to convey an entire unencumbered fee simple. The creation of potentially infinite successive future interests was eventually curbed by the development of the common law rule against perpetuities. The rule therefore represented a compromise between the policy of assisting the prudent management of family wealth across generations on the one hand, and the prevention of schemes for tying up property for unacceptably long periods on the other.

Perpetuity rules and their modification over time
Since its original inception, however, the policy behind the rule has undergone modification. Although it was originally developed in the context of settlements of

land, in the twenty-first century the rule has come to apply in respect of all kinds of interests in property, both real and personal. Since nowadays settlements of land are very rare, mainly for reasons which are unconnected with perpetuities and which are considered in chapter 1, it could be argued that early fears about tying up land for generations should no longer govern modern policy. This is certainly very strongly present as an argument throughout the Law Commission documentation from 1993 and 1998.

The chief scope of the rule today is in fact within settlements of personalty (i.e., property which is not land), which are mostly set up with a view to tax saving. But because fiscal law alters fairly rapidly, there is in any case an in-built disincentive to create long-term, immoveable arrangements. The Law Commission recognised this as valid critique of such a rigid prohibition against such settlements, and by the same token therefore, as potentially less of a justification for a stringent rule against perpetuities.

6.4.1 Continuing development in the rule against perpetuity

A closer examination of the Law Commission Report provides insight into why the rule against perpetuities is often characterised as anachronistic, and why there have been frequent calls for its abolition. The Law Commission does concur that the rule against excessive accumulations should go—which it admits has very little purpose, and actually creates a number of practical difficulties. And although the Law Commission insisted that some provisions against perpetuity must remain in force, it did recommend that the law as it is is in need of considerable overhaul. This view in turn rested on a conclusion that the current law was complicated and even inaccessible. Here, the Law Commission accepted (at 2, 1998) that the current law is 'needlessly complicated' and so to the point that it can 'only be understood by specialists' and even that 'In a number of situations it is uncertain whether or how it applies'.

6.4.2 The modern law: how does it apply and how does it 'work'?

The modern law hinges on whether or not the disposition in question came into being before 16 July 1964, the date on which the Perpetuities and Accumulations Act 1964 came into force.

Before looking at the provisions of the common law and of the 1964 Act, generally the thrust of the provisions under the statute and at common law alike concern what are known as 'future' interests in property. Much complicated discussion could follow around the nature and reach of future interests, but the purpose here is to give a very simple explanation, and to relate them to the law's desire to restrict the dead hand rule at the heart of perpetuities law. An interest which is a future interest is, at this extremely basic level of operation and understanding, an interest in property which is not created and does not take effect immediately. And, following on from this idea of a future interest, as distinct from one which is immediate, the rule against perpetuities operates to restrict the time within which future interests can be created. It is this in turn which has the effect of limiting the life of the trust.

Future interests and their creation: the significance of time
At common law, the rule against perpetuities operates so that a future interest in any type of property is only valid where there is no possibility that the interest may vest or commence outside the perpetuity period. And where there is the possibility that it may do so outside the perpetuity period, the interest is void from the date that the instrument purporting to create it takes effect. In this respect, the 'perpetuity period' referred to consists of one or more 'lives in being' plus a period of 21 years, and where relevant a period of gestation (as the Law Commission explains in para. 1.7, a child *in utero*, or *en ventre sa mere* is treated as a life in being for the purposes of the rule against perpetuities; explained in para. 4.11). It is from this measure of the 'life in being' that the 'royal lives' clause has become central. This became a favoured device of those drafting settlements since its effect is to terminate the period applicable to the vesting of the gift 21 years after the death of the survivor of all those members of the royal family who are alive at the date of the disposition. Such a clause always validates the gift, since it cannot vest more than 21 years after the death of somebody living at the date of the disposition, and doubtless royal lives clauses became significant because royalty tend to be long-lived!

Understanding the common law: guidance from law reform, and reasoning backwards
This position is not easy to grasp, and even the Law Commission policy documentation castigating the law's complexity 'explains' its current position with only limited clarity. This itself is in many respects the most appropriate precursor to explain *why* things are going to change. Shortly, it will become apparent how original reforms in 1964 tried to improve on the common law position. Looking at the Act's provisions does in a backward-reasoning way actually explain the common law position better than the act of trying to put it into words alone does. But first, there is the need to consider the idea of an 'interest' to make sense of the central notion of a 'future' interest. In so doing, you will need an appreciation of interests which are 'vesting' and ones which are 'contingent'.

Vesting and contingent interests
In order for an interest to vest to arise, three factors must be present (see, e.g., the similar definition in Law Com. 251, at para. 4.2). First, the person who is to have the interest must be in existence, and identifiable as the person entitled. Secondly, the size of the interest must be known for certain. Thirdly, nothing further must need to happen before the person in question becomes entitled to the interest. For example, an interest can vest where the person is a living human who is identified by name in the settlement; and the size of his interest is certain (e.g., a fee simple in remainder); and there are no conditions which have to be fulfilled beyond this. It would be different if, for example, the interest could only be obtained if the intended recipient were to marry (since, unlike death, marriage need not occur); or complete study for a degree and graduate from university. Where the obtaining of an interest is dependent on certain conditions coming into play, the interest is known as a *contingent interest*.

6.4.3 Common law: problematic development and calls for reform

The common law provisions are highly complex, and it is difficult even to formulate a basic understanding of them, even in the comparatively clear way in which they are set out in the Law Commission Report. It is also the case that criticism of the common law arose from its harsh operation, as much as its complex nature. A basic appreciation of how the common law can operate harshly can be gleaned by reference to the provision as it was explained above. This requires appreciation of the way in which a future interest in property is rendered void *ab initio* if there is any possibility that it might vest outside the perpetuity period. This meant that a future interest could and indeed would be rendered void at the outset if vesting outside the perpetuity period were even a possibility (without establishing when it might actually vest). This has the effect of 'killing' a number of future interests which might not violate the perpetuity rule at all.

Both criticisms of complexity and also undue harshness started to gather momentum in the 1950s and reforms were introduced in 1964 for dispositions taking effect prospectively (after 15 July of that year) by the enactment of the Perpetuities and Accumulations Act 1964.

6.4.4 Statutory perpetuity requirements and the common law position: an outline

This legislation introduced two key changes to the common law. One sought to avoid harshness resulting from a future interest being void from the outset simply on account of the possibility that it might vest outside the perpetuity period. The other substituted a fixed perpetuity period for the common law life in being plus 21 years. The Law Commission Report statutory provisions are summarised as follows (at 4, 1998):

Where an instrument creates a future interest after 15 July 1964—

(1) That instrument will only be void where it (the interest) must vest or take effect (if at all) outside the perpetuity period;

(2) It is therefore necessary to 'wait and see', if need be for the whole perpetuity period, to determine whether the instrument is valid; and

(3) An alternative perpetuity period of up to 80 years may be employed instead of a life in being plus 21 years.

Future interests and 'wait and see'
The 1964 Act's 'wait and see' principle sought to address the way in which, at common law, a future interest would be void from the outset simply on account of the possibility that it *might* vest outside the perpetuity period. This was perceived as a cause of undue harshness, on account of the 'hardest line' taken on future interests just on the possibility that they might infringe the perpetuity period, and regardless of the way in which many would doubtless not actually do so. 'Wait and see' completely altered the vista by focusing not on the possibility that an interest *may* vest outside the perpetuity period, but by switching emphasis completely to situations where it *must actually* do so. Thus 'wait and see' ensures that an interest will not be void until such time as it becomes apparent that it *must* vest outside the perpetuity period. In addition, the provision of a fixed statutory maximum perpetuity period of (not exceeding) 80 years, replacing the life in being plus 21 years at common law, was extremely radical—not so much because of the apparent extended period of time for vesting, but because it brought to the rules some much needed certainty.

Common law and statutory regimes

Although the statutory provisions were intended to respond to the complexity and harshness of the common law, the two regimes exist side by side even in dispositions taking effect post-1964. Indeed, the 'wait and see' sections in the 1964 Act apply only to those which are void under the common law rule. The result is therefore a two-stage process, in which the common law rules must be applied first. If the disposition is valid at common law, that is the end of the matter. Only if it would have been void at common law do the provisions of the Act apply, in which case a 'wait and see' operation is triggered. This means that time is allowed to run to see whether the gift does in fact vest within the permitted period.

6.4.5 Relationship between common law and statutory provisions: more detail

The interrelationship between the regimes can be quite complicated, however, because if the gift is valid at common law the Act never applies. Under the Act, the donor may expressly stipulate for a period not exceeding 80 years, which it was envisioned would replace the use of 'royal lives' clauses, but this does not actually appear to have occurred. It used to be thought this had to be done expressly and it would not be enough simply to fix a date, so that, for example, a gift 'to be given equally to the issue of X, living on 1 January 2030' would be void even in the case of a 1980 disposition. However, in *Re Green's WT* [1985] 3 All ER 455, Nourse J upheld a similar disposition, made in 1976, for the establishment of a charitable foundation on 1 January 2020 unless an event stated in the gift had occurred before then. A mother believed that her son who, as one of the crew of a bomber, had been killed in the Second World War, was still alive, and the gift to the charity took effect only if he had not claimed the property by the date stipulated. The court held that the gift to charity was not void for perpetuity.

Where the Act applies, the period during which the trustees may wait and see is calculated as follows, assuming that the 80-year period or other express choice has not been made. A list of all those who count as 'lives' by virtue of s. 3(5) is made and, on the death of the last survivor of them all, a further 21 years is added. This gives the maximum time for which wait and see is permitted. If at any time before the expiry of that period it becomes evident that a disposition cannot vest in time, then and only then is it treated as being void. Otherwise, the period is allowed to run its course to see if it will vest in time.

6.5 Proposals for reform and the position of the common law

Mapping common law and statutory provisions: concerns and future directions

If the Law Commission's proposals for reform are accepted (and it is suggested that the issue is more likely to be a case of *when* rather than whether) then the common law will cease to have any relevance, at least in a prospective sense. However, it is not intended that any legislation should have any automatic retroactive effect, so the common law is likely to continue to be relevant at least for one more lifetime.

But the common law *is* very difficult to grasp with much confidence, and by the Law Commission's own admission, it is not simply complicated but actually 'needlessly complicated'. This accusation in the 1998 Report was accompanied by its accusation that the current law is actually out of touch with modern uses of property rights. This is because, as explained above, the rules originated with wills and trusts around family settlements, but their application has not remained so confined. Key difficulties in the current law can be seen in situations where property interests spring from contexts outside these traditional ones, itself a reflection of the dynamism of property and proprietary interests. It is also in some respects a reflection of changing adaptations of trusts and their applications.

Family settlements and continuing justification of the rule against perpetuities
Family settlement trusts are of course very uncommon today, while commercial transactions and dealings with property much more readily typify use made of interests arising in respect of property. And while the justification for the rule against perpetuities developed around the paradigm of the family trust, what has happened is that, without critical appraisal of the rule and its justifications, it has become applied to interests which are far removed from this model. The Law Commission accepted that the justifications surrounding the family-type trust simply did not extend to these newer manifestations of proprietary interest. And in addition to the fact that its extended reach was created by accident, exporting the rule to a much wider range of interests is actually capable of creating considerable practical difficulties in commercial transactions. To this end, the Law Commission made a series of recommendations in its 1998 Report. These are set out in brief below, considered alongside and against the proposed benefits which such direction in reform can achieve.

6.6 Conclusions of the Law Commission's enquiries

The 1998 Report sets out in great detail why reform is due in this sphere, and the way in which the new proposals are envisaged to bring much-needed improvement to the current operation of the rule against perpetuities. These are set out in outline below, but the most appropriate starting point is the fundamental premise on which the reforms are explained. The remit of the Law Commission's 1993 Consultation offered four possible options in light of concerns about the current state of the law. First was the option of no change to existing law, and at the other extreme rested the possibility of abandoning the rule against perpetuities. Other options arose in the shape of replacement of the rule against perpetuities with a new rule, or reforming the rule against perpetuities. Thereafter, the subsequent Report is premised on the need to keep some control over the 'dead hand rule'.

The Law Commission did not think that control over perpetuities should be abolished altogether, and in its assessment of the issues, it concluded that some limits on the power of property owners to dictate its future use should remain. This is a matter which should remain within the law's reach, and this was itself premised on the idea that greater appropriateness had to be built into reform. But the actual reasoning behind the Law Commission's assessment that some form of the rule should remain (and not actually be abolished, or replaced with something completely different) is worthy of attention before an examination is made of the actual direction of the proposals for reform.

6.6.1 A rule which should remain within the law's reach?

There are a number of references in the 1998 Report, both of a direct and indirect nature to the way in which some control should be maintained over attempts by one generation to restrict the free application and devolution of property by successive generations. The proposed reformed rule will now only apply to interests in property arising under wills and family settlements, but it is deemed to be necessary and desirable to maintain its reach in such situations. Restricting the rule against perpetuity to 'successive estates and interests in property and to powers of appointment' in this way will, according to the Law Commission restore the original function of the rule. It removes from the reach of the rule circumstances where 'that justification is absent'. In the outline of the principal recommended reforms, the Law Commission did acknowledge that there was no universal agreement even that the rule should remain at all, even in its original context. According to the Report (at 8, 1998) there was a 'distinguished minority' of respondents to the consultation process calling for the rule to be abolished rather than reformed, on grounds which were grouped by the Law Commission under limitations which were no longer necessary, or where such limitations could be achieved by alternative means (e.g., statutory powers of sale; legislation relating to taxation; and legal facilities for the variation of trusts).

6.6.2 Retention not abolition: scope of reform

Notwithstanding the arguments against retaining the rule against perpetuities, the Law Commission nevertheless concluded that it should be retained in some form. The case in favour of controlling the 'dead hand rule' outweighed arguments against its continuing application, but the Law Commission acknowledged that this should be framed in reference to an approach which is described as **inclusionary** rather than **exclusionary**. The Law Commission explained this focus as one which defines interests which *should* be subject to the rule against perpetuities, rather than those which should not. This is an approach in which the 'test' is whether there is need to control the dead hand rule: where there is, the rule will apply; where there is not, the rule shall not.

The 'dead hand rule', and balance in the law's approach
The question which arises from this new approach (and even 'test') is whether the Law Commission has given sufficient and appropriate consideration to the much vaunted negativity of the 'dead hand rule'? It is suggested that there is much which points to this in the affirmative, and that in terms of interests and estates created by trusts and under wills, it is not in the interests of beneficiaries nor society in general that the present is ruled by the minds, prejudices and wisdoms of the past. In terms of making an assessment of the relationship between past and present, and achieving the most appropriate degree of consonance between the two, many historians approach this through use of the principle of historical process. In this framework,

'the present' is regarded as being part of a continuing evolution of societal processes, and part of a trajectory which is still unfolding. Indeed, in a directly applicable manifestation of this, the Law Commission itself acknowledges in the 1998 Report that it is not possible to rule against new kinds of property rights arising in the future. If this is the case, then it must follow that even very well-intentioned ancestral views on the 'best ways' of managing property cannot be accorded equal let alone greater value than current understanding of property and optimising its use.

6.6.3 New law: a rule with direction, purpose and rationale

More limited but more appropriate application

What remains by adopting such an inclusionary approach is according to the Law Commission, a rule with more limited application, but with clear purpose. The Law Commission accepted that the rule against perpetuities was being applied to a number of transactions where it was wholly inappropriate given its origins in familial wealth preservation, and that because of this, it should have a restricted ambit and reach. Here, it should only apply to rights arising under wills and trusts. Pension schemes should be exempt from the rule's applications, and it should not apply to certain rights over property such as options, and rights of first refusal, future easements etc. created after the enactment of new perpetuities legislation.

To address the current situation whereby there is often uncertainty as to whether the rule applies and the consequent degree of expertise required for advising clients, the Law Commission has proposed that the circumstances in which a transaction is subject to any new rule against perpetuities be set out clearly in statute. This is of course the realisation of the new law's proposed inclusionary approach.

New single statutory perpetuity period to offer certainty and flexibility

The Law Commission has recommended that there should be one fixed perpetuity period of 125 years. Under the proposed scheme, a future interest or right would only be void for perpetuity when it became clear that it would not take effect within 125 years from the date on which the instrument creating it took effect. This incorporates the virtues of the 1964 Act evident in its 'wait and see' provisions, which acts as a device to prevent future interests being struck out *ab initio* (on grounds of possibility of vesting outside the perpetuity period) as is the case under the common law. The fixed statutory maximum period is more generous than the current statutory provisions, and as such will help to promote flexible and confident dealings with property. The manner in which it is fixed also removes the clumsiness and certainty arising in the common law, and may actually at last sound the death knell of 'royal lives clauses'.

Key perceived benefits of reform

Following the main body of the document, the Law Commission sets out the intended beneficial effects of the reforms at length. These cluster around promoting greater confidence in dealings with property and thus facilitation of them; encouraging greater flexibility in dealings with property and drafting trusts; provision of greater access to the law and reduction of scope for error in respect of stating the law; and facilitating the production of documents which are simplified and less lengthy, with the result of a reduction of costs incurred for legal and related professional services.

6.7 **Rule against excessive accumulations**

Very much as it sounds, the notion of 'accumulation' of property can be found strongly rooted in ideas of wealth preservation. It is the term given when any profits which are produced by property subject to a trust are added to its original value, rather than being distributed to beneficiaries under the trust. Accumulations are a very common feature of modern trusts, and are premised on the desirability of being able to provide a healthy capital sum for beneficiaries on their coming of age, or other event which reflects their entitlement to the trust (such as marriage), and the facilitation of this. However, the law requires that the time during which accumulation (rather than distribution) is directed to take place is limited to one of the periods permitted. It is another mechanism by which the law places limits on how property can be 'tied up'.

If an accumulation is directed for longer than the common law perpetuity period of a life plus 21 years, the direction is void *ab initio* and no accumulation can be undertaken at all. If, however, the direction does not infringe this rule, it is subject to additional control, and it will only be allowed to take place for a period not exceeding one of the periods specified by statute. Should it overrun, it will be void with regard to the excess, and in this event the surplus accumulated income will pass to the persons who would have been entitled to receive that income if the accumulation had not been directed.

The control of accumulations is statutory, originating in the Accumulations Act 1800, this legislation believed to be an over-zealous response to the decision in *Thellusson* v *Woodford* (1799) 4 Ves 227; (1805) 11 Ves 112; 31 ER 117; 32 ER 1030. In this case, a direction to accumulate for what was then the full perpetuity period (thought at that time to be lives in being only) was upheld as lawful at common law. The amount of the moneys to be accumulated was very large, and Parliament considered it undesirable that so large a proportion of the nation's wealth should be tied up for such a long period.

The present statutory periods are contained in the Law of Property Act 1925, ss. 164 to 166, and in the Perpetuities and Accumulations Act 1964, s. 13. In terms of functioning, s. 164 of the 1925 Act sets out four periods and only these can apply to pre-1964 dispositions, while in the case of post-1964 dispositions the additional two periods contained in s. 13 of the 1964 Act are available. Only one period can be used and it is usual in a modern, professionally drafted trust, to specify which it should be. In any other case, the court will determine which period is most appropriate on proper construction of the instrument.

Four possible measures of time determining permitted accumulation of income
The four periods found in the 1964 Act are as follows. First, there is the life of the grantor or settlor; then a period marked as 21 years from the death of the grantor or settlor. The remaining two are: the minority or respective minorities only of any person or persons living or *en ventre sa mère* (unborn) at the death of the grantor,

settlor or testator; and finally the minority or respective minorities only of any person or persons who would, under the limitations of the instrument directing the accumulation, for the time being, if of full age, be entitled to the income directed to be accumulated. In addition (s. 13 of) the Act tries to remedy the peculiarity of s. 164 (which allows periods two and three to run only from the death of the settlor and not from the date of the instrument, and becomes unnecessarily restrictive) by adding 21 years from the making of the disposition the minority or respective minorities only of any person or persons who, under the limitations of the instrument directing the accumulation, would for the time being, if of full age, be entitled to the income directed to be accumulated. In summary, the four periods in s. 164 are:

(i) the life of the grantor or settlor;

(ii) 21 years from the death of the grantor or settlor;

(iii) the minority or respective minorities only of any person or persons living or *en ventre sa mère* at the death of the grantor, settlor or testator;

(iv) the minority or respective minorities only of any person or persons who, under the limitations of the instrument directing the accumulation, would for the time being, if of full age, be entitled to the income directed to be accumulated.

6.7.1 Reform proposals: a much restricted application of the rule against excessive accumulations

The Law Commission in its consideration of the rule against perpetuities and excessive accumulations has recommended that this rule should be abolished except in relation to charitable trusts. It has already been noted (in chapter 1) that charitable trusts can exist perpetually (i.e., they do not infringe the rule against perpetuity), but in reforming the rule against excessive accumulations, charitable trusts which have a power or duty to accumulate income should only be capable of doing so for a period of 21 years. Given their perpetual nature, the ability to accumulate income indefinitely (rather than applying it to its purposes) could operate contrary to benefiting the public. It is very hard to envisage a 'private familial context' *Thellusson* v *Woodford* (1799) situation arising today, but the issues arising in respect of charitable trusts are perhaps more current than ever, the ability of charitable trusts to accumulate assets as distinct from applying them to their purposes is very much a 'live' issue.

6.8 Rule against inalienability: rule against perpetual trusts

In the earlier chapter dealing with certainty requirements and the 'beneficiary principle' note was made of the rule against inalienability. This is more commonly known as the rule against perpetual trusts.

6.8.1 A final point of reference

In terms of relating the rule against inalienability to the very similar sounding 'rule against perpetuity' it should be clear that while the latter relates to future vesting of interests and estates, the former rule against perpetual trusts does something quite different. Confusion between the two is easier to avoid where reference is made to the rule against perpetuities as the rule against 'remoteness in vesting'. At this point the rule against perpetual trusts sounds quite different, and of course it is. This is even more clear when using its term as the rule against inalienability.

Point of revision
The rule against perpetual trusts relates to the duration of trusts for non-charitable purposes. These instruments are usually void for want of a beneficiary in a position to enforce the trust, under the authority provided by *Re Astor's ST* [1952]. But even for those dispositions where validity is upheld notwithstanding violation of the beneficiary principle, an additional problem with their validity comes from the way in which they may be perpetual or ever-lasting. To avoid this, as it was explained earlier they are only valid for the perpetuity period (even dispositions which are valid without a beneficiary).

Difficulties created by perpetual trusts and the need to avoid their operation
It should have been clear in chapter 4 that the litigation which arises reveals these trusts as highly problematic in terms of enforcement and monitoring performance of them. In this respect, as the Law Commission notes in its 1998 documentation, the rule against inalienability is a device to limit the operation of such trusts in light of these difficulties, and certainly to curtail their development. The materials in chapter 4 did intend to invite a more critical appraisal of the 'private purpose trusts' than the Law Commission actually engages in, although the discussion in the Report does proceed to explain why the rule against inalienability has not been considered within the provinces of the enquiry.

6.8.2 Law Commission's exclusion of the rule against inalienability

This rule has been expressly excluded from the Law Commission's remit because, in the Commission's words, it 'belongs more properly in a review of the law governing non-charitable purpose trusts'.

online
resource
centre

FURTHER READING

R. Deech (1981) 'Lives in Being Revisited' 97 LQR 593.

A. Ogus (1986) 'The Trust as a Governance Structure' 36 UTLJ 187.

C. Harpum (2000) 'Perpetuities, Pensions and Resulting Trusts, 64 Conv 170.

7

Introduction to resulting and constructive trusts

The attention given in this text to constructive and resulting trusts arises from the way in which their characteristics and operation necessarily require extensive and thorough treatment. The starting point is the fundamental principle of trusts law which emerged from the principle in *Westdeutsche Landesbank Girozentrale v Islington London Borough Council* [1996] AC 669 that the basis for all trusts is conscience. It is from this premise that we can now consider the creation and operation of trusts which arise from ways other than the settlor's express intention to create a trust.

7.1 Resulting trusts

It was stated earlier in the brief introduction to resulting trusts that they are difficult to pin down, mainly because they can be found in a number of very diverse factual situations.

7.1.1 Introduction

It was also suggested in that introduction that at the heart of all resulting trusts could be found a fundamental characteristic which overarches all their different factual manifestations and applications. This common factor is that the settlor and the beneficiary are the same person.

Settlor and beneficiary are the same person
So, what is common to all resulting trusts is that although legal title is vested in a trustee, the settlor and the beneficiary are actually the same person. In the brief introduction in chapter 2 it was suggested that this arose from the occurrence of two broad scenarios. The trust in favour of the settlor-beneficiary might arise where the settlor has tried to create a trust in favour of a third party beneficiary, but failed to do so. This has the consequence that the equitable interest which is created on the transfer of legal title never actually leaves him. It can also arise where property has been divested from the settlor, but for some reason equitable interest in it is at a later date returned back to him. This latter position, whereby the equitable interest is actually returned to the settlor can be illustrated by the occurrence of an event which has not been foreseen by the donor and hence (or perhaps because of bad drafting) this 'contingency' has not been provided for.

In due course (at the end of the chapter on remedies), greater attention shall be given to the creation of the resulting trust on account of the *Westdeutsche* determination that unless and until there is separation of titles, while one person holds property absolutely, no distinct equitable title actually exists (and it and the rights it confers are until the point of separation), and district equitable ownership is instead encompassed within the legal title which is held. It is the position post-*Westdeutsche* that equitable title is actually created, and this occurs when legal title is transferred to another—because the conscience of its recipient is affected. For the sake of simplicity, at this point it is best to try to keep in your mind that equitable interest created in property as a result of the transfer of legal title *remains with* the settlor, or it is *returned to* him. In this manner a resulting trust can be seen to provide the basis of a claim for the recovery of one's own property. This is vital because what follows is a brief consideration of a number of factual situations to which this 'remains with–or returns to' model can be applied.

7.1.2 Classification of resulting trusts

Re Vandervell's Trusts (No. 2) and the categorisation of 'automatic' and 'presumed' resulting trust
In this case ([1974] Ch 269) Megarry J distinguished between presumed and automatic resulting trusts:

(a) The first class of case is where the transfer to B is not made on any trust . . . there is a rebuttable presumption that B holds on resulting trust for A. The question is not one of the automatic consequences of a dispositive failure by A, but one of presumption: the property has been carried to B, and from the absence of consideration and any presumption of advancement B is presumed not only to hold the entire interest on trust but also to hold the beneficial interest for A absolutely. The presumption thus establishes both that B is to take on trust and also what that trust is. Such resulting trusts may be called 'presumed resulting trusts'.

(b) The second class of case is where the transfer to B is made on trusts which leave some or all the beneficial interest undisposed of. Here B automatically holds on resulting trust for A to the extent that the beneficial interest has not been carried to him or others. The resulting trust here does not depend on any intentions or presumptions, but is the automatic consequence of A's failure to dispose of what is vested in him. Since *ex hypothesi* the transfer is on trust, the resulting trust does not establish the trust but merely carries back to A the beneficial interest that has not been disposed of. Such resulting trusts may be called 'automatic resulting trusts'.

7.1.3 Resulting trusts and the *Westdeutsche* reclassification

A similar but not identical categorisation was adopted by Lord Browne-Wilkinson in *Westdeutsche Landesbank Girozentrale* v *Islington London Borough Council* [1996] AC 669, at p. 708. In what must now be regarded as a reclassification, under existing law, a resulting trust arises in two sets of circumstances:

(A) where A makes a voluntary payment to B or pays (wholly or in part) for the purchase of property which is vested either in B alone or in the joint names of A and B, there is a presumption that A did not intend to make a gift to B: the money or property is held on trust for A (if he is the sole provider of the money) or in the case of a joint purchase by A and B in shares proportionate to their contributions. It is important to stress that this is only a presumption, which presumption is easily rebutted either by the counter-presumption of advancement or by direct evidence of A's intention to make an outright transfer . . .

(B) where A transfers property to B on express trusts, but the trusts do not exhaust the whole of the beneficial interest: . . . *Quistclose Investments Ltd* v *Rolls Razor Ltd* [1970] AC 567.

Both types of resulting trust are traditionally regarded as examples of trusts giving effect to the common intention of the parties. A resulting trust is not imposed by law against the intentions of the trustee (as is a constructive trust); but gives effect to his presumed intention. Megarry J in *Re Vandervell's Trusts (No. 2)* suggests that a resulting trust of type (B) does not depend on intention but operates automatically. We are not convinced that this is right. If the settlor has expressly, or by necessary implication, abandoned any beneficial interest in the trust property, there is in my view no resulting trust: the undisposed-of equitable interest vests in the Crown as *bona vacantia*: see *Re West Sussex Constabulary's Widows, Children and Benevolent (1930) Fund Trusts* [1971] Ch 1.

7.2 Category (B) resulting trusts

7.2.1 Incomplete disposal of the equitable interest

The settlor may have made it clear that property is intended to be held on trust and may even have transferred the legal title to the trustee. There may be some reason, however, why the equitable interest is not properly disposed of. Obviously the trustee cannot keep the trust property for himself and so he holds it on resulting trust for the settlor. There is nowhere else for the equitable interest to go.

7.2.1.1 *Formalities, certainty and public policy*

Sometimes this can arise for technical reasons. For example, we saw in chapter 5 that formalities may be required for the disposal of an equitable interest. If these formalities are not complied with, there will be no effective disposal. In that case the equitable interest never leaves the settlor, and there is a resulting trust. A similar result obtains if the certainty of object requirement (see chapter 4) is not complied with: e.g., *IRC* v *Broadway Cottages Trust* [1955] Ch 20 (chapter 4).

A trust can also fail for public policy reasons, for example where equity has not allowed a person to retain the fruits of criminal activities. In *Cleaver* v *Mutual Reserve Fund Life Association* [1892] 1 QB 147, the executors of a person who had effected an insurance on his life for the benefit of his wife were held by the Court of Appeal to be able to maintain an action on the policy where the wife had murdered the insured; the trust in favour of the wife was unenforceable, for public policy reasons. There are a number of cases where persons guilty of murder or manslaughter have been prevented from obtaining the property of the victim, either through intestacy (*Re Crippen* [1911] P 108), or through the right of survivorship (*Re K (dec'd)* [1985] 2

WLR 262, affirmed on other grounds [1986] Ch 180, although there relief was granted against forfeiture by the Forfeiture Act 1982).

The result in *Cleaver* was that the executors held the insurance money for the estate of the insured. The result is exactly the same as in any other failed trust case; there is a resulting trust, as in the other cases in this section. In short, this is a category (B) *Westdeutsche* resulting trust.

7.2.1.2 *Equitable interest undefined*

Another possibility is where property is settled on trust but details of the trust are left unclear (i.e., the terms of the trust fail to provide for the totality of the beneficial interest). In *Vandervell v IRC* [1967] 2 AC 291 (a case considered in greater detail in chapter 5) Mr Vandervell made arrangements to endow a chair of pharmacology by transferring shares to the Royal College of Surgeons, to enable it to take the dividends declared on those shares. He did not wish to make an out-and-out transfer, however, and so gave an option to purchase (at a nominal cost) to a trustee company which was under his control. He left no clear instructions with the trustee company as to the terms on which the option was to be held by them.

As explained in chapter 5, Vandervell's liability to surtax on the dividends depended on whether he had divested himself of his entire interest in both the shares and the option. The Revenue failed to show that he had not divested himself of the entire interest in the shares. The point that arises in the present context, however, is that they succeeded in showing that he had not divested himself of his equitable interest in the option, the legal title to which was now in the trustee company. The option was therefore held on resulting trust for him along with liability to pay surtax on the dividends.

Lord Wilberforce said that the trusts upon which the option was supposed to be held were undefined and in the air, possibly to be defined later. The trustee company itself was clearly not a beneficiary. An equitable interest cannot remain in the air and so the only possibility was a resulting trust in favour of the settlor. This is an example, then, of the trust being insufficiently defined.

To counter the Revenue's claims to surtax on the dividends declared on the shares, Mr Vandervell in 1961 instructed the trustee company to exercise the option, and repurchase the shares. The shares were then placed by the trustee company on the trusts of the children's settlements. The Court of Appeal held in *Re Vandervell's Trusts (No. 2)* [1974] Ch 269, that Vandervell had now succeeded in divesting himself of the entire interest in these shares, there being no longer a resulting trust in his favour. The later trusts were precisely defined, in favour of the children's settlements, so it was no longer necessary for this reason for the equitable interest to remain in the settlor.

7.2.1.3 *Necessary pre-condition absent*

There can be other reasons, apart from a defective trust instrument, for a failure to dispose of an equitable interest. One possibility is that the body on which money or property is settled has never existed or has ceased to exist. If a general or paramount charitable intention is shown on the part of the donor, a cy près scheme may be applied (considered later in the context of charitable trusts). Otherwise the property will be held on resulting trust for the settlor.

Another situation is where money or property is given for a purpose, and the circumstances necessary to achieve the purpose fail to materialise. For example, in *Essery* v *Coulard* (1884) 26 Ch D 191, a trust for the parties to an intended marriage, and the issue of the marriage, could not take effect when the parties decided to live together without marrying, so Pearson J held that the property was to be held on resulting trust for the settlor. The intention of the settlor (the intended wife) had been to provide for all the issue of the relationship, and this was inevitably defeated by failure to marry, even if a marriage were later to take place: children had already been born, and at that time illegitimate children could not benefit from such a trust. Since a subsequent marriage would not legitimate the children who had already been born, the settlor's intention to provide for all the children had been irrevocably defeated by the failure of the parties to marry.

A similar result was reached in *Re Ames' Settlement* [1946] Ch 217. Property was settled expressly on trusts, declared as part of a marriage settlement, which gave the husband an income for life, with remainder to his wife for life or until her remarriage, with remainder to the issue of the intended marriage. However, although Mr Ames and Miss Hamilton went through a ceremony of marriage, and lived together as if married, the Supreme Court of Kenya later declared the marriage void *ab initio*, a decree of nullity having at that time retrospective effect. In other words, the position was as if there had never been a valid marriage. Nor was there any issue. The income was paid to Mr Ames until his death, and the question arose as to what to do with the capital. The settlement had provided for an ultimate trust of the capital, for an artificial class of the husband's next-of-kin, in the event of failure of issue of the 'intended marriage', but Vaisey J held that the property should be held on resulting trust for the settlor (or rather, his representatives). *Re Ames* was distinguished by the House of Lords in *Westdeutsche* v *Islington BC* [1996] AC 669.

The same result would not obtain on the same facts today: since 31 July 1971, a decree of nullity in respect of a voidable marriage has not had retrospective effect, so the marriage would not be regarded as void *ab initio*.

7.2.1.4 *Partial disposal of equitable interest*

Sometimes the settlor disposes of some, but not all, of the equitable interest. Usually this occurs because some contingency is unprovided for, perhaps because it is unforeseen, or perhaps because of sloppy drafting. In this case also, the undisposed of residue 'results' to the settlor.

A good example is *Re Cochrane* [1955] Ch 309, which concerned a marriage settlement of funds for the wife:

. . . during her life so long as she shall continue to reside with the said W.J.B. Cochrane . . . and after [her] decease or the prior determination of the trust in her favour . . . upon trust to pay the said income to the said W.J.B. Cochrane (if then living) during his life and after the decease of the survivor of them . . . in trust for such of their issue as they should jointly or as the survivor of them should appoint, and in default of appointment equally at the age of 21, or in the case of daughters, earlier marriage.

The draftsman appears to have assumed that even if Mrs Cochrane ceased to reside with Mr Cochrane, Mr Cochrane would live long enough either for an appointment to be made, or for his children to take in default of appointment. In the event, however, this did not happen, the timing of events being as follows. First, Mrs Cochrane stopped living with Mr Cochrane. Her interest accordingly terminated. Then

Mr Cochrane died, before either any appointment in favour of the children had been made, or the default conditions had occurred. The issue before the court was what should happen to the income from the fund between Cochrane's death and the children reaching 21 or, in the case of daughters, their marriage if earlier.

It can be seen that the contingency that occurred had simply not been provided for, so that for a time there was no clear disposition of the equitable interest. Not only had it not been provided for, but the deed gave no guidance to the court as to what could have been intended. Harman J held that for the unprovided for period there was a resulting trust of the income to the settlor.

7.2.2 **Necessary condition ends**

7.2.2.1 *General position*

It may be that the trust pre-supposes the existence of a condition which comes to an end. In that case, again there will be a resulting trust of any surplus. For example, in *Hussey* v *Palmer* [1972] 1 WLR 1286 a payment of £607, for improvements to property to enable a widow to live with her daughter and son-in-law, was held on resulting trust for her when differences arose and she had to leave the house.

In this situation, however, there will be a resulting trust only if the surplus is undisposed of at the end of the precondition. Another possibility is that the donor made an unconditional gift, and did not intend to retain any interest in the surplus should the necessary conditions for the gift cease.

In *Re the Trusts of the Abbott Fund* [1900] 2 Ch 326, a fund was collected for the relief of two deaf and dumb ladies (who had been defrauded out of their rights under an earlier settlement). No provision was made for disposal of the fund on the death of the survivor. A surplus of some £367 remained when they died, and Stirling J held that this should be held on resulting trust for the contributors to the fund. It can be seen that the case is not unlike *Re Cochrane* [1955] Ch 309 (see chapter 8), in that the contingency of the death of the ladies had not been provided for.

In reaching his decision in *Re the Trusts of the Abbott Fund*, Stirling J held that the ladies themselves never became absolute owners of the fund. Nor did the trustees once the purposes were accomplished. No resulting trust occurs if either beneficiary or trustee is intended to take absolutely, however.

The fund in *Abbott* was subscribed to by various friends of the Abbotts. On the other hand, where the whole of a specific fund is left by a single individual for the maintenance of given individuals, the courts are more likely to construe the transaction as an absolute gift to those individuals, even where the fund is expressed to be left for a particular purpose (although it depends, of course, on the intention of the donor, which is ultimately a question of fact). An example is the Court of Appeal decision in *Re Osoba* [1979] 1 WLR 247, where a testator left the whole of a fund on trust for the education of his daughter up to university level. On completion of the daughter's university education she was held entitled to the surplus beneficially, the educational purpose being regarded merely as a statement of the testator's motive—in other words, there was no resulting trust in favour of the testator's estate.

The other possibility is a gift to the trustee. *Re the Trusts of the Abbott Fund* applies only where the property was intended to be held on trust, and so does not apply where the intention is to make an out-and-out gift subject to trusts (as opposed to a gift 'on trust', which is subject to the *Abbott* principle). In such cases the trustee is clearly intended to keep the surplus. An example is *Re Foord* [1922] 2 Ch 519, where the testator left in his will: 'all my effects including rubber and other shares I leave absolutely to my sister on trust to pay my wife £300 p.a., etc.'.

7.2.2.2 *Anonymous subscriptions to funds*

Where money has been given to a fund, say a disaster appeal fund, one might infer the donor's intention from, among other considerations, whether the donation was anonymous (e.g., small change in a street collecting box). If so, and no means of tracing the donor exists, then the contribution might be construed as an out-and-out gift. Clearly the donor cannot have intended that any surplus left over be held on resulting trust for him, when he has left the organisers no means of finding him in the event of there being a surplus. If there is a surplus left over after the fund has fulfilled his purposes, therefore, and the fund is not charitable, that part of the surplus attributable to his donation will have no owner. It therefore goes to the Crown as *bona vacantia*.

Note that the position is different where the purpose of the fund is charitable. In that event the Charities Act 1960, s. 14 applies (see 14.5), and a cy près scheme could be invoked. For present purposes, however, we are assuming that the purpose of the fund is not charitable.

In spite of the general principle suggested above, *Re the Trusts of the Abbott Fund* [1900] 2 Ch 326 was followed in *Re Gillingham Bus Disaster Fund* [1958] Ch 300 (upheld on a different issue [1958] 2 All ER 749), and such donations were directed to be held on resulting trust. The case concerned a fund collected to defray funeral and other expenses incurred as a result of a disaster involving the deaths of 24 Royal Marine cadets in Gillingham. The town clerk of Gillingham wrote a letter to *The Daily Telegraph* in the following terms:

Cadets' memorial. To the editor of '*The Daily Telegraph*'. Sir, The mayors of Gillingham, Rochester, and Chatham have decided to promote a Royal Marine Cadet Corps Memorial Fund to be devoted, among other things, to defraying the funeral expenses, caring for the boys who may be disabled, and then to such worthy cause or causes in memory of the boys who lost their lives, as the mayors may determine.

Harman J held that this was not a charitable purpose, and that the last purpose, 'to such worthy cause or causes in memory of the boys who lost their lives, as the mayors may determine', was void for uncertainty (see further chapter 5). The purposes were therefore taken to be defraying the funeral expenses of the boys who lost their lives, and caring for the boys who were disabled.

Far more money (about £9,000) was collected than was necessary for these purposes, especially as there were common law actions available against the bus company. The question therefore was who owned the surplus: was it the donors, represented by the Official Solicitor, or the Crown (represented by the Treasury Solicitor), as *bona vacantia*? Harman J, following *Re the Trusts of the Abbott Fund*, held that the surplus should be held on resulting trust for the donors.

The difficulty was that, although some of the money had been provided by identifiable people, most had been obtained from street collections. So many of the donors were anonymous and the trustees were therefore required to hold the fund on resulting trust for unknown people. Obviously, this is most inconvenient administratively. As we will see in chapter 13, had the gifts been charitable the cy près doctrine could have provided a way of avoiding this difficulty, but the gifts in *Gillingham* were not charitable. As explained above, if people give money in an anonymous collection, surely it can be assumed that they do not intend to see it back again (a view taken, in a slightly different context, by Jenkins LJ in *Re Ulverston and District New Hospital Building Trusts* [1956] Ch 622). In other words, an out-and-out gift seems a more sensible inference than a gift on trust. Had that inference been drawn by Harman J, the surplus would of course have gone to the Crown as *bona vacantia*. He was, however, reluctant to draw the inference that 'the small giver who is anonymous has any wider intention than the large giver who can be named', and in any case observed that the resulting trust 'doctrine does not rest, in my judg-ment, on any evidence of state of mind of the settlor' but arises automatically by process of law. The last part of this reasoning cannot survive *Westdeutsche*.

Moreover, doubt was also cast by Goff J, in *Re West Sussex Constabulary's Widows, Children and Benevolent (1930) Fund Trusts* [1971] 1 Ch 1, on Harman J's inferences about the donor's actual intention, since in the later case the out-and-out gift con-struction was adopted. The case concerned a fund for widows and dependants, to which the members contributed, but there were also outside contributions. Here we are concerned only with the outside contributions (the division of the surplus among the members themselves is considered in chapter 4, and at the beginning of this chapter).

The purpose of the fund was to provide allowances for the widows and depend-ants of deceased members. Some of its revenue was derived from contributions from its own members. Some was also raised from outside sources, by:

(a) entertainments, raffles and sweepstakes;

(b) collecting boxes;

(c) donations, including legacies.

The fund was wound up at the end of 1967, upon the amalgamation of the con-stabulary with other police forces, and the question arose as to how to divide it up.

Goff J held that the outside contributions raised from category (c) were held on resulting trust for the contributors. Those raised by categories (a) and (b) were clearly intended to take effect as out-and-out gifts to the fund, and therefore the resulting trust doctrine did not apply to them.

So far as identifiable donations and legacies were concerned (category (c)), Goff J thought these indistinguishable from *Re the Trusts of the Abbott Fund* (but see further 5.3), so the proportion of the surplus attributable to that source was held on result-ing trust. But there were also identifiable collections from raffles and sweepstakes (category (a)), which Goff J thought were out-and-out payments subject only to a (contractual) hope of receiving a prize. Third, however, there were the proceeds of street collecting boxes (category (b)), and here Goff J declined to follow Harman J's earlier judgment, again on the grounds that the intention to be inferred was also that of an out-and-out gift. Thus, nobody could lay claim to the proportion of the surplus attributable to the last two categories, so it went to the Crown as *bona vacantia*.

Clearly, the *West Sussex* case is easier to justify in conceptual terms than the earl-ier case, and of the two *West Sussex* is, we suggest, more likely to be followed in the future. Understandably, however, Harman J was concerned in the earlier case to ensure that the Crown was not the main beneficiary of a fund collected in highly publicised and tragic circumstances.

7.3 Category (A) resulting trusts: from voluntary conveyance

Broadly, this type of trust arises where there is a voluntary transfer of legal title to property (i.e., a transfer which is not one for value). Here, it is provided that *unless* there is a presumption of advancement, the presumption is that equitable title does *not follow* legal title to the transferee, but will instead remain with the transferor. Now there is a trust; legal title has been transferred to another, but because there has not been a transfer for value, equitable title has not passed to the new legal owner of property.

In other words, where there is a transfer of legal title to property, but the transfer has not been one for value, then although legal title has been transferred, equitable title remains with the transferor.

That is, unless there is a presumption of advancement. The presence of a presumption of advancement will alter the outcome significantly, as a presumption of advancement means that equitable title will follow legal title.

7.3.1 Authority for the operation of a resulting trust in voluntary conveyances

The presumption of a resulting trust in such situations goes back at least as far as the late eighteenth century, and its most often cited authoritative basis is the case *Dyer v Dyer* (1788) 2 Cox Eq Cas 92. In this case Eyre CB remarked that:

The trust of a legal estate, whether . . . taken in the names of the purchasers and others jointly, or in the names of others without that of the purchaser; whether in the name of one or several; whether jointly or successive results to the man who advances the purchase money. This is a general proposition supported by all the cases, and there is nothing to contradict it; and it goes on a strict analogy to the rule of common law, that where a feoffment is made without consideration, the use results to the feoffer [the transferor].

In terms of linguistic clarity, the feoffment translates into 'transfer' for our purposes and feoffer becomes the 'transferor'. The effect of the presumption of a resulting trust is that equitable title effectively never leaves the transferor.

7.3.1.1 *presumption of advancement*

The presumption of advancement has already been mentioned in Megarry J's *Vandervell* classification of resulting trusts and also in Lord Brown-Wilkinson's reclassification in *Westdeutsche*. It is alluded to in *Dyer* in Eyre CB's articulation of nothing which might contradict the operation of the resulting trust as a result of the rule of common law whereby if a transfer is made without consideration, it results (remains with/returns to) the transferor.

7.3.1.2 *Resulting trust and advancement: presumptions compared*

At its most simplistic, the presumption of advancement produces an operation which is the complete opposite to that of a resulting trust. The presumption of a resulting trust is that equitable title will not follow (a) legal (transfer of) title, and will remain with the transferor of the property. The presumption of advancement provides the reverse, and ensures that on the occurrence of a transfer, equitable title will not remain with the transferor, and will actually 'follow' legal title and become vested (like legal title) with the transferee.

7.3.1.3 *When does the presumption that equitable title follows legal title on a transfer arise?*

Once again, this concept is rooted in history and in the ideologies of a society very different from today's. Presumptions of advancement are historically coupled with moral obligation. The most obvious examples of moral obligations are the ones which exist in respect of a husband for his wife, and a father for his children.

The operation of a presumption of advancement means that where there is a voluntary transfer—one that is effectively a gift, as a result of no consideration being given, then equitable title *will* follow legal title to the transferee, but that it will do so in order to fulfil a moral obligation. Here the existence of such a moral obligation will transform the transfer effectively to an out-and-out gift.

Gifts, moral obligations and a context directed by the past

By looking at the nature and direction of the moral obligations which will give rise to a presumption of advancement, it becomes clear just how old this principle is. It is clear that the presumption that equitable title follows legal title in furtherance of a moral obligation will apply only as between husband and wife (and then only moving in the direction of husband to wife, and not from wife to husband!); and in a transfer from a father to his children (or any other person for whom he stands *in loco parentis*).

(a) Gifts, moral obligations and limits to the presumption of advancement The presumption of advancement does not apply between couples who are unmarried, and, as has been indicated, it will not even in the case of a married couple in the direction of wife to husband.

(b) Gifts, moral obligations and (traditional) male/female parenting roles Further limitation of the presumption of advancement can be seen within the very powerful obligations flow from parental responsibility in respect of children. The presumption's operation appears to differentiate between the expectations of fathers and mothers. Whilst there is absolutely no doubt that there is such a moral obligation so as to ensure the operation of a presumption of advancement between a father and his children, the exact position and scope of a presumption of a gift in furtherance of an obligation is less clear cut in relation to the mother of children. In *Bennett v Bennett* (1879) 10 Ch D 474, Sir George Jessel MR oriented his judgment around the proposition that the presumption of a gift arises from the moral obligation to give. The judgment reiterated the unquestionable moral obligation that falls upon a father in relation to his children, stating that all that needs to be established is that he is the father of the children concerned. Thereafter, the father's moral obligation is without question.

[T]he father [of a child] is under that obligation from the mere fact of his being the father, and therefore no evidence is necessary to shew the obligation to provide for his child. In the case of a father, you have only to prove that he is the father, and when you have done that the obligation at once arises.

However, in relation to the position of the mother he added that: 'In the case of a mother . . . it is easier to prove a gift than in the case of a stranger: in the case of a mother very little evidence beyond the relationship is wanted, there being very little additional motive required to induce the mother to make a gift to her child'. This is quite a complex passage, but basically Sir George Jessel made the point that a weaker form of the presumption of advancement need apply in the case of the mother of a child. The essence of this passage is that it is far easier to establish that a mother intended to make a gift to her children than it would be to establish that a stranger intended to make a gift.

Presumption of advancement founded on intention
The presumption that equitable title should follow legal title can therefore be rebutted. We can see how this intention can be rebutted in two cases; one very old and one more modern case, both of which illustrate the same point:

(a) In *Marshal* v *Crutwell* (1875) LR 20 Eq 325, a wife was allowed to draw cheques on a joint bank account for the convenience of her husband because he was ill. There was in these circumstances clearly no intention to make a gift to the wife.

(b) In *Re Figgis* [1969] 1 Ch 123, an otherwise very similar arrangement to *Marshal* concerning a joint bank account which was not merely for convenience.

It also appears that bank guarantees, e.g., where a husband guarantees his wife's overdraft, do not attract the operation of the presumption, with *Anson* v *Anson* [1953] 1 QB 636 standing as authority that instead the ordinary rules of contract apply.

Why do we need the presumption of advancement?
One might reasonably ask *why* there is a need for presumption of advancement especially in light of the view in *Dyer* that the normal rule of common law is one whereby 'where a feoffment [transfer] is made without consideration, the use results to the feoffer [the transferor]'. The need, of course, arises on account of the way in which people do not always make their intentions clear. Indeed, there would be no need whatsoever for such a rebuttable presumption if all intentions were made clear. However, life is not that simple, and if it were there would be a considerably reduced need for lawyers! Indeed, the position whereby intentions are not always clear is particularly pointed as far as evidential problems are concerned, and this arises most acutely where the donor has actually died. It is of course very difficult to second-guess intention in such circumstances, and the presence of a rebuttable presumption is meant to help to clarify such uncertainties surrounding intention.

Modernity, social and economic equality
Given that both the presumption of a resulting trust and the presumption of advancement have a long tradition in history, it might be wondered what application they might have in modern times. Indeed, this is especially so in the case of the

presumption of advancement which reflected a society in which there were huge social and especially economic differences between the positions of men and women. The presumption of advancement was constructed around the perceived needs and values of a society in which men were regarded as 'providers' for their families, and this of course included their wives who would not have had any economic independence of their own. The huge social and economic changes which took place, particularly following the Second World War in the second half of the twentieth century, have transformed earning power and capability, and within this the changed position of women is particularly striking. The role of the presumption of a resulting trust and the presumption of advancement in modern times will be considered in chapter 9 which looks at trusts of the family home as illustrations of the operation of resulting and constructive trusts.

7.4 **Constructive trusts**

7.4.1 **Introduction**

Constructive trusts are a very difficult area of law, and this can be seen to operate at all levels of their consideration. Indeed, they are not to be found easily defined anywhere, and many works in the area as well as the law itself point to the conclusion that they are not susceptible to easy definition and illumination. On a positive note, such uncertainties can be recast as constituting flexibility, and in this manner may even be seen to represent their strength. What is beyond dispute in academic writings and in case law alike is that the constructive trust is a very flexible and indeed adaptable instrument. There are many accounts of this adaptability and capability to meet a variety of situations—even ones which are ever changing in our society.

In search of definition and illumination
As indicated, constructive trusts cannot easily be defined. This is clear from the case *Carl Zeiss Stiftung* v *Herbert Smith (No. 2)* [1969] 2 Ch 276, where (at p. 300) in the words of Edmund Davies LJ 'English law provides no clear and all-embracing definition of a constructive trust. Its boundaries have been left perhaps deliberately vague, so as not to restrict the court by technicalities in deciding what the justice of a particular case may demand.' Rather, they have traditionally been found to exist in a series of disparate and changing situations. This passage from Edmund Davies LJ's judgment also ties into the notions of flexibility and adaptability which were considered at the outset, as does the later case *Sen* v *Hedley* [1991] Ch 425 where (at p. 40) Nourse LJ commented that the constructive trust had been a 'ready means of developing our property law in modern times'.

Issues of intention, and the courts' 'imposition' of a constructive trust
Remember that the constructive trust, although capable of arising in numerous and diverse circumstances, has as its fundamental basis an imposition by the courts which operates irrespective of the intention of the owner (of what becomes the 'trust property').

Consequences where a constructive trust arises

Immediately below, and by way of an introduction to a more extensive and detailed consideration of constructive trusts (along with resulting trusts) in subsequent chapters, examples will be given of situations in which constructive trusts arise. This does not actually by itself spell out the effect of the court determining that a constructive trust has arisen. For example, it will become clear that strong arguments have been advanced advocating the differences between the constructive trust and the doctrine of proprietary estoppel (as well as more recent ones highlighting their commonality).

7.4.2 Situations where constructive trusts have been found to exist

Again like the resulting trust, constructive trusts have come to be applied to numerous and diverse factual situations from which a number of illustrative examples can be drawn.

7.4.2.1 *Constructive trusts and analysis of constructive and resulting trusts*

Imposition of a constructive trust

(a) Cohabitation of the family home In the case study which appears later in chapter 9, it will become clear that the constructive trust has become central in the 'battleground' of difficulties created where strict principles of property law may leave a party, who is not the owner of the property at law, disadvantaged. It will become clear that constructive trusts have traditionally been imposed to come to the aid of a party who is not the legal owner of property, and where representations are made to them in respect of the property by its legal owner. In this respect, in the modern law relating to shared beneficial ownership, the constructive trust was at the heart of the landmark decision in *Lloyds Bank* v *Rosset* [1991] 1 AC 10. However, more recently, *Oxley* v *Hiscock* [2004] 3 All ER 703 is an important indicator of the growing significance of proprietary estoppel in relation to disputed ownership of family homes. Thus in this edition, chapter 9 gives considerable emphasis to the changing dynamics of dispute resolution and the 'interplay' between constructive trust and proprietary estoppel principles in light of this.

(b) Creation of 'mutual wills' The case study which follows on equitable fraud as a context for the imposition of a constructive trust by the courts will include the example provided by mutual wills. Mutual wills arise in situations whereby two people (usually couples) agree by the creation of mutual wills to effect the situation whereby on the death of the first of them, their property shall be enjoyed by the survivor, and thereafter (on the death of the second will-maker) to pass to beneficiaries which have been nominated. It shall become apparent that the constructive trust becomes an issue in response to questions of whether, and to what extent their original 'mutual' agreement does actually control and even dictate the distribution of their property.

(c) Secret trusts During the extensive consideration of constructive and resulting trusts which follows, 'case study' consideration is given to trusts which are made outside the formalities requirements of the Wills Act 1837, and the significance which constructive trusts may have in this context.

(d) Killing There are good reasons of policy which suggest that a perpetrator of a crime should be prevented from benefiting from it. At its most extreme, this would operate to ensure that a murderer is not able to benefit from his killing of a testator under whose will he will benefit. The most famous illustration of this principle is the case of Dr Crippen, whose conduct is considered in the discussion of fraud.

7.4.2.2 *Trusteeship and liability following breach of trust*

Unauthorised profit by a trustee or other fiduciary
The materials in chapter 15 will explain that any occupant of a fiduciary position (including, but not confined to, the trustee) must act unequivocally in the interests of the person in respect of whom the fiduciary position arises. This means that a fiduciary will not be able to keep for his own use property acquired directly or indirectly from his position. In this respect, chapter 15 will explore the use which is made of the constructive trust in making such a trustee liable 'to account' to the trust for any such 'unauthorised profits' (with further, albeit brief, reference also being made to this in chapter 18).

Liability of third party 'strangers' in breach of trust situations: the basic idea
The chapter on remedies, chapter 19, is essentially a consideration of the remedies which are available to a beneficiary where trust property has been applied by a trustee acting in breach of trust. In considering this, it will become clear that an area of particular difficulty is the liability which can be incurred by those other than the trustee himself. It does of course follow that the beneficiary should be able to pursue a remedy in respect of trust property against a trustee acting in breach of trust, but it is also the case that persons other than the trustee may come into possession of misapplied trust property, or may even have assisted the trustee's initial breach.

Where persons who have not been appointed trustees find themselves in receipt of trust property (usually on account of it being 'taken' from the trust in breach of trust), or otherwise 'interfere' with the proper administration of a trust, they may find themselves constituted 'constructive trustees'. Other forms of action available to beneficiaries in such circumstances will be considered later in chapter 19. The purpose of flagging up remedies following a breach of trust at present is to consider very basically the *facilitation* of liability for breach of trust through the machinery of the constructive trust.

Third parties and liability following a trustee's breach of trust
Traditionally, the liability of strangers to a trust has been divided into two categories of 'knowing receipt' (of trust property) and 'knowing assistance' (of a breach of trust). The reason for attaching third-party liability to **receipt of trust property** will be explained fully in chapter 19, but for present purposes, it pertains to the way in which the proprietary remedies available to a beneficiary in these circumstances depend on the continuing existence of identifiable or 'traceable' trust property. Tracing *is* sufficiently flexible that the property need not be *physically* identifiable as such, because it may well have been sold: in these circumstances, it may still be possible to trace the *proceeds* of sale, subject to the rules which apply to tracing trust money which has become 'mixed' with other funds. This is why the significance of recipient liability requires some basic understanding of alternatives to proprietary remedies: here claims which attach to the *receipt* of trust property help to ensure that there is a remedy even where property no longer exists in an identifiable form. For example,

trust money which has been spent with nothing identifiable to show for it will not be 'traceable'. In these circumstances, a recipient of trust property can become a constructive trustee of it, on account that he receives trust property with some degree of knowledge of the trust. It will become apparent that there is contention as to the degree of knowledge which is required, with current favour being for a recipient's state of knowledge to be such as to make it 'unconscionable for him to retain the benefit of the receipt' (*per* Nourse LJ in *Bank of Credit and Commerce International (Overseas) Ltd v Akindele* [2001] Ch 437). But fundamentally, receipt-based liability is complete *upon* receipt, and does not require property to remain in the recipient's hands in order for him to incur liability. Here, constructive trusteeship will arise upon receipt, and what happens to the property thereafter is immaterial.

In a similar vein, a stranger to a trust is also able to incur liability on the basis of his **assistance of a trustee's breach of trust**. This was traditionally known as 'knowing assistance' but the important Privy Council decision of *Royal Brunei Airlines v Tan* [1995] 3 WLR 64 set in motion a new approach in which it is now deemed more accurate and appropriate to characterise the latter category as 'accessory liability': acting as an accessory to a trustee's breach of trust.

In any event, liability as an accessory is distinguishable from recipient liability, because it is only in the latter situation that the stranger concerned actually receives trust property. Strictly speaking, therefore, it may be argued that in the case of knowing assistance or 'accessory liability' there is actually no trusteeship because no property is actually received in respect of which a (constructive) trust could attach. Notwithstanding this obvious difference, and on account of their otherwise similar nature in relation to liability, the two categories—of liability for the receipt of trust property, and that arising from assisting a breach of trust—have generally been treated together, and remain so.

Thus, as already indicated above, more detailed consideration of both forms of constructive trusteeship (along with leading cases including *Royal Brunei Airlines v Tan; BCCI v Akindale, Twinsectra v Yardley* [2002] 2 All ER 377, and most recently *Barlow Clowes International Ltd (in liquidation) v Eurotrust International Ltd* [2006] 1 All ER 333) will be made in chapter 19.

7.4.2.3 *Other situations which can give rise to a constructive trust*

Where there is a specifically enforceable contract
A contract is specifically enforceable where (common law contractual) damages would not be an adequate remedy. Although contracts for the sale of personal property are seldom specifically enforceable, because of their 'unique' nature, contracts for the sale of land are. How this translates into the creation of a constructive trust is illustrated in *Lysaght v Edwards* (1876) 2 Ch D 499. This case proposes that on account of equity's willingness to enforce such contracts specifically, on the conclusion of the sale the purchaser is considered the owner in equity, and accordingly, the vendor becomes a trustee of the land (property) for the purchaser. The concept of constructive trusteeship arising from specifically enforceable contracts was considered very briefly in chapter 5. Beyond this very broad proposition, theorisation of the way in which specific enforceability engaged a trust situation is not pursued further, save to point out that while there is an element of 'conscience' present there is arguably a lesser exhibition of improper conduct on the part of the purchaser than in other situations in which constructive trusts are seen to arise.

Where a trust is constituted under the 'rule in Re Rose'?

As we suggested earlier in chapter 3, the precise mechanism operating in *Re Rose, Rose* v *IRC* [1952] Ch 499 is unclear, but one explanation might lie in the imposition of a constructive trust by equity during the period *after* the transfer had occurred in equity, but *before* it could take place in common law. We expressed concern about this as a possibility because of the apparent inconsistency between the conferment of a gift, and the more usual manner in which a constructive trust is invoked in order to impose on the conscience of the legal owner of property on account of his conduct. If this is the case then the constructive trust in *Re Rose* must be regarded as anomalous with the other situations listed above in as much as the donor in *Rose* had clearly done nothing wrong, and was actively demonstrating generosity in both his intended outright gift and in the express trust which he did seek.

7.4.3 **Is the constructive trust too flexible and too adaptable?**

The earlier introduction to constructive trusts pointed to the difficulties entailed in defining them. We aligned this very closely to the flexibility of the constructive trust, and pointed to case law which suggested that it was an extremely useful and adaptable instrument. Although there is much intellectual respect for such views within judicial and academic circles alike, it is not a universal view and certainly not one which is beyond question. Indeed, there is a strong view that during the 1970s and 1980s the constructive trust became too flexible, and Lord Denning's 'new model' constructive trust became (in his Lordship's own words, in his judgment in *Hussey* v *Palmer* [1972] 1 WLR 1338) employed 'wherever justice and good conscience require it'. This use of the constructive trust might be regarded as an approach based on outcomes and result rather than principle or sound theory, as indicated by the statement of Sir Peter Millett (in (1995) *Trust Law International*, 35) that ' . . . the language of constructive trust has become such a fertile source of confusion that it would be better if it were abandoned'. While not all reaction has been so extreme, much academic and judicial commentary has advocated greater employment of the great adversary of flexibility—the need for certainty.

7.4.4 **A place in English law for the remedial constructive trust?**

The constructive trust in English case law can be seen as a substantive institution which operates to vindicate an existing property right. But this is not the case in many other jurisdictions (including Commonwealth jurisdictions such as Australia, New Zealand and Canada) which accept also alongside the *substantive* institutional constructive trust, the existence of a different *remedial* type constructive trust which at its most radical may operate to create a new proprietary interest for the claimant, rather than simply to formalise and provide validity for an interest which already exists and which the courts will give recognition to. While the existence of the remedial constructive trust in English law has been left open, it is clearly a principle which is regarded with suspicion in the highest judicial circles. Indeed, the commentary of Lord Millett (1995, above) suggests that it is a device for which there is no room in English law and one which is actually capable of causing much mischief:

In my view it is a counsel of despair which too readily concedes the impossibility of propounding a general rationale for the availability of proprietary remedies. We need to be more ready to categorise wrongdoers as fiduciaries and to extend the situations in which proprietary remedies are made available, but we can still do all this while adhering to established principles.

7.4.5 **Trusts, conscience and 'overlapping' of resulting and constructive trusts**

There is at present much confusion in the law between resulting trusts and constructive trusts. Consequently, the theoretical differences between them are not clear cut and it can be difficult, on particular fact situations, to determine which type of implied trust will arise. This will become particularly plain in the later analysis of trusts arising from cohabitation and family arrangements. But for present purposes the way in which confusion is easily reached in an analysis of constructive and resulting trusts is illustrated by reference to an extract from Lord Denning's judgment in *Hussey* v *Palmer* [1972]:

Although the plaintiff alleged that there was a resulting trust, I should have thought that the trust in this case, if there was one, was more in the nature of a constructive trust; but this is a matter of words than anything else. The two run together.

The ways in which this 'blurring' of distinctions can be seen to operate, as well as an assessment of the view that it is a distinction only in rhetoric shall be carried over into the area in which it can be illustrated most graphically—trusts relating to the family home, considered in chapter 9.

 online resource centre

FURTHER READING

This can be found under substantive consideration of resulting and constructive trusteeship in chapters 8, 9, 10 and 11.

8

Resulting trusts, gifts to non-charitable unincorporated associations and pension funds

A number of the chapters in this book which follow previous chapters' introductions to constructive and resulting trusts, are case studies which require us to look at constructive and resulting trusts closely alongside each other. All the 'case studies' focus on the features and characteristics of constructive or resulting trusts which were introduced in the previous chapter. The case studies also try to communicate how these instruments work in operation, and consider critically whether, and in what ways their operation 'in reality' reflects textbook assessments which are made of them. In the same vein, this chapter on unincorporated associations and pension funds follows one introducing constructive and resulting trusts and as such is a case study on the features and operation of trusts which are 'resulting'. By way of reminder, although resulting trusts arise in a number of different contexts, what is common to all is that although legal title is vested in a trustee, the settlor and the beneficiary are actually the same person. This position will arise on account of two broad situations. It will follow a failed attempt to create a trust in favour of a third party beneficiary (because equitable interest which is created upon the transfer of legal title to the trustee never actually leaves him); or where property is divested from the settlor, but for some reason equitable interest in it returns to him (e.g., on the occurrence of an event which has not been provided for because it was unforeseen or the trust instrument was poorly drafted).

8.1 The question of ownership

Moving into a more substantive consideration of resulting and constructive trusts, and following on from our earlier discussion of the beneficiary principle and purpose trusts, this chapter considers difficulties which arise where property is conveyed to an unincorporated association—for example, this to a society, a social club or religious group. Such associations will exist to use property for a particular purpose. Un*incorporated* associations cannot own property themselves because they lack the legal personality to do so. In*corporated* bodies, such as companies, do have requisite legal personality, and can thus own property in their own right. The difficulties (and possible solutions) we shall consider in this chapter will only arise in situations where the unincorporated body itself is non-charitable. Indeed, as you will see when we consider the position of charities later, there is no difficulty whereby a gift is made to an unincorporated body with charitable purposes, because in these circumstances, the association's officers can hold the property as charitable trustees.

Non-lawyers might well be astonished at the legal difficulties to which a transaction as simple as giving property to a club or other unincorporated association gives rise. The problem is that analyses based on trusts do not work very well, whereas a contractual analysis, which can usually be made to work, seems very unfair. In this scenario, the donor of the property has to give up all interest in the gift he is making. In a contractual analysis, the donor cannot make his gift conditional, nor prevent the club members using the property for any purpose they please, whether or not it is for the original purposes of the club.

Advantages of a Re Denley-style purpose trust
At first sight, it might be thought that a *Denley*-style purpose trust (considered in chapter 4) might be a good method of allowing property to be conveyed to a non-charitable unincorporated association; the property would be held in trust for the members of the association, for the purposes of the association, and it would be necessary only that the identity of those members was sufficiently certain. This would certainly have advantages for donors, since the property could be constrained to be used for the association's purposes, and members would not be able (for example) to dispose of it for their own benefit. If the purposes of the association were fulfilled (e.g., vivisection abolished where the association in question was the National Anti-Vivisection Association), or became impossible (e.g., where a gun club was prohibited by legislation from carrying out its previously lawful activities), the donor would obtain any property not already used on resulting trust. Unfortunately, however, a gift to members for the time being (i.e., present and future, assuming a fluctuating membership) will usually infringe the perpetuity rules (another difficulty in *Leahy* seen in chapter 4), so the trust solution is not generally appropriate. It should be noted that in *Denley* itself the grant was only effective until 21 years from the death of the last survivor of a number of specified persons (with a gift over to a hospital), so no perpetuity difficulty arose. There are also, of course, no perpetuity difficulties where the association is charitable.

The perpetuity problem
The nature of the perpetuity problem depends on which analysis of *Denley* is correct. If gifts for non-charitable purposes are valid, as long only as persons exist with *locus standi* to enforce the trust, even where they do not have a full beneficial interest, then the applicable rule is the rule against inalienability (see 6.6). In that case the common law rules must be satisfied, and the Perpetuities and Accumulations Act 1964 will (almost certainly) not apply. If *Denley* is just an ordinary trust for beneficiaries then the rule against remoteness applies. The problem arises where there is a fluctuating membership, because of the need to vest beneficial interests in new members as the membership varies; and if this could occur outside the perpetuity period (on which, see chapter 6 generally), then at common law any disposition on this basis will be void, as will any condition re-vesting property in the donor (e.g., achievement of the club's purposes, or their subsequent impossibility). This is subject to three qualifications. First, it is possible for an association, by appropriate drafting of its rules, to avoid the perpetuity problem (see, e.g., Warburton [1985] Conv 318, at 321); but most existing associations have not done this. Second, the donor can constrain a gift so that it satisfies the perpetuity rules; but most donors do not do this (Gardner [1992] Conv 41, especially at pp. 49*ff*, suggests that donors can choose the manner of their gift, but does not dwell on the perpetuity difficulties).

Third, on this analysis the 1964 Act may save the disposition, but 'wait and see' would surely be very difficult to operate in practice, and most of the cases, even now, involve at least some donations made prior to 16 July 1964.

Another limitation on a *Denley* analysis is that the recipients must benefit, directly or indirectly, sufficiently to give them *locus standi*. Warburton observes that there may be difficulties in this regard with altruistic societies, such as an anti-vivisection society, where there is no tangible benefit for the members.

Avoiding perpetuity difficulties

Perpetuity difficulties can be avoided by construing the gift to present members only. The problem is that, if it is construed simply as a gift to them as joint tenants, then retiring members (or indeed any member) are perfectly at liberty to sever and sell their shares. New members could only obtain any benefit from association property by acquiring shares (or part shares) from existing members. No doubt it would be theoretically possible to run an unincorporated association on that basis, but it would be very inconvenient.

Before the contractual solution considered below had become widely adopted, courts strove, in a line of authorities beginning with *Cocks* v *Manners* (1871) LR 12 Eq 574, to construe a gift as being to the members of the society, and it was often observed that, if all the members of the association could join together to dispose of its property, the rule against inalienability (see 6.6) was not infringed. This is no doubt correct, as long as 'members of the association' means members at the time of the gift. The analysis implied, of course, that conditions could not be attached to the gift. The main problem with the analysis, apart from its artificiality, was that it provided no mechanism for moving beneficial interests as the members of the association changed.

Importance of the contractual analysis

For this reason gifts to non-charitable unincorporated associations are usually construed as being to existing members only, but subject to their contractual duties as members of the society or club. These will be determined by the rules of the association, but usually a member will be prevented from severing his share, and it will accrue to other members on death or resignation. Thus, although present and future members of a fluctuating body will benefit *de facto*, because the gift is construed as one to existing members alone, there is no perpetuity problem.

This was Cross J's analysis in *Neville Estates* v *Madden* [1962] Ch 832, where (at pp. 849–50) he analysed in detail the methods by which property can be conveyed to a non-charitable unincorporated association:

The question of the construction and effect of gifts to or in trust for unincorporated associations was recently considered by the Privy Council in *Leahy* v *Attorney-General for New South Wales* [1959] AC 457. The position, as I understand it, is as follows. Such a gift may take effect in one or other of three quite different ways. In the first place, it may, on its true construction, be a gift to the members of the association at the relevant date as joint tenants, so that any member can sever his share and claim it whether or not he continues to be a member of the association. Secondly, it may be a gift to the existing members not as joint tenants, but subject to their respective contractual rights and liabilities towards one another as members of the association. In such a case a member cannot sever his share. It will accrue to the other members on his death or resignation, even though such members include persons who became members after the gift took effect. If this is the effect of the gift, it will not be open to objection on the score of perpetuity or uncertainty unless there is something in its terms or circumstances or in the rules of the association which precludes the members at any given time from dividing the subject of the gift between them on the footing that they are solely entitled to it in equity.

Thirdly, the terms or circumstances of the gift or the rules of the association may show that the property in question is not to be at the disposal of the members for the time being, but is to be held in trust for or applied for the purposes of the association as a quasi-corporate entity. In this case the gift will fail unless the association is a charitable body.

Trusts for purpose valid only if charitable

This passage is interesting in a number of respects. Cross J (whose views are technically *obiter*, because the property was in the event held on charitable trusts: see chapter 13) first sets out the difficulties of construing a gift to an unincorporated association as a gift to the members of the association at the relevant date as joint tenants. Second, he sets out the usual solution to the problem, that of a gift to the existing members not as joint tenants, but subject to their respective contractual rights and liabilities towards one another as members of the association. In that case, he points out that a member cannot sever his share. Third, he reiterates the orthodox position that a trust for purposes is valid only if charitable.

It is also essential to the analysis that the members at any one time own the entirety of the fund: that they can, if they wish, dissolve the association and divide the property among themselves. Donors can place no conditions on their donation, for fear of infringing the perpetuity rules (and remember that *Neville Estates* was decided prior to the Perpetuities and Accumulations Act 1964). In *Re Lipinski's Will Trusts* [1976] 1 Ch 235, Oliver J gave effect to a gift to the Hull Judeans (Maccabi) Association to be used solely for construction and improvements of the association's buildings, despite having rejected charity arguments, but only by striking out the condition relating to buildings and holding that the present members of the association were absolutely entitled and could use the property in any way they liked. He could thus bring the case within the second *Neville Estates* category.

The limits of the contractual analysis became apparent from Brightman J's judgment in *Re Recher's WT* [1972] Ch 526. The testatrix left some of her residuary estate to a non-charitable unincorporated association which, on the construction of her will, was identified as the London and Provincial Anti-Vivisection Society. By the date of the will, however, that society had ceased to exist, but had amalgamated with the National Anti-Vivisection Society. The question was whether the gift could take effect in favour of the National Anti-Vivisection Society.

Brightman J held that the gift could not be construed as a trust for the purposes of the London and Provincial Anti-Vivisection Society. It would have been possible to construe the gift, on the basis of Cross J's views in *Neville Estates*, as a gift to the members of the London and Provincial Anti-Vivisection Society, subject to the contract towards each other to which they had bound themselves as members, had the Society been in existence at the date of the testatrix's will. By then it had been dissolved, however, and the contract between the members terminated. The gift could not be construed as a gift to the members of a different association (i.e., the National Anti-Vivisection Society) and, accordingly, failed.

Re Grant: division between local and national control

A slightly different difficulty arose in *Re Grant's WT* [1980] 1 WLR 360, where a grant to the Chertsey and Walton Constituency Labour Party failed. The difficulty in *Re Grant* was that the members of the Chertsey and Walton Constituency Labour Party (CLP) did not have control over their own property, because they were also bound by the rules of the Labour Party nationally. Thus, a gift to the CLP could not be construed as a gift to the members of the CLP beneficially, since they could not direct that the bequest be divided among themselves as beneficial owners. The gift could take effect, if at all, only as a private purpose trust, in which case it infringed the rule against perpetuities.

This merits further examination, since the relationship between national and local Labour Parties was unusual, in that the local association appeared to have virtually no control over its own funds. Indeed, the national Party could itself take direct control of the local Party's funds, and it is not at all surprising, therefore, that Vinelott J held that the funds were owned by the national, rather than the local Party. However it does not follow that gifts can never be made to local branches of federated societies. In *News Group Newspapers Ltd* v *SOGAT 1982* [1986] ICR 716, the local branch of SOGAT could unilaterally secede from the national union (Society of Graphical and Allied Trades) and was therefore held still to control its own property. Presumably, therefore, it would have been possible to make a donation to the local branch. Many federated societies adopt an intermediate position where, although the local branches cannot unilaterally secede, the national society has no direct control over the local funds, the local society instead paying an annual membership subscription and agreeing to be bound, to a greater or lesser extent, by national rules. It is uncertain whether the reasoning in *Re Grant's WT* applies in this situation.

Limitations of the contractual analysis
It is clear, then, that there are serious limitations on the contractual analysis. Trust analyses were even more fraught with difficulties, as we have seen, mostly because of the common law rule against perpetuities. Since the 1964 Act, dispositions that would have failed for perpetuity may be saved by 'wait and see' (see chapter 6). The gift in *Recher* pre-dated the Act, but that in *Grant* did not; even so, it might have been difficult to identify beneficiaries had the testator clearly settled the property in trust in *Grant*, especially as the purpose was altruistic, and the case suggests that the courts will not struggle to find a trusts analysis, even where a contractual one does not work, unless the settlor makes the trust explicit.

8.2 Winding up unincorporated associations

The correct analysis of a gift to an unincorporated association, such as a club or society, also controls the distribution of its assets when it is wound up, since that question depends on who are the owners of the fund.

8.2.1 When is a fund wound up?

It is necessary first to consider when a fund may be wound up. According to Brightman J in *Re William Denby & Sons Ltd Sick & Benevolent Fund* [1971] 1 WLR

973, winding up of a fund is not at the discretion of the treasurer or trustees of the fund, but may occur only when:

(a) the rules allow for dissolution, or

(b) all interested parties agree, or

(c) a court orders dissolution, or

(d) the substratum upon which the fund is founded is gone (e.g., *Re St Andrew's Allotment Association* [1969] 1 WLR 229, where an allotment association was wound up when the land for allotments was sold to developers for £70,000).

Many of the cases arise when the club or association has simply been inactive for a number of years, but no positive moves have been made to wind it up. The courts are reluctant in these circumstances to infer that the substratum has gone. In *William Denby* itself the substratum had not disappeared, although after an industrial dispute many of the company's employees left, and for some time (about four and a half years) nobody had contributed to the fund. But before the dispute the fund was viable, and indeed increasing, and mere inactivity by the members did not necessarily lead to the conclusion that they had acquiesced in the dissolution of the fund, since a less drastic interpretation was possible, namely that they had acquiesced in the temporary suspension of contributions and grants.

A similar dispute arose in *Re GKN Bolts and Nuts Ltd Sports and Social Club* [1982] 2 All ER 855, noted at [1983] Conv 315, where Megarry V-C allowed what he called 'spontaneous dissolution', that is to say, the winding up of a club without any resolution or court order to that effect. He observed, however, that mere inactivity is not enough, unless it is so prolonged that dissolution is the only reasonable inference. A cataleptic trance, he said, may look like death without being death, and suspended animation may be continued life, not death. Here, however, spontaneous dissolution had occurred, but it required a positive act, in this case a resolution to sell the club's only remaining asset, the sports ground.

8.2.2 Basis on which funds are held

The types of fund with which this section is concerned are Members' clubs or friendly societies, which are unincorporated associations. As we saw in 5.2, the property of unincorporated associations is not normally held in trust for the members. Instead, the relationship between the members is contractual. Members' contributions or subscriptions are regarded as out-and-out gifts, each member retaining contractual rights (based on the rules) to use the property of the club or society. On resignation from the club or society, although the gift of the subscriptions remains (otherwise a retiring member could claim back a share of these), the retiring member gives up any contractual claim on the property of the association.

It ought to follow, therefore, that when such an association is wound up, only existing members have a right to claim any part of the fund. The basis of their claim is a contractual right to share in the property, and the method by which the division is calculated is considered in the next subsection.

It is nevertheless possible in theory for funds to be held by trustees on trust for the members, even though this is rare in practice. The main difficulty is the rule against perpetuities (see chapter 6), at any rate if membership is likely to fluctuate, since dispositions in favour of future members might fall outside the perpetuity period. This difficulty will not necessarily apply where the fund is intended only for the benefit of existing members or is of short-term duration (e.g., limited to 21 years from the death of the last survivor of a number of specified persons, like the trust in *Re Denley's Trust Deed* [1969] 1 Ch 373, considered in chapter 4). Otherwise, the normal requirements for constitution of an express trust will apply.

Surplus contributions and the operations of a resulting trust
If such a fund is dissolved, the *surplus of the contributions themselves* will be held on resulting trust. All contributors, including those who have ceased to contribute, will be entitled to a share, and division will be in proportion to the *total amount* they have contributed. Thus, assuming everyone pays subscriptions at the same rate, a person who has contributed for ten years is entitled to twice as much of the share of the proceeds as someone who has contributed for only five.

   This was the basis of division in *Re Hobourn Aero Components Air Raid Distress Fund* [1946] Ch 86, affirmed at [1946] Ch 194. From 1940 to 1944, employees of a company in Coventry made weekly contributions to a fund to assist employees who had suffered damage as a result of air raids. Only contributors to the fund could benefit. The fund was closed in 1944, and the question arose as to what to do with surplus moneys. The Crown did not claim the fund as *bona vacantia*. The contributors wanted the surplus back. The Charity Commissioners wanted to adopt a cy près scheme, which they could do only if the fund was charitable (see chapter 14).

   At first instance, Cohen J held that the purposes of the organisation were not charitable, since there was an insufficient element of public benefit. It followed that a cy près scheme could not be directed. That being so, the contributors were entitled to distribute the fund among themselves, in proportion to the total amount each had contributed, on resulting trust principles:

[The] basis on which the contributions are returned is that each donor retained an interest in the amount of his contributions except so far as they are applied for the purposes for which they were subscribed.

In other words, a proportion of the *total* contribution of each individual contributor is held on resulting trust, the assumption being that he retains an interest in his contribution. On a contractual analysis, however, anyone ceasing to contribute to the scheme loses any benefits they had under the scheme, and also loses any property interest in the fund. All those who are still contributors at the date of closure of the fund are usually entitled to an *equal* share in the surplus, not a share which is based on their past contributions (see further below).

   The Crown in *Hobourn Aero* appealed on the issue of the charitable status of the fund alone, and the Court of Appeal upheld Cohen J's decision. On this aspect of the case, see further chapter 13. However, nothing was said in the Court of Appeal about the distribution of the funds.

   One of the problems with Cohen J's analysis is that the rule against perpetuities appears to be infringed, unless either the fund is expressly limited in duration, or there are no fluctuations in membership. Arguably the fund in *Hobourn Aero* did not infringe the rule, although there were fluctuations in the identity of the individual contributors, because of its essentially temporary nature. Presumably, however, nobody knew how long the fund would continue at its inception, and no express limit appears to have been put on its duration.

Re West Sussex and the analysis in Re Bucks
In *Re West Sussex Constabulary's Widows, Children & Benevolent (1930) Fund Trusts* [1971] Ch 1, Goff J thought that it was not part of the *ratio* of the case, but we would

suggest that it was. He also pointed out that there were no contractual benefits in *Hobourn*, so that the usual contractual analysis may well not be applicable, but that does not in any way answer the perpetuity difficulties inherent in Cohen J's analysis.

We would respectfully suggest that Cohen J's analysis set out above is wrong. At any rate, the case cannot be regarded as laying down any principle applicable to the majority of fund cases, since their duration is not limited, and fluctuating membership is assumed.

Walton J's analysis in *Re Bucks Constabulary Widows' & Orphans' Fund Friendly Society (No. 2)* [1979] 1 WLR 936 will usually be more appropriate. The case involved a fund which was made up of voluntary contributions from its members, for the relief of widows and orphans of deceased members of the Bucks Constabulary. In April 1968 the Bucks Constabulary was amalgamated with other constabularies to form the Thames Valley Constabulary, and in October 1968 the society was wound up. The trustee applied to court to determine how the funds were to be distributed. Walton J thought that the Members' rights to share in the fund were governed by their contractual rights and duties *inter se* and that, in the absence of evidence to the contrary, members who resigned lost all claim on the fund. Therefore, division should be made among only those who were still members at the time of the dissolution of the fund and, in the absence of evidence to the contrary, they were entitled to an equal share in the fund. Accordingly, he held that the surplus should be held by the trustees for the members at the time of dissolution in equal shares.

Contractual v resulting trust analyses: final resolution?
It cannot be assumed, however, that the courts have finally resolved the issue in favour of a contractual basis for the holding of funds. In *Re West Sussex Constabulary's Widows, Children and Benevolent (1930) Fund Trusts* [1971] Ch 1, Goff J held that the proportion of the surplus attributable to identifiable donations and legacies was held on resulting trust. He thought these indistinguishable from *Re the Trusts of the Abbott Fund*. Presumably, then, before the dissolution of the constabulary, the donations and legacies had been given to the association on trust. The problem is that this is not at all like *Re the Trusts of the Abbott Fund* (considered in chapter 4) which concerned a trust for two identifiable ladies, living at the time the trust was set up. There could not possibly be any perpetuity problems with such a trust. Nor could there be, we would suggest, in *Re Gillingham Bus Disaster Fund* [1958] Ch 3000, where the purposes (or at any rate, the valid purposes), were taken to be defraying the funeral expenses of the identifiable boys who had just died, and caring for those living who in light of the disaster were left disabled. But if there was a trust of donations in *Re West Sussex Constabulary's Widows, Children and Benevolent (1930) Fund Trusts*, the beneficiaries would have been a fluctuating body of present and future members, and exactly the same perpetuity problems would arise as in the *Hobourn Aero Case* (above).

Introduction to pension funds: Davis v Richards and Wallington Industries Ltd
Similar reasoning was adopted by Scott J in *Davis v Richards and Wallington Industries Ltd* [1991] 2 All ER 563, which concerned the winding up of a pension fund. The *ratio* of the case was that distribution of the assets was by a definitive deed which was executed by the trustees, but Scott J went on in his judgment to consider the position if he were wrong. Employers, employees and money transferred from other funds were the three main sources of contributions to the fund. Scott thought

that the employers' contributions should be held on resulting trust for them, on account of their similarity with the *West Sussex* legacies. There was no reason to rebut the conclusion that there was a resulting trust. But the problem is exactly the same as above. What was the trust upon which the funds were held prior to the winding up of the fund? It must have been a trust for a fluctuating body of individuals. Surely similar perpetuity problems arise as before? (Although perhaps in this case the trust could have been saved by the Perpetuities and Accumulations Act 1964 (considered in chapter 6) in a manner which is illustrated below.)

Re Bucks Constabulary Widows' and Orphans' Fund Friendly Society (No. 2) was not mentioned by Scott J, although according to the report the case was cited, and there was some consideration given to a contractual analysis (at pp. 589–90). No obvious reason was given for the rejection of this latter analysis. We would suggest however that in such a situation (which is distinct from the more general position of pension funds) that a trust analysis simply cannot work. It is greatly hoped therefore that the courts will adopt the analysis of Walton J in *Re Bucks Constabulary Widows' and Orphans' Fund Friendly Society (No. 2)*.

8.3 Conclusion: the general position of unincorporated associations and support for the contractual basis for the calculation of shares

Notwithstanding the alternative approaches considered in relation to the general position of unincorporated associations, it is suggested that a contractual basis for the division of funds is the only tenable mechanism. This is of course the solution provided for by the *Re Bucks Constabulary* case. In this situation, if the rules provide for the contingency of dissolution of the fund, division will be according to the rules, as they will form the basis of the contract.

Often the rules do not so provide, however, and in this event the courts are left to imply terms. In accordance with normal contractual doctrine, this will be on the basis of inferred intention and, since this is largely a question of fact, no rigid rules of law can be stated. Nevertheless, certain presumptions appear to apply:

(1) Only existing members can claim, because it is assumed that past members gave up all claims on the fund on resignation (*Re Bucks Constabulary Widows' & Orphans' Fund Friendly Society (No. 2)* [1979] 1 WLR 936). Sometimes the rules expressly so provide, as in *Re West Sussex Constabulary's Widows, Children & Benevolent (1930) Fund Trusts* [1971] Ch 1.

(2) Generally speaking, in the case of Members' clubs, division is equally among existing members. In mutual benefit or friendly society cases, the *prima facie* rule also appears to be equal division (*Bucks Constabulary*), although there have also been cases where division has been proportional to total contributions— this seems appropriate where the benefit contracted for while the fund subsists is also proportional to total contributions. In *Re Sick & Funeral Society of St John's Sunday School, Golcar* [1973] Ch 51, there were two distinct classes of membership, one class of which (adults) paid and received twice the benefit of the other (children). Division was such that adults received twice as much

as children. It must be emphasised, however, that inferred intention is a question largely of fact, and that it would be a mistake to deduce rigid principles of law from these cases.

(3) If the assumption can be made that a contributor has made an out-and-out gift of his contributions, retaining no rights in the fund at all, then the property will go to the Crown as *bona vacantia*, because nobody has a claim on it. This conclusion has sometimes been drawn where only third parties could benefit from the fund (e.g., in *Cunnack* v *Edwards* [1896] 2 Ch 679, where only the widows of contributors were entitled to benefit). The same result was reached in the *West Sussex* case: Goff J thought that the contributors had parted with their property out-and-out, and had retained no interest in the fund since it was held for the benefit of third parties (the widows and dependants of the deceased members), but on this point the case was criticised in the *Bucks Constabulary* case. In the later case, Walton J observed that merely because the members have contracted between themselves to provide benefits for third parties does not mean (in the absence of a valid trust in favour of the third parties) that they have relinquished their property in the fund. They can still, after all, collectively agree to distribute the fund among themselves, or to vary the benefits under the scheme. The position is essentially analogous to *Beswick* v *Beswick* [1968] AC 58, where although two parties had contracted to provide a benefit for a third party, they could at any time agree to vary the benefit to be provided for the third party, and the third party had no enforceable claim against either of them. If they had set up enforceable trusts in favour of the third parties, of course, the position would be different, but in that case the third parties would have the beneficial interest in the surplus. In neither case should the property go to the Crown as *bona vacantia*.

8.4 Perpetuities since 1964: general principles

This final section brings together a number of the central issues raised in this chapter, and also positions them alongside the brief study made of perpetuities made earlier. From this earlier study it will have been clear and apparent that the law relating to perpetuities is very, very complicated, and can give rise to some truly bizarre considerations and results. While this was explained as a broad idea in the earlier work, the precise extent of such difficulties and bizarreness is actually very difficult to capture, especially given chapter 6's brevity. Nevertheless, the law is due to change—precisely on account of these considerations, which is why chapter 6 has been very much reduced in extent. This section is designed to bring together the different ways of analysing unincorporated associations, oriented very strongly towards the articulation of a contractual analysis as that which should be preferred. And this brief consideration of perpetuities does explain some of the difficulties of applying a trusts analysis to such bodies. It also provides a working example of just how complicated the perpetuities rules are!

Earlier it was suggested that there are perpetuity difficulties with the trusts cases, such as *Hobourn Aero* and *West Sussex*, because with a fluctuating membership it is necessary to provide for transfers of beneficial interests into the indefinite future, unless a maximum duration is placed on the fund. Where a donation is made to a non-charitable unincorporated association, therefore, and it is not expressed to be by way of trust, in principle the courts ought to adopt the contract analysis in order to validate the gift.

Unfortunately, the contract analysis in *Neville Estates* (considered elsewhere) depends on the members of the society at any time having the entire beneficial interest in the funds, so that they can, if they so wish, dissolve the society and use the assets as they wish. Furthermore, because since 1964 reverters after a condition subsequent are subjected to the rule against perpetuities, by s. 12 of the Perpetuities and Accumulations Act 1964, donors cannot impose any conditions on their donation to prevent dissolution, for example by making a gift for the purposes of the association unless those purposes are charitable. In *Re Hopkins* [1965] Ch 669, a gift was made to the Bacon–Shakespeare Society, not out-and-out but for the purposes of finding the Bacon–Shakespeare manuscripts. In order to validate the gift, Wilberforce J had to hold finding the Bacon–Shakespeare manuscripts to be charitable for the advancement of education (considered below). Otherwise, either the donation will not take effect at all, or the courts will (if they can) validate the gift by striking out the condition; in *Re Lipinski's WT* [1976] 1 Ch 235, Oliver J was able to give effect to a gift to the Hull Judeans (Maccabi) Association to be used solely for the construction and improvements of the association's buildings, but only by striking out the condition relating to buildings, and holding that the present members of the association were absolutely entitled and could use the property in any way they liked.

It is sometimes argued (e.g., *Gardner* [1992] Conv 41) that if donors wish to make gifts on trust, or conditional gifts to unincorporated associations, they should be free to do so, but, at any rate prior to 1964, the law did not allow this (note that both *Hobourn Aero* and *West Sussex* involved pre-1964 dispositions which, if made on trust, ought to have been void). The Perpetuities and Accumulations Act 1964, as explained in the earlier chapter, relaxed the position in two respects, namely by providing for the possibility of stipulating an 80-year perpetuity period and for the 'wait and see' principle. The application of 'wait and see' could lead to considerable difficulties at the end of the period, however, if it became clear that the rule against perpetuities would indeed be infringed. And, although it may be useful to validate temporarily gifts expressed to be made on trust, it is not a satisfactory solution where the gift is silent as to how it is to take effect. Since the contractual analysis clearly works, it should be used in preference to a trust analysis, except where the donor has made it quite clear that a trust is intended.

8.5 Resulting trusts and pension funds

Pension funds and a workable resulting trust analysis
The rise of the pension fund in recent times has ensured that issues of operation and regulation have come sharply into focus on a number of social, economic and legal

fronts. The discourses which have taken place in furtherance of creating a workable legal framework for the operation and safe-guarding of pension assets demonstrate clear favour for the trust as the most appropriate mechanism for ensuring this. The favourable view of the trust was confirmed in the Report of Sir Roy Goode's Pension Law Review Committee (1993, Cmnd 2342). The Committee's recommendations resulted in the passage of the Pensions Act 1995. The 1995 Act sought to reflect the importance of rigorous regulation and supervision of pension schemes, and one of its principal tenets was its accommodation of the reality that the beneficiaries under a pension scheme differed from the normal trust position of volunteers; indeed, the entitlement of beneficiaries under a pension scheme could be seen to arise from contractual origins (provided by their contracts of employment). This aside, the trust was the device which was strongly favoured in the promotion of the expedient and safe use of such schemes. Here, even perpetuities difficulties which are usually fatal in other examples of unincorporated associations do not arise thanks to specific consideration made in pensions legislation.

Pensions, trusts and the future: a clawback to fundamental principles
As a result of this topical interest in pension funds and the primacy of place given to the trust, it is perhaps not surprising that academic commentators are enthusing in the way which is evident in Charles Harpum's [2000] Conv 170 article. Harpum suggests that these are most interesting and even exciting times for trusts lawyers and pensions lawyers alike.

One source of this excitement can be attributed to a theme which runs through-out this text—hailing the trust as one of the most flexible and adaptable, and also most useful, instruments in English law. Much is made of the way in which its application cuts across domestic and commercial contexts, providing certainty and protection in relation to property rights in commercial relationships as much as private familial ones. The use of the trust instrument in the context of pensions operation and pensions law also indicates something in addition to this, and which has up to now been implied rather than made explicit. The issue of pensions and their operation in contemporary society is one of the most important socio-economic issues of today. To recap, with the combination of declining birth-rate, longer life expectancy and a broader global context signalling the dismantling of the welfare state, the focus on privately-funded pensions outside state provision have come increasingly to the fore. Today's issues arise very strongly from the need to plan for tomorrow, and private pension schemes (occupational and otherwise) are very much concerned with planned long-term personal asset management.

Indeed, it has already been suggested that while the trust's traditional associations are strongly with wealth and its preservation, it is nevertheless significant that it is these age-old principles which are envisioned as the blueprint for this personal asset management into the twenty-first century. This is a testament to the trust's versatility, adaptability, and also to its endurance. This is so notwithstanding that demonstrating how pension funds are modelled on the trust instrument will reveal some crucial departures from 'ordinary' trust principles.

Clearly the huge shifts in social and economic demography have contributed to the rise of the pension fund, but it is the very characteristics which provided the introduction to this subject right at the outset of this book which form its back-bone. It is the fundamental principles of fiduciary responsibility and (from the beneficiaries' perspective) the proprietary rights conferred upon the equitable owners of property which have ensured that the trust has shaped the pension fund, and will remain central to its evolution.

Trust parties and pension situations

The term 'trust' parties in this context is used to illustrate how the parties which are central to the trust—as understood by text—can be applied to the pensions scenario. In this situation, the trust is a pension scheme and trust property arises in the form of contributions made to it, which ultimately become payable under it. In this respect, the term 'trust party' is used to 'locate' the settlor, the trustee and the beneficiary (parties central to the trust's operation) in the pension context. It does not of course refer to parties *to* the trust, because the beneficiary of a properly constituted trust has rights to enforce the trust, but is not party to its creation. But the settlor, the trustee and the beneficiary are all central to the operation of a private trust, and will now be explained in the operation of the pension trust.

In the case of an occupational pension trust, the employer is the settlor, and the members of the scheme, typically employees, and their dependants occupy the position of beneficiaries. The scheme will have trustees, which may well include the employer, and or other key organisational figures (e.g., from the board of directors) from the particular occupational culture concerned, or are appointed from a separate specialist trustee company. The involvement of the employer in the scheme confers even greater (theoretical at least) power than would subsist in the employer–employee relationship alone, in a 'structural' power sense. But in addition to this more abstract sense of power (which *is* regarded as a significant consideration, and is reflected as such in the Pensions Act 1995's provision that a proportion of trustees are to be nominated by members of the scheme), the position of the employer as trustee will vest in him *trust* powers in a real sense under the scheme. A glance back to the work on certainty and the introduction to the nature of trusts in chapter 2 will provide a reminder of the nature of powers—clearly, the powers conferred to trustees of such a scheme will be fiduciary powers, and will include the power to appoint any surplus (in the fund).

Duties and powers of trustees under a pension scheme

Just as in the case of any express private trust, trustees under a pension scheme are duty-bound to protect the trust assets and to administer the trust in accordance with its terms. This is a gross oversimplification, as there are a number of legal considerations reflecting the differences between pension funds and other trust instruments. In terms of protecting the trust assets, the trustees must ensure that settlor contributions falling due under the scheme are paid to it. Duties arising from administration are more complicated, and different issues will arise according to whether the scheme continues to operate and is due to remain operational, or whether it is being wound up. Other factors which will affect the administration of pensions trusts flow from the way in which they are likely to be operational for a long duration of time. On one level, this would ensure important perpetuity implications were it not for the way in which the 1995 Act exempts 'approved schemes' from perpetuities provisions. On another, the long-term management of assets which is required has resulted in pension trustees having powers of investment which are wider and more delegable than would normally be the case. Investment policy is also required to be formalised through the production of a formal statement of investment strategy. Statutory requirements exist requiring trustees to select investments, diversify portfolios and to observe their operations, and to take advice and review them. The trustees of a pension scheme are also under a duty to seek recovery of funds where pension funds become 'lost' (usually on account of a breach of trust), with potential implications flowing from liabilities of fellow trustees and previous ones, and where property applied in breach of trust has come into the hands of third parties.

Members as beneficiaries and key entitlements
It is the members of the pension scheme (along with their relatives and dependants) who are its beneficiaries. And in terms of being 'beneficially entitled' to the fruits of the fund, the members of the pension scheme are no different from the beneficiary under an 'ordinary' private trust. As was noted earlier, the key crucial difference lies in the contributions which comprise the basis of the pension entitlement. Contributions of this nature will include ones made by the beneficiary himself, directly and also indirectly. This is not the position in many ordinary private trusts, and in this respect the beneficiary has provided consideration for the benefit ultimately due under the scheme. However, this does not necessarily give the beneficiaries any additional rights to be informed about decisions taken by trustees (in respect of their own rather considerable obligations arising) regarding the fund, and the 'normal' position on this is considered below in the discussion of trusteeship. It is also the case that the remedies available to the pension fund beneficiary against trustees and 'strangers' (those not parties to the trust) are identical to those arising in any other private express trust—as explained in chapters 18 and 19.

Workable resulting trusts: Davis v Richards and Wallington
At this point, it might be wondered how this view of the trust can be squared with the analysis given to *Davis* above, and the important pensions case of *Air Jamaica* v *Charlton* (considered shortly) does distinguish *Davis*. Furthermore, it is especially important to note at this stage that the scheme in *Davis* was unusual in as much as such schemes will normally provide for the allocation of surplus assets on winding up of such a fund. This was not the case in *Davis*, and this is what triggered the operation of the general law relating to unincorporated associations (and the conclusion offered that the correct analysis to be applied was the one in *Re Bucks Constabulary*).

The resulting trust in action: Air Jamaica v Charlton
Air Jamaica Charlton [1999] 1 WLR 1399 (PC) concerned a contributory pension fund which was started in 1969. The fund was wound up following the company's privatisation upon which all the employees were made redundant. Many employees were re-engaged, but under new pension arrangements. The (original) scheme (and subject of the litigation) had been funded from (compulsory) deductions made from employees' salaries, and from matching payments which had been made by the employer. However, whereas each employee became a member of the pension scheme by virtue of his employment, his entitlement to a pension arose under the trusts of the scheme, and not under his contract of employment.

The case concerned two key provisions relating to the scheme. The first was Clause 4 of the trust deed. This provided *inter alia* that: 'No moneys which at any time have been contributed by the Company under the terms thereof shall in any circumstances be repayable to the [airline] company.' The second was s. 13 of the pension plan which authorised the airline to amend the plan or discontinue it, but not in a way which was incompatible with the exclusive use of the fund for the members and families and dependants also entitled under it. The fund was to be used for making annuity purchases for existing and future beneficiaries, and any surplus was to be directed to the provision of additional benefits for dependant beneficiaries following a member's death (to be applied to them at the discretion of the trustees).

Air Jamaica and a familiar problem: disputes arising from distributed funds
The litigation concerned the issue of the disposition of the large balance in the original fund when the company was privatised in 1994. As a result of new conditions of employment, no further contributions were made to the original fund, nor deductions made from the members of the scheme. The sum remaining was $400 million, and was surplus (i.e., not subject to any liability under the scheme). The members of this pension plan sought declaration that the plan had been discontinued, and in accordance with s. 13 of the plan, that the balance of the fund should be distributed for the benefit of the intended beneficiaries (the employees and their dependants). Almost immediately, the airline sought to amend the trust deed and plan to try to ensure that the surplus subject of the beneficiaries' claims would return to it, rather than be distributed among the beneficiaries. A royal lives clause was introduced to try to counter claims that the scheme (and its underlying trusts) was void for perpetuity. Meanwhile the Attorney-General alleged that the scheme was void for perpetuity, and that the surplus funds should pass to the Crown *bona vacantia*.

Distribution of the fund and direction of distribution: three parties in dispute
In the Privy Council (following a decision in the Jamaican Court of Appeal that the rule against perpetuities did not apply to the scheme, which arising out of the contract of employment was correctly the province of the law of contract), the Board concluded that the scheme had been established as a trust fund. It was found that membership of the scheme had arisen from the contract of employment, but entitlement to it flowed from the trust nature of the scheme. The scheme was subject to the rule against perpetuities and was found to be in infringement of the common law perpetuity rules. The Perpetuities and Accumulations Act 1964 does not form part of the law of Jamaica, so the common law perpetuity rules applied. This meant that there was no 'wait and see' facility, and the effect of this on the operation of the 'class gift' (in favour of members, their widows and dependants) was that this would be governed by common law. Under this scheme this meant that some (of the class) were not 'lives in being' at the time of the settlement, and it followed that there was the possibility that the gift might vest outside the perpetuity period (21 years after the death of a member).

Partial failure, distribution and operation of the resulting trust
As a consequence of the partial failure of the trusts (explained below), determination had to be made about the surplus and to whom it must be directed. It was held that there was a resulting trust in operation in favour of the member contributors and for the airline (on account of its 'matched employer' contributions under the scheme). The share to be returned to the members on resulting trust was to be on a *pro rata* basis, according to the contributions which individual members had made, but without reference to the time (dates) on which contributions had been made, or any benefits received under the scheme.

This case, its decision and its reasoning can be summarised as follows:

(a) Although the common law perpetuity period applied to this scheme, it did not follow that it was altogether void. The view of the Law Commission (in (1998) Law Com. 251, at para. 353) was adopted. The trusts took effect as separate settlements entered into by each employee. Each separate settlement comprised the contributions made in respect of the employee either by him or by the employer. This would satisfy the common law rule with the employee as the 'life in being'.

(b) The pension plan was discontinued when the employer ceased to deduct contributions from its employees and to pay matching contributions to the trustees.

(c) The surplus was held on resulting trust, being treated as provided as to one half by the employer and one half by the employees. Clause 4 did not negative the inference of a resulting trust; it is a failure of the company to dispose of the funds similar to *Vanervell* v *IRC* [1967] 2 AC 691. As for the employees' contributions, *Davis* v *Richards and Wallington Ltd* [1991] 2 All ER 563 could be distinguished since here they had not received all they had bargained for, but in any case the inferences as to intention drawn in *Davis* were disproved.

8.5.1 The regulation of pensions trusts: the Pensions Act 2004

The text immediately above has provided a brief introduction to the special features which pertain to pension trusts, and the special rules which apply to them as a reflection of this. Indeed, in due course (in chapter 18) you will come across the reference made by the Law Commission, in its 2006 *Report on Trustee Exemption Clauses*, to pension trusts as ones which are 'to a great extent a law unto themselves'. By way of brief explanation, the Law Commission suggested that such trusts are 'conceptually different from other types of trusts and operate in a distinct manner', and note has already been made of the way in which they are quite unlike other trusts in many respects, including the relationships between the parties, and the way in which beneficiaries thereunder are not volunteers, for example.

In many respects, the Pensions Act 2004 is best understood by reference to the Pensions Act 1995 as legislation enacted to protect the position of beneficiaries in light of the possibilities for maladministration and fraud, and also insolvency. In this respect, requirements that trustees must keep proper records; that contributions received by them must be placed in a separate account within an authorised institution; and that an offence can be committed where an employer fails to pay over contributions which have been deducted from members, are well established in the framework of modern pension trust law. However, this legislation has also sought to 'unpack' still further, and respond to, the rather unusual position of pension trusts and the different 'interests' and relationships which arise between the key parties.

Although many provisions of the 1995 Act remain in force, the 2004 Act has also introduced a number of changes. A detailed discussion of the new Act is beyond the scope of this text, where the consideration given to pensions trusts is very brief and basic. However, it is probably worthy of note that the background to the 2004 Act was one of numerous perceived shortcomings in the 1995 Act, both in terms of its scope and utility, and also in the nature of its operation. Thus, very brief reference will be made to the provisions for new funding requirements under the Act, and also to those relating to enhanced professionalism among the trustees of pension funds. It is also the case that the new Act has created the office of Pensions Regulator.

The 'special nature' of trusteeship under pension funds

The 'special nature' of pension trusts and the trusteeship which arises from them is recognised in the provisions of the 2004 Act which relate to enhanced expectations of trustees. Under the new provisions, a trustee must (pursuant to s. 249) have the requisite degree of knowledge and understanding to enable him to exercise his functions in accordance with the scheme of which he is a trustee. Accordingly, in *general*, trustees must have knowledge and understanding of the law relating to pensions and trusts, and the principles of scheme funding and investment. In furtherance of s. 247 and s. 248, trustees must also be conversant with a number of key matters relating to their *specific* scheme; namely the trust deed itself, and rules of the scheme in question, the scheme's statements of investment and funding principles, and any documents recording policy adopted by the trustees relating to the scheme.

Pension trusts and their new Regulator

In the spirit and direction of the 2004 legislation—to continue to emphasise the importance of protecting pension trusts and to recognise shortcomings in the regime provided by the 1995 Act—the new Act has created a new office of Pensions Regulator. The Pensions Regulator now holds all the powers which were originally vested in the Occupational Pensions Regulatory Authority by virtue of the 1995 Act. Accordingly, the new Pensions Regulator has powers under the 1995 Act, many provisions of which remain in force alongside the 2004 Act, as well as the 2004 Act. For example, powers relating to the appointment of 'replacement' trustees originally contained within s. 7 of the 1995 Act have now been vested in the new Regulator. Similarly, provisions which allow the Regulator to prevent a person not considered 'fit and proper' from acting as a trustee (in relation to specific trusts, or more generally), originally located in the 1995 legislation, can now be found in s. 33 of the 2004 Act. Elsewhere, provisions relate to the removal of trustees who become bankrupt or against whom there are proceedings which relate to accusations of dishonesty or deception (pursuant to s. 34). The Pensions Regulator also has the power to impose financial penalties on trustees and others in relation to breaches of their statutory duties (by virtue of s. 256); and to seek injunctions to prevent the misuse or misappropriation of assets, and to apply to the court for restitution in respect of assets misapplied or misappropriated (within s. 15 and s. 16 respectively). Furthermore, although the objective of seeking to prevent losses to pension trusts arising from fraud or maladministration is clear in this very brief overview of some of its key functions and powers, this body—the Pensions Regulator is a corporate body—is intended to be proactive in promoting good practice in pension trust administration, such as, for example, in publishing codes of practice.

Like its predecessor, the Pensions Regulator can order that an occupational scheme is wound up or, where it is appropriate to do so, to replace an existing scheme with a different one, but the new winding-up powers include the power (contained within ss. 23–32) to make a freezing order in response to an 'immediate risk' which might be presented to members of the scheme. The Pensions Regulator also has the power (by virtue of s. 17) to recover an employer's contributions to a fund which are unpaid by him, and to issue an 'improvement notice' (under s. 13) to any person where it appears that requirements of pensions legislation are not being complied with, and also to enter and inspect business premises (pursuant to ss. 73–76).

Pension trusts and the need to protect assets from maladministration
It is also the case that funding requirements have been tightened up by the 2004 Act, with these new provisions also illustrating the role of the Pensions Regulator created under the legislation. The provisions of the 1995 Act relating to scheme funding were, like their successors in the 2004 legislation, designed to try to prevent inadequacies in funding which might otherwise arise in this very complex, and in many respects highly intangible 'long-term' trust arrangement. The underlying purpose of so-called scheme funding rules was always to try to ensure that any inadequacies could be exposed through regular monitoring, which would allow remedial action (such as increased contributions either from employee or employer) to be taken.

The 1995 Act sought to achieve this by providing a 'minimum funding rule' for occupational pension schemes, which has now been replaced by a more strict scheme of funding rules by virtue of the 2004 legislation. However, while this regime is stricter, it is also more flexible inasmuch as it is one which applies in a 'scheme-specific' manner. Fundamentally, it remains rooted in the most elemental consideration of pensions law: this is of course the need to ensure that each scheme must have sufficient assets to cover its liabilities (2004 Act, s. 222). In furtherance of this strict, but flexible, scheme-specific approach, trustees must (under s. 223) prepare a statement of funding principles setting out their policy for ensuring that these funding objectives are met, and obtain an actuary's valuation of the scheme's assets and liabilities at regular intervals (under s. 224). Trustees must also prepare (under s. 227) and keep under review a schedule of contributions made by employers and also employees, which the actuary must certify.

The significance of the new Pensions Regulator lies in the way in which the Regulator must (by the provisions of ss. 225 and 227) be informed by the actuary if the valuation carried out on the scheme shows that the trustees are failing to meet their funding objectives, or if he is unable—for any reason—to certify the schedule of contributions required under s. 227. If this happens, the Pensions Regulator is also at the heart of the plan for recovery which must then be drawn up (by the provisions of s. 226), detailing the steps which will be taken to meet the statutory funding objective (under ss. 229–231): the Regulator will oversee this, inasmuch as trustees must report any failures in this process, and ultimately the Regulator has the power to wind up the scheme.

online resource centre

FURTHER READING

Harpum [2000] Conv 170.
Gardner [1992] Conv 41.
Warburton (1985) Conv 321.

9

Beneficial interests in the family home: a case study

This chapter is an important point of reference for a number of themes covered in this text thus far. Initially, chapter 1 introduced the nature of the trust, and its respective treatment of beneficial interests and legal title, and at that point it was noted that the instrument is widely used across human interactions; increasingly in the commercial sphere, and that it has long been used in relation to family property and financial arrangements. This theme was explained further in chapter 2, which signposted cohabitation of the 'family home' directly. In respect of both these initial chapters, this chapter's discussion of ownership of family homes now brings sharply into focus the everyday significance of trusts and trusts law, and in a context to which almost everyone can relate directly or indirectly. Fundamentally this is through consideration of central issues flowing from legal ownership of a home, and the ways in which a party who is not the legal owner of a home can nevertheless acquire a proprietary interest in it.

In this respect, the materials in this chapter also resonate with coverage given to the constitution of trusts in chapter 3: this is where consideration was given to the ways in which legal title becomes vested in the trustee, who then holds that property subject to the entitlements of the beneficiaries (and with these considerations shaping his responsibilities in relation to the trust property). This will become very significant to the subject matter which follows, as will closely connected questions of formality requirements considered in chapter 5, which pointed to the differing positions of trusts on account of whether or not they are 'express'.

In many respects this 'case study' chapter follows directly from chapters 7 and 8. Chapter 7 did, of course, introduce non-express trusts, which are classified as constructive and resulting, while chapter 8 provided a case study of the operation of resulting trusts, through examining unincorporated associations, and also pension funds. This case study of the family home, and those immediately following (on equitable fraud and secret trusts), examines trusts best described as constructive—at any rate, because the trust is imposed against the will of the trustee—but it will also consider the resulting trust in a way which follows on directly from its introduction in chapter 7.

Case study in the working of constructive and resulting trusts
Most of the trusts considered in this chapter can, like those in the following chapters, be categorised as constructive; but equally, however, some of the cases are clearly based on resulting trust principles. Furthermore, even where there is a constructive trust, it does not necessarily follow that it has an independent existence, and that better reasoning comes from the way it may well be used solely to avoid the formality provisions of s. 53(1)(b) of the Law of Property Act 1925. It will

become clear that in the case of a constructive trust, all the features of an express trust will be present, except for the statutory requirement that the declaration of trust is in writing.

This is a case study of the operation of constructive and resulting trusts, and illustration of their essential features. It also provides a point of reference for considering where they arise; and whether their use in operation always observes the conceptual distinctiveness which 'textbook' accounts of them emphasise. It will become apparent in this chapter that legal disputes surrounding ownership of the family home cluster very strongly around constructive and resulting trusts, along with (increasingly) proprietary estoppel.

A hypothetical model for the case study

This discussion on the issues arising from disputed home ownership is going to be pursued with reference to the following hypothetical problem 'scenario'. This concerns Mr A and Miss B, an unmarried couple, who purchase a home in which they intend to live together. Legal title is conveyed to Mr A alone. The issues thus pertain to in what circumstances can Miss B claim an equitable interest in the home and, if she can, how large is her interest? The context for such considerations of interest in the family home is very much that of relationship breakdown, and it will become apparent that many of the cases examined concern disputes between the parties to the relationship themselves. In this respect, the parties in this hypothetical example are unmarried because, as it will become clear at the end of this chapter, by virtue of the Matrimonial Causes Act 1973 (as amended) the courts have the power to alter significantly the property interests of married couples in the event of divorce, a decree of nullity of marriage or a decree of judicial separation. In such an event, the importance of the prior property interests of the spouses is reduced, since they will no longer be conclusive in the face of the court's discretion. In this vein, the assumption made that A is the male partner and B the female is simply one of convenience, and it does appear to be the one most commonly found in the cases, but also that it makes no difference if the sexes' position is reversed in the 'A and B' model.

Previous editions of this text have added at this point that it also makes no difference if the couple in question is a same-sex couple, or whether a couple is—in the parlance of the Law Commission's recent commentary on home-sharing—a 'non-conventional' couple. This was to make the point that the basic issue which arises across the spectrum of personal relationships is that only one party has legal title to a disputed home. What this edition needs to clarify in the hypothetical assumptions which are made in this chapter is that the Civil Partnership Act 2004 alters the position of same-sex couples who elect to register their 'civil partnership'. Upon doing so, partners in a registered arrangement will acquire rights to financial interests and those relating to property which are broadly similar to those of married couples. The implications of this in relation to property adjustment orders upon the dissolution of a civil partnership are considered below, alongside the position of divorcing couples seeking ancillary relief. What needs to be stressed at this point is that the general hypothetical examples given in this chapter now apply only to same-sex couples who have not registered a civil partnership. For same-sex couples who have not registered a civil partnership, the issues arising around acquiring an interest in property vested in their partner remains the same as that of an unmarried heterosexual couple, or a couple in any other kind of 'unconventional' relationship.

The reasons underlying the hypothetical model and current policy movements
It is of course possible for the above position, which at heart concerns the way in which only one party has legal title to a disputed home, to be avoided. Indeed, the courts have frequently expressed the view that it is desirable for the transfer of the property to contain an express declaration of trust concerning the beneficial interests. It is also worth observing that the law in this area is widely regarded as unsatisfactory, and in 1995 the Law Commission announced that it was to examine the property rights of home-sharers (Item 8, Sixth Programme of Law Reform: Law Com. 234). The Report commented (at 34) that 'the present legal rules are uncertain and difficult to apply and can lead to serious injustice'.

In 2002 the Law Commission published a Discussion paper entitled *Sharing Homes*, which suggested the need for new approaches to the issues arising from a variety of personal relationships. Further consideration of this project is made later in this chapter, but it is commonly referred to as a highly disappointing exercise which failed to translate into proposals for reform. What can be added to this edition is reference to the Law Commission's Cohabitation Project announced in July 2005. By way of brief overview, the project is in many respects a continuation of the findings of *Sharing Homes*, because the Law Commission is continuing to highlight the need for the law to accommodate and respond to a variety of different living arrangements within which relationships of 'intimacy and exclusivity' arise, and to provide fairness to the people concerned which is reflective of the nature of their relationships. The Law Commission published Consultation Paper No. 179, *Cohabitation: The Financial Consequences of Relationship Breakdown*, on 31 May 2006 in light of the Government's instruction to 'examine the options for reforming the law that applies to cohabiting couples on separation or death'. More is said about the Consultation towards the end of the chapter, and the Law Commission is due to report by August 2007.

For present purposes, the position of non-legal owners of homes continues to be characterised by the 'uncertain and difficult' legal rules which are also in the Law Commission's view capable of leading 'to serious injustice'. And while most earnest encouragement might be given by the courts for parties to make their intentions clear, for the purposes of this chapter, it is assumed that this has not been done.

9.1 Uncertainty in the law, and the significance of *Lloyds Bank plc* v *Rosset*

Until 1990, the law in this area was indeed very difficult to state with any degree of certainty. The House of Lords then stepped in, with a remarkably clear statement by Lord Bridge in *Lloyds Bank plc* v *Rosset* [1991] 1 AC 107. The starting point for discussion will therefore be this important House of Lords' decision, but before we examine it there are some preliminary points to make. Following *Rosset*, since the mid 1990s, the law has once again become unsettled and uncertain. This commenced with the Court of Appeal decision in *Midland Bank plc* v *Cooke* [1995] 4 All

ER 562 (noted by Glover and Todd [1995] 4 Web JCLI), which muddied the waters regarding quantification of beneficial interests. This was so, it has been argued in this text, given its apparent conflicts with other Court of Appeal decisions, including, in particular, *Springette* v *Defoe* (1992) 24 HLR 552, [1992] 2 FCR 561, noted at [1992] Conv 347 and *Huntingford* v *Hobbs* [1993] 1 FCR 45. *Midland Bank* v *Cooke* allows the courts a great deal of flexibility over quantification and benefits the person claiming the beneficial interest, who is Miss B in our hypothetical example.

Although this text has staunchly maintained that it is difficult to reconcile with a correct application of trusts law, a number of cases have followed the essence of *Midland Bank* v *Cooke*. It is also the case that its rationale has become central to current policy movements. Alongside this, a number of decisions have cast much more fundamental doubt on the continuing operation of trusts law in determining interests in family homes. Since the closing years of the 1990s, the courts have started to show a preference for an approach based on considerations of fairness and justice associated with a proprietary estoppel analysis. This is a contrast from the period immediately post-*Rosset*, during which the case of *Baker* v *Baker* (1993) 25 HLR 408 stood out against what appeared to be a clear preference for a trusts model. Now a number of decisions post 2000, including a series of Court of Appeal judgments—the most recent of which is *Oxley* v *Hiscock* [2004] 3 All ER 703—are showing a distinct leaning towards proprietary estoppel. It is hard to predict how the law will now develop, but a definite preference for a proprietary estoppel approach to quantification of beneficial interests is being signalled.

Alongside this, on the policy front, the Law Commission's Cohabitation Project is also seeking to alter the position of parties within intimate and personal relationships which are not formally recognised legal partnerships. This is currently at Consultation stage, and is being pursued through the proposed introduction of a framework of remedies available upon the cession of a relationship which will give the courts discretion to make orders relating to financial provision.

Beneficial interests and a new leading case
The discussion which now follows on determinations of the **existence** of and **quantification** of interests in a shared home acknowledges that the leading case for *quantification* of beneficial interests is now *Oxley* v *Hiscock*. Notwithstanding, this chapter continues to be written around the touchstone case of *Lloyds Bank* v *Rosset* [1991] 1 AC 107. This is to emphasise the utmost significance which is attached to the presence (or otherwise) of an agreement which subsists between parties as to the ownership of their home, and how the courts determine whether there is such an agreement subsisting. In questions which follow on from this, relating to how the parties' respective beneficial interests should be quantified, the text considers *Oxley* as important authority for the courts' current preference for approaches based on fairness and justice.

In so doing, this chapter continues to assert that Lord Bridge's speech in *Rosset* as authority for the ability of parties actually to establish an interest in a disputed home. This is so notwithstanding that, in light of *Oxley*, the courts are continuing their current favour for remedies calculated on the basis of a proprietary estoppel analysis. Closely related to this, *Oxley* also appears to continue the trend set in motion by *Midland Bank* v *Cooke*, whereby distinctions between so-called 'category 1' and 'category 2' cases (as explained below) are becoming blurred. This is because agreement or common intention to share property beneficially remains at the heart of being able to establish an interest in property owned by another. Indeed, in *Oxley* itself, Chadwick LJ proposed that in *Rosset* 'Lord Bridge was addressing the primary question' of 'was there a common intention that each should have a beneficial interest in the property?'. In one respect, this was clearly being used by Chadwick LJ to support his suggestion that 'the better view' of Lord Bridge's references to agreement to share in *Rosset* was that it did not extend to the secondary question— 'what was the common intention of the parties as to the extent of their beneficial interests?'. However, even having regard to this, it suggests *Oxley* is seeking to preserve the need to find an intention to share before questions of size can arise. Thus, this aspect of Lord Bridge's speech remains at the heart of establishing a cause of action, if not necessarily the remedy. This is because *Oxley* must now be regarded as the leading authority on quantification, and its rationale is quite different from *Rosset's* observations in this respect.

9.2 Two different types of case

The following passage, which distinguishes between two completely different types of case, is taken from Lord Bridge's speech in *Lloyds Bank plc v Rosset*:

The first and fundamental question which must always be resolved is whether, independently of any inference to be drawn from the conduct of the parties in the course of sharing the house as their home and managing their joint affairs, there has at any time prior to acquisition, or exceptionally at some later date, been any agreement, arrangement or understanding reached between them that the property is to be shared beneficially. The finding of an agreement or arrangement to share in this sense can only, we think, be based on evidence of express discussions between the partners, however imperfectly remembered and however imprecise their terms may have been. Once a finding to this effect is made it will only be necessary for the partner asserting a claim to a beneficial interest against the partner entitled to the legal estate to show that he or she has acted to his or her detriment or significantly altered his or her position in reliance on the agreement in order to give rise to a constructive trust or proprietary estoppel.

In sharp contrast with this situation is the very different one where there is no evidence to support a finding of an agreement or arrangement to share, however reasonable it might have been for the parties to reach such an arrangement if they had applied their minds to the question, and where the court must rely entirely on the conduct of the parties both as the basis from which to infer a common intention to share the property beneficially and as the conduct relied on to give rise to a constructive trust. In this situation direct contributions to the purchase price by the partner who is not the legal owner, whether initially or by payment of mortgage instalments, will readily justify the inference necessary to the creation of a constructive trust. But, as we read the authorities, it is at least extremely doubtful whether anything less will do.

In this passage Lord Bridge clearly distinguished between two types of case. The first type is where there is evidence of an agreement to share the property beneficially. The agreement need not be formal and its terms need not be particularly precise, but it appears that it must be based on evidence of express discussions between the partners (but see further below). More importantly, the evidence of the agreement must be independent of the conduct of the parties in the course of sharing the house as their home (conduct for this category is any detrimental reliance and is wider than that for the second category, considered later). If there is such evidence, then in principle it is not necessary to look at the conduct of the parties in order to establish either the existence of a beneficial interest, or its size. The agreement tells you both of those.

The second type of case is where there is no evidence, independently of the conduct of the parties (e.g., contributions to the home), of any such agreement. *Rosset* itself was such a case. Here, if any inference is to be drawn of an intention to share the beneficial interests, it can be drawn only on the basis of the contributions themselves. Thus, the contributions are used to establish the existence of Miss B's beneficial interest, and also (we shall argue) its size, there being no other evidence for either. Lord Bridge is of the opinion that in this situation, it is likely that only direct contributions to the purchase price by the partner who is not the legal owner, whether initially or by payment of mortgage instalments, will do (see further below).

The conduct of the parties is also relevant in the first type of case, but it is of far less importance than in the second type. Also, the conduct need not necessarily be in the form of direct contributions to the purchase price. Since the agreement to share is shown independently of the parties' conduct, the only function of the conduct is to get around the formalities requirements of s. 53(1)(b) of the Law of Property Act 1925. It should be borne in mind that there is unlikely to have been any written agreement in this type of case, and the inference to be drawn is that Mr A has declared himself trustee for himself and Miss B. Section 53(1)(b) of the Law of Property Act 1925 requires such a declaration to be in writing, unless there is an implied, resulting or constructive trust, in which case by virtue of s. 53(2), the provisions of s. 53(1)(b) do not apply. There will be a constructive trust if the female cohabitee has acted to her detriment or significantly altered her position in reliance on the agreement. All that is required, therefore, is to show detrimental reliance, in order to get round the formality provisions.

This is made clear elsewhere in Lord Bridge's speech in *Rosset*:

Even if there had been the clearest oral agreement between Mr and Mrs Rosset that Mr Rosset was to hold the property in trust for them both as tenants in common, this would, of course, have been ineffective since a valid declaration of trust by way of gift of a beneficial interest in land is required by s. 53(1) of the Law of Property Act 1925 to be in writing. But if Mrs Rosset had, as pleaded, altered her position in reliance on the agreement this could have given rise to an enforceable interest in her favour by way either of a constructive trust or of a proprietary estoppel.

It also follows from this analysis that no detrimental reliance is required if the agreement is in writing, for example where the parties communicate by signed letters, or where the property is not land (e.g., a caravan or houseboat).

It is a matter of some importance to establish into which of the two categories a particular case falls, since generally speaking Miss B will do better under the first category than under the second. We are now going to expand on the fundamental distinction drawn by Lord Bridge, but in reverse order. It is easier to first consider cases where there has been no independent agreement, and then to look at the independent agreement cases by way of contrast.

Before that, however, we need to consider some general principles. Much (but not all) of the second category can be explained in terms of resulting trusts, and it is there that we need to turn next. We will begin with an explanation in general terms, and then apply that explanation to the second category in *Lloyds Bank* v *Rosset*.

9.3 *Rosset* second category

9.3.1 Presumption of resulting trust

A definition of a resulting trust is where 'the beneficial interest "results" to the set-tlor or his estate' (see, e.g., A.J. Oakley, *Parker & Mellows, The Modern Law of Trusts*, 6th edn, Sweet & Maxwell (1994), at p. 189). It follows that for Miss B to obtain an interest by way of resulting trust, she must settle property; or, in other words, she must start with legal and equitable title to some property, legal title to which she transfers to Mr A. One possibility would be where she starts off with legal and equit-able title to the home itself, and transfers the bare legal title to Mr A, as in *Hodgson* v *Marks* [1971] 1 Ch 892. This is clearly not the normal *Rosset* situation, but it is easy to see how a resulting trust can arise from Miss B's contributions to the purchase money. If Miss B pays the purchase money (in which she has legal and equitable title) over to Mr A, then in the absence of a presumption of advancement or con-sideration moving from him, she is presumed to retain equitable ownership in the money: *Dyer* v *Dyer* (1788) 2 Cox Eq Cas 92, *per* Eyre CB, at p. 93. If the money is referable to the acquisition of property, then on its acquisition by Mr A, Miss B's interest in the money becomes converted into an interest in the property (on the principles stated by Sir George Jessel MR in *Re Hallet's Estate* (1880) 13 Ch D 696 at p. 708, an equitable tracing case considered at 19.2). Alternatively, if both Mr A and Miss B separately pay the vendor, V, then V becomes trustee of the money for him and her in the proportions in which he and she has paid it, until such time as the property is conveyed, when again the equitable interests are converted into inter-ests in the property.

   For these purposes the origin of the money advanced by Miss B is irrelevant. If it is obtained by a loan, with her undertaking liability to repay the loan, the position is exactly the same; and similarly if she obtains the money through a mortgage on the property itself, accepting liability to repay the mortgage debt. This explains, for example, *Huntingford* v *Hobbs* [1993] 1 FCR 45, where the entirety of Mr Huntingford's under-taking to repay the mortgage debt was taken into account in calculating his share, although he had not actually paid off any of the capital.

9.3.2 Presumption of advancement

If the presumption of advancement is applicable to this area of law, it can be rele-vant whether or not the parties are married. Suppose, for example, a matrimonial home is purchased in the name of the husband alone, but his wife has contributed to the purchase price (either the deposit or mortgage repayments). There being no presumption of advancement from wife to husband, on the principles discussed above, the equitable interests remain in proportion to the contributions, and the husband will therefore hold the legal estate on trust for both himself and his wife in proportion to their contributions. They will thus hold the land as joint tenants or tenants in common in equity, and a statutory trust of land will arise under the provisions of the Trusts of Land and Appointment of Trustees Act 1996 (see further chapter 1). The same result obtains, of course, if the parties are living together but not married.

Suppose instead, however, that the man contributes to the purchase money, the property being conveyed into the woman's name alone. It now matters whether the parties are married. If they are, and if the presumption of advancement applies, the wife will obtain both legal and equitable title. If the parties are unmarried, the opposite result obtains, the presumption being that the man retains an equitable title under a resulting trust.

Modernity, changing social conditions and a continuing role for the presumption of advancement?

All this presupposes that the presumption of advancement has any application in this area of law (there is no doubt that the presumption of resulting trust applies— see *Tinsley* v *Milligan*, below). Obviously, the justification for the presumption (below) applies to a set of circumstances very different from that being considered here. Indeed, the presumption may well be regarded as very old fashioned. In *Pettitt* v *Pettitt* [1970] AC 777, a cottage was purchased in the name of the wife, Mrs Pettitt providing the entirety of the purchase money. The husband significantly improved the property, using his own labour and money. He claimed an equitable interest, but the House held that he had no interest in the cottage (see further 8.6.1). The House refused to decide the case simply on the basis of the presumption of advancement, however, which would have led them to the same conclusion. Lord Diplock did not think the presumption applied at all in shared home cases, observing that:

It would, in my view, be an abuse of the legal technique for ascertaining or imputing intention to apply to transactions between the post-war generation of married couples 'presumptions' which are based on inferences of fact which an earlier generation of judges drew as to the most likely intentions of earlier generations of spouses belonging to the propertied classes of a different social era.

The other judges appeared to favour a weak presumption, so that as Lord Diplock observed in *Gissing* v *Gissing* [1971] AC 886 (see below):

. . . as I understand the speeches in *Pettitt* v *Pettitt* four of the members of your Lordships's House who were parties to that decision took the view that even if the 'presumption of advancement' as between husband and wife still survived today, it could seldom have any decisive part to play in disputes between living spouses in which some evidence would be available in addition to the mere fact that the husband had provided part of the purchase price of property conveyed into the name of the wife.

In *McGrath* v *Wallis* [1995] 2 FLR 114, Nourse LJ began his judgment as follows:

Ever since the decision of the House of Lords in *Pettitt* v *Pettitt* [1970] AC 777, it has been my understanding that, in its application to houses acquired for joint occupation, the equitable presumption of advancement has been reclassified as a judicial instrument of last resort, its subordinate status comparable to that of the *contra preferentem* rule in the construction of deeds and contracts; see *per* Lords Reid, Hodson and Diplock at pages 793, 811 and 824 respectively; see also *Gissing* v *Gissing* [1971] AC 886, *per* Lord Diplock at page 907 . . . For myself, I have been unable to recollect any subsequent case of this kind in which the presumption has proved to be decisive, even where one of the parties has since died.

He continued:

> In *Pettitt* v *Pettitt* Lord Upjohn, more loyal to the presumption of advancement than the others of their Lordships, while maintaining that that presumption and the presumption of a resulting trust, when properly understood and properly applied to the circumstances of today, remained as useful as ever in solving questions of title (see page 813H), nevertheless accepted that they were readily rebutted by comparatively slight evidence (see page 814H).

In that case the presumption between father and son was easily rebutted, there being no evidence that the father intended to make a gift of the house to his son.

Presumption of advancement in matrimonial cases

It is clear, therefore, that the presumption of advancement will rarely, if ever, be decisive in matrimonial property cases, but whether there is no presumption at all, or a very weak presumption, a matter on which the courts have reached no definite conclusion, can make a difference. In *Tinsley* v *Milligan* [1994] 1 AC 340, Stella Tinsley and Kathleen Milligan jointly purchased a home which was registered in Tinsley's name alone. On the principles set out above, the beneficial interest would have been shared between Tinsley and Milligan in equal shares, but to both Tinsley and Milligan's knowledge, the home was registered in Tinsley's name alone to enable Milligan to make false claims to the Department of Social Security for benefits. After a quarrel, Tinsley moved out and claimed possession from Milligan. Milligan counterclaimed, seeking a declaration that the house was held by Tinsley on trust for both of them in equal shares. Tinsley argued that Milligan's claim was barred by the common law doctrine *ex turpi causa non oritur actio* and by the principle that he who comes to equity must come with clean hands.

The House of Lords held (Lord Keith and Lord Goff dissenting) that because the presumption of resulting trust applied, Milligan could establish her equitable interest without relying on the illegal transaction, and was therefore entitled to succeed. However, it is also clear that if she had had to rebut a presumption of advancement, however weak, she would have failed, because she would have had to plead the fraud in order to do so. In *Tribe* v *Tribe* [1995] 4 All ER 236, the Court of Appeal allowed evidence to rebut a presumption of advancement where the fraud had not actually been carried out, but this decision will not apply where the fraud has been carried out. Where a husband has conveyed a house to his wife (for example) to perpetrate a capital gains tax fraud, and the fraud has been successfully perpetrated, it does matter whether there is a weak presumption or none at all.

9.3.3 Contributions definitely outside the second category

The exact scope of the second category in *Lloyds Bank* v *Rosset* is considered below, when its juristic basis is made clearer, but the important point about this category is that apart from the contributions of the parties, there is no independent evidence of their intention. It is therefore not surprising that only contributions which are referable to the property, and indeed to its acquisition, count. These will usually (perhaps necessarily) be financial contributions, as in the previous sections.

Capital and the value placed by the law on non-financial contributions

By comparison, other contributions are arguably undervalued. Generally speaking, this operates to the disadvantage of the woman living in the home, since it is still far more likely that the man will earn more money than the woman, and it is accordingly likely that his financial contributions will be the greater. On the other hand, the woman may contribute in other ways. She may, for example, give up her job to bring up children, pay the household expenses, or provide furniture or domestic services. Because it undervalues these other contributions, the law appears to work unjustly against the woman (which is presumably why legislation was thought necessary for married couples—see further below).

Yet (subject to possible new developments considered later) the courts appear to attach little weight to non-financial contributions. In the 1970s it was argued that the courts should exercise a discretion based on some abstract notion of justice. It was also argued that equity is a flexible instrument. 'Equity', said Lord Denning MR in *Eves* v *Eves* [1975] 1 WLR 1338, at 1340, 'is not past the age of child bearing'. The facts of *Eves* v *Eves* are set out in due course.

It is now reasonably clear that the courts will not exercise the sort of discretion envisaged by Lord Denning MR in *Eves* v *Eves* (although the actual decision in the case was implicitly approved in *Lloyds Bank* v *Rosset*). Indeed, a rigidly property-based approach was taken by the House of Lords in *Pettitt* v *Pettitt* [1970] AC 777 and *Gissing* v *Gissing* [1971] AC 886. Mrs Gissing had been married to Mr Gissing for 16 years and had paid a substantial sum towards furniture and the laying of a lawn, but the house had been conveyed into the name of Mr Gissing alone, and Mrs Gissing had made no direct contributions towards its purchase. On their divorce, the House of Lords held that she had no interest (the position would possibly have been different after the enactment of the Matrimonial Causes Act 1973—set out at 9.7.3). The main importance of the case is that the House refused to exercise a discretion simply in order to do 'justice'. The interests of the parties were determined on the basis of their intentions at the time of acquisition of the property, and not by their subsequent conduct. It was also clear that normal principles of property law would be applicable.

In *Eves* v *Eves*, Lord Denning MR relied on the following passage from Lord Diplock's speech in *Gissing* v *Gissing* [1971] AC 886, as authority that the courts had a great degree of flexibility. The nature of the interest depended on all the equities of the case, and the law might consider not merely financial contributions at the time of acquisition of the property, but all types of contribution, whether at that time or subsequently:

A resulting, implied or constructive trust—and it is unnecessary for present purposes to distinguish between these three classes of trust—is created by a transaction between the trustee and the *cestui que trust* in connection with the acquisition by the trustee of a legal estate in land, whenever the trustee has so conducted himself that it would be inequitable to allow him to deny to the *cestui que trust* a beneficial interest in the land acquired. And he will be held so to have conducted himself if by his words or conduct he has induced the *cestui que trust* to act to his own detriment in the reasonable belief that by so acting he was acquiring a beneficial interest in the land.

The quotation was taken out of context, since from the previous paragraph in Lord Diplock's speech it is clear that he was referring to the constructive trust here merely as a device to get round s. 53(1)(b) of the Law of Property Act 1925, where all the other requirements of a trust are already present. In other words, this passage merely referred to what has now become detrimental reliance for the purposes of the first category in *Rosset* (set out shortly), and Lord Diplock did not intend this reasoning to be used to create a trust in the first place.

Burns v Burns: restatement of the conventional view

The Court of Appeal restated the conventional view in *Burns* v *Burns* [1984] Ch 317, the facts and result of which were similar to *Gissing*, except that though the parties had lived together as husband and wife for many years, they were unmarried. The claimant, Valerie Burns, had been living with the defendant for 19 years, 17 in the house which was the subject of the dispute. She and the defendant, Patrick Burns, had never married. The house had been purchased in the name of the defendant, and he paid the purchase price. The claimant made no contribution to the purchase price or the mortgage repayments, but had brought up their two children, performed domestic duties and recently contributed from her own earnings towards household expenses. She also bought various fittings and a washing machine, and re-decorated the interior of the house. The claimant left the defendant and claimed a beneficial interest in the house.

Since the couple had never married the provisions of the Matrimonial Causes Act 1973, ss. 24–25 did not apply, and the Court of Appeal held that the claimant's case rested on orthodox property principles. In the absence of a financial contribution which could be related to the acquisition of the property, for example to the mortgage repayments, or a contribution enabling Patrick Burns to pay the mortgage instalments, Valerie Burns was not entitled to a beneficial interest in the house. *Burns* v *Burns* was upheld by the House of Lords in *Winkworth* v *Edward Baron Development Co. Ltd* [1988] 1 WLR 1512. There the House refused to infer that Mrs Wing had an equitable interest in the matrimonial home, which was owned by a company of which she and her husband were sole directors, where she had used the proceeds from her share of her former matrimonial home to pay off the company overdraft, because the payment was not referable to the acquisition of the house (in Hayes Lane).

Lloyds Bank v Rosset: a landmark decision

Lastly, there is *Lloyds Bank plc* v *Rosset* [1991] 1 AC 107 itself. Mr and Mrs Rosset decided to purchase a semi-derelict farmhouse for £57,000. Mrs Rosset understood that the entire purchase money was to come out of a family trust fund, the trustees of which insisted that the house be purchased in the husband's sole name (this appears to have been the only reason for the legal title being vested in Mr Rosset alone). The house required renovation, and it was intended that this should be a joint venture. The vendors allowed Mr and Mrs Rosset to enter the property a number of weeks before completion in order to begin repairs and render the house habitable.

During this period, Mrs Rosset spent a lot of time at the house, urging on the builders and attempting to co-ordinate their work (until her husband insisted that he alone should give instructions), going to builders' merchants to obtain material required by the builders, delivering the materials to the site, assisting her husband in planning the renovation and decoration of the house (she was a skilled painter and decorator), wallpapering two bedrooms, arranging the insurance of the house, arranging a crime prevention survey, and assisting in arranging the installation of burglar alarms.

Unbeknown to Mrs Rosset, Mr Rosset was unable to fund the purchase and repairs entirely from the trust fund, and obtained an overdraft of £18,000 from Lloyds Bank, executing a legal charge on the property in their favour on the same day as completion. He later defaulted on the repayments and the bank sought possession. Mrs Rosset claimed a beneficial interest in the property, binding the bank by virtue of her actual occupation as an overriding interest under the Land Registration Act 1925, s. 70(1)(g).

In the Court of Appeal in *Rosset*, most of the discussion revolved around whether Mrs Rosset was in actual occupation when the charge was created, in order to be able to rely upon s. 70(1)(g). The House of Lords were able to avoid all discussion of s. 70(1)(g), simply holding that Mrs Rosset had no beneficial interest. There was no evidence of any agreement between the parties to share the beneficial interest, and the wife's contributions were regarded as *de minimis*. The principles discussed in this section were applied.

The cases suggest, then, that for a beneficial interest to be acquired in this type of case, the contributions must be referable to the *initial* acquisition of the property. There is no such requirement under the first category in *Rosset*, where there is independent evidence of the intentions of the parties.

The resulting trust reasoning explained above also suggests that for the second category, the extent of Miss B's interest depends solely on her contributions (but see further below).

9.4 *Rosset* first category

9.4.1 Calculating beneficial entitlements: trust or estoppel?

By contrast with the second category in *Lloyds Bank v Rosset*, where the intention of the parties is inferred from the contributions themselves, under the first category there *is* independent evidence of intention.

Lord Bridge does not make clear, however, whether the analysis should be in terms of constructive trust or proprietary estoppel, or even whether the concepts are intended to be the same or distinct. Professor Hayton, for example, argues that Lord Bridge is equating these concepts ([1990] Conv 370, at p. 376), a view apparently shared by Morritt LJ in *Lloyds Bank plc v Carrick* [1996] 4 All ER 630, and Lord Oliver of Aylmerton in *Austin v Keele* (1987) 61 AJLR 605, at p. 609. However, this is by no means clear from the judgment itself (see P. Ferguson, (1993) 109 LQR 114, at p. 118), and even Morritt LJ in *Lloyds Bank plc v Carrick* seemed prepared to accept that estoppel might raise different issues, and actually dealt with estoppel separately when considering (and rejecting) the *Rosset* argument advanced by Mrs Carrick, on the ground that her estate contract precluded the co-existence of a *Rosset* interest.

Unfortunately, an investigation of the cases cited by Lord Bridge throws little more light on the issue, and both estoppel and constructive reasoning can be found, for example, in *Grant v Edwards* [1986] 1 Ch 638 (set out shortly). The courts have tended to prefer trusts to estoppel reasoning, as in *Ungurian v Lesnoff* [1990] 1 Ch 206, decided a few months prior to *Lloyds Bank plc v Rosset*, and *Stokes v Anderson* [1991] 1 FLR 391. However, Professor Hayton argues for a pure estoppel approach to the first category, and estoppel reasoning was adopted in *Baker v Baker* [1993] 25 HLR 408. It is suggested that some cases within the first category are properly categorised as trust cases, while for others estoppel is a more appropriate classification. The traditional view taken in this text has been that facts which give rise to an estoppel will not necessarily suffice for a trust, and the consequences of trusts and estoppel reasoning are different. This edition has looked at this again in light of a number of recent cases.

9.4.2 Constructive trust requirements

The trust requirements were analysed by Lord Diplock in *Gissing* v *Gissing* [1971] AC 886, at pp. 904H–05D, in terms of a declaration of trust by Mr A for Miss B. The declaration would (if verbal) be void for want of writing, which is required by s. 53(1)(b) of the Law of Property Act 1925, unless it were acted upon by her so as to render it inequitable to allow him to deny the trust. It would then take effect as a constructive trust, to which, by virtue of s. 53(2), s. 53(1)(b) has no application. The explanation in *Lloyds Bank plc* v *Rosset*, at p. 129C, is similar: see also *Re Densham* [1975] 1 WLR 1519. As was observed earlier, it follows that there is no need for detrimental reliance by Miss B if either s. 53(1)(b) is satisfied, or the property is not land.

The important point about this analysis is that the constructive trust does not have any independent existence, in that it assumes that all the incidents of an express trust are also present. If the trust is in writing then you do not even need detrimental reliance, and if not then the only function of detrimental reliance is to invoke s. 53(2), and hence avoid the formality requirements. This is similar to the analysis in chapter 10, where again all the elements of an express trust (apart from writing) are present, and the constructive trust is imposed as a device to avoid a formality requirement. It is not like the analysis in chapter 11, where a constructive trust is imposed although there is no declaration of trust, but in those cases legal title is only obtained at all on the strength of an express representation, and the courts hold representors to their representations. By contrast, in these cases legal title passes to Mr A wholly independently of any representation, and the effect of the representation is only to induce detrimental reliance on the part of Miss B. Lord Denning MR's view in *Eves* v *Eves* [1975] 1 WLR 1338, that the constructive trust might exist on its own, is inconsistent with *Gissing* v *Gissing*, and has received no support from later authorities.

A consequence of all the incidents of an express trust being present is that Miss B's interest ought to be capable of binding a third party, such as a purchaser or mortgagee. A second consequence is that the quantification of Miss B's interest ought to depend on the discussions alone, and not on the extent of her detrimental reliance, since the function of the detrimental reliance is simply to avoid the formality provisions of the Law of Property Act 1925. Quantification is discussed separately below, however, since there is recent authority suggesting that a broad brush can be taken to quantification (though not to acquisition, which remains governed by the rigid principles discussed here).

Lloyds Bank v Rosset and the significance of earlier authorities
The leading cases cited by Lord Bridge as examples of this category were the Court of Appeal decisions in *Grant* v *Edwards* [1986] 1 Ch 638 and *Eves* v *Eves* [1975] 1 WLR 1338. In *Grant* v *Edwards*, a house was purchased in 1969 for the claimant, Mrs Linda Grant, and the defendant, George Edwards, to live in as if married (although

Linda Grant was actually married to someone else). The house was purchased in the name of Edwards and his brother. Edwards told Grant that her name would not go on the title for the time being because it would cause prejudice in the matrimonial proceedings pending between Mrs Grant and her husband. In reality, Edwards had no intention of conveying any legal title to the claimant.

The defendant paid the deposit on the house and most, but not all, of the repayments on the two mortgages. He paid the deposit and all the mortgage instalments on the first mortgage, but Mrs Grant paid some instalments under a second mortgage. The claimant also made substantial contributions towards general household expenses, provided housekeeping and brought up the children. In 1980 the couple separated, and the claimant claimed a beneficial interest in the property.

The Court of Appeal held that Edwards's statement that Mrs Grant's name would have appeared on the title except that it could cause prejudice in the matrimonial proceedings was evidence of a common intention that Mrs Grant should have a beneficial interest (a half share) in the property. Mrs Grant had relied to her detriment on the common intention, so that she was entitled to a half share on a resulting or constructive trust.

It must be observed that Linda Grant's contributions were not particularly significant, and would certainly not have justified a half share, or probably any share, on the principles discussed in the previous section. The crucial element in the case was the statement by the defendant as to why the claimant's name would not go on the title. The Court of Appeal took the view that this statement could be explained only on the basis of a common intention that she was to have a half share. At first sight this seems rather a surprising conclusion, since Edwards clearly intended no such thing, but the representation was interpreted (in effect) as meaning: 'Your name would go on the title but for the fact that it would prejudice your matrimonial proceedings.' Had Edwards intended to say 'The house is to be mine alone', there would have been no need for an excuse. By this somewhat tortuous reasoning, therefore, the Court was able to infer, independently of her contributions, a common intention that Mrs Grant was to have a half share, and the case depended on this.

Because there was evidence of a common intention (independent of the contributions themselves), Linda Grant's contributions (unlike those of Valerie Burns), were relevant only in order to get round the formality provisions of s. 53 of the Law of Property Act 1925. It was only necessary for Grant to show that she had relied on the agreement to her detriment, by acting in a manner which was explicable only on the basis that she was to have an interest in the house, for a constructive trust to arise in her favour.

This is a far less stringent requirement than that adopted in *Burns* or *Rosset*, where there was no outside evidence of any agreement so that evidence of intention could be inferred only from the contributions themselves. Furthermore, the value of the beneficial interest was determined by the common intention (as evidenced by the defendant's statement) and not by the value of Linda Grant's contributions.

Eves v Eves and Grant v Edwards: constructive trusteeship and intention

Mention has already been made (in the previous section) of *Eves v Eves* [1975] 1 WLR 1338. In that case, Lord Denning MR reasoned that equity was still capable of developing, and that the courts had a discretion to depart from strictly property-based criteria in order to achieve what they saw as 'justice'. It is now clear that the case cannot be explained on that basis, but while in *Grant* v *Edwards* Lord Denning MR's reasoning in *Eves* v *Eves* was expressly rejected, the decision itself was upheld, and in *Lloyds Bank* v *Rosset* the case was explained as one of the type where there is evidence of a common intention that beneficial interest in the home should be shared.

Janet Eves, who was under 21 and separated from her husband, went to live with a man whose marriage had also broken down. They had a child together and shortly afterwards found a house with the intention that they would live there together. The man told her that if she had been 21 he would have arranged for the house to be conveyed into their joint names, but in reality this was simply an excuse for having the house conveyed into his name alone. The house was in a dilapidated state and Janet did a great deal of heavy building work improving it, including wielding a 14lb sledge-hammer to break up the concrete in the front garden so that it could be levelled and turfed. When the relationship broke down, Janet Eves was held to be entitled to a quarter share. As in *Grant* v *Edwards*, the case depended on the representation made by the man: there would have been no need for him to make an excuse had he intended to say: 'The house is to be mine alone.' As Brightman J explained (at p. 1345): 'The defendant clearly led the plaintiff to believe that she was to have some undefined interest in the property, and that her name was only omitted from the conveyance because of her age.'

Grant v *Edwards* and *Eves* v *Eves* were explained by Lord Bridge in *Rosset*, who also made clear what inference was to be drawn from the representations and what was the importance of the subsequent conduct of the female partner:

Outstanding examples on the other hand of cases giving rise to situations in the first category are *Eves* v *Eves* [1975] 1 WLR 1338 and *Grant* v *Edwards* [1986] Ch 638. In both these cases, where the parties who had cohabited were unmarried, the female partner had been clearly led by the male partner to believe, when they set up home together, that the property would belong to them jointly. In *Eves* v *Eves* the male partner had told the female partner that the only reason why the property was to be acquired in his name alone was because she was under 21 and that, but for her age, he would have had the house put into their joint names. He admitted in evidence that this was simply an 'excuse'. Similarly, in *Grant* v *Edwards* the female partner was told by the male partner that the only reason for not acquiring the property in joint names was because she was involved in divorce proceedings and that, if the property were acquired jointly, this might operate to her prejudice in those proceedings. As Nourse LJ put it (at p. 649):

Just as in *Eves* v *Eves*, these facts appear to me to raise a clear inference that there was an understanding between the plaintiff and the defendant, or a common intention, that the plaintiff was to have some sort of proprietary interest in the house otherwise no excuse for not putting her name onto the title would have been needed.

The subsequent conduct of the female partner in each of these cases, which the court rightly held sufficient to give rise to a constructive trust or proprietary estoppel supporting her claim to an interest in the property, fell far short of such conduct as would by itself have supported the claim in the absence of an express representation by the male partner that she was to have such an interest. It is significant to note that the share to which the female partners in *Eves* v *Eves* and *Grant* v *Edwards* were held entitled were one-quarter and one-half respectively. In no sense could these shares have been regarded as proportionate to what the judge in the instant case described as a 'qualifying contribution' in terms of the indirect contributions to the acquisition or enhancement of the value of the houses made by the female partners.

In *Grant* v *Edwards*, Nourse LJ (at p. 647) drew the following distinction, which essentially summarises the above discussion, between the relevance of the woman's conduct in *Grant* v *Edwards* itself, and its relevance in a case like *Burns* v *Burns*:

In most of these cases the fundamental, and invariably the most difficult, question is to decide whether there was the necessary common intention, being something which can only be inferred from the conduct of the parties, almost always from the expenditure incurred by them respectively. In this regard the court has to look for expenditure which is referable to the acquisition of the house (see . . . *Burns* v *Burns* [1984] Ch 317). If it is found to have been incurred, such expenditure will perform the two-fold function of establishing the common intention and showing that the claimant has acted upon it.

There is another and rarer class of case, of which the present may be one, where, although there has been no writing, the parties have orally declared themselves in such a way as to make their common intention plain. Here the court does not have to look for conduct from which the intention can be inferred, but only for conduct which amounts to an acting upon it by the claimant. And although that conduct can undoubtedly be the incurring of expenditure which is referable to the acquisition of the house, it need not necessarily be so.

Elaborating on the question of what conduct would suffice, he referred to *Eves* v *Eves* and said (at p. 648):

So what sort of conduct is required? In my judgment it must be conduct on which the woman could not reasonably have been expected to embark unless she was to have an interest in the house. If she was not to have such an interest, she could reasonably be expected to go and live with her lover, but not, for example, to wield a 14lb sledge-hammer in the front garden. In adopting the latter kind of conduct she is seen to act to her detriment on the faith of the common intention.

The requirement for this type of case is detrimental reliance, therefore. In *Burns* v *Burns*, by contrast, the court had to look for expenditure which was referable to the acquisition of the house. It is obvious that it is far easier to satisfy the requirement in *Grant* v *Edwards* than it is to satisfy the requirement in *Burns* v *Burns*.

These cases have been criticised on the grounds that the agreement is entirely fictitious, because in each case the man clearly did not intend the woman to have any interest in the property. Thus, Simon Gardner has written ((1993) 109 LQR 263, at p. 265):

But the fact that the men's statements were excuses (i.e., neither objectively valid nor even sincerely uttered) does not mean that the men were thereby acknowledging an agreement whereby the woman should have a share. If I give an excuse for rejecting an invitation to what I expect to be a dull party, it does not mean that I thereby agree to come: on the contrary, it means that I do not agree to come, but for one reason or another find it hard to say so outright. The fallacious quality of the reasoning in *Eves* v *Eves* and *Grant* v *Edwards* is thus clear. It is hard to think that the judges concerned really believed in it . . . .

He contrasted these cases with *Hammond* v *Mitchell* [1991] 1 WLR 1127 (below), where it appears that Hammond really did intend Vicky Mitchell to have a share (Vicky Mitchell obtained a half share on the basis of statements that had been made to her by Hammond, which are set out below).

Simon Gardner, constructive trusteeship and objective and subjective intention
Gardner's objection (above) is clearly valid if a subjective view is taken of intention, but the cases considered in chapter 3 on declaration of trusteeship suggest that intention is judged objectively. The courts appear to adopt the position of a reasonable observer. In *Richards* v *Delbridge* (1874) LR Eq 11, Sir George Jessel MR

concentrates on the words used, as opposed to the actual intention, observing that 'however anxious the Court may be to carry out a man's intention, it is not at liberty to construe words otherwise than according to their proper meaning'. This suggests that the actual intention is irrelevant. In *Re Kayford Ltd* [1975] 1 WLR 279, Megarry J, at p. 282A, also talks in terms of an intention being manifested, rather than merely held.

It was for these reasons that Paul Todd and Nicola Glover (Glover and Todd [1995] 5 Web JCLI) felt that Gardner's objection was misplaced. To take *Grant v Edwards* as the example, what George Edwards was saying, in effect, was that although legal title must be vested in himself alone, this was for purely formal reasons (so as not to cause prejudice in the matrimonial proceedings pending between Linda Grant and her husband), and the reality was that the property (i.e., equitable title) was to belong to both of them. Once it is accepted that the test is objective, and does not depend on what George Edwards actually thought, it is difficult to imagine a clearer declaration of trusteeship than that.

Constraints on the constructive trust analysis
There are, however, other constraints on the constructive trust analysis. A trust operates as an immediate and irrevocable commitment, so that statements as to future intention will not suffice. The cases in chapter 3 show that before a trust can be inferred, Mr A must evidence an intention to deal with the property in such a way as to deprive himself of his beneficial ownership, and to declare that he will hold it from that time forward on trust for Miss B. Another limitation of some importance is that the property must be identified as existing property: *Re Ellenborough* [1903] 1 Ch 697. A trust analysis should not work, therefore, where the property has not been identified (i.e., where the statement concerns a house to be purchased at some future time). On this basis, there are difficulties with *Ungurian v Lesnoff* [1990] 1 Ch 206, which is surely wrongly categorised as a constructive trust case.

Mrs Lesnoff, who was a Polish academic, gave up a flat in Poland (which she could have occupied for life), as well as her Polish nationality and her career, in order to live with Mr Ungurian. Ungurian bought a house in London, registered in his sole name, in which he and Mrs Lesnoff lived as man and wife for four years. During that time Mrs Lesnoff installed or supervised the installation of central heating, and the re-wiring and replumbing of the house, in addition to other works of improvement and redecoration (had this been a second category case, she would probably have failed to get an interest). Mrs Lesnoff remained in occupation and when Ungurian brought an action for possession and the case finally came to court many years later, Vinelott J held that Mrs Lesnoff had an interest, but clearly did not want to give her the fee simple. Perhaps for this reason, he did not think that Mr Ungurian's words when handing over a cheque for the balance of the purchase price ('This is your house; you had better sign it') constituted a declaration of trusteeship (at pp. 214F and 220F). If they had done, and it is not at all clear why they did not, Vinelott J would have had no option but to grant Mrs Lesnoff the fee simple. Instead, he relied on obscure recollections of conversations which had occurred over 20 years before the case was heard, in Beirut. We would suggest, however, that unlike the statement made when the cheque was handed over, the conversations relied on cannot, in principle, amount to a declaration of trust, both because there was no trust property at the time they were made, and because they were statements of future intention, not therefore amounting to a present irrevocable commitment. The Beirut conversation were: 'We will have to look for and buy a house for us in London so that you will feel secure and happy, having lost your house in Poland', and 'You'll have to decide and find the house which you like. I want you to feel that you have something to rely on if anything happens to me.'

Ungurian v *Lesnoff* is also notable in showing how substantial property interests can depend on obscure recollections. Coming as she did within the first category, Mrs Lesnoff obtained a life interest, with all the powers thereby conferred by the Settled Land Act 1925, whereas without the Beirut conversations she would have come within the second category and obtained little or nothing.

The criticism here of *Ungurian* v *Lesnoff* is based on the following assumptions: first, all the features of an express trust of land should be present apart from writing, and, secondly, an express trust requires existing trust property. There is, we would suggest, ample authority (already referred to in this section) for both these propositions. However, there is also authority discussed in 10.4, in a slightly different context, that identification of existing trust property is not a requirement for a constructive trust (in some of the cases discussed there, the trust crystallised on property which was identified only at a future time). There is limited authority (in particular in Nourse LJ's judgment in *Stokes* v *Anderson* [1991] 1 FLR 391) that similar reasoning can be applied in this area of law, in which case the assumptions made at the start of the paragraph are incorrect; instead we should assume merely that all the features of an express trust of land should be present, apart from writing and identification of existing trust property. The courts in the cases discussed in chapter 11 seem to be quite attracted to the floating trust concept, so the possibility that the law will develop in this direction cannot be ruled out.

By contrast with *Ungurian* v *Lesnoff*, both types of statement (future intent and present irrevocable commitment) were present in *Hammond* v *Mitchell* [1991] 1 WLR 1127, noted at [1992] Conv 218. On its own, Hammond's promise (at p. 1131E): 'Don't worry about the future because when we are married it will be half yours anyway and I'll always look after you and [the boy]'—is a statement of future intent which ought not (subject to the views tentatively advanced in the previous paragraph) to lead to the inference of a trust. However, Hammond also said (at p. 1131D):

I'll have to put the house in my name because I have tax problems due to the fact that my wife burnt all my account books and my caravan was burnt down with all the records of my car sales in it. The tax man would be interested, and if I could prove my money had gone back into a property I'd be safeguarded.

This is similar to the statements in *Eves* v *Eves* [1975] 1 WLR 1338 and *Grant* v *Edwards* [1986] Ch 638, considered above, where a trust analysis is entirely appropriate. In both cases the property was identified, and in *Eves* v *Eves* the statement appears to have been made at the time of purchase, so that the declaration of trust is of existing property. The statement may have been made earlier in *Grant* v *Edwards*, but there is no problem in construing the defendant's intention as continuing until title was conveyed to him, at which point it became irrevocable. This would also therefore be a declaration of trusteeship of existing property.

9.4.3 **Estoppel requirements**

From the above discussion it will be seen that a trusts analysis will not always be appropriate, but this will not necessarily preclude the alternative of an estoppel. Estoppels differ from constructive trusts in a number of significant respects. Whereas a trust is based on an irrevocable commitment, estoppel is based on the notion of A misleading B, and A is prevented from going back on his or her assurances only to the extent necessary to do justice to B. The commonly-accepted formula for proprietary estoppel, adopted by Oliver J in *Taylors Fashions Ltd v Liverpool Victoria Trustees Co. Ltd* [1982] QB 133, at pp. 151H–2A, requires only that 'it would be unconscionable for a party to be permitted to deny that which, knowingly or unknowingly, he has allowed or encouraged another to assume to his detriment', and in *Moorgate Mercantile Co. Ltd* v *Twitchings* [1975] QB 225 Lord Denning MR took the view (at p. 241) that encouragement can be by words or conduct.

In the third edition of this book, it was suggested that this 'is less stringent than the requirements for a declaration of trusteeship. A statement as to future intent will suffice, even where the property is not as yet identified (*Re Basham* [1986] 1 WLR 1498, at pp. 1508–09).' Although it is suggested that this statement is still broadly correct, it cannot stand without qualification, since doubt has since been cast on the width of *Re Basham*. The correctness of some of the remarks in the case has been questioned by two decisions in the Chancery Division in *Taylor* v *Dickens* [1998] 1 FLR 806 and *Gillett* v *Holt* [1998] 2 FLR 1. And although the requirements for estoppels and trusts still require extensive consideration, those for estoppels appear to be more stringent than had been previously thought. In *Taylor* the requirement for unconscionability was re-emphasised, and it was also held that the promises made must be irrevocable. However, nothing in either of these cases suggests that a statement of future intent will not suffice for an estoppel, nor that the property must yet have been identified, as long as the promise is irrevocable and it would be unconscionable to renege upon it.

More recently *Gillett* v *Holt* has gone to the Court of Appeal, and there has also been the decision in *Yaxley* v *Gotts* [2000] 1 All ER 711. The judgment of Robert Walker LJ emphasises the points of commonality between the two, and defends Lord Bridge's articulation of them as interchangeable:

[T]he species of constructive trust based on 'common intention' is established by what Lord Bridge in *Lloyds Bank plc.* v *Rosset* [1991] 1 AC 107, 132, called an 'agreement, arrangement or understanding' actually reached between the parties, and relied on and acted on by the claimant. A constructive trust of that sort is closely akin to, if not indistinguishable from, proprietary estoppel. Equity enforces it because it would be unconscionable for the other party to disregard the claimant's rights.

Gillett v *Holt* [2000] 2 All ER 289 is authority for the proposition that the detriment which is required to give rise to an estoppel, and forms the basis of the remedy which must follow from this (depending on the nature and extent of the detriment) is not a 'narrow or technical concept'. It is instead part of the 'broader enquiry as to whether repudiation of an assurance is or is not unconscionable in all the circumstances'. Indeed, the detriment pointed to does not need to entail fiscal expenditure, nor be represented by 'quantifiable financial detriment', and 'something substantial' will suffice. What the judgment also makes reference to in relation to calibrating proprietary estoppel alongside constructive trusteeship is the Court of

Appeal decision in *Wayling* v *Jones* (1995) 69 P & CR 170, which considered *Re Basham* above. The judgment of Balcombe LJ was cited in respect of the principles pertaining to reliance and detriment, which also drew attention to equation between constructive trusteeship and proprietary estoppel (at p. 173):

(1) There must be a sufficient link between the promises relied upon and the conduct which constitutes the detriment—see *Eves* v *Eves* [1975] 1 WLR 1338, in particular per Brightman J; *Grant* v *Edwards* [1986] Ch 638 . . . *per* Nourse LJ and per Browne-Wilkinson V-C and in particular the passage where he equates the principles applicable in cases of constructive trust to those of proprietary estoppel. (2) The promises relied upon do not have to be the sole inducement for the conduct: it is sufficient if they are an inducement—*Amalgamated Property Co.* v *Texas Bank* [1982] QB 84 . . . (3) Once it has been established that promises were made, and that there has been conduct by the plaintiff of such a nature that inducement may be inferred then the burden of proof shifts to the defendants to establish that he did not rely on the promises—*Greasley* v *Cooke* [1980] 1 WLR 1306; *Grant* v *Edwards* . . .

However, *Yaxley* v *Gotts* also harbours reference to the way in which regard must be had to important differences which nevertheless remain for critical consideration. Such ideas are discussed in reference made to 'those cases in which a supposed bargain has been so fully performed by one side'. The significance of such cases can be found in the way in which 'the general circumstances of the matter are such, that it would be inequitable to disregard the claimant's expectations, and insufficient to grant him no more than a restitutionary remedy'. This points to important differences which are visible in terms of the outcome which the two mechanisms deliver. It reveals that the extent of the equity awarded depends on the circumstances of the case, and will be the minimum necessary to achieve justice.

Shared homes, agreement, and Yaxley v Gotts and Gillett v Holt
While neither of these decisions arose directly in the context of disputed home ownership, both did engage in extensive discussion of the 'shared homes' authorities. The influence that these cases might bring to bear in the sphere of beneficial ownership (as distinct from their authority for consideration of the differences and similarities between the concepts of estoppel and constructive trust) can be found below.

The quantification of B's interest is considered in greater detail below, but it will not always be the same for estoppels as for constructive trusts. The main difference between the two, however, is in the extent to which they can affect third parties. This is especially a problem where a mortgagee is involved since, as Ferguson states (1993, at p. 122), 'the consensus of opinion favours' the view that estoppels do not bind third parties, at any rate until the extent of the interest has been crystallised by a court. The consensus is by no means unchallenged, and Morritt LJ took a different view in *Lloyds Bank plc* v *Carrick* [1996] 4 All ER 630, but this has been considered in greater detail elsewhere: Glover and Todd [1995] 5 Web JCLI.

9.5 Further consideration of *Lloyds Bank* v *Rosset*

The essence of this section is to consider *Lloyds Bank* v *Rosset* further, working from its status as the clearest statement of law in this very important sphere of ascertaining beneficial entitlements to family homes. It will consider how much *Rosset* has clarified the law, and important questions which remain in its wake.

9.5.1 **Category 1 *Rosset* cases: trust or estoppel? (*Yaxley* v *Gotts* and *Gillett* v *Holt*)**

This postscript considers the attention drawn to the principles of constructive trust and proprietary estoppel in Lord Bridge's speech in *Lloyds Bank* v *Rosset* [1991], in reference to the outcomes of agreements made in relation to shared homes. The presence of an agreement does of course establish the case as a 'category 1' Rosset one, and once an agreement to share the home has been found, an interest in it can, according to Lord Bridge, arise on account of either a constructive trust or proprietary estoppel. This was of course this chapter's substantive starting point, before we proceeded to illuminate the workings of both principles, highlighting their similarities and differences, and posing questions about the appropriateness of Lord Bridge's reference to them as interchangeable. In addition, this was couched with reference to the way in which the law had actually developed, as distinct from the way in which Lord Bridge suggested it could.

This highlighted the way in which, notwithstanding the availability of both constructive trust and proprietary estoppel mechanisms to resolve disputes where there was evidence of agreement, in practice the courts were consistently showing preference post *Rosset* favouring the constructive trust—rather than proprietary estoppel—route. The text also emphasised that one important exception to this came in 1993 in the decision in *Baker* v *Baker* (1993) 25 HLR 408 which, shortly after *Rosset* could have hailed a different direction. As the law has developed, *Baker* did not signal such a movement, but it did highlight the stark contrasts in the two mechanisms, evident in the interest which was awarded to the claimant, and firmly rooted in estoppel's approach of the 'minimum (equity) to achieve justice'. Based on this mantra, reliance was obviously key to demonstrating an entitlement to an interest, but the extent of the claimant's reliance also determined the size of the interest.

Thereafter, the courts have continued to favour the trust mechanism. In this scenario, in reliance on an 'agreement' which the parties are deemed to have reached, a constructive trust is invoked, which is exempt from normal formality requirements for trusts of land. And, in contrast with the estoppel approach, a presumption of equal share was the starting point for determining quantification.

Support for this approach is by no means universal, however, and this chapter has shown how a great deal in terms of entitlement can turn on very little. Here, the two recent decisions *Yaxley* v *Gotts* [2000] 1 All ER 711 and *Gillett* v *Holt* of the Court of Appeal may trigger a rethinking of the courts' approach to giving effect to agreements reached between parties. The cases both point to the way in which the detriment acts as the 'measure' for the most appropriate remedy to be meted, which will depend on the circumstances present, but they also point to the proposition (*per* Robert Walker in *Yaxley*) that the 'two doctrines sometimes overlap'. Robert Walker LJ's judgment continues to explain that, at a high level of generality, there is much common ground between the doctrines of proprietary estoppel and the constructive trust. This is evident through the concepts' shared concern with equity's intervention to provide relief against unconscionable conduct, in a variety of commercial and domestic situations. And, in the area of a joint enterprise for the acquisition of land (which may be, but is not necessarily, the matrimonial home) the two would coincide (citing Lord Diplock in *Gissing* v *Gissing* as authority for this proposition).

Reference was also made to Sir Nicolas Browne-Wilkinson V-C in *Grant* v *Edwards* (at p. 656) who stated that:

I suggest that in other cases of this kind, useful guidance may in the future be obtained from the principles underlying the law of proprietary estoppel which in my judgment are closely akin to those laid down in *Gissing* v *Gissing* [1971] AC 886. In both, the claimant must to the knowledge of the legal owner have acted in the belief that the claimant has or will obtain an interest in the property. In both, the claimant must have acted to his or her detriment in reliance on such belief. In both, equity acts on the conscience of the legal owner to prevent him from acting in an unconscionable manner by defeating the common intention. The two principles have been developed separately without cross-fertilisation between them: but they rest on the same foundation and have on all other matters reached the same conclusions.

While neither *Yaxley* nor *Gillett* arose directly in the context of disputed home ownership, it is nevertheless still possible that, against a backdrop of criticism of the current state of the law, these decisions might become influential cases directly arising from shared home ownership. In this respect they might well have triggered a reassessment of the use being made of the constructive trust and a reconsideration of it more critically alongside (a more stringent approach to?) proprietary estoppel in terms of the share which is ultimately awarded to the claimant. This trend is now strongly evident in light of *Oxley*.

9.5.2 Exact scope of second category

Reference has already been made to the way in which certain types of contribution are incapable of giving rise to the inference necessary to create a trust. It is also clear that direct contributions to the purchase price will give rise to the necessary inference. There are, however, grey areas, such as indirect financial contributions and improvements to the property.

In the passage from *Lloyds Bank* v *Rosset* already quoted, Lord Bridge observes that:

. . . direct contributions to the purchase price by the partner who is not the legal owner, whether initially or by payment of mortgage instalments, will readily justify the inference necessary to the creation of a constructive trust. But, as I read the authorities, it is at least extremely doubtful whether anything less will do.

This passage, which is not part of the *ratio* of the case, may appear at first sight clearly to state what is, and what is not, within the second category; but not only does Lord Bridge not analyse the authorities to which he refers, but he is not absolutely ruling out a lesser contribution. Other authorities (and in particular statements by Fox and May LJJ in *Burns* v *Burns* [1984] Ch 317) suggest that indirect financial contributions, referable to the acquisition of the property will also suffice. The following passage is taken from Fox LJ's judgment in *Burns* v *Burns*, at p. 327:

What is needed, I think, is evidence of a payment or payments by the plaintiff which it can be inferred was referable to the acquisition of the house . . . If there is a substantial contribution by the woman to the family expenses, and the house was purchased on a mortgage, her contribution is, indirectly, referable to the acquisition of the house since, in one way or another, it enables the family to pay the mortgage instalments. Thus, a payment could be said to be referable to the acquisition of the house if, for example, the payer either (a) pays part of the purchase price or (b) contributes regularly to the mortgage instalments or (c) pays off part of the mortgage or (d) makes a substantial financial contribution to the family expenses so as to enable the mortgage instalments to be paid.

This is obviously wider than Lord Bridge's view, in that Lord Bridge would not recognise category (d) as justifying the inference necessary for the creation of a trust. Lord Bridge does not however make clear whether his intention is to alter the law or merely to re-state it, a point made by Patricia Ferguson (1993) 109 LQR 114, at p. 116:

[Lord Bridge's] requirement of 'direct contributions' where there is no express agreement runs contrary to previous authorities which held that indirect financial contributions which were 'referable to the acquisition of the house'—such as F's payment of all household expenses to free M's income for mortgage instalments—were sufficient. It is difficult to know . . . whether he intends to depart from this view of the law or not.

Contributions, Lloyds Bank v Rosset and 'improvements' to the home

Another area on which *Lloyds Bank* v *Rosset* is inconclusive (indeed silent) is that of improvements by Miss B to Mr A's property.

Where authorities conflict (as in the case of Fox LJ's category (d)), or are silent (as in the case of improvements), it is necessary to examine the juristic basis of the category and deduce from that what should be included and what should not.

It is clear from earlier discussions that where Miss B provides cash contributions to the purchase price, the interest that she obtains can be explained in resulting trust terms. It does not matter where the money comes from, so that if, for example, she obtains the money by accepting liability to repay a mortgage debt, the entire capital liability can be explained in resulting trust terms. It is not possible, however, to explain the whole of the second category in this way. It is also noteworthy that Lord Bridge's analysis in the above passage is in constructive, rather than resulting, trust terms.

Contributions, mortgage payments and difficulties with the resulting trusts analysis

Thus, even on Lord Bridge's view, payment of mortgage instalments (and not merely undertaking liability to repay the mortgage) counts, but there are serious difficulties in analysing these in resulting trust terms. For example, where Miss B pays the instalment to Mr A, Miss B might be presumed to retain beneficial title to the money, which will be converted into an interest in the property as each mortgage instalment is made by A. This would result in the undesirable situation where the extent of B's interest alters every month, but in any event, the explanation works only where B pays the instalment to A, who then pays it to the mortgagee. If both parties pay the instalments directly to the mortgagee, then it is impossible to devise a resulting trust mechanism.

There is also Court of Appeal authority, which nobody has seriously doubted, that Miss B can obtain an interest even if her contribution is in the form of a discount from the purchase price, rather than an actual cash payment. In *Springette* v *Defoe* [1992] 2 FCR 561, in assessing the size of her share the Court of Appeal took into account Springette's 41 per cent discount, attributable to her council tenancy under a 'right to buy' scheme. Although the Court purported to adopt a resulting trust analysis, it is difficult to see how Springette settled anything. In *Springette* v *Defoe*, her discount arose from a legal chose in action enforceable against the council, and it might be possible to argue that she had transferred the bare legal title to the chose in action; but even this could not explain *Marsh* v *Von Sternberg* [1986] 1 FLR 526, where the discount depended on increased bargaining power as a statutory tenant under the Rent Act 1974, and did not arise from a cause of action at all. It follows that resulting trust reasoning cannot explain the discount cases.

So the resulting trust adequately explains neither mortgage repayments nor discounts from the purchase price, both of which are generally accepted as falling under the second category. Let us first consider mortgage repayments, aided by the following example. A and B purchase a house, paying a 10 per cent deposit and obtaining a mortgage advance of 90 per cent, repayable over 25 years. Let us assume also that the mortgage is an ordinary repayment mortgage, where the monthly repayments are made up partly of income and partly of capital. A and B share the deposit, paying 5 per cent each. The house is conveyed into A's name alone, and A undertakes liability to repay the mortgage, perhaps because A is earning and B is not. For the next five years, the parties live together happily, with A and B sharing the mortgage repayments, half and half. The relationship then terminates, the house is to be sold, and the issue arises as to the extent of B's interest. Even if a resulting trust mechanism can be made to work at all, certainly no more than a fifth of the mortgage will have been repaid, probably less, since interest always claims a higher proportion of early payments. It is unlikely, in fact, that the total payments, including the deposit, will amount to more than about 20 per cent of the total at this stage, B's contribution therefore amounts to a mere 10 per cent. A resulting trust analysis (if it could be made to work) would give her 10 per cent. Yet all the indications here are that the couple intended to share on a 50:50 basis, and if the house has increased in value, for B to be awarded only 10 per cent would constitute a tremendous windfall for A. Surely a better analysis is, as Fox LJ observed in *Burns* v *Burns* (at p. 327D), that 'subsequent events may throw light on the initial intention'. Lord Diplock in *Gissing* v *Gissing* also thought that 'what [the parties] said and did after the acquisition was completed is relevant if it is explicable only on the basis of their having manifested to one another at the time of the acquisition some particular common intention as to how the beneficial interests should be held.' Surely, therefore, this is the correct analysis of the situation here. The parties' behaviour is explicable only on the basis that from the start they intended to share 50:50; the mortgage repayments are actually performing exactly the same role as the discussions in first category cases.

A similar analysis of discounts can be found in Staughton LJ's judgment in *Evans* v *Hayward* [1995] 2 FCR 313, at p. 319D:

> . . . I do consider that the facts as to the existence of a discount and the source from which it is derived must be taken into account, and are capable of leading to the inference that the parties have made an agreement as to how the purchase price is provided.

In other words, the discount leads to the inference that the parties made an agreement, at the time of acquisition, that they are to be treated as having provided the purchase price in proportions which take into account the discount. Conceptually, this is far closer to the analysis we have already seen, in the first category, than it is to the resulting trust. Notice also that in both the mortgage repayment and discount cases, it is the payments themselves which give rise to the inference as to intention; no further evidence of intention is required since, after all, what other inference could you reasonably draw from payments of this type?

Resulting trust: 'discount' cases and repayments on other grounds
Once it is accepted that the true explanation of the discount cases, and of mortgage repayments, is in terms of an inferred agreement, and does not depend on a resulting trust, then we can see that similar reasoning can also apply to the non-financial contributions mentioned in *Burns*. In principle, therefore, it may seem that there is no particular reason to prefer Lord Bridge's views to those of Fox LJ. However, the requirements of the second category are that B's interest can be inferred from the contributions alone, in the absence of other evidence of an agreement to share. Whereas in the discount and mortgage repayment cases this inference can be made automatically, nothing in *Burns* v *Burns* suggests that any automatic inference should be drawn from indirect contributions. They could lead to many different types of inference, depending on the other evidence available. In terms of the categorisation in *Lloyds Bank* v *Rosset*, therefore, indirect financial contributions are not correctly placed in the second category, since the court cannot rely entirely on the conduct of the parties to infer A's intention. Nor do these contributions fit happily into the first category, since there may be no evidence of express discussions between the parties.

If Lord Bridge's categories are exhaustive, therefore, indirect financial contributions cannot create an interest outside the first category. In principle, however, surely such contributions should nevertheless be capable of being taken into account in inferring A's intention; to refuse to do so is to place artificial constraints on the evidence that will be accepted.

The same arguments can be used in the case of capital improvements. It is difficult to see why they should be ruled out, but it is clear that no automatic inference can be drawn, since all sorts of inferences can be reached in the absence of further evidence. Clearly, if Miss B improves Mr A's property without his permission, B should not obtain an interest in that property (*Ramsden* v *Dyson* (1866) LR 1 HL 129). Even if A gives permission, or acquiesces, a possible inference is that B makes a gift of the work. This was the view taken by the House of Lords in *Pettitt* v *Pettitt* [1970] AC 777 (see 8.4.1), where the husband as improver failed to obtain an interest in his wife's property. A stronger case is *Thomas* v *Fuller-Brown* [1988] 1 FLR 237, where the Court of Appeal held that a man had no interest in the house in which he lived with a woman (who had legal title), although in the view of Slade LJ (at p. 240):

[The work he did] was obviously quite substantial . . . *inter alia*, he designed and constructed a two-storey extension, created a through lounge, carried out minor electrical and plumbing works, replastered and redecorated the property throughout, landscaped and reorganised the garden, laid a driveway, carried out repairs to the chimney and the roof and repointed the gable end of the property, constructed an internal entry hall at the property, rebuilt the kitchen and installed a new stairway.

Again, however, the inference must have been that he intended to make a gift of his work.

It does not necessarily follow that this will always be the inference, however. Another possibility is an implied contract for reimbursement of the value of the work done, a solution which was apparently adopted by the Court of Appeal in

Huntingford v *Hobbs* [1993] 1 FCR 45 (see 8.4.1) in respect of the money spent on the conservatory. Another possibility would be to give Miss B an estoppel interest, as was envisaged by Lord Oliver of Aylmerton in *Austin* v *Keele* (1987) 61 AJLR 605, at p. 609. He also drew another distinction, between capital improvements and the other types of contribution, which clearly fall within the second category, observing that there is no reason why the interest should be acquired at the time of acquisition of the property.

There is indeed no reason in principle why a full beneficial interest might not be inferred, either from the time of acquisition or from a later date, an approach contemplated by Lord Reid in *Pettitt* v *Pettitt* [1970] AC 777, at pp. 794–5. Although, as we have seen, he rejected Pettitt's claim to a beneficial interest, this was solely on the ground that his improvements were of an ephemeral character and that it would be unreasonable for him to obtain a permanent interest in the house in return for making improvements of this nature: at p. 796E. Other views expressed in *Pettitt* are more equivocal, particularly that of Lord Upjohn (whose views were expressly adopted by the Court of Appeal in *Thomas* v *Fuller-Brown*). However, an inference that improvements to the property could give rise to a beneficial interest was actually adopted by Karminski LJ in *Cooke* v *Head* [1972] 1 WLR 518, where Miss Cooke, who had contributed only about one-twelfth of the purchase price, was nevertheless granted a third share, one of the factors in assessing Miss Cooke's share (from acquisition) being the value of her labour, and by the majority of the Court of Appeal in *Hussey* v *Palmer* [1972] 1 WLR 1286 where the inference here must have been a declaration of trust by Mr A post-acquisition. It cannot be said, therefore, that improvements to property can never give rise to the inference of a trust.

However, it follows from so many different approaches being possible that although the work may provide relevant evidence of intention, it cannot be conclusive, and that the approach which is adopted will depend on all the facts of the case. As with indirect contributions, to rule out entirely this type of contribution would seem to be an unnecessary and artificial limitation.

9.5.3 **Communication requirements: first category**

For the first category, Lord Bridge stated that 'The finding of an agreement or arrangement to share in this sense can only, I think, be based on evidence of express discussions between the partners, however imperfectly remembered and however imprecise their terms may have been.' A similar view was adopted by the Court of Appeal in *Springette* v *Defoe* (1992) 24 HLR 552, [1992] 2 FCR 561 (see further above). There Miss Springette and Mr Defoe purchased a house, Miss Springette being able to obtain a 41 per cent discount under a 'right to buy' scheme under Part V of the Housing Act 1985, the discount being based on her 11 years as a tenant. The property was conveyed into joint names, there being no declaration of trust in the transfer, and both were liable to repay the mortgage instalments, and in fact both contributed equally to the repayments. Both Springette and Defoe also provided other moneys, the result being that, taking into account her 41 per cent discount, Miss Springette's financial contributions were about 75 per cent, and Mr Defoe's 25 per cent.

Silences in parties' communications: who benefits?
The relationship broke down and proceedings were commenced to determine the respective beneficial interests of the parties. Miss Springette claimed a 75 per cent share on the basis of her financial contributions, whereas Mr Defoe claimed 50 per cent on the basis that the couple understood that they were to share the property equally. Mr Defoe claimed that the case should be decided on the basis of the first category in *Lloyds Bank plc* v *Rosset*.

The Court of Appeal held in Miss Springette's favour, applying Lord Bridge's remarks in *Rosset* that the finding of such an agreement, arrangement or understanding could only be based on evidence of express discussions between the partners. Steyn LJ observed that '[o]ur trust law does not allow property rights to be affected by telepathy. *prima facie*, therefore, the alleged actual common intention was not established' ((1992) 24 HLR 552, at p. 558).

Springette v *Defoe* was distinguished in *Savill* v *Goodall* [1993] 1 FLR 755. Mrs Goodall was entitled to a 42 per cent discount under a 'right to buy' scheme, the entirety of the remainder of the purchase money being raised on a mortgage for which Mr Savill accepted liability to repay. As in *Springette* v *Defoe*, the property was transferred into the joint names of the parties. The Court of Appeal held, on the basis of express discussions between the parties, that the beneficial interests should be divided equally, but also accepted that Mr Savill's *quid pro quo* for being granted a beneficial interest was his agreement to repay the mortgage capital and costs of redemption. The net proceeds, after repayment of the mortgage by him, were therefore divided equally.

The only substantive difference between *Springette* v *Defoe* and *Savill* v *Goodall* was the absence of any discussion in the former and its presence in the latter case.

In *Midland Bank plc* v *Cooke* [1995] 4 All ER 562, however, Waite LJ did not regard *Springette* v *Defoe* as laying down any general principle, for the following reasons: that Dillon LJ, who had given the leading judgment in *Springette* v *Defoe*, had taken a very different approach in *McHardy & Sons* v *Warren* [1994] 2 FLR 338; that no such requirement for express discussion could be gleaned from *Gissing* v *Gissing* [1971] AC 886 or *Grant* v *Edwards* [1986] 1 Ch 638; and that the couple in *Springette* v *Defoe* were 'a middle aged couple already established in life whose house-purchasing arrangements were clearly regarded by the Court as having the same formality as if they had been the subject of a joint venture or commercial partnership'.

If Waite LJ is correct, we can no longer assume that the presence or absence of discussions will be decisive. In principle, however, it is not easy to see how a declaration of trusteeship can occur without at least some form of communication (there was none at all in *Midland Bank* v *Cooke*). In any case, in order to render it fraudulent for Mr A to deny the existence of the trust, Miss B must rely on the declaration, or significantly alter her position. Again, this necessitates communication between the parties, and is again a justification for the requirement for discussion. There are also certainty arguments for requiring communication. Waite J's decision in *Hammond* v *Mitchell* [1991] 1 WLR 1127 shows how much can turn on A's declaration of trusteeship: Vicky Mitchell obtained a half share under the first category in *Lloyds Bank plc* v *Rosset*, having contributed nothing at all to the house itself, solely because of statements that had been made to her by Hammond. Any beneficial interest thereby created will also bind third parties. It should also be borne in mind that a declaration of trusteeship constitutes an irrevocable and onerous commitment. Prior to an act of commitment, it ought to be possible for A to change his or her mind, however much, at that time, he or she is determined to become a trustee. It is not unreasonable to require the act of commitment to be in some sense public, or at any rate to be communicated to the other party.

There is nothing in the *Springette* v *Defoe* line of cases to indicate what needs to be communicated. It follows from the above that Mr A needs to communicate something which leads Miss B to suppose that A is making an immediate and irrevocable commitment, whether or not this is A's actual intention (see the discussion of Gardner, above at 8.5.2). But in *Re Kayford Ltd* [1975] 1 WLR 279 (see 8.5.2), Megarry J required only that the intention to declare oneself trustee be manifested. While detrimental reliance requires some form of communication, it may not necessarily require words. If the evidence showed that the parties really were capable of communicating by telepathy, there is no obvious reason why the law should not allow this method of communication to be used to create beneficial interests within this category.

In *Savill* v *Goodall*, the Court of Appeal distinguished *Springette* v *Defoe* on the basis that there were discussions in the later case. The Court did not pay particular regard to the nature of the discussions, however, and it is surprising, we would suggest, that they led to the inference of a beneficial interest. The content of the discussions was tenuous, and certainly there was no substantial discussion of beneficial interests in the property. We would suggest, therefore, that there were no obvious grounds for distinguishing *Springette* v *Defoe*, and that the case was incorrectly decided.

The requirement in *Lloyds Bank* v *Rosset* (at p. 132F) was for evidence of express discussions, not express evidence of discussions. This suggests that inferred evidence of discussions ought to be sufficient, and indeed, in *Gissing* v *Gissing* Lord Diplock suggested (at p. 906A) that the parties' intentions could be inferred from their conduct, even in the absence of express words. No doubt is thereby cast on the correctness of *Springette* v *Defoe*, where there was no evidence at all of discussions.

All of the above applies a trust analysis. The commonly-accepted formula for proprietary estoppel, adopted by Oliver J in *Taylors Fashions Ltd* v *Liverpool Victoria Trustees Co. Ltd* [1982] QB 133, at pp. 151H–2A, requires only that 'it would be unconscionable for a party to be permitted to deny that which, knowingly or unknowingly, he has allowed or encouraged another to assume to his detriment'. There is no express communication requirement in this formula, and there is authority for the proposition that encouragement can be by words or conduct: e.g., *Moorgate Mercantile Co. Ltd* v *Twitchings* [1975] QB 225, *per* Lord Denning MR at p. 241.

Indeed, it is universally accepted that Oliver J's formulation is intended to broaden the definition of estoppel, and there is no doubt that it still suffices to satisfy Fry J's five *probanda* from *Willmott* v *Barber* (1880) 15 Ch D 96, at pp. 105–6, recently applied by Roch LJ in *Matharu* v *Matharu* (1994) 26 HLR 648, at pp. 656–7. Fry J's fifth element, encouragement of B in the expenditure of money, or in other acts, can be satisfied by A merely abstaining from asserting a legal right. A can therefore be estopped, in theory, having taken no positive acts to communicate at all. So although in many cases communication will be necessary to establish an estoppel, we cannot assert that it will be necessary in every case. It will, however, remain necessary to establish reliance by Miss B to her detriment.

To conclude, then: for a trust to arise there must be communication between the parties, but the requirement for express discussion may be too stringent. Any form of communication which is fully understood by both parties ought to suffice. It should not be necessary to use express words. To allow a complete lack of communication, however, as in *Midland Bank* v *Cooke*, seems impossible to justify, especially as it was common ground that there had been no discussions between the parties. For an estoppel, it is possible, albeit exceptionally, to envisage circumstances where the communication requirement is unnecessary, but there still has to be reliance by the representee to her detriment.

9.6 Quantification

In *Lloyds Bank plc* v *Rosset*, Lord Bridge set out the two methods where the person without legal title could acquire a beneficial interest, and traditionally this text has proposed that these remarks did not expressly address the issue of quantification because in *Rosset* itself, Mrs Rosset failed to establish an interest in the property. Thus, the analysis given on quantification in this text has always proceeded by reference to the *dicta* in *Rosset* and first principles drawn from pre-*Rosset* case law and also general understandings of trusts law and its operations. This has in turn been applied to cases deemed to be category 2 and category 1 respectively.

9.6.1 Quantification and *Rosset* Category 2

This has always commenced with a consideration of the way in which, on the reasoning proposed in this chapter, on the applications of ordinary trusts law, for cases analysed as *Rosset* Category 2:

- The decision in *Huntingford* v *Hobbs* [1993] 1 FCR 45 is authority for the proposition that (in the words of presiding Sir Christopher Slade):

In the absence of any declaration of trust, the parties' respective beneficial interests in the property fall to be determined not by reference to any broad concepts of justice, but by reference to the principles governing the creation or operation of resulting, implied or constructive trusts which by section 53(2) of the Law of Property Act 1925 are exempted from the general requirements of writing imposed by section 53(1).

This approach is founded on the proposition that a non-legal owner retains the equitable interest in her contribution, and is hence entitled to a share in the house which will be in proportion to her contribution. It has been suggested that this analysis can be applied even in situations where resulting trust reasoning is inappropriate, such as in the discount cases like *Springette* v *Defoe*, and the payment of mortgage instalments: here the contributions are the only evidence for her share, and the courts again calculate shares in proportion to the contributions.

- This 'strict property' approach was departed from in *Midland Bank plc* v *Cooke* [1995] 4 All ER 562.

In this case, Mrs Cooke was granted a half share in the property, although she had contributed only 6.47 per cent of the purchase price, and there were no discussions about beneficial interests. The case provided early authority for a 'broad brush' approach to quantification, once the existence of the beneficial interest has been established (on the basis of actual contributions made), to account for the 43.53 per cent share she received with no declaration of trust in her favour.

• Continuing the pattern set in motion by *Midland Bank v Cooke*.

Midland Bank v *Cooke*'s approach to quantification continued in *Le Foe* v *Le Foe* [2001] 2 FLR 970, in which Nicholas Mostyn QC held that the wife had a 50 per cent share in the home because of her indirect contributions to the mortgage, which revealed an intention that she should have an interest. And, taking into account all the circumstances of the case (including her much later, and substantial) capital contributions, this share should be quantified as one half.

Nicholas Mostyn determined that the family economy had depended on the contributions which she had made and that the division of the financial responsibilities between the spouses was an arbitrary one. He went on to observe that he did not believe Lord Bridge (in *Lloyds Bank v Rosset*) to have intended to exclude such financial arrangements from succeeding in raising an interest under the second limb of *Rosset*. He relied on *dicta* from *Gissing* v *Gissing* and *Burns* v *Burns* in support of the view that such indirect contributions might provide grounds for inferring an intention to share beneficial interest in shared homes. Were the law otherwise (at p. 982) '. . . these cases would be decided by reference to mere accidents of fortune, being the arbitrary allocation of financial responsibilities as between the parties', and the distinction which cases post-*Rosset* made between direct and indirect contributions 'appear more unjust and arbitrary than ever'.

9.6.2 **Quantification and *Rosset* Category 1**

In respect of *Rosset* category 1 cases, the following observations were made:

• Quantification is measured by a declaration of trust, not on reliance.

Applying a trusts analysis to this type of case, quantification should be determined from the declaration of trust, or in other words from the discussions or representation (with contributions being relevant only to s. 53(1)(b), and not to quantification itself). This can be seen in cases such as *Hammond v Mitchell* [1991] 1 WLR 1127, which itself followed *Grant v Edwards* [1986] 1 Ch 638. See also *Gissing* v *Gissing*.

• Quantification to be fixed at some point in the future.

There are other cases where there is a declaration of trust, but shares are not determined by this, and this question is to be settled at some point in the future (and possibly even depending upon the extent of contributions made). Thus, in cases like *Stokes v Anderson* [1991] 1 FLR 391 and (probably) *Passee v Passee* [1988] 1 FLR 263 a non-legal owner's contributions will be relevant to her share, but only because the parties have so agreed from the outset.

• The possibility that *no* share can be inferred from A's declaration.

In *Grant* v *Edwards* the Court of Appeal presumed a half share, but the presumption can be rebutted in appropriate circumstances. A quarter share was awarded in *Eves* v *Eves*, but it is difficult to discern why the presumption was rebutted in that case.

- The application of 'broad brush' approaches to quantification in Category 1 cases.

In *Drake* v *Whipp* [1996] 1 FLR 826, Mrs Drake was awarded a third share. Peter Gibson LJ observing that 'in constructive trust cases, the court can adopt a "broad brush" approach to determining the parties' respective shares'. This appears similar to the reasoning in *Midland Bank* v *Cooke*, discussed above, and is subject to the same criticisms on a trusts analysis. In *Drake* v *Whipp*, however, Whipp's intention was not clear from his declaration, and Mrs Drake's share appears to have been determined from all the evidence, including the respective contributions of the parties. Since she had never claimed more than a 40 per cent share, it would clearly have been reasonable to rebut the half share presumption in the light of contrary evidence. The parties' entire course of conduct together was considered relevant, and maybe this can be justified on an analysis similar to that in *Stokes* v *Anderson* above, in which case *Drake* v *Whipp* broke no new ground.

- Quantification on an estoppel reasoning rather than a trusts analysis.

In this scenario, it has been suggested that the quantification of B's interest may not depend on the representation which is made alone, but also on the extent of reliance which was placed upon it by the other party. In these circumstances A's representation is undoubtedly relevant in that B cannot get more than was contemplated by the parties: see, for example, *Baker* v *Baker* (1993) 25 HLR 408. However, while B's entitlement cannot be more than would be accorded on the basis of A's representation, it can certainly be less, as in *Dodsworth* v *Dodsworth* (1973) 228 EG 1115, and in principle there seems no reason why in satisfying the equity it would be inappropriate to consider the extent of B's reliance.

9.6.3 *Oxley* v *Hiscock*, and assessing the current state of play in law and policy

Before considering the decision in *Oxley* v *Hiscock* and its possible implications, reference will be made to two distinct but closely related trends of which *Oxley* might be seen as a culmination. They are respectively apparent continuing judicial favour for an estoppel-based approach to disputed home ownership, and movement away from drawing strict distinctions between the two categories in *Rosset*.

Current patterns and preferences in judicial approaches

- Continuing preference for proprietary estoppel approach to quantification of beneficial interests.

A number of recent cases have pointed to the courts' adoption of an estoppel-based approach to resolving disputes in home ownership; for example *Gillett* v *Holt* and *Yaxley* v *Gotts* have both been noted above. Interests in property were awarded in both *Campbell* v *Griffin* [2001] WTLR, 981 and *Jennings* v *Rice* [2003] 1 P & CR, 8 with the Court of Appeal reversing the first instance decision in the former, and affirming the initial decision in the latter. Both these cases were determined on the basis that some assurances were given and the claimant in each case relied to their detriment upon this: and, in *Jennings* Aldous LJ suggested the approach which was adopted was discretionary but was made to achieve a proportionate solution with due regard to the nature of expectation.

In *Ottey* v *Grundy* [2003] WTLR 1253, the test adopted to establish detrimental reliance was held (in the words of Arden LJ) not to be that 'the claimant would have left the maker of the assurance if the promise had not been made, but only that he would have left the maker of the assurance if the promise had been withdrawn'. This was the test adopted in *Wayling* v *Jones* (1995) 69 P & CR 170. Under *Wayling*, once the claimant shows that a promise was made, the burden of proof falls upon the maker to show that the claimant did not, in fact, rely on the promise. Upon determining this, *Jennings* v *Rice* could be applied to satisfy the equity. *Jennings* affirms that in this manner, questions of relief are approached with caution, and amounts to the minimum equity to do justice, and this must also be proportionate to the detriment.

All these cases point to achieving justice to the parties and a remedy which is pro-portionate to the determinant which has been suffered. They all thus point to estoppel as a rounded approach which seeks a remedy which is appropriate in all the circumstances. The decision in *Ottey* made reference to the earlier decision in *Re Basham* [1987] 1 All ER 405 in which it was suggested that:

... the purpose of proprietary estoppel is not to enforce an obligation which does not amount to a contract nor yet to reverse the detriment which the claimant has suffered but to grant an appropriate remedy in respect of unconscionable conduct.

In this vein it was suggested in *Ottey* v *Grundy* itself that estoppel is a remedy 'in the round' and which does not only have regard to financial detriment and benefit. According to Arden LJ:

It is common ground that proprietary estoppel can arise where an owner of property encour-ages another to rely to his detriment in the belief that he will obtain an interest in that prop-erty. The underlying rationale is that it would be unconscionable for the maker of the assurance not to give effect to his promise. The matter must be looked at in the round.

- Continuing blurring of distinction between category 1 and category 2 cases.

Previous editions of this textbook have always been critical of the decision in *Midland Bank* v *Cooke* notwithstanding its apparent connotations of fairness, and also despite its favour in the courts in decisions like *Le Foe*, and evident support for approaches which emphasise fairness in 'policy' discourses. The objections which have been made to *Cooke* in this text have suggested that while providing solutions which are fair and just is a laudable pursuit, that 'broad brush' approaches to quantification also encourage uncertainty and arbitrariness in determinations of valuable property interests. Fundamentally, it has also been maintained that *Midland Bank* v *Cooke* undermines *Rosset* and the trusts analysis at the heart of cases where there is no evidence of an agreement between the parties to share a family home beneficially. Equally, as the 'broad brush' approach to quantification has become infiltrated into category 1 cases where there is evidence of agreement, a number of commentators have suggested that the cases of *Midland Bank* v *Cooke* and

Drake v *Whipp* are difficult to reconcile: indeed, in these two cases, a smaller contribution in the former gave rise to a larger interest, in absence of independent evidence of an agreement to share property beneficially.

It has of course been suggested that *Drake* v *Whipp* can be explained on reasoning flowing from *Stokes* v *Anderson*, and thus, this text is not unduly concerned with the decision. However, a number of more recent cases are appearing to suggest that the courts are becoming less concerned with at least *some* of the aspects which, for Lord Bridge in *Rosset*, distinguished category 1 cases from those found to be category 2. After *Oxley*, the courts continue to emphasise the need to find an agreement to share in order to establish a claim in equity, but the probable significance of this distinction for the remedy awarded (namely the size of the beneficial interest awarded) is now much less certain. In this vein, reference to 'probable' significance *Rosset* continues to be emphasised because, as it was observed above, in *Rosset* itself no interest was found to subsist, and so the issue of quantification did not arise.

The decision in *Oxley* v *Hiscock*

Oxley concerned a home shared by the claimant and her former partner the defendant. Initially the parties lived in a council house occupied by the claimant and her children from a former marriage, and in September 1987 the claimant exercised her right to buy the council property, and the purchase was funded by the defendant from proceeds of the sale of his property. In 1991 a larger house (the disputed property) was purchased using £61,500 represented by the proceeds of sale from the original former council house and by a further contribution of £35,500 from the defendant, and a mortgage loan of £30,000. The new property was registered in the defendant's name, notwithstanding the claimant had been advised by her solicitor to protect her interest through joint registration. Thereafter both parties contributed towards the maintenance and improvement of the property, and pooled resources more generally in the belief that each had a beneficial interest. By 2001 the mortgage had been paid off, but the relationship between the parties had broken down and the home sold.

The claimant sought a declaration that the proceeds of sale of the property were held on trust for both parties in equal shares. At first instance it was found that in absence of express agreement, both parties had evinced an intention to share benefits and burdens of the property jointly and equally, declaring the claimant was entitled to a half share of the proceeds of sale. On appeal the defendant claimed that because there had been no discussion about the parties' respective beneficial interests at the time of the purchase, the presumption of a resulting trust was not displaced and the property was thus held on trust for both parties, but in beneficial shares proportionate to their contributions. In concluding that an agreement to share the property beneficially *could* be found, Chadwick LJ nevertheless insisted that 'it does not follow from the fact that the parties live together in a house they both regard as their home that they share the ownership of that house equally'. In ordering a 40 per cent–60 per cent share in favour of the defendant in absence of 'evidence of any discussion between the parties as to the amount of the share each was to have' Chadwick LJ suggested that declaring that the parties were entitled in equal shares would be 'unfair to Mr Hiscock'. This was so notwithstanding the 'classic pooling of resources' by the couple found by the judge at first instance, and was founded upon Hiscock's contribution of £60,000 being significantly greater than the £36,500 made by Oxley (with the couple being treated as having made roughly equal contributions to the discharge of the mortgage).

The position of the law in the aftermath of Oxley
At present, the precise extent of *Oxley*'s impact is not entirely clear, because it is part of a continuing picture of emerging trends, which have not yet become ossified. This is itself occurring within a broader setting of uncertainty as to the continuing operation of trusts law in the determination of ownership of disputed homes. That having been said, *Oxley* points to a number of things which are becoming more clear.

- *Rosset*'s significance on agreement to share: the continuing significance of finding 'common intention'.

The essence of finding between the parties a common intention in relation to the beneficial interests of their home remains, but Chadwick's reading of Lord Bridge's references to it in *Rosset* is that it applies only to the primary question of *whether* there was 'a common intention that each should have a beneficial interest in the property?'. In Chadwick LJ's view, this was a better reading than one which extended to the secondary question—'what was the common intention of the parties as to the extent of their beneficial interests'.

- A broad acknowledgement remains of the existence of two categories of case from *Rosset*.

Chadwick LJ makes direct and explicit reference to them in saying that '[i]n many such cases—of which the present is an example—there will have been some discussion between the parties at the time of the purchase which provides the answer to that question. Those are cases within the first of Lord Bridge's categories . . .' and adding '[i]n other cases—where the evidence is that the matter was not discussed at all—an affirmative answer will readily be inferred from the fact that each has made a financial contribution. Those are cases within Lord Bridge's second category.'

- Broad acknowledgement of two categories remains, but for quantification purposes, it appears that distinction is being made between two different types of category 1 case.

Oxley is authority for the proposition that in some category 1 *Rosset* cases, the agreement to share a property beneficially will also determine the size of the parties respective interests: this is because the couple will agree (prior to the sale of the property, or the breakdown of their relationship) that the property will be shared, and will also agree it is to be shared in a particular way (e.g., equally). However, in absence of this, even within category 1 cases, there could be no presumption that the parties intended beneficial interests to be shared equally.

- In the case of category 1 cases where *quantification* is not fixed in advance of the sale of the property or the breakdown of the parties' relationship, and a remedy is sought, it is for the courts to determine the extent of beneficial interests.

This proposition follows on from the way in which *Oxley* argues that *Rosset*'s 'common intention' does not apply to the secondary question of 'what was the common intention of the parties as to the extent of their beneficial interests?' unless the parties have agreed the size of their respective interests. Thus, Chadwick LJ suggested that even in category 1 cases there could not be a presumption of equal shares where the parties had themselves left the question open. Pointing explicitly to *Stokes* v *Anderson* (and this text suggests *Passee* v *Passee* appears to be another example), Chadwick LJ suggested that in these circumstances it is up to the court to 'supply' the parties' common intention regarding size of share to be received by both parties. The basis for the court's determination is, according to Chadwick LJ, that which is 'fair having regard to the whole course of dealing between them in relation to the property' (the significance of which is considered below).

- For the purposes of *quantification*, the position of *Rosset* category 2 cases is that it is up to the courts to determine the extent of beneficial interests.

In cases where there is no agreement to share, under *Rosset* this could be inferred from direct financial contributions made by a non-legal owner. Up to this point *Oxley* is consistent with *Rosset*. However, *Oxley* appears to suggest that where there is no discussion at all (i.e., *Rosset* category 2) but where intention can be inferred by direct contributions, that the contributions establish detrimental reliance, and that each party 'is entitled to a share which the court considers fair having regard to the whole course of dealing between them in relation to the property' (on which see further below). This is a significant departure from that which was envisioned by *Rosset*, which appeared to suggest that contributions in absence of agreement to share not only established reliance but also measured the extent of the interest which arose on the operation of a resulting trust. Chadwick LJ acknowledged that the cases in this area showed that 'the courts have not found it easy to reconcile that final step' (of awarding a share considered to be fair in all the circumstances) 'with a traditional property-based approach'. This is probably on no small account that this 'final step' makes category 2 cases, as envisioned by Lord Bridge, virtually indistinguishable from all but the most clear and unambiguous cases in category 1.

However, while suggesting that the entitlement of each party to a share which the court considers fair 'must be accepted . . . at least in this court and below' (thus pointing to an apparent strengthening of authority in absence of a House of Lords' ruling), the displacement of resulting trust principles in category 2 cases is technically *obiter* because *Oxley* itself was actually a category 1 case.

- In relation to quantification, the position of category 2 cases would now appear to be the same as all category 1 cases where the parties have not agreed the extent of their share by effectively declaring an express trust to that end.

In so far as the remedial outcome of disputed homes cases is concerned, by making these observations on category 2 cases, Chadwick LJ effectively aligns them with those which fall into a *sub-category* of category 1 where there *is* common intention that each should have some beneficial interest in the property, but the question of size of share remains open upon the end of the relationship or the sale of the property. In these circumstances, which points to absence of evidence that any thought was given to quantification, 'the necessary inference is that they must have intended that question would be answered later on the basis of what was then seen to be fair'. It is between category 2 cases and this sub-category of category 1 that determination of quantification appears to be becoming merged.

- A continuing preference for principles of estoppel to be applied once an agreement is found to determine the size of a beneficial interest.

Chadwick LJ's statement that 'at least in this court and below' questions of quantification—in cases where the parties have not agreed this—will be determined by the position that 'each is entitled to that share which the court considers fair having regard to the whole course of dealing between them in relation to the property' must now be regarded as authoritative. Furthermore, clarification was given that what this amounted to will include a range of outgoings (not just mortgage repayments, but also council tax payments and utilities bills, repairs, insurance and housekeeping) 'which have to be met if they are to live in the property as their home'. This points to the courts' continuing preference for resolving disputed home ownership by applying principles of proprietary estoppel. This is so notwithstanding that Chadwick LJ also conceded that time had come to accept that in cases of this nature 'the outcome is actually likely to be the same, whether the true analysis lies in constructive trust or proprietary estoppel', on account of the factors which clearly now inform what is fair having regard to the 'whole course of dealing between them in relation to the property'.

In summary, it is clear from *Oxley* that once an intention to share has been found (with direct financial contributions readily inferring this in absence of express discussion to *share*) the court will 'read in' or 'supply or impute' the parties' common intention as to what their respective shares will be, and this will be measured on the basis of what is fair in the circumstances. On this reasoning, a common intention to share does not thus automatically give rise to a presumption that equal shares were intended. At this point it would appear that conduct such as paying household expenses or contributions to housekeeping, which would not be capable of establishing an interest under *Rosset* (category 2), will be part of the calculus of what is fair in the circumstances in respect of quantification.

Thus, it would appear that the position which this text has always maintained—highlighting the differences between the trusts approach and one arising in estoppel—is now swimming against the tide of judicial decisions which include a number of Court of Appeal authorities. These decisions show that interests of fairness and justice are becoming ever more entrenched in approaches to disputed home ownership which concern quantification. And while *Oxley* must now be considered the leading case relating to quantification of beneficial interests in light of an agreement, it is also the case that this approach—emphasising fairness and justice, in light of a range of potential 'contributions'—has yet to be considered by the House of Lords. But there is now strong Court of Appeal authority that actually the principles of trusts law and those of proprietary estoppel are becoming increasingly intertwined. In *Yaxley v Gotts*, for example, Robert Walker LJ proffered that:

At a high level of generality, there is much common ground between the doctrines of proprietary estoppel and the constructive trust [because both, along with the doctrine of part performance] are concerned with equity's intervention to provide relief against unconscionable conduct . . . Plainly there are large areas where the two concepts do not overlap . . . But in the area of a joint acquisition of land (which may be, but is not necessarily, the matrimonial home) the two concepts coincide.

In respect of the cause of action, namely establishing the existence of an interest, *Rosset* appears to remain intact: *Oxley* continues to emphasise the need to find an agreement *to share*. However, beyond this, the distinctions which *Rosset* would have drawn between category 1 and category 2 cases do appear to be becoming less significant. This is so on account that direct financial contributions in absence of an agreement to share are, according to *Oxley*, to be given the same remedial treatment as category 1 cases where the parties have left open the question of the size of beneficial interest. Although *Oxley*'s observations on category 2 are strictly *obiter*, this apparent blurring of *Rosset* distinctions is plausibly part of a bigger trend of blurring strict property principles into broader considerations of fairness and justice. Thus, while the law may be seen as becoming more focused on fairness and justice, it is also going to become increasingly difficult to predict; that is beyond a highly likely further decline of the application of trusts law to disputed home ownership which is increasingly becoming clear in the cases.

9.7 Shared homes, beneficial interests, and proposals for reform

The rules governing the acquisition of equitable interests under *Pettit*, *Gissing* and *Rosset* have caused a great deal of controversy. And for the views which are expressed in support in the application of strict property principles in the promotion of certainty, at least as much concern has been directed towards the injustice that such an approach can cause (and indeed, has been demonstrated to cause). In seeking to respond to such concerns the Law Commission produced a discussion paper called *Sharing Homes* in July 2002.

In the paper, the Law Commission sets out a proposed scheme which it devised in an attempt to replace the current system of property entitlement, while also providing a useful analysis of the current law and a discussion of the ways in which it might be improved. Discussion revolved around providing fairness in a variety of different relationships and in response to a number of differing manifestations of contribution. The paper can be viewed in full on the Law Commission website: *www.lawcom.gov.uk/library/lcspecial-1/sharing_homes.pdf*

Notwithstanding the criticisms which can be raised by *Midland Bank plc* v *Cooke*, as an application of trusts law, its flexible approach was adopted in *Le Foe* v *Le Foe* [2001] 2 FLR 970, and was simultaneously visible in the Law Commission's castigation of current law as uncertain, difficult to apply, and capable of serious injustice. The concurrence of *Le Foe* v *Le Foe* with the Law Commission's 2002 Discussion Paper captured a sense of optimism about new approaches to home sharing which were flexible, around disputed entitlement, and accommodating of a variety of social living arrangements.

Despite this apparent zeal, however, in *Sharing Homes* the Law Commission ultimately came to the view that it was not going to be possible to devise reforms which could operate fairly and even-handedly across the envisaged very ambitious spectrum of diverse social home-sharing arrangements. The Discussion Paper's Executive Summary made a number of key points, alluding to why the law is in need of reform, and how this might have been achieved, but it also warned that this had not been possible under the *Sharing Homes* auspices. Thus, prominence was given to the way in which parties involved in home sharing can best protect their interests, emphasising the desirability of execution of a deed of trust. Interestingly, it also implored the courts to continue to effect reform through greater application of the approach adopted in *Cooke* and *Le Foe*.

It is also interesting to note the Law Commission's views on marriage as a status 'deserving of special treatment'. Closely alongside this, the discussion of 'broader based approaches to personal relationships' across a range of partnerships through-out society (e.g., recognition of certain civil partnerships, and the ability of legal rights and obligations to arise in respect of individuals in relationships outside marriage) is also noteworthy. The scope of the Law Commission's concerns and its interest for lawyers interested in co-ownership was especially apparent in the entreaty which the Law Commission makes to the Government to 'attempt to define a status which would lead to the vesting of rights and obligations' in this way. The Law Commission concluded that this was not only beyond the scope of the project before it, but actually that it was outside its remit as a law reform body.

9.7.1 **Moving on from** *Sharing Homes*: **the Law Commission's Cohabitation Project**

In many respects, the disappointment felt by many following *Sharing Homes* extends beyond the Discussion Paper's failure to formulate proposals for reform, and fundamentally to its appreciation of just how complicated this task ultimately will be in light of the diversity of relationships which can be found across society. Recently, aspects of this have re-emerged in the Law Commission's Consultation Paper *Cohabitation: The Financial Consequences of Relationship Breakdown*, published in May 2006, arising from the Cohabitation Project announced in 2005. This project is concerned with the position of cohabitants and their children in the event of death or relationship breakdown, but in many ways its essence reflects the concerns identified in *Sharing Homes* relating to the variety of personal relationships found across society.

Thus *Cohabitation* continues to be concerned with people who live together in relationships which are characterised by intimacy and exclusivity but are not married or have not formed civil partnerships (and are not relationships between blood relatives or 'caring' relationships, or ones which are 'commercial' in nature, such as a landlord and tenant relationship or a 'lodging' arrangement). The Consultation is set to look at issues of financial hardship arising from relationship breakdown or death, and concerns a number of questions of asset distribution between cohabitants.

Consultation No. 179: financial relief and the position of cohabitants
The Consultation Paper points to the case of *Burns v Burns* [1984] Ch 317 to illustrate why the current legal rules are in need of reform. The Law Commission noted (at para. 2.2) that although it is over 20 years since Mrs Burns went to court, 'the law has not changed significantly in the interim, and it is likely that if Mrs Burns' case were heard today, the result would be exactly the same as it was then'.

Pointing to the way in which the current law relating to cohabiting couples is unsatisfactory, upon announcing the Consultation's Publication, the Commissioner leading the project, Stuart Bridge, also pointed to the way in which '[m]ore people live together outside marriage than ever before'. This provides especial impetus to try to resolve the current position whereby 'the general law of contract, property, and trusts' determines the position of parties (para.1.19). The Law Commission has suggested at this point that a new approach is desirable in which the court would have discretion to:

> ... examine the contributions and sacrifices made by each party during the course of the relationship. It would seek to share the benefits and losses created by the relationship and experienced on separation, more fairly between the couple than the current law is able to do.

At the outset in 2005, when the Cohabitation Project was announced, the Law Commission pointed to a number of 'Key Issues' which would define its remit. These were questions of entitlements to financial remedies upon separation, including property transfer; intestacy and inheritance upon death; and whether contracts setting out how property should be distributed in the event of a break-down in relationships of cohabitation should be enforceable, and if so, in what circumstances. And in 2006 (at para. 1.22) the Law Commission confirmed that the current project is not intended to be a comprehensive review of all the law as it applies to cohabiting couples, and it is specifically confined to the 'financial conse-quences of the termination of cohabiting relationships, whether by separation or by death'.

Furthermore, while the Law Commission clearly perceives the law to be in need of reform, and has made initial recommendations accordingly, it is unlikely that in respect of these financial consequences, cohabiting couples will be conferred the same protection as couples who are married (and that which analogously applies to same-sex couples who have registered a civil partnership under the Civil Partnership Act 2004). Although the Consultation will allow respondents to express views on this, the Law Commission stressed (at para. 1.21):

> we have provisionally rejected the suggestion made by some commentators that the law applying to married couples in terms of financial relief on divorce should be extended to cohabiting couples upon separation . . . we consider that there is a difference between rela-tionships in which the couple have made a public and legal commitment to each other and relationships in which they have not.

The position of cohabitants and the Law Commission's initial recommendations
The initial recommendations made by the Law Commission for reform of the finan-cial position of persons currently cohabiting, upon the end of their relationship, are set out in Part 3 of the Consultation. The actual way in which the proposals are set out is far more extensive than coverage in this text permits, but, as indicated briefly above, essentially the Law Commission proposals hinge on a new scheme which would enable the courts to make orders for financial relief between cohabitants on termination of the relationship, taking into consideration the contributions and sacrifices made by each party, and determining the best way to apportion benefits and losses accordingly.

The Law Commission accepted that it would be up to Parliament 'as a matter of social policy' to determine whether it is appropriate to introduce laws which would enable the courts to act in this way in relation to the financial positions of cohabiting couples (see para. 3.6). After making this primary observation, the Law Commission added that if Parliament were willing to do so, then how this would proceed could be conducted on two possible models: a scheme by which couples could 'opt in' or one where couples could 'opt out' of a new set of remedies being applicable to their relationship.

In respect of **'opting in'** the Law Commission pointed to a scheme whereby this new set of remedies would be available only to those who had expressly consented to the application of the scheme to their relationship. In an alternative **'opting out'** scheme, a set of remedies could be made available to cohabitants who are 'eligible' under the scheme, but which would not apply 'if and to the extent that the parties had made their own arrangements or had agreed that they would opt out (of the new scheme of remedies)'.

Responses have been invited on the Law Commission's proposals, which include its provisional view (in para. 3.9) that the 'opt out' scheme is a better route. This is on the basis that all eligible cohabitants should be automatically entitled to apply for remedies under such a new scheme without having to 'opt in' beforehand, thus helping to ensure that those who might be most vulnerable and in need of seeking financial relief have proper protection. In coming to this view, the Law Commission accepted that this then required consideration of which cohabitants should be 'eligible' as envisaged, and whether parties can, by agreement, determine that their relationship is not to be subject to the new remedies framework.

In anticipation of a Law Commission Report: the challenges of cohabitation
Defining eligibility is part of a wider question of giving meaning to the term 'cohabitant' which should apply to the Law Commission's proposals, and the Consultation has invited views on this very important underlying question. And while the Law Commission accepted that a wide range of relationships currently subsist within the broad umbrella of 'cohabitation', it also proposed that not all cohabitating couples should necessarily be eligible for the new remedies framework. Currently it is exploring how eligibility should be measured, looking at factors such as how definitions of 'cohabitating couple' might be framed from their **analogous position with marriage** (paras 3.20–3.24) and why this might be rejected; the way in which 'cohabiting couple' suggests a couple living together in a **shared household** (paras 3.25–3.32); and how a definition of cohabitation might be framed around the concept of **commitment** (paras 3.37–3.39). Other considerations relating to eligibility include whether there should be a **minimum duration** of relationship requirement (see paras 3.45–3.51).

While the Law Commission appreciates the enormity of its task arising from diversity of living arrangements, its focus is very clearly relationships of a personal and intimate, and 'exclusive' nature (and it specifically excludes interest in commercial relationships and ones between blood relations). In this respect, it is determined to keep the project focused upon cohabitation and to 'produce recommendations closely tailored to the particular needs of this category of relationship'. In this vein, the Law Commission appears to be especially mindful that any scheme of reform must not only accommodate diversity in living arrangements found across society, but also 'respect parties' autonomy' and that intervening too readily 'may undermine cohabitants' confidence' in the integrity of the agreements which are reached between the parties concerning their relationship. However, this must itself also be weighed against the law's responsibility to 'protect the vulnerable and to take adequate account of the inherent difficulty of providing for future events' (para. 6.13). Given the conclusions drawn about the challenges arising from diversity in *Sharing Homes*, what the Law Commission feels can be realistically achieved from this project remains to be seen.

This is perhaps especially so considering the current caselaw developments most recently manifested in *Oxley*, which show the courts appearing to be less interested establishing whether a case is 'category 1 or 2 *Rosset*' and more interested in achieving fairness and justice for the parties. Thus, it must be asked whether the scheme currently being pursued by the Law Commission will be able to provide a system of determining and apportioning interests in shared homes which is any more flexible and appropriate than that which is currently emerging in the general law?

9.8 Some postscript considerations

9.8.1 Particular problems with life interests

In the third edition of this book, this section was devoted to problems caused by cases such as *Ungurian v Lesnoff* [1990] 1 Ch 206 where Vinelott J held that Mrs Lesnoff was entitled to a life tenancy. The problem with such cases, and also cases such as *Bannister v Bannister* [1948] 2 All ER 133 and *Binions v Evans* [1972] 1 Ch 359 (considered in chapter 10), was that because (in *Ungurian v Lesnoff*) Ungurian's interest was subject to Mrs Lesnoff's prior life interest, there were thereby necessarily successive interests in the property, and the house therefore became settled land within the Settled Land Act 1925 (considered in chapter 1). The result of this was that Mrs Lesnoff as tenant for life was entitled to call for the execution of a vesting deed and the appointment of trustees, and, once the house was vested in her, to sell it and to re-invest the proceeds in the purchase of another house or to enjoy the income therefrom. This is a consequence infinitely more far-reaching than anything envisaged in the obscurely-recollected conversation that took place in Beirut in December 1968.

It was also perfectly clear that the draftsmen of the 1925 legislation never intended this result, which was an accidental consequence of legislation the original purpose of which had nothing to do with the problem in *Ungurian v Lesnoff*, and which indeed was enacted in response to social conditions which simply no longer exist.

Interesting though these problems were, they are no longer relevant, at any rate for interests created in the future, because the Settled Land Act 1925 regime has been replaced by the trust of land under the Trusts of Land and Appointment of Trustees Act 1996, which no longer gives the life tenant the extensive powers which he or she would have had under the Settled Land Act 1925.

9.8.2 Effect of legal joint tenancy

Discussion so far rests on the assumption that legal title vests in A alone. In many of the cases it vests jointly in A and B. It surely cannot be the case, however, that the dispositions of the equitable interests depend on the whereabouts of legal title. It is therefore suggested that a joint tenancy makes no difference, except perhaps to the reliance requirement.

The starting point where A and B have joint title, and where the conveyance does not state the whereabouts of the equitable title, is that A and B share equally. Also, the effect of rebutting the resulting trust presumptions will be that the parties share equally: the equitable title then following the legal. One effect of this is that for Miss B to obtain a 50 per cent share where A has paid more requires only rebuttal of the normal resulting trust presumptions. There is no need for A to declare himself trustee of any part of his share. Consequently, no reliance is required on B's part (excepting where her claim is based on estoppel) where she claims a 50 per cent share.

If Miss B is claiming a share greater than 50 per cent, assuming that she has not paid more than 50 per cent of the purchase price, and again apart from estoppel, A must declare himself trustee of part of his share. The same problem can arise in a case like *Midland Bank plc v Cooke* [1995] 4 All ER 562, if the analysis is accepted that Miss B definitely has a share (having contributed something to the purchase price), but claims a greater share.

In the third edition of this book, the argument was examined that even in this situation the writing requirement of s. 53(1)(b) did not apply, even assuming no reliance by B. The argument was that the existence of a joint tenancy at common law necessarily required a statutory trust for sale, and that the equitable doctrine of conversion (see chapter 1) converted A's interest into an interest in personalty, to which, of course, s. 53(1)(b) does not apply. The effect of this would again be to remove the need for detrimental reliance by Miss B.

In that edition we expressed doubts as to whether that analysis was correct, on the ground that the courts have never taken the logic of the equitable doctrine of conversion to its logical conclusion (see chapter 1). The conversion doctrine has, at any rate in this context, now been abolished by s. 3 of the Trusts of Land and Appointment of Trustees Act 1996, with retrospective effect (see chapter 1). The issues discussed in the previous edition are therefore no longer relevant.

9.8.3 Legislation affecting spouses and property interests under the Civil Partnership Act 2004

The legislature reacted to the House of Lords decisions in *Pettitt v Pettitt* [1970] AC 777 and *Gissing v Gissing* [1971] AC 886, by enacting legislation which allows the courts to take into account additional considerations when the parties are married.

Section 37 of the Matrimonial Proceedings and Property Act 1970, entitled 'Contributions by spouse in money or money's worth to the improvement of property', was a reaction to *Pettitt v Pettitt*. It allows for the beneficial interests of husbands and wives (and by virtue of s. 2(1) of the Law Reform (Miscellaneous Provisions) Act 1970 and fiancées, but not those of other unmarried couples) to be varied by substantial contributions 'in money or money's worth to the improvement of real or personal property in which . . . both of them has or have a beneficial interest'.

Sections 24 and 25 of the Matrimonial Causes Act 1973 were a reaction to *Gissing v Gissing*. The sections allow the courts significantly to alter the property interests of married (but not unmarried) couples in the event of divorce, a decree of nullity of marriage or a decree of judicial separation. In such an event, the importance of the prior property interests of the spouses is reduced, since they will no longer be conclusive. The Matrimonial Causes Act 1973 applies only on the breakdown of marriages, however, and if the question of the existence or otherwise of a beneficial interest arises during the course of the marriage (as is usually the case, for example, where a third party is involved, as in *Lloyds Bank plc* v *Rosset* itself), the issue will be determined on the basis of the ordinary principles of equity discussed in this chapter.

Property interests and the Civil Partnership Act 2004

In contrast with the uncertainty which continues to prevail in relation to unmarried couples generally—and the scope for injustice which is recognised both judicially and in policy discourses—there has been reform in the position of same-sex couples specifically. The Civil Partnership Act 2004 allows same-sex couples to register their partnership, and upon doing so, rights relating to property are broadly similar to those of married couples. The way in which this impacts on matters of inheritance and survivorship, administration of estates, and pension entitlements is beyond the scope of this text, but there are some important observations to make concerning the family home. It is now possible for persons within a registered civil partnership to acquire an interest, or a greater share, in a shared home (in which one or both has an interest) by making a substantial improvement to the property concerned. In this respect, s. 65 of the Civil Partnerships Act is analogous with s. 37 of the Matrimonial Proceedings Act 1970. In a similar vein, when the partnership is terminated, the court is able to make property adjustment orders with the same discretion as applies to married couples pursuant to Matrimonial Causes Act 1973, as amended by the Family Law Act 1996.

 online resource centre

FURTHER READING

Ferguson (1993) 109 LQR 114.

Glover and Todd [1995] Web JCLI.

Hayton [1990] Conv 370.

Pawlowski [2002] Fam Law 190.

Thompson [2000] 64 Conv 245.

Thompson [2002] 66 Conv 273.

Thompson [2003] 67 Conv 411.

Wells [2001] 65 Conv 13.

10

Secret and half-secret trusts
(and constructive and resulting trusts)

10.1 What are secret and half-secret trusts?

10.1.1 Formality requirements of the Wills Act 1837, section 9 (as amended)

As with *inter vivos* transactions (see chapter 5), there are formality requirements where property is left by will. To be valid, under s. 9 of the Wills Act 1837 (as amended by s. 17 of the Administration of Justice Act 1982) wills have to be made in writing, and properly signed and witnessed. The full text of s. 9, as amended, is as follows:

No will shall be valid unless—

(a) it is in writing, and signed by the testator, or by some other person in his presence and by his direction; and

(b) it appears that the testator intended by his signature to give effect to the will; and

(c) the signature is made or acknowledged by the testator in the presence of two or more witnesses present at the same time; and

(d) each witness either—

    (i) attests and signs the will; or

    (ii) acknowledges his signature, in the presence of the testator (but not necessarily in the presence of any other witness),

but no form of attestation shall be necessary.

If the provisions of s. 9 are not complied with, the will is completely void and any trusts which it purports to create will be invalid also. As will be seen, however, a secret or half-secret trust may take effect on the death of the testator without any need to specify the terms of the trust in the will, or even to reveal its existence.

The purpose of s. 9 (as amended) is to prevent fraud. To make a will is to enter into a major transaction. This must not be done in a light-hearted manner but must be the result of a deliberate act. Formality requirements are supposed to ensure this. It is also more important than with *inter vivos* gifts to remove the possibility of false claims as the testator himself obviously cannot refute them. As in other areas, however, formalities can sometimes encourage fraud. But 'equity will not permit a statute to be used as a cloak for fraud' (see the equitable maxims in 1.4.1) and the doctrines of secret and half-secret trusts have evolved in this area to prevent this.

10.1.2 **Reasons for testators wishing to avoid formality requirements**

There are at least two reasons why a testator may wish to avoid formality provisions (see, e.g., Sheridan (1951) 67 LQR 314).

First, he may wish the identity of the beneficiary to remain secret. This was espe-cially common in the 19th century, if a gift of land to a charity was intended, when the Statutes of Mortmain (which prevented testamentary gifts of land to charities between 1736 and 1891) were in force. Another common situation was (and still is) where the beneficiary is to be a lover or mistress, or illegitimate child. Possibly the need for secrecy in this situation has diminished since 1969, because until then there was a pre-sumption that a gift to 'children' in a will excluded illegitimate children. Thus, it was necessary to identify them to include them. That presumption was reversed in 1969, so that a gift to 'children' on its own will now include illegitimate children (the rele-vant provisions can now be found in the Family Law Reform Act 1987). Even so, secrecy may still be desired if the testator wishes to keep their very existence secret.

Second, the testator may simply not have made up his mind at the time of mak-ing the will about the details of all the dispositions. It has been argued (e.g., Watkin [1981] Conv 335) that whereas the law should indulge secrecy, it should discourage indecision, and to at least a partial extent, it has taken this line.

10.1.3 **Methods of avoiding formality provisions of Wills Act**

There are two methods by which the Wills Act can effectively be avoided. A can leave property by will to B, in a manner which complies with the provisions of the Act, but having come to an (unwritten) understanding with B that he is merely trustee of it in favour of C. The understanding does not, of course, comply with the formality requirements of the Act. This is called a fully secret trust.

Alternatively, A can leave property by a valid will 'to B on trust', but where the beneficial interest under the trust (for example, in favour of C) is undeclared. This is called a half-secret trust because, while the details of the trust are secret, it is made clear that B holds as trustee and not beneficially.

For clarity, A, B and C will be used in the same fashion throughout the chapter.

In general, the principles for the enforcement of fully secret and half-secret trusts are probably the same (although some argue otherwise). Thus, most of what follows in the next section (on fully secret trusts) applies equally to half-secret trusts. However, because it is necessary to refute arguments that their basis of enforcement is different, and because there are respects in which half-secret trusts are treated differently, there is also a separate section on half-secret trusts.

10.2 **Enforcement of fully secret trusts**

Subject to the constraints on the doctrine outlined in the remainder of this section, fully secret trusts will be enforced by the courts—C can enforce the trust against B. The question therefore arises: on what basis does equity allow the clear provisions of the Wills Act to be avoided?

10.2.1 **Fraud theory**

The leading authority on fully secret trusts is the House of Lords decision of
McCormick v *Grogan* (1869) LR 4 HL 82 which clearly states that the basis of their
enforcement is fraud. The precise nature of the fraud is discussed shortly but at the
very least, if it would be fraudulent for B to take beneficially, he will be required to
enforce the trust in favour of C. This would be the case, for example, if the only
reason why the property was left to B in the will was because of the unwritten
understanding that he would hold it on trust for C.

The facts in *McCormick* v *Grogan* were that in 1851, the testator had left all his
property by a three-line will to his friend Mr Grogan. In 1854 he was struck down
by cholera. With only a few hours to live he sent for Mr Grogan. He told Mr Grogan
in effect that his will and a letter would be found in his desk. The letter named
various intended beneficiaries and the intended gifts to them. The letter concluded
with the words:

I do not wish you to act strictly on the foregoing instructions, but leave it entirely to your own
good judgment to do as you think I would, if living, and as the parties are deserving.

An intended beneficiary (an illegitimate child) whom Mr Grogan thought it right to
exclude sued.

The House of Lords held that although in principle the courts will enforce secret
trusts, the terms of the letter in this particular case were not such that equity would
impose on the conscience of Mr Grogan, and the secret trust alleged would not be
enforced.

McCormick v *Grogan: different facts and a different result*
Although in *McCormick* v *Grogan* itself it was held that no secret trust was created in
favour of C (an illegitimate child), but merely a moral obligation imposed on B, the
court made it clear that had the facts been different a fully secret trust would, in
principle, have been enforceable by C, in spite of the provisions of the Wills Act. In
fact, the principles of enforcement of secret trusts go back at least as far as *Thynn* v
Thynn (1684) 1 Vern 296.

It is by no means self-evident that equity should uphold a trust despite a clear
statutory provision to the contrary. In *McCormick* v *Grogan*, Lord Hatherley LC and
Lord Westbury emphasised that the justification for the doctrine is personal fraud.
In several places in his speech, Lord Westbury in particular emphasised the need for
a *'malus animus'* to be 'proved by the clearest and most indisputable evidence' (at
p. 97):

. . . the jurisdiction which is invoked here . . . is founded altogether on personal fraud. It is a
jurisdiction by which a court of equity, proceeding on the ground of fraud, converts the party
who has committed it into a trustee for the party who is injured by that fraud. Now, being a
jurisdiction founded on personal fraud, it is incumbent on the court to see that a fraud, a *malus
animus*, is proved by the clearest and most indisputable evidence.

Fraud and a deliberate intention to deceive
On one view, this means that a deliberate intention to deceive must be shown on
B's part (for example, where B had deliberately induced the testator to leave the
property to him in the will, on the clear representation that he would hold it in
trust for C), and it could also be argued that the standard of proof is as in common

law fraud; in other words, a very high standard indeed is required. It may well be that this was what Lord Westbury meant. However, the statement has recently been explained in different terms. As will be explained below, *malus animus* may mean no more than the state of mind required for equity to impose a constructive trust on B's conscience, a very different proposition from common law fraud. Further, clearest and most indisputable evidence may mean no more than the standard of proof which the court will require before rectifying a written instrument. This is, at any rate, how the passage was interpreted by Brightman J in *Ottaway* v *Norman* [1972] Ch 698 (see Chapter 11).

How 'fraud enforcement' might work
The fraud basis of enforcement could operate in one of two ways. Either equity imposes upon the conscience of the secret trustee, B, and forces him to hold the property received under the will on constructive trust for the secret beneficiary, C, or alternatively secret trusts are express trusts to which the Wills Act 1837 does not apply, because equity will not allow a statute intended to prevent fraud to be used as a cloak for fraud (see the equitable maxims in chapter 1). The question whether secret or half-secret trusts are express or constructive is considered shortly.

10.2.2 Why no resulting trust?

The principles enunciated in *McCormick* v *Grogan* (1869) LR 4 HL 82 beg an important question. If the only basis of the doctrine is to prevent B from fraudulently keeping the property for himself, why is it necessary to enforce the trust in C's favour? If the defeat of the intended trustee's (B's) fraudulent profit is all that was desired, surely it should be sufficient merely to compel him to hold the property on a resulting trust for the testator's estate? This solution would deprive B of his personal gain and the policy of the Wills Act 1837 would appear to be effected. Why should equity further disregard the requirements of the Wills Act 1837 to the extent of giving effect to the testator's oral instruction that the property should go to someone not named in the will?

Clearly, however, the House of Lords in *McCormick* v *Grogan* would have been prepared to enforce a secret trust on its terms (although on the facts no trust was held to have been created). Indeed, even long before *McCormick* v *Grogan* it was clear that the courts did not favour the resulting trust solution and that equity would enforce the trust in favour of C. There are in fact three answers to the resulting trust argument.

10.2.2.1 *The residuary legatee argument*
A historical reason why a resulting trust would not have provided a satisfactory solution is that, prior to the Executors Act of 1830, an executor was entitled to take as residuary legatee all property not specifically disposed of in the will. If, as might well happen, the intended trustee (B) was also the executor, a resulting trust would merely have the effect of granting him indirectly what the court refused to allow him to take directly.

An early example is *Thynn* v *Thynn* (1684) 1 Vern 296. The testator (A) had made his wife sole executrix. The son (B) persuaded the wife to make him sole executor instead, upon a completely fraudulent pretext. The Lord Keeper held that the property must be held in trust for the wife (C). If the court had not enforced the trust but allowed the property to result to the estate, the fraudulent son B (as executor) would himself have benefited from that as residuary legatee and indeed would have taken beneficially. Clearly, therefore, this solution would have been inappropriate and the only way to prevent personal fraud was to enforce the secret trust.

McCormick v Grogan and the significance of the Executors Act 1830
By the time *McCormick v Grogan* was decided, the Executors Act 1830 had altered the rule. Nowadays, the effect of a resulting trust in favour of the testator's estate will be to pass the property to the person named as residuary legatee, or if there is none, to those persons (usually close relatives of the testator) who are entitled to take in the event of his total or partial intestacy.

Hence, were the same facts to have arisen as in *Thynn v Thynn* today, B may not have personally benefited in the same way from a resulting trust. Yet *McCormick v Grogan* applied the same principles to a case under the Wills Act 1837. This appears to go further than necessary and to defeat the intention behind the Act. There can still be similar problems today, as in *Re Rees* [1950] Ch 204, where the intended trustee, B (the solicitor who had drafted the will), was also the *named* residuary legatee. Where B is named as residuary legatee the arguments advanced in *Thynn v Thynn* retain their full force. Any argument favouring a resulting trust must at any rate make an exception to cover this situation, therefore.

10.2.2.2 *The policy argument*
It is also possible to justify enforcing the secret trust on policy grounds. A common reason for setting up a secret trust is the desire to benefit someone whose existence the testator would prefer to keep hidden from his family, such as a mistress or, as in *McCormick v Grogan* an illegitimate child. A resulting trust in favour of the estate would divert the property to the very last people whom the testator wished to benefit (his legitimate family).

But for the court to give weight to this sort of consideration involves accepting that the testator's wishes are of sufficient importance to justify ignoring the clear terms of a statute in order to enforce the trust. The policy argument alone cannot justify enforcement, as opposed to a resulting trust, although if there are other justifications as well, it is a significant additional factor.

10.2.2.3 *The nature of the fraud*
More importantly, however, we must examine the nature of the fraud upon which the doctrine is based. Just because Lord Westbury insisted on an element of intention to deceive, it does not follow that the nature of that deceit rests only in the personal gain of B.

Hodge [1980] Conv 341 has a different explanation. It should be remembered that the gift to B depended in the first place on B's promise to carry out the wishes of the testator. Hodge argues that the nature of B's fraud lies not simply in keeping the property personally, but in the fact that it was the promise to carry out the testator's wishes *in their exact terms* which induced him to leave his property to the intended trustee. It is the intended trustee's (B's) failure to do this which makes the fraud, not the element of greed.

B's fraud then, in equity, lies in the defeat of the testator's wishes, not necessarily in his own personal gain. He would be just as fraudulent with regard to the testator's confidence if he gave the property to a charity as he would be if he kept it for himself. And the testator would be no less defrauded if the intended trustee were (say) to hand over the gift intended for the testator's mistress to his innocent and long-suffering wife. A deception practised out of high moral principle is still deceit. Therefore, nothing less than the enforcement of the testator's wishes will suffice to avert a fraud in this situation.

McGormick v Grogan: the consequences if the circumstances had suggested fraud
On this argument, had the facts in *McCormick v Grogan* suggested fraud, it could only have been resolved by the enforcement of the trust in C's favour: a resulting trust would not have sufficed.

This line of reasoning is not universally accepted, but is clearly the basis on which at any rate *Blackwell v Blackwell* [1929] AC 318 was decided in the House of Lords (see further 9.4). A similar statement can be found in Lord Sterndale's judgment in *Re Gardner* [1920] 2 Ch 523 (at p. 529): 'The breach of trust or the fraud would arise when [the secret trustee] attempted to deal with the money contrary to the terms on which he took it.' It is not necessary for him to attempt to keep it beneficially, and indeed, in *Re Gardner* itself, he had no intention of so doing.

10.2.3 Developments since *McCormick v Grogan*

Lord Westbury's requirement in *McCormick v Grogan* was for a *malus animus* to be proved by clearest and most indisputable evidence. This seems to suggest that a deliberate intention to deceive must be shown on the legatee's part (for example, where he had deliberately induced the testator to leave the property to him in the will, on the clear representation that he would hold it in trust for the secret beneficiary). It also appears that the standard of proof is as in common law fraud; in other words, a very high standard indeed is required.

There is limited authority that since *McCormick v Grogan* (1869) LR 4 HL 82, their Lordships' stringent requirements concerning *malus animus* have been relaxed. Before considering the law itself, however, which is not yet clear, it is useful to consider why Lord Westbury was so concerned to limit the doctrine as he did, and what has altered since 1869.

As we have seen, *McCormick v Grogan* concerned an attempt to make a secret gift in favour of an illegitimate child. Secret trusts were also frequently used, however, in providing for charity. Testamentary gifts of land in favour of charities were, at that time, void. The practice therefore grew up whereby A left property to B, who was a trusted friend, on the understanding that he would later give the property to the charity (C).

It must be appreciated that it was not the intended beneficiary (C) in these cases who brought the action. Rather, it was A's family who attempted to show that the secret trust was enforceable. This can be seen from *Wallgrave v Tebbs* (1855) 2 K & J 313, where the secret trust failed, for reasons discussed in the next section.

The reason for this extraordinary state of affairs was this. If the secret trust was unenforceable, B took the property beneficially, and he could be relied upon, as a friend of the testator, to carry out A's wishes. If, however, it was enforceable, then by virtue of the Statutes of Mortmain, it was void. Thus, there would be a resulting trust to the estate (i.e., A's family)! This accounts for the surprising circumstance that it was the very last people who might at first sight be expected to benefit from the secret trust being enforceable, who argued that it was. On the other hand, it was in the interests of the charity for it not to be enforceable, because the charity could rely on B carrying out A's wishes.

McGormick v Grogan: its strict limitations

It is likely that the House of Lords in *McCormick v Grogan* did not wish to allow gifts to charities to be defeated in this way. On the other hand, if B had procured a bequest dishonestly, they did not wish to see a mistress or illegitimate child deprived of his or her rightful interest because of the provisions of the Wills Act 1837. In the first case B was far from being fraudulent—indeed, he only wished to carry out the trust. In the second case, he was. Hence, the stringent limits placed on the doctrine in that case.

The position changed in 1891, and the last vestiges of the mortmain legislation disappeared in 1960. Only the second type of secret trust remains today, therefore. Arguably, their lordships' limits to the doctrine are no longer appropriate. Their status is, of course, *obiter dicta*, albeit from the House of Lords, because in the event C lost on other grounds, and there is some authority that the limitations will no longer be stringently applied.

Equitable fraud and 'other' fraud

For example, although it seems that the basis of enforcement is still based on fraud, in so far that equity will not allow a statute intended to prevent fraud to be used to perpetrate fraud, it is possible that fraud in equity is nowadays a wider concept than it was in 1869. Today, there is some authority that it bears little relation to the common law or criminal law concept of the same name. It imposes on B's conscience, but may not necessarily demand the same degree of *mens rea* as fraud in the common law or criminal sense. Because of this, it may also demand a lower standard of proof.

Lord Westbury's remarks were not essential to the decision in *McCormick v Grogan*, and indeed, seem not to have been adopted in later cases. For example, in the later House of Lords authority, *Blackwell v Blackwell* [1929] AC 318, Lord Buckmaster thought that all that was required to show a fraud was:

(a) the intention of the testator to subject the intended trustee to an obligation in favour of the intended beneficiary;

(b) communication of that intention to the intended trustee; and

(c) the acceptance of that obligation by the intended trustee, either expressly or by acquiescence.

Blackwell v Blackwell concerned a half-secret trust, but it is clear that the reasoning was intended to apply equally to fully secret trusts.

10.2.3.1 Ottaway v Norman

In *Ottaway v Norman* [1972] Ch 698, Brightman J enforced an oral secret trust of land without any suggestion that the intended trustee (B) had procured her prior life interest by deceit. Miss Hodges's (B's) employer, Mr Ottaway (A), left her his bungalow in his will, on terms that she would leave it by her own will to Mr Ottaway's son (C). Brightman J was prepared to enforce that agreement by imposing what he described as a constructive trust upon the bungalow in the hands of Miss Hodges's executor (she having later changed her mind and left her property to a cousin).

At the time of the arrangement between Miss Hodges (B) and the testator Ottaway (A), she clearly intended to carry out her promise to leave the land to Ottaway's son (C) in her own will. Although she later changed her mind, there was no evidence that she had procured the bequest by deceit: certainly, the evidence was insufficient to surmount the stringent standard of proof required for common law fraud. Her failure in the event to carry out her promise is clearly a fraud in the sense that it defeats the intention of the testator, but no question of *malus animus* arose. Far from requiring fraud in the sense required by Lord Westbury, Brightman J held that enforcement of a secret trust in C's favour depended only on those criteria derived from *Blackwell* v *Blackwell* [1929] AC 318 (see 10.2.3). Brightman J also thought that it was immaterial whether these elements precede or succeed the will. This seems correct in principle: if acceptance of an obligation by B persuades A not to revoke an existing will in B's favour, for B to break this obligation is quite as clearly a fraud on A, as it would have been had A been persuaded by B's acceptance of the obligation to make a will in his favour.

Nor did Brightman J see any reason to depart from the ordinary civil standard of proof, i.e., balance of probabilities.

Blackwell v *Blackwell and the imposition of a constructive trust*

Brightman J called the trust which he imposed upon the legatee of the (by then deceased) trustee a 'constructive' trust. This is a description of the mechanism by which secret trusts are enforced, not the basis of their enforcement. The constructive trust is simply a device of equity to protect beneficiaries where trust property has found its way into the hands of someone who, even if personally innocent, cannot assert a better right to that property.

The fact that the trust (of land) was oral was not a bar to its enforcement, despite the Law of Property Act 1925, s. 53(1)(b), because the executor was held to be a constructive trustee of the bungalow. Whether or not this analysis was correct, in principle a fully secret trust of land should be enforceable despite the absence of writing, either on the assumption that such trusts are to be regarded as constructive since they are imposed on the ground of conscience or because equity will not allow a statute intended to prevent fraud to be used as a cloak for fraud.

So much for the trust of land in *Ottaway* v *Norman*. According to the evidence given by the son and his wife, Miss Hodges also undertook to leave them the furniture and other contents, including her money. Brightman J accepted that the secret trust comprised such furnishings and fixtures as Miss Hodges had received under Mr Ottaway's will, but not that it included all Miss Hodges's other property and cash from whatever source.

In respect of the last, it seems that he was not convinced that so far-reaching an obligation had in fact been envisaged in the agreement, but if the intended trustee (B) has clearly accepted such an obligation, it would appear, on analogy with mutual wills (on which, see chapter 11), that this obligation also could be enforced against her estate.

What is the status of the Ottoway trust?

This raises the issue of the status of the trust during Miss Hodges's lifetime. In *Ottaway* v *Norman*, Brightman J employed the concept of a 'floating trust', derived from the Australian case of *Birmingham* v *Renfrew* (1937) 57 CLR 666, which would remain in suspense during the life of the trustee and crystallise on her death, attaching to whatever property was comprised within her estate. This, as the learned judge noted, would seem to preclude Miss Hodges from making even a small pecuniary legacy in favour of her relatives or friends. This reasoning is similar to that of Nourse J in *Re Cleaver* [1981] 1 WLR 939 in the context of mutual wills.

10.2.3.2 Re Snowden

Sir Robert Megarry V-C partially dissented from Brightman J's view in *Re Snowden* [1979] Ch 528. He thought that a higher standard of proof was required where fraud (which he seemed to view in the narrower Lord Westbury sense) had to be proved, as was necessary for some, but not all secret trusts. In other words, in his view, there are two classes of secret trusts, some of which require a more stringent burden of proof than others. Unfortunately, he did not go on to elaborate on the distinction, which appears to have been a desperate attempt to reconcile Brightman J's views with the apparently irreconcilable views of Lord Westbury, but perhaps he had in mind that if the only way that a would-be beneficiary can assert the existence of a trust in his favour is to allege facts which necessarily impute fraud to the alleged trustee, then the higher standard of proof applies. If the three elements listed earlier can be shown without proof of fraud, however, presumably he may succeed on the ordinary civil standard of balance of probabilities.

In the event, it was not necessary for Sir Robert Megarry V-C to elaborate, because there was really no evidence at all on which a secret trust could be established. His views are therefore *obiter*. In any case, if the criteria in *Blackwell* v *Blackwell* and *Ottaway* v *Norman* are sufficient, it is difficult to see why it is ever necessary to allege fraud in the Westbury sense, in which case the higher standard ought never to be required. If, on the other hand, Lord Westbury is correct, it is difficult to see why the higher standard is not always required.

10.3 Limitations on enforcement of secret trusts

The limitations on the enforcement of half-secret trusts are mainly concerned with the time of communication of the terms of the trust. It appears to be necessary for the existence of the secret trust to be communicated to the trustee before the death of the testator, and there is some authority that the terms also have to be communicated before the testator's *death*. Whether or not these communications precede or succeed the date of the *will* is irrelevant to the enforcement of a fully secret trust (although it is probably different in the case of half-secret trusts).

The authorities are *Wallgrave* v *Tebbs* (1855) 2 K & J 313, and *Re Boyes* (1884) 26 Ch D 531.

10.3.1 Wallgrave v Tebbs

Whether the stringent limitations of *McCormick* v *Grogan* (1869) LR 4 HL 82 still apply, or whether the law was correctly stated by Brightman J in *Ottaway* v *Norman* [1972] Ch 698, it is clear that once B has received a gift absolutely, any subsequently imposed obligations cannot deprive him of that gift. Apart from the principle that gifts are irrevocable, there is no reason, in such a case, to impose on B's conscience.

Thus, in *Wallgrave* v *Tebbs* (1855) 2 K & J 313, the existence of the secret trust, in favour of a charity, was not communicated to B until after A's death. B was entitled to the property absolutely. The testator had left property to close friends (B) without informing them in his lifetime that he wished the land to be used for a religious charitable purpose (i.e., in favour of C). The court held that the friends (B) were entitled to the property beneficially—a decision which, surprisingly enough, was most likely to give effect to the wishes of the testator, since if a secret trust had been found to exist it would have been void under the (now repealed) Statutes of Mortmain.

As it was, the friends were free to carry out the testator's wishes. If, as the testator's relatives had argued, a secret trust had been created, they would have had to hold the property on resulting trust *for those relatives*, the purpose of the trust being unlawful. Hence the surprising situation that the very last people who might be expected to argue for a secret trust (the relatives) did so in that case, and in other cases to which the Statutes of Mortmain applied.

The case is authority for the proposition that for a fully secret trust to be enforced, the intended trustee must be told of the existence of the trust before the testator's death. There is no particular difficulty in justifying the decision in *Wallgrave* v *Tebbs*, since if the intended trustee knew nothing about the trust until after the testator's death, there could have been no fraud in the procuring of the bequest, and thus no reason for the court to compel the intended trustee to do anything in particular with what is now his own property.

Another justification is that any other decision would have permitted the testator (A) to derogate from his grant. A bequest ought not to be 'snatched back' after it has been made, any more than a birthday present could be later reclaimed.

10.3.2 *Re Boyes*

A more difficult case is *Re Boyes* (1884) 26 Ch D 531. Here, the intended trustee (B) was told of the existence of the trust before the testator's death, but was not told its terms until after the death of the testator.

A legacy was given to the testator's solicitor, who was told, before the testator's death, that he was to hold the residuary estate upon trust. However, he was not told its terms until a letter was found, after the death of the testator, which directed him to hold the residuary estate on behalf of a lady who was not the testator's wife. The solicitor wished to carry out the testator's wishes, but the validity of the trust was challenged by the testator's family. Kay J held that the solicitor held the property as trustee, but on resulting trust for the testator's estate.

If *Re Boyes* is correct, then not only the existence, but also the terms of a fully secret trust must be communicated to the trustee before the death of the testator. Kay J said (at p. 536):

If the trust was not declared when the will was made [i.e., fully secret trust], it is essential in order to make it binding, that it should be communicated to the devisee or legatee in the testator's lifetime and that he should accept that particular trust.

This is a difficult case to fit into the general scheme of things, and the result was arguably a fraud on the testator, because A obviously did not intend the property to go to his estate, but it is clear from Kay J's judgment that his understanding of the basis of enforcement was substantially that outlined in the previous sections:

The essence of [the early cases on secret trusts] is that the devisee or legatee accepts a particular trust which thereupon becomes binding upon him, and which it would be a fraud in him not to carry into effect.

Fraud and the knowledge of the intended trustee
There is nothing in the fraud basis of enforcement, however, which would require that an intended trustee must know the terms of the trust *by the time the will is executed*. There is no real difference between making a bequest on the strength of the intended trustee's promise, and leaving that bequest unrevoked on the strength of his later assurance. So, there is no reason to refuse to enforce the trust where the intended trustee becomes aware of its terms only after the execution of the will. All that is necessary is that he should be aware of them, or where they are to be found, before the bequest takes effect, i.e., *upon the testator's death.*

Further, in *Re Boyes* the intended trustee (B) was willing to carry out those terms. It seems that the case must be explained as one in which the scope of any possible fraud was limited to denying the existence of the trust. The intended trustee could hardly be said to have procured the bequest by a promise to adhere to its terms since he did not know them. All he knew was that the testator wished him to take the property in the capacity of trustee and not beneficially, so by compelling him to hold as trustee the court had done all it needed to in order to make him comply with the terms on which the bequest had been granted.

There may also be sound policy considerations for not enforcing a trust on its terms in a *Re Boyes* situation, sufficient to outweigh that of enforcement of the trust in C's favour. In particular, to enforce the trust would sanction indecision by A, which is arguably bad policy, since to allow a testator to establish a trust whose terms he may change from moment to moment is to permit the very luxury of indecision which the Wills Act 1837 sought to circumscribe. Furthermore, the court has to set a limit on the time for which trustees are required to hold property without knowing who the objects are, and it is a reasonable solution to insist that they know from the outset (although this may be not until the estate has been administered, i.e., later than death, so arguably this rather than death should be the deadline).

Is Re Boyes correct?
Another possibility is that the case is simply wrong: after all, it is a High Court case only, which has not been followed. We suggest that *Re Boyes* is correct, however, and is explicable on one or both of the bases outlined above.

It is enough, incidentally, for the intended trustee (B) to be aware of where the terms of the trust could be found (for example, if the terms of the trust are to be placed in a sealed letter to be opened only after the testator's death). Then it could be said that he accepted those terms and was bound by them. In this situation, he would hold the property on the terms of the secret trust (*Re Keen* [1937] Ch 236, 242). Further, although B is not informed of them until after A's death (as in *Re Boyes*), the policy reasons discussed above against enforcing the secret trust in C's favour do not apply. A is not being indecisive and B is not being asked to hold property for any length of time as trustee without knowing the identity of the objects of the trust.

10.4 **Half-secret trusts**

Half-secret trusts are also valid in principle, and like secret trusts, can be enforced by the intended beneficiary. The leading House of Lords authority is *Blackwell* v *Blackwell* [1929] AC 318. The justification for enforcement of half-secret trusts is exactly the same as that for fully secret trusts, that equity imposes upon the conscience of the secret trustee for the prevention of fraud. This is clear from the speech of Viscount Sumner in *Blackwell* v *Blackwell* (at pp. 335–6):

For the prevention of fraud equity fastens on the conscience of the legatee a trust, a trust, that is, which otherwise would be inoperative; in other words it makes him do what the will in itself has nothing to do with; it lets him take what the will gives him and then makes him apply it, as the court of conscience directs, and it does so in order to give effect to wishes of the testator, which would not otherwise be effectual.

From the quote three propositions can be gleaned. First, the reason equity fastens on the conscience of the legatee is for the prevention of fraud. Second, the effect of the trust is to make the legatee 'do what the will in itself has nothing to do with'; in other words, the trust operates independently of the will. Third, in order to prevent fraud, equity directs the legatee to give effect to wishes of the testator. This point is of some importance. The fraud whose commission is being prevented is not the taking of the property beneficially by the legatee, but having taken it, not giving effect to the wishes of the testator.

The facts of *Blackwell* v *Blackwell* were that, by a codicil to his will a testator transferred £12,000 to five trustees, to apply the income 'for the purposes indicated by me to them', with power to pay over the capital sum of £8,000 'to such person or persons indicated by me to them'. He had given detailed oral instructions on the codicil to one of the trustees, and all five knew the general object of the codicil before its execution. The trustees accordingly proposed to pay the income to a lady who was not the testator's wife. The testator's legitimate family challenged the validity of the half-secret trust. The House of Lords held that the half-secret trust was valid.

10.4.1 **Fraud theory**

It is sometimes argued that the fraud theory ought to draw a distinction between fully and half-secret trusts, on the ground that there is no possibility of an intended trustee of a half-secret trust claiming the property for himself since the fact of the trust is plain from the will. All that is needed to avert fraud, therefore, is to compel him to hold on resulting trust for the testator's estate.

Some writers have argued that fraud cannot be the justification because B cannot in any event take beneficially himself, whereas he could if fully secret trusts were not enforced. This is because half-secret trusts differ from the fully secret variety in that the will makes it clear that B takes as trustee only. So, if half-secret trusts are not enforced, B holds the property, not beneficially, but on resulting trust for the residuary legatee. Therefore, there is no possibility of personal gain by B (unless, of course, B is also residuary legatee).

It is no answer to say that a resulting trust would be a fraud on C, the intended beneficiary. As an argument in favour of enforcement, the reasoning is circular, because if a half-secret trust is not enforceable there is no beneficiary to make the argument work. C is only a beneficiary if the conclusion has already been reached that half-secret trusts are to be enforced.

The answer to the resulting trust argument, however, is exactly the same as that for fully secret trusts. The resulting trust is a fraud on the testator (A), and the property has only been given to B because of an express or implied promise, made by B to A. This is clear from the facts of *Blackwell v Blackwell* itself. A intended to benefit his mistress and illegitimate son. A resulting trust would have given the property to his wife and legitimate child—indeed, it was they who argued for a resulting trust. Clearly, A did not intend that they should benefit. He would not have settled the property on B had he thought that the result would be a gift in favour of his wife and legitimate child. B's acceptance of the property would have been a fraud on A unless the trust was enforced in favour of C. The justification for the enforcement of half-secret trusts, therefore, is exactly the same as that for fully secret trusts.

It is in any case clear from Viscount Sumner's speech that the basis of the enforcement of half-secret trusts is fraud, and that the fraud lies not in the personal gain of the intended trustee (B) but in not giving effect to the promise made to the deceased testator.

The case also contains statements to the effect that the law does not distinguish between enforcement of fully and half-secret trusts.

10.5 Limitations on enforcement of half-secret trusts

10.5.1 *Re Keen*

It appears, however, that half-secret trusts differ from their fully secret cousins in one respect. It is necessary for their enforcement for B to have accepted the obligation before the will is made. This distinction is difficult to justify in principle because a will is a revocable instrument having no legal status until death. And if it is argued that the contrary result allows the testator to alter the identity of the beneficiaries every day, at any time up to his death, then why not have the same rule for fully secret trusts?

Nevertheless, there are *dicta* which appear to support the distinction in *Blackwell v Blackwell* itself, where Viscount Sumner observed (at p. 339):

A testator cannot reserve to himself a power of making future unattested dispositions by merely naming a trustee and leaving the purposes of the trust to be supplied afterwards, nor can a legatee given testamentary validity to an unexecuted codicil by accepting an indefinite trust, never communicated to him in the testator's lifetime . . .

What does the dicta in Re Blackwell stand for?
It is possible that Viscount Sumner meant no more here than to restate the general principle that there must be acceptance by the secret or half-secret trustee and that such acceptance must take place within the lifetime of the testator, but this passage clearly can be taken to support the distinction made in the previous paragraph.

Blackwell v *Blackwell* was used as authority for that distinction in *Re Keen* [1937] Ch 236. It is arguable that the time of communication was not the true basis of the decision in *Re Keen*, since the alleged communication did not in any way match the description given in the will, but the rule derived from *Re Keen* has since been applied in *Re Bateman's WT* [1970] 1 WLR 1463.

In *Re Keen*, a clause in the testator's will gave £10,000 on trust to two persons, who were directed to dispose of it 'as may be notified by me to them or either of them during my lifetime'. In fact, some months prior to the will, the testator had given one of the two trustees a sealed envelope containing a sheet of paper on which he had written the name and address of the proposed secret beneficiary (a lady to whom the testator was not married).

The Court of Appeal held that no valid half-secret trust had been created, and the £10,000 fell into residue. One reason was that, simply as a matter of construction, the clause in the testator's will referred to a *future* direction, whereas the direction had by then *already* been communicated to one of the two trustees. Therefore, the express terms of the will were inconsistent with the terms of the trust being contained in the sealed envelope. Had that been the only ground for the decision, the case would have created no difficulties, and the position for half-secret trusts would have been identical to that for fully secret trusts.

Re Keen and the timing of the finalisation of the trust
Lord Wright MR also said, however, that the testator, having declared the existence of the trust in the will, should not be able to reserve to himself the power of making future dispositions without a duly attested codicil simply by notifying them during his lifetime. If that is correct, it follows that the terms of a half-secret trust must be finalised by the date of the will. In *Re Bateman's WT*, the trustees were directed by a clause in the will to pay the income from the testator's estate 'to such persons and in such proportions as shall be stated by me in a sealed letter in my own handwriting and addressed to my trustees'. As in *Keen*, this refers to a *future* direction, but unlike *Keen*, the trustees in *Bateman* received their instructions by means of a sealed letter after the will, but before the death of the testator. Therefore, the express terms of the will were not inconsistent with the timing of the communication.

Nevertheless, the Court of Appeal held that the direction to the trustees was invalid. The only possible explanation for the case, and indeed the one actually adopted by Pennycuick V-C, was that as a general principle, a half-secret trust is enforceable only where its terms are known at the date of the will.

The distinction drawn in *Keen* and *Bateman* has not been adopted in the Republic of Ireland: *Re Prendiville (dec'd)*, Irish High Court, 5 December 1990, noted [1992] Conv 202, where the alternative view of the *Blackwell dictum*, above, was adopted.

10.5.2 Justifications for *Re Keen*

10.5.2.1 *Analogy with incorporation by reference*
A possible explanation is that there is a second principle at work in addition to the fraud principle already discussed. This is that where reference is made in a will to a document, that document must already be in existence, otherwise the possibility exists of testators creating unattested codicils. It may be that of the two principles, the latter prevails where there is conflict.

With fully secret trusts, the question does not arise because the will is silent. It only applies to half-secret trusts because the existence of a half-secret (but not fully secret) trust is openly declared in a formal testamentary bequest. The argument proceeds that the testator having availed himself of this luxury, later additions or changes to the statement that the property is to be held on trust must also be made in a properly attested will or codicil. Therefore, if the testator chooses to declare the terms of his trust later than the date of executing his will, he is committed to using the correct formalities. Thus the distinction between half and fully secret trusts is justified.

This argument has a superficial attraction, taking account as it does of the fact that the problem of adequate proof is one which bedevils the whole area of secret trusts. If a testator has blandly asserted that property is to be held on trust, it is obviously vital to ensure that any other statements he may have made regarding the precise terms of that trust are indeed referable to that particular trust and no other. B. Perrins [1985] Conv 248 explains the timidity of the courts in accepting evidence which post-dates the will.

In this, they appear to have been influenced by the probate doctrine of incorporation by reference. This, in brief, permits the incorporation into the will of any document which was in existence at the time the will was executed, and was referred to as such in the will itself. It is a useful doctrine in that it saves the bother of copying out lengthy trust documents in the will itself merely for the purpose of adding a fresh sum to those trusts by way of bequest. The testator can instead simply refer to those documents and rely on a short declaration that the bequest is to be held on the terms set out in those documents. He cannot, however, incorporate a document which is not yet in existence at the time of making the will: to allow this would be to tempt fraudulent claims that this or that document was the one to which the testator meant to refer.

Policy for the limitations upon half-secret trusts
It is therefore easy to see why the courts, conscious of the wisdom of these limits to the doctrine of incorporation by reference, may have thought it prudent to import those limits into the enforcement of half-secret trusts. But as a principled justification for the communication rules, the explanation has defects.

For example, it is not necessary to the enforcement of a half-secret trust that any document at all should exist to declare the terms of the trust. So long as he communicates the terms before signing his will, the testator is free to rely on a purely oral communication, which must be even more susceptible to later misrepresentation than a document. If the courts are prepared to accept the existence of fully secret trusts on quite slender evidence, e.g., *Ottaway v Norman*, it would be odd if they refused to accept oral evidence to show the terms of a half-secret trust, where the chance of fraud is, if anything, less.

In any case, to argue that the testator, having once committed himself to formality, remains bound by the need for further formality if he wishes to expound the terms of his trust later than the date of making his will, is merely to penalise him for partial compliance with the Wills Act 1837, while allowing the testator who ignores that Act entirely (by creating a fully secret trust) to have his wishes enforced. This seems to fall short of being a rational justification, therefore.

10.5.2.2 *Policy against indecision*

Another, related argument which was stated in *Blackwell* v *Blackwell*, and repeated in *Re Keen*, is that to permit a testator simply to state the existence of a trust and communicate its terms at his leisure would be to permit a will to be freely altered by unattested dispositions, thus defeating the policy of the Wills Act 1837.

Thus, for example, Watkin [1981] Conv 335 argues for the *Bateman* position on policy grounds, namely that whereas the law should not and does not object to secrecy, it should not encourage indecision. A testator should have made up his mind by the time the will is made.

The argument reflects a respect for the policy of the Wills Act 1837, and the logic of this reasoning (if correct) applies to fully secret trusts also. Indeed, Watkin argues that they should be brought into line by statute. This, it is argued, would allow the testator who has made up his mind where he wants his property to go, but wishes its destination to be secret, to fulfil his desires by making his communication prior to the will, while defeating the testator who is merely indecisive and wants the luxury of changing his will without the trouble and expense of making fresh testamentary provisions. As Watkin acknowledges, however, the practice of permitting indecisive behaviour via a fully secret trust is so firmly entrenched that a statute would be required to effect the change.

10.5.3 **Codicils**

As we have seen in 10.5.1, half-secret trusts must be communicated prior to, or contemporaneously with, the execution of the will. Suppose that the trusts are communicated after the date of the will but before a later codicil. This raises the question of the effect of the codicil. Another issue is whether additional property can be added to an existing secret or half-secret trust by codicil.

In *Blackwell* v *Blackwell* [1929] AC 318 itself, the gift which was subject to the half-secret trust was contained in a codicil, but in that case the gift was created for the first time by the codicil and the trustees had been duly informed in advance. Suppose, however, that the half-secret trust is originally created earlier, in the will, and the intended trustee (B) has not been informed in advance. There is no direct authority whether the later reference to that trust in the codicil will suffice first to create the trust contained in the will and secondly to add extra property to this trust.

In favour of allowing the trust, it can be argued that the policy of the *Re Keen* rule ([1937] Ch 236) is merely to ensure that the trust is communicated prior to some properly executed testamentary disposition which indicates its terms, and that therefore the mention of the trust in the codicil should be good enough. A codicil has the effect of republishing a will, in other words it is as though the will itself had been made at the date of the later codicil.

The position is different where additional property is added by the codicil, since the trustees may not have accepted any obligations regarding the additional property. In *Re Colin Cooper* [1939] Ch 811, a testator had left £5,000 to trustees on half-secret trust in his will, having duly informed them in advance and obtained their agreement, and later added a further £10,000 to this trust in a codicil. The Court of Appeal held that only the first amount mentioned in the will could be subject to the half-secret trust, and that the amount added by the codicil fell into residue. In *Re Colin Cooper*, the trustees had agreed to hold £5,000, and that was the limit of their obligation, since they never knew of the further obligation imposed in the codicil. As Sir Wilfred Greene MR said (at p. 818):

it was not with regard to any sum other than the £5,000 that the consciences of the trustees (to use a technical phrase) were burdened.

He seemed to envisage, however, that if the agreement had been that the trustees would hold £5,000 or whatever sum the testator finally chose to bequeath, it would have been enforceable on those terms. This also accords with the view taken by the courts that a sealed envelope may be sufficient communication, despite the fact that the terms are, *ex hypothesi*, unknown to the trustee, who assents to carry them out whatever they might turn out to be.

10.6 **Secret and half-secret trusts take effect independently of the will**

It is also clear from *Blackwell v Blackwell* [1929] AC 518 that secret and half-secret trusts operate independently of the will. It is possible that they operate as express trusts created *inter vivos* by the agreement reached between the testator and the intended trustee, the function or relevance of the will being to vest the property in the intended trustee at the agreed time for the assumption of his office. From the passage in Viscount Sumner's speech, however, to which allusion has already been made (at 10.4), it seems more likely that after the will has transferred legal title to the legatee, the court fastens on the conscience of the legatee by imposing on him a trust. This is probably best analysed as a constructive trust, imposed in order to prevent fraud.

A similar analysis was adopted by Lord Westbury in *McCormick v Grogan* (at p. 97):

The court of equity has, from a very early period, decided that even an Act of Parliament shall not be used as an instrument of fraud; and if in the machinery of perpetrating a fraud an Act of Parliament intervenes, the court of equity, it is true, does not set aside the Act of Parliament but it fastens on the individual who gets a title under that Act, and imposes upon him a personal obligation, because he applies the Act as an instrument for accomplishing a fraud.

Whichever analysis is correct, whether secret and half-secret trusts are express *inter vivos* trusts or constructive trusts imposed once the legatee has received the property (on which, see further shortly), the will does no more than constitute the trust, transferring the legal property to the secret trustee. It seems likely that the trust could also be constituted by intestacy, in the absence of any will, if the settlor refrains from making a will in the knowledge that the property will pass to the intended trustee by virtue of the Administration of Estates Act 1925, rather than using a more usual form of transfer for an *inter vivos* trust.

It is sometimes argued that if secret and half-secret trusts are ordinary *inter vivos* trusts, the Wills Act has no application to them. If this is so, then fraud ought not to be strictly necessary for their enforcement. The mere fact of an existing trust should be enough for equity to intervene to enforce it, irrespective of any '*malus animus*' on the part of the trustee.

Yet, while it is undoubtedly correct to say that the *mechanism* by which secret and half-secret trusts are enforced has nothing to do with the will, merely to describe the mechanism is not the same thing as providing a reason for their enforcement. The reason that equity imposes on the conscience of the legatee is fraud, and the mere fact that the mechanism operates independently of the will in no way affects that requirement.

The operation of secret and half-secret trusts independently of this will does have other consequences, however. In *Re Young* [1951] Ch 344 a half-secret trust was enforced despite the fact that the beneficiary had witnessed the will, which, under s. 15 of the Wills Act 1837, would normally have the effect of invalidating the gift to the witnessing beneficiary. Since he took outside the will, however, this rule did not apply. Danckwerts J commented:

The whole theory of the formation of a secret trust is that the Wills Act has nothing to do with the matter . . . , since the persons do not take by virtue of the gift in the will, but by virtue of the secret trusts imposed upon the beneficiary, who does in fact take under the will.

In *Re Gardner (No. 2)* [1923] 2 Ch 230, a secret trust in favour of a beneficiary who had predeceased the testator was upheld. It is not possible to leave property to a dead person by will, and it is difficult to justify this decision even on the basis that the will has nothing to do with the matter. The usual analysis is that, at the very least, the will constitutes the trust by transferring legal title to the secret trustee, but Romer J saw no reason why a declaration of trust by the secret trustee should not have occurred at the moment of communication of the trust to him (at p. 233):

The rights of the parties appear to me to be exactly the same as though the husband [secret trustee], after the memorandum had been communicated to him by the testatrix . . . , had executed a declaration of trust binding himself to hold any property that should come to him upon his wife's [settlor's] partial intestacy upon trust as specified in the memorandum.

If Romer J's view is correct, then the consequences are not limited to an ability to make a secret or half-secret trust in favour of a beneficiary who predeceases the testator. If the trust comes into force from the moment of communication, then it must also follow that it is irrevocable from that moment, and that neither the testator nor the secret trustee would be able later to change his mind. This would be an unfortunate consequence if the communication was made many years before the testator's death and circumstances had changed radically in the meantime. Suppose, for example, the secret beneficiary ran off with the secret trustee's wife. Could not the secret trustee inform the testator that he was no longer prepared to accept the property on the original terms? Or, if he were no longer able to get in touch with the testator, could he not refuse to take the property under the will? One would have thought that, in principle, he should be able to change his mind, but if Romer J is right, and the trust is created from the moment of communication, then it may well be that he cannot.

Romer J's view is in any case inconsistent with views expressed in the Court of Appeal in *Re Maddock* [1902] 2 Ch 220, to the effect that the trust only becomes binding once the legatee accepts the legacy. For example, Collins MR said (at p. 226):

But the right of the [beneficiary] is wholly dependent on whether the legatee accepts the legacy with knowledge of the mandate, and no right for them arises at all unless and until the legatee has, with notice, accepted the legacy.

Cozens-Hardy LJ took a similar view (at p. 231):

Now, the so-called trust does not affect the property except by reason of a personal obligation binding the individual devisee or legatee. If he renounces and disclaims, or dies in the lifetime of the testator, the persons claiming under the memorandum can take nothing against the heir-at-law or next-of-kin or residuary devisee or legatee.

These statements clearly imply that the trust is not constituted until the testator has died, and the legatee has accepted the trust property.

There is another difficulty with Romer J's analysis. The secret trustee must be declaring himself trustee of after-acquired property, since only on the testator's death is legal title vested in him. The conventional view is that trusts of future property are void (see further chapter 3).

The orthodox view is that *Gardner (No. 2)* is wrong.

10.7 Miscellaneous issues

10.7.1 *Re Stead*

In *Re Stead* [1900] 1 Ch 237, Farwell J (at p. 241) made various distinctions where property was given to two or more persons (let us call them B1 and B2) as joint tenants or tenants in common, but where only one (B1) had promised to hold the property on a secret trust. The question at issue is whether B2 is bound by the trust.

Where a gift is made to trustees as joint tenants, the orthodox view, as stated in *Re Stead*, is that if communication is made before the execution of the will, all will be bound, whereas if communication is made after the execution of the will but before the death of the testator, only those who have accepted the trust are bound by it, on the basis that the gift to an intended trustee who does not consent is not tainted with any fraud in procuring the execution of the will. Where the gift is to the intended trustees as tenants in common, only those who are aware of the trust are bound, whether they obtain this knowledge before or after the will is executed.

The distinctions were said to be based on older cases but are difficult to support as a matter of policy. However, B. Perrins (1972) 85 LQR 225 argues, at p. 228, that Farwell J's distinctions are wrong and that the true rule rests on the principle of *Huguenin* v *Baseley* (1807) 14 Ves Jr 273, that no man may profit from the fraud of another. On this argument, B2 would be bound if the testator was induced to leave the property to him on the strength of B1's promise, but not otherwise, and the question of when communication occurred would be a matter of evidence only. The argument has much to commend it, and if Perrins is correct then these cases fit into the general scheme of things, so long as the criteria for enforcement advanced in *Ottaway* v *Norman* [1972] Ch 698 are correct.

10.7.2 Absence of intended trustee, or renunciation by him of the legacy

Suppose B has died before A. This makes it necessary to consider whether a secret trust can be enforced in the absence of the intended trustee (B). It is undoubted law that a legacy cannot take effect where the legatee predeceases the testator, and the statements already considered from *Re Maddock* [1902] 2 Ch 220 (see 10.6), and in particular that of Cozens-Hardy LJ, suggest that the trust will not be enforced in this case, nor where the secret trustee renounces the legacy.

On the other hand, the fraud on the testator is no less in these cases than in the conventional situation, and there is a general principle that 'equity will not allow a trust to fail for want of a trustee'. It might be thought, therefore, that where the intended trustee has predeceased the testator, a trust should be imposed upon the property in the hands of A's executor.

There are also *dicta* of Lord Buckmaster in *Blackwell* v *Blackwell* [1929] AC 318, at p. 328, that the intended trustee will not be allowed to defeat the testator's purpose by renouncing the legacy.

The *dicta* in *Re Maddock* cannot be reconciled with those of Lord Buckmaster in *Blackwell* v *Blackwell*. It is true that *Re Maddock* concerned a fully secret trust, whereas the trust in *Blackwell* v *Blackwell* was half-secret. One could argue for a distinction on that basis, since the trust is plain on the face of the will in the latter, but not the former case. It is clear, however, that both sets of *dicta* are intended to apply to both types of trust, and we can only conclude that neither issue has been finally decided.

If the secret trustee cannot renounce the legacy, then on the assumption that the trust is not fully constituted before the death of the testator (but see 9.6), there must be a general principle that a trustee cannot renounce his obligations once he has accepted trusteeship, even before the trust is fully constituted. There appears to be no authority for or against the existence of such a general principle, but I have already suggested (see 9.6) that significant problems could arise if there was a long period of time between acceptance of the trust and the death of the testator, and circumstances had changed radically in the meantime.

10.7.3 **Residuary legatees**

Suppose B is directed to dispose of only some of the property acquired under the will and to keep the rest for himself. In effect, the will makes him residuary legatee.

The issue seems to turn on the construction of the will. If it can be said that the will creates a conditional gift then the trustees may take, subject to fulfilling the condition. If, however, on its true construction it imposes a trust, the courts have shown themselves reluctant to allow the trustees to introduce evidence to contradict its terms. In other words, the trustees will be unable to adduce evidence that they were intended to take as residuary legatees.

In *Re Rees* [1950] Ch 204, the testator had left his whole estate on half-secret trust and privately informed his trustees (B) that they were to make certain payments and retain the surplus for themselves. Since one of the trustees was the solicitor who had drafted the will, the court was, perhaps, especially disposed towards caution in this case, holding that on the proper construction of the will, the half-secret trust was imposed upon the entire estate. The trustees would not therefore be allowed to introduce extrinsic evidence to contradict this by showing that they were intended to take beneficially subject only to making the payments.

The reasoning in *Re Rees* applies only to half-secret trusts, since with a fully secret trust the will itself will be silent. There can therefore be no question of additional evidence *contradicting* the will. *Re Rees* was doubted in *Re Tyler* [1967] 1 WLR 1269, but *Re Tyler* was distinguishable because the trustees were claiming only a specified sum (£500), and were not claiming to take as residuary legatees: the £500 was apparently treated as a conditional gift. In any case, this was a fully secret trust, so that in principle *Re Rees* should not have been applicable.

10.8 Express or constructive trusts: does it matter?

We have seen that the basis of enforcement of both fully and half-secret trusts is B's fraud, defined in a wide equitable sense. Additionally, both varieties implement the express intentions of the testator, even though those intentions may not be expressed correctly, in writing, signed and attested, etc. Each takes effect outside the will. It is said that it matters whether they are classified as express or constructive trusts because the formality requirements of the Law of Property Act 1925, s. 53(1) (see chapter 5) apply to express, but not (by virtue of s. 53(2)) constructive trusts.

Section 53(1)(b) requires express trusts of land to be declared in writing, yet a fully secret trust of land was enforced in *Ottaway* v *Norman* [1972] Ch 698 despite being oral. Further, that case ostensibly rested on constructive trust principles. This is therefore apparently authority that fully secret trusts at least are constructive. Yet some writers distinguish between the two varieties, and argue that *Ottaway* v *Norman* applies only to fully secret trusts. Indeed, *Re Baillie* (1886) 2 TLR 660 suggests that writing is required for half-secret trusts of land, although perhaps not too much emphasis should be placed on cases prior to *Blackwell* v *Blackwell* [1929] AC 318, and there can be no justification for the distinction if the basis of enforcement of half and fully secret trusts is the same.

We would suggest that writing is never required for any secret trust of either variety. The mechanism appears to be that B obtains property under the will and that equity, operating outside the will, imposes on his conscience and requires him to hold as constructive trustee for C. On this basis, both fully and half-secret trusts are constructive.

We would also suggest that the issue is wholly academic and of no practical importance whatever. The classification is relevant only to the formality requirements of s. 53. Yet the validity of half and fully secret trusts depends on a principle of equity, which is not defeated by s. 9 of the Wills Act 1837. Surely it will also not be defeated by s. 53 of the Law of Property Act 1925 or any other statutory formality provision intended to prevent fraud. If equity will not permit a statute intended to prevent fraud to be used as an instrument for fraud, there is no reason why it should distinguish between statutes for these purposes. The principle applies as much to the Law of Property Act 1925, s. 53, as to the Wills Act 1837, s. 9. This will be so however secret trusts are classified because it is not therefore necessary that they fall within the s. 53(2) exception to avoid the requirements of s. 53(1). See further on this point, Perrins [1985] Conv 248, 256–7.

Further support for the view that s. 53(1)(b) is treated in a similar fashion to the Wills Act itself can be found in *Sen* v *Headley* [1991] Ch 425.

The conclusion is, then, that whether secret and semi-secret trusts are express or constructive, they are not affected by any statute requiring formality.

online resource centre

FURTHER READING

Kincaid [2000] Conv 420.
Meager [2003] Conv 203.
Perrins [1985] Conv 248.
Sheridan (1951) 67 LQR 314.
Watkin [1981] Conv 335.

11

Equitable fraud and the constructive trust

This chapter is concerned primarily with constructive trusts, differentiating them from other types of trust—namely, express and implied trusts. Previous chapters have described the way in which the express trust and the implied trust will give effect to the express or implied wishes of the settler respectively, with resulting trusts also arising as a consequence (albeit in a less direct sense) of the settlor's intentions. In contrast, constructive trusts are imposed by the courts as a matter of law. They depend on principles of equity and conscience, and are independent of the settlor's intention.

Constructive trusteeship arising from representations
A number of the cases considered in sections 11.2 to 11.4 involve representations, where equity holds representors to their representation. In 11.3 and most of the cases in 11.4, the representor has either obtained the trust property on the strength of the representation, or at any rate obtained it on terms different from those upon which he or she would have obtained it had the representation not been made. Note that in none of these cases does equity require representors to return the property; the effect of the constructive trust is always to hold them to their representation.

Representations that are relied on by others, to their detriment, can give rise to estoppels as well as constructive trusts, and, as chapter 9 case studying the family home revealed, the consequences of imposing a constructive trust can be greater than the consequences of estoppels (although, recent authorities suggest that the requirements for an estoppel appear to be more stringent than was once thought). This 'consequences' approach suggests that a constructive trust will not necessarily arise in all cases of detrimental reliance. And the reality appears to be that it arises only in a few rigidly defined and discrete categories of case, and that there is no generalised equitable fraud jurisdiction.

Thereafter, in 11.5 a different type of case comes to the fore: a situation for which there is limited but growing authority. These may be (but are not necessarily) cases where the trust is imposed because of unconscionable conduct by the trustee. Here, legal title is obtained by someone who either knows from the outset that she is not entitled to the property, or who does not know from the outset but discovers later. In such situations, where a constructive trust is imposed, the legal owner appears to be required to hold the property on trust for the transferor. It appears that, in contrast to many situations considered within this chapter (where anything beyond holding those who make representations to that which has been represented would be inappropriate), such conduct (knowing that one is not entitled to property, or discovering so later)—will actually have the effect of requiring the return of the property.

In 11.6 consideration is given to whether any generalisations can be made from the categories emerging from progression through the chapter, and as to whether the courts are moving towards a principled jurisdiction based on the defendant's conduct. This will be set against an oppositional proposition that the categories are exhaustive, and that the constructive trust has no wider role in cases of misconduct.

11.1 Defining fraud: the starting point

In this chapter the focal point is fraud which can be classified as *equitable* fraud. The significance of labelling it in this manner lies in the proposition that fraud which is equitable denotes a meaning that is different from, and actually wider than, fraud at common law.

Common law fraud and equitable fraud compared and contrasted
The distinction and difference between common law and equitable fraud was noted in two comparatively recent decisions in *Armitage* v *Nurse* [1998] Ch 241, and *Walker* v *Stones* [2001] QB 902. The significance of *Armitage* v *Nurse* is considered immediately below, but for immediate purposes, the classic definition of fraud at common law hails from Lord Herschell in *Derry* v *Peek* (1889) 14 App Cas 337. At p. 374, Lord Herschell observed that in the context of representations:

fraud is proved when it is shown that a false representation has been made (i) knowingly, or (ii) without belief in its truth, or (iii) recklessly, careless whether it be true or false. Although I have treated the second and third as distinct cases, I think the third is but an instance of the second, for one who makes a statement under such circumstances can have no real belief in the truth of what he states.

The significance of starting with the **common law definition** in this discussion on **equitable fraud** is that in many of the cases considered within this chapter, fraud in the common law sense is not proved. Indeed, for example, in the discussion that will follow concerning *Bannister* v *Bannister*, the claimant may well have believed the representations he made, at the time when they were made, but later he changed his mind. This certainly did not amount to fraud in a common law sense, but as far as equity was concerned, a different set of considerations applied. For equity it was sufficient that the defendant had been induced to rely on the claimant's representations; that she had actually relied on them, and that it was unconscionable for him therefore to renege on his promises. In the discrete sets of circumstances considered in this chapter, equity holds people to the representations they have made, when it would be unconscionable for them to renege. A similar principle operated in *Ottaway* v *Norman* (in chapter 10), where again there was no fraud in the common law sense.

Beyond 'civil fraud' arising from Derry v Peek: explaining 'actual' and 'equitable' fraud
This very brief introduction to the significance of identifying and distinguishing fraud at common law and fraud in equity will develop into a much fuller discussion shortly. At this stage attention must be drawn to the important observations made

on the interpretation of the meaning of 'fraud' in *Armitage v Nurse* [1998] Ch 241. Crucially, the judgment of Millett LJ distinguished equitable fraud from 'actual fraud'.

This arose in the context of determining the validity of a trustee exemption clause: the significance and operation of trustee exemption clauses will be considered in due course in chapter 18 as part of this text's study of trusteeship. For present purposes, it will suffice to note simply that this is a mechanism designed to protect trustees from liability which can be incurred should they commit a breach of trust. The clause in *Armitage* itself purported to exclude the trustee's ability to incur liability under the trust 'except for losses and damage which is caused by his own actual fraud'. It was in respect of this that Millett LJ explained the meaning of **actual fraud** by distinguishing it from **equitable fraud**. In determining that reference to 'actual fraud' connoted behaviour which was different from equitable fraud, Millett LJ considered that 'actual fraud' required 'proof of dishonesty', and that in this context it:

connotes at the minimum an intention on the part of the trustee to pursue a particular course of action, either knowing that it is contrary to the interests of the beneficiaries or being recklessly indifferent whether it is contrary to their interests or not.

In contrast, the species of 'equitable' fraud:

covers breach of fiduciary duty, undue influence, abuse of confidence, unconscionable bargains and frauds on powers. With the sole exception of the last, which is a technical doctrine in which the word 'fraud' merely connotes excess of views, it involves some dealing by the fiduciary with his principal at the risk that the fiduciary may have exploited his position to his own advantage.

It is with this latter equitable fraud that this chapter is concerned. In this vein, the themes which have been attributed to Millett LJ immediately above will provide the basis for much of the material which will be used in the discussions which follow.

11.2 Equity will not allow a statute to be used as a cloak for fraud

This principle was developed by the courts of equity to prevent people from taking unfair advantage of statutory formality provisions, which are of course intended to prevent rather than encourage fraud. We have already seen examples of this, fraud certainly being the basis of the part performance doctrine, which has usually been used to prevent reliance on the now-repealed s. 40 of the Law of Property Act 1925. It is probably also the principle that operates to avoid s. 53(1)(b) of the Law of Property Act in first-category *Rosset* cases. It might be argued that secret trusts are also based on the same principle here preventing reliance on s. 9 of the Wills Act 1837, as subsequently amended. However, for reasons that appear below, this may not explain cases such as *Ottaway v Norman*, where the principle operating is that in the following section.

A principle with general application
The principle is also of more general application, applying whenever there is an attempt to use a statute intended to prevent fraud as a means of perpetrating fraud.

In *Rochefoucauld* v *Boustead* [1897] 1 Ch 196, the claimant (Comtesse de la Rochefoucauld) owned some estates producing coffee in Ceylon (present-day Sri Lanka), but these properties were subject to a considerable mortgage, which the Comtesse was having difficulty in repaying. In order to stop the mortgagee from foreclosing, an arrangement was made whereby the defendant purchased the estates subject to the mortgage. The precise circumstances of this transfer were disputed, but the Court of Appeal accepted on the basis of both oral evidence and letters that the defendant took the land as trustee for the claimant.

He treated the land as if it were his own, however, and raised more money on it by way of mortgage without the claimant's consent. The claimant later asserted her equitable title, and claimed an account of profits, but the defendant claimed that he was beneficial owner of the property.

Various arguments were advanced by the defendant, all of which were rejected, but the interesting one for our purposes was that the trust claimed by the claimant was not evidenced in writing signed by the defendant, as required by the Statute of Frauds 1677, s. 7, which was the precursor of the Law of Property Act 1925, s. 53 (on which, see chapter 6). This argument was rejected on the principle that equity will not allow a statute to be used as a cloak for fraud.

The principle illustrated

Another case which is probably an example of the same principle, is *Hodgson* v *Marks* [1971] 1 Ch 892 which was considered in the family homes case study (chapter 9). Here, an old lady (Mrs Hodgson) was cajoled into making a voluntary conveyance (i.e., not for value) of her house to her lodger (Evans). Evans told her that the conveyance was just a device to protect him against her nephew, who disapproved of him. Evidence that the transfer to Evans was on express oral trust for Mrs Hodgson (who remained in occupation) was accepted, but there was no writing (and an oral express trust of land is void by virtue of s. 53(1)(b) of the Law of Property Act 1925). Evans then sold the property to a third party (Marks). Two issues arose: first, did Mrs Hodgson have an equitable interest in the property; and, second, did that interest bind Marks? Both issues were decided in favour of Mrs Hodgson in the Court of Appeal. The second issue is of more importance to land law than trusts, because of the application of s. 70(1)(g) of the Land Registration Act 1925. This concerns the first consideration arising from equitable fraud.

In the Court of Appeal Russell LJ, who gave the only substantive judgment, and with whom Buckley and Cairns LJJ agreed, thought that Mrs Hodgson's interest was by way of resulting trust, in which case the decision would be of no help for this discussion, since resulting trusts are expressly exempted from the operation of s. 53 (by virtue of s. 53(2)). A different explanation must, however, be found in the light of Lord Browne-Wilkinson's speech in *Westdeutsche* v *Islington LBC* [1996] AC 669 (which has been noted already in chapters 1, 2, and 7). In any case, Mrs Hodgson did not argue a resulting trust; there was evidence of an express oral trust, and this was the basis of Ungoed-Thomas J's decision in the High Court, who relied on *Rochefoucauld* v *Boustead* to avoid s. 53(1)(b). (Although Ungoed-Thomas J was reversed in the Court of Appeal, the reversal was only as to the interpretation of the Land Registration Act 1925, not on the question of the existence of a trust.)

Russell LJ seemed unsure whether the *Rochefoucauld* v *Boustead* principle could apply to Marks, the third party purchaser. This is why he preferred to base his decision on resulting trust reasoning, but he would have been happy to apply Ungoed-Thomas J's reasoning to Mr Evans, the original lodger: 'Quite plainly Mr Evans could not have placed any reliance on section 53, for that would have been to use the section as an instrument of fraud.'

Equitable fraud: understanding its limits
Though the doctrine can be generalised beyond secret trusts and the *Rosset* first-category cases considered earlier, it is important to appreciate its limits.

(a) The principle operates only where all the requirements for a trust (or contract) are already present, apart from writing. The part performance doctrine operates only where the contract is in all respects otherwise valid, and would be enforceable if in writing. The case study in chapter 9 provides illustration that all the elements of a trust (apart from writing) must be present in a first-category *Rosset* case. In secret trust cases, all the elements of a valid trust (apart from the formalities) are often present; where they are not (as, e.g., in *Ottaway* v *Norman*, where the property was probably not taken by the legatee on trust) the principles in the next section operate.

(b) The doctrine probably applies only to formality provisions, the purpose of which is to prevent fraud.

(c) In all the cases considered, the nature of the fraud is a representation relied on by another party, where it would be unconscionable for the person making the representation to renege upon it. Fraud certainly does not appear to be generalised to include all instances of bad faith. In *Midland Bank Trust Co. Ltd* v *Green* [1981] AC 513 a very important land law case, a sham sale between husband and wife, intended specifically to defeat their son's option to purchase a farm, succeeded in its purpose, solely because the option had not been properly registered under the Land Charges Act 1925. This makes quite a contrast to the cases considered here, but the statute relied on was intended to simplify conveyancing, not to prevent fraud. Moreover, Mrs Green made no representations of any kind to her son, and Lord Wilberforce observed (at p. 531) that in general it is not 'fraud' to rely on legal rights conferred by Act of Parliament.

In the discussion in chapter 10, it was suggested that the mechanism upon which the doctrine operated, at least for secret and half-secret trusts, was the imposition of a constructive trust, and a similar explanation was adopted in chapter 9, in the later case in order to trigger s. 53(2). However, the fact that constructive trusts are not exempted from the Wills Act 1837 suggests that it would have made no difference in chapter 10 had s. 53(2) never been enacted. The mechanism by which the part performance operates may also be the constructive trust; certainly a constructive trust arises, on the principles considered earlier. It is interesting that s. 2 of the Law of Property (Miscellaneous Provisions) Act 1989, which is often said to have abolished the part performance doctrine as far as it related to land, does not apply (by virtue of s. 2(5)) to the creation or operation of resulting, implied or constructive trusts. This strengthens the argument we advanced in chapter 10—i.e., to the extent that part performance is a fraud-based doctrine, it survives the enactment of the 1989 Act.

However, it is not clear beyond doubt that the mechanism is always the imposition of a constructive trust; it could, as previously observed, simply be an interpretation of a statute which was intended to prevent fraud—it cannot be used to promote fraud. For similar reasoning to that advanced at in chapter 10, it probably does not matter whether the mechanism is one of constructive trust or not, unless it were intended to use these cases to advance a more general principle connecting fraud with constructive trusts.

11.3 Obtaining legal title expressly subject to rights of another

There is now a clear line of authority that where somebody obtains legal title to property by agreeing to take it expressly subject to the rights of another party, equity will require him to hold the property as constructive trustee, to give effect to the rights of the other party.

As in the previous section, equity holds the representor to his representation, where it would be unconscionable to allow the representor to renege. There the unconscionable element was reliance upon a statute the purpose of which was to prevent fraud; here it is the use of the representation to obtain property. It is also an alternative explanation of the secret trusts cases considered in chapter 10.

This development is not particularly startling, and can again be seen as a generalisation of the secret trusts doctrine. It is also not that dissimilar to ordinary express trusteeship, since trustees ordinarily accept legal title subject to the terms of the trust, except of course that in these cases, formality provisions are avoided. In so far as these cases cause problems, it is because the trusts which thereby arise are full property interests capable of binding third parties. The problems of life tenancies are considered in chapter 1. Conveyancing problems might also arise where a bare trust is created, since this would not require registration under the Land Charges Act 1972 and, since the beneficiary would often be in occupation, could be an overriding interest under s. 70(1)(g) of the Land Registration Act 1925. That would seem to be an argument for amending the conveyancing provisions, however, rather than curtailing the development of the equitable doctrine.

Fraud and conscionability: case law illustrations
In *Bannister* v *Bannister* [1948] 2 All ER 133, the claimant, who was the defendant's brother-in-law, was able to obtain two cottages from the defendant, at well below their market value, on the understanding that after the sale the defendant would be able to continue to live in one of the cottages rent-free for as long as she wished. She relied on his oral statement—'I do not want to take any rent, but will let you stay [in one of the cottages] as long as you like rent free'—and consequently the claimant obtained the cottages for only £250, as compared with their true market value of around £400. No written agreement to this effect was included in the conveyance. The claimant thereafter occupied the whole cottage save for one room which was occupied by the defendant. Troubles arose between the parties a few years later and the claimant sought possession of the cottage, claiming that the defendant was a mere tenant at will. The Court of Appeal took the view that although the claimant

had not actually obtained the property by fraud, since he probably meant what he said at the time, it would now be unconscionable for him to retain it with vacant possession, and therefore decided that he held it as constructive trustee of the defendant for her life.

In *Binions* v *Evans* [1972] 1 Ch 359 Mrs Evans's husband was employed by the Tredegar Estate (near Newport in South Wales) and lived rent free in a cottage owned by the estate. The husband died when the defendant (Mrs Evans) was 73. The trustees of the estate then entered into a written agreement with the defendant that she could continue to live in the cottage during her lifetime as tenant at will rent-free; she undertook to keep the cottage in good condition and repair. The trustees later sold the cottage to the claimants, Mr and Mrs Binions, expressly subject to Mrs Evans's 'tenancy agreement'. The claimants, having thereby obtained the cottage more cheaply, six months later sought possession from Mrs Evans, claiming that she was a tenant at will. The Court of Appeal held in favour of Mrs Evans but, although the decision was unanimous, the reasoning of the Master of the Rolls was quite different from that of Megaw and Stephenson LJJ.

Lord Denning MR started with the assertion that Mrs Evans had a contractual licence, which bound the purchasers with notice. This is inconsistent with the later Court of Appeal decision in *Ashburn Anstalt* v *Arnold* [1989] 1 Ch 1 (see further below) and is almost certainly incorrect. Indeed, Stephenson LJ doubted whether this line of reasoning was correct in *Binions* v *Evans* itself.

Lord Denning MR's alternative grounds were that because Mr and Mrs Binions had purchased expressly subject to the agreement, equity would impose on their conscience and require them to hold the property on constructive trust for Mrs Evans. This approach, based on *Bannister* v *Bannister*, differs from the views of the other two judges, in that the trust arose not under the original agreement, but only on the sale of the property to the claimants.

Lord Denning: the legacy of a radical judge

Lord Denning MR's constructive trust approach, narrowly interpreted, is probably the *ratio* of *Binions* v *Evans*, and has been followed in subsequent cases. However, parts of Lord Denning's judgment are more radical. He thought that to take property *impliedly* subject to an enforceable agreement would also be enough, and that a constructive trust could be imposed whenever the trustee had conducted himself in an inequitable manner. As with the contractual licence reasoning, this part of the judgment probably cannot survive the criticism in *Ashburn Anstalt* v *Arnold*.

The reasoning of Megaw and Stephenson LJJ was entirely different. In their view, the original agreement between the trustees and the defendant created a life tenancy. Thus, even at this stage the trustees held the property on trust for Mrs Evans for her life, thereafter for the Tredegar Estate in fee simple. Because this was a succession of equitable interests, Mrs Evans had an interest in land coming within the provisions of the Settled Land Act 1925 (see 8.8). The purchasers were therefore bound by an existing trust, on the ordinary principles of the equitable notice doctrine (see chapter 1).

The majority view has never been followed and there is a problem with it—i.e., that it is difficult to see why the sale to the claimants was not caught by the 'paralysing section' which should have prevented the sale to Mr and Mrs Binions from taking effect: Settled Land Act 1925, s. 13. On the Settled Land Act question, however, we saw at 8.8 that in *Ungurian* v *Lesnoff* [1990] Ch 206, Vinelott J preferred the view of the majority to that of Lord Denning MR (who thought that the Act did not apply to interests created under a constructive trust). It is reasonably clear, therefore, that the imposition of a trust creates a property interest so as to trigger the Settled Land Act 1925.

Cases subsequent to *Binions* v *Evans* suggest that the very broad views of Lord Denning MR, that a constructive trust could be imposed whenever the trustee had conducted himself in an inequitable manner, have not gained favour. However, there is now a reasonable body of authority supporting his view that a constructive trust may be imposed on a purchaser (probably of land or chattels: see, e.g., Browne-Wilkinson J's judgment *Swiss Bank Corporation* v *Lloyds Bank Ltd* [1979] 1 Ch 548) who purchases expressly subject to a prior agreement.

Lord Denning MR's view was adopted by Dillon J in *Lyus* v *Prowsa Developments Ltd* [1982] 1 WLR 1044, but Dillon J limited *Binions* v *Evans* to the situation where the purchaser took *subject to* a right. It is not enough that he merely knew of it.

The decision of the Court of Appeal in *Ashburn Anstalt* v *Arnold* [1989] 1 Ch 1, comprehensively noted by M. P. Thompson ([1988] Conv 201), is probably more important to students of land law than to those of trusts, but nevertheless it contains important *dicta* which bear on the present discussion. Fox LJ thought that contractual licences are not interests in land and do not bind third-party purchasers. The relevance of this point to the present discussion is that if Lord Denning MR's judgment in *Binions* v *Evans* can be justified, it can only be on the basis of constructive trust reasoning, and not on the basis of contractual licence reasoning alternatively advanced.

Ashburn as an illustration of a constructive trust argument
A constructive trust was argued in *Ashburn Anstalt* v *Arnold* on the basis of Lord Denning MR's reasoning in *Binions* v *Evans*. The court, however, took the view that it would be imposed only where it was satisfied that the conscience of the purchaser was affected. This required more than mere notice, even express notice of the contractual licence. Even a purchaser who took 'subject to' a contractual licence would not necessarily be bound. There must be a clear undertaking on the part of the purchaser, and the obligation must be imposed expressly in the conveyance. While Fox LJ supported the decision in *Binions* v *Evans*, he would virtually have limited it to its facts. On his view, a constructive trust will be imposed only where the conveyance to the purchaser is made *expressly* subject to the contractual licence, and he also thought the fact that the purchaser had paid a reduced price in *Binions* v *Evans* was significant. None of these factors was present in *Ashburn Anstalt*, so no constructive trust arose.

The actual decision in *Ashburn Anstalt* has been overruled by the House of Lords in *Prudential Assurance Co.* v *London Residuary Body* [1992] 2 AC 386, but no doubt has been cast on the statements in the previous paragraph, which were *dicta* and not necessary for the decision; the Court of Appeal's decision in *Ashburn Anstalt* was that there was a valid lease, and that aspect of the case can no longer be supported.

Unconscionable dealings in land; no legally binding agreement
The case of *Ashburn* regardless of its lack of authority in its own right does provide illustration of a broader principle which is interesting in this examination of constructive trusts. This is a 'chapter setting' which has a very strong orientation

towards domestic arrangements. This is so whether the dispute arising is as between the parties themselves, or in respect of a third party who becomes involved (on account of the possibility of having to take property subject to the interests of another): constructive trusts which arise from interests in land are very much dominated by the 'shared homes' scenario. What cases like *Lyus* and *Ashburn* illustrate is the application of a constructive trust in the context of commercial relationships and agreements arising from these relationships. This was also seen in the more recent decision in *Banner Homes Group plc. v Luff Development* [2000] Ch 372.

Banner Homes v Luff Development concerned a proposed joint venture between Luff and Banner, both commercial parties, and in respect of a development of a commercial land site. There had been extensive negotiations between the parties, and there had been much reference within these negotiations to the creation of a joint venture company for undertaking the purchase of the land, and to the idea that each party would have equal shares in the company. On this understanding a company was purchased by Luff through which the joint venture would be operated, but although these negotiations were kept up ostensibly, Luff started to think about finding a different partner for the venture. Luff decided to keep Banner 'on board' whilst pursuing other partner possibilities, fearing that Banner might act similarly and make an independent bid for the purchase. Banner, meanwhile, unaware of Luff's 'forked tongue' and anticipating that formal agreement would in due course arise in respect of the joint venture, continued to conduct itself with a view to this eventuality. The company made the purchase of the site, and it was only at that point that Luff revealed that the joint venture as between the parties was not going ahead. Banner argued that it was entitled to half shares in the company by virtue of a constructive trust, and at first instance this allegation was rejected. The judge concluded that there was no binding agreement actually reached between the parties. This in turn negated there being requisite common intention to give rise to an equity to which a constructive trust could become attached. It was also found that there was no evidence that Banner had acted to its detriment in reliance of the agreement coming to fruition, because it was not clear it would have made an independent bid if it had been aware of Luff's intention to find a different partner. This was so notwithstanding the judge's view that Luff *had* behaved badly.

In the Court of Appeal a different view was taken, and the conclusion was reached that an equity did arise on account of Luff's conduct. This operated to make it unconscionable for Luff to assert beneficial entitlement to the proceeds of a venture which was pursued on the understanding of a joint venture between the parties concerned. This was so notwithstanding that this understanding arose in the absence of an actual binding contract between them. What *Banner v Luff* suggests is that the equity arose from the inequitable conduct of Luff, and that this was itself manifested in the detriment suffered by Banner. This detriment took the form of it not being in a position to secure a new partner, on account of not even realising its proposed venture with Luff was in jeopardy. In other words, Banner's reliance on what it *believed* was an agreement which *would* come to fruition was the key to the detriment it suffered for the constructive trust to operate. Indeed, the judgment suggests that a different finding would have followed had Banner been informed that the venture was being abandoned before the detriment arose.

11.4 **Mutual wills and the imposition of constructive trusts**

Until fairly recently, the principles behind mutual wills could be viewed as merely another application of those that operated in the previous section, but recent cases have extended the equitable jurisdiction in two major respects. First, there is the notion of the floating trust, which crystallises on the death of the survivor, on all his or her property. Secondly, unlike the cases in the previous section, it does not appear to be necessary for the trustee to have received any property on the strength of the representation made.

If the principles operating in this section were generalised across the law of trusts, that would amount to a very radical extension of equitable fraud jurisdiction. However, the recent judgments considered here, which have made explicit the existence of a wider jurisdiction than that in the previous section, are merely wide interpretations of previous mutual wills cases; they do not purport to be applicable outside mutual wills. Moreover, mutual wills are in fact a special case, as will be argued more fully below.

What is a 'mutual will'?
Mutual wills are agreements, usually (but not necessarily) between husband and wife. Wills are made (or the parties agree to make them) by each party in (usually) the same terms, and there is a mutual agreement that neither party will revoke, but the essence of the transaction is an agreement that each party will settle his or her property in a particular (usually the same) way.

Mutual wills and the creation of an enforceable contract
Mutual wills create enforceable contracts, the importance of which will be examined further below. The question which arises at this point is how far the analysis in the previous section, which does not of course depend on the existence of enforceable contracts, can be sustained. This is now pursued through imagining an agreement between A and B. B is the survivor. B accordingly receives property under A's will, but he receives it only because he has agreed to settle it in a certain way. If the condition attaches merely to the property received under A's will, then the principles of the previous section, or indeed those discussed in chapter 10, suffice. B has taken property expressly subject to conditions, and equity will, by the device of the constructive trust, require him to carry out those conditions.

Suppose, for example, that as with the land in *Ottaway* v *Norman* [1972] Ch 698, B has agreed that he will leave the property received to C. B simply obtains a life interest in the property. This is also a possible explanation of *Re Oldham* [1925] Ch 75, a mutual wills case. A more problematic situation is where A and B agree that each will leave all his property to the survivor on the understanding that the survivor will leave all his property to C. *Re Hagger* [1930] 2 Ch 190 suggests (contrary to *Re Oldham*) that a trust attaches to all the survivor's property, as long as the survivor accepts the legacy under the other's will. This is an extension of the reasoning explained thus far, in that the obligation extends beyond the property actually received by B. It also suggests that unlike express trusts, constructive trusts can cover future as well as existing property.

Constructive trusts covering future property: the 'floating' trust

A similar concept was envisaged in *Ottaway* v *Norman*, in respect of the furniture and other contents, including Miss Hodges' money. In fact, Brightman J thought that the obligation extended only to such furnishings and fixtures as Miss Hodges had received under Mr Ottaway's will, but also thought that if the agreement had included all Miss Hodges's other property and cash from whatever source, this obligation also could be enforced against her estate. He employed the concept of a 'floating trust', derived from the Australian case of *Birmingham* v *Renfrew* (1937) 57 CLR 666, which would remain in suspense during the life of the trustee and crystallise on her death, attaching to whatever property was comprised within her estate. This, as the learned judge noted, would seem to preclude Miss Hodges from making even a small pecuniary legacy in favour of her relatives or friends.

Similar reasoning was adopted, by Nourse J in a mutual wills context, in *Re Cleaver* [1981] 1 WLR 939. However, it is not clear from the report whether the trust imposed actually bound any property not received under Arthur Cleaver's will. If it did not then the *ratio* goes no further than *Re Oldham* [1925] Ch 75 (the widow, who survived her husband, would simply have enjoyed a life interest in the property received under Arthur Cleaver's will). But in *Re Dale* [1994] Ch 31, Morritt J applied the mutual wills doctrine in a situation where the second testator had received no benefit at all under the first testator's will, the mutual agreement having been that their children should share equally. There the trust clearly applied to the whole of the widow's estate, since the widow had received no property to which it could apply.

Fraud and floating trusts: two important extensions

There appear to be two important matters here. The trust can apply to future property, and there is no need for the constructive trustee to have obtained legal title to any property. The issue is, then, the extent to which, if at all, it is legitimate to generalise these extensions beyond mutual wills. It is suggested that this is not legitimate at all, firstly because the cases themselves reason entirely from earlier mutual wills cases, and secondly because there are unusual factors operating here. The Court of Appeal in *Re Goodchild* [1997] 3 All ER 63, affirming Carnwath J [1996] 1 All ER 670, accepted the notion of the floating trust, holding also that the floating trust so created was not destroyed by the remarriage of the second testator after the death of the first, but also held that it is not enough for wills to be made in the same terms; there must be a specific agreement that the wills were to be mutually binding (in other words, an enforceable contract between the parties) and there was insufficient evidence of such in the case itself. It also appears (in particular from the judgment in *Re Dale*) that A's refraining from revoking his will prior to his death constitutes consideration in equity, in which case the analysis becomes virtually identical to that in *Pullan* v *Koe* [1913] 1 Ch 9 in chapter 3. The difference between these cases and those discussed in the previous section, therefore, is the existence of the contract enforceable in equity, which can crystallise on future property, just as that in *Pullan* v *Koe* did.

Conclusions

Two conclusions follow from this. First, the floating trust and other developments in this section apply only where there is a contract enforceable in equity. Second, however, in the cases discussed at the start of this section, where the floating trust concept is not needed, and where the trust property is limited to that actually received by B, the principles in the last section suffice, and there is no need for the enforceable contract, required by the Court of Appeal in *Re Goodchild*. Note that in *Ottaway* v *Norman*, the trust was imposed only on the property that had devolved to Miss Hodges, and that the floating trust would only have applied if there had been an enforceable agreement relating to other property.

The issues arising in respect of mutual wills have been considered most recently in the decision in *Healey* v *Brown* [2002] EWCH 1405 (Ch). A typical 'mutual wills scenario', Mr and Mrs Brown made wills which were to be their 'last' and each spouse undertook not to 'revoke or amend', each leaving their estate to the survivor in their relationship. On the death of the surviving spouse, the property under these 'mutual wills' was to pass to Mr Brown's son Paul in part, and also to the claimant, Mrs Brown's niece. Mrs Brown died first, and after her death, her husband transferred the family home, a flat, into the joint names of himself and Paul in consideration of natural love and affection. This ensured that upon Mr Brown's subsequent death Paul became the property's sole owner. This operation of the doctrine of survivorship meant that the property did not pass as Mr and Mrs Brown's original wills had determined. The claimant asserted that through the doctrine of mutual wills, the flat was held by Paul on trust for her. It was found that a constructive trust arose in the claimant's favour, in respect of Mrs Brown's original share of the property. Paul therefore held the flat on trust for himself and the claimant, in equal shares.

The way in which a constructive trust arose only in respect of Mrs Brown's share of the property was explained by the judge as arising from the decision in *Re Goodchild*, which was considered above. This decision had asserted that in the absence of a binding contract, there was no basis for imposing a constructive trust over property already owned by the survivor. Quoting Morritt LJ in *Re Goodchild* that there was 'a consistent line of authority [requiring] that for the doctrine of mutual wills to apply there must be a contract between the two testators', Donald Davidson QC found in *Healey* v *Brown*, that while some degree of arrangement or understanding short of a binding contract was sufficient for the mutual wills doctrine, the property of the second testator which was not acquired from the first testator (i.e. the survivor's original share) could not be bound by a constructive trust arising in these circumstances. In this case, this outcome appears to have followed precisely the nature of the parties' original intentions. Here, difficulties following from this analysis could conceivably arise where the outcome was not reflected in this way, which would raise issues about the promises made in the original wills, and about how parties to wills made in this way might be able to protect future interests relating to 'mutual' property.

11.5 Returning property to the transferor

In all of the cases considered so far, the effect of a constructive trust has been to hold representors to their representations. In none of the cases in 11.3 or 11.4, where property has been obtained on the strength of the representation, have the courts required that it be returned (indeed, in many of the cases this would have been wholly inappropriate). There is, however, now a line of authority suggesting that this can happen in some cases.

In *Westdeutsche* v *Islington LBC* [1996] AC 669, Lord Browne-Wilkinson thought that a thief of money, who mixed the money with his own, would thereby obtain legal title to the money, but would hold it as constructive trustee for the victim of the theft. Although this statement is not part of the *ratio* of the case, it probably represents good law. However, the reasoning adopted by Lord Browne-Wilkinson in reaching this result is unconvincing. He goes on to say: 'Although it is difficult to find clear authority for the proposition, when property is obtained by fraud equity imposes a constructive trust on the fraudulent recipient . . . '.

This statement is, in general terms, correct. However, in a way which Lord Browne-Wilkinson himself clearly appreciated, its possible limitations are borne out by the discussions above in 11.3 and 11.4, which showed that where a con- structive trust has been imposed, there has been no requirement on the part of the guilty partly actually to return the property. In *McCormick* v *Grogan* for example (considered in chapter 10; which Lord Browne-Wilkinson actually cites in *Westdeutsche*), had the facts supported the imposition of a constructive trust, it would have been wholly inappropriate for the trustee to return the property to the estate. This would appear to apply equally to Lord Browne-Wilkinson's thief; but, unlike the thief example, a constructive trust in a 'representation' situation arises from a representation actually made. So, what is the basis of Lord Browne- Wilkinson's 'thief conclusion' that property is held on constructive trust for the victim (from which the return of property result follows)?

Justification via a different route
However, it is possible to justify the thief conclusion by a different route. Another case analysed by Lord Browne-Wilkinson is *Chase Manhattan Bank NA* v *Israel-British Bank (London) Ltd* [1981] Ch 105, where a bank which had already been paid was accidentally paid a second time. Although Lord Browne-Wilkinson did not agree with the reasoning in *Chase Manhattan*, he did agree with the result, taking the view that the recipient bank would become a trustee for the transferring bank as soon as it discovered the mistake. The case bears some similarities to *Bankers Trust Co.* v *Shapira* [1980] 1 WLR 1274, cited in *Westdeutsche*, where the Court of Appeal appears to have assumed that a bank which had been advanced money because of forged cheques presented by its customers became a trustee for the transferring bank when it learned of the mistake. In *Westdeutsche* itself, it was assumed that the local authority would have become trustee had it known that the swap agreement (under which the disputed money had been transferred to it) was void before that money had ceased to exist (having been spent).

There appears, therefore, to be some authority at least for a principle that a recipient of property who discovers that he is not entitled to it becomes trustee for the transferor. Obviously, Lord Browne-Wilkinson's thief is an extreme example of this principle, but note that the general principle has nothing to do with the jurisdiction discussed earlier, and indeed can operate against a recipient who has done nothing wrong.

11.6 **A wider conduct-based doctrine?**

The cases and the analysis which has been made of them would appear to suggest that the equitable fraud doctrine is probably limited to the cases we have considered. It may be argued that this is unsatisfactory, since there appears to be no clear underlying principle, but the law is perhaps not unlike the law of tort before 1932; the courts do not appear to have taken the step that they took in *Donoghue* v *Stevenson* [1932] AC 562, of bringing together all the strands within a general umbrella. Perhaps they are worried about 'proprietary overkill', since the constructive trust is more than merely a remedy in English law. Perhaps it is simply too difficult to develop a generalised conscience-based doctrine, except by developing specific factors, as in the examples in this chapter.

There have, however, been attempts to extend the jurisdiction beyond that considered so far in this chapter. In two cases the courts have almost gone so far as to hold that whenever a representation is made, certainly where the representation is to the effect that the representee is to have rights in property, that that can give rise to a constructive trust. First, in *Re Sharpe (a bankrupt)* [1980] 1 WLR 219, an 82-year old lady, who was in poor health, loaned a large sum of money (£12,000) to her nephew to enable him to purchase a house in which they could both live. The nephew later went bankrupt, and the question arose whether the old lady's money was secured, or whether it formed part of the nephew's assets, to be divided among his general creditors. Browne-Wilkinson J found for the old lady, on the basis that she was a beneficiary under a constructive trust which bound the trustee in bankruptcy. He thought that a constructive trust can be imposed simply because a licensee expends money or otherwise acts to his detriment. If the reasoning in this case is correct, almost any reliance on a promise relating to the occupation of property could give rise to a constructive trust, and the constructive trust could exist in a pure form in the situations discussed earlier.

Re Sharpe: confusing constructive trusts and proprietary estoppel
This seems to be confusing the constructive trust with a proprietary estoppel (see Jill Martin [1980] Conv 207), and indeed we argued earlier that trust and estoppel concepts are entirely different. *Re Sharpe* looks wrong as an estoppel case, if the earlier reasoning is correct, since it ought not to be capable of binding a trustee in bankruptcy. Indeed, Sir Nicholas Browne-Wilkinson himself took this view in his Holdsworth Club Address 1991, observing that 'only if the third party's conduct is such as to raise an estoppel against the third party individually will the third party be affected'. If this is correct, the trustee in bankruptcy as the third party could hardly have been affected by an estoppel in *Re Sharpe*.

Ashburn and Re Sharpe rebuffed?
The constructive trust reasoning in *Re Sharpe* was treated dismissively by Fox LJ in *Ashburn Anstalt* v *Arnold* [1989] 1 Ch 1, but he did not elaborate, since the case before him was sufficiently different not to be affected directly by *Re Sharpe*.

Nonetheless, the confusion between trust and estoppel concepts appears wrong in principle, and *Re Sharpe* is unsupported by other authority and is probably wrong.

The second case is *Re Basham (deceased)* [1987] 1 All ER 405, where the claimant was induced to do various things for the deceased, on the understanding that he would obtain the property under the will of the deceased when the deceased died. Edward Nugee QC, purporting to follow *Re Cleaver* [1981] 1 WLR 939 (see 11.4), held that a proprietary estoppel giving rise to a constructive trust arose, the claimant thereby obtaining the conveyance of the estate to her. He said that proprietary estoppel was a form of constructive trust which arose when A acted to his detriment on the faith of a belief known to and encouraged by B that he had or was going to have a right over B's property, so that B was prevented by equity from insisting on his strict legal rights if to do so would be inconsistent with A's belief. If this case is correct, then any act by the claimant, in reliance upon an alleged agreement (or even a mere representation by the defendant), would enable the claimant to succeed on constructive trust reasoning, but the judgment has been criticised recently in *Taylor* v *Dickens* [1998] 1 FLR 806 and *Gillett* v *Holt* [1998] 2 FLR 1 (considered earlier), and like *Re Sharpe*, is probably best regarded as wrong.

Floating trusts outside the context of mutual wills

There have also been cases, such as *Stokes* v *Anderson* [1991] 1 FLR 391 and *Ottaway* v *Norman*, which apply the floating trust concept outside the context of mutual wills. We saw in the previous section that *Ottaway* v *Norman* is probably consistent with the principles in that section. *Stokes* v *Anderson* is a first-category *Lloyds Bank* v *Rosset* case where the declaration of trust occurred while Stokes was still negotiating to purchase the share that he eventually obtained in the property, and Nourse LJ, founding upon *Birmingham* v *Renfrew*, saw no reason in principle why a constructive trust could not 'attach to an after-acquired estate or interest in property, whether legal or equitable'. Note that unlike the mutual wills cases, there was no enforceable agreement between Stokes and Anderson because of lack of writing (unless interests under a statutory trust for sale could have been regarded as personalty for these purposes: see chapter 1), but it is doubtful whether *Birmingham* v *Renfrew* reasoning was needed in the case, or indeed adopted. All that is needed is to hold (surely quite reasonably?) that Stokes' intention continued until he actually acquired his interest, and that the declaration of trust therefore occurred at that time. *Stokes* v *Anderson* therefore probably does not represent an extension of the equitable jurisdiction considered in this chapter.

 online resource centre

FURTHER READING

Yondon [1984] CLJ 306.

Thompson [1988] Conv 201.

Thompson [2001] 65 Conv 265.

Davies [2003] 67 Conv 238.

12

An introduction to charity

12.1 Charities and the trust

It is usual to deal with charities as an integral part of the law of trusts. It is not necessarily the most appropriate classification, however, because though many charities exist in the form of a trust, this is not universal. Also, historically the law has recognised charities for even longer than the trust itself.

In its earliest institutional form, charity was the province of the medieval Church, and its supervision the responsibility of the ecclesiastical courts. It was the secularisation of charitable donation during the Tudor period and the contemporaneous growth of the jurisdiction of the Court of Chancery by way of the Use which brought the administration of charity under the control of the Chancellor. He began to enforce Uses for 'pious purposes' at around the same time as he began to enforce Uses relating to land. Because of the attractive simplicity of the Use, and later of the trust, for philanthropic donors, coupled with the effectiveness of equitable remedies, the trust rapidly became the commonest method of dedicating property to worthy causes.

The charitable trust as a variety of purpose trust
Charitable trusts are, of course, a variety of purpose trust and, as we have seen, there are difficulties in the enforcement of purpose trusts, especially as with charities there will probably not be easily identifiable human beneficiaries. However, since the early seventeenth century the Attorney-General has undertaken the enforcement of charitable trusts, as representative claimant, and since 1960 the Charity Commissioners have been given supervisory powers over charities (the present powers are contained in the Charities Act 1993). Because the Attorney-General has powers of enforcement, there is no need for charitable trusts to be subject to the same certainty of objects requirements as private purpose trusts, and they are not. Indeed, because of the public character of charitable trusts, they are also exempt from other requirements to which private trusts are subject and in addition enjoy certain privileges.

Charities and the trust instrument
Although not all charities exist in the form of a trust, the trust is still the most common medium of charity today, both in terms of the quantity of trusts in existence and in terms of the value of their funds. The trust seems to be most favoured on the one hand by private individuals and on the other by the largest and wealthiest of charitable enterprises, the foundations which often originate within international commercial corporations.

From the viewpoint of the private donor, the trust form is simple to create and sufficiently flexible to allow for a degree of individuality to be expressed in its provisions. For a large and well-funded organisation, the trust form offers the opportunity to maintain large capital funds producing high levels of income, which can be distributed on a discretionary basis. For these reasons the trust will probably remain the most usual form of charitable enterprise and charity law will continue to take its direction from the doctrines developed in equity. Indeed, the courts have always shown a preference for treating all charities as partaking in the nature of a trust, even where their institutional arrangements are of a quite different sort.

The most common alternative forms for charity are the charitable corporation and the unincorporated association.

12.1.1 Charitable corporations

An increasing number of charitable ventures nowadays operate within a corporate structure and this form is particularly well suited to collective, active enterprises. A corporate charity will usually be a company limited by guarantee and will usually have a constitution forbidding the distribution of profit among its members. Otherwise, the establishment of a company limited by guarantee is broadly similar in terms of formality to the setting up of an ordinary commercial company. As with a commercial company, the liability of the charity is limited to its assets, thus protecting its members from unlimited personal liability in the event of the charity becoming insolvent.

The advantage of corporate status is that the charity can operate as a legal person. So it has the capacity to make contracts, incur liabilities and hold property in its own right without the need to involve trustees. Also, it does not need to effect alterations in the documents of title to its property at every change in personnel. Corporate status is therefore well suited to charities which undertake extensive long-term operations. These often have considerable assets, sufficient to make the expense of incorporation worthwhile.

12.1.2 Unincorporated associations

These are the other most common form, which may convert to corporate status if and when it becomes convenient to do so. The less rigid framework offered by this form makes it attractive to groups of people wishing to undertake active charitable work in accordance with broadly democratic and flexible policies which may change and develop over time. Control of the organisation and its funds, if any, will typically be vested in a committee of managers who will probably be elected in conformity with the wishes of the current membership.

The earlier 'case study' on unincorporated associations (in chapter 8) has already shown that the basis of this form of organisation is usually a contract between the members, formulated as rules which are contained in the constitution of the association. This carries the advantage of extreme flexibility, allowing the terms of the contract to be modified to meet new situations. The main disadvantage is that the managers and members are exposed to unlimited personal liability incurred in the course of the organisation's activities. Nevertheless, the unincorporated association accounts for a moderate proportion of old established charities, as well as some of the newer and most active charitable undertakings.

12.1.3 Other, unusual forms

Mutual benefit organisations maintaining funds collected by subscription from members, and being intended to provide benefits during sickness, old age, etc., may be registered under the Friendly Societies Act 1974, and those which qualify as charitable according to the legal definition of that term (see chapter 13) may have the status of 'benevolent societies'. However, their significance appears to be declining in view of the growth in state welfare provision.

Another form available to charities, and apparently favoured by the growing number of housing associations, is *the industrial and provident society*, a kind of hybrid with some of the features of both the friendly society and the guarantee company, and registrable under the Industrial and Provident Societies Acts 1965 to 1978.

Finally, there is the *charitable corporation*, which is not related to the guarantee companies discussed above. These include universities, hospitals and the British Museum, and they are established either by charter from the Crown or else by legislation (e.g., the Charitable Trustees Incorporation Act 1872 and the British Museum Act 1963). Such institutions are diverse in nature, and there is no standard form—each is endowed with a constitution specific to its own requirements. These charities are generally considered to enjoy high prestige by virtue of their unique character, and represent something of an elite category within the range of charitable organisations.

12.2 Legal regulation of charities: consequences of charitable status

Before considering the legal definition of charity in the next chapter some attention needs to be given to the consequences that flow from charitable status. The cases considered in the following chapters have arisen for a diversity of reasons, and this may have led to a confusion on the part of the courts as to the policy they should adopt.

For the consequences outlined below to apply it is necessary to show that the property is to be held beneficially for charitable purposes. It is insufficient for the recipient merely to covenant to use the property for purposes which happen to be charitable purposes. In *Liverpool City Council v Attorney-General* (unreported), *The Times*, 1 May 1992, Allerton Hall had been conveyed (in 1926) to Liverpool City Council subject to covenants that it would be used only as a public park. It was accepted that the provision of a public park or recreation ground was a charitable purpose (presumably on the principles illustrated below). The Attorney-General nevertheless failed in his contention that the land was held on charitable trusts, so that the City Council were able to treat it as part of its corporate property. No doubt the covenants remained valid, but presumably since the original covenantees had long-since died, there was nobody in a position to enforce them.

12.2.1 Tax advantages

Charities enjoy exemption from income tax on all income, rents, dividends and profits, provided these are applied for charitable purposes, and may reclaim from the Revenue any income tax already paid prior to receipt of the income. Nor is income tax chargeable on the profits of any trade carried out by the charity, so long as these are applied for charitable purposes only and the trade is either exercised in carrying out the primary purposes of the charity or the work is carried out mainly by its beneficiaries (e.g., workshops for the disabled). Charitable corporations are exempt from corporation tax.

Gifts to charity are largely exempt from inheritance tax, and capital gains tax is not payable where gains are applied to charitable purposes. All charities are exempt from half of the rates on premises occupied in connection with the charity, including charity shops, and premises used for religious purposes are entirely exempt from rates. Generally, charities must pay VAT on goods and services, but certain goods, such as some equipment for the disabled, are zero rated.

Some conception of the importance of the taxation consequences of charitable status may be gleaned from the number of cases considered in the next chapter involving the Inland Revenue. In addition, charitable status is often claimed for rates advantages: e.g., in *Re South Place Ethical Society* [1980] 1 WLR 1565 and *United Grand Lodge of Ancient Free & Accepted Masons of England and Wales* v *Holborn Borough Council* [1957] 1 WLR 1080 both considered shortly.

The annual cost to the Revenue of these tax concessions is of the order of half a billion pounds or, to put it into perspective, about £50 for every average-sized family in the UK.

12.2.2 Validity

Another common reason for litigation on charitable status is to ascertain whether the gift is valid at all. Probably the commonest situation is where the next-of-kin challenge the validity of a testamentary bequest (e.g., *Re Shaw* [1957] 1 WLR 729; *Re Pinion* [1965] Ch 85; and *Re Koeppler's WT* [1986] Ch 423). Charitable status has three main consequences for validity.

Charitable trusts in relation to the beneficiary principle
First, charitable trusts are trusts for purposes, which would often be void if non-charitable. Yet as we have seen, charities are public trusts enforceable at the suit of the Attorney-General, and are supervised by the Charity Commissioners, so their lack of human beneficiaries is not fatal, as it is to private trusts. Indeed, only the Attorney-General can establish an action against to establish the existence of a charitable trust, which will commonly arise from a challenge to a testamentary gift (purportedly made in favour of a charity) brought by the deceased's next-of-kin. This is the official position, although the Attorney-General can be substituted as claimant for individuals: *Hauxwell* v *Barton-on-Humber UDC* [1974] Ch 432, where

he was substituted as claimant by two individuals. The supervision powers of the Charity Commissioners are now set out in ss. 32–33 of the Charities Act 1993, which also give powers to 'the charity trustees, or [to] any person interested in the charity, or [to] any two or more inhabitants of the area of the charity if it is a local charity, but not [to] any other person'. For a discussion of the meaning of 'any person interested' under s. 33(1), see *Scott* v *National Trust* [1998] 2 All ER 705, where local huntsmen and tenant farmers were held to have *locus standi* to challenge a decision of the National Trust to ban deer-hunting with hounds on its estates, because they had an interest materially greater than or different from that possessed by ordinary members of the public in securing due administration of the charity.

Second, it is not necessary for the purposes of a charitable trust to be defined with certainty. A gift on trust 'for charitable purposes' will be valid, and the court and Charity Commissioners have jurisdiction to create a scheme for the application of the property donated. A gift to charity which is not expressed as a trust will be similarly disposed of by the Crown.

Third, charitable trusts, unlike private trusts, may exist indefinitely. This being so, a gift over from one charity to another may take effect at any time in the future: *Christ's Hospital* v *Grainger* (1849) 1 Mac & G 460. Once property is dedicated to charity, there is no infringement of the perpetuity rules merely because it passes from one charitable body to another. However, the rule against perpetuities applies as usual to prevent a too remote vesting of a gift to a charity in the first instance, and also to a gift over from a charity to a non-charity.

12.2.3 Registration of charities

Though the definition of charitable status is at the end of the day a matter for the courts, the process of obtaining recognition as a charity today is primarily administrative, and largely outside the direct control of the courts. Currently, under provisions of the Charities Act 1993 an organisation seeking charitable status must normally apply for registration to the Charity Commissioners, who have power under the Act to grant or withhold registration according to their decision as to whether the proposed purposes are, in law, charitable. The modern Charity Commission, charged with supervising charitable endowments, came into being in 1853, although originally it was given only limited powers. Even in the current regime under the Charities Act 1993, the Charity Commission has no legal existence as a body, with the functions of the Commission actually being held by the Charity Commissioners themselves personally. However, changes pursuant to the recently enacted Charities Act 2006 inserts into the 1993 Act provisions that create a new body corporate called the Charity Commission for England and Wales: this has the effect of conferring upon the Commission the status of a non-ministerial government department. Further information relating to the key changes relating to the new Act can be found located on the ORC website which accompanies this text (and can also be found on the extremely impressive website maintained by the Charity Commission at http:www.charity-commission.gov.uk).

The Charity Commission and the registration of charities

Until the 2006 Act comes into force, the duty to maintain the register of charities is placed on the Commissioners themselves by virtue of s. 3(1) of the 1993 Act, while a duty to apply for registration is also placed on the charity trustees by virtue of s. 3(7). Registration is conclusive evidence of charitable status.

Therefore, the workings of the Charity Commissioners is significant on account of their quasi-judicial function in this area. In reaching their decisions, they may consult with other bodies, such as the Inland Revenue, which may also be called upon to judge the validity of claims to be treated as a charity. The overall effect of the procedure has been to reduce the number of reported court decisions on the boundaries of charity to a handful of test cases which raise significant issues of law.

Commissioners' refusal to register an organisation as charitable

Refusal by the Commissioners to register an organisation gives rise to a right of appeal, under s. 4 of the Charities Act 1990, which is in the first instance an informal appeal to the board of Charity Commissioners. Such appeals are rare—usually in single figures each year. Further appeal lies through the courts (as in, e.g., *Incorporated Council of Law Reporting for England and Wales* v *Attorney-General* [1972] Ch 73, and *McGovern* v *Attorney-General* [1982] Ch 321), initially through the High Court, and thence to the Court of Appeal and House of Lords.

Viewed from the perspective of the saving thus effected in money and time, the registration process must be regarded as an improvement upon ad hoc litigation as a method of establishing charitable credentials. From the standpoint of the well-meaning donor or charity activist, however, the process of registration may appear as a system of gate-keeping, limiting the range of altruistic enterprises to settled and uncontentious fields already blessed by judicial decisions and the precedents of the Commission. This is one respect in which the creation of a new Charity Tribunal by the Charities Act 2006 is highly significant. The new Tribunal is seen as a 'court of first instance' for decisions relating to appeals and applications made originally to the (new) Charity Commission.

Charity Commissioners' supervisory powers

The supervisory powers of the Commissioners, and their powers of inquiry, have been strengthened by the Charities Act 1992 and 1993, and it appears that the main arm of these provisions (as with a great deal of charities legislation over the centuries) is to curb abuses by and maladministration of charitable bodies.

Further, although achieving charitable status carries numerous advantages, it also has the effect of bringing the organisation under the supervision of the Commissioners, who are given wide-reaching powers by the Act. Under existing law, a large number of charities are exempted from requiring registration (and can be found within Sch. 2 of the Charities Act 1993). However, the new Charities Act 2006 signals an important policy change in this regard, providing (in s. 9) that as a general rule every charity must be registered and within reach of the Charity Commission. There are some exceptions and exemptions which remain, but these are intended to be much narrower and more tightly controlled than is currently the case. Once again, more detail can be found on the ORC website which accompanies this text.

Under the new regime intended by the 2006 Act, the Charity Commission must continue to keep the register of charities, but the new provisions (located within s. 9) prescribe the contents of the register and the circumstances in which the Commission must or may remove charities or institutions which are no longer considered to be charities from the register.

The Charity Commission maintains an extremely impressive website at: *www. charity-commission.gov.uk*

12.2.4 Cy près

If a charitable organisation is wound up, any surplus property may be applied cy près. If, on the other hand, the organisation is not charitable, any surplus property will go to the Crown as *bona vacantia*, or to the donors on resulting trust, or in the case of an unincorporated association, to the members of the association, both discussed in chapter 8. In *Re Hobourn Aero Components Ltd's Air Raid Distress Fund* [1946] Ch 194, the sole consequence of the fund being held non-charitable was that a cy près scheme was not directed, and that the surplus was distributed among the contributors.

12.2.5 Political dimension

The political dimension to charities has possibly influenced their development and cannot be altogether avoided.

The role adopted by charities 100 or so years ago has to some extent been superseded by state provision for the least fortunate in society. Some might even go so far as to argue that charities have no value alongside a state-funded system. Most, however, would probably hold that the freedom of individuals to decide whether to distribute any of their property to philanthropic purposes, and if so which purposes, is an important freedom, which is in no way in opposition to the welfare state provision (in which, of course, individuals have very little direct say).

Politics, welfare and the relief of poverty: a continuing justification for charities?

At the very least, however, it is more difficult nowadays to justify tax concessions to charities, when at the same time many of the least fortunate are provided for by the welfare state. Also, if the state has decided not to fund a particular purpose through the welfare scheme, it is odd that it should be required to fund it through the back door, by virtue of the tax concessions given to charitable enterprise. Probably such an argument has to some extent been taken on board by the courts and the legislature, the former by laying down more stringent conditions for charitable status, and excluding 'undesirable' forms of altruistic activity, the latter by requiring registration and to some extent supervision by a public body, viz. the Charity Commissioners.

There is also no doubt that the terms of a gift to charity are controlled by the donor, and some might argue that, at any rate where very large sums are concerned, the power that goes with such control is better administered by public bodies than private individuals.

12.3 The law of charity: conflicting policies adopted by the courts

12.3.1 Charities and their operations today

Courts today are generally unwilling to frustrate the wishes of a settlor and prefer to deem gifts to be valid if they can. This leads to a tendency to expand the legal definition of charity. On the other hand, jealousy of the tax concessions tends towards the opposite result. In other words, there is a tension between two conflicting tendencies, which to some extent explains the haphazard development of the law.

The jealousy over the tax position may also explain why the public benefit requirement for charitable status figures so largely. Lord Cross of Chelsea in *Dingle v Turner* [1972] AC 601, a case where only the validity of the trust was at issue, would have preferred different tests for validity on the one hand and tax concessions on the other. The law adopts the same test, however.

It is not only today that tensions between conflicting policies are felt, and it should be remembered that the legal definition of charity is the result of the development of several centuries, at any rate from the Statute of Charitable Uses 1601 onwards. At certain periods, charity was viewed with extreme suspicion, particularly where, as in the case of the medieval Church, the power of charitable donation could be seen in rivalry to the claims of the then nascent secular state, or where, as in the seventeenth and eighteenth centuries, charity was blamed for taking away the rightful expectations of heirs.

12.3.2 Elizabethan times to the eighteenth century

With the decline during this period of the influence of the Roman Catholic Church, and other economic factors, poor relief during Elizabethan times became something of a problem for the state. Statutory provision for the poor, to be administered by the parish and paid for out of local rates, was introduced in 1572, and comprehensive Poor Codes were enacted in 1597 and 1601. However, it was in the interests of the state to encourage charitable donation in order to reduce the burden of poor rates. The development of charity law at this time, therefore, was geared primarily towards relief of the poor, rather than other forms of philanthropic enterprise.

This can clearly be seen by examination of the preamble to the Statute of Charitable Uses 1601, set out in full in the following chapter. The primary purpose of this Act was to provide for commissioners to be appointed to investigate administration of charities, and in particular misappropriation of trust property. This procedure continued in operation for about 200 years.

Of greater importance for present purposes, however, was that a number of charitable uses (or, in other words, charitable purposes) are listed in the preamble to the Act, and the preamble was later used by the courts to provide the basis for the legal definition of charity. Indeed, under the fourth head of charity, this is still the case today.

The preamble in fact contains quite a divergent list of charitable purposes, sufficiently diverse to provide for the expanding definitions of charity in the eighteenth and nineteenth centuries. However, the list as a whole is clearly intended to be confined to provision for the poor, to reduce the burden of the poor rates, and early development of charity was heavily influenced by this bias.

The notion of public benefit also appears clearly in the preamble.

12.3.3 Eighteenth and nineteenth centuries

This period of development is important because it was then that the legal definition of charity was consolidated. The modern law of charity is based on developments during this period. The two main influences are the decline in importance of genuine poverty charities and the influence of the mortmain legislation (Mortmain and Charitable Uses Act 1736).

The decline in the importance of poverty relief in charitable giving was partly connected with notions of the 'undeserving' poor. At the same time, there was a move towards other types of charitable donation. For example, the NSPCC, Dr Barnardo's Homes and the National Trust are all creatures of this period.

A major influence on the law of charity at this time was judicial hostility to bequests for charitable purposes which threatened to deprive testators' families from their 'rightful due'. It might be thought that this judicial hostility would lead to a narrowing of the legal definition of charity, but in fact the reverse was often the case. It should not be forgotten that the mortmain legislation made many testamentary gifts of land to charity void during this period (from 1736 to 1891), and this may paradoxically have resulted in a *wider* definition of charity being adopted in order not to frustrate the claims of disappointed relations (if the gift was held void, there was a resulting trust of the property for the estate).

Definition of charity and the emergence of 'public benefit'
Examples of cases where the adoption of a wide definition of charity led to a gift being struck down under the mortmain legislation were *Townlee* v *Bedwell* (1801) 6 Ves Jr 104, on the establishment of botanical gardens; *Thornton* v *Howe* (1862) 31 Beav 14, on the advancement of religion; and *Tatham* v *Drummond* (1864) 4 De G J & Sm 484, on animal charities.

Also during this period, the original notion of public benefit underwent a change. Originally a benefit to the poor was required, but now almost any public purpose would do. For example, it became clear that a school to educate the sons of gentlemen may be charitable, whereas it had previously been thought that the preamble covered only free schools. Also apparent, even at the height of philanthropic activity in the nineteenth century, was that middle-class social values of the time were strongly in evidence in an attempt to limit the distribution of charity to the 'deserving'. Hence, the modern definition of relief of poverty for charitable purposes is by no means limited to the relief of the destitute.

12.3.4 **Late nineteenth and twentieth centuries**

Two further developments are important during this period: first, the growing tie between tax concessions and charitable status, and secondly further changes in the nature of charitable donation, especially with the development of increased welfare provision.

In *Commissioners for Special Purposes of the Income Tax* v *Pemsel* [1891] AC 531 (set out later), the case which really forms the basis of the present-day definition of heads of charity, it became clear for the first time that relief from taxation might be tied in to the definition of charity. The judges themselves do not appear to have appreciated the importance of the connection, however.

There was an exemption in the Income Tax Act 1842 for rents and profits of lands vested in trustees for 'charitable purposes', and the House of Lords held (by a 4:2 majority) that this exemption applied to a trust for the maintaining, supporting and advancing of missionary establishments (known as Unitas Fratrum, or United Brethren, whose purpose was to convert people among the 'heathen nations' to Christianity).

Modern charity law and the categorisation of validity

That case (*Pemsel*) laid down the heads of charity as relief of poverty, advancement of education, advancement of religion, and other purposes beneficial to the community. These heads are described in detail in the following chapter.

There has also been a further change in the nature of charitable donation. In the twentieth century, relief of poverty has become more clearly a state function, and accordingly charities for the relief of poverty have declined to a greater extent even than in the nineteenth century. On the other hand, gifts to social welfare, disaster appeals, and especially pressure groups, have increased. Also, a far greater proportion of charitable income comes from fees and government grants, as opposed to voluntary donations.

It is questionable whether the law has altered significantly to take account of these developments, although Lord Cross clearly faced the taxation issue in *Dingle* v *Turner* in chapter 13. On the changing emphasis of charity, the Recreational Charities Act 1958 added a new head of charity, in line with the greater emphasis on social welfare. Also, the fourth head of charity (considered below) may still be developing, in line with modern social conditions. For example, Lord Wilberforce said in *Scottish Burial Reform & Cremation Society Ltd* v *Glasgow Corporation* [1968] AC 138, 154 (a case on the fourth head):

But three things may be said about [the *Pemsel* classification], which its author [Lord Macnaughten] would surely not have denied: first that, since it is a classification of convenience, there may well be purposes which do not fit neatly into one or other of the headings; secondly, that the words used must not be given the force of a statute to be construed; and thirdly, that the law of charity is a moving subject which may well have evolved even since 1891.

Similar statements can be found, also in the House of Lords, in *IRC* v *McMullen* [1981] AC 1, a case concerning the playing of football at schools and universities, and discussed below. This is a case on the second head of charity, and again it is clear that the legal concept of charity is not static but changes with ideas about social values.

12.3.5 **Validity of non-charitable purposes**

Lord Cross's desire to see different tests for validity on the one hand, and tax conces-sions on the other, to some extent presupposes that it is difficult to achieve valid dis-positions for purposes which are not charitable. It is by no means impossible, however, and the methods by which this can be achieved are described in chapter 4. It is, for example, common nowadays for disaster appeals to be expressly made non-charitable, to free them from the fetters of Charity Commissioners' supervision, and in particular the requirement that the funds must be distributed so as to relieve poverty.

That being so, the main consequence of charitable status today may well be taxation privileges. Perhaps the law should not be too free in the granting of those privileges. This probably explains the personal nexus rule in *Oppenheim* v *Tobacco Securities Trust Co. Ltd* [1951] AC 297 considered in due course.

The position is more difficult for pure purpose trusts, like *Re Astor's ST* [1952] Ch 534 in chapter 4, where trustees were instructed to hold a fund upon various trusts including 'the maintenance of good relations between nations [and] ... the preser-vation of the independence of newspapers'; or *Re Shaw* [1957] 1 WLR 729, involv-ing a trust to research the development of a 40-letter alphabet. Both were void, and such trusts can still only be validated by being charitable.

In conclusion, it should come as no surprise that the legal definition of charity has fluctuated over the centuries, depending on the prevailing social philosophies of the time, and that this, coupled with the conflicting policies of the present law, has resulted in a less than logical legal position obtaining today.

12.4 **The operation of charities: a 'live' issue**

Many of the consequences of charitable status considered up to this point, as well as the law relating to charity which has been introduced through brief reference to its evolution in modern times, draw attention to key themes which will dominate the work now being commenced on charitable trusts and their operation. It has been observed that the legal definition of charity has fluctuated over the centuries, very much a consequence of—or at the very least a reflection of—the prevailing social philosophies of the time. Important points of continuity and change have been identified. It is also the case that today's dominant social and cultural interests ensure continuing focus on the consequences of charitable status. Illustration of the 'live-ness' of the operation of charity comes in the high levels of activity in this sphere in policy circles. In May 2004 a draft Charities Bill was published, and thereafter a Charities Bill was presented in Parliament in December 2004. After being 'timed out' of the opportunity for progress through Parliament by the General Election of May 2005, it was almost immediately reintroduced. In late October 2006, the Bill then entered the last and very heated phase of its journey through Parliament, and received Royal Assent on 8 November 2006. The Charity Commissioners' website reports that in the 'timetable' for implementing the new Act, some aspects will be implemented within a matter of months, while other aspects will require 'further work before they come force'. However, even at this point, and in contemplation of implementation of the new provisions, the Charities Bill as it originally appeared in 2004 can be considered an 'end result' of considerable energy which has been given to charities in policy circles. Thus, the following chapter will not only analyse the current position of the legal definition of charity, but will also signal important imminent changes. In doing so, it will highlight key changes being pursued, and attempt to trace their significance within our broader cultural consideration of charity and its position in UK society.

12.4.1 The Charities Bill 2004: introduction and background

The starting point for the examination which will be made of the Charities Bill is recognition of it as *an* 'end' point for an extensive exercise in policy-making and in many respects, this is even the case with the new Act itself on account of the 'timetable' for implementation. But returning initially to the very appearance of the Bill in 2004 as an end point, this is because this did *itself* reflect a wealth of accompanying policy documentation, which, alongside the Bill itself, reveal charities very much as a 'live' issue. There is extensive documentation which will enrich appreciation of this, including the following key works. NCVO (2001) 'For the public benefit? A Consultation Document on Charity Law Reform': the National Council for Voluntary Organisations works with and for the voluntary sector in England by providing information, advice and support and by representing the views of the sector to government and policy-makers. There is also the Report of the Scottish Charity Law Review Commission (the McFadden Report), published in May 2001, making numerous recommendations for the reform of charity law and regulation in Scotland.

Following this, a further two key publications preceded the Bill. The first is the publication of the Strategy Unit of the Cabinet Office, known in government circles as 'the Review'. This publication, entitled 'Private Action and Public Benefit', was presented to the Government in 2002 with a series of recommendations to be considered by the Government. The second is the Government's response to these recommendations, published via the Home Office in 2003 as *Charities and Not-for-Profits: A Modern Legal Framework: the Government's Response to 'Private Action, Public Benefit'*. Within the document, the original recommendations of the Strategy Review are presented alongside the Government's response to them, thus providing a comprehensive and convenient 'one-document' representation of much of the key debate in this area. It draws clear and detailed attention to the central tenets of the proposed changes in law: modernisation and effectiveness, transparency, accountability, and regulation. These considerations provide the essence of the Charities Bill, which will be considered extensively in the next chapter.

online
resource
centre

FURTHER READING

Reading materials relating to charity and trust laws can be found referenced in the following two chapters, which relate to the legal definition of charity and cy près as appropriate.

13

The legal definition of charity

13.1 Introduction

Following on from the previous chapter, this one is focused on the legal definition of charity itself. Although there are many respects in which the Charities Act 2006 is highly significant for the way in which charity is to be defined in English law, the previous chapter also drew attention to the way in which it would be some time before the new provisions across the Act will actually come into force and affect existing laws. In this vein, the discussion which is made of the legal definition of charity remains that which still subsists until the new Act is implemented, and references made to 'exisitng law' relate to that which is not represented by the Charities Act 2006. The reference made immediately above to the new law affecting existing law is also a 'marker' for a theme which is going to become very prominent as the new Act is implemented. This rests on the way in which it will become apparent that as well as inculcating some very important new policy directions in charity law, the new definitions of charity derive much of their direction and authority from existing law. Thus, at this point, it is not very clear how the new provisions will interact with existing law in many respects. Constraints of space mean it is not possible to explore the parameter of uncertainty in the text itself, and so some of the key issues can be found on the accompanying ORC website.

13.1.1 Sources of law; identifying the legal definition of charity

In previous editions this section has opened with the statement that 'There is no formal statutory definition of charity, despite occasional proposals'. In this very important respect, the Charities Act 2006 will formally place the legal definition of Charity on a statutory footing. However, it is also highly significant that the statutory definitions of categories of charity do to a large extent represent a legislative consolidation of much of the developments to charity law which have occurred over four centuries.

This development over time has given prominence to the consideration of charity made by the courts, with little statutory intervention at the level of definition (save the Recreational Charities Act 1958 which will be considered in due course). The courts in turn have taken their lead from the Statute of Elizabeth 1601, otherwise known as the Statute of Charitable Uses 1601. It is the preamble to this piece of legislation which the courts have drawn on so extensively as a guideline to simplify their task of determining which purposes could be considered charitable.

The preamble listed purposes which were regarded as charitable at the time. Purposes which fell within the 'spirit and intendment' of the preamble were accepted by the courts as being charitable. Those which did not were not—however much they may have been regarded as beneficial to the public. By operation of the doctrine of precedent, what had originally been simply a convenient practice by the courts crystallised into rigid legal doctrine, and thus the preamble came, in effect, to have direct legal force. This was most unusual, because preambles to statutes usually have no legal force. Of course, the authority for the present law cannot be the preamble itself, but the cases which subsequently adopted it.

Elizabethan 'spirit' and nineteenth century formalisation: Pemsel
The Statute of Elizabeth's preamble is set out at a later point in this chapter, but for the present, it is sufficient to say that purposes laid down in it are many and diverse. Fortunately for this consideration of the legal definition of charity, a more modern 'base point' of reference exists by virtue of the decision of the House of Lords in *Commissioners for Special Purposes of the Income Tax* v *Pemsel* [1891] AC 531. In this case, Lord Macnaughten categorised charitable purposes under four main heads ('The *Pemsel* heads'):

(1) Purposes for the relief of poverty.

(2) Purposes for the advancement of education.

(3) Purposes for the advancement of religion.

(4) Other purposes which are beneficial to the community.

Noting the different classification 'heads' at this point is simply a marker for the discussion which is to come. More extensive discussion of each of them will commence shortly, and for present purposes, apart from noting the classification itself, it should also be appreciated that any given charitable purpose may, of course, fall within more than one of these heads.

Pemsel: a statement of modern law; evolution and change
Generally, therefore, there is no need to go back before 1891 for a judicial definition of charity. But it is also the case, for reasons which will become clear, that for head 4 the test still depends on the spirit and intendment of the preamble. An illustration of this can be found in the case of the *Scottish Burial Reform & Cremation Society Ltd* v *Glasgow Corporation* [1968] AC 138. This case also provides authority for the essence of charitable purposes as matters of continuing evolution and development. As an idea this was flagged up in the previous chapter, and in this very case Lord Wilberforce sounded a general note of caution about over-rigorous application of the *Pemsel* heads. He anchored this to his suggestion that the law of charity is a moving subject which may well have evolved even since 1891.

Evolving definition of charity and Charities Bill 2004
There will be some consideration of the Charities Bill throughout this chapter, and alongside the attention which will be drawn to its implications for the 'public nature' of charities, and the activities which charitable trusts engage in during the operation of their purposes, will be explanation of the import of the new Act for the definition of, and classification of charitable purposes themselves. As the very ending of the previous chapter suggested, reference will be made to a wealth of policy materials surrounding this particular movement for reform, and in particular the key Home Office publication from 2003. It was explained that in this particular document, the recommendations of the Strategy Review are presented along with the Government's response to them. This and the subsequent Bill of 2004 contain

important changes to the legal definition of charity, which are going to be key to this latest phase of its evolutionary development.

1601 preamble and its continuing life

The Statute of Charitable Uses 1601 was *itself* repealed by subsequent legislation, so that for a time only the preamble remained. The preamble itself was repealed by the Charities Act 1960 and was not replaced. This repeal had no legal effect, however, because the cases which used the preamble as a guideline can still be taken to be authoritative. Indeed, Lord Wilberforce in the *Scottish Burial Reform* case, mentioned above, used the spirit and intent of the preamble as a test of charitable status as late as 1968.

Because reference still therefore occasionally needs to be made to the preamble, it is here set out in full:

Whereas Lands, Tenements, Rents, Annuities, Profits, Hereditaments, Goods, Chattels, Money and Stocks of Money, have been heretofore given, limited, appointed and assigned, as well as by the Queen's most excellent Majesty, and her most noble Progenitors, as by sundry other well disposed persons; some for Relief of aged, impotent and poor People, some for the Maintenance of sick and maimed Soldiers and Mariners, Schools of Learning, Free Schools, and Scholars in Universities, some for the Repair of Bridges, Ports, Havens, Causeways, Churches, Sea-Banks and Highways, some for the Education and Preferment of Orphans, some for or towards Relief, Stock or Maintenance for Houses of Correction, some for the Marriages of Poor Maids, some for Supportation, Aid and Help of young Tradesmen, Handicraftsmen and Persons decayed, and others for the Relief or Redemption of Prisoners or Captives, and for Aid or Ease of any poor Inhabitants concerning Payments of Fifteens [a tax on moveable property], setting out of Soldiers and other Taxes; which Lands, Tenements, Rents, Annuities, Profits, Hereditaments, Goods, Chattels, Money and Stocks of Money, nevertheless have not been employed according to charitable Intent of the givers and Founders thereof, by reason of Frauds, Breaches of Trust, and Negligence in those that should pay, deliver and employ the same: For Redress and Remedy whereof, Be it enacted . . .

Pemsel as the source of modern law

In spite of the caution sounded in *Scottish Burial Reform*, the main source of the modern law can be taken to be Lord Macnaughten's classification in *Pemsel*. In addition to judge-made law, a body of precedent has now been built up by the Charity Commissioners in exercising their jurisdiction under s. 4 of the Charities Act 1960. This body of precedent is not technically authority but may be assumed to govern the process of registration in practice, unless and until it is successfully challenged in a court.

Recreational charities are a special case, by virtue of the Recreational Charities Act 1958, which provides a limited extension to the general law.

13.1.2 Requirement of public benefit

The previous chapter introduced the public nature of charitable trusts, identifying them as purposes which are publicly enforced and controlled, and have certain tax concessions. There is also a requirement that to be charitable a purpose must, in addition to falling within the *Pemsel* heads outlined above, involve a public benefit. There are therefore two requirements for a purpose to be charitable. It must confer a benefit upon those who are directly the objects of the charity, and it must also confer an additional benefit upon the public at large.

For example, if a charitable purpose such as education is to be advanced, it must not only confer a benefit on those in direct receipt of the education, but must also be advanced in some way that benefits the public, or at least a substantial section thereof, rather than providing benefits for some artificially limited class of people. However, as we shall see later, this requirement is not applied with the same rigour to each of the four heads of charity, and in the case of the relief of poverty, its role is minimal. For this reason, the public benefit requirement will be dealt with separately under each head.

13.1.3 **Charitable status and overseas benefits**

There is no rule of law which prevents the benefits of a charity being directed overseas, as opposed to being confined within the UK or primarily directed within the UK. For example, in *Re Niyazi's WT* [1978] 1 WLR 910, a trust to construct a hostel for working men in Cyprus was held charitable as being for the relief of poverty. Missionary societies operating abroad always seem to have been regarded as religious charities, and these will also often involve advancement of education. There are, however, three qualifications concerning overseas benefits.

(a) Although the Charity Commissioners (Annual Report for 1963, paras 69–76) take the view that trusts to relieve poverty or to advance religion will be charitable wherever found, a trust which falls within the fourth head must involve a benefit, even if indirect, to persons within the UK.

(b) Charity must not be tainted with political activity, and the large-scale charities which aim at assisting developing nations must avoid this pitfall. It seems that whereas it can be charitable to provide direct relief of observable poverty among a population, it is not charitable to seek to raise the total economy of an overseas country, or to alter its laws in order to alleviate poverty.

(c) An institution established under the laws of another legal system cannot be charitable under UK law, because the courts cannot administer a foreign charity, or settle a cy près scheme for such a charity, since they have no means of controlling an institution established in another country and administered by trustees there: *Gaudiya Mission* v *Brahmachary* [1998] 2 WLR 175 (CA).

13.1.4 **Purposes must be exclusively charitable**

A further point to be noted is that a trust must not merely be capable of application to charitable purposes; it must be exclusively so. If it is possible to benefit an object which is not charitable, then the trust will not be exclusively charitable, and will fail unless the courts feel able to sever the offending objects from the main corpus of the otherwise charitable purpose, or to declare that the non-charitable purposes are merely subsidiary.

Charitable exclusiveness and the construction of language
A great deal therefore depends on whether drafting of the trust is construed conjunctively or disjunctively. For example, if a purpose is described as 'charitable *and* benevolent', it is probable that these will be construed conjunctively: 'benevolent' merely qualifies 'charitable', so only charitable purposes are included. But in *Chichester Diocesan Fund and Board of Finance* v *Simpson* [1944] AC 341, the words 'charitable *or* benevolent' would have permitted the trustees to devote all the funds to benevolent ends which were not also charitable. The trust therefore failed,

leading to further litigation because funds had already been distributed by the trustees (*Ministry of Health* v *Simpson* [1951] AC 251). A gift to 'benevolent, charitable and religious' purposes was treated in *Williams* v *Kershaw* (1835) 5 Cl & F 111 as allowing the trustees to select purposes which were benevolent, but not necessarily charitable and religious. In other words, the comma was treated as allowing the trustees to select alternatives (i.e., as '*or*').

Although each case calls for independent construction, as a general guide it may be said that a comma, or the word 'or', is likely to lead to the listed purposes being interpreted disjunctively (i.e., as alternatives), while the word 'and' is usually read conjunctively. 'Charitable and ... ' succeeds; 'charitable or ... ' fails.

Towards a uniform rule of construction?
This is not invariably the case. In *Attorney-General of the Bahamas* v *Royal Trust Co.* [1986] 3 All ER 423, the Privy Council held not charitable a bequest for 'any purposes for and/or connected with the education and welfare of Bahamian children and young people', on the grounds that education and welfare should be interpreted disjunctively, and that a trust for welfare was not charitable. Therefore, although it may be possible to draw up guidelines to construction, categoric statements should be treated with caution.

In *Chichester Diocesan Board of Finance* v *Simpson*, it was impossible to construe the gift as being confined to charitable purposes, rather than benevolent purposes. Sometimes it is possible to construe the gift as a whole as being to charitable purposes, however, and as a matter of construction to exclude all purposes which are not charitable: see, e.g., *Re Hetherington* [1990] Ch 1. If so, the trustees will be restrained from using trust property for purposes which are not charitable, even where by so doing they are not contravening the *express* terms of the donation. In *Webb* v *O'Doherty* (unreported), *The Times*, 11 February 1991, the officers of a students' union were restrained from making any payments to the National Student Committee to Stop War in the Gulf, or to the Cambridge Committee to Stop War in the Gulf, whose purposes were not charitable. The union was an educational charity, and the officers were therefore entitled to use its property only for charitable purposes, even though there was nothing in the constitution of the union itself prohibiting such payments.

13.1.5 Profit-seeking

Generally speaking, it is incompatible with charitable status actively to seek profit as a primary objective, although fees may be charged, and incidental acquisition of profit should not disqualify. In *Scottish Burial Reform & Cremation Society Ltd* v *Glasgow Corporation* [1968] AC 138, the House of Lords held a society charitable for rating purposes (under the fourth *Pemsel* head: see 13.1.1) whose main object was the promotion of sanitary methods of disposal of the dead. The society charged fees but was not profit-making.

13.1.6 Charitable purposes

This general introduction to the legal definition of charity has introduced key sources of law, and provided a reminder that key changes are imminent in the form of the newly enacted Charities Act 2006. It has also identified key features flowing from the nature of charitable status which have influenced the development of the law relating to charities up to this point, and which are essential for appreciating why and how this has occurred in the manner it has. It will also become clear that understanding the introductory matters set out above will also enhance appreciation of the proposed future directions which are imminent. What needs to follow now, before consideration is made of the new provisions is substantive consideration of each of the classifications of charitable purposes laid out in *Pemsel*.

13.2 Purposes for the relief of poverty

13.2.1 What is poverty?

The courts have not attempted to define poverty in precise terms (e.g., a particular level of income), but, it is clear that this has been influenced by notions of 'the deserving poor'. Hence, poverty is not as extreme a concept as destitution (i.e., people can be poor who are not destitute) and it varies depending on one's status in life. People who are sufficiently well off to be able to live without state aid can be regarded as being poor for these purposes. Paradoxically, it is nowadays actually very difficult to relieve poverty among the poorest sections of society, because a claimant of state benefit can suffer a reduction in that benefit if he receives more than a small donation from charity.

13.2.1.1 *Relative nature of poverty*
In *Re Coulthurst* [1951] Ch 661, Evershed MR said of poverty (at pp. 665–6):

It is quite clearly established that poverty does not mean destitution: it is a word of wide and somewhat indefinite import; it may not be unfairly paraphrased for present purposes as meaning persons who have to 'go short' in the ordinary acception of that term, due regard being had to their status in life, and so forth.

Poverty, therefore, is a relative matter, depending on one's status in life, and the courts have been willing to allow trusts to assist such categories as 'distressed gentle folk'. In *Re De Cartaret* [1933] Ch 103, a trust for annual allowances of £40 each to widows and spinsters 'whose income otherwise shall not be less than 80 or more than 120 pounds per annum' was held charitable, even though there was a minimum income qualification, and £80 a year was at any rate a moderate income then.

Purposes exclusively for the poor
Subject to the width of the definition of poverty, it is essential that poverty should be imposed as a qualification for benefit and that only the poor can benefit. Whereas a trust under any of the other four heads can be charitable even where affluent people can enjoy its benefits, a trust which may benefit rich persons as well as poor will fail under this head. This is the reason why disaster fund appeals are often not charitable (see below), but the organisers of recent appeals have sometimes preferred to forgo charitable status, and the consequent tax exemptions, rather than limit compensation expressly to the poor.

The rich must usually be expressly excluded, the courts being very reluctant to infer their exclusion even where the nature of the benefit is unlikely to make it attractive except to the destitute. Thus it will become clear that in *Re Gwyon* [1930] 1 Ch 255, a clergyman had provided in his will for the distribution of trousers to the boys in the Farnham area. Though the trousers were described in such a way as to be unlikely to appeal to any but the very needy, because the rich were not expressly excluded, the provision was not charitable, and therefore failed. Another case is *Re Drummond* [1914] 2 Ch 90, where a bequest of shares on trust to provide holidays for employees failed, even though the actual wages received by those employees was very low. In *Re Sanders's WT* [1954] Ch 265, Harman J thought that the provision of dwellings for 'the working classes' in the Pembroke Dock area was not sufficient to limit the benefit to poor persons. Nor will a gift for 'deserving' persons, or 'those in need of financial assistance' suffice, but 'indigent' and 'needy' can be regarded as synonyms for poverty. Poverty can also often be implied in the case of gifts to elderly or disabled recipients.

Construction: the trend against hard-and-fast rules

As with any question of construction, however, no hard-and-fast rules can be laid down. Whereas the courts are reluctant to infer exclusion of the rich in the absence of an express limitation to the poor, it would be wrong to assume that they never do so. For example, in *Powell* v *Attorney-General* (1817) 3 Mer 48, it was assumed that the widows and children of Liverpool seamen would necessarily be poor, even though the word 'poor' itself was not used. More recently it will be seen that in *Re Niyazi's WT* [1978] 1 WLR 910, Megarry V-C held charitable a bequest of £15,000 'for the construction of or as a contribution towards the cost of a working men's hostel' in Famagusta, Cyprus, although there was no express limitation to the poor. He accepted that persons requiring such accommodation would necessarily be poor. *Re Niyazi's WT* is probably not of general application, however. The amount of money left for the purpose was relatively small, and the word 'hostel', rather than 'dwelling' suggested very inferior accommodation. 'Working men' is more limited than 'working classes', excluding, for example, battered wives and students, and Megarry V-C had regard to the deplorable housing shortage in Famagusta. It follows that it would be inadvisable for settlors to rely too heavily on this decision, and an express limitation to the poor is safer.

13.2.1.2 *Methods of relieving poverty*

The measures must actually relieve poverty, so merely to provide amusement for the poor will not suffice under this head, although it might under the second head, if educational.

It used to be thought that relief of poverty had to be ongoing, rather than by way of an immediate distribution of property. It was thought that an immediate distribution was indistinguishable from an ordinary private bequest. It is now clear from the Court of Appeal decision in *Re Scarisbrick* [1951] Ch 622 that this is no longer the case and that it is possible to relieve poverty by way of one-off payment or distribution. The question of whether or not a trust is perpetual in nature could, in the view of Jenkins LJ in that case, be relevant to the question of public benefit (which is set out later) because an immediate gift would be less likely to be in favour of a class of persons, as opposed to individuals. But on the assumption that the public benefit test is satisfied, it is not fatal that the disposition is once and for all rather than perpetual.

Indeed, the growth in state welfare provision has reduced the attractiveness of 'hand-outs', for reasons explained at the beginning of the section. Yet many old trusts to relieve poverty still bind trustees to distribute money or goods. This problem and the solution to it are considered in chapter 14.

Relief need not even necessarily be in the form of direct hand-outs of money, goods or services, but could, for example, allow access to necessary amenities at reduced cost. So it was accepted in *Joseph Rowntree Memorial Trust Housing Association Ltd* v *Attorney-General* [1983] Ch 159 that the sale of homes to elderly persons at 70 per cent of cost was charitable.

13.3 'Advancement of education'

13.3.1 What constitutes education?

The scope of charitable educational activities is surprisingly wide. In other areas a wide definition of charitable activity has been motivated by the mortmain legislation but this legislation rarely affected educational charities, many of which were incorporated by royal charter. The preamble to the Act of 1601 speaks only of 'schools of learning, free schools, scholars in universities' and the 'education and preferment of orphans', but in modern times this category has grown to cover a very wide range of educational and cultural activities extending far beyond the administration of formal instruction.

Definition beyond teaching
Schools and universities are clearly charitable, and so now are nursery schools, adult education centres and societies dedicated to promoting training and standards within a trade or profession. Education is not limited to teaching, however, and learned societies which bring together experts in a field to share and exchange knowledge may be charitable. Museums, zoos and public libraries may be educational to the public at large, quite apart from their research activities. Even cultural activities such as drama, music, literature and fine arts can come within this head, on the ground that they have a role in the cultivation of knowledge and taste.

As with other heads of charity, it is essential that the organisation should not be profit-seeking and the purposes must be exclusively charitable. Thus, a trust for 'artistic' purposes may be too wide (see *Associated Artists Ltd* v *IRC* [1956] 1 WLR 752).

Education must be advanced
It is also necessary that education be 'advanced', so that although research can be charitable, probably it will not be if, for example, it is carried on in secret. Scholarship for its own sake is also not charitable, and this is one of the reasons why researching the advantages of a new 40-letter alphabet was held non-charitable by Harman J in *Re Shaw* [1957] 1 WLR 729. The validity of a bequest under George Bernard Shaw's will, which also provided for the transcription of *Androcles and the Lion* into the proposed 40-letter alphabet, was also successfully challenged.

Learned societies are charitable, and professional and vocational bodies which advance education, such as the Royal College of Surgeons, are also charitable, even though one of the ancillary purposes is the protection and assistance of its members. Other examples include the Royal College of Nursing, the Institution of Civil Engineers, and the Incorporated Council of Law Reporting (in *Incorporated Council of Law Reporting for England and Wales* v *Attorney-General* [1972] Ch 73, the Attorney-General tried unsuccessfully to argue that the citation of law reports in court could not be educational because judges are deemed to have complete knowledge of the law). Bodies whose chief purpose is to further the interests of the members and to promote the status of the profession will not, however, be charitable; for example, the General Nursing Council (see *General Nursing Council for England & Wales* v *St Marylebone Borough Council* [1959] AC 540).

13.3.1.1 *Issues arising from physical education*

It will shortly become apparent that physical activity which is of a purely recreational nature will not be charitable unless it falls within the provisions of the Recreational Charities Act 1958. Games and other leisure-time pursuits can be charitable under this head, however, if educational. Thus, in *Re Marriette* [1915] 2 Ch 284, a gift to provide squash courts at a public school was held charitable, Eve J remarking (at p. 288) that the playing of games at boarding schools was as important as learning from books, and that the proper education of young people can include a physical element:

No one of sense could be found to suggest that between those ages [10 to 19] any boy can be properly educated unless at least as much attention is given to the development of his body as is given to the development of his mind.

On the same principle, the provision of toys for small children can be charitable (the National Association of Toy Libraries is a registered charity) as are youth movements, such as the Boy Scout Movement, or trusts to provide school outings. In *Re Dupree's Deed Trusts* [1945] Ch 16, Vaisey J held charitable a chess contest for young men in the Portsmouth area, though leaving the issue open for less intellectually demanding pursuits:

I think that the case before me may be a little near the line, and I decide it without attempting to lay down any general propositions. One feels, perhaps, that one is on a slippery slope. If chess, why not draughts; if draughts, why not bezique, and so on, through to bridge and whist, and, by another route, to stamp collecting and the acquisition of birds' eggs? Those pursuits will have to be dealt with if and when they come up for consideration in connection with the problem whether or no there is in existence an educational charitable trust.

These cases have been approved and followed by the House of Lords in *IRC* v *McMullen* [1981] AC 1, a case involving the playing of football at schools and universities. The House, holding that the Football Association Youth Trust was charitable, also made it clear that the legal conception of charity was not static but changed with ideas about social values.

All the above cases concerned the education of children or young persons. There is no reason, in principle, why adult education should not also be charitable, but a different approach seems to be taken to adult *physical* education: a police athletic association was held to be a trust for recreational purposes, and therefore not charitable. Nor has it been suggested that driving schools or flying schools should be charitable, although their purposes are undoubtedly, in a sense, educational.

13.3.1.2 *Value judgements*

Inevitably, with a wide definition of educational purposes, the courts and Commissioners may be involved in subjective value judgements as to whether a particular purpose falls within or outwith the definition. There appear to be two separate issues. First, does the activity have any educational value at all? Second, in the case of research, on the assumption that any discoveries made will be of value, to what extent should the courts take account of the likelihood of finding nothing?

Education, research and value judgements
It is clear that the courts are prepared to embark upon value judgements on the first question. The views of the donor will of course not be conclusive, and expert evidence will be admitted in order to assist in evaluating the merit of artistic and cultural work.

In *Re Pinion* [1965] Ch 85, for example, the testator left his 'studio' for the purposes of a museum to display his collection of what were claimed to be 'fine arts'. However, expert witnesses thought that the paintings were 'atrociously bad', and one 'expresse[d] his surprise that so voracious a collector should not by hazard have picked up even one meritorious object'. The question arose as to the validity of the trust, and this depended on whether it was charitable. Harman LJ described the collection as 'a mass of junk' and, reversing Wilberforce J, the Court of Appeal held the trust void. In *Re Hummeltenberg* [1923] 1 Ch 237 the court held void a trust to train spiritualistic mediums (though perhaps disciplined research into the paranormal, undertaken on scientific principles, could be charitable). On the other hand, in *Re Delius* [1957] Ch 299 a trust for the appreciation of the works of the composer was held charitable, but Roxburgh J made it clear that the undoubted merit of Delius's music was crucial, and the same view would not be taken of a 'manifestly inadequate' composer.

Research and the limitations of an 'outcomes' test
Where research is concerned, the courts will also presumably assess the value of the ultimate aim of the project, but on the assumption that any findings would be of value, it does not seem to be a bar to charitable status that nothing might be found at all. Of course, it is often difficult to know in advance whether or not the results of research will be useful (after all, if you did know the conclusions, the research would be pointless).

Perhaps this point was in Wilberforce J's mind in *Re Hopkins* [1965] Ch 669, where he upheld as charitable a bequest to the Francis Bacon Society for the purposes of finding the Bacon–Shakespeare manuscripts. Though he observed that, if found, the discovery would be 'of the highest value to history and to literature', the search could equally have been futile, as not only were the manuscripts not known to exist, but Wilberforce J thought their discovery unlikely. Value judgements are very difficult to operate when the outcome of the quest is uncertain, as will usually be the case where genuine research is concerned.

13.3.1.3 *Education and political purposes*

A trust for the advancement of political purposes will not be charitable. Education, however, can undoubtedly cover political theory and philosophy. The borderline appears to fall at the point where partisan propaganda is seen to be masquerading in the guise of instruction. In *Re Hopkinson* [1949] 1 All ER 346, a trust for adult education in socialist principles fell foul of the line. The political angle was another reason why the trust in *Re Shaw* [1957] 1 WLR 729 failed. The Charity Commissioners commented on the problem in their Annual Report for 1967, para. 8, but seem to take a fairly generous view, regarding, for example, the promotion of racial harmony as charitable. Greater attention will be paid later to the problem of political purposes generally.

13.4 'Advancement of religion'

13.4.1 Religion, but what religion?

The law adopts a tolerant stance towards religion, and seems reluctant to enter into value judgements in this area. As Cross J remarked in *Neville Estates* v *Madden* [1962] Ch 832, a case already considered in another context in 5.2, in which a trust for the members of the Catford Synagogue was held charitable: 'As between different religions the law stands neutral, but it assumes that any religion is at least likely to be better than none.' Another example is *Church of the New Faith* v *Commissioner of Payroll Tax* (Victoria) (1983) 83 AJC 4652, a case concerning Australian Scientology, where the High Court of Australia held that:

There can be no acceptable discrimination between institutions which take their character from religions which the majority of the community recognises as religions and institutions which take their character from religions which lack that general recognition.

Neutrality
Generally speaking, it seems, the courts are unprepared to engage in value judgements as to the relative worth of different religions.

In *Bowman* v *Secular Society Ltd* [1917] AC 406, Lord Parker of Waddington thought that a trust for the purpose of any kind of monotheistic theism would be a good charitable trust.

The preamble to the Statute of Charitable Uses 1601 gave little support for the tolerant approach the law has taken, the only reference to religion within it concerning the repair of churches. It may be that the explanation lies in the mortmain legislation in force from 1736 to 1891 which as we have seen rendered many gifts to charity void. Religious tolerance in this area, therefore, may have been used simply as a device to strike down testamentary gifts, though the authorities from that period still have validity today.

In *Thornton* v *Howe* (1862) 31 Beav 14, for example, charitable status was extended to a devise of land to promote the writings of Joanna Southcote, the founder of a small but fervent sect in the West of England, who had proclaimed that she was with child by the Holy Ghost and would give birth to a second Messiah. The practical effect of the decision was to bring the trust within the invalidating provisions of the mortmain legislation, but the case is still seen as a landmark in establishing that any theistic belief, however obscure or remote, will fall within the meaning of religion for the purposes of charity law. A recent example to the same effect is *Re Watson* [1973] 1 WLR 1472, where Plowman J held charitable a trust to publish the religious writings of a retired builder who was virtually the sole remaining adherent of a small, fundamentalist group of believers. Expert testimony regarded the theological merits of the works as very small but confirmed the genuineness of the writer's beliefs.

It is not necessary that the religious beliefs in question should be Christian. Certainly, the Jewish, Sikh, Hindu and Muslim faiths have been accepted. Faith healing was held to be a charitable purpose in *Re Le Cren Clarke* [1996] 1 WLR 288. In *Re South Place Ethical Society* [1980] 1 WLR 1565, however, Dillon J remarked that religion is concerned with man's relations with God, so it seems therefore that one qualification is the need for a belief in some kind of God (or gods). The South Place Ethical Society was held not to be a religious charity, because although its objects included 'the study and dissemination of ethical principles', and 'the cultivation of a rational religious sentiment', its beliefs were non-theistic. Dillon J observed:

> Religion, as I see it, is concerned with man's relations with God, and ethics are concerned with man's relations with man. The two are not the same, and are not made the same by sincere inquiry into the question, what is God? If reason leads people not to accept Christianity or any known religion, but they do believe in the excellence of qualities such as truth, beauty and love, or believe in the Platonic concept of the ideal, their beliefs may be to them the equivalent of a religion, but viewed objectively they are not religion.

In an old case in the Privy Council, *Yeap Cheah Neo* v *Ong Cheng Neo* (1875) LR 6 PC 381, a provision for the performance of ancestor worship was held non-charitable. High ethical principles or moral philosophy, being concerned with man's relations with man, cannot amount to a religion, though they may of course be educational and so charitable under that head. Plowman J also thought in *Re Watson*, considered above, that doctrines which were averse to the foundations of all religion, and subversive of all morality, would not be charitable under this head.

It seems that the gift must be exclusively for religious purposes, so that a gift for 'missionary work' or 'parish work' will be too wide, since such work may involve elements not wholly religious. On the other hand, in *Re Simson* [1946] Ch 299, a gift to a named clergyman 'for his work in the parish' was held to be impliedly confined to his religious duties.

Buddhism poses a problem in this context, since although it is generally accepted as being a religion, it is not clear (at any rate to the judiciary) whether or not Buddhists believe in a supernatural or supreme being. It is possible that it should be treated as an exception, since a trust to advance Buddhism is clearly charitable. Difficulties could also presumably arise where a human being sets himself up as a deity, and is worshipped as such—such religions exist, and it is unclear whether or not their advancement is charitable.

13.4.2 *Advancement* of religion

It is not enough merely to practice religion. Religion must also be advanced. As with education, the means by which religion may be advanced may be many and various. Apart from the provision and maintenance of churches, and provision of or for the benefit of clergymen, such matters as church choirs, Sunday school prizes, and even exorcism, have all been held to advance religion.

The advancement of religion seems also to require some positive action. For example, in *United Grand Lodge of Ancient Free & Accepted Masons of England and Wales* v *Holborn Borough Council* [1957] 1 WLR 1080, Donovan J, in denying charitable status to freemasons (who attempted to claim rates advantages), commented that:

There is no religious instruction, no programme for the persuasion of unbelievers, no religious supervision to see that its members remain active and constant in the various religions they may profess, no holding of religious services, no pastoral or missionary work of any kind.

Religion may have been a necessary qualification for membership of the lodge, as it might be for a church squash club, for example, but the lodge did not advance religion any more than a church squash club would.

13.4.3 Religion, society and reform of the law?

The Government, in its White Paper *Charities: A Framework for the Future*, HMSO (May 1989), the recommendations of which led to the enactment of the Charities Act 1992, later consolidated in 1993, considered whether the law in this area should be altered. The White Paper noted that:

Anxieties have been expressed, in particular, about a number of organisations whose influence over their followers, especially the young, is seen as destructive of family life and, in some cases, as tantamount to brainwashing.

Nevertheless, although considerable sympathy was expressed for these anxieties, reform of the law was not recommended, mainly because it was considered too difficult to formulate adequate proposals. Removal of charitable status from all trusts established for the advancement of religion was rejected because of the difficulties in which it would leave many existing trusts. Denial of charitable status only to new organisations, established after the legislation came into force, was rejected on the grounds that it would be difficult to justify denying charitable status to new trusts for religious purposes of an existing denomination. Replacing the presumption of public benefit with a positive test of 'worth' considered later which those seeking charitable status would need to satisfy, was rejected on the grounds that it would be difficult to define any criteria upon which a test of worth could be based. Problems would also occur where there was a single objectionable feature in a complex body of doctrine. The Paper also notes that the public anxieties which have been expressed have generally been addressed to the *conduct* of a movement rather than its *objects*, and that these matters can be dealt with administratively by the Charity Commissioners.

The result is, therefore, that the substantive law in this area has been unaffected by the Charities Act 1993.

13.5 'Other purposes beneficial to the community'

The consideration given to this final category which arises from Lord Mcnaughtan's *Pemsel* classification will show that it does, as its 'title' suggests, provide a residual category of charitable purposes. This is where a vast number, and very diverse purposes, can be found 'grouped', and as a reflection of this as much as its imprecise title itself, it is a head and classification which it is almost impossible to define precisely. The first point to note relating to this is that not every purpose which might, by common consensus, be considered beneficial to the community can come within this head. What the law admits as charitable under this head is still governed by the general statement of charitable purposes which was set out in the preamble to the Statute of Charitable Uses 1601, for although this has itself been repealed, the cases which have relied upon its guidance over centuries are still themselves authority. If some wholly novel purpose appears, the question is not whether it is beneficial in some general sense, but whether it falls within the 'spirit and intendment' of the preamble, or can be held to do so by analogy with the principles developed through the cases.

A 'catch-all' category

It should therefore be obvious that it is not always possible to state whether a particular purpose is charitable under this head or not. Some cases are expressly mentioned in the preamble, however, and there are also classes of trust which have been specifically considered by the courts. About these, at least, it is possible to state conclusions.

13.5.1 Purposes specifically included in the preamble

The preamble makes specific mention of the relief of aged, impotent (meaning disabled) and poor people; and it has never been necessary to show that the recipients possess all three characteristics simultaneously. Trusts to assist the elderly are common, as are trusts for the disabled, and no further requirement of poverty in the recipients is imposed. In other words, this head is wider than the relief of poverty head.

It must be the case, however, that the proposed purpose will offer some relief to the recipients. Since many of the disadvantages which accompany age or general disability can in fact be eased by material provision in the form of money or special equipment, this general requirement usually poses no problems. Probably, however, a gift of money which was wholly confined to such elderly or disabled people as are already wealthy could not be charitable, because it would fail to relieve the disadvantage of their condition. It is also likely that the class of recipients would not amount to a section of the public so as to satisfy the additional public benefit requirements.

Trusts for the benefit of the sick

Trusts to benefit the sick are *prima facie* charitable and before the introduction of the National Health Service in 1946, charitable gifts were the main source of provision for those needing hospital care but unable either to afford it or to insure against illness or injury. Today, gifts to private hospitals will still be charitable, since they help to ease the pressure on public services, as was noted in *Re Resch's WT* [1969] 1 AC 514. It is no objection that such hospitals tend to be of direct benefit to those who are relatively rich, though as under other heads a purely profit-making institution will not be charitable. There is no need to confine the benefits of the trust directly to the patients, and gifts which improve the efficiency of the service by providing homes for nurses, or accommodation for visiting relatives, are included under this head. Even organisations offering help with family planning, and those which seek to promote health by encouraging temperance, have been accepted for registration, but the Commissioners have found difficulty (see their Annual Report for 1975, para. 70) with fringe methods of healing, not generally recognised by the medical profession. Methods which are widely recognised, such as acupuncture, osteopathy and faith healing, are acceptable, but in other cases some evidence of the method's effectiveness will be demanded.

Trusts for the benefit of soldiers

Another category of benefits mentioned in the preamble was the 'setting out of soldiers', which has been extended to include the wellbeing and morale of the forces, or specific units thereof; charities for ex-servicemen; and the promotion of the efficiency of the police and the maintenance of law and order. Gifts to the Inland Revenue and for 'my country England' have been held charitable (*Re Smith* [1932] Ch 153), but gifts expressed to be for 'public' or 'patriotic' purposes have failed as being too wide and not exclusively charitable.

Anomalies: purposes prea without modern counterparts

Gifts for the 'repair of bridges, ports, havens, causeways, sea-banks and highways' were included in the preamble, and now that the state assumes responsibility for such matters, this category has grown to include such miscellaneous amenities as the National Trust, museums, art galleries, parks and community centres. In *Scottish Burial Reform & Cremation Society Ltd* v *Glasgow Corporation* [1968] AC 138, a crematorium was held charitable. And while it is not charitable to erect a monument to oneself, the commemoration of significant people or events (e.g., war memorials) will qualify. The Earl Mountbatten of Burma Statue Appeal Trust has been registered as being 'likely to foster patriotism and good citizenship' (Charity Commissioners' Annual Report 1981, paras 68–70).

Old ideas and modern applications: bringing the preamble up to date

The 'preferment of orphans' mentioned in the preamble has its modern counterpart in the provision of orphanages and local authority homes, but in *Re Cole* [1958] Ch 888 a majority of the Court of Appeal held non-charitable a trust for the general welfare and benefit of children in such a home out of fear that this might permit the provision of amenities not of an educational nature, such as radios or television sets, and this decision was followed in *Re Sahal* [1958] 1 WLR 1243. In this respect, therefore, purposes are unlikely to succeed under this head unless they will also succeed under the educational head.

Trusts to aid the rehabilitation and reform of prisoners have been accepted as charitable since the nineteenth century, but it is not easy to envisage circumstance in which the reference in the preamble to the 'ransom of captives' has any application today, unless perhaps hostages taken by terrorists are encompassed within the term 'captives'.

A gift for the benefit of a locality such as a town, county or parish, or for its inhabitants, will be charitable although one might have expected it to fail either because of failure to specify exclusively charitable purposes or on the ground that there is an insufficient public benefit. The explanation may lie in an analogy with gifts to local authorities. These have long acted in the capacity of trustees of various charities and so such gifts may be *impliedly* confined to charitable purposes. In any event, gifts to localities were probably within the spirit of the reforms of 1601 historically as these reforms were largely directed towards easing the burden of local poor rates. The trust must, it seems, be cast in terms of benefit for an area or its residents for the time being (not, e.g., a trust for expatriate Welshmen, unless the purposes were charitable for some other reason).

13.5.2 Animal charities

Animal charities are among the most popular with the public. Their inclusion within this head of charity owes nothing to the preamble to the Statute of Charitable Uses 1601 but rests upon a process of reasoning by analogy. As with religious toleration, the motive may well have lain in the mortmain legislation, but precedents of that period are of course still followed today.

In *London University* v *Yarrow* (1857) 1 De G & J 72, a trust to study the diseases of animals useful to mankind was held charitable, but this would probably have been a valid educational charity anyway. A more general authority is *Tatham* v *Drummond* (1864) 4 De G J & Sm 484, in which a bequest for the relief and protection of animals taken to be slaughtered was held charitable so that the gift failed under the mortmain legislation. Romer J also held a gift to a named lady to aid her work in caring for cats and kittens to be charitable in *Re Moss* [1949] 1 All ER 495.

Animal charities

It is not, however, the benefit to the animals themselves which has been fastened upon, to provide principled justification for the inclusion of animal charities under this head (although in Ireland, the good of animals requires no further justification). Rather, the assumed benefit is to humans, by encouraging them in 'feelings of humanity and morality generally' (see the judgment of Swinfen Eady LJ in *Re Wedgwood* [1915] 1 Ch 113, at 122).

Homes for lost dogs, needy horses, donkeys etc., have been accepted as charitable, along with well-known organisations such as the RSPCA and the PDSA. On the other hand, the need to benefit humans leads to the conclusion that the protection of creatures harmful to man could not be charitable under this head, nor, according to the Court of Appeal in *Re Grove-Grady* [1929] 1 Ch 557, would be the creation of a sanctuary where animals would be protected from all human intrusion. No doubt, however, both these could, in the case of trusts appropriately drafted, be valid as educational charities, for example, by the inclusion of a provision that the wildlife be studied.

Animal welfare and judgements of competing merits

Whereas it is usually assumed that a purpose falling under the first three heads of charity is a benefit, no such assumption is made for purposes falling under the fourth head, and indeed, sometimes the courts will be faced with value judgements as to the relative merits of competing benefits. On the issue of whether the abolition of vivisection might be a public benefit, for example, the House of Lords in *National Anti-Vivisection Society* v *IRC* [1948] AC 31 was not prepared to depart from the view of the Special Commissioners for Income Tax, that any assumed public benefit in the suppression of vivisection, in the advancement of morals, was outweighed by a detriment to medical science and research, which was itself of undoubted public benefit. The purposes of the National Anti-Vivisection Society not therefore being charitable, it was not entitled to exemption from income tax. This case will be further considered later.

Private trusts for pet animals are not charitable because there is no public benefit, but they may nevertheless be valid as private purpose trusts as an anomalous category as seen in chapter 4.

13.5.3 **Purposes beneficial to the community;**
Pemsel **and continuing evolution**

Although one would be wise to give due regard to the views of Lord Wilberforce expressed in the *Scottish Burial Reform* case of the dynamic nature of charity and charity law, it is not surprising that the fourth 'dustbin' *Pemsel* head has been a particular hub of activity. This can be illustrated by a number of examples whereby the Charity Commissioners have made determinations on such 'topical' issues as unemployment, questions of rural and urban regeneration and conservation, corporate social responsibility and fair trade. The references made to Charity Commission documents can be followed up on its extremely informative (and even quite straightforward) website (see *www.charity-commission.gov.uk*). This is also a reflection of the discussion which will follow about the new Charities Act and the changes it will make to the way in which charity is defined, which are discussed immediately hereafter—following discussion of the Recreational Charities Act 1958.

Relief of unemployment
Trusts for the relief of unemployment (directly, rather than through the traditional routes such as the alleviation of poverty) have recently been considered in the review of the Register of Charities. The Charity Commission ruled that such purposes can be charitable if they are able to establish that they are seeking to address unemployment generally for a community or for a section of it. Examples of addressing or tackling employment which would satisfy the Charity Commissioners would include giving advice or training to those who are unemployed, and initiatives to help business 'start ups' (including, e.g., subsidised rents and capital advances, etc.).

Promotion of urban and rural revival
This purpose has recently been recognised as one which is charitable where it can be shown that the organisation seeking charitable status can demonstrate that it is seeking to improve 'physical, social and economic infrastructure' and assist to alleviate disadvantage which has arisen on account of social and economic circumstances. Such purposes can include the provision of financial assistance or the promotion of improving standards in housing; the provision of education or (re)training; the provision and maintenance of infrastructure (a modern day counterpart for the Statute of Elizabeth's 'repair of bridges' etc.!?); the provision of recreational facilities and public amenities and their maintenance; and the preservation of historic buildings and places of interest.

Preservation of national heritage and conservation of the environment
Closely related to the promotion of rural and urban revival is the preservation of national heritage and the environment. For example the National Trust has a long tradition of being charitable, and in 2001 the conservation of the environment was recognised as a charitable purpose in its own right. However, the Charity Commission has made it clear that charitable status shall only follow the provision of public access to the site or habitat or building in question (in order to satisfy the public benefit requirement). If there are good reasons for restricting public access, public benefit can be satisfied with the provision of alternative means of providing the public with information.

Promotion of business ethics and responsibility
Recently the Charity Commission has determined that organisations which promote the incorporation of ethics into their business practice, and which provide
advice or protection for employees faced with ethical difficulties encountered in
their work can be recognised as charitable.

Promotion of fair trade
Trusts for the promotion of fair trade have been recognised as charitable since the
'fair trade mark' received charitable status in 1995. Whilst the motivation for reliev-
ing poverty and promoting better standards of living in Third World countries might
appear to be a trust for the relief of poverty it will of course provide benefit for those
who are not poor in addition, and thus would not be exclusively for the poor (illuminating the need for charitable status to be sought and conferred by head 4).

13.5.4 Recreational purposes

Until the 1950s it was assumed that while some recreational purposes, such as boys'
clubs, women's institutes and parish halls, were potentially charitable, sporting
facilities were not, unless they were either educational or promoted efficiency in the
armed forces. A series of cases in the 1950s, however, suggested that no recreational
purpose will be charitable at common law. As we shall see shortly, however, a fifth
(limited) head of recreational charities has now been added by statute.

Recreation, charity and the 'big three'
In *IRC* v *Glasgow Police Athletic Association* [1953] AC 380, the encouragement and
promotion of athletic sport and general pastimes for officers and ex-officers of the
City of Glasgow police force was held non-charitable, although it might have been
allowed had the purpose been merely incidental to improving police efficiency. It
had been found as a fact that the athletic association played an important part in the
maintenance of health, morale and *esprit de corps* within the police force, and in
attracting recruits to the force. The leisure element 'bulked too large', however, to be
merely incidental to maintaining the efficiency of the police force. Lord Reid said:

> I do not doubt that the purpose of increasing or maintaining the efficiency of a police force is
> a charitable purpose within the technical meaning of those words in English law. It appears to
> me to be well established that the purpose of increasing the efficiency of the army or a part of
> it is a charitable purpose. It may be that in some cases the facts hardly justified the conclusion
> that this was the purpose of the gift in question, but that does not affect the principle. I can
> see no valid distinction between the importance or character of the public interest of main-
> taining the efficiency of the army and that of maintaining the efficiency of the police.
>   But it is not enough that one of the purposes of a body of persons is charitable: the Act
> requires that it must be established for charitable purposes only. This does not mean that the
> sole effect of the activities of the body must be to promote charitable purposes, but it does
> mean that that must be its predominant object and that any benefits to its individual mem-
> bers of a non-charitable character which result from its activities must be of a subsidiary or
> incidental character.
>   . . . I have come to the conclusion that conferring such benefits [leisure and enjoyment] on
> its members bulks so large in the purposes and activities of this association that it cannot
> properly be said to be established for charitable purposes only. . . .

In *Williams's Trustees* v *IRC* [1947] AC 447, the London Welsh Association, whose
objects were to promote social and recreational purposes among Welsh people

living in London had also been held non-charitable, partly on the basis that purely social activities could not be charitable within the spirit of the preamble to the Statute of Charitable Uses 1601. Finally, in *IRC* v *Baddeley* [1955] AC 572, a reduction in stamp duty on a conveyance of land was refused because the purposes of the conveyance were not charitable. The conveyance was to a Methodist mission and the purposes were essentially those of promoting the 'religious, social and physical wellbeing' of residents of an area by providing facilities for 'religious services and instruction; and for the social and physical training and recreation' of such people. The inclusion of purely social purposes prevented these purposes from being exclusively charitable.

13.6 Problems with 'other purposes' and the Recreational Charities Act 1958

The discussion immediately above explains how doubt was cast by a number of decisions in the 1950s on the charitable status of a number of social trusts which had always been assumed to be charitable. The Recreational Charities Act 1958 was enacted to restore what was assumed to be the *status quo ante* in respect of those trusts. The London Welsh Association, for example, was validated by the Charity Commissioners in 1977.

Section 1 states that it shall be, and be deemed always to have been, charitable to provide, or assist in the provision of, facilities for recreation or other leisure-time occupation, if the facilities are provided in the interests of social welfare. A proviso adds that nothing in the section shall be taken to derogate from the principle that to be charitable a trust or institution must be for the public benefit. Under s. 1(2), the requirement that the facilities are provided in the interests of social welfare will not be satisfied unless the facilities are provided with the object of improving the conditions of life for the persons for whom the facilities are primarily intended, and either:

(a) those persons have need of such facilities as aforesaid by reason of their youth, age, infirmity or disablement, poverty or social and economic circumstances, or

(b) the facilities are to be available to the members or female members of the public at large.

Subject to the requirement of social welfare, there is specific reference to the provision of facilities at village halls, community centres and women's institutes, and to the provision and maintenance of grounds and buildings to be used for the purposes of recreation or leisure-time occupation, extending to the provision of facilities for these purposes by the organising of any activity. There is also express provision (in s. 2) for miners' welfare trusts.

Where the Act applies, the spirit of the preamble to the Statute of Charitable Uses 1601 seems no longer to be relevant, and it must therefore be taken that the statute has added a fresh head of charity.

Section 1(2)(b) above allows for the provision of facilities for recreation or other leisure-time occupation where the facilities are made available to the public at large, but under s. 1(1) they have also to be provided in the interests of social welfare. In *IRC* v *McMullen* (considered in a different context earlier), Walton J at first instance ([1978] 1 WLR 664, [1978] 1 All ER 230) held that the requirement of social welfare in s. 1(1) implied that for a charity to succeed under the Act, the recipients must be limited to those who are in some way 'deprived persons'. The Court of Appeal ([1979] 1 WLR 130, [1979] 1 All ER 588) split on the issue, the majority (Stamp and Orr LJJ) holding that the class to be benefited must be disadvantaged in such a way as to have a special need for the facilities. There was no such limitation in *McMullen* itself, where the gift was to the Football Association Youth Trust. Bridge LJ dissented, preferring a wider view that social welfare may be promoted by benefits which extend to the better off as well as the socially deprived, observing that he could:

see no reason to conclude that only the deprived can have their conditions of life improved. Hyde Park improves the conditions of life for residents in Mayfair and Belgravia as much as for those in Pimlico or the Portobello Road, and the village hall may improve the conditions of life for the squire and his family as well as for cottagers.

The House of Lords ([1981] AC 1) left the issue open, allowing the appeal on the grounds that the trust was charitable under head 2. Indeed, their lordships expressly refused to decide which of the approaches adopted in the Court of Appeal was correct, but the issue has now been resolved in *Guild* v *IRC* [1992] 2 AC 310, where the House of Lords came down in favour of Bridge LJ's view. It is therefore not fatal that benefits are not limited to deprived persons.

Presumably, social welfare indicates some element of provision for others, so that a group acting purely to benefit themselves would fail to qualify. In any event, such an enterprise would lack the necessary element of public benefit preserved by the Act.

13.7 **The Charities Act 2006 and reform in the definition of charitable purposes**

It will quickly become obvious and apparent to anyone who studies the text of the original 2004 Bill that an exhaustive consideration of it is simply not possible in terms of space. What *is* provided in this chapter is a basic outline of the way in which the Bill relates to the legal definition of charity. Thus, at this point, attention is paid only to how the Bill will impact on the legal definition of charitable purposes. Accordingly, its implications for the 'public benefit' requirement for charitable status is held over to be discussed alongside the current provisions relating to public benefit, which follow immediately below.

In looking at proposed changes to the legal definition of charity (and in due course the provisions relating to public benefit), attention is of course drawn to the relevant sections within the new Act itself. These proposed reforms are themselves positioned alongside the issues which underpinned the policy of 'Private Action and Public Benefit', and the subsequent Home Office Publication from 2003 which contained the Government's response to that Review publication. Reference will also be made as appropriate to more recent Parliamentary consideration of the then Charities Bill dating from 2005 and 2006.

At this stage there is one very important element to understanding the provisions of the new Bill, which will place the legal definition of charity on to a new statutory footing. It is essential to appreciate that in many respects the new provisions represent a consolidation of much of the development of charities law at common law. This is so both in respect of the actual classification of charitable purposes themselves and in the way in which an accompanying framework focused on the general character of charitable operation has been developed alongside this. This latter 'frame work' does of course include matters such as that, in order to be charitable, purpose must be 'exclusively charitable'.

13.7.1 The Bill's starting point: the meaning of charity

The first sections of the Charities Bill as it was published in 2004 attend to what, for the purposes of the proposed new statutory footing for charitable trusts, will be meant by the terms 'charity' and 'charitable purpose'. Two important related considerations flow from the new Act's direction in these matters. These relate to the import which has been accorded to the courts' development of charity law over the past 400 years. In defining what is meant by charity, s. 1(1)(a) provides that the term 'charity' means an institution *'which is established for charitable purposes only'*, and by s. 1(1)(b) one which (accordingly) *'falls to be subject to the control of the High Court in the exercise of its jurisdiction with respect to charities'*.

The references within s. 1(1)(a) are very clearly to the 'framework' adopted in the development of the current law relating to charities which has enabled the courts to develop and refine principles governing charitable purposes themselves. This is thus affirmation that the notion of purposes which are exclusively charitable remain at the heart of English charity law. In this spirit of 'conservation' between current and future directions, s. 1(3) provides authority for the continuing operation of the essence of the legal basis of charity law for the past 400 years: *'A reference in any enactment or document to a charity within the meaning of the Charitable Uses Act 1601 or the preamble to it shall be construed as a reference to a charity as defined by this section.'*

An analysis of the Act's new approach, which signals consolidation and confirmation, and importantly clarification, rather than substantive new direction, can be seen in the explanation given to what is meant by charitable purposes as provided by s. 2. Section 2(1) provides that *'For the purposes of the law of England and Wales, a charitable purpose is a purpose which—(a) falls within subsection (2), and (b) is for the public benefit (see section 3)'*. Accordingly, a purpose is charitable if it falls within any of the following descriptions of purposes listed there under s. 2(2):

(a) the prevention and relief of poverty;

(b) the advancement of education;

(c) the advancement of religion;

(d) the advancement of health;

(e) the advancement of citizenship and community development;

(f) the advancement of the arts, heritage or science;

(g) the advancement of amateur sport;

(h) the advancement of human rights, conflict resolution or reconciliation;

(i)   the advancement of environmental protection or improvement;

(j)   the relief of those in need, by reason of youth, age, ill-health, disability, financial hardship or other disadvantage;

(k)   the advancement of animal welfare;

(l)   any other purposes within subsection (4).

The first three categories of purposes within s. 2(2)—purposes (a) (b) and (c)—are instantly recognisable as three of the *Pemsel* heads of charitable purposes. Indeed, the provisions of s. 2(3) even mimic concerns which have arisen in the interpretations given to advancement of religion: according to s. 2(3)(a) *religion includes (i) religion which involves belief in more than one god; and (ii) a religion which does not involve belief in a god'*. Thus, although in many respects the new Act is an exercise in consolidation and confirmation, it does signal a certain degree of new direction.

However, it is also the case that consolidation and confirmation is particularly strong in analysing the intended direction of the new Act. The remaining 10 heads comprise a mixture of purposes which are recognisable within current understandings of 'charitable purpose' and others which *could* potentially be brought within the scope of the current fourth head in *Pemsel* relating to 'other purposes beneficial for the community', by being in the 'spirit and intendment' of the 1601 Act. Section 2(3) continues to provide clarification of s. 2(2) beyond the position relating to religion in the following ways:

• Section 2(3)(b) provides that in respect of paragraph (d) 'the advancement of health' includes *'the prevention or relief of sickness, disease or human suffering'*.

• Section 2(3)(c) provides that paragraph (e) includes *'(i) rural or urban regeneration, and (ii) the promotion of civic responsibility, volunteering, the voluntary sector or the effectiveness or efficiency of charities'*.

• Section 2(3)(d) provides that for the purposes of paragraph (g) 'sport' means *'sport which involves physical skill or exertion'*.

• Section 2(3)(e) provides that paragraph (j) includes *'relief given by the provision of accommodation or care to the persons mentioned in that paragraph'*.

The spirit of confirmation and consolidation is further indicated in the provisions of s. 2(4)–(8). In this respect, attention has been drawn to the following:

• By the provisions of s. 2(4)(a), purposes which are not included within the statutory categories contained within s. 2(2) can nevertheless still be charitable where they are *inter alia* recognised as purposes under existing charity law.

By these new provisions they may accordingly be regarded as analogous with any purposes in the new statutory list, or under existing charity law. Here, existing charity law is defined as that which is in force immediately before the date at which the new section (of the new Act) comes into force. This reference to recognition of purposes which are charitable under existing law will include the purposes made charitable by the Recreational Charities Act 1958.

• By the provisions of s. 2(5) where any term used in the definitions of s. 2(2), or s. 3's provisions for public benefit, has particular meaning under charity law, in the new legislation the term will be taken as having the same meaning where it appears in that provision.

- By the provisions of s. 2(8), references made in s. 2 to 'charity law' denote *'the law relating to charities in England and Wales'* and 'existing charity law' means *'charity law as in force immediately before the day on which this* [new] *section comes into force'*.

13.8 Legal definition after classifying purposes: public benefit requirement

In addition to the manner in which purposes must be able to be classified in order to achieve charitable status, as the introduction made clear, there is an additional requirement for all charities that they must confer a 'public benefit'.

What follows at this point is a consideration of how public benefit is accommodated in the current law's requirements, and as a matter of logic which will become apparent, the requirement or 'test' for public benefit will be considered under each charitable 'head', and will be so in the order of heads 2, 4, 1 and 3 respectively. The reason for starting with head 2 is that the test of public benefit for educational charities has been clearly stated, and one of the main issues is the extent to which that test also applies to the other heads of charity. Most of the cases are on head 4, which is why this head is dealt with immediately after head 2.

Following this consideration of the law as it is, the discussion will then move to the significance of public benefit in the new Charities Act 2006, signalling future direction.

13.8.1 Public benefit and educational charities

In the case of relief of poverty, even benefiting a small number of people may be regarded as conferring a public benefit. Yet whereas education is clearly a benefit to those in immediate receipt of it, it is not self-evident that educating a few people constitutes a benefit to the general public. Indeed, given that many of the cases under this head are in reality disputes over tax relief, it would be quite wrong if the education of a privileged few were to be regarded as charitable. Under this head it is therefore necessary that there is some additional benefit to the general public or some appreciable sector thereof.

That is not to say that a particular form of education has to be capable of being enjoyed by everyone, so long as access to it is reasonably open. Thus public schools may be charitable as long as they are not operated as profit-making ventures, although their fees may place them beyond the means of the majority. Even scholarships or endowed chairs, which can be enjoyed only by one person at a time, present no difficulty. The problems arise where it is sought to limit the potential beneficiaries within a class which is insufficiently wide to constitute a section of the public.

It is clear that it may be charitable to provide, e.g., scholarships, open to:

(a) persons following a common profession or calling, or their children and dependants, or

(b) people of common nationality, religion or sex, or

(c) the inhabitants of a given area, provided this is reasonably large, such as a town or county.

Special provisions for disabled people are also permissible, since they are a section of the public in a meaningful sense.

13.8.1.1 *The Oppenheim personal nexus test*

However, under this head, and probably under all the *Pemsel* heads except relief of poverty, it will be fatal if the class of potential beneficiaries (however large) is defined in terms of relation to particular individuals or a company. This approach originated in *Re Compton* [1945] Ch 123, where charitable status was denied to a trust to educate the children of three named families. It is understandable that the courts are reluctant to allow an essentially private arrangement to enjoy charitable privileges, especially tax advantages, but it seems that the principle extends to cases where the class of potential beneficiaries is defined in terms of a relationship with an employer, even were the employer is a substantial concern.

The most authoritative statements, however, are those of Lord Simonds in *Oppenheim* v *Tobacco Securities Trust Co. Ltd* [1951] AC 297, where *Re Compton* was approved in the House of Lords. Lord Simonds said that first, the number of possible beneficiaries must not be negligible, and secondly, that the class must not be defined so as to depend on any relationship to a particular individual or employer:

> Then the question is whether that class of persons can be regarded as such as a 'section of the community' as to satisfy the test of public benefit. The words 'section of the community' have no special sanctity, but they conveniently indicate first, that the possible (I emphasise the word 'possible') beneficiaries must not be numerically negligible, and secondly, that the quality which distinguishes them from other members of the community, so that they form by themselves a section of it, must be a quality which does not depend on their relationship to a particular individual. . . . A group of persons may be numerous, but, if the nexus between them is their personal relationship to a single *propositus* or to several *propositi*, they are neither the community nor a section of the community for charitable purposes.

In the trust with which the House of Lords was concerned, the number of potential beneficiaries (at least in theory) was certainly not negligible. The income of the trust fund was directed to be applied 'in providing for . . . the education of children of employees or former employees of the British-American Tobacco Co. Ltd . . . or any of its subsidiary or allied companies in such manner . . . as the acting trustees shall in their absolute discretion . . . think fit'. The number of present employees alone exceeded 110,000, so it was only the personal nexus rule which was fatal (because they were all connected with the same company).

As Lord MacDermott pointed out in his dissenting speech, however, the rule is by no means easy to apply, and produces odd results when the '*propositus*' is an employer. For example, a trust to educate the sons of railwaymen, not expressed as limited to a single company, would have been valid before the nationalisation of the railways, and void when British Rail became the sole employer. In any case the test is arguably inappropriate in large companies. Though perhaps the special tax concessions of charitable status should not be given to any arrangement for a private class, the personal link between employees is not as obvious as that between members of a family, among whom considerations of mutual interest might be considered to negate the altruistic status of the trust.

Justifying Oppenheim

Perhaps the real, if unstated, justification for the result in *Oppenheim* was the extent of the trustees' discretion in that case. The benefit to 110,000 or more people may in fact have been entirely theoretical—e.g., if the trustees had used the funds to pay 15 per cent of fees to those employees who sent their sons to boarding school, only the relatively small number who could afford the other 85 per cent would actually have benefited. The problem is that the test in *Oppenheim* may not achieve the desired result in all cases; the House of Lords should have concentrated, we would suggest, on the extent of the trustees' discretion to limit the number of people who could in practice have benefited, rather than the nexus with the company.

The personal nexus test

Nevertheless, the personal nexus rule is law, certainly for trusts under this head. There may however be loopholes, as for example in *Re Koettgen's WT* [1954] Ch 252, in which an educational trust succeeded despite a direction that the trustees should give preference to the families of employees, up to a maximum of 75 per cent of income. On the other hand, doubts have been expressed and, for example, a preference for the grantor's family rendered a gift non-charitable in *Caffoor v Income Tax Commissioner* [1961] AC 584. In *IRC v Educational Grants Association Ltd* [1967] Ch 123, affirmed [1967] Ch 993, between 76 per cent and 85 per cent of the income of a fund (varying from year to year) was paid out for the education of persons connected with the Metal Box Co. Ltd. In a dispute with the Inland Revenue, it was held that the money had not been paid exclusively for charitable purposes. Pennycuick J found 'considerable difficulty in the *Koettgen* decision' and thought that a preference for a private class might always be fatal (although he did not actually need to decide that). The problem with laying down a clear rule of this nature would be that extreme cases could be envisaged (e.g., a *preference* up to 5 per cent of income) where its application would further no obvious policy (unless again, of course, an objection is taken in principle to charitable status for an arrangement with any purely private content).

   This problem is similar to that in *Oppenheim* itself, i.e., that the rule is arguably too rigid. The real problem in *Oppenheim*, as has been seen, was the extent of the trustees' discretion to limit the number of people who could in practice have benefited rather than the nexus with the company (unless again, objection is taken to *any* private arrangement). It would have been difficult to formulate a clear rule on trustees' discretion, however, where the problem is essentially one of where to draw the line, just as it is difficult to draw the line in the *Koettgen* situation. In both cases, therefore, a rigid rule may well be the only answer.

13.8.1.2 *Class must be a section of the community*

Oppenheim v Tobacco Securities Trust Co. Ltd [1951] AC 297 also required that it must be possible to describe the class genuinely as a section of the community, rather than simply a body of private individuals. There are in effect two separate requirements. First, the class must be capable of being genuinely described as a section of the community, rather than simply a fluctuating body of private individuals. Persons following a common profession or calling, people of common nationality, religion or sex, or the inhabitants of a town or county can be described as a section of the community. Special provisions for disabled people are also permissible, since they are a section of the public in a meaningful sense. But in *Davies v Perpetual Trustee Co. Ltd* [1959] AC 459, the Privy Council held non-charitable a trust which was confined to Presbyterian youths who were descended from settlors in New South Wales who had originated from the North of Ireland. Although quite large in number, this category of potential beneficiaries was held not to be a section of the public. It was merely a fluctuating body of private individuals.

13.8.2 Public benefit under the fourth head

Lord Simonds thought in *Oppenheim v Tobacco Securities Trust Co. Ltd* [1951] AC 297 that the test of public benefit may vary between the four heads of charity (in particular he excluded the 'poor relations' cases entirely from consideration). It is clear that the personal nexus test applies to the fourth head, but arguably the requirement that the trust benefits a section of the public is more stringent under the fourth head than under the second.

For example, in *Williams's Trustees v IRC* [1947] AC 447, doubt was expressed by Lord Simonds about whether Welsh people living in London could be a section of the public under the fourth head. In *IRC v Baddeley* [1955] AC 572, the House of Lords held that the persons to be benefited must either be the whole community or the inhabitants of a particular area. If some further restriction is imposed, thus creating in effect a class within a class, the test of public benefit will not be satisfied.

Viscount Simonds in *IRC v Baddeley* thought 'that a different degree of public benefit is requisite according to the class in which the charity is said to fall', and that public benefit considerations 'have even greater weight [than in the case of educational trusts] in the case of trusts which by their nominal classification depend for their validity upon general public utility': it is possible, particularly in view of the so-called 'poor relations' cases, the scope of which may one day have to be considered, that a different degree of public benefit is requisite according to the class in which the charity is said to fall. But it is said that if a charity falls within the fourth class, it must be for the benefit of the whole community or at least of all the inhabitants of a sufficient area.

Baddeley: a different and additional test
The *Baddeley* test seems therefore to be a different, and additional, test to that adopted in *Davies v Perpetual Trustee Co. Ltd* [1959] AC 459 for the second head. Indeed, the very definition of charity under the fourth head (purposes beneficial to the community) would seem to demand a more stringent test of public benefit than under any other head. However, Lord Reid thought otherwise in his dissenting speech in *IRC v Baddeley*.

'Section of the public' and the significance of the trust's purposes
It is also likely that what constitutes a section of the public depends on the purposes of the particular trust, and the courts are more likely to strike down arbitrary restrictions which are irrelevant to those purposes, but which simply serve to exclude other sections of the public. For example, in *IRC v Baddeley*, the limitation was to Methodists living in West Ham and Leyton, and the trust included the provision of playing-fields. Lord Simonds clearly thought that the restriction to Methodists living in West Ham and Leyton was completely irrelevant to the provision of playing-fields. Referring (at p. 592) to a rhetorical question put in argument: 'Who has ever heard of a bridge to be crossed only by impecunious Methodists?' he went on to say that what is true of a bridge for Methodists is equally true of any other public purpose falling within the fourth head, and of the adherents of any other creed. The limitation merely operated to prevent the purpose from being a public purpose; it could have had no other effect. A purpose which is not a public purpose cannot be charitable within the fourth head.

Variation within the heads of charity as well as between them?

There is some authority that the test of public benefit can vary even within the fourth head itself. In *Re Dunlop* [1984] NI 408 (noted by Norma Dawson [1987] Conv 114), Carswell J upheld as charitable a bequest 'to hold the remainder of my residuary estate for the Presbyterian Residential Trust ... to found or to help to found a home for old Presbyterian persons', and a cy près scheme (see chapter 14) was ordered. There was earlier Northern Irish authority that the Presbyterians of Londonderry were not a sufficient section of the public under the fourth head, and it was accepted that there was no difference between Irish and English definitions of charity. Carswell J took the view, however, that public benefit depended on the nature of 'the advantage which the donor intends to provide for the benefit of all of the public'. A 'bridge to be used only by Methodists should clearly fail to qualify, whereas a gift for the education of the children of members of that church might be a valid charity'. But he was also prepared to distinguish between purposes within the fourth head itself.

It should perhaps finally be observed that neither *IRC* v *Baddeley* nor *Williams's Trustees* v *IRC* actually turned on the issue of public benefit. In the former case the purposes were not exclusively religious, but included social purposes and the provision of playing-fields, and in the latter case purposes were exclusively social and recreational. They would therefore have failed because of the inclusion of a social content, whatever view had been taken on the public benefit issue.

13.8.3 Public benefit and the relief of poverty

It is unquestioned law that to relieve poverty is to confer a benefit upon the public at large, if only by mitigating the burden of support for the poor which would otherwise fall upon the community. The House of Lords in *Oppenheim* v *Tobacco Securities Trust Co. Ltd* [1951] AC 297 exempted 'poor relations' cases as anomalous and left open the question whether the personal nexus test applies to them.

The 'poor relations' anomaly stems from the practice of Chancery in the nineteenth century when faced with trusts expressed to be for poor relations; rather than allow these to fail for uncertainty (at a time when the class ascertainability test applied: see 4.4.5) or perpetuity, the courts rescued such trusts by holding them charitable. The 'poor relations' cases have been consistently followed, which is probably why the House of Lords left them alone in *Oppenheim*. The House of Lords has considered them directly in *Dingle* v *Turner* [1972] AC 601, and expressly upheld them. In that case a trust for 'poor employees of E. Dingle & Co.' was held charitable, although it would have failed under the personal nexus test. The same reasoning must apply to 'poor relations'. It is clear, therefore, that the personal nexus test does not apply to this head of charity.

A less strict test, subject to limitations

In order for a trust to be charitable under this head, it is, however, necessary that the trust should be intended to benefit a class of persons, and not simply to make a gift to an individual, or group of individuals, who happen to be poor. In *Re Scarisbrick* [1951] Ch 622, Jenkins LJ stated the rule thus:

I think the true question in each case has really been whether the gift was for the relief of poverty amongst a class of persons, or ... a particular description of poor, or was merely a gift to individuals, albeit with relief of poverty amongst those individuals as the motive of the gift, or with a selective preference for the poor or poorest amongst those individuals.

This statement received the approval of Lord Cross of Chelsea in the leading case of *Dingle* v *Turner*, considered below, and recently applied in *Re Segelman* [1996] 2 WLR 173. In *Re Scarisbrick* itself the class of potential recipients was sufficiently wide to be incapable of exhaustive ascertainment ('such relations of my said son and daughters as shall be in needy circumstances ...') so the trust was charitable.

Assuming that Jenkins LJ's test is satisfied, however, the public benefit requirements are less stringent under this head than under the others and the class to be benefited can be quite small.

13.8.4 **Public benefit and the advancement of religion**

There are *dicta* in *Oppenheim* that the public benefit tests advanced in that case apply to all heads of charity except the relief of poverty. Certainly, for religious charities, there must also be an element of public contact. Private salvation, however commendable, is not charitable. This is another explanation of *Yeap Cheah Neo* v *Ong Cheng Neo* (1875) LR 6 PC 381 because a provision for the performance of ancestor worship could benefit only the family group. The leading case is *Gilmour* v *Coats* [1949] AC 426, where the House of Lords had to consider a gift of £500 towards a Carmelite priory. The priory housed about 20 cloistered nuns who devoted themselves to intercessory prayer and had no contact at all with the outside world. This was held non-charitable on the grounds that there was no contact with the outside world. Arguments based on Catholic doctrine, to the effect that everyone benefited from the intercessory prayers, were rejected as being not susceptible to legal proof. Nor could any benefit be found merely in the example of the piety of the women, as it was too vague and intangible. The House of Lords also rejected the argument that, entry being open to all women, the priory should be treated on analogy with an educational institution offering scholarship entry, holding that an educational establishment which required its members to withdraw from the world and leave no record of their studies would not be charitable either.

On the other hand, in *Re Caus* [1934] Ch 162, Catholic masses for the dead were held charitable. This case was doubted in *Gilmour* v *Coats*, but in principle the case seems correct, and *Caus* was applied by Browne-Wilkinson V-C in *Re Hetherington* [1990] Ch 1. The point is that Catholic masses are open to the public at large even where a private function, such as a funiary rite, is incorporated into the celebration, so in principle *Caus* is distinguishable from *Gilmour* v *Coats*.

Re Hetherington: a review of the authorities
In *Re Hetherington*, Browne-Wilkinson V-C was called upon to consider a gift for the saying of masses, which did not exclude the possibility that the masses would be said in private. In practice, however, all or most of the masses would be open to public. Reviewing the cases, he said (at pp. 134–5):

(1) A trust for the ... advancement of religion is *prima facie* charitable, and assumed to be for the public benefit ... This assumption of public benefit can be rebutted by showing that in fact the particular trust in question cannot operate so as to confer a legally recognised benefit on the public, as in *Gilmour* v *Coats*.

(2) The celebration of a religious rite in public does confer such a benefit because of the edifying and improving effect of such celebration on the

members of the public who attend. As Lord Reid said in *Gilmour* v *Coats* [1949] AC 426 at 459:

> 'A religion can be regarded as beneficial without it being necessary to assume that all its beliefs are true, and a religious service can be regarded as beneficial to all those who attend it without it being necessary to determine the spiritual efficacy of that service or to accept any particular belief about it.'

(3) The celebration of a religious rite in private does not contain the necessary element of public benefit since any benefit by prayer or example is incapable of proof in the legal sense, and any element of education is limited to a private, not public, class of those present at the celebration: see *Gilmour* v *Coats* itself . . .

(4) Where there is a gift for a religious purpose which could be carried out in a way which is beneficial to the public (i.e., by public masses) but could also be carried out in a way which would not have sufficient public benefit (i.e., by private masses) the gift is to be construed as a gift to be carried out only by the methods that are charitable, all non-charitable purposes being excluded . . .

Applying these principles to the case before him, he concluded that:

a gift for the saying of masses is *prima facie* charitable, being for a religious purpose. In practice, those masses will be celebrated in public, which provides a sufficient element of public benefit . . . The gift is to be construed as a gift for the saying of public masses only . . . private masses not being permissible since it would not be a charitable application of the fund for a religious purpose.

In other words, he construed the gift in such a way as to exclude purposes which were non-charitable.

Public and private: distinguishing Gilmour v Coats
It follows that the mere attendance by the public at a prayer service is sufficient to distinguish *Gilmour* v *Coats*. Suppose, on the other hand, the religious organisation conducts all its affairs in private, but unlike *Gilmour* v *Coats* its members have not cut themselves off entirely from the outside world, but mix with it. This also seems sufficient to distinguish *Gilmour* v *Coats*. In *Neville Estates* v *Madden* [1962] Ch 832 (considered in a different context earlier), Cross J held charitable a trust for the members of Catford Synagogue. He thought that the rejection of example as a benefit in *Gilmour* v *Coats* would not apply to a restricted religious group if its members lived in the world and mixed with their fellow citizens, because they could thereby extend their example of religious living to the public at large:

The trust with which I am concerned resembles that in *Gilmour* v *Coats* in this, that the persons immediately benefited by it are not a section of the public but members of a private body. All persons of the Jewish faith living in or about Catford might well constitute a section of the public, but the members for the time being of the Catford Synagogue are no more a section of the public than the members for the time being of a Carmelite Priory. The two cases, however, differ from one another in that the members of the Catford Synagogue spend their lives in the world, whereas the members of a Carmelite Priory live secluded from the world. If once one refuses to pay any regard—as the courts refused to pay any regard—to the influence which these nuns living in seclusion might have on the outside world, then it must follow that no public benefit is involved in a trust to support a Carmelite Priory. As Lord Greene said in the Court of Appeal ([1948] Ch 340, at p. 354): 'Having regard to the way in which the lives of the members are spent, the benefit is a purely private one.' But the court is, I think, entitled to assume that some benefit accrued to the public from the attendance at places of worship of persons who live in this world and mix with their fellow citizens.

On this view, religion can be advanced by example, so long as one mixes in the world in a *physical* sense. *Neville Estates* is authority that no more is required (however, see also *Re Warre* [1953]; but the *Neville Estates* view seems more in accord with recent High Court decisions and the Charity Commissioners).

13.9 **Public benefit: future direction under the Charities Act 2006**

Although the new Charities Act is a lengthy and extensive project relating to charity law, once again, consideration here is directed towards the provisions relating to the legal definition of charity. And following the brief explanation of the new classifications of 'charitable purposes', and the framework for the meaning of the term 'charity', what remains now is for some consideration to be made of what the Act says in respect of the public character of charitable activity, and the requirement of public benefit which currently reflects this. The public benefit requirement is at the heart of the current law's legal definition of charity, and thus of the ability of purposes to acquire charitable status. This spirit continues within the new Act, where it can be found in s. 3.

It has been suggested that the new Act, in respect of its treatment of the core meaning of charity and the classification of charitable purposes, represents an important project of consolidation and clarification, and one which accords considerable respect to existing charity law. This has already been suggested in relation to the statutory list of charitable purposes, and it is reflected in the retention of a public benefit requirement: according to s. 3(1), a purpose must be for the public benefit if it is to be considered charitable. The new section does not actually define what is meant by public benefit, but once again anchors this firmly to existing charity law in s. 3(3). At one level this can be explained in the language of continuity and with conservation of current law in a way that mirrors the approach taken to the statutory definition of charitable purposes: in this respect it should not be too difficult to align what are effectively existing charitable purposes with current approaches to public benefit. However, there are important questions surrounding what test (for public benefit) might actually accompany the 'heads' of charitable purpose which are actually new and are not to be found in existing law. This is one important respect in which it is not obvious how new law and existing law might actually map coherently onto one another, and this is likely to result in much more extensive consideration in the next edition of this text. For now the issue is noted in the text and considered a little further in the accompanying ORC, but how it actually 'shakes out' as the new law is implemented very much remains to be seen.

Futhermore, the provisions in s. 3(2) do represent a new direction, because there is no longer to be a presumption of public benefit operating in favour of a purpose wishing to secure charitable status. As the Explanatory Notes accompanying the new Act explain, '[u]nder existing law there is a presumption that purposes for the relief of poverty, the advancement of education, or the advancement of religion ... are for the public benefit ... The effect of this presumption is that ... [an] organisation's purpose is presumed charitable unless there is evidence that it is not...' Currently all other purposes must demonstrate their public benefit and the effect of the new Act is to remove this presumption by placing all charitable purposes on an equal footing in having to demonstrate their public benefit in order to achieve charitable status. In implementing this new approach—in which *all* purposes falling into *all* categories of the new statutory definitional framework will have to demonstrate the 'public benefit' dimensions of their purposes—it will fall to the Charity Commission to issue guidance on demonstrating this. Some indication of this is given below, but at present there is little 'hard and fast' information on how this is likely to work.

The continuing significance of public benefit for the legal definition of charity
The task of determining whether or not a particular purpose is charitable, and thus, assessing the merits of a purported public benefit is vested in the Charity Commission by the provisions of s. 4, and both the Strategy Review document and the Government response to it emphasised the desirability that the Charity Commission should carry out ongoing checks on public character. The Government's support of this as desirable rested on its observation of structural weakness in the current system whereby the only time at which systematic check is made on a charity's public character is at the point of its registration. A move to checks which are ongoing could be used to assess any doubts which might arise in respect of the public character of the purpose during a registered charity's operation. Very interestingly, in addition, the Government suggested that ongoing checks could be instrumentally used to monitor the 'performance' of certain types of charity, which may accrue benefits for 'under-performing' charitable purposes to be aware of their own positions. What this monitoring proposal does not explicitly point to—but the implication is clearly present in the documentation—is the way in which 'performance' is not being directed towards under-performance alone, or even in the main. The import appeared instead to be concerns that might arise from a charity which is appearing to be *too successful* and therefore difficult to reconcile with charitable status. An obvious point of reference for this might well be the charitable status of independent schools, and this is considered in more detail shortly.

The operation of the public benefit requirement under the Charities Act 2006
What can be concluded at this point is that, notwithstanding that the term has not been defined in the intended statute and that lack of statutory clarification is capable of being problematic, English charity law remains grounded in the concept of 'public benefit'. It is set to continue to be central in securing charitable status under the proposed new regime of charity law, in spite of the extensive and often controversial attention which it has attracted at all stages of the Bill's genesis. Although the requirement of public benefit is to be enshrined in statute, along with the way in which there will be no presumption of charitable status, what potentially charitable purposes actually must establish is not being given a clear legal test within the imminent Act. The preferred approach appears instead to be framing its meaning in reference to existing, more generalised notions of public benefit, and from the provisions of clause 4 it becomes clear that the Charity Commission will be at the heart of determining this; acting as *regulator* of charitable purposes through being responsible for their *registration*. Accordingly, the provisions of s. 4 are, *inter alia*, as follows:

- Under s. 4(1), the Charity Commission for England and Wales '*must issue guidance in pursuance of its public benefit objective'*.
- Under s. 4(2), the 'public benefit objective' of s. 4(1) is '*to promote awareness and understanding of the operation of the requirement'* mentioned in s. 3(1) of the Charities Act 1993.

- Under s. 4(3), the Commission may from time to time revise any guidance on the public benefit requirement, but must (under s. 4(4)) carry out public consultation before issuing guidance or making revisions to such guidance, and (under s. 4(5)) must publish any guidance issued or revised as it considers appropriate.

- And, the trustees of a charity must (under s. 4(6)) '*have regard to any such guidance when exercising any powers or duties to which the guidance is relevant*'.

13.9.1 Continuing problems for public benefit: the Charities Act 2006 and the position of 'public' schools

During Parliamentary debates in the House of Commons during June 2006, Minister for the Cabinet Office Hilary Armstrong proposed (as recorded in *Hansard* (26 June 2006), col. 21) the following to explain the significance of the Charities Bill. The Bill sought to acknowledge that charities 'play a fundamental role in the fabric of our society', and 'provide a vital service to individuals and communities'. The Government thus wished to 'break down the barriers that face the charitable sector', and to promote their growing importance within society 'by helping to release charities' potential for further public good'. However, as well as increasing charities' potential in an evolving modern world, it was also important to ensure that charities were accountable to 'the public whom they serve' in a way which reflects the 'significant economic and social weight' which the sector wields.

Accordingly, alongside the purposes of providing charities with a legal and regulatory environment which is enabling, and encouraging a vibrant and diverse sector, the new Charities Act is also concerned to sustain 'high levels of public confidence in charities', which is to be achieved through 'effective regulation'. The Minister clarified that the requirement that charitable organisations conferred a public benefit had to remain for these reasons, because (at col. 25) the Act is partly about 'securing public confidence in charitable status' *itself*.

This text has always made note of the way in which controversy over public benefit is frequently directed at the position of independent schools as charitable purposes. In current law the operation of a presumption of public benefit (in the first three *Pemsel* heads) ensures that very exclusive educational establishments— which are in common parlance somewhat ironically described as 'public schools'— have a presumption in favour of them being charitable. This is notwithstanding perceptions that access to many of these establishments is substantially enjoyed by only a very few, and closely related ones that in many ways this position under- mines quite fundamentally notions of 'publicness'. Since the first appearance of the Charities Bill in 2004, it has commonly been thought among academics and policy- makers that the new requirement to demonstrate public benefit is going to be most keenly felt by these establishments, which in many respects eschew accepted understandings of publicness.

This perception has been borne out most recently during Parliamentary consid- eration during 2006. While Members and Peers have expressed concerns about the position of religion (e.g., Andrew Selous MP, *Hansard* (26 June 2006), col. 21), and sporting pursuits (e.g., Richard Burden MP, *Hansard* (26 June 2006), col. 24), and have sought reassurance (at col. 22) that 'research and knowledge transfer' in the university and higher education sector will 'remain charitable activities for the pub- lic benefit', most consideration of public benefit in both Houses has concerned the controversial position of public schools.

Indeed, while the views of MPs Daniel Kawczynski and Andrew Turner were very much in support of the continuing (*presumptively*) charitable status of public schools, their commentary is also indicative of why the charitable position of such establishments is so controversial. According to Mr Kawczynski (*Hansard* (26 June 2006), col. 37) 'one of the best public schools in the country—Shrewsbury—is in my constituency. It does a lot for charity and is very good for the community in Shrewsbury. These plans will affect it, and I am worried about the impact on it of the extra bureaucracy involved in meeting these requirements.' Furthermore, fundamentally, according to Andrew Turner:

[w]ho can argue that education is not for public benefit? The principal argument for education being provided at the taxpayers' expense is that it is in everyone's interest that we have a better educated nation ... How can it be argued that education that people pay for—those of us who can afford to do so—is of less benefit than other benefits?

In a manner which both acknowledges that this is a critical point in time for such establishments, and also opposes much of the support which was subsequently offered in favour of them in the House of Commons above, in the House of Lords in 2005, Lord Best (*Hansard* (7 June 2005), col. 821) remarked that this might be an appropriate point in time to 'drop the term "public school" '. This was a 'term which so inaccurately describes' educational establishments which are 'clearly distinct from the public sector in their governance and funding'; and in respect of them new charity law is intending to import that 'charitable status means an obligation to reach out to the community outside the school gates, offering bursaries to pupils from less affluent families and joining in partnerships with local education authorities'.

It is uncontentious to suggest that Parliamentary discussion of the new Act was dominated by the highly contentious position of public schools, and it is the view of this text that actually debates have even become hijacked by the issues arising in contemplation of such establishments having to demonstrate their public benefit. Indeed, in the House of Lords in 2005 it was suggested by Lord Best (*Hansard* (7 June 2005), col. 820) that '[t]he best illustration of the public benefit debate, and the most controversial ingredient of the Bill relates to the treatment of independent schools that charge high fees, but are registered as charities'. It is clear from the commentary immediately above that the continuing 'problem' of (in many ways inappropriately termed) public schools continued to follow the Bill right up until its passage into law, and is likely to continue.

13.10 Purposes which create problems under any head

13.10.1 Political purposes

A trust cannot be charitable under any head if its purposes are, directly or indirectly, political. A trust to promote the aims of a particular political party is clearly not capable of being charitable, and attempts to disguise such objectives as educational trusts have generally failed.

What amounts to 'political purposes'?
The definition of 'political' in this context is somewhat wider than the layman might expect, however. Where the objectives involve attempting to bring about a

change in the law, they will be considered political and therefore non-charitable, unless change in the law is merely ancillary to the main purpose of the trust. This was one of the reasons for the failure of the National Anti-Vivisection Society to achieve charitable status in *National Anti-Vivisection Society* v *IRC* [1948] AC 31. Lord Simonds gave as the ostensible rationale that it is for Parliament, not the courts, to decide whether any change would be for the public benefit. He also rejected the contention that alteration in the law was merely ancillary to the purposes of the trust, since in order to abolish vivisection it would have been necessary to repeal the Cruelty to Animals Act 1876 (since replaced by the Animals (Scientific Procedures) Act 1986) and pass an Act prohibiting vivisection altogether. He said at pp. 61–3:

Here, the finding of the Commissioners is itself conclusive. 'We are satisfied', they say, 'that the main object of the society is the total abolition of vivisection ... and (for that purpose) the repeal of the Cruelty to Animals Act 1876 [now replaced by the Animals (Scientific Procedures) Act 1986], and the substitution of a new enactment prohibiting vivisection altogether.' This is a finding that the main purpose of the society is the compulsory abolition of vivisection by Act of Parliament. What else can it mean? And how else can it be supposed that vivisection is to be abolished? Abolition and suppression are words that connote some form of compulsion. It can only be by Act of Parliament that that element can be supplied. . . .

I would remind your lordships that it is the King as *parens patriae* who is the guardian of charity and that it is the right and duty of his Attorney-General to intervene and inform the court, if the trustees of a charitable trust fall short of their duty. So too it is his duty to assist the court, if need be, in the formulation of a scheme for the execution of a charitable trust. But, my Lords, is it for a moment to be supposed that it is the function of the Attorney-General on behalf of the Crown to intervene and demand that a trust shall be established and administered by the court, the object of which is to alter the law in a manner highly prejudicial, as he and His Majesty's government may think, to the welfare of the State? ... I conclude upon this part of the case that a main object of the society is political and for that reason the society is not established for charitable purposes only.

Changes in the law

It follows, therefore, that any trust whose main object includes a change in the law of the UK cannot be charitable. In *Re Bushnell* [1975] 1 WLR 1596, money was left to advance awareness of the benefits of socialised medicine and to show that its realisation was fully possible only in a socialist state. The testator had died in 1941, before the introduction of the National Health Service. One of the grounds upon which the trust was held void was its political bias in favour of socialism. Another ground for the failure of the trust in *Re Bushnell* was that in 1941 legislation would have been needed (and was of course later enacted) to introduce socialised medicine.

This was also an additional reason for the failure of Shaw's 40-letter alphabet (see 13.3.1.4), and accounts for the inability of, e.g., the Campaign against Racial Discrimination and the National Council for Civil Liberties to be registered. Charities may, however, campaign *against* changes in the law, which may enable some political purposes of a generally conservative nature to obtain registration.

Political objects and changes in the law overseas

Lord Simonds's reasoning in *National Anti-Vivisection Society* v *IRC*, above, applies only to changes to the law in the UK, but in *McGovern* v *Attorney-General* [1982] Ch 321, Slade J frustrated Amnesty International's attempt to procure charitable status for some of its activities by creating a trust of those parts which were thought most likely to be accepted as charitable, on the grounds that a main object of the trust was to secure the alteration of the laws of foreign countries. The objects of the trust were as follows:

(a) The relief of needy persons within any of the following categories:
   (i) prisoners of conscience;
   (ii) persons who have recently been prisoners of conscience;
   (iii) persons who would in the opinion of the trustees be likely to become prisoners of conscience if they returned to their country of ordinary residence;
   (iv) relatives or dependants of the foregoing persons; by the provision of appropriate charitable (and in particular financial educational or rehabilitational) assistance.

(b) Attempting to secure the release of prisoners of conscience.

(c) Procuring the abolition of torture or inhuman or degrading treatment or punishment.

(d) The undertaking promotion and commission of research into the maintenance and observance of human rights.

(e) The dissemination of the results of such research by (i) the preparation and publication of the results of such research (ii) the institution and maintenance of a library accessible to the public for the study of matters connected with the objects of this trust and of the results of research already conducted into such matters (iii) the production and distribution of documentary films showing the results of such research.

(f) The doing of all such other things as shall further the charitable purposes set out above *provided always* that the foregoing objects shall be restricted to those which are charitable according to the law of the UK but subject thereto they may be carried out in all parts of the world.

The trustees applied to the Charity Commissioners for registration as a charity under s. 4 of the Charities Act 1960, and the Commissioners refused. Amnesty International unsuccessfully appealed to the High Court under s. 5(3). The problem was the inclusion of objects (b) and (c), seeking release of prisoners of conscience and the abolition of torture, which necessarily involved securing changes in the laws of foreign countries.

The decision represents an extension of the principles laid down in the House of Lords in *National Anti-Vivisection Society* v *IRC* [1948] AC 31. The reasoning adopted by Lord Simonds could not be applied directly here, but Slade J thought that to grant charitable status to such purposes might prejudice the relations of the British Government with foreign countries, and this consideration of policy could not be overlooked by the court:

The point with which I am at present concerned is whether a trust of which a direct and main object is to secure a change in the laws of a foreign country can ever be regarded as charitable under English law. Though I do not think that any authority cited to me precisely covers the point, I have come to the clear conclusion that it cannot.

I accept that the dangers of the court encroaching on the functions of the legislature or of subjecting its political impartiality to question would not be nearly so great as when similar trusts are to be executed in this country. I also accept that on occasions the court will examine and express an opinion on the quality of a foreign law.... .

Furthermore, before ascribing charitable status to an English trust of which a main object was to secure the alteration of a foreign law, the court would also, I conceive be bound to consider the consequences for this country as a matter of public policy. In a number of such cases there would arise a substantial *prima facie* risk that such a trust, if enforced, could prejudice the relations of this country with the foreign country concerned.... .

Any political taint will suffice

A political taint will in any case be fatal to charitable status, whether or not a trust's direct and main object is to secure a change in the law of the UK, or of a foreign country. This can apply even to trusts seeking to promote aims which most civilised nations hold to be high aspirations. In *Re Strakosch* [1949] Ch 529, the promotion of racial harmony between English and Afrikaans communities in South Africa was held non-charitable, and registration of community councils is refused where their principal aims are the promotion of interracial accord. The same will apply where the aims are harmony and peace, if such movements overtly or covertly call upon governments to promote specific policies, such as disarmament. One reason sometimes given for denying charitable status to attempts to promote moral objectives is that they necessarily involve a propagandist element biased in favour of only one side of the argument.

13.10.1.1 *Discussion of political issues, and campaigning*

On the other hand, it is legitimate for an educational charity to discuss political issues, and a political object which is merely incidental will not be fatal. In *Re Koeppler's WT* [1986] Ch 423, a testamentary gift to Wilton Park, whose main function was to organise educational conferences, was upheld by the Court of Appeal as a gift for charitable purposes, although the Wilton Park's objects included the promotion of informed international public opinion and the promotion of greater co-operation between East and West. The objects of the trust were:

(1) An enquiry into the 'quality of life'; ecology and the environment; participation in government and industry; tensions in free societies; (2) Europe and the emergent pattern of superpower relationships; (3) the unification of Europe; a balance sheet; (4) the requirements of Western defence and the possibilities of arms control; (5) the European Community and its external relations; (6) the media, public opinion and the decision-making process in government; (7) security issues as a factor in domestic and international politics; (8) labour and capital and the future of industrial society.

In upholding the trust, Slade LJ distinguished *McGovern* v *Attorney-General* on the grounds that a political purpose which is merely incidental to the objects of a trust will not necessarily be fatal where the purposes are otherwise educational. In *McGovern* v *Attorney-General*, by contrast, alteration in the law was not incidental to the objects of the trust, but was essential to Amnesty International's aims:

the activities of Wilton Park are not of a party political nature. Nor, so far as the evidence shows, are they designed to procure changes in the laws or governmental policy of this or any other country: even when they touch on political matters, they constitute, so far as I can see, no more than genuine attempts in an objective manner to ascertain and disseminate the truth. In these circumstances I think that no objections to the trust arise on a political score, similar to those which arose in the *McGovern* case.

Another authority that discussion of political issues is not necessarily fatal to charitable status is *Attorney-General* v *Ross* [1986] 1 WLR 252, where Scott J commented at p. 263 that 'there is nothing the matter with an educational charity in the furtherance of its educational purposes encouraging students to develop their political awareness or to acquire knowledge of and to debate and to form views on political issues'. He also observed that there is no reason why a charitable student organisation should not affiliate to a non-charitable organisation if that enables it to further its own charitable activities for the benefit of students. That is the basis upon which student unions are entitled to affiliate to the National Union of Students, a non-charitable organisation. It is, however, essential that the purpose of the affiliation should be to benefit the student body in their capacity as students.

It may also be that it is legitimate to go beyond discussion and take tentative steps into the arena of persuasion. The following passage is taken from the White Paper, 'Charities: A Framework for the Future', HMSO (May 1989):

Charities can, for example, quite properly respond to invitations from Government to comment on proposed changes in the law. Where a Bill is being debated, they can legitimately supply members of either House with such relevant information and arguments as they believe will assist the attainment of their objects. Where this kind of action is in furtherance of their purposes, charities are free to present to government departments reasoned memoranda advocating changes in the law.

The White Paper continues a few paragraphs further on:

Ministers welcome the advice and the guidance which charities offer to Members of Parliament, to central and local government, and to other public authorities on a wide range of social problems. Charities should feel free to take the initiative in offering advice and opinions and in proposing changes to the law and should not need to wait to be invited to do so.

There is the qualification, however, that such activities must remain ancillary to the charity's primary purposes.

Distinguishing political discussion from campaigning
There are limits to the extent to which a charity can go in this direction, however. Political discussion may not be fatal to charitable status, but campaigning, in the sense of seeking to influence public opinion on political matters, undoubtedly is. In *Webb* v *O'Doherty*, (unreported) *The Times*, 11 February 1991, Hoffmann J, distinguishing *Attorney-General* v *Ross*, granted an injunction restraining the officers of a students' union, which was an educational charity, from making any payments to the National Student Committee to Stop War in the Gulf, or to the Cambridge Committee to Stop War in the Gulf. The union had passed a resolution in January 1991 which mandated the executive in the following terms:

(1) To affiliate to the National Student Committee to Stop the War in the Gulf and the Cambridge Committee to Stop the War in the Gulf. (2) To campaign on the above issues. (3) To support and publicise national and local demonstrations, speaker meetings and non-violent direct actions organised by CND and Committee to Stop War in the Gulf. (4) To support the teach-in on the Gulf Crisis organised by the Student Committee to Stop War this Thursday. (5) To allocate £100 from the Campaign budget to the anti-Gulf War campaign. (6) To write to the Prime Minister and Ministry of Defence outlining this policy.

In restraining the officers from making the payments, Hoffmann J observed:

There is ... a clear distinction between the discussion of political matters, or the acquisition of information which may have a political content, and a campaign on a political issue. There is no doubt that campaigning, in the sense of seeking to influence public opinion on political matters, is not a charitable activity. It is, of course, something which students are, like the rest of the population, perfectly at liberty to do in their private capacities, but it is not a proper object of the expenditure of charitable money.

The Charity Commissioners exercise supervisory control over charities, and one area is the permissible limits to political involvement by charities. Their Annual Reports of 1969 and 1981 point out that charity trustees who engage in political activities risk personal liability to repay trust funds expended in breach, and that charities whose purposes are found to be wide enough to permit political action may be de-registered. Charities may aid governments on particular issues by giving information and by rational persuasion, but must avoid seeking to remedy the causes of poverty which lie in social, economic and political structures, or to eliminate other social injustice.

The advice of the Commissioners has also been published in the form of a booklet, 'Political Activities by Charities', which is intended for the guidance of trustees. In the White Paper 'Charities: A Framework for the Future', the Government summarises the position as follows:

The Charity Commission's guidance is, broadly, to the effect that:
governing instruments should not include a power to exert political pressure except in a way which is ancillary to a charitable purpose;
the powers and purposes of a charity should not include the power to bring pressure to bear on the Government to adopt, to alter, or to maintain a particular line of action, although charities may present reasoned argument and information to Government;
where the objects of a charity include the advancement of education or the power to conduct research, care must be taken that both objectivity and balance is maintained and that propaganda is avoided.

13.10.1.2 Law reform?

Since reform of this aspect of the law has recently been considered and rejected, it is perhaps pertinent to make reference to criticisms that have been levelled at the law in this area. In his excellent contextual work, *Charities, Trusts and Social Welfare* (1979), Chesterman observes (at pp. 357–8) that it has ultimately conservative implications, particularly where a welfare organisation takes the view that its role is that of a catalyst, its long-term aim being to encourage state funding:

The irony here, however, is that if they are too vociferous in urging the state to take over from them, they risk being deemed non-charitable because they are 'political' in one of the senses which charity law does not recognise. In the eyes of the law, a statement by a charity such as Shelter that 'it exists to put itself out of business' has non-charitable implications.

He also observes that overseas welfare charities, such as Oxfam and War on Want, are restricted by the law to distribution of food and other basic amenities, which is unlikely to have any long-term impact on the problems being addressed. They cannot, under the present law, become involved in projects of a more strategic nature, such as stimulation of local food production, or attempts to persuade a foreign government to distribute the country's resources more equitably or the British government to grant more foreign aid. In short, they cannot do that which would be most effective.

The Government took a different view in 1989, commenting in 'Charities: A Framework for the Future' that:

... the safeguards which the law provides are indispensable to prevent what are essentially political factions or pressure groups from assuming the guise of charity. It is vital, in the long-term interests of the public and charities alike, that political and charitable purposes should remain distinct. It would be wrong if taxpayers, through the Government, were to find themselves unwittingly distorting the democratic process by subsidising bodies whose true purpose was to campaign not so much for their beneficiaries as for some political end. Nor do the Government believe that the public would for long continue to display their generosity if charities were to ally themselves to causes with which individual donors might well differ strongly on political grounds.

13.10.1.3 *Charities and political activities: recent developments*

Previous editions of this book have noted that although no substantive change to this area of the law was made by the Charities Acts 1992 or 1993, it might be the case that changes to the political activities of charities could be achieved through the strengthening of the Charity Commissioners' powers of investigation by legislation.

The booklet referred to earlier—*Political Activities by Charities*—was updated in 1999 by the Charity Commissioners as *Political Activities and Campaigning by Charities*. In this, the Charity Commissioners acknowledged that whilst political objects would always be fatal for charitable purposes, there were activities which may be of a political nature which fell considerably short of this, and which were actually necessary for achieving the organisation's purposes. It also conceded that *Re Keoppler* type distinctions between encouraging and facilitating proper debate and political activities which were improper were not always clear-cut.

The advice given to organisations is that, in seeking to accommodate political activity within charitable purposes, any political activity must be in furtherance of but ancillary to the organisation's (dominant non-political) purposes. It defines legitimate political activity as campaigns to mobilise public opinion providing that this is not directed towards (in favour or against) a political party. Information which is provided to the public must be accurate and sufficient to support the organisation's position, and must not be merely emotive. A charity may seek to influence government, but only through well-founded and reasoned argument. It is permitted to provide and publish comments on possible or proposed changes in law or policy 'which can reasonably be expected to achieve its purposes' or oppose changes in the law which might reasonably hinder this.

Finally, it is perfectly legitimate for groups to split up their activities among various distinct organisations with their own separate legal structures. This would allow for the situation whereby some (but not all) of the group's organisations could engage in political activities, which would allow for charitable status to be claimed in respect of those which did not. This is what Amnesty International tried to do in *McGovern* v *Attorney-General* by claiming charitable status only for their Prisoners of Conscience Fund. However, this failed because even the purposes of that sub-group were held to be non-charitable.

13.10.2 **Problems with charitable status and the Charities Bill**

The discussions immediately preceding have focused on the way in which certain activities have long caused 'compatibility difficulties' with the definition and spirit of charitable activity. These are not confined to, but include thorny issues arising from trading activities by charitable trusts. Difficulties also arise when charitable purposes interface with political activism. In respect of campaigning, the Government concluded that there is no evidence that change is warranted, either to allow greater scope for charities to partake in campaigning, or to reduce this scope, and that no change to current permissions and limitations would be pursued. In respect of trading activities by charities, the Government did not agree with recommendations which would have made it easier for charities to trade in a less restricted way than at present, with the benefit of tax considerations and relief from a number of 'burdens' experienced by private business. In this respect, the 2003 publication does reveal the Government's discomfort with the ability of charities to trade outside the context of 'minor' trading activities.

13.11 Charitable status and 'self-help'

Although self-help organisations may possibly have been regarded as charitable in the nineteenth century when, for example, friendly societies contributed considerably to the then limited provisions for welfare, Hall V-C held in *Re Clark* (1875) 1 Ch D 497 that a friendly society was not charitable because of the absence of any stipulation that benefits should be restricted to those members who were poor as well as old, disabled or sick.

If they are not poverty charities, self-help organisations clearly fail on the *Oppenheim* personal nexus test. Hall V-C envisaged that they may succeed as poverty charities, where as we have seen public benefit tests are less stringent, but there may be a second principle that the benefits of charity must be provided by bounty and not bargain. Where, as is the case with many friendly societies, the beneficiaries have, in effect, bought their entitlement in a contractual arrangement, the element of altruism essential to charity is lacking.

In *Re Hobourn Aero Components Ltd's Air Raid Distress Fund* [1946] Ch 194, a fund established by employees to relieve members suffering in consequence of air raids on Coventry was held by the Court of Appeal to be non-charitable on the ground that the employees among whom benefit was confined could not be a section of the public. It was not argued as a poverty charity, and the issue was left open whether it could have been charitable had it been so limited. Nevertheless, there are passages in Lord Greene MR's judgment which suggest that it could not have been charitable even as a poverty charity because the Members' entitlement to benefit turned on the fact of their having subscribed to the fund. This was, in his view, a private trust. If this is correct, then no self-help organisation will be charitable.

It should perhaps be observed that the contributors did not want the fund in *Re Hobourn Aero Components Ltd's Air Raid Distress Fund* to be charitable, since if it had been the Charity Commissioners would have applied their contributions cy près (in the next chapter) when the fund was wound up.

13.11.1 Disaster appeals

These will be valid if for the relief of poverty, otherwise, like self-help organisations, they will fail on the grounds of public benefit. This leaves the organisers of such funds with two alternatives. One possibility is that they can apply a means test criterion to the receipt of benefit, which they may regard as invidious. For example, in the Aberfan coal-tip disaster of 1966, the majority of victims were children, and far from it being easy to show that their deaths produced material deprivation among the relatives, one could actually argue that the cost of rearing the children was saved. In fact, the Commissioners eventually held that the fund was charitable, when money was paid to enable people to move away from the area altogether. Chesterman, *Charities, Trusts and Social Welfare*, gives an extremely comprehensive coverage of this appeal (pp. 339*ff*) and see also (1982) NLJ 223.

The other possibility, often favoured by fund organisers (e.g., Penlee lifeboat disaster fund in 1982), is to avoid the means test and draft the appeal in such a way as to avoid charitable status altogether. In that event, of course, the tax concessions will also be forgone. Perhaps more importantly, the cy près doctrine described in chapter 14 will not apply and there may be difficulties over distribution of any surplus left over after the purposes have been achieved (see chapter 8). It may even be that the Crown will take some or all of the surplus as *bona vacantia*, not perhaps the most fitting consequence of the altruism of the donors.

One of the problems with disaster appeals is that they are usually set up very quickly after the disaster has occurred, often before the full legal consequences have been considered. They may well be described as charitable, and donors may believe that their contributions are going to a charitable fund, only for the organisers later to change their minds and draft the purposes so as to avoid charitable status. An interesting question might then arise as to what happens to the money already contributed, in the (probably unlikely) event of a dispute (e.g., if somebody who had contributed on the assumption that the fund was charitable objected when he discovered that it was not).

 **online resource centre**

FURTHER READING

Chesterton [1979] *Charities, Trusts and Social Welfare.*
Dunn [2000] 20(2) *Legal Studies* 222.
Morris [2000] 20(3) *Legal Studies* 409.

14

Cy près

14.1 General principles

The Anglo-Norman phrase cy près (which is sometimes hyphenated) meant something like 'as near as possible', and the doctrine of cy près in charity law lays down that where property given on trust for charitable purposes cannot be used in the precise manner intended by the donor, the court (and since about 130 years ago the Charity Commissioners) may make a scheme for the application of the property to purposes resembling as closely as possible the donor's original intention. The idea, in other words, is not to frustrate the intention of the donor (who cannot be consulted if the gift is testamentary) any more than necessary. The doctrine dates back at least as far as the 17th century. It only applies to charities—if private purposes fail, the results are as discussed in chapter 4.

Where the donor's wishes cannot be fulfilled
The question whether cy près can be applied can arise either because it is clear from the outset that the donor's intention cannot be fulfilled, as where the organisation which he has singled out for benefit has already ceased to exist, or because at some later time, during the continuance of the trust, it turns out that the purposes cannot be achieved. Cy près is more easily invoked in the latter case, for once property has been dedicated to charity, there is no possibility of a resulting trust to the donor.

Initial failure and ascertaining the donor's intentions
Where, however, a gift fails from the start, the courts have since the early nineteenth century insisted that before the property can be applied cy près, a general or 'paramount' charitable intention must be shown.

The application of the doctrine has been significantly widened by the Charities Act 1960. This may reflect a difference of emphasis. The equitable doctrine was probably based on the presumed intention of the donor, and could in some circumstances militate against the efficient operation of charitable enterprises. The 1960 Act, on the other hand, is concerned more with the efficient running of charities, even at the expense of the donor's intentions.

Cy près and the Charities Act 2006
Following on from the consideration which has been made to the Charities Act 2006, it is sufficient to say at this point that apart from some minor amendments being made to the Charities Act 1993 by the Act 2006 (pursuant to sections 15–18), the cy près doctrine will continue to operate in respect of charitable gifts which cannot be applied to the original purposes envisioned by their donor. Further consideration is given to the new provisions within the ORC.

14.2 **Initial failure**

The question turns on whether the intention of the donor was specific or general. If it was to further some specific purpose which cannot be carried out, or benefit some specific institution no longer in existence, then the gift fails and the property will return to the settlor, or his estate, on a resulting trust, as discussed in chapter 7.

If, however, the intention is a more general one, which might be satisfied by applying the property to a purpose or institution similar to that specified, a cy près scheme may be ordered. The test, then, is whether a general or 'paramount' charitable intention can be found.

14.2.1 **Gift to a charity which has never existed at all**

14.2.1.1 *Operation of cy près doctrine: general charitable intention*

In *Re Rymer* [1895] 1 Ch 19, a gift for a specific seminary which had ceased to exist failed. This is the general position where no paramount (or general) charitable intention can be found. Whether a general charitable intention can be shown is a question of fact. The cases in this section are illustrations of the factors that can be taken into account but do not lay down general rules.

If the charity specified by the donor has never existed at all, it is usually easier to discover a general charitable intention than where the charity once existed but has since ceased (as in *Re Rymer*), since only a general intention can be attributed to the donor who fails correctly to specify the beneficiary. For example, in *Re Harwood* [1936] Ch 285, a gift was made to the Peace Society in Belfast, which could not be shown ever to have existed. Farwell J found that there was an intention to benefit societies aimed at promoting peace, and the gift was therefore applied cy près. A second gift in the will, in favour of the Wisbech Peace Society, which had once existed but had ceased to do so prior to the testatrix's death, was held, however, to have lapsed. Although the case is a good illustration of the operation of the cy près doctrine, doubt may perhaps be cast on the assumption that the promotion of peace is in fact capable of being charitable.

Finding a general paramount charitable intention: the approach of the courts

In *Re Satterthwaite's WT* [1966] 1 WLR 277, a will listed a number of organisations concerned with animal welfare. The list had been thoughtlessly compiled from the London telephone directory, the testatrix's chief concern being to divert her estate to animal charities, because she hated the whole human race. One of the named institutions, the London Animal Hospital, had never existed as a charity. The Court of Appeal held that the gift to the London Animal Hospital should be applied cy près: a general charitable intention could be inferred from the testatrix's known attitude towards the human race, and from the fact that all but one of the other dispositions were made in favour of genuine animal charities. In the opinion of Russell LJ, therefore, a general intention to benefit animal charities could easily be inferred.

Harman LJ expressed 'the gravest doubts', however, and a better explanation of this case may be that, as with the Peace Society in Belfast in *Re Harwood* [1936] Ch 285, the London Animal Hospital had never existed as a charity. Sir Robert

Megarry V-C refused to apply what he described as the doctrine of 'charity by association' in *Re Spence's WT* [1979] Ch 483, on the grounds that *Re Satterthwaite* only applied where the body had never existed. It is also necessary for the other donations to be to charitable organisations of the same type; merely for a non-charitable body to be included among a general list of charities is not evidence of a general charitable intent. In *Re Jenkins's WT* [1966] Ch 249 Buckley J declined to hold that a gift to the British Union for the Abolition of Vivisection (which did exist but was not charitable) could be taken as charitable simply by being included in a list of gifts to unquestionably charitable organisations.

It must be emphasised, however, that the question is ultimately one of fact, and the above cases should not be treated as authorities.

14.2.1.2 *Non-existent body, but no initial failure*

Even where the charity specified does not exist, it may be possible to save the gift if the institution can be said to continue to exist in some other form. In recent years many small charities have amalgamated, and it is sometimes possible to regard the new body thus formed as being the same as the old. In *Re Faraker* [1912] 2 Ch 488, for example, a gift to 'Mrs Bailey's charity, Rotherhithe' (which was taken to mean 'Hannah Bayly's Charity') passed to the new charity formed by an amalgamation of Hannah Bayly's Charity with several others.

Gifts which are made to a charitable purpose and not to a charitable body
Another approach is to find that the gift was made for the *purpose* of the named charity, rather than for the body itself. If the body is unincorporated then by definition the gift cannot be to it but must be to its purposes, and if those purposes can still be fulfilled the gift will not fail. Since there is no failure there is no need to show a general charitable intention. Indeed, this is not an application of cy près as such, but rather an instance of finding a substitute trustee to carry out the purposes of the trust. Where the body is a corporation, however, a gift to it will *prima facie* lapse if the corporation has ceased to exist, just as a gift to a human individual would lapse if the person concerned had died before the gift was made. The gift may be rescued only on the cy près principles already outlined, i.e., if the court is able to find a general charitable intention going beyond the specific aim of benefiting the named corporate charity.

Distinguishing incorporated and unincorporated bodies: Re Fingers WT
In *Re Finger's WT* [1972] Ch 286, for example, testamentary gifts were made to the National Radium Commission, an unincorporated association, and to the National Council for Maternity and Child Welfare, which was a corporate charity. Both had ceased to exist by the time the testatrix died. Goff J held that the gift to the National Radium Commission was interpreted as a gift to its purposes, and since these still continued, the gift did not fail. The gift to the National Council for Maternity and Child Welfare would have failed, as a gift to a corporate charity, in the absence of a general charitable intention, which in the event it was, however, possible to discern.

Similar principles were applied in *Re Koeppler's WT* [1986] Ch 423 (considered earlier), where Slade LJ construed a gift to a non-existent body as a valid trust for educational purposes. The case concerned the validity of a testamentary gift to the warden of the institution known as Wilton Park. At the time of the testator's death there was no entity called Wilton Park, nor was there a warden of Wilton Park, but there was a Wilton Park project, which organised a series of conferences. The gift was construed as a gift for the purposes of the Wilton Park project, the non-existent body in *Re Koeppler's WT* being treated as analogous to the National Radium Commission in *Re Finger's WT*.

14.2.2 **Gifts with conditions attached**

Even where the institution to which the donation is made exists there may be an initial failure if there is a condition in the gift which the donee body finds unacceptable. In *Re Lysaght* [1966] Ch 191, the testatrix left £5,000 to the Royal College of Surgeons in order to establish and maintain one or more studentships. There was a condition, however, which would have disqualified Jews and Roman Catholics, and the College declined to accept the gift on these terms. The gift was saved because the court found a general charitable intention on the part of the testatrix, to establish medical studentships. The cy près doctrine therefore operated; the condition could be deleted as not being essential to the fulfilment of the general intention. A scheme was ordered on the terms of the will as it stood without the condition.

Recently, in *Re Woodhams* [1981] 1 WLR 493, a general charitable intention to foster musical education was found, allowing the court to remove the restriction which would have limited scholarships to boys from two named children's homes and would have also prevented the donees from accepting the gift.

Why should a gift fail at all?: Equity will not let a trust fail for want of a trustee
It may be wondered why the gift fails unless the conditions are deleted. After all, a trust should not fail merely because the trustee refuses to accept the trust property. 'Equity will not allow a trust to fail for want of a trustee', and in principle it might be thought that the court should find a trustee who is prepared to carry out the terms of the trust on the settlor's terms. In other words, it should not be necessary to delete the repugnant condition.

In a case like *Re Lysaght*, however, the identity of the donee is essential to the purposes of the trust, and were the Royal College to decline the gift another trustee simply could not be found to carry out the testatrix's intention. As Buckley J pointed out in the case:

Obviously a trustee will not normally be permitted to modify the terms of his trust on the ground that his own opinions or convictions conflict with them. If his conscience will not allow him to carry out the trust faithfully in accordance with its terms, he must make way for a trustee who can and will do so. But how, if the identity of the trustee selected by the settlor is essential to his intention? It is of the essence of a trust that the trustees selected by the settlor and no one else shall act as the trustees of it and if those trustees cannot or will not undertake the office, the trust must fail.

14.3 **Subsequent failure**

Cy près has a much wider application in the event of a subsequent failure, and none of the difficulties which arise in the event of an initial failure arise here.

Once property has been dedicated to charitable purposes, it remains so, and if those purposes cease to be capable of achievement, there can be no resulting trust to the settlor or his estate unless the terms on which the gift was originally made provide for this to happen. It is not necessary to search for a general charitable intention on the part of the settlor. The only relevant consideration is whether there was an outright disposition in favour of charity. Where this is so, funds which cannot be applied to the original purpose, whether because that purpose is impossible, or because there is a surplus left over after the purposes have been achieved, may be applied cy près.

The importance of timing

In *Re Slevin* [1891] 2 Ch 236, a legacy had been left to the Orphanage of St Dominic, Newcastle-upon-Tyne. The orphanage ceased to exist after the date of the donor's death, but before the legacy could be paid over. Since the orphanage had survived its benefactor, by however short a time, the gift was effective in favour of charity and could be applied cy près. In *Re King* [1923] 1 Ch 243, a surplus was left after the purpose (the setting of a stained-glass window in a church) was carried out. Finding that the whole fund, and not just the sum sufficient for the window, had been dedicated to charity, Romer J applied the surplus cy près (to the setting of a second window).

Timing of subsequent failure and gifts which are postponed

Nor will it matter that the gift to charity was intended to be postponed until some future date under the terms of the will or gift. In other words, the relevant date is that of the original donation, even though the charity may only at that time obtain a future interest in the property. If A dies leaving property to B for his life, thereafter to C (a charity), and C ceases to exist after A's death but before B's, this is regarded as a subsequent, not an initial, failure.

Thus, in *Re Moon* [1948] 1 All ER 300, the testator directed that a legacy should be paid to the trustees of a Methodist church for the purposes of missionary work after the death of his widow. The purposes were no longer practicable by the time of the widow's death and Roxburgh J held that the question of whether the gift had lapsed must be resolved in relation to the time when the gift was made, that is, at the death of the testator. Since the purposes would have been practical then, there was an effective gift to charity at that time, and the failure was subsequent and not initial. A similar result was reached in *Re Wright* [1954] Ch 347, where a testamentary gift for the founding of a convalescent home was to take effect after a life interest, at the end of which time the property was insufficient for this purpose. The date of the testatrix's death was taken to be crucial in determining the question of whether the gift was practicable.

In *Re Welsh Hospital (Netley) Fund* [1921] 1 Ch 655, a surplus of £9,000 remained after the winding up of a (charitable) hospital erected at Netley, and the question arose what to do with the surplus. P.O. Laurence J held that it should be applied cy près, but only after concluding that the donors must be taken to have parted with their donations out and out to charity (much of the money had been derived from anonymous sources, and the issues were essentially those discussed in chapter 8). There was no suggestion, in other words, that a cy près scheme ought to have been automatic, on the basis of subsequent failure. However, in *Re Ulverston and District New Hospital Building Trusts* [1956] Ch 622, Jenkins LJ explained *Re Welsh Hospital (Netley) Fund* as a straightforward case of subsequent failure. The earlier case was distinguished because, in *Re Ulverston*, the hospital had never been built and none of the funds ever expended, so the failure was regarded as an initial failure. There being no evidence of general charitable intention, the fund was not applied cy près.

14.4 Altering charitable objects

14.4.1 At common law

Whereas no difficulties have ever arisen in the case of a clear failure, such as a charitable body ceasing to exist, when the cy près doctrine could operate on the subsequent failure, there could be problems before 1960 where a charitable purpose simply became outdated and obsolete although the original charitable body continued in existence. There was no effective system whereby moribund charities could be modernised and of course the cy près doctrine could not apply if there was no failure.

Until the reforms introduced by the Charities Act 1960, the courts' only jurisdiction was their inherent jurisdiction to apply funds cy près, but the inherent jurisdiction is confined to rather narrow limits, being available only where it is 'impossible' or 'impracticable' to carry out the terms of the trust. Some very peculiar trusts were kept on foot by the limits of the cy près doctrine before 1960, obliging trustees to distribute bread, linen, stockings, boots, etc., among the poor. One old trust specified the distribution of green waistcoats in memory of the testator's surname. The courts' main concern was not to depart too far from the original wishes of settlors, rather than to promote the efficient administration of charities.

The common law and a restrictive approach to the alteration of charitable purpose
For example, in *Re Weir Hospital* [1910] 2 Ch 124, a testator left two houses to be used as a hospital. The premises were not suitable, and the Charity Commissioners approved a scheme to use them as a nurses' home instead, perpetuating the testator's name by renaming a hospital in his honour. The Court of Appeal held that the scheme was *ultra vires*, since the original purpose was not impossible to fulfil, merely difficult. Sir Herbert Cozens-Hardy MR's view (at p. 131) was that the court's primary duty was to give effect to the charitable intentions of the donor, rather than to seek the most beneficial application of the property:

The first duty of the Court is to construe the will, and to give effect to the charitable directions of the founder, assuming them not to be open to objection on the ground of public policy. The Court does not consider whether those directions are wise or whether a more generally beneficial application of the testator's property might not be founded.

Similar sentiments were echoed by Kennedy LJ at pp. 140–1:

But neither the Court of Chancery, nor the Board of Charity Commissioners, which has been entrusted by statute, in regard to the application of charitable fund, with similar jurisdiction, is entitled to substitute a different scheme for the scheme which the donor has prescribed in the instrument which creates the charity, merely because a coldly wise intelligence, impervious to the special predilections which inspired his liberality, and untrammelled by his directions, would have dictated a different use of his money ... If the charity can be administered according to the directions of founder or testator, the law requires that it should be so administered.

The scope of the courts' inherent jurisdiction

It is permissible under the courts' inherent jurisdiction, however, to eradicate a condition of the trust which, with the passage of time, has become inimical to its main
purpose. In *Re Robinson* [1923] 2 Ch 332, a condition in a gift of an endowment for an
evangelical church requiring a preacher to wear a black gown in the pulpit was cut
out, since it was thought likely to offend the congregation and reduce attendance:
with the passage of time, the condition had become inimical to the main purpose of
the gift. Another example is *Re Dominion Students' Hall Trust* [1947] Ch 183, where a
colour bar was removed from a trust for the maintenance of a hostel for male students
of the overseas dominions of the British Empire, since the main purpose of the trust
was to promote community of citizenship among members of the Commonwealth.

Re Robinson was applied by Buckley J in *Re Lysaght* (considered shortly), the same
test being used there in an initial failure case to strike out a condition. Unlike
Robinson, of course, which is a subsequent failure case, in *Lysaght*, it was necessary
to find a general charitable intention, in order to invoke the cy près doctrine in the
first place.

In *Re J.W. Laing Trust* [1984] Ch 143, Peter Gibson J was prepared to strike out a
term requiring trustees to distribute, within 10 years of the settlor's death, a fund
which by then had risen significantly in value (from some £15,000 in 1922 when
the trust was set up, to over £24 million in 1982). The increase in value had been
quite unforseen when the trust was set up, partly because the settlor had lived much
longer than expected (to the age of 98). The recipients of the income from the charity (Christian evangelical bodies) had come to depend upon it, whereas it would
have been impossible to distribute such a large amount of capital in such a way as
to ensure continuance of the causes which the settlor wished to support. The term
was struck out on the basis that it was 'inexpedient in the very altered circumstances of the charity since that requirement was laid down 60 years ago'. It is not
entirely clear whether this expediency test is the same as that being applied in the
earlier cases, or whether a wider principle is being adopted.

Situations where no cy près scheme is required

There may also be situations where no scheme is required. In *Oldham Borough
Council* v *Attorney-General* [1993] Ch 210, the Clayton Playing Fields in Oldham had
been conveyed to the council (or more accurately, to the bodies which preceded it
prior to the local government reorganisation in 1974) in 1962, for recreational purposes. The Borough Council proposed to sell the land for development, but also to
provide a new site which (it was assumed) would be used for exactly the same charitable purposes. The council expressly disclaimed reliance on the Charities Act
1960, since clearly none of the heads (enumerated below) could apply in this case.
Dillon LJ, who gave the only substantive judgment in the Court of Appeal, took the
view that the sale of the land would have been approved prior to the Charities Act,
since there was no requirement to use *that particular land*. Since the charitable purposes would still be carried out, there was no need for a scheme, and the court was
prepared to approve the sale.

14.4.2 **Charities Act 1993, section 13**

Following a recommendation of the Nathan Committee on the Law and Practice
Relating to Charitable Trusts (1952, Cmd 8710), para. 365, s. 13 (which replaces a

similar provision in the 1960 Act) extends, presumably in the interests of more efficient administration of charities, the circumstances in which property may be applied cy près.

The modernisation of outmoded trusts

The purpose of this section is to modernise outmoded trusts; as we have seen this was difficult using only the inherent jurisdiction of the courts. Section 13(5) places a duty upon trustees to seek the application of property cy près if and when appropriate circumstances arise. Much of the work of the Commissioners consists in settling and approving schemes of this kind.

The precise circumstances are set out in s. 13(1). No longer is it necessary to show that it is 'impossible' or 'impracticable' to carry out the terms of the trust. It is enough that the original purpose has been fulfilled as far as possible, or cannot be carried out according to the directions given and the spirit of the gift, or if there is a surplus left over, or if the purposes have been adequately provided for by other means, or become useless or harmful to the community. Cy près may also apply where the original purposes relate to an area, or class of persons, which has ceased to have any relevance, having regard to the spirit of the gift. There are also provisions for the amalgamation of small charities if that is more efficient.

Section 13(1) is in the following terms:

(1) Subject to subsection (2) below, the circumstances in which the original purposes of a charitable gift can be altered to allow the property given or part of it to be applied cy près shall be as follows:—

(a) where the original purposes, in whole or in part—

(i) have been as far as may be fulfilled; or

(ii) cannot be carried out, or not according to the directions given and to the spirit of the gift; or

(b) where the original purposes provide a use for part only of the property available by virtue of the gift; or

(c) where the property available by virtue of the gift and other property applicable for similar purposes can be more effectively used in conjunction, and to that end can suitably, regard being had to the spirit of the gift, be made applicable to common purposes; or

(d) where the original purposes were laid down by reference to an area which then was but has since ceased to be a unit for some other purpose, or by reference to a class of persons or to an area which has for any reason since ceased to be suitable, regard being had to the spirit of the gift, or to be practical in administering the gift; or

(e) where the original purposes, in whole or in part, have, since they were laid down—

(i) been adequately provided for by other means; or

(ii) ceased, as being useless or harmful to the community or for other reasons, to be in law charitable; or

(iii) ceased in any other way to provide a suitable and effective method of using the property available by virtue of the gift, regard being had to the spirit of the gift.

Subheads (a) to (e) of s. 13(1) will generally be wider than the pre-1960 definition of failure, and apparently supersede it; in *Oldham Borough Council* v *Attorney-General* [1993] Ch 210, Dillon LJ took the view that the s. 13 heads were exhaustive, at any rate where alteration of the 'original purposes' is sought (on which, see further below):

Broadly the effect of that section is that an alteration of the 'original purposes' of a charitable gift can only be authorised by a scheme for the cy près application of the trust property and such a scheme can only be made in the circumstances set out in subheads (a) to (e) of subsection (1) of section 13.

The scope of s. 13 and the definition of failure
Section 13 defines failure and arguably applies to define initial as well as subsequent failure. However, the section begins by talking of 'the original purposes of a charitable gift', which supposes that a charitable gift has taken place. It will not have in many cases of initial failure. In that case the question of whether there has been a failure will be determined on the basis of the pre-1960 law.

In any case, s. 13 (by virtue of s. 13(2)) only affects the definition of when failure occurs for cy près purposes, and all the other requirements of the doctrine remain. Thus, for example, it is still necessary to show a paramount charitable intention in the case of an initial failure.

In interpreting the section, the Commissioners attempt, so far as possible, to effect the intentions of the donor, these being understood in the context of modern conditions (see their Annual Report 1970, para. 41).

In *Re Lepton's Charity* [1972] Ch 276, Pennycuick V-C invoked ss. 13(1)(a)(ii) and 13(1)(e)(iii) (above) to increase payment to a church minister from £3 per year to £100 per year. Under the original will of 1715 the testator left land, the profits of which amounted to £5 a year, with a direction to trustees to pay £3 a year to the minister, and the residue to the poor of Pudsey. In 1967 the income from the investments representing the land was £791 14s 6d. Pennycuick V-C approved an application under s. 13 to increase the income of the minister to £100 a year, the residue going, as before, to the poor of Pudsey. The court felt that after the change the relative distribution between the minister and the poor of Pudsey remained as in the spirit of the gift. The main argument in the case was whether s. 13 applied to the trusts in the will as a whole, or to each of the two trusts separately (a trust to pay the £3 a year to the minister, and a separate trust to pay the residue to the poor of Pudsey). Only if (as Pennycuick V-C held) the spirit of the gift related to the will as a whole could the court alter the relative proportions of each part.

Another case falling within s. 13(1)(e)(iii), but where the original purposes were neither impractical nor impossible to achieve is *Varsani* v *Jesani* [1998] 3 All ER 273 (CA). The case concerned a charity, established in 1967 by a declaration of trust, the purpose of which was to promote the faith of a Hindu sect. In 1984 the sect split into two factions, with each side accusing the other of having departed from the true faith. As long as either faction in fact adhered to the true faith, it remained possible to achieve the original purposes, but the effect of the schism was that only one of the factions was making use of the main asset of the charity, a temple in London, to the exclusion of the other faction. The Court of Appeal, upholding the decision of Carnworth J, felt that the framework within which the faith was practised in 1967 (i.e., the original purposes) had ceased to provide a suitable and effective method of enabling the property to be used in accordance with 'the spirit of the gift'; therefore the court had jurisdiction to order a cy près scheme. Only the jurisdictional issue was before the court, and it is not reported what was actually done (or will be done) with the property.

Distinguishing substantive purposes from administrative matters
Section 13 allows only the original purposes of a charitable gift to be altered, and for this reason it could not be used in *Re J.W. Laing Trust* [1984] Ch 143 to delete a provision relating to distribution, which was essentially administrative in nature. Peter Gibson J observed (at p. 153) that 'it cannot be right that any provision, even if only administrative, made applicable by a donor to his gifts should be treated as a condition and hence part of its purpose'. The same view was taken in *Oldham Borough Council* v *Attorney-General* [1993] Ch 210, above, where Dillon LJ considered that the requirement that the actual land given should be used as playing fields was not part of the 'original purposes' within s. 13. In *J.W. Laing*, the condition was struck out under the inherent jurisdiction, whereas in *Oldham* there was no need for a scheme at all, so these are both cases where the common law applied but the statute did not.

14.4.3 Limit to Commissioners' scheme-making powers

One of the problems perceived with the Charities Act 1960 was the inability of the Commissioners to make a scheme of their own volition where no trustees could be found who were able or willing to apply for one. It is true that under s. 18(6), the Commissioners can apply to the Secretary of State to refer to them cases where the trustees have unreasonably refused or neglected to make a scheme, but apparently this provision has never been invoked. The Commissioners have also since 1960 had wide-ranging powers under s. 20 in the event of misconduct or mismanagement in the administration of the charity, for example to suspend trustees and to appoint additional trustees as necessary for the proper administration of the charity, but under the original legislation they had no power to make a cy près scheme themselves. This has now been catered for by the Charities Act 1993, s. 18.

14.5 Charities Act 1993, section 14

Section 14 provides reform to cope with the problems which may arise if property is given for charitable purposes which fail and where it is difficult to find the donors. This is a form of initial failure and often there will be no paramount charitable intention. This most frequently arises in disaster appeal funds.

14.5.1 Position in the case of non-charitable trusts

In the case of private (non-charitable) trusts, the operation of the resulting trust doctrine usually results in a proportion of the funds passing to the Crown as *bona vacantia*. This is because where a donation to such a fund is anonymous (e.g., small change in a street collecting box) and no means of tracing the donor has been left, it is reasonable to construe the contribution as an out-and-out gift. It is difficult to infer that the donor intended any surplus left over to be held on resulting trust for him since he has left the organisers no means of finding him. That part of the surplus attributable to his donation will therefore have no owner and so goes to the Crown as *bona vacantia*.

It is true that in *Re Gillingham Bus Disaster Fund* [1958] Ch 300, such donations were directed to be held on resulting trust, so that such a result was avoided, but apart from being administratively inconvenient this result is probably wrong. Undoubtedly the usual inference would be that if people give money in an anonymous collection, they intend an out-and-out gift, not to see it back again.

This result (i.e., the out-and-out gift construction) was in fact reached by Goff J in *Re West Sussex Constabulary's Widows, Children & Benevolent (1930) Fund Trusts* [1971] Ch 1. The fund was not a disaster fund but was for widows and dependants, and there were outside contributions in addition to those of the members themselves. It came to an end upon amalgamation with other police forces in 1968, and the court was asked to decide how to distribute the surplus.

So far as identifiable donations and legacies were concerned, the proportion of the surplus attributable to that source was held on resulting trust. But there were also the proceeds of street collecting boxes and in relation to those Goff J declined to follow Harman J's earlier judgment on the ground that the intention to be inferred was also that of an out-and-out gift (see further chapters 7 and 8). Thus, nobody could lay claim to the proportion of the surplus attributable to the last two categories, so it went to the Crown as *bona vacantia*.

14.5.2 Position where purposes charitable

The *West Sussex* result will be the norm not only in the case of non-charitable donations where a surplus is left over after the fund is wound up or its purposes achieved but also where money is given for charitable purposes which initially fail (unless a paramount charitable intention can be found). It does not apply where a charitable fund *subsequently* achieves its purposes because this will be a subsequent failure and there will be no difficulty applying the cy près doctrine. So had the Gillingham Bus Disaster Fund been charitable, cy près would have applied in the normal way on a subsequent failure.

14.5.3 Operation of section 14

Section 14 of the Charities Act 1993, replacing a similar provision from the 1960 Act, is intended to prevent the *West Sussex* result where money is given for charitable purposes which fail. The section has application only in the case of initial failure, as in the case of subsequent failure (as we have seen) no question of returning the gifts to the donors would arise.

Section 14(1) allows the application of such property cy près, regardless of charitable intention, when the property has been given:

(a) by a donor who, after such advertisements and inquiries as are reasonable, cannot be identified or cannot be found (donors may claim within one year of the scheme); or

(b) by a donor who has executed a written disclaimer of his right to have the property returned.

There is a conclusive presumption (in s. 14(3)) that property raised by cash collections by way of collecting boxes or other methods which make it hard to tell one gift from another, or as the proceeds of lotteries, competitions, sales, entertainments or similar fund-raising activities, belongs to unidentifiable donors without the need for instituting any inquiries:

(3) For the purposes of this section property shall be conclusively presumed (without any advertisement or inquiry) to belong to donors who cannot be identified, in so far as it consists—

  (a) of the proceeds of cash collections made by means of collecting boxes or by any other means not adapted for distinguishing one gift from another; or

  (b) of the proceeds of any lottery, competition, entertainment, sale or similar money-raising activity, after allowing for property given to provide prizes or articles for sale or otherwise to enable the activity to be undertaken.

Allowance must, however, be made for property given to provide prizes or articles for sale, or otherwise to allow the activity to be undertaken, and the donors of such items are entitled to the return of the property or its proceeds, should they so wish.

In any other case, the court may direct the property to be considered as belonging to unidentifiable donors if it would not be reasonable to return it in view of the amounts involved or the lapse of time since the gift was made.

It would seem then that the law is thus improved to the degree that it is no longer necessary to impute a fictitious general charitable intention to the donors or else attempt the return of the property—a result which, as has been seen, often results in the fund passing to the Crown as *bona vacantia*.

However, David Wilson has argued ([1983] Conv 40) that s. 14 is 'a dead letter of English law', and it is indeed arguable that it made no difference to the pre-1960 law. The argument essentially is that s. 14(1) applies only where the property belongs to a donor. But if Goff J was correct in *Re West Sussex Constabulary's Widows, Children and Benevolent (1930) Fund* [1971] Ch 1, doubting Harman J in *Re Gillingham Bus Disaster Fund* [1958] Ch 300, anonymous contributors do not intend to retain any interest in the property, and hence s. 14 is never triggered. It might be thought that the presumption in s. 14(3) cures the problem, but arguably the presumption goes only to the question of identification, rather than to whether the property also 'belongs to donors'. Indeed, it is natural to read s. 14(3) as applying to identification only. In that case, the property will, as in *West Sussex*, still go to the Crown as *bona vacantia*, and s. 14 will make no difference.

If, on the other hand, any of the fund has actually been applied towards a charitable purpose, then on Jenkins LJ's views in *Re Ulverston and District New Hospital Building Trusts* [1956] Ch 622, the failure would be a subsequent failure, and a cy près scheme would be ordered. In that case, there would be no need for s. 14 anyway. If this argument is correct, in the only situation where s. 14 is needed, it is worded in such a way that it cannot operate.

14.6 Small poverty charities

There are particular problems with old charities for the relief of poverty. Many of these required trustees to distribute money or goods, but the growth of State welfare has reduced the attractiveness of these, and even rendered them counter-productive in some cases, because hand-outs can lead to a reduction in State benefit. As long ago as 1967 the Annual Report of the Charity Commissioners (paras 17–20 and App. B) recognised the problem involved in cash hand-outs by commenting on the undesirability of using charity funds to relieve the burdens of the DHSS and local authorities and, instead, suggested other schemes; for example, outings or home decoration.

Yet many old trusts to relieve poverty bound trustees to distribute money or goods. One example required the trustees to spend the income in buying bread and linen for the poor of East Barning—in 1983, the fund available was £5.12p! Obviously, by the 1980s a trust of this type had come to serve little useful purpose.

A possible solution to this problem obviously existed under the provisions of the Charities Act 1960, but the mechanisms for the full scheme-making powers contained therein were arguably too complicated for very small charities. Following a report of a House of Lords Select Committee in 1984, the Charities Act 1985 addressed this problem. Section 2 allowed trustees of charities more than 50 years old, by a simplified procedure, to change the objects to more suitable ones, so long as they were within the spirit of the original donor's intentions. Under s. 3, where the annual income of a charity was less than £200, the trustees could transfer its property to another charity having similar aims, or if its income was less than £5 a year, the trustees under s. 4 could wind it up, by spending the capital as if it were income.

The Government, in its White Paper *Charities: A Framework for the Future*, HMSO (May 1989), proposed to extend the policy of the 1985 Act, by standardising the application of ss. 2 and 3, and applying both these sections to all charities with an income of less than £1,000 a year, without distinction of age, locality or purpose, the sole exception being those holding land for the purposes of the charity. It was proposed that trustees wishing to modify their objects or amalgamate with another charity need to be satisfied:

that the original purposes had, since they were laid down, ceased to provide a suitable and effective method of using the property; and

   that the new objects specified, or the objects of the charity to which property was being transferred, were as similar as practicable to the charity's original objects having regard to the spirit of the gift.

The Charities Act 1993 has for the most part put these recommendations into effect, but the ss. 2 and 3 financial limits have been raised to £5,000 per year (rather than £1,000 as recommended), and the s. 4 limit has been raised to £1,000. Section 74 of the 1993 Act replaces the old ss. 2 and 3, and s. 75 replaces the old s. 4.

Trustees are required to act by unanimous resolution and with the Commissioners' concurrence, and to give reasonable public notice of their intentions. Transfers of property under what used to be s. 3 obviously require the consent of the trustees of receiving charities.

 **online resource centre**

FURTHER READING

Wilson [1983] Conv 40.

15

The office of trustee: commencement and termination

Up to now, we have examined trusts which are private (non-charitable), looking at them in one of two ways. The first has been to draw attention to the nature of the trust on a general level by looking at its particular features and characteristics, and the way in which core features can be found grouped around different types of trusts and the requirements which must be in place for a trust to be said to be operational. The second has been to try to glean an appreciation of how these more generalised features 'work' through consideration of a number of case studies. What follows now is an examination of how those key characteristics of the trust and its operation are reflected in the responsibilities placed upon those who are involved in their operation. This is a study of how trusts are administered, and as such examines the nature of trusteeship itself, and the duties and responsibilities which must be carried out in furtherance of this. It will also ultimately examine the consequences of a trustee's failure to fulfil his responsibilities to the trust.

What follows therefore in chapters 15, 16 and 18 is an examination of the nature of the office which characterises a trustee's responsibilities and duties; a fairly comprehensive consideration of how the office of trustee arises; and the consequences of it coming to an end. Chapter 16 provides an examination of the actual administration of the trust, and in particular of the nature of trustee duties, and the entitlements of the beneficiaries which flow from this. Chapter 18 looks at the essence of functions which are to be performed by the trustee; the consequences of a trustee not acting in the manner which is demanded of him; and the position in which this leaves the beneficiaries.

In respect of this initial consideration of trusteeship, a few points need to be made by way of introduction.

Onerous nature of trusteeship
It will soon become clear how onerous the office of trusteeship is. Legal title, without its equitable counterpart is by no means a privilege. It is no wonder that the courts require very clear evidence that in the creation of a trust, a trust was what was actually intended (instead of a gift, for example), as is illustrated by the case law surrounding the settlor's self-declaration of trust (considered in chapter 3). Nor will it come as a surprise that trusteeship is often undertaken on a professional basis and that the charges for such services can be very high.

The law, and fall-back provisions
Whereas some of what will follow in these next few chapters is inherent in the nature of any trust, many of the powers and duties which are described represent

simply a fall-back or default position where nothing to the contrary is provided in the trust instrument which has given rise to the trust. In reality, the precise scope of such powers and duties will, in the case of most express trusts, be governed by the terms of the trust instrument and not the fall-back legal position. Provision is also frequently made in trust instruments for the remuneration of trustees, and it is usual for example to include clauses which are designed to limit trustees' liability for breach of trust.

This is not to deny the importance of the general law. As long as people set up trusts without taking proper legal advice the legal fall-back position remains of utmost importance. Also, of course, trust instruments can be considerably short-ened to the extent that powers and duties are provided anyway, in the absence of provision to the contrary.

Constructive trustees of property
It is less certain how far these legal rules apply to constructive trustees, whose powers and obligations may depend on the circumstances in which the trust arises.

Quite a lot of the material on the administration of trusts is statutory, but usually the provisions only restate the previous law, or re-enact earlier provisions either exactly, or only slightly differently. Thus you will notice that there are on occasions cases which are cited as authority on the interpretation of a section of legislation where the cases actually pre-date the section currently in force.

15.1 The office of trustee: continuity and change

It will become clear that much of the law relating to the conduct of trustees in rela-tion to the trust's operation originates from the nineteenth century. You will have noticed throughout this book the way in which the nineteenth century can be seen to represent the origins of many aspects of modern trusts law, and the implicit and more explicit questions which have been raised concerning the appropriateness of continuing application of principles which were forged and refined in a society very different from today's. Along with some of the principles which underpin the determination of shares in shared homes considered earlier in chapter 9, the law relating to trusteeship is itself an excellent illustration of many of these questions and issues. Indeed, there has for some time been considerable dissatisfaction with the persistence of principles of law which clearly date from times long gone. In 1997, and in its Consultation Paper on Trustees Duties (Law Com. 146) the Law Commission carried out wholesale consideration of the role of trustees in modern times, against a backdrop of its belief that '... the law governing the powers and duties of trustees has not kept pace with the evolving economic and social nature of trusts—indeed the default powers which trustees have under the present law are generally regarded as seriously restrictive'. In July 1999 its proposals for reform were published. The resulting Trustee Act 2000 was given the Royal Assent on 23 November 2000, containing provisions in respect of investment, the acquisition of land, the appointment of agents nominees and custodians, trustees remuneration, and also a new statutory duty of care for trustees.

15.2 **Standard required of trustees**

15.2.1 **Creation of the trust**

Upon creation of the trust, the trustees become the legal owners of the trust property. Where the trust is created *inter vivos*, they will normally be parties to the deed which creates it, with the effect of vesting in them the trust property. In the case of a testamentary trust, it is usual to appoint the same persons to be executors and trustees, so the acquisition of the legal title to the testator's property is automatic inasmuch as it vests in his personal representatives from the moment of death. Upon completion of the administration of the estate, it may be necessary depending on the nature of the property to execute additional formalities signifying that they now hold in the capacity of trustees, or if other persons are to act as trustees, to vest property in them.

In any event, it is the duty of those who take the property as trustees to familiarise themselves with the nature of the property and the terms of the trusts upon which it is held. They must also ensure that all formalities necessary to vest the property have been complied with. As this stage it might also be necessary to consider the conversion and disposal of any unproductive assets, and the settling of any liabilities outstanding against the trust estate. Trustees appointed to an existing trust (replacing a retiring trustee) must satisfy themselves that the affairs of the trust are in order and that no breach of trust has occurred. If it has, steps must be taken as soon as possible to put matters right and recoup any loss.

15.2.2 **Duty of care and day-to-day running of the trust**

The duty of the trustees in the day-to-day running of the trust is to manage the property so as to preserve the value of the capital and produce an income for the beneficiaries. In effecting administrative functions, they may employ the services of agents such as solicitors, accountants and stockbrokers, but there are also functions which a trustee must perform personally.

In the Trustee Act 2000 is a statutory duty of care applicable to trustees when carrying out their functions under the Act. Although the idea of a duty of care is not itself new, what *was* new about the 2000 Act's duty is, in the words of the Law Commission, the creation of a 'uniform duty' with the aim of providing 'certainty and consistency to the standard of competence and behaviour expected of trustees'. This works by applying the same standard of care across each of the functions to which the duty applies. In terms of what the legislation should be, it is clear that the Law Commission envisioned a context of increased professionalism and a diverse business environment within which trusteeship can increasingly be seen to operate.

The wording of the new statutory duty of care is as follows:

1. —(1) Whenever the duty under this subsection applies to a trustee, he must exercise such care and skill as is reasonable in the circumstances, having regard in particular—

   (a) to any special knowledge or experience that he has or holds himself out as having, and

(b) if he acts as trustee in the course of a business or profession, to any special knowledge or experience that it is reasonable to expect of a person acting in the course of that kind of business.

The duty of care applies only in the circumstances listed in Sch. 1, which are the statutory functions of the Act, and thus arise in the following instances:

(a) when exercising the general power of investment (or any other power of investment howsoever conferred), or when exercising statutory duties relating to exercise of a power of investment or to the review of investments;

(b) when exercising the acquiring of land or exercising any power in connection with land so acquired;

(c) when entering into arrangements for the appointment of agents, custodians or nominees or when carrying out the reviewing duties pertaining to such appointments;

(d) when exercising the powers under s. 15 of the Trustee Act 1925, or any similar power to compound liabilities;

(e) when exercising powers of insurance under s. 19 of the Trustee Act 1925 or any similar power;

(f) when exercising the powers under s. 22(1) or (3) of the Trustee Act 1925, or other similar powers relating to reversionary interests, valuations and audit.

Accordingly, where a trustee acts in a way whereby he fails to take reasonable care, but does so in circumstances not covered by the ambit of Sch. 1, his failure is actionable not under the new law but under pre-existing legal provisions. Moreover, the Act provides in Sch. 1, para. 7 that 'The duty of care does not apply if or in so far as it appears from the trust instrument that the duty is not meant to apply'.

Standard of care and the paid professional trustee
The duty to exercise such care and skill as is reasonable in the circumstances is the basic statutory duty; and the provisions of s. 1 clarify that what amounts to reasonable skill and care in the circumstances will depend on the facts of the case. Indeed, this is the essence of the specific regard which must be given to the factors within s. 1(1)(a) and (b).

The s. 1 criteria give rise to what is often referred to as a combination subjective/objective test. Here, the essence of (a) is directed towards the trustee concerned, and operates in relation to the qualities which he is representing that he possesses. The trustee's own representations are then pitched alongside and against the objective criteria in (b) drawn from the standards which can reasonably be expected from a practitioner within the trustee's own business or profession.

On this model it is clear that a higher standard is expected from a specialist professional, and indeed this principle subsisted at common law. In *Bartlett* v *Barlcays Bank Trust Co. Ltd (No. 1)* [1980] Ch 515 Brightman J thought that a higher standard of care was required from paid trustees than from unpaid and non-professional trustees, with the former category being judged against the standards of skill and expertise which they claim to possess.

15.2.3 **Duty of care and termination of trusts: distribution among beneficiaries**

Sooner or later a private trust will come to an end and the trustees will be required to distribute the property among the beneficiaries. Needless to say, they must distribute it to those who are properly entitled, and failure in this regard will be a breach for which they may be liable.

The onus is heavy, and trustees have been held liable where they made payment on the strength of a forged marriage certificate (*Eaves* v *Hickson* (1861) 30 Beav 136) or in the erroneous belief that a valid charitable trust was created (*Ministry of Health* v *Simpson* [1951] AC 251). They may even be liable where they acted on legal advice (*National Trustee Co. of Australia Ltd* v *General Finance Co. of Australasia Ltd* [1905] AC 373), although this may be a factor which would induce the court to exercise its discretion under s. 61 of the Trustee Act 1925 to exempt the trustees from liability.

The problems of wrongful payment are dealt with more fully in chapter 18, but it may be noted here that trustees may apply to court for directions in doubtful cases or, in the last resort, protect themselves by paying money into court.

Section 27 of the Trustee Act 1925 gives trustees power to advertise for claimants, in accordance with certain formalities, and to distribute the whole of the fund to those who come forward. By this procedure they obtain the same protection as if they had administered the trust under a court order. The rights of those properly entitled to the property (see chapter 18) are not thereby prejudiced. Other potential liabilities can be met by setting aside a fund, distributing under a court order, or obtaining an indemnity from the beneficiaries before distributing.

A special problem may arise by virtue of the statutory reforms made by the Family Law Reform Act 1987, which gave new rights to illegitimate children in some circumstances. The trustees or personal representatives could be unaware of the existence of such children and the legislation therefore provides protection for the trustees without diminishing the rights of the person entitled to recover their property.

15.3 **Personal nature of trusteeship, delegation and law reforms**

Throughout this book emphasis is given to the way in which the duty of trustees in the exercise of their discretions is one of a personal nature. Yet although trustees have a hugely onerous job, they will not necessarily be experts in everything which is needed for the safe and profitable running of a trust. Thus, it is obviously very important for trustees to be able to employ others to carry out the more specialised aspects of the management of the trust.

Equity has therefore always allowed the employment of agents in effecting specialised administrative functions, the most common examples of which are solicitors, stockbrokers and accountants. Prior to the enactment of the Trustee Act 1925 two principles had been established by the House of Lords in *Speight* v *Gaunt*

(1883) 9 App Cas 1. First, under *Speight* v *Gaunt* it was permissible to employ an agent where this was reasonably necessary, or in accord with normal business practices. Second, where such an agent was employed, trustees would not be liable for conduct attributable to the agent, so long as proper care was taken in the agent's selection, and the agent was employed within his proper sphere and exercised reasonable general supervision over his work.

This power to delegate has been widened considerably by legislation, and in the following sections we will be considering the Trustee Act 1925, the Trustee Delegation Act 1999 and the Trustee Act 2000. It is fair to say that the position relating to the delegation by a trustee of his functions has long attracted criticism. For example, in 1990 Professor David Hayton published his 'Developing the Law of Trusts for the Twenty-First Century' in the *Law Quarterly Review*. Professor Hayton argued in this piece the necessity of wider powers for the delegation of trustees' functions on account of rapidly changing economic conditions and investment choices. Of particular interest within this discussion (and especially in light of more recent developments) were Professor Hayton's considerations of wider powers of delegation for investment managers, and also for the accompanying need for trustees not to become vicariously liable for the defaults of the manager. In 'Trustees' Powers and Duties', the Law Commission echoed the need for wider powers of delegation. Much of the thrust of the Law Commission's findings was anchored to particularly scathing attacks upon the principle stemming from *Speight* v *Gaunt* distinguishing between so-called ministerial and fiduciary functions, in a social and economic climate which makes personal overseeing of many aspects of running of the trust (and particularly in relation to investment choice and management) impracticable at best and difficult to justify. The Law Commission's recommendations and more recent changes to the law will be considered further under subsequent headings.

15.3.1 Trustee Act 1925: the statutory right to delegate, and pressure for reform

The 1925 Act retained the distinction between ministerial and fiduciary powers in respect of a trustee's right to delegate, but it did relieve the requirement at common law that delegation must be reasonably necessary or in the ordinary course of business. Sections 23 and 30 of the 1925 Act provided for these wider powers of collective delegation by trustees, the two sections working in tandem (although in a manner which over time became widely regarded as confused and difficult to ascertain). Section 23 (now repealed) allowed for the facility of delegation and provided that there would be no responsibility for the default of an agent 'if employed in good faith' while s. 30 relieved the trustees from potential responsibility for the default of an agent by insisting that a trustee was to be 'accountable only for his own acts ...' and not for those of another unless this occurred through the trustee's 'own wilful default'.

The Law Commission's recommendation for 'root and branch' reform can be seen in this extract from their 1997 Consultation Paper.

We consider that there is no longer any continued justification for the existing restrictions on trustees' powers of collective delegation. The principal objection to the present law is that trustees' powers of investment and certain of their powers of management (such as the power to sell, lease or mortgage trust property) are regarded in all respects as fiduciary. As such they must be exercised by the trustees alone and are non-delegable. This position was the product of a time when decisions which trustees had to take were comparatively straightforward and infrequent. However, it is increasingly unrealistic, given that many of these tasks (particularly in relation to investment) now arise regularly and often require speedy professional advice and execution. We consider the 'exigencies of business' now justify the delegation of these discretions because adherence to the present restrictions is likely to frustrate the trustees' paramount duty to act in the best interests of the trust.

15.3.2 Delegation and the current statutory framework

The Trustee Act 2000 breathed completely new life into the position of delegation by throwing out an approach concentrated on specifying circumstances in which a trustee can delegate and putting in its place one which conferred a general power to delegate. It combined this with a prescription of functions which cannot be delegated. The relevant provisions are to be found in s. 11 of the 2000 Act, and the general power can be found in s. 11(1) 'Subject to the provisions of this Part, the trustees of a trust may authorise any person to exercise any or all of their delegable functions as their agent'. What amounts to a delegable function is considered in s. 11(2) which states that a delegable function is one which consists:

'of any function other than—

(a) any functions relating to whether or in what ways any assets of the trust should be distributed,

(b) any power to decide whether any fees or other payment due to be made out of the trust fund should be made out of the income or capital,

(c) any power to appoint a person to be a trustee of the trust, or

(d) any power conferred by any other enactment or the trust instrument which permits the trustee to delegate any of their functions or to appoint a person to act as a nominee or custodian.'

The Trustee Act 2000 adopts the same approach to the liability of trustees as was present at common law. Here, trustees are obliged to exercise reasonable care in the appointment of agents and also in their supervision. This is achieved through the operation of the new statutory duty of care.

Individual delegation and the Trustee Delegation Act 1999
Traditionally, individual trustees could delegate all their powers, including fiduciary powers, under s. 25 of the Trustee Act 1925 (as substituted by the Powers of Attorney Act 1971, s. 9). While this must now be seen in light of the Trustee Delegation Act 1999, the traditional position was a reflection of the assumption that the trustee would only want to do this in circumstances where he was actually absent. Indeed, originally, this section only applied where the trustee was away from the UK, and in such a situation it would of course be necessary for the trustees to have the power of the absentee in his absence. This facility was limited to a period of 12 months, and there were other important limitations (including no survivorship of delegation arising from a delegating trustee's mental incapacity (because it was by power of attorney), and a prohibition on delegation to a trustee's only other co-trustee). Of particular significance also is the position in respect of liability for delegation, which as s. 25(5) of the Trustee Act 1925 illustrates, is in stark contrast to the position in respect of collective delegation. Section 25(5) provides that 'A donor of a power of

attorney given under this section shall be liable for the acts or defaults of the donee in the same manner as if they were acts or defaults of the donor'.

The limits to individual delegation under the old regime have been considered in some depth in Paul Todd's *Cases and Materials on Equity and Trusts*. Here it will suffice to say that criticism of the restrictive qualities (alluded to above) of the 1925 Act (as amended in 1971) resulted in the passage of the Enduring Powers of Attorney Act 1985, which sought to remedy the difficulties by allowing for general powers of individual delegation by virtue of s. 3(3), as long as a prescribed form was used, and (by s. 3(4)) subject 'to any conditions or restrictions contained in the instrument'.

However, the 1985 enactment created as many difficulties as it solved, and can in many ways be seen as a piece of reactionary legislation. Clearly, it was intended to address the limitations of the 1925 Act (as amended), but equally, the general power of delegation effectively operated without any safeguards at all for the beneficiaries. Indeed, this was one of the concerns subsequently raised in respect of individual delegation in the Law Commission's 1991 Paper (*Delegation by Individual Trustees*, Law Com. 118). These were eventually discussed alongside possibilities for reforming powers of collective delegation in the later 'Trustees' Powers and Duties' (Law Com. 146) 1997.

The 1997 Consultation Paper in its principal focus on collective delegation was extremely critical of the law as it stood. It made many far-reaching and radical recommendations for reform, seeking amongst other things to establish a relationship between trustees' responsibilities with the nature of various aspects of trusteeship (perhaps especially investment), at the heart of which was abolition of the distinction traditionally drawn between ministerial and fiduciary powers, and introduction of a more general right to delegate, subject to appropriate safeguards. While it was true that all the trustees, by using their powers of individual delegation, could in effect collectively delegate, the Law Commission recommended the enactment of a new and rational system of collective delegation. Their proposal was that, subject to any contrary intention expressed in the trust instrument, trustees should have authority to delegate their powers to administer the trust, including their powers of investment and management, but (except in relation to trust property abroad) should have no authority to delegate their powers to distribute the income or capital of the trust.

In recognition of the considerable width of these proposed powers, the Law Commission also recognised the need for a number of safeguards. At one level this highlighted the need to review the employment of delegation regularly, and especially to consider the appropriateness of any proposed delegation at the outset. There was also the need to draw up and review, at reasonable intervals, a written statement of trustees' policy in relation to the exercise of the powers delegated, reflective of their fiduciary obligations to ensure that the trust is administered in the best interests of its objects, informing the agent(s) of that policy. Particular account was to be taken of the need for such to apply in the delegation of powers relating to the selection of investments, the sale, lease or charging of trust property; granting of options or rights of pre-emption over trust property, and the acquisition of property for the benefit of the trust.

The Trustee Delegation Act 1999 reformed individual delegation, but did so by tackling some of the specific problems identified in the dual regimes provided for under the 1925 Act (as amended) and the 1985 Act, such as trusts of land—through effective repeal of the Enduring Powers of Attorney Act 1985 and amendments to s. 25 of the Trustee Act 1925.

15.4 **Fiduciary nature of trusteeship**

At the heart of the 'fiduciary nature of trusteeship' are questions of *which* relationships are fiduciary, and *what* is their nature? The nature of a trustee's duty towards a beneficiary is fiduciary. In this book primary concern is with the duties of trustees, but to understand this, some appreciation that the trustee–beneficiary relationship as one of a number of so-called 'fiduciary relationships' which the law recognises, is essential. For example, the relationship between agent and principal in the law of agency is fiduciary, as is the relationship between co-partners in a partnership; another can be found in the relationship between company director and his company. Indeed, many of the cases considered in this section relate to fiduciary relationships other than trustee–beneficiary, and a number of them are actually 'company–director' illustrations. Nevertheless, all these cases are also authoritative on the position of trustees.

Trustees, beneficiaries and the distinguishing feature of all fiduciary relationships
The exact scope of the fiduciary relationship is also recognised as not necessarily exhaustive, and thus its precise extent is not clear. But for present purposes, what *is* clear and certain and beyond doubt is the way in which all fiduciary relationships are underpinned by one fundamental principle. This principle is that of 'fiduciary integrity' which sets out the expectation that the fiduciary is expected to act impartially in the interests of his principal. Classic expression of this principle of fiduciary integrity is found in Lord Herschell's judgment in *Bray* v *Ford* [1896] AC 44.

It is an inflexible rule of equity that a person in a fiduciary position ... is not, unless otherwise expressly provided, entitled to make a profit ... It does not appear to me that this rule is ... founded upon principles of morality. I regard it rather as based on the consideration that, human nature being what it is, there is danger, in such circumstances, of the person holding a fiduciary position being swayed by interest rather than by duty, and thus protecting those whom he is bound to protect. It has, therefore, been deemed expedient to lay down this positive rule.

This can be distinguished from ordinary commercial relationships, where parties act independently in their own interests and are not fiduciary relationships. In *Re Goldcorp Exchange Ltd* [1995] 1 AC 74, the Privy Council refused to recognise the existence of any fiduciary relationship between a company which had sold gold bullion for future delivery, and its customers. Lord Mustill observed that 'the essence of a fiduciary relationship is that it creates obligations of a different character from those deriving from the contract itself' and that that was not the case here. One effect of the lack of a fiduciary relationship between the parties was that the customers were unable to trace the property in equity (see chapter 19).

It is of the essence of any fiduciary relationship that the fiduciary has no personal interest in the way the duty is performed. Thus, where a fiduciary has a discretion, he must not have a personal interest in exercising the discretion in a particular way. A trustee, for example must be motivated to benefit the trust and not himself. That is not to say that fiduciaries are not entitled to receive benefit for their services. Banks, accountants and lawyers are not accustomed to working for nothing, and trustee-ship is clearly an onerous business. What is clear though is that the amount of their reward must not depend on the manner in which their discretion is exercised.

Trustees, beneficiaries and a 'core liability with several facets'
The essence of Lord Herschell's judgment will be found throughout the cases examined in this chapter, and in many throughout this study of trusteeship. This can be seen, for example, in *Bristol and West Building Society* v *Mothew* [1998] Ch 1 CA, arising in the context of breaches of duty committed by professionals working in the broad sphere of commercial activity. In the course of explaining the need to identify and distinguish within these commercial relationships ones which *were* of a fiduciary character and ones which were not, Millett LJ explained that:

A fiduciary is someone who has undertaken to act for or on behalf of another in a particular matter in circumstances which give rise to a relationship of trust or confidence. The distinguishing obligation of a fiduciary is the obligation of loyalty. The principal is entitled to the single-minded loyalty of his fiduciary. This core liability has several facets. A fiduciary must act in good faith; he must not make a profit out of his trust; he must not place himself in a position where his duty and interest may conflict; he may not act for his own benefit or for the benefit of a third person without the informed consent of his principal. This is not intended to be an exhaustive list, but it is sufficient to indicate the nature of fiduciary obligations.

15.4.1 Payment of trustees

The remuneration of trustees raises a number of interesting issues flowing from their position as fiduciaries, as introduced and explained above. In many parts of the US statutory rates of payment are established, but in the UK only the Public Trustee and a number of other trustees acting in an official capacity have any statutory entitle-ment to charge fees. And, in linking the subject of remuneration of trustees to the discussion of appropriate fiduciary conduct above, much flows from the rather tricky starting point that in English law, the general position (which is subject to exceptions) is that trustees are not entitled to benefit from their fiduciary position, and thus have no automatic right to be remunerated at all.

General principle and two justifications
The general principle (which is subject to the exceptions considered in the follow-ing section) that trustees (and other fiduciaries) are not entitled to benefit from their fiduciary position, does as it is suggested above, lead to the position that trustees have no automatic right to be remunerated for their service in this respect. There are two possible justifications for this position, flowing from the principle of 'no benefit'. First, there is the argument that payment should not be allowed if the prospect of payment affects, or has any possibility of affecting the manner in which the fiduciary's duties are performed. A fiduciary must act in a manner which is dis-interested, and there should be no conflict of interest, or even possibility of conflict of interest with their duties, which are created by the prospect of reward. Secondly, all money and the property acquired by the trustee when acting in his capacity as trustee rightfully belongs to the trust. As we shall see, these two justifications lead to slightly different conclusions, and it is not clear whether the courts have fully adopted the second.

Losses, gains and liability to account (to the trust)

It follows from the general principle (subject to the exceptions set out shortly), that trustees are not entitled to claim remuneration for the performance of their duties. Moreover, it is also clear from case law that should it transpire that they do obtain a benefit from their trusteeship, they are required to account for it to the trust. Unlike the situations considered in the chapter dealing with liability arising from breach of trust, many of the cases which stand as authority for this liability to account are cases where there has actually been no loss experienced by the trust, and only gain made by the trustee. While the work on breach of trust below deals with the position whereby an incompetent trustee is required to make good losses which have been experienced by the trust, this chapter is concerned with preventing unauthorised gains by the trustee. In this latter situation, the remedy of account is focused on the defendant's gain rather than the claimant's (the trust's) loss. In this respect a trustee is in a position quite different from an ordinary contract breaker who can generally keep profits which he has gained from the breach so long as he compensates the other party for his losses.

15.4.1.1 *Reform, modernisation and entitlement to payment: a departure from the general principle?*

Unsurprisingly perhaps in light of the discussions on modernisation and professionalism in trusteeship, the general principle has come under fire. The Law Commission's 1997 Report on 'Trustees' Powers and Duties' insisted that the position set out above was incompatible with the increased professionalisation of trusteeship, and it was accordingly recommended that in the absence of express contrary provision, professional trustees should be entitled to charge as long as the charges are reasonable and do not exceed the amount which trustees would charge in the ordinary course of their business. This entitlement has now been enacted as s. 28 of the Trustee Act 2000 which provides in s. 28(1) that a trustee is entitled to payment (except to the extent that this is inconsistent with the trust instrument) if '(a) there is a provision in the trust instrument entitling him to receive payment out of the trust funds in respect of services provided by him to or on behalf of the trust, and (b) the trustee is a trust corporation or is acting in a professional capacity'. Section 29 provides an entitlement to remuneration for 'certain trustees' where there is no provision elsewhere (i.e., in the trust instrument or by any enactment or secondary legislation), where the trustee is a trust corporation (but not a trustee of a charitable trust), or the trustee is one who acts as a professional trustee. The entitlement which arises is to 'reasonable remuneration out of the trust funds for any services he provides to, or on behalf of, the trust *if each other trustee has agreed in writing that he may be remunerated for the services*'.

This must be regarded as an important addition to the well-established situations in which a trustee is entitled to receive remuneration.

Circumstances in which there is a right to remuneration

These situations along with the very important entitlement for professional trustees introduced by the 2000 Act, should be regarded as exhaustive.

(1) The right to remuneration is fixed by contract at the outset. This will of course be by contract between the settlor and trustee at the outset. Prior to the enactment of s. 28, this will have been the mechanism used by banks and

accountants and other professionals which became associated with trust administration. It is also the way in which a director of a company (who stands as a fiduciary in respect of the company) will fix his entitlement to remuneration, by contract at the outset. This mechanism has as its basis the way in which it removes a possible conflict of interest because as his remuneration is fixed *ab initio*, it creates no incentive to act in a particular manner. However, the contract must be one which the company is entitled to make. In *Guinness plc* v *Saunders* [1990] 2 AC 663, two Guinness directors (Thomas Ward and Ernest Saunders) claimed that they were contractually entitled to fees of £5.2 million for advice and services rendered to Guinness in connection with a takeover bid for Distillers Co. plc. The purported contract was made by a committee of three of Guinness's directors (two of whom were Ward and Saunders), but under Guinness's articles of association the committee had no power to authorise reimbursement, and the House of Lords held that the directors were not entitled to keep the £5.2 million that they had received.

(2) Section 31 of the Trustee Act 2000 entitles a trustee to reimbursement for expenses from trust funds. This is wholly restitutionary in nature, and does not allow the trustee any payment for his services as such.

(3) The courts have an inherent jurisdiction to authorise payment, even where no remuneration is provided by the trust instrument. Originally the courts were prepared, if it was in the interests of the beneficiaries and if the trustee felt unable gratuitously to devote his time to trust affairs, to authorise payment of remuneration to him. The authorities and the basis of the jurisdiction were thoroughly reviewed in *Re Duke of Norfolk's ST* [1982] Ch 61, where the Court of Appeal appeared to have accepted as its justification ensuring the efficient administration of trusts. An alternative, implied contract view was expressly rejected by the Court.

(4) In *Re Duke of Norfolk's ST* (above), the Court of Appeal exercised the jurisdiction to increase the remuneration of a trustee over the amount agreed in the original settlement (the case broke new ground because previously the jurisdiction had been exercised only where no remuneration at all was provided by the trust instrument). The quantity of work had increased because new property had been added to the settlement, and the tax position had been substantially altered by the introduction of capital transfer tax in 1975 (see further on the effects of this tax in chapter 17). The trustee was held entitled to extra remuneration for the increase in work. The Court saw no difference in principle between increasing an already-agreed remuneration and granting remuneration where none was agreed, whereas this would obviously have been difficult had the implied contract justification for the jurisdiction been accepted.

(5) In many of the cases considered in this chapter the trust has suffered no loss, and in many cases it may indeed have gained from the activities of the trustee (or other fiduciary), who may have put in a considerable amount of work, well beyond his normal duties, or taken a substantial financial risk. It is arguable that the trust would be unjustly enriched if the trustee were required to account the entirety of his profits, but the trustee (or other fiduciary) may

(assuming he has acted in good faith throughout) claim under a common law jurisdiction based on *quantum meruit*, and an equitable jurisdiction to award an allowance.

In one of the cases involving a breach of fiduciary duty considered below, *Boardman v Phipps* [1967] 2 AC 46, although a solicitor as fiduciary to a family trust was not entitled to keep profits received as a result of his position, he was held at first instance to be entitled to an equitable allowance of remuneration, 'on a liberal scale', for his work and skill, and there was no appeal from this aspect of the decision. The Court of Appeal took a similar view in *O'Sullivan v Management Agency and Music Ltd* [1985] QB 428, another case involving a breach of fiduciary duty. Dunn LJ observed that: 'Although equity looks at the advantage gained by the wrongdoer rather than the loss to the victim, the cases show that in assessing the advantage gained the court will look at the whole situation in the round.'

The basis of the jurisdiction therefore appears to be a discretion in calculating the profit made by the defendant, in cases where he has benefited the claimant through hard work. *O'Sullivan* extended the law in two respects: first, the Court of Appeal invoked the equitable jurisdiction even though the defendant was not, as he was in *Boardman v Phipps*, morally innocent; secondly, the remuneration in *O'Sullivan* included even a reasonable profit element (but note that it was not related to the *actual* profits obtained in breach of fiduciary duty, which had to be accounted).

Rewarding trustee zeal; the common law quantum meruit award
There is also a common law jurisdiction, based on *quantum meruit*, where the claimant has been enriched at the defendant's expense. A possible justification for the *quantum meruit* claim is that it is founded on an implied contract, in which case it is simply a variation on the express contractual provision already considered (in (a) above). In that case, it ought not to be possible for a fiduciary to claim on a *quantum meruit* basis where the express contract would be void. The directors in *Guinness plc v Saunders* (above) claimed an alternative *quantum meruit* entitlement, because they had after all through their skill brought about a takeover (of Distillers Co.) on favourable terms from which Guinness had undoubtedly benefited. They failed, in Lord Templeman's view, for precisely the same reasons that their claim in contract failed (that the company had no power to authorise payment): Guinness were no more empowered to enter into an implied contract to pay for the services of the two directors, than they were to enter into an express contract for the same.

However, in *Westdeutsche Landesbank Girozentrale v Islington London Borough Council* [1996] AC 669, Lord Browne-Wilkinson, disapproving the reasoning in the earlier House of Lords decision in *Sinclair v Brougham* [1914] AC 398, doubted whether a personal claim of money 'had and received' (explained in chapter 19), for total failure of consideration, was based on implied contract. Instead, he said, it is based on unjust enrichment, and is therefore entirely independent of the underlying contract. It is difficult to see why similar reasoning should not apply to the *quantum meruit* claim in *Guinness plc v Saunders*. An alternative ground for rejecting the *quantum meruit* claim in *Guinness plc v Saunders*, particularly in Lord Goff's view, was that it contradicted the long-established principle that a director (or other fiduciary) may not make an unauthorised profit out of his position (see further below).

The problem with this is that Saunders also failed in *Guinness v Saunders* to claim an equitable allowance, the criteria for which appear to have been accepted in the case as being similar to those for a *quantum meruit* claim. This aspect of *Guinness* v *Saunders* has to be reconciled with *Boardman* v *Phipps*, and *O'Sullivan* v *Management Agency and Music Ltd*, where a similar restitutionary claim succeeded, although there may have been a conflict of interest. It is not satisfactory to argue that the directors in *Guinness* were dishonest, although the later well-known criminal proceedings cast doubt upon their honesty, because the case proceeded on the assumption that they had acted in good faith. One (not very satisfactory) possibility is that it is a matter of degree: the conflict of interest was much more extreme in *Guinness* than in the other two cases (indeed, it is questionable whether there was really any conflict at all in *Boardman* v *Phipps*). See further generally on this problem, Burrows, *The Law of Restitution*, Butterworths (1993), p. 308.

Final considerations of payment

It is clear from the previous section that there are a limited number of circumstances where trustees and other fiduciaries are entitled to payment. In none of these cases, however, is the amount of remuneration dependent on the manner in which the discretion (if any) of the trustee is exercised. Thus, there can be no conflict between the interests of the trust and the personal interests of the trustee.

15.4.2 **Trustees and making profit from the trust**

15.4.2.1 *Profiting from the trust: old and new cases*

We now move on to consider the converse situation, where the trustee (or other fiduciary) in fact gains from his position, and the question now becomes, is he entitled to keep his gain? If one starts from the premise that a trustee should not put himself in a position where there is any possibility that his duty and interest might conflict then he should be required to account (i.e., pay over to the trust) his profit when there is *any possibility* that a conflict of interest may occur. Whether any conflict occurs in fact is not relevant. In other words, it should be immaterial that the trust does not suffer, or even that it gains, from the activities of the trustee. However, if no possibility of a conflict arises, the trustee should not be required to account.

If, on the other hand, we start from the premise that any gains made by a trustee in the course of his duties are the property of the trust, the trustee should be required to account profits even if there is no possibility of a conflict of interest. The trustee should have to go further, and show that there is no causal connection between his position and any profit made by him (outside the payment categories outlined above). It is reasonably clear, but not certain, that the law has adopted this stricter position.

Whichever of these positions the law has adopted, it is at least clear that the law is extremely strict. Some argue that it is too strict and can stifle entrepreneurial spirit; and in some of the cases below such stifling appears indeed to have occurred. This is inevitable if the law insists that a trustee is to exercise truly independent judgment, but it is arguable that the law accords too high a value to the principle of independence, and too little to the encouragement of initiative by trustees. It should be remembered that many equitable principles developed in the days when family settlements were the main variety of trust, and initiative was not therefore an especially valued asset in a trustee. Some would argue that to apply similar principles today is inapposite.

On the other hand, the law has the advantage of certainty. It is fairly clear what trustees may and may not do, and it is possible for prospective trustees to negotiate terms freely before accepting appointment.

The essence of the way in which trustees are not to make profit from the trust in their charge is well entrenched in cases old and new alike (as seen above in the examples provided by *Bray* v *Ford,* and *Bristol and West* v *Mothew*). And, apart from the methods described above whereby a trustee (or other fiduciary) becomes entitled to payment, a trustee will rarely, if ever, be allowed to profit from the office of trusteeship. The words 'rarely, if ever' are used deliberately, because it is not clear whether the law ever allows a trustee to profit from his trusteeship. It is just about arguable that the law prevents only profits being obtained by wrongdoing, or where there is a clear conflict of duty and interest; but it is also arguable that profits made by trustees are never permitted.

Breach of a fiduciary duty is a breach of trust, so where profits are wrongfully obtained all the remedies in chapter 18 also apply here. Often, however, the trust will have suffered little or no loss; but where a trustee has obtained incidental profits from his office, to which he is not entitled on the basis of the principles discussed below, he can be required to 'account' (i.e., pay over to the trust) those profits. In most of the cases discussed in this chapter the remedy sought is account of profits. Moreover, since it is assumed that the fiduciary will have invested the profits made, compound interest is payable on them (see further chapter 19).

Trustees' profit and liability to account to the trust

Account of profits is, however, a personal remedy, which is of no use if the trustee is bankrupt. Further, although the trustee is assumed to earn compound interest on any profits made, if the trustee invests the profits which have been wrongfully obtained, the account of profits remedy on its own does not allow the trust to claim the investment, which may have increased in value. However, any profits so acquired can be regarded as being trust property, which should have been paid over to the trust. Since equity treats as done that which ought to be done, the profits will therefore also be held on constructive trust by the trustee. The effect of this is that the trust can claim any investment into which the profits can, on the principles discussed in chapter 19, be traced in equity, thereby protecting the trust in the event of the trustee's bankruptcy, and also giving the trust any increase in the value of the investment, as in *Attorney-General for Hong Kong* v *Reid* [1994] 1 AC 324.

Limitations on liability to account?

Much of the law in this section is very clear, but the precise limits of the requirement to account profits are not. It is clear that a wrongdoing fiduciary must account profits, and there are also two well-defined conflict of interest scenarios: first, a trustee may not purchase trust property (or sell property to a trust); second, he must not set himself up in competition with the trust. It is reasonably clear that these are merely examples of a wider proposition that a trustee must not put himself into a position where his duty and interest might conflict. Less clear is whether a trustee is allowed to make any profit by virtue of his position, even where there is no possibility of a conflict between his duty and his interest. Lastly, there is the question of whether information acquired by a trustee can be regarded as trust property, in which case not only the fiduciary but also third parties who profited from the information might be required to account those profits to the trust.

15.4.2.2 *Profits made by trustees from 'wrongdoing'*

There is at any rate no doubt that where the trustee, or other fiduciary, has acted in bad faith, he will not be allowed to benefit from his wrongdoing. In *Reading* v *Attorney-General* [1951] AC 507, Reading had been a sergeant in the British army and had made at least £19,000 illegally by helping smugglers to transport smuggled goods, by riding in the lorries in his uniform. Unfortunately for Reading, the £19,000 was confiscated and he was forced into the role of claimant, petitioning for its return. He failed because as a fiduciary he was liable to account for his profits to the Crown. An army sergeant would probably not normally be regarded as a fiduciary, but the use in the case of the uniform to deceive the authorities may have been the decisive factor.

Reading v *Attorney-General* was considered and followed in *Attorney-General* v *Guardian (No. 2)* [1990] 1 AC 109 (the *Spycatcher* case, where *The Sunday Times* was required to account the profits that it had received from Peter Wright's deliberate breach of confidence). It was also followed in *Attorney-General for Hong Kong* v *Reid* [1994] 1 AC 324, where a fiduciary who accepted bribes was required to hold them on constructive trust for the Crown (his employer). Because he held them on constructive trust, the Crown's claim was not limited to the value of the bribes, but extended to any property purchased with the secret commissions. Thus the Crown was able to obtain the value of three houses, which had substantially increased. There was old Court of Appeal authority, including in particular *Lister & Co.* v *Stubbs* (1890) 45 Ch D 1, to the contrary, which was disapproved by the Privy Council in *Reid*.

Reid and the requirement of a fiduciary relationship

The principles in *Reid* apply only where there is a fiduciary relationship between the parties. In *Halifax Building Society* v *Thomas* [1996] 2 WLR 63, the defendant mortgagor had obtained a 100 per cent mortgage advance from the claimant building society to finance the purchase of a flat, having made fraudulent misrepresentations as to his identity and creditworthiness. He fell into arrears and the building society exercised its power of sale, but because of a rising property market, there was a surplus after discharging the mortgage. The building society claimed this, arguing on the basis of *Attorney-General* v *Reid* that the defendant was constructive trustee for the mortgagee of all the profits made as a result of his fraud. The Court of Appeal held that the remedy of account of profits, and the imposition of a constructive trust were not applicable where there was no fiduciary relationship between the parties. Accordingly, the defendant was not required to account to the claimant for the profit he had made from the rising market.

A requirement for bad faith?

Where there is bad faith there need not be any harm to the claimant. Indeed, in none of the above cases had the Crown suffered any obvious loss. In *Industrial Development Consultants* v *Cooley* [1972] 1 WLR 443, the defendant, a managing director for the claimant company, had been negotiating on its behalf a contract with the Eastern Gas Board. The negotiations failed and it was apparent from the circumstances that the Eastern Gas Board was not at all happy about entering into dealings with Industrial Development Consultants (IDC) under any circumstances. Thus it appeared that whatever Cooley himself had done, the negotiations between IDC the company and EGB would have broken down. This meant that the claimant company IDC had actually suffered no loss from the personal gain which Cooley ultimately achieved for himself after the original negotiations between IDC and EGB ceased.

After these original negotiations ceased, the Eastern Gas Board then began negotiations with the defendant personally, with whom they wanted to work. The end result was that he terminated his contract with the claimant company, obtaining a release on the false representation that he was ill, and contracted with the Eastern Gas Board himself, on terms similar to those originally proposed on behalf of the claimant company. Roskill J held that the defendant was constructive trustee of the benefit of the contract for the benefit of the claimant company.

It is noteworthy that the claimant company had lost nothing, and as a result of the case gained only as a result of the defendant's breach of duty.

15.4.3 **Trustees' profit illustrated by conflict of interest cases**

The wrongdoing cases may be an application of a wider principle that a fiduciary should not put himself into a position where his duty and interest conflict. After all, it is obviously not in the interests of someone accepting bribes or secret commissions to act in an impartial, or fiduciary, manner. A conflict of interest was also assumed to exist in *Industrial Development Consultants* v *Cooley*, since the defendant had negotiated for his own benefit in the claimant's time.

But conflicts of interests can arise even in the absence of *mala fides*. There are two other clear situations where a conflict of interest may arise between the trust and the personal interest of the trustee, which the law therefore prevents from arising. First, a trustee may not purchase trust property (or sell property to a trust). Secondly, he must not set himself up in competition with the trust.

15.4.3.1 *Trustees may not purchase trust property*

It is possible, particularly in the light of Harman LJ's views at least in *Holder* v *Holder* [1968] Ch 353 (below), to distinguish self-dealing (trustee purchasing trust property for himself) from fair dealing (trustee purchasing from beneficiary). Self-dealing renders the transaction voidable at the option of the beneficiaries. Fair dealing renders the transaction voidable only if the trustee has behaved unfairly.

The distinction is not universally accepted, and both are arguably part of a wider principle that a trustee should not profit from his office as trustee (on which again, see further below).

Conflict of interest: distinguishing 'self' and 'fair' dealing
The rationale for the self-dealing rule is that if a trustee purchases trust property, he can abuse his position and buy at less than the best price obtainable. Similarly, if he sells to the trust, he may be able to demand too high a price.

The self-dealing rule is very strict where trustees are concerned, so that there must be no *possibility* of the trustee taking advantage of his position, whether he does so in fact or not. The lengths to which the law goes are shown by *Wright* v *Morgan* [1926] AC 788, where a trustee who had resigned his trusteeship purchased trust property at a price that had been fixed by independent valuers. One might have thought that not even a possibility of conflict arose here. The arrangements had been made while he was still trustee, however, and the Privy Council held that this sale must be set aside.

It is possible for purchases by trustees to be valid, but only in very exceptional cir-cumstances. It is essential not only that the trustee paid a fair price, as he had in *Wright* v *Morgan*, but also that he took no advantage of his position and made full disclosure of his interest. For example, in *Holder* v *Holder* [1968] Ch 353, an executor (Victor) purchased two farms that were part of an estate at a fair price at auction. The Court of Appeal refused to set aside the sale, although as executor Victor was acting in a fiduciary capacity. It was clear, however, that Victor had not been active in his role as executor, had indeed purported to renounce it and had acquired no information as a result of it. He took no part in instructing the valuer who fixed the reserves or in the preparations for the auction. Additionally, the claimant beneficiary had accepted his share of the purchase money in full know-ledge of the facts, and so was disentitled from taking the action on the grounds of acquiescence.

Limits of self-dealing
Both Sachs and Danckwerts LJJ expressed doubt whether the self-dealing rule should apply today where trust property is sold at public auctions, at least in a case where the sale is arranged by trustees other than the purchasing trustee. However, *Holder* v *Holder* was limited almost to its own unusual facts by Vinelott J in *Re Thompson's Settlement* [1986] Ch 99, a case which concerned the purchase of leases of farms owned by a trust, by a company whose director was one of the trustees. Vinelott J explained *Holder* v *Holder* on the narrow ground that the defendant had never acted as executor in a way which could be taken to amount to acceptance of a duty to act in the interests of the beneficiaries under his father's will. He said that the self-dealing rule is an application of the wider principle that a man must not put himself in a position where duty and interest conflict, or where his duty to one conflicts with his duty to another. If Vinelott J is right, *Holder* v *Holder* should not be regarded as laying down more than the narrowest of exceptions to the rule.

The same principles apply to sales of property to trusts by trustees.

15.4.3.2 *Trustees must not set themselves up in competition with the trust*
Similar principles apply here, because the trustee may gain for himself the benefit of any goodwill acquired by the trust, and possibly also useful information. It is not necessary to show that he has in fact done so, however.

In *Re Thomson* [1930] 1 Ch 203, an executor was restrained from carrying out a yacht-broking business in competition with the estate. The substantive issue did not come before Clauson J, because the executor had, as a consequence of an earlier interlocutory injunction granted by the Court of Appeal, transferred the business to the sole beneficiary. The question of costs was still outstanding, however, and depended on whether the original action was justified.

Conflict, competition and resigning from fiduciary office
The point of interest about *Re Thomson* is that Clauson J, in finding against the executor, did not think it would have made any difference if he had resigned his executorship, as long as he had contemplated starting a competing business while still an executor. There is a logic in this approach, because such contemplation may have affected the manner in which his duties as executor were performed. It has been argued that Clauson J's view depends on the specialist nature of the business, but it is difficult to see why this should make any difference.

15.4.3.3 *Examples of conflict of interest and duty which might be different?*

It is not clear whether the above cases are all part of a wider principle, that a trustee (or other fiduciary) may not make any profit from his position. If so, then all that should be necessary is to establish a causal connection between the profit and the position. It should not be necessary to go further and show either *mala fides* or a conflict of interest.

In *Re Macadam* [1946] Ch 73, trustees who used their position to appoint themselves to directorships of a company were held liable to account to the trust for all the fees they received as directors. This type of situation can commonly arise in private companies, because eligibility for appointment to directorships can depend on the legal ownership of a minimum number of shares, and indeed trustees may be under a duty to procure their representation on the board if it is necessary in order to safeguard the value of the trust shares.

Establishing causation: nothing else required

Arguably, all that is necessary is to establish the causal connection between position and profit. No such connection was established in *Re Dover Coalfield Extension* [1908] 1 Ch 65, a case similar to *Re Macadam*, but where a trustee had already become a director before becoming trustee. *Re Gee* [1948] Ch 284 is similar, where a trustee became a director after refraining from using his vote, which he had by virtue of holding trust shares. He would have been elected anyway, due to the votes of the other shareholders, however he had voted himself; he would even have been elected if he had voted against himself. Harman J held that the remuneration received as director was not accountable to the trust. In neither of these cases could it be said that the trustees had made any profit by virtue of their position.

A closer examination of these cases suggests that they are, in reality, conflict of interest cases, since clearly a trustee who stands to gain from the choice of himself as director cannot advise the trust impartially as to the choice of who to appoint.

Keech v Sandford: position, profit and a stronger case

A stronger case is *Keech v Sandford* (1726) Sel Cas Ch 61, where the trustee took over the benefit of a lease which had been devised to the trust when that lease expired. Since the lease had expired, this is not a case of dealing in trust property. The causal connection between position and profit was presumably established, in that he would not have been in a position to take the lease had he not been trustee. The lessor had refused to renew the lease for the trust, on the ground that the beneficiary was an infant against whom it would be difficult to recover rent. The trustee thereupon took the lease for his personal benefit, and profited from it.

There cannot have been any actual conflict of interest, because the trust itself could not have benefited, given the views of the lessor. Nor would Lord King LC say that there was any fraud in the case. Yet he held that the trustee had to assign the benefit of the lease to the infant, and account for profits received. The trustee was the one person in the world who could not take the lease for his own benefit, because by so doing he would be profiting from his position. The same principle may apply where a trustee of a lease purchases for himself the freehold reversion: *Protheroe v Protheroe* [1968] 1 WLR 519 (CA) (but there are contrary authorities).

Conflict of interest: absence of bad faith

There was no *mala fides* in *Regal (Hastings) Ltd* v *Gulliver*, originally reported in [1942] 2 All ER 378 and only in the official reports in [1967] 2 AC 134n. Regal were considering applying for shares in a subsidiary company, but was unable to afford them, so the directors subscribed themselves and made a profit. The directors would not have been in a position to profit had they not been directors, but arguably there was no conflict of interest, given that Regal was not in a position to subscribe for itself. Yet the directors were held liable to account. Lord Russell of Killowen said:

> The rule of equity which insists on those, who by use of a fiduciary position make a profit, being liable to account for that profit, in no way depends on fraud, or absence of *bona fides*; or upon such questions or considerations as whether the profit would or should otherwise have gone to the plaintiff, or whether the profiteer was under a duty to obtain the source of the profit for the plaintiff, or whether he took a risk or acted as he did for the benefit of the plaintiff, or whether the plaintiff has in fact been damaged or benefited by his action. The liability arises from the mere fact of a profit having, in the stated circumstances, been made.

This is a fairly clear statement that all that needs to be established is the causal connection between position and profit. Arguably, however, there was in fact a conflict of interest, as the directors themselves must have determined that the company could not afford to subscribe for the shares. It would have been difficult for them to advise impartially where they intended to subscribe for themselves, and hence obtain a profit.

Cornerstone of law or hard case?: Boardman v Phipps

The leading case is *Boardman* v *Phipps* [1967] 2 AC 46, but it is not clear on what principle it was decided. Boardman was solicitor to a trust, which owned 8,000 of 30,000 shares in a private textile company with whose performance Boardman was dissatisfied. The trust had no wish to buy the remaining shares, and in any case was unable to buy them, although it could have applied to court for power to do so. Boardman decided to purchase them himself, undoubtedly benefiting from information he had received in his fiduciary capacity (in knowing what price to offer), and did not obtain the consent of all beneficiaries (on which see further chapters 16 and 18). The shares later increased in value (partly perhaps because of Boardman's management in selling off some of the assets of the newly acquired company), so Boardman made a large profit for himself. Additionally, however, because the trust still had a large share in the same company, his activities resulted in a large profit for the trust. There was no claim of bad faith, or any obvious conflict of interest, since the trust did not have the power to purchase the shares itself; and in any case, the trust had positively benefited from Boardman's intervention.

By a 3:2 majority, the House of Lords nevertheless held that Boardman held the shares as constructive trustee for the trust, and was therefore liable to account profits. It is not easy to discern the *ratio*, although it seems that whereas the majority thought it enough simply to profit from the trust, Viscount Dilhorne and Lord Upjohn (dissenting) thought that this was insufficient in the absence of a clear conflict of interest. They took the view that there was no conflict or possibility of a conflict between the personal interests of the appellants and those of the trust. Unfortunately, the position is muddied because the majority also took the view that there was a (somewhat theoretical) conflict of interest also: the trust might have changed its mind and sought to buy the shares itself, in which case Boardman as solicitor to the trust would have had to advise on the application to court. It may be, therefore, that the case does not extend existing principles, except in showing how willing the courts are to find even the most theoretical possibility of a conflict of interest.

Is information trust property?

A further difficulty about *Boardman* v *Phipps* is that in the Court of Appeal ([1965] Ch 992), Russell LJ had decided the case on an entirely different ground, that all the information acquired by Boardman in his fiduciary capacity became trust property. Lords Hodson and Guest also seemed to be of this view. Lord Cohen appeared less sure about the trust property point, but was happy to decide the case on causation alone.

The property reasoning raises serious difficulties (see, e.g., Gareth Jones (1968) 84 LQR 472), especially where information is obtained by somebody who is trustee to several trusts, or where the information is passed on to other, innocent recipients who also profit from it. Partly for these reasons, Viscount Dilhorne, adopting the views of Lindley LJ in *Aas* v *Benham* [1891] 2 Ch 244, said that information was not the property of the trust, and Lord Upjohn's views were similar. Certainly, the 'information as trust property' reasoning is not part of the *ratio* in the House of Lords.

15.4.4 **Conflict of interest and duty: conclusion and clarification?**

Although the *ratio* of *Boardman* v *Phipps* is not very clear, the weight of authority probably supports the proposition that all that is required is to find a causal connection between the fiduciary's position and the profit obtained. If Boardman would have purchased the shares anyway, even without the information acquired by virtue of his fiduciary position, there would have been no causal connection between the position and the profit, and the case would have been like *Re Gee*. If not, the case is similar to *Re Macadam*, and Boardman was properly held to account.

It may be objected that the law deters entrepreneurial activity which may well benefit the trust. However, Boardman was liberally rewarded on a *quantum meruit* basis for benefiting the trust, on the principles discussed earlier. What he could not do was to keep any additional profits he made. The law allows private speculators to do so, but takes the view that those who are acting as fiduciaries accept, by taking on fiduciary positions, that their remuneration is limited to the categories described earlier, however much they benefit the other party. Though this view may appear harsh, it at least has the merit of ensuring that their discretion will be exercised in an independent manner.

15.4.5 **Trusteeship, integrity and entrepreneurialism: new thoughts on *Boardman* v *Phipps***

The arguments surrounding the continuing operation of the no profit rule as exemplified in the House of Lords' decision in *Boardman* v *Phipps* (in the context of the unauthorised use of property or opportunities rightfully belonging to the trust) fit essentially into two broad interpretations of the result of the case; namely, its justifications and its implications. The rule against profiting from a position as fiduciary arises where the justifications in favour of it are strongly outweighed by the opposing position in which it can be seen to unnecessarily stifle entrepreneurial activity. This might have the result of actually depriving the trust of the benefit of business expertise and acumen from which it might otherwise benefit greatly, as was the case in *Boardman* itself. On this reasoning, the operation of the rule against profit will ensure that the potential (and possibly considerable) benefits for the trust will not be forthcoming in light of the fact that trustees have no incentive to act in a manner which is entrepreneurial, as they are not able to benefit personally from doing so. Indeed the rule represents an active disincentive for trustees to act in such a way. The alternative reading of the rule against profiting by virtue of the position of fiduciary is that such a strict 'no profit' rule is required in the interests of certainty and preservation of the principle of fiduciary integrity; or the principle of disinterest.

Entrepreneurialism v integrity: the same arguments?
The case law in the area of the governance of fiduciary relationships has consistently put at its heart the principle of disinterest. This is promoted as the only position that the law can realistically adopt in order to ensure fiduciary integrity. Indeed, if it were the case that some profits were regarded as being 'authorised' and others not, it would not only become more difficult on a conceptual level to defend the principle of fiduciary integrity, but it would also become impossible to demark such distinctions appropriately on a practical level. On such a line of argument (against interference with the principle of fiduciary integrity), this impossible middle way of regarding some profits as authorised whilst others remain unauthorised is also actually unjustifiable in light of trustees' ability to fix remuneration in advance, so as to avoid 'disappointment' (this was always possible through provision in the trust instrument, even before the enactment of the express power conferred by s. 28 of the Trustee Act 2000). There are no right answers to the existence of the rule against unauthorised use of trust property, information and opportunities, what is instead needed are new approaches which can be added to the two well-worn broad and opposing ideas.

Departing from the position of fiduciary integrity
Making the case for a more entrepreneurial reading of the use of trust information and opportunities would take as its starting point the view that the 'no profit' rule requires reconsideration. Trusteeship is becoming less restrictive as exemplified in the widening powers of investment in the 2000 legislation—e.g., in the general power of investment in s. 3(2), on which see chapter 16. The rationale for this arises from recognition of a greatly expanded financial market from which investments can potentially be made and the concomitant increased opportunity that this represents for enhancing the wealth of the trust. Thus, the law relating to trusteeship is becoming generally more entrepreneurial, and discouraging trustees from acting in an entrepreneurial manner is inconsistent with this development. Following this trend towards entrepreneurialism, the policy of the current New Labour Government is the promotion of 'enterprise culture'. Enterprise culture does of course have its roots in the challenges presented by the onset and progression of globalisation, which has itself provided the inspiration of the politics of the Third Way. The broad message of the Third Way, and the way in which it has become attached to New Labour's own reforming zeal, requires all people to be entrepreneurial so as to equip individuals and nation states to meet the new economic conditions created by globalisation. At this point, it may be asked how the anti-entrepreneurial approach of trusts law as exemplified in the 'no profit' rule can sit comfortably alongside the broad trend towards entrepreneurial behaviour. And while the law of trusts is concerned to safeguard the position of those whose interests the occupants of fiduciary office are bound to protect, can it be readily assumed

that trusts and their operation are to remain exempt from this new and never static direction which is sweeping the world? This must surely be a crucial question in view of the Trustee Act 2000 which was itself strongly oriented towards the need to modernise trusts law taking into account twenty-first century reality.

There is also new blood which can be added to the opposing position advocating the preservation of fiduciary integrity. This comes from the work of the American scholar Susan Shapiro. Shapiro works mainly in the field of white collar crime scholarship, and it is through this work that she has actually made some very important points in relation to the law of trustees and fiduciaries. In 1987, Shapiro argued in the *American Journal of Sociology*, that scholarly consideration of white collar crime is really a study of the maintenance and abuse of trust in society. This work potentially has important applications for the study of trusts, and here it can be applied to the operation and implications of the 'no profit' rule. As has already been suggested, there is a line of respected authorities which stand as authority for the position of maintaining fiduciary integrity. Shapiro's work means arguments from very old cases can be strengthened by applying to them a new theoretical consideration of integrity, which argues against further empowering fiduciaries (here exemplified in enabling them to profit from their activities).

In defence of the principle of fiduciary integrity
Power imbalances in the trust relationship Shapiro argues in a different piece in 1990 that because of the nature of their functions, occupants of fiduciary office operate in circumstances which are integrally highly advantageous to them. Indeed, she describes the relationship between fiduciary and principal (here, the position occupied by the beneficiary under a trust) as 'asymmetrical', and proposes that the huge power imbalances between the parties (which operate in the favour of the fiduciary) arise from the reliance created by inequalities in ability in a particular relevant area. She proposes moreover that the asymmetries which are thus created are further skewed by information which is used by the fiduciary in the performance of his actions, and which is 'hidden' from the beneficiary on grounds of his lack of expertise or other contextual references. This is also exacerbated by the 'moral hazard' which can be translated into behaviour which is committed by the fiduciary in the course of performing his duties, but which is concealed from the beneficiary.

Misconceptions about the 'burden' of trusteeship Shapiro also argues that the much-vaunted burdens which seemingly attach to the fiduciary's performance of his duties are not only more than compensated for in the remuneration he receives, but that characteristically high levels of remuneration also build in protection against temptation for abuse of position which the fiduciary might otherwise experience (i.e., the 'moral hazard', and how to protect against it). She argues that occupants of fiduciary office are further empowered because the way in which trust and trust relationships are organised in society ensures that abuses of trust are difficult to detect. In this manner, Shapiro's work could be used to assert that the fiduciary position is in many respects advantageous to those who occupy it, and accordingly, fiduciaries should not be allowed to derive yet further benefit from their positions than they already do. Indeed, although classical statements of the principle of fiduciary integrity (e.g., in *Regal (Hastings) v Gulliver*) acknowledge asymmetries in the fiduciary/principal relationship, and the emphasis placed on the duty of protection strongly implies the need not to prejudice the interests of the weaker party, Shapiro adds to this by making direct connection between the occupation of fiduciary office and the active advantages that this confers for the fiduciary.

A more convincing view?

How persuasive these arguments appear is a matter of personal choice, and simply advancing new ways of considering the tensions created by the relationship between trustee and beneficiary does not necessarily mean that a conclusion in favour of one view or another will necessarily be forthcoming. However, what the advancement of new approaches to the problems which are believed to characterise the trust relationship does provide is scope for its consideration in light of factors other than a line of respected, and also old authorities. Just as the Trustee Act 2000 finds its *raison d'être* in the need to provide a modern legal regime, its passage must surely signal the need at least *to consider* new approaches to the questions and difficulties which will from time to time arise within it.

15.5 Trusteeship and its commencement: the appointment of trustees

Usually, trustees will be appointed by the document which brings the trust into existence, and this document ought also to make provision for any additional appointments which may be necessary during the continuance of the trust. In addition, however, the Trustee Act 1925 makes provision for any additional appointments which may be necessary, unless the operation of the Act is expressly excluded. The Trustee Act 2000 provisions are necessary if the trust instrument does not make the necessary provision or if there is no trust instrument at all.

The settlor will usually name those whom he wishes to act as trustees, and where the settlement is *inter vivos*, the trustees themselves will normally be parties to the deed of settlement, since the purpose is both to declare the trusts and to vest the property in the trustees. In the uncommon case where the settlor simply declares his intention henceforth to hold some of his property on trust, he will himself be the sole trustee. Alternatively, he may decide to appoint other trustees as well and take steps to vest the property in himself and his co-trustees jointly.

Where trusts are created by will, it is usual to appoint the same persons to be both executors and trustees. The fiduciary duties of executors are very similar to those of trustees, but they are not identical and it may be important to know at what point an executor has ceased to act as such and become a trustee. Generally, this will occur when the executors assent to the vesting of property in themselves as trustees, although in the case of personalty, this assent may be implied since no formalities are necessary. In the case of land, an assent in writing is required, since this is an essential document of title.

15.5.1 No trustee available

It may happen that for some reason a trust comes into existence without there being anyone able or willing to act as trustee, for example, if the trustees appointed by the will have predeceased the testator or if the trust arises by operation of law.

An instance of the latter is where an outright bequest of property is made to a minor, who cannot give a good receipt for the property until she comes of age. The absence of trustees will not invalidate the trust. If the trust is *inter vivos*, the settlor himself will be the trustee. If it arises by will, the personal representatives of the testator will hold the property on trust. Where an instrument creating the trust names someone as having power to appoint trustees, he may use that power to fill the gap. If all else fails, the court will appoint trustees.

15.5.1.1 *Acceptance once and for all*

No one can be compelled to accept office as a trustee under an express trust, although a person may find himself a trustee against his will by operation of law, e.g., a constructive trustee. Once the office is accepted, it cannot later be renounced, although retirement is possible under certain conditions. In theory, the office of trustee is lifelong, and if a trustee dies in office, any liabilities which he has incurred will persist against his estate. Should the trustee wish to disclaim his role as trustee for any reason, he should do so as soon as possible, and preferably by deed, for failure to disclaim may lead to a presumption that he has accepted. Acceptance will also be presumed once the trustee has started to act in relation to the property.

15.5.1.2 *Who may be trustee?*

Anyone who has the legal capacity to hold the legal title to property may be appointed a trustee of that property. A corporation may thus be a trustee provided its constitution authorises it so to act. An infant may become a resulting or constructive trustee of personalty (*Re Vinogradoff* [1935] WN 68) although not of land, as s. 20 of the Law of Property Act 1925 declares the express appointment of an infant trustee void (and s. 36(1) of the Trustee Act 1925 permits her replacement by a person of full age). These restrictions apart, the settlor may appoint as he pleases. Traditionally, certain appointments, such as that of a beneficiary or one of his relatives, or the solicitor to the trust, have been regarded as undesirable by the courts, but they are not invalid and are commonly made in practice.

Certain special categories of trustee exist, the most important in practice being the trust corporation, usually but not always the executor and trustee company of a bank. The main advantages of appointing a trust corporation are its longevity, financial stability and expertise, and the fact that it may act alone in circumstances where two individual trustees would be necessary. The chief disadvantage is that its fees are likely to be high. The qualifications necessary for a company to be a trust corporation are contained in the Public Trustee Rules 1912 (SR&O 1912 No. 348), r. 30, as amended.

Other special trustees include custodian trustees, the public trustee and judicial trustees. They perform specialist functions which in practice are rare.

Appointment of new trustees during the continuance of the trust
If an occasion for the appointment of new trustees arises during the continuance of the trust, rather different considerations apply than those governing the initial appointments.

15.5.1.3 *Role of settlor*

It should be recalled that once a settlor has completed the steps necessary to create a trust, he has no further interest in the trust property. It follows that he retains no rights in regard to the appointment of trustees in the future. If he wishes to control future appointments, he must nominate himself in the trust instrument as being the person having power to appoint new trustees, and any appointments that he makes will be in this capacity and not by virtue of his being settlor.

Alternatively, he may prefer to nominate some other person to exercise the power of appointing trustees, particularly where the trust is intended to extend beyond his lifetime. A well-drafted trust instrument will be required for this, because the terms of any power to appoint will be strictly construed. It is usual nowadays, when nominating a person in the trust instrument to exercise the power of appointing new trustees, to draft the power in very simple terms, since in the event of an inconsistency between the terms of the trust instrument and the statutory power considered below, the latter will prevail.

15.5.1.4 *Trustee Act 1925, section 36*

It is obviously desirable that there should always be some person with power to appoint new trustees, and usually such powers will be contained in the trust instrument itself. Even where there are no powers in the instrument itself, however, s. 36(1) of the Trustee Act 1925 makes provision for new appointments. As with other sections of the Act, however, its operation can be expressly excluded. Trustee Act 1925, s. 69(2) states that:

The powers conferred by this Act on trustees are in addition to the powers conferred by the instrument, if any, creating the trust, but those powers, unless otherwise stated, apply if and so far only as a contrary intention is not expressed in the instrument, if any, creating the trust, and have effect subject to the terms of that instrument.

Where s. 36 applies, its effect is to create a hierarchy of categories of persons having power to appoint. There is an order. Persons falling into the first category have the first right to make the appointment, and only if there is no one in that category, or no one able and willing to act, will the power become exercisable by the persons within the next category. By virtue of the section, the following persons, in this order, may appoint:

(a) The person(s), if any, nominated in the trust instrument.

(b) The existing trustees, if any.

(c) The personal representatives of the last, or only surviving trustee.

If there is no one in any of these categories who is able and willing to act then the power given by s. 36(1) cannot be exercised at all (although the court may have jurisdiction to appoint under s. 41 of the Act).

The circumstances which give rise to a power under s. 36(1), on the part of the appropriate person to appoint fresh trustees in replacement for the original trustees, are also specified in the section, and are as follows:

(a) *Where a trustee has died.* This covers not only the situation of a trustee dying while in office, but also that of a trustee dying before assuming office, as where a trustee named in a will predeceases the testator. The Act makes no provision for the perhaps unlikely case of all trustees dying before the will comes into effect, as noted above.

(b) *Where a trustee remains outside the UK for more than 12 months.* The absence must be for a continuous period, so that a trustee who occasionally returns for short visits cannot be removed under this head (*Re Walker* [1910] 1 Ch 259). As long as the absence is continuous, its cause is immaterial, so that a trustee who remains abroad involuntarily by reason of illness or imprisonment may be replaced. Where it is intended that the trust should operate in another jurisdiction, care should be taken expressly to exclude the operation of this part of s. 36(1), to protect the tenure of foreign residents who have been specifically selected as trustees.

(c) *Where a trustee desires to be discharged* from all or any of the trusts or powers reposed in or conferred on him. Although it is not permitted to disclaim in relation to part only of the trust before assuming office, a trustee who accepts office and later seeks to be discharged may be relieved of his duties with regard to a part only of the trust, while retaining a say in the management of those parts in which he has an interest.

(d) *Where a trustee refuses.* It seems apt to permit an appointment to be made in replacement of a trustee who disclaims, although strictly, of course, such a person never becomes a trustee. Old authorities on the predecessor of s. 36 favour this interpretation.

(e) *Where a trustee is unfit to act.* This appears to refer to defects of character, and although no precise description can be given of the circumstances in which a trustee can be described as unfit for the purposes of s. 36(1), the courts will remove a trustee as unfit where she has been convicted of a crime of dishonesty, or has become bankrupt and her continuation in office is opposed by the beneficiaries, or she has been imprudent in the management of her own affairs. A bankrupt trustee who is free from moral blame may, however, be permitted to remain in office.

(f) *Where a trustee is incapable of acting.* This covers the case where a trustee is unfit due to mental or physical incapacity, and also where some legal incapacity is imposed, as where wartime regulations forbid certain foreign nationals to hold property in this country. Special provisions apply where a trustee has also a beneficial interest under the trust and is a patient under the Mental Health Act 1983. In this case, the leave of the authority having jurisdiction over him under Part VII of the Act will be required before a new trustee can be appointed in his place.

(g) *Where the trustee is an infant.* The express appointment of an infant trustee is void, but a trust could be deprived of an active trustee because of the infancy of a person named as a trustee, and the section appears to cover this contingency.

(h) By virtue of s. 36(3), *where a corporate body acting as trustee has been dissolved.* It is deemed to be incapable of acting from the date of dissolution.

In addition to the power of appointing new trustees by way of replacement, there is also power to appoint additional trustees, the existing trustees remaining in office. Where there are currently three trustees or fewer, none of whom is a trust corporation, and it is thought desirable to have more, appointment may be made by the person nominated in the trust instrument for the purposes of appointing new trustees, or by the existing trustee or trustees, in that order. The total number of trustees must not be raised beyond four, although more than one at a time may be appointed. The power is contained in s. 36(6), and is independent of the power to appoint replacement trustees under s. 36(1).

An appointment under s. 36 must be in writing, and in practice it will be made by deed to take advantage of the vesting provisions of s. 40 (as considered below).

15.5.1.5 *Trustee Act 1925, s. 41: trustee appointments by the court*

The court has an inherent power to appoint trustees as part of its supervisory jurisdiction over trusts, which is supplemented by s. 41 of the Trustee Act 1925. Under this section, the court may appoint whenever it is expedient that an appointment should be made and it is inexpedient, difficult or impracticable to bring this about without the assistance of the court.

Application to the court may be made by a beneficiary or by a trustee, but if it is possible to appoint under a power in the trust instrument or under s. 36, this should be done in preference. If there is some person having power to appoint and seeking to exercise that power in good faith, the court will not interfere even if the proposed appointment is not one which it would itself have made.

Where allegations of misconduct against a trustee are being made, the court may act under its inherent jurisdiction, but the proper course is to begin the action by writ so that the trustee knows what accusations he has to meet.

The court's assistance may properly be sought when no one has power to appoint, or no one is willing and able to exercise it, or where there is some doubt about whether the power has become exercisable. Recourse to the court may be the only way of replacing elderly or sick trustees who have become incapable of acting for the trust (as in *Re Phelp's ST* (1885) 31 Ch D 351, where the sole trustee was 85 years old, deaf, and failing in intellect); or of meeting the case where the only person having power to appoint is too old or ill, or too young, to be able to exercise it. In practice, application is sometimes made by trustees who wish to avoid later argument over the propriety of a particular appointment.

Certain principles govern the court's selection in appointing trustees. At one time, a beneficiary, or even one of his relations, would have been unsuitable because of the possibility of a conflict between duty and self-interest. Nor would the family solicitor be chosen, ostensibly to avoid the indelicate task of assessing the probity of a member of the legal profession. Both kinds of appointment are commonly made out of court, however, and the attitude of the courts appears to be changing.

The court will not, however, make an appointment which favours the interests of certain beneficiaries above others, nor will it willingly appoint against the known wishes of the settlor. For example, in *Re Tempest* (1866) LR 1 Ch App 485 a trustee had predeceased the testator, and there was strong disagreement between the surviving trustee and a faction among the beneficiaries over who should replace him. It was clear that the surviving trustee would be unwilling to act with the person appointed by the court at first instance. Turner LJ considered that it would be going too far to say that a court would refuse to appoint a person with whom the existing trustees refuse to act since that would amount to giving them a veto. The court should inquire whether the objection is well founded and act accordingly. Regard will be had to whether a proposed appointment will promote or impede the execution of the trust.

Persons permanently resident abroad will not normally be suitable, but where the beneficiaries have emigrated and the trust property is situated abroad, the court may make such an appointment (*Re Windeatt's WT* [1969] 1 WLR 692).

15.5.1.6 *Role of beneficiaries*

Where a sole beneficiary is absolutely entitled to the entirety of the trust property, or where all the beneficiaries are *sui iuris* (i.e., not children or people who are mentally incapacitated) and together so entitled, the rule in *Saunders* v *Vautier* (1841) 10 LJ Ch 354, considered in greater detail in chapter 17, permits the beneficiaries to terminate the trust. They may then, if they so wish, set up a new trust to which they, now as settlors, have the right to appoint the trustees. This course of action, however, will require transfers, which may well give rise to liability for capital transfer or other tax on the dissolution and fresh settlement.

However, although the beneficiaries may make new appointments in this roundabout fashion, equity did not allow them to do so directly. In *Re Brockbank* [1948] Ch 206, a trustee wished to retire and the beneficiaries sought to have a trust corporation appointed in place of the remaining trustees, who opposed the change on the ground of the cost to the trust of the trust corporation's fees. The beneficiaries argued that since they were all *sui iuris* and collectively entitled, the trustees were obliged to appoint in accordance with their wishes. Vaisey J rejected this argument. The beneficiaries might terminate the trust if they so wished but they were not entitled to control the trustees' exercise of their statutory power to appoint while the trust subsisted.

Further, it seems that those who have the right to appoint under s. 36 may do so regardless of the wishes of the beneficiaries. In *Re Higginbottom* [1892] 3 Ch 132, an illiterate lady of no means, and having no interest in the trust, became executrix of the last survivor among the trustees, and therefore was entitled by virtue of the statute to appoint new trustees. The majority of the beneficiaries opposed this and requested the court to appoint trustees of their choosing, but Kekewich J refused to interfere with the lady's right to make the appointment herself.

The Trusts of Land and Appointment of Trustees Act 1996 gave additional powers to the beneficiaries, effectively overruling *Re Brockbank*, where they are all of full age and capacity, and are together absolutely entitled to the trust property. Section 19 empowers the beneficiaries, by written direction to the trustees, to appoint a person or persons as trustee(s), and to direct the retirement of a trustee. Section 20 allows them to substitute for a trustee who is incapable by virtue of mental disorder of exercising his functions as trustee.

15.6 **Formalities for vesting of trust property in new trustees**

As we saw in chapter 2, where a settlement is created *inter vivos*, the trust property will be vested in the trustees as part of the transaction. If the settlor declares herself sole trustee, there is of course nothing more to be done. In a testamentary trust, where the same persons are appointed as executors and trustees, the change of role involves the executors in vesting the property in themselves as trustees, which is notional in the case of most kinds of personalty (personal property; not real property) but requires a formal assent in the case of land. If other persons are to take over as trustees, the property must be vested in them with whatever degree of formality is appropriate to that property. Similarly, when new trustees are appointed to an existing trust, the property must be vested in them so that they hold it jointly with the existing trustees.

15.6.1 **The formalities themselves**

In brief, formalities are required as follows (all those relating to land are dealt with in greater detail in land law textbooks):

(a) *unregistered freehold land*: a conveyance must be executed;

(b) *unregistered leasehold land*: the lease must be assigned;

(c) *registered land*, either freehold or leasehold: the appropriate transfer and its registration at the land registry must be completed (Land Registration Act 1925, s. 47);

(d) *stocks and shares*: must be formally transferred, and the transfer registered in the books of the company or other body issuing the shares;

(e) where the property is a *debt*, it must be formally assigned and notice given to the debtor, to secure priority over future assignees;

(f) *negotiable instruments* (e.g., cheques): must be delivered and (unless payable to bearer) endorsed;

(g) *personal chattels* (i.e., ordinary goods): may be physically handed over unless there are specific documents of title to be transferred, e.g., a car or an aeroplane.

15.6.2 **Consequences of improper vesting**

Proper vesting is vital, since the trustees may be held personally liable for any loss arising from failure in this regard. A newly appointed trustee must satisfy himself that all is in order and cannot say that it should have been attended to by the other trustees. However, in the case of a newly appointed trustee, some of the formalities of vesting are obviated by s. 40 of the Trustee Act 1925. The effect of this section is that where he is appointed by deed containing a declaration in appropriate terms, the trust property vests automatically in the new trustee and his co-trustees as joint tenants.

Unfortunately, certain types of property are excluded from the operation of s. 40. This is inconvenient, since they include the most common types of property held in trust, but there are good reasons for the exclusion. These are:

(a) *Land held by way of mortgage*. The reason for requiring formality is probably simply to ensure that the mortgagor knows who to pay.

(b) *Land held under a lease which contains a covenant against assignment* (i.e., transfer of the lease to any but the original lessor), unless permission to assign was obtained prior to executing the deed of appointment. This is because, if vesting was automatic upon appointment of new trustees, there would necessarily be a breach of the covenant against assignment, and this might render the lease liable to forfeiture (i.e., termination by the landlord).

(c) *Stocks and shares* must be formally transferred and registered in the company's books. This is because, under the Companies Acts, legal title to stocks and shares depends on registration, and companies can recognise as shareholders only those who appear in their books.

15.7 Termination of trusteeship

15.7.1 Retirement

In principle the office of trustee is lifelong. Nevertheless, a trustee may voluntarily retire in one of several ways. First, he may take advantage of any power to retire contained in the trust instrument, although such a power is nowadays uncommon. Second, if someone can be found to replace him, he may retire under the provisions of s. 36(1) of the Trustee Act 1925.

Third, he may retire under the provisions of s. 39 of the Act even without replacement, under the following conditions:

(a) His retirement must leave the trust with not less than two individual trustees or a trust corporation to act for it; and

(b) The remaining trustees must consent to his retirement; and

(c) Anyone empowered to appoint trustees must consent.

Retirement, and any necessary consents, must be in the form of a deed. Unlike s. 36(1), s. 39 does not permit retirement from part only of a trust.

Fourth, the beneficiaries may consent to his retirement, so as to debar themselves from holding the trustee accountable for any event arising after the date of such consent. This is only an aspect of the rule that a beneficiary who consents to a breach of trust has no right of action in respect of that breach. Unless all are *sui iuris* (i.e., suffering from no incapacities, such as infancy or mental incapacity) and collectively entitled to the entire trust property, the trustee will not obtain his discharge from the trust. It will also be prudent to obtain the consents of the other trustees, to avert any claim by them to an indemnity.

Fifth, the court may discharge a trustee without replacing him under its inherent jurisdiction, but will not do so if this would leave the trust without a trustee. In such a case it may make an order for administration of the trust by the court, so that the trustee remains in office but is relieved of responsibility. Alternatively, if the trustee pays the entire trust fund into court, he thereby loses the right to exercise any of his discretionary powers in the trust, which amounts to virtual retirement. He remains in office for the purpose of receiving notices of dealings with the trust property, however, and may be made a party to any action brought by the fund.

Although the once-and-for-all nature of trusteeship looks harsh in theory, in practice the statutory provisions for retirement are almost always sufficient.

15.7.1.1 *Death of a trustee*

Trustees hold their office, and the trust property, jointly. There is a right of survivorship so that upon the death of a trustee, his office and the trust estate devolve on the survivors. As we saw in 1.2.6, one of the attractions of the early Use was its ability to allow estates to pass from generation to generation with few conveyances of legal titles. This was achieved in part by vesting the legal title in a number of feoffees to use jointly, and relying on the right of survivorship on the death of any one of them. Trusts today operate in the same way and for essentially similar reasons.

The equitable rule was codified in s. 18(1) of the Trustee Act 1925, which provides:

> Where a power or trust is given to or imposed on two or more trustees jointly, the same may be exercised or performed by the survivors or survivor of them for the time being.

If one trustee dies, then, the rest may carry on the trust without interruption, subject to the possible need to appoint a replacement if the numbers have been reduced below what is required for effective management.

Although the trust property vests automatically in the survivors, due steps should be taken to ensure that any register or document of title is brought up to date.

When a sole surviving trustee dies, the trust property devolves on his personal representatives and is held by them on the terms of the trust. Section 18(2) enables the personal representatives to exercise all the powers of the former trustee, although they are not obliged to do so. The personal representatives can only act until new trustees are appointed. Often, they will themselves be the persons having the power to appoint.

15.7.1.2 *Enforced removal of trustee*

A trustee may be removed against his will in any of the following ways:

(a) Under an *express power in the trust instrument.* Such power is almost never inserted in a domestic trust, and if it exists it will be strictly construed. More commonly it is found in certain commercial transactions. A common example is an equitable mortgage effected by depositing the title deeds with the lender, where the mortgagor may declare himself a trustee of the legal estate for the lender. In turn, the lender is likely to reserve a power to remove and replace the mortgagor as trustee—simply a means of protecting himself.

(b) He may be removed under s. 36(1) if he *remains outside the UK for more than 12 months, refuses, or is unfit to act or incapable of acting,* by the appointment of some other person to act in his place.

(c) He may be removed by the court either in the exercise of its jurisdiction under *s. 41,* where the appointment of a new trustee may involve removing an existing trustee, or under its *inherent jurisdiction* where an action for the administration of the trust is brought.

(d) Under the provisions of the *Trusts of Land and Appointment of Trustees Act 1996.*

online
resource
centre

FURTHER READING

All reading which relates to the consideration given to trusteeship across chapters 15, 16 and 18 can be found detailed at the end of chapter 18 .

16

Powers, discretions and duties of trustees

16.1 General description and overview

16.1.1 Powers and duties

Equity equips trustees with a number of powers and also imposes a range of duties, most of which may be modified or excluded by the express terms of the particular trust in question. Modern trusts created by deed or settlement or will, and prepared under expert legal advice, generally seek to give the trustee the widest possible powers, being almost invariably drafted with tax saving in mind. It is important to bear in mind that the powers described in this chapter are generally subject to the terms within the trust instrument itself.

The distinction between trusts and powers was considered in chapter 2. This is useful to recall at this point because a similar distinction exists between the duties of the trustee's office on the one hand, and his powers and discretions arising from it on the other. Trustees have a discretion as to whether or not they will exercise a power, and if after proper consideration they decide in good faith not to exercise it, then the beneficiaries have no ground for complaint. Generally speaking however there will be a duty to undertake such consideration where it would be appropriate. There is of course no discretion as to whether to fulfil a duty, and the new statutory duty of care in the Trustee Act 2000 will of course apply in the exercise of duties laid down in Sch. 1.

16.1.2 What are the powers and duties?

In view of the different types of situations in which trusts come into being, it is only to be expected that powers and duties will vary according to the character of the trust, for example, whether the trustees are required to accumulate or distribute the income and so on.

However, it will be seen that some kinds of power are in principle widely available to trustees. Most of these are now statutory and they are chiefly concerned with facilitating the management of the trust.

For example, there will be much attention given to the trustees' obligation to invest the funds of the trust according to powers of investment conferred them by the trust instrument or the newly enacted Trustee Act 2000. They must also ensure the proper payment of tax, and at some stage they may well have to consider matters such as the sale of trust property, or making provision for infant beneficiaries. Accounts of trust business must be kept and copies supplied to the beneficiaries, and in this vein, it is usual and desirable for trustees to meet in order to transact trust business, and records of such meetings must be minuted in a diary or minute book.

The trust instrument will usually give additional powers appropriate to the trust. In the case of the modern tax-saving trust, these are likely to be extensive, and by and large the statutory powers have more application in older and less professionally oriented trusts.

Although the duties of trustees will vary considerably, there are nevertheless certain fundamental duties which are fiduciary in character (for example the duty of loyalty, namely the duty not to profit from the trust) which apply to all trustees. Other common duties will include the safe-keeping of trust property, the proper custody of documents of title, and investment, etc. It will also become clear later that trustees also have in addition duties towards the beneficiaries. These include the duty to inform them of their rights and provide information regarding the affairs of the trust, and the duty to distribute the property in accordance with entitlements to it. They must also consider the need to maintain fairness between the beneficiaries.

Duties, trust instruments and the scope for modification
Some duties can be and indeed are frequently modified by the trust instrument. Others such as the duty to make proper distribution are inherent in the nature of any trust, although even here the trust instrument may limit the personal liability of the trustees in the event of breach of trust.

Trusts and the professional context of their operation
It will be apparent that the administration of all but the simplest of trusts calls for a considerable degree of business competence, and nowadays most trusts of any size will have a professional trustee such as a bank or trust corporation to act for them. The professional may act either as a sole trustee or in conjunction with one or more individuals. This sort of mixture can be useful in family settlements, combining the expertise of the professional with the more intimate knowledge of family circumstances supplied by the private trustee.

16.1.3 Constructive trustees

The powers and duties described in this chapter apply to express trusts. Constructive trustees are in a peculiar position because of the fact that they hold property under a trust which has been imposed upon them from the operation of law. The duties of constructive trustees are uncertain, and key in the application of the Trustee Act 2000 and the statutory duty of care which it lays down. The difficulties in ascertaining how and to what extent the new statutory duty can be applied can be seen to flow from the huge variety of circumstances in which constructive trusteeship arises. One view of this might propose against the application of the duty of care on account of the fact that at the most extreme of the constructive trust's operation, a person can become such a trustee without knowing it and remains ignorant until the matter is determined by the court. In the absence of definitive guidance, it must also be noted that an argument in favour of the duty applying to a constructive trustee can be made from the way in which the legislation expresses the duty of care applying to trustees exercising the powers prescribed 'however conferred'.

16.2 **Sale of trust property**

A power to sell some or all or the trust property is usually given by the trust instrument, either expressly or by implication, and even in the absence of such power, trustees will often be permitted to sell by statute, or as a last resort by order of the court. Some specific cases require consideration.

16.2.1 **Land governed by the Settled Land Act 1925**

Settled land is very rare today and the creation of a statutory trust for sale under the Settled Land Act 1925 is a very unusual type of trust. Here the sole function of the trustees of the settlement is to take the proceeds if the land is sold, so as to protect the (overreached) interests of the beneficiaries under the trusts of the settlement. The legal estate (fee simple absolute in possession) and the powers of sale are not vested in trustees but in the tenant for life. Further, very little limit is placed on the power of the tenant for life to sell the land, who has far more extensive powers than a normal trustee in this regard. Although strict settlements still in existence on 1 January 1997 are unaffected by new powers conferred by s. 8 of the Trustee Act 2000 (see below), the Act has made some changes to the operation of strict settlements. Firstly under s. 75(2) of the Settled Land Act (as amended by the 2000 Act), the investment or other application of capital monies is no longer the province of the tenant for life and discretion as to how the trust fund should be invested is now vested in the trustees. In addition, a new s. 75 (4)(c) provides that anyone authorised to exercise trustees' functions under s. 11 (in respect of the application or investment of capital money) will not be subject to the obligation to consult with the tenant for life and give credence to his wishes.

16.2.2 **Trusts for the sale of land**

Statutory trusts for sale have been abolished by the Trusts of Land and Appointment of Trustees Act 1996. It is still possible (but rarely appropriate) to set up express trusts for the sale of land, in which case the duty to sell will be contained in the trust instrument, and a power to postpone shall be implied.

16.2.3 **Other trusts of land**

Apart from existing strict settlements, all trusts of land are now governed by the Trusts of Land and Appointment of Trustees Act 1996 which gives trustees wide powers of sale, but (unlike the predecessor trust for sale), not duties to sell.

16.2.4 **Personal property**

The Trustee Act 1925 contained a number of provisions for the sale which authorise sale of trust property by trustees (including its s. 16) for situations where no such power was expressly or impliedly given in the trust instrument itself. However, under the new regime, there is no statutory power of sale except in the case of trusts of land, and the Trustee Act 2000 does not include any provision authorising the sale of (personal) property except for the purposes of varying investment.

16.2.5 Power to give receipts

The power to sell or otherwise deal with trust property is of little value unless the purchaser can obtain a valid receipt for the transaction. Thus, s. 14 of the Trustee Act 1925 gives a power notwithstanding anything to the contrary in the trust instrument, to give an effective receipt. The receipt of such a receipt in writing from a trustee operates to exonerate the purchaser from any obligation to ensure that the trustees apply the money received in accordance with the trust. This is very important from the perspective of the purchaser, because his awareness that the property which he has purchased was the subject of a trust might otherwise be taken to ensure that he holds it as constructive trustee under the equitable notice doctrine.

16.3 Power to insure

Section 34 of the Trustee Act 2000 gives trustees wide powers to insure trust property. The enactment of s. 34 marks the repeal of the previous provisions regarding insurance as laid out in s. 19 of the Trustee Act 1925. The 1925 provisions were regarded as being restrictive in that they gave trustees limited power to insure against loss or damage by fire, but not against other very important insurable risks. This very limited power stemmed from the way in which 1925 predated many forms of insurance which are available to (and increasingly regarded as being indispensable within) commercial dealings. The exercise of this power is now subject to the statutory duty of care.

16.4 Power to employ nominees or custodians

Part IV of the Trustee Act 2000 creates a new regime for the appointment of agents, custodians and nominees. Under this trustees can collectively authorise an agent to carry out 'delegable' functions. The definition of delegable functions can be found in s. 11 of the Act. Furthermore, the 2000 Act confers upon trustees wide powers for the holding of trust property by custodians and nominees. Perhaps most important under this head is the new statutory duty in Sch. 1, para. 3, under which trustees must labour in the appointment of agents, custodians and nominees, while s. 22 places upon trustees the duty to review the activities of this category of delegatee. Over and above compliance with these duties for the appointment and review of such persons, by the provision of s. 23 of the Trustee Act 2000, trustees incur no liability for any default committed by agents, custodians or nominees so appointed. Trustees are subject to the statutory duty of care in this respect.

16.5 Power to compound liabilities

As the legal owner of the property, a trustee has the right to maintain an action with regard to the trust property. Where the claim itself is a legal claim, it will be the case that it is only the trustee as legal owner who can sue. This is very important, particularly where debts are owed to the trust. Notwithstanding, litigation is still a risky business, perhaps especially so in the pursuit of debts owed, where it is far from clear that there will be recovery of what is owed, and there is expense entailed in the debts pursuit. To this end s. 15 of the Trustee Act 1925 gives discretion to trustees in their dealings with persons who are in contention with the trust (commonly because they owe the trust money). When exercising this power under s. 15 of the Trustee Act 1925 (or any corresponding power, however conferred), trustees are subject to the statutory duty of care as provided by s. 1 of the Trustee Act 2000.

16.6 Power to acquire land

The power to acquire land is conferred by provisions within Part III of the Trustee Act 2000. These new powers are extensive and apply to the purchase of leasehold and freehold land. By the provision of s. 8, such purchases can be made for the purposes of investment; for occupation by a beneficiary; or for any other purpose. By the provisions of s. 8(3) the trustee is given all the powers of an absolute owner. The trustee is subject to the duty of care in s. 1 in the exercise of these powers.

16.7 Powers of maintenance and advancement

Powers of maintenance and advancement are appropriate to family type settlements, and they have the object of providing for infant beneficiaries who are not as yet entitled to the benefit of any income of capital, but who will still require financial support during their minority. In addition to the statutory powers conferred by the Trustee Act 1925, the court has inherent jurisdiction to provide both maintenance and advancement.

16.7.1 Power of maintenance

The statutory power of maintenance under s. 31 of the Trustee Act 1925 can only arise where the beneficiary is entitled to receive intermediate income under the trust. This will be the case either where his interest is vested or where it is a contingent interest which carries the intermediate income. If there are prior interests, or if the beneficiary's interest is as a member of a class of discretionary beneficiaries the power will not be available at all.

The discretion to maintain and the trustees' guiding principle

Where income is available and the trustees have the discretion as to whether to maintain the beneficiary, s. 31 provides guidance on such matters as the age of the infant and the requirements he may have and the general circumstances of his case. Subject to contrary intention in the trust instrument the power to maintain ceases where the infant obtains majority. This is the 'contingency'. Even if his interest is still contingent, the trustees must pay the whole of the income to him until he obtains a vested interest or dies.

16.7.2 The power of advancement

The power of advancement permits trustees to pay capital sums to, or on behalf of a beneficiary some time before he is entitled to claim the fund. The power may be given by the trust instrument or, subject to a contrary intention, s. 32 of the Trustee Act 1925 may be invoked. The statutory power allows trustees at any time to pay or apply capital money for the 'advancement or benefit' of any person entitled to that capital or a share thereof. Subject to that limitation the powers are wide and apply whether the interest is vested or contingent, or whether it is in possession, in remainder or in reversion. Up to one half of the beneficiary's share may be advanced.

16.7.2.1 *The significance of the power of advancement and its context*

The trustees' discretion whether to exercise their power of advancement is absolute, so long as it is for the 'advancement or benefit' of the beneficiary. The ambit of the power is very wide, and it is popular in schemes which are designed as tax saving devices. In this context, it can be seen as a device which operates for schemes which are designed to avoid tax on capital transfers. Capital Transfer Tax (or CTT) is due on transfers of capital taking place *inter vivos* as well as ones which occur upon death. It is a tax which was designed to circumvent the avoidance of Estates Duty (by ensuring that gifts were made more than seven years before death), and was designed to tax family capital at least once per generation.

The power of advancement, CTT and the significance of
Pilkington v IRC [1964] AC 612

This case arose from a proposed advancement of part of a contingent share of Penelope Pilkington, who was an infant beneficiary, under the terms of a fund established by her uncle so long as she attained majority (of 21 years). The trustees of the settlement wished to advance to Penelope a sum of £7,600, which was to be settled on other trusts for her and this was for the purpose of avoiding duty payable on death. It was held in the House of Lords that this course of action was a proper exercise of the statutory power of advancement and there was benefit to the infant in the avoidance of tax. In this respect, it did not matter that the purpose of the advancement was for its resettlement on different trusts for the benefit of the infant.

16.7.3 Advancement must be for the benefit of the advancee

However widely expressed the statutory power of advancement might be, it was held by the Court of Appeal in *Re Pauling's ST* [1964] Ch 303 that the trustees must be satisfied that the advancement is for the benefit of the advancee. Further, should trustees decide to make an advance for a particular purpose, then they must ask themselves whether the beneficiary is likely actually to carry out the intended purpose. Following this, no payment should be made for such a purpose where the trustees will then leave him free to do with it what he pleases. The question was left open as to whether the trustees can actually recover money which the beneficiary requests for a particular purpose and then applies to something quite different.

16.8 Duty to protect the trust assets: the duty of investment

There is a continuing duty which begins with the collection of the assets upon a trustee's assumption of office and ends only with the final distribution of the property amongst those entitled to it.

16.8.1 Initial duties

From the outset, trustees must acquaint themselves with the terms of the trust and the state of the property they are to hold. They must also ensure that funds are appropriately invested and see that all securities and chattels are in proper custody. If there is property which is outstanding, all proper steps must be taken to gather it in.

Initial duties and trustees' liabilities
In *Re Brogden* (1888) 38 Ch D 546, trustees were held liable where they refrained from suing to enforce a covenant to pay £10,000 into the settlement. This was so even though their motivation was reluctance at endangering the family business of which the covenantor's estate formed a major part. On the other hand, in *Ward* v *Ward* (1843) 2 HL Cas 777, trustees were not liable for failure to sue a beneficiary who might have been ruined by the action along with his family who were also beneficiaries. However, *Ward* is regarded as an extreme case.

Failure to sue and 'excuses' made
In *Re Brogden*, the Court of Appeal found that the only excuse for the trustees' failure to sue was that the action was considered to be fruitless. This was not an appropriate reason for failing to enforce payments due to the trust. However, there is now s. 15 of the Trustee Act 1925 which comes to the aid of trustees in weighing up litigation risks. And subject now to the statutory duty of care, trustees in the exercise of their powers, are able to compound liabilities and allow time for the payment of debts will not incur liability.

16.8.2 The protection of assets by investment

16.8.2.1 *General principles*
Once assets have been 'collected' in this manner by the trustees they must then be protected, and at the heart of this lies the selection by the trustees of proper investments. In this regard two central principles can be seen to operate. First trustees have a general duty to act fairly as between the beneficiaries, and second the trustees must make investments which are appropriate.

The duty to act with an even hand amongst the beneficiaries

This principle will dictate that, in the selection of investments, the trustee must be mindful of those for whom the property must provide an income and also those who have ultimate entitlement to the property.

The duty to make appropriate investments

In respect of this, the enactment of the Trustee Act 2000 signals the arrival of a new approach to investment which is radically different from the traditional caution of the law relating to investment by trustees in contrast with normal investment culture and practice. The law will provide the fall-back position whereby it will apply in absence of express powers of investment conferred in the trust instrument. It is very common for professionally drafted trusts to contain such express powers, but it might well be that the enactment of a general power to invest by the Trustee Act 2000 might reduce the need for such express provisions.

16.8.2.2 *Departure from the restrictive nature of trustees' powers of investment*

The policy of the law until the recent changes introduced in the 2000 Act was that of restriction and the need for caution. This can be seen exemplified in the 2000 Act's predecessor, the Trustee Investments Act 1961, which demanded that trustees were limited to safe investments in their choice for investment. Extensive criticism of the 1961 regime was made in the Law Commission's 1997 Consultation Paper 'Trustees' Powers and Duties' (Law Com. 261) describing it as 'over cautious and restrictive'. Indeed, the paper argued that such a regime placed huge and unnecessary burdens upon trustees, and that there was evidence of serious under-performance by some trusts on account of it. The Law Commission suggested that instead, trustees should have the same power as individuals in the making of investments, and that the operation of a duty of care would compel them to have regard to the need for diversification and suitability, and that further safeguard would be achieved in the way in which trustees would have to seek proper professional advice in such matters.

16.8.3 Trustees and investment, and the Trustee Act 2000: the introduction of a more modern regime

In response to the criticism levelled at the regimes governing trustees' investment activities contained within the Trustee Act 1925 and the Trustee Investment Act 1961, s. 3 of the Trustee Act 2000 provides trustees with new wide statutory powers. The old regime was regarded by the Law Commission as being outmoded and restrictive, and not at all reflective of the tremendous opportunities offered in the diversified investment market of the late twentieth century. The opening of s. 3 of the new Act is illustrative of the new legislation's intent to sweep away much of what is outmoded and replace it with a more appropriate and facilitative legal framework governing investment.

16.8.3.1 *The general power of investment: s. 3*

Section 3(1) states that:

Subject to the provisions of this Part, a trustee may make any kind of investment that he could make if he were absolutely entitled to the assets of the trust.

While the remainder of the discussion of the new legal regime now in place will focus on the limitations of trustees' powers of investment as well as their scope, this statement of intent should remain foremost a matter of context. Indeed s. 3(2) defines this statement of intent as the 'general power of investment'.

Significantly, unlike in the provisions of the Trustee Investment Act 1961, there is no requirement under the new legislation that there should be any division of the trust fund, but the general power of investment is subject to the 'safeguards' prescribed by sections 4 and 5. These safeguards essentially refer to the duty of trustees to have regard to the 'Standard Investment Criteria', and the obtaining and consideration of proper advice.

16.8.3.2 *Section 4 and the Standard Investment Criteria*

Neither the idea of 'standard investment criteria' nor its precise composition within the Trustee Act 2000 can be regarded as new, and they have in essence been re-enacted from the Trustee Investment Act 1961. According to the provisions of s. 4(1) trustees must have regard to the Standard Investment Criteria when exercising any power of investment whether this is part of the general power of investment conferred by the 2000 legislation or is from a different source (for example, the trust instrument itself, when the power will be an express one provided, rather than a general one available to all trustees). Indeed, in this respect, the general power of investment operates subject to restrictions or exclusions on such activity which are contained within the instrument which has created the trust. Under s. 4(2), trustees must take into account the Standard Investment Criteria when exercising *any* investment powers. And, as part of this process they should from time to time review whether or not investments made should in any way be varied from their original composition. Again, this need to review is defined in terms of reference to the Standard Investment Criteria, and provides the benchmark against which such an assessment must be made.

The Standard Investment Criteria: a twin set of objectives
The Standard Investment Criteria is composed of two measures of the appropriateness of any given investment, and this is reflected within the legislation. The *suitability* to the needs of the particular trust of the type of investment which is being considered is enshrined in s. 4(3)(a), while the need for *diversification* in so far as this is appropriate to the needs of the individual trust, is sign-posted within the provisions of s. 4(3)(b).

Trustees' investment choice: explaining suitability and diversification
The requirement that the type of investment chosen should be suitable for the nature of the trust requires that the trustee should look at the type of investment that they are wishing to make to judge its appropriateness for the needs of the particular trust, and for an assessment of suitability to be made. The needs of individual trusts will of course vary considerably, and accordingly so will the factors which will influence questions arising in the assessment of suitability. But it is clear from authorities such as *Cowan* v *Scargill* [1985] Ch 270 that the calculus of suitability can include within its ambit questions of ethical or moral suitability.

The requirement of diversity is of essence in 'portfolio theorisation' of investment, which takes as its standard of risk assessment the risk level of the *entire portfolio* and not of *individual investments* within it. It is this global consideration of assessing risks taken in investments which articulates that trustees must ensure that investments are appropriately spread, and thus risk is evened out. It would be surprising therefore if the duty to ensure diversification were not applicable to the exercise of all powers of investment (and not simply the general power provided in the 2000 legislation), and indeed it is so applicable to all powers of investment. Whilst this is a duty which cannot be excluded or restricted, and notwithstanding its general policy of promoting the spirit of portfolio in all exercisings of investment power, by the provisions of s. 4(3)(b) the duty to ensure diversification applies (only) 'in so far as is appropriate to the circumstances of the trust'. Thus whilst the import of diversification is within the legislation without dispute, its provisions recognise that there are nevertheless limitations on its appropriateness (for example on grounds of size of the trust and its assets).

16.8.3.3 *Section 5 and the duty to take advice in the exercise of the power of investment*

Under s. 5(1), before exercising power of investment (irrespective of its source) the trustee must (subject to the exception provided in s. 5(3)) obtain and consider proper advice. This proper advice refers to the way in which the power of investment (from whatever source) should be exercised, when regard is had to the Standard Investment Criteria. By the provisions of s. 5(2), when a review is being made of the suitability of investments (by reference to the Standard Investment Criteria, and in furtherance of s. 4(2) of the 2000 Act), the trustee must obtain and consider proper advice as to the way in which the investments should be varied. This requirement marks a considerable point of departure from the 1961 legislation whereby the duty to seek and consider advice was much narrower, while s. 5(3) seeks to deal with the situation whereby the trustee is himself an experienced financial advisor, by providing that 'a trustee need not obtain such advice if he reasonably concludes that in all the circumstances it is unnecessary or inappropriate so to do'.

The question of what amounts to 'proper advice' is provided for in its definition in s. 5(4) as 'the advice of a person who is reasonably believed by the trustee to be qualified to give it by his ability in and practical experience of financial and other matters relating to the proposed investment'. This definition has been lifted from the provisions of the 2000 Act's predecessor, the Trustee Investment Act 1961.

16.8.4 **The 'general power of investment' and its exception**

The important exception to the ability provided by the legislation for a trustee to make any investment as he could do if he were absolutely entitled, is the power to invest in land other than loans which are secured on land. However, this will make little difference in practice because the power for purchases of land (including for the purposes of investment) is expressly provided in s. 8 of the 2000 Act.

16.9 **The duties of trustees towards beneficiaries**

16.9.1 **General principles of control by the beneficiaries**

Although the ultimate benefit under a trust goes to the beneficiaries the trustees are concerned not only with their wishes, but also with those expressed by the settlor in the creation of the trust. There is therefore no general principle which permits the beneficiaries to control the way in which the trustees exercise their discretions. Were it otherwise, the trustees would be hopelessly handicapped in fulfilling their overriding duty towards the trust as a whole, and the court will never compel the trustees to act under orders from the beneficiaries where a power or discretion has been entrusted to the trustees alone. This will hold as long as the trust continues, although if the beneficiaries collectively wish, they can bring the trust to an end and resettle the property on any terms they wish, under the *Saunders* v *Vautier* doctrine (see further chapter 17).

Tempest v *Lord Camoys* (1882) 21 Ch D 571 shows the position while the trust continues. The beneficiaries desired the trust to purchase an estate but one of the trustees objected. Jessel MR refused to interfere with that trustee's bona fide decision. Strictly, the trustees are under no obligation even to consult with the beneficiaries as to how a power or discretion should be exercised, although of course they will often do so in practice.

An exception arises by virtue of the Trusts of Land and Appointment of Trustees Act 1996, which requires trustees of land under a statutory trust for sale to consult beneficiaries in possession and to give effect to their wishes so far as is consistent with the general intentions of the trust. The reason is, as we saw in chapter 1, that these are really fictitious trusts, whose main purpose is to simplify the conveyancing of shared land, but even in this limited case there is no overriding obligation to follow the beneficiaries' directions.

16.9.2 Disclosure of reasons for decisions

The need to protect trustees from importuning beneficiaries is evident. However, the courts have gone further and established that trustees will not be compelled to disclose the reasons behind the exercise of a discretion. In *Re Beloved Wilkes's Charity* (1851) 3 Mac & G 440, charity trustees were required to select a boy to be educated for the ministry, preference to be given to boys from four named parishes if a fit candidate could be found. The trustees, without giving reasons, selected a boy who did not come from one of the named parishes but whose brother had put forward his merits to the trustees. It was held that in the absence of evidence that the trustees had exercised their discretion unfairly or dishonestly, the court would not interfere.

This poses an obvious problem for any beneficiary wishing to challenge a decision made by trustees. If trustees are not required to give reasons for their decisions, it will generally be impossible to know whether they have exercised their discretions in a proper manner.

Where trustees declare their reasons
If on the other hand the trustees choose to disclose their reasons, then the court may consider their adequacy. In *Klug* v *Klug* [1918] 2 Ch 67, a trustee whose daughter was a beneficiary refused to consider the exercise of a power of appointment in her favour, and from the correspondence it appeared that her reason was annoyance that the daughter had married without her consent. Neville J held that the trustee had not exercised her discretion at all, and that it was the duty of the court to interfere. Where the trustees take steps to keep the basis of their decisions private, however, there appears to be little that a beneficiary can do if the decision is not obviously unreasonable or fraudulent.

This leads to the question of whether the beneficiaries are entitled to have access to any written records of how the trustees have conducted the trust business. It is usual practice for trustees to keep a trust diary or minute book in which decisions affecting the trust are kept, but there is no requirement that the reasons for trustees' decisions should be recorded. The beneficiaries are, however, entitled to access to documents connected with the trust, known as 'trust documents', and indeed have a proprietary interest in such documents. If those documents disclose the reasons for a decision, this would seem to offer the beneficiaries a way round the difficulty that trustees will not be compelled to disclose reasons.

Trust documents and 'closing the door'
The Court of Appeal, however, in *Re Londonderry's Settlement* [1965] Ch 918, effectively closed this door. In that case a beneficiary, dissatisfied with the sums appointed to her by trustees, pressed them to disclose various documents connected with the settlement. The trustees sought directions from the court. The Court of Appeal found that the category of 'trust documents' had not previously been defined with any degree of clarity, but concluded that all documents held by trustees *qua* trustees are *prima facie* trust documents, but that documents containing confidential matters which a beneficiary is not entitled to know about should not be disclosed, either (in the view of Harman J) because they are protected by analogy with the rule that trustees need not disclose reasons, or (according to Salmon LJ) because a document which a beneficiary is not entitled to see cannot be a trust document.

It would appear, then, that the only way in which a beneficiary can gain sight of documents disclosing the trustees' reasons is to bring a hostile action against the trustees, as a preliminary to which an order for discovery of documents can be sought from the court. Unless the beneficiary already has substantial evidence of misconduct, this course will be fraught with difficulties.

16.9.3 Trust accounts

There is no argument here: beneficiaries are entitled to be informed of the condition of the trust property and trustees must be ready at all times to produce trust accounts. Normally, the beneficiaries will be supplied with copies, perhaps in a simplified form, although strictly they are entitled to see the original accounts and to have copies made at their own expense. Income beneficiaries (e.g., life tenants under a family settlement) are entitled to see the accounts relating to the entire property of the trust, but remaindermen are entitled only to those accounts which relate to capital transactions and may therefore affect their interests.

It is not obligatory or even usual to have trust accounts subjected to an audit, but this may be done, at the absolute discretion of the trustees, who may employ an independent accountant and charge the costs to the trust fund. By s. 22(4) of the Trustee Act 1925, an audit is not to be carried out more frequently than once every three years, unless the nature of the property or other special difficulties so require. Any trustee or beneficiary may apply for an investigation and audit of the trust accounts by virtue of s. 13 of the Public Trustee Act 1906. A copy of the auditor's report is supplied to the applicant and to each trustee.

16.9.4 **Apportionment**

The general duty of trustees to act even-handedly as between the beneficiaries entails the necessity, where there are successive interests under a trust, to take certain steps to ensure that a fair balance is maintained between the capital and income of the trust, so that the former is preserved for those entitled in the future while at the same time allowing a reasonable income to those currently entitled. The rules relating to apportionment are an instance of this principle, and although it is nowadays usual practice to exclude their operation where possible, they are by no means without relevance, particularly in their application to accretions to the trust fund. It has been said that in special circumstances the court itself may direct an apportionment (*Re Kleinwort's Settlement* [1951] Ch 860), but this does not appear to have been done in practice.

16.9.5 *Howe v Earl of Dartmouth*

Some types of property are inherently unsuited to being held for successive interests. A wasting asset, which will soon be used up, provides no benefit to the remaindermen, while a reversionary interest which may not accrue for many years will provide no present income for the life tenant. The obvious way to achieve fairness as between the beneficiaries is therefore to sell the property and invest the proceeds so as to produce an income for the life tenant and an addition to capital for the benefit of the remainderman.

Obviously no problem arises if the trust instrument so directs, e.g., in the case of a trust for sale, but *Howe* v *Earl of Dartmouth* (1802) 7 Ves Jr 137 compels trustees to sell in other circumstances, even if there is no express direction, in some testamentary trusts of personal property (not land). The principle in the case only applies to settlements of the types of property considered in the previous paragraph, and where there is no contrary intention expressed in the will.

Where a duty to convert (i.e., sell) arises under this principle, the normal date at which the property should be converted is one year from the death of the testator, that is, at the end of the 'executors' year' allowed for the administration of the estate to be carried out. If there is power to postpone the sale and conversion, however, this cannot apply, and the valuation for the purposes of apportionment is taken to be the date of the death.

It will usually not be possible to convert and reinvest on either of these specific dates, so some principle is needed for apportioning the income from the asset until actual conversion. This is unnecessary if there is a clear intention that the tenant for life should have the actual income, or if the property is realty (and so not subject to the rule in *Howe* v *Earl of Dartmouth*) and no contrary intention appears, in which event the life tenant will receive the actual income.

Otherwise complex actuarial calculations are required, which turn on the precise nature of the property. For property which produces no present income, such as a reversionary interest, the principles deriving from the decision in *Re Earl of Chesterfield's Trusts* (1883) 24 Ch D 643 apply, and apportionment between capital and income is calculated by a formula. In effect, an assumption is made of 4 per cent interest, compounded annually. Thus, suppose the property produces £1,000 at sale. The capital element will be the amount which if invested at 4 per cent compound interest would have produced £1,000. This will be less than £1,000, and the income will be the rest.

Where the asset produces income, the life tenant is entitled to 4 per cent of its value as interest, and if extra income is actually produced, it accrues to capital.

There is also a formula, based on an assumption of 4 per cent compound interest, for apportioning the payments of liabilities out of the fund (e.g., funeral expenses, debts of the testator) to capital and income. This formula derives from *Allhusen* v *Whittell* (1887) LR 4 Eq 295.

It seems likely that none of these formulae could easily be applied without employing the services of an accountant, to the obvious detriment of the fund. Perhaps for this reason, they are in fact frequently ignored. Another difficulty is that 4 per cent is a very low rate of return today, and it is possible that if the issue were to come again before a court, a higher rate would be considered appropriate, on the principles discussed in chapter 18. This in turn gives rise to a third problem, which is that until that occurs, trustees do not know which interest rate to apply.

It is no surprise, therefore, that the Law Reform Committee, reviewing these principles in its 23rd Report (1982), advocated their replacement with a statutory duty of a more general nature, to hold a fair balance between beneficiaries, with express power to trustees to convert capital to income and vice versa, and a duty to have overall regard to the investments of the trust. The effect of this if enacted would simplify the actuarial calculations required in these situations.

16.9.6 Duty to distribute

This has already been mentioned, and the remedies available to those who suffer as a result of wrongful distribution are considered in chapter 18.

16.10 Trustees' powers and duties in investment and law reform

In 2004 the Law Commission published Consultation Paper No. 175 on *Capital and Income in Trusts: Classification and Apportionment*. This is a very important project in light of this study of trustees' powers and duties relating to investment.

It is described by the Law Commission as a project to reform the complicated rules governing (1) classification of trust receipts and outgoings as 'capital' or 'income', and (2) the requirement that trustees apportion capital and income in order to keep a fair balance between different beneficiaries.

The Consultation's remit and underlying context
The Consultation's remit in this respect has arisen from the reappraisal of trusteeship which arose from the Trustee Act 2000. This text has already made many references to this far-reaching modernisation of the office of trustee, which did of course include provisions relating to investment of trust assets. However, the Law Commission noted in Consultation Paper No. 175 (at para. 1.5) that at the time

when the (then) Trustee Bill was heading towards becoming law, concerns were expressed as to whether the Act would 'tackle the difficulties caused in the management of trust estates by the distinction which trust law draws between income and capital'.

In the Consultation Paper, the Law Commission identified as the principal issues arising from its consideration of how income and capital are classified in trusts law as follows. First, in relation to private trusts:

- appraisal of the rules which govern trusts receipts as income or capital; and
- consideration of the statutory and equitable rules which require conversion of the original trust property or apportionment between the capital and income accounts.

And thereafter, the impact of these rules on charities.

Appraisal of existing rules and proposals for reform
Following publication of the Consultation Paper, the Law Commission has stressed that work on this project has currently been suspended until 2007, to allow the completion of the Cohabitation Project to take place. In the meantime, the provisional recommendations made in the Consultation Paper which relate to *private* trusts are as follows:

- In absence of any contrary provision in the terms of the trust, that the current rules relating to the classification of corporate receipts by trustee-shareholders as income or capital should be replaced by **a simpler alternative based on the form of receipts** (with the rules relating to the classification for other receipts and expenses remaining unaltered).
- To make available to trustees a new '**power of allocation**' in respect of investment returns and trust expenses **as income or capital in so far as is necessary to maintain a balance between income and capital**.
- To **abrogate** all existing **equitable rules of apportionment** (namely, the rules in *Howe* v *Earl of Dartmouth* etc.).
- To **replace** the provisions of the Apportionment Act 1870 in so far as they relate to trusts **with a discretion to apportion periodic payments which accrue from day to day**, when it is just and expedient to do so (and there is no contrary intention shown in the terms of the trust).

 online resource centre

FURTHER READING

All reading which relates to the consideration given to trusteeship across chapters 15, 16 and 18 can be found detailed at the end of chapter 18.

17

Variation of trusts

17.1 Inherent equitable jurisdiction

As a general rule, as we have seen, trustees are bound to carry out the settlor's wishes, and any deviation from the terms of the trust will amount to a breach of trust. Nonetheless, circumstances may arise in which an extension of the trustees' powers, or even a substantial alteration in the beneficial interests of the trust, would be desirable in the interests of efficient administration, or for the sake of preserving the value of the beneficiaries' entitlements.

The main reason for wishing to vary trusts is to reduce liability to taxation, and that is what this chapter is really about. Yet although equity permits trustees discretion, as we have seen, in many aspects of performing the trust, it does not generally allow them to recast its terms. Until recent statutory reforms, therefore, powers to vary have been extremely limited, especially where tax planning is the motive.

There are nevertheless circumstances apart from those provided for by statute where variation is possible.

17.1.1 Express powers to vary

Obviously the trust instrument itself may have been drafted so as to confer upon the trustees powers far wider than those contemplated by the general law. Modern trust instruments generally contrive to allow the trustees considerable discretionary powers, and not uncommonly provide for variation of the beneficial interests themselves, by means of suitably drafted powers of appointment. The terms of such powers must, of course, be strictly observed, but it is often possible through careful drafting to obviate the need for recourse to more complex variation procedures. Reliance upon express powers contained in the trust instrument, needless to say, creates no exception to the duty not to deviate from the terms of the trust, for such powers are themselves among the terms of the trust.

17.1.2 *Saunders v Vautier*

In the absence of express powers, it may be possible to effect a variation in the trust by taking advantage of the rule in *Saunders* v *Vautier* (1841) 10 LJ Ch 354. Collectively, the beneficiaries, so long as they are all adult, *sui iuris* and between them entitled to the entirety of the trust property, can bring the trust to an end and resettle the property on any terms they wish. Thus, in a simple settlement of property upon a life interest for X with remainder for Y, X and Y may agree to end the trust and divide the capital between them immediately. More complex settlements may require more sophisticated measures, involving perhaps the actuarial valuation of future entitlements, and possibly the need for insurance against any risk of loss, but the principles are basically the same.

Variation with the collective consent of the beneficiaries
The beneficiaries can also collectively consent to any act by the trustees which has the effect of varying the terms of the trust, without going through the process of dissolving and resettling the property which may involve a number of separate conveyances, all attracting stamp duty. It is very important, however, to appreciate the limits of the *Saunders* v *Vautier* doctrine.

First, it depends on the beneficiaries all being collectively entitled. Thus, donees under a power cannot use it, and though beneficiaries under a discretionary trust usually can, they will not be able to unless the entire class of objects is ascertainable. Second, it turns upon all the beneficiaries being able to consent to dissolve the trust, or to what would otherwise be a breach of trust by the trustees. If some of the beneficiaries are infants, or if the settlement creates any interests in favour of persons who are not yet born or ascertained, variation of the trust upon this basis will not be possible. This is a serious limitation when dealing with family settlements of the usual type, which almost invariably give interests to non *sui iuris* persons. As will appear below, this is the difficulty tackled by the Variation of Trusts Act 1958.

Third, unless the trustees also agree, the beneficiaries cannot vary an existing trust, and keep it on foot, instead of dissolving it and resettling the property. *Re Brockbank* [1948] Ch 206 has already been discussed in 15.1.4.4. Although the *ratio* of the case (which does not survive the enactment of the Trusts of Land and Appointment of Trustees Act 1996) is confined to the appointment of new trustees under s. 36 of the Trustee Act 1925, there are remarks by Vaisey J of a much wider scope:

> It seems to me that the beneficiaries must choose between two alternatives: either they must keep the trusts of the will on foot, in which case those trusts must continue to be executed by trustees ... not ... arbitrarily selected by themselves; or they must, by mutual agreement, extinguish and put an end to the trusts.... .

Walton J expressed similar views in *Stephenson* v *Barclays Bank Trust Co. Ltd* [1975] 1 WLR 88. One of the reasons he gave was that otherwise the beneficiaries could force upon the trustees duties quite different to those they had originally accepted. This reasoning would seem to survive the 1996 Act.

17.1.3 Limited inherent jurisdiction of courts to vary trusts

The problem arises with persons unable to give consent, especially children and unborn persons. As will shortly be explained, the Variation of Trusts Act 1958 confers upon the court a discretion to give its approval to a proposed variation on behalf of such persons if the court is satisfied that such a variation would be for their benefit. Before considering the effect of that Act and other statutory provisions, however, it is necessary to outline the extent to which the courts have traditionally been willing to permit a variation of trust under their inherent jurisdiction, where not all beneficiaries are adult and *sui iuris*.

It has long been recognised that the court may, in the case of necessity, permit the trustees to take measures not authorised by the trust instrument. In *Chapman* v

Chapman [1954] AC 429, the House of Lords indicated that this inherent jurisdiction is narrow, encompassing for the most part only emergency and salvage. Originally, this seems to have been confined to cases where some act of salvage was urgently required, such as the mortgage of an infant's property in order to raise money for vital repairs. Gradually, it was widened to cover other contingencies not foreseen and provided for by the settlor, but the House of Lords reaffirmed in *Chapman* v *Chapman*, unanimously approving the formulation of Romer LJ in *Re New* [1901] 2 Ch 534, that some element of emergency still needs to be shown.

Chapman v *Chapman* applies only to variations in the *beneficial interests* as such. There is a wider inherent jurisdiction regarding the administration of the trust fund. For example, as seen earlier, in *Re Duke of Norfolk's ST* [1982] Ch 61, the court authorised payment of remuneration to a trustee under its inherent jurisdiction (considered in chapter 15).

The courts may also approve compromises of disputes regarding the beneficial entitlements on behalf of infant or future beneficiaries. Arguably, this is not a matter of genuine variation of the trust, since by definition its terms are not clear: hence the dispute. The courts, however, showed a willingness to extend the term 'compromise' to cover situations where no real dispute had arisen, and approval was sometimes granted to what were, in reality, mere variations worked out between the beneficiaries. This broad conception of the inherent jurisdiction was firmly disapproved by the House of Lords in *Chapman* v *Chapman*, and held to be confined to instances where a genuine element of dispute exists.

Thus, in *Re Powell-Cotton's Resettlement* [1956] 1 All ER 60, the Court of Appeal decided that there were no disputed rights where an investment clause was ambiguous and it would have been advantageous to the beneficiaries to replace it with a new clause. In *Mason* v *Farbrother* [1983] 2 All ER 1078, genuine points of difference were found to have arisen where two contending interpretations of an investment clause had widely different implications for the permitted range of investments. The court, however, was reluctant to approve the substitution of a new clause under its inherent jurisdiction, preferring to rely upon s. 57 of the Trustee Act 1925. In *Allen* v *Distillers Co. (Biochemicals) Ltd* [1974] QB 384, the court was asked to approve a settlement of the claims of the child victims of the drug thalidomide, and the question arose as to whether the court could postpone the vesting of capital in the children to an age greater than 18. Eveleigh J, on the basis of the rule in *Saunders* v *Vautier*, held there was no inherent jurisdiction to order such a postponement, but found it to be authorised by the terms of the settlement itself.

Clearly, therefore, the inherent equitable jurisdiction is of limited value to those whose main motive for variation is to reduce liability for taxation.

17.2 Statutory powers to vary trusts apart from the Variation of Trusts Act 1958

17.2.1 Matrimonial Causes Act 1973

The narrowness of the court's inherent jurisdiction to give approval to variations in the terms of trust is offset by several statutory provisions. A particularly useful and important addition to the jurisdiction was made by the Matrimonial Causes Act 1973, which, by ss. 24 and 25, gives a wide power to make orders affecting the property of parties to matrimonial proceedings, so as to avoid the unfairness which sometimes arose where the property of a married couple, in particular the matrimonial home, came under the rules governing resulting trusts (see chapter 9). The court may order provision for either spouse to be made by payments in cash, by transfers of property or by the creation of a settlement for the benefit of a spouse and children.

More important in the context of variation, s. 24(1)(c) and (d) allow for variation of an ante or post-nuptial settlement, including settlements made by will or codicil, and also permit the making of an order extinguishing or reducing the interest of either of the spouses under such a settlement. The term 'settlement' has been widely interpreted to include any provision (other than outright gifts) made for the benefit of the parties to a marriage, whether by themselves or by a third party, and the acquisition of a matrimonial home has been held to be a settlement (*Ulrich v Ulrich* [1968] 1 WLR 180). Further, the court has the power to vary or discharge any order for a settlement or variation under s. 24(1) made on or after a decree of judicial separation if the separation order is rescinded or the marriage subsequently dissolved.

17.2.2 **Mental Health Act 1983**

The power given by s. 96(1)(d) of the Mental Health Act 1983 to the Court of Protection to make a settlement of a patient's property also allows the judge to vary the settlement as he thinks fit if it transpires that some material fact was not disclosed when the settlement was made, or if substantial changes in circumstances arise.

17.2.3 **General powers in the 1925 legislation**

The above provisions are designed to meet rather special situations. More general powers may be made available to trustees by virtue of provisions contained in the Trustee Act 1925 and the Settled Land Act 1925. Section 57(1) of the Trustee Act 1925 in effect widens the inherent jurisdiction with regard to 'emergency' by making the jurisdiction available in any case where it is 'expedient':

(1) Where in the management or administration of any property vested in trustees, any sale, lease, mortgage, surrender, release or other disposition, or any purchase, investment, acquisition, expenditure, or other transaction, is in the opinion of the court expedient, but the same cannot be effected by reason of the absence of any power for that purpose vested in the trustees by the trust instrument, if any, or by law, the court may by order confer upon the trustees, either generally or in any particular instance, the necessary power for the purpose, on such terms, and subject to such provisions and conditions, if any, as the court may think fit and may direct in what manner any money authorised to be expended, and the costs of any transaction, are to be paid or borne as between capital and income.

The section operates as though its provisions were to be read into every settlement, but it is clearly limited to matters falling within the management or administration of the trust property and does not permit the alteration of beneficial interests under the trust.

Applications under the section are usually heard in chambers and so are not generally reported, but the few reported cases show that it has been used to authorise a sale of settled chattels, to partition or sell land where necessary consents had been refused, to purchase a residence for the tenant for life, and to sell prematurely a reversionary interest.

Settlements of land do not fall within s. 57(1) of the Trustee Act 1925, but they may be varied by recourse to s. 64(1) of the Settled Land Act 1925, which allows the court to make an order authorising the tenant for life to effect any transaction affecting or concerning the settled land or any part of it, if the court is of the opinion that the transaction would be for the benefit of the settled land or any part of it, or of the persons interested under the settlement. The transaction must be one which could have been effected by an absolute owner. The section is not confined to cases of management or administration alone, although it includes such purposes and allows alteration of the beneficial interests with a view to reducing tax liability. In the days of estate duty, the especial vulnerability of the strict settlement to onerous charges might be mitigated by rearrangement of the beneficial interests under this section.

This section was invoked by Morritt J in *Hambro* v *Duke of Marlborough* [1994] Ch 158, to allow the eleventh Duke of Marlborough (as tenant for life) to execute a conveyance the effect of which was to disinherit the Marquis of Blandford, who (the trustees had concluded) displayed unbusinesslike habits and lack of responsibility.

The Settled Land and Trustee Acts (Court's General Powers) Act 1943, as amended by the Emergency Laws (Miscellaneous Provisions) Act 1953, permanently extends the court's jurisdiction to authorise the expense of any action taken in the management of settled land or land held on trust for sale in the context of ss. 57 and 64 to be treated as a capital outgoing where the action is beneficial and the income insufficient to bear the expense.

The inherent jurisdiction to make provision for infants is somewhat extended by s. 53 of the Trustee Act 1925, which allows the court to authorise dealings with the infant's property with a view to application of the capital or income for the infant's maintenance, education or benefit. 'Benefit' has been interpreted to cover dealings having the effect of reducing estate duty for the benefit of the infant (*Re Meux* [1958] Ch 154).

In that case, the proceeds of sale of property were to be resettled upon the infant, and so could be regarded as an 'application' for the infant's benefit. However, in *Re Hayworth's Contingent Reversionary Interest* [1956] Ch 364, a proposal to sell an infant's contingent reversionary interest to the life tenant for cash, thus ending the trusts, was thought not to be for the 'benefit' of the infant. Other types of dealing approved under the section have included the barring of entails to exclude remote beneficiaries (*Re Gower's Settlement* [1934] Ch 365) or to simplify a proposed application to the court for approval of a further variation under the Variation of Trusts Act 1958 (*Re Bristol's Settled Estates* [1965] 1 WLR 469).

17.3 **Variation of Trusts Act 1958**

The decision of the House of Lords in *Chapman* v *Chapman* [1954] AC 429 curtailed, as explained above, the broad approach previously developed by the courts in the exercise of the inherent jurisdiction to approve compromises or 'disputes', and the

Law Reform Committee was asked to consider the question of the court's powers to sanction variations (see Law Reform Committee, *Court's Power to Sanction Variation of Trusts* (Cmnd 310, 1957)). The Variation of Trusts Act 1958 was based on these recommendations and provides a new statutory jurisdiction independent of the Trustee Act 1925 or the Settled Land Act 1925.

Under s. 1(1) of the 1958 Act, the court has discretion to approve, on behalf of the following categories of person, any arrangement varying or revoking all or any of the trusts, or enlarging the trustees' powers of management and administration over the property subject to the trusts. The categories are as follows:

(a) infants or people who are mentally incapacitated; or

(b) people who have a mere expectation of benefiting under the trusts, but those with interests, whether vested or contingent, should consent on their own behalf (see further below); or

(c) any person unborn; or

(d) any person with a discretionary interest under a protective trust.

Proposals to vary the beneficial interests under a trust may be approved, provided (except in the case of para. (d) persons) that the court is satisfied that such variation will be for the benefit of the persons on behalf of whom approval is given. In deciding whether to approve a proposed settlement, the court will consider the arrangement as a whole since it is the arrangement which has to be approved and not just those aspects of it which happen to affect a person on whose behalf the court is being asked to consent.

17.3.1 Use of the 1958 Act

Where an extension of the trustee's powers of management is sought, the jurisdiction of the Act is invoked in preference to s. 57 of the Trustee Act 1925 wherever possible. The courts have shown themselves willing to approve the insertion of powers of advancement or a period of accumulation, or to terminate an accumulation, among other matters.

So far as investment is concerned, in *Trustees of the British Museum* v *Attorney-General* [1984] 1 WLR 418, Sir Robert Megarry V-C took the view that the powers conferred by the (then in force) Trustee Investments Act 1961 were becoming outdated, and that the effects of inflation and the character of the trust may amount to special circumstances in which it would be proper to give approval under the 1958 Act. The decision was based on the changes of investment pattern, including the movement from fixed interest investments to investments in equities and property, that had occurred between 1961 and 1983.

The reasoning is by no means of universal application, however, and indeed, Sir Robert Megarry V-C's judgment is in quite restricted terms. At the time of the case, investing in equities was relatively risk-free, and there had been a more or less continuous bull market for some eight years. That is not the case today. Sir Robert Megarry V-C also said:

The size of the fund may be very material. A fund that is very large may well justify a latitude of investment that would be denied to a more modest fund; for the spread of investments possible for a larger fund may justify the greater risks that wider powers will permit to be taken.

The main application of the Variation of Trusts Act 1958 has been to vary the beneficial interests for tax-saving purposes, and this has been assumed to be its natural sphere of operation. Some would argue that those who, like infants and the unborn, cannot give a valid consent to schemes which would be for their benefit, should not be deprived of the advantages which their adult counterparts could obtain on *Saunders* v *Vautier* principles; nor should their incapacity prevent the opportunity of gain to the trust as a whole.

17.3.2 Persons on whose behalf the court may give its approval

The way in which the statute works is to allow the court to give consent on behalf of *non sui iuris* beneficiaries, but the principles underlying the rule in *Saunders* v *Vautier* were preserved by the Act inasmuch as the court will not provide a consent which ought properly to be sought from an ascertainable adult, *sui iuris* beneficiary. Hence, the limits placed on para. (b) of s. 1(1).

The difficulty with para. (b) arises with interests which are very remote, such as interests in default of appointment, or in the event of a failure of the trust. The subsection allows the court to consent on behalf of:

any person (whether ascertained or not) who may become entitled, directly or indirectly, to an interest under the trusts as being at a future date or on the happening of a future event a person of any specified description or a member of any specified class of persons, so however that this paragraph shall not include any person who would be of that description, or a member of that class, as the case may be, if the said date had fallen or the said event had happened at the date of the application to the court.

It is the words after 'so however' which cause the problem since those persons have to consent on their own behalf: the court cannot consent for them. There is no problem over, for example, potential future spouses, since they clearly have a mere expectation of succeeding. They clearly come within the first part of para. (b) and the court can consent on their behalf. But if somebody is named in the instrument as having a contingent interest, however unlikely that contingency is to arise, the court cannot consent on his or her behalf. They must consent themselves to any variation.

The scope and limitation of the 1958 Act
This can seriously limit the scope of the 1958 Act. For example, in *Re Suffert's Settlement* [1961] Ch 1, the court could not consent on behalf of a cousin who benefited only if Miss Suffert died without issue, and even then subject to a general testamentary power of appointment. Other examples are *Re Moncrieff's ST* [1962] 1 WLR 1344, and *Knocker* v *Youle* [1986] 1 WLR 934. In the latter case the court could not consent on behalf of sisters who would benefit only in the event of failure or determination of the trust, and Warner J felt constrained to adopt a fairly literal interpretation of the Act.

The application should be made by a beneficiary, preferably by the person currently receiving the income, but the settlor may also apply, and as a last resort the trustees may apply if no one else will apply and the variation is in the interests of the beneficiaries. Otherwise, it is undesirable for trustees to apply, as their position as applicants may conflict with their duty impartially to guard the interests of the beneficiaries. The settlor, if living, and all the beneficiaries, including minors, should be made parties, special attention being paid to ensure proper representation for minors and the unborn.

17.3.3 What is benefit?

The general scheme of the 1958 Act is to give a wide discretion to the courts, but the one limit on the discretion is that, except for persons within para. (d), the court may not approve a variation unless it is satisfied that such variation will be for the benefit of those persons on behalf of whom approval for the variation is given. Stamp J took the view in *Re Cohen's ST* [1965] 1 WLR 1229 that the benefit must be to those persons considered as individuals and not merely as members of a class.

The benefit requirement does not extend expressly to a variation proposed on behalf of a beneficiary under a discretionary protective trust (para. (d)) but the court has an unfettered discretion as to the exercise of its powers under the Act, and in *Re Steed's WT* [1960] Ch 407 the Court of Appeal refused its consent in such a case where it thought no benefit was shown (see further below).

17.3.3.1 *Nature of benefit*

It is not possible to state categorically what the court will regard as benefit, except that it will adopt the test of what a reasonable *sui iuris* adult beneficiary would have done in the circumstances.

Financial benefit is clearly included, and most tax-saving schemes will satisfy the requirement since such saving preserves the total quantum of property available for distribution among the beneficiaries.

Assessing financial benefit: long term considerations v short term considerations
In assessing financial benefit, the court may have to balance short-term against long-term factors, and take account of the character of the persons on whose behalf approval is sought. In *Re Towler's ST* [1964] Ch 158, Wilberforce J was prepared to postpone the vesting of capital to which a beneficiary was soon to become entitled, upon evidence that she was likely to deal with it imprudently. In *Re Steed's WT* [1960] Ch 407, the proposed scheme was for the elimination of the protective element in a trust relating to land. The principal beneficiary, who was a life tenant (but not *sui iuris* because of the protective element), wanted a variation such that the trustees held the property on trust for herself absolutely. Clearly, this was in theory to her financial advantage, but evidence suggested that advantage would in fact be taken of the life tenant's good nature by the very persons against whose importuning the settlor had meant to protect her, and the Court of Appeal refused its consent (considered shortly).

Though it will be rare for the court to look beyond the financial advantages contained in the proposed arrangement, the unfettered discretion given by the Act to the courts can lead them to refuse a variation where there is a clear financial benefit. In *Re Weston's Settlements* [1969] 1 Ch 223, the Court of Appeal refused to approve a scheme which would have removed the trusts to a tax haven (Jersey), where the family had moved three months previously, on the ground that the moral and social benefits of an English upbringing were not outweighed by the tax savings to be enjoyed by the infant beneficiaries. Harman LJ said that 'this is an essay in tax avoidance naked and unashamed', and Lord Denning MR noted (at p. 245) that:

There are many things in life more worth while than money. One of these things is to be brought up in this our England, which is still 'the envy of less happier lands'. I do not believe it is for the benefit of children to be uprooted from England and transported to another country simply to avoid tax ... Many a child has been ruined by being given too much. The avoidance of tax may be lawful, but it is not yet a virtue.

Re Weston is perhaps atypical, and the court will not always refuse approval to the removal of a trust from the jurisdiction. It will depend on the circumstances. In *Re Windeatt's WT* [1969] 1 WLR 692, a similar scheme was approved by Pennycuick J, but there the family had already been in Jersey for 19 years and the children had been born there: there was no question of uprooting them. Similarly, in *Re Seale's Marriage Settlement* [1961] Ch 574, Buckley J approved a scheme removing the trusts to Canada, to which country again the family had moved many years previously, with no thought of tax avoidance, and had brought up the children as Canadians.

In reality, the use of the 1958 Act to export trusts is quite common, but *Re Weston* shows that all circumstances will be taken into account, and that the existence of a clear financial benefit will not necessarily be conclusive.

Another possibility, included for the sake of completeness, is that some beneficiaries will benefit at the expense of others. An example is *Re Remnant's ST* [1970] Ch 560, where Pennycuick J approved the deletion of a forfeiture clause in respect of children who became Roman Catholics. Some of the children were Protestant and others Roman Catholic, but the court approved the deletion of the clause on policy grounds (as being liable to cause serious dissension within the family) although this was clearly to the disadvantage of the Protestant children. The settlor's intentions were also not considered conclusive (indeed, they were overridden).

The courts may go further and approve schemes where there is a positive disadvantage in material terms. In *Re CL* [1969] 1 Ch 587, the Court of Protection held that there was a benefit to an elderly mental patient in giving up, in return for no consideration, her life interests for the benefit of adopted daughters. This was, in effect, giving approval to a straightforward gift by the beneficiary, from which in strictly material terms she could not possibly benefit. The lady's needs were otherwise amply provided for, however, and the court, in approving the arrangement, took the view that it was acting as she herself would have done, had she been able to appreciate her family responsibilities.

These cases should not be regarded as typical, however. Assuming that a proposed arrangement is otherwise unobjectionable, it will be rare for the court to look beyond the financial advantages contained therein.

17.3.3.2 *Extent of court's discretion*

The only constraint on the court's discretion under the Act is the requirement that it must be satisfied of a benefit, except in the case of para. (d) persons. However, even if it is clear that the court has *jurisdiction* to consent to a variation, it has an unfettered discretion to exercise its powers under the Act '*if it thinks fit*'. Thus, whereas the court cannot approve a variation except where the Act so provides, it has an unlimited discretion to refuse its approval where it is given jurisdiction under the Act.

It follows that, even where a benefit is clearly shown for the persons on whose behalf approval is sought, the court is not required to approve. For para. (d) persons, it is not even required that a benefit be shown, yet the court, in its discretion, refused to approve a variation in *Re Steed's WT* [1960] Ch 407.

17.3.3.3 *Relevance of settlor's views*

In *Re Steed's WT* [1960] Ch 407, the Court of Appeal was undoubtedly influenced by the views of the settlor, who in his will had clearly expressed his concern about the welfare of the beneficiary under the protective trust, for whom approval was sought. Yet though the settlor's views can be relevant, they are rarely paramount; they were overridden in *Re Remnant's ST* [1970] Ch 560, and it was the settlor who applied for the variation in *Re Weston's Settlements* [1969] 1 Ch 223 (see above). Moreover, the Court of Appeal held in *Goulding* v *James* [1997] 2 All ER 239 that they have no relevance at all unless they relate to someone on whose behalf the court's approval is required. In *Goulding* v *James*, the proposed variation (which was clearly for the benefit of the testatrix's unborn great grandchildren for whom approval was sought) would have frustrated her desire to restrict the ability of two adult, *sui iuris* beneficiaries to touch the capital of the estate. Since the court's approval was not required for the adult beneficiaries, however, who were able to consent for themselves, the settlor's views were entirely irrelevant.

17.3.3.4 *Risks*

Sometimes, a proposed arrangement may involve some element of risk to the beneficiary for whom the court is asked to consent. An element of risk will not prevent the court from approving the arrangement if the risk is one which an adult beneficiary would be prepared to take. Such a test was applied by Danckwerts J in *Re Cohen's WT* [1959] 1 WLR 865.

In *Re Robinson's ST* [1976] 1 WLR 806, the fund was held on trust for the claimant for her life, with remainders over to her children, one of whom was under 21 (the age of majority at the time). The claimant was 55 and expected to live for many years. The variation proposed was to divide up the fund, giving the claimant an immediate capital share of 52 per cent (the actuarial capitalised value of her share), the children dividing the balance in equal shares. The children who got their share immediately, and those who were over 21 consented to the variation. The court was asked to approve variation on behalf of Nicola (who was 17).

Before the introduction of capital transfer tax in 1975, division of the fund in this way, by giving the children their interests immediately rather than on the death of the life tenant, was almost certain to reduce liability to estate duty, because at that time there was no liability to estate duty on any advance made more than seven years before the death of the life tenant. The same is true today under inheritance tax. However, for a short period following the Finance Act 1975, which introduced capital transfer tax, all *inter vivos* gifts were also taxable, albeit that liability was lower so long as the transfer was made more than three years before the death of the life tenant.

At the time of *Re Robinson's ST*, therefore, the division would not necessarily have favoured Nicola. The transfer would have been taxed immediately so that the value of the fund would be reduced. On the other hand, Nicola would get her share immediately and not have to wait for the death of her mother. Whether this would be to her benefit or not would depend entirely on how long her mother was likely to live. If she died immediately, Nicola's share would be less than she would have received under the unvaried trust since tax would have been paid on it. It was calculated, however, that, given the mother's life expectancy, the deficiency would be made up in income on her share between the date of the variation and her mother's death.

Templeman J took the view that the court should require evidence that the infant would at least not be materially worse off as a result of the variation. He adopted as the test whether an adult beneficiary would have been prepared to take the risk: a 'broad' view might be taken, but not a 'galloping, gambling view'. The arrangement was approved subject to a policy of insurance to protect the infant's interests, but Templeman J did not require the entirety of the possible loss to be covered, the view being taken that the saving in premium on a lesser cover was worth the small risk.

A diagramatic representation of *Re Robinson's ST* can be found in figure 17.1.

A different type of case was *Re Holt's Settlement* [1969] 1 Ch 100. The trust provided for a life interest of personal property for Mrs Wilson, and then to her children at 21 in equal shares. The variation proposed was that Mrs Wilson should surrender the income of one half of her life interest to the fund, but another effect of the proposed variation was to postpone the vesting of the children's interests until 30. The court was asked to approve the variation on behalf of Mrs Wilson's three children who were 10, 7 and 6.

The surrender of the income (whose real purpose was to reduce Mrs Wilson's liability to surtax) was also clearly to the advantage of the children, since the value of the trust property would be increased. However, the postponement to 30 (on the grounds that it would be undesirable for Mrs Wilson's children to receive a large income from 21) was clearly to their disadvantage. Megarry J approved the variation on the same test adopted in *Re Robinson*.

17.3.3.5 *Benefit must be to individuals, not just class as a whole*

In *Re Cohen's ST* [1965] 1 WLR 1229, Stamp J held that in considering questions of benefit under the 1958 Act, the court was being asked to consent on behalf of *non sui iuris* beneficiaries considered as individuals, and not merely as members of a

		Mrs Robinson	Children
Before proposed variation	Capital	Life interest on 100%	Remainder on all, but subject to CTT
	Income	Income on all until death	Income on all, but only after Mrs R's death
After proposed variation	Capital	52% immediately	48% immediately, maybe lower CTT
	Income	Immediate income on 52%	Immediate income on 48%

Figure 17.1 *Re Robinson's ST* [1976] 1 WLR 806

class. It follows that if only one member of the class can be envisaged who cannot possibly benefit from the proposed variation, even if the class as a whole will benefit, the court will refuse its consent.

In *Re Cohen's ST*, the variation sought, with a view to saving estate duty, was to substitute for the death of the life tenant (who was an elderly lady), a specified date (30 June 1973) for the vesting of her grandchildren's interests. It was very unlikely that the life tenant would survive beyond 30 June 1973, although of course it was a theoretical possibility. Consent was sought on behalf of infant and unborn beneficiaries.

There was no problem regarding the infant beneficiaries, although even here, an element of risk was involved. They all stood to gain from the tax advantages of the proposed variation. If, however, the life tenant died before 30 June 1973, any infant grandchild who died between her death and the specified date would inevitably lose out (the grandchild would have taken under the unvaried, but not under the varied settlement). Also, the share of all the infant beneficiaries would be reduced if further grandchildren were born between her death and the specified date. On balance, however, these risks would be worth taking given the likely saving in estate duty (the principles applicable being those considered in the previous section).

Risks beneficiaries and unborn grandchildren
The difficulty concerned unborn grandchildren. Although it was unlikely, it was theoretically possible for the life tenant to live beyond the specified date. Had she done so, it was also theoretically possible for an unborn grandchild to be born after 30 June 1973, but before the life tenant's death. Any such grandchild would take under the unvaried settlement, but not under the proposed variation, and therefore could not possibly benefit from the variation. Of course, the chances of *both* these events occurring were very low, and it may well be thought that the class of unborn grandchildren, as a whole, might be prepared to take the risk of the life tenant living beyond the specified date, and having further grandchildren before she died. Weighed against the tax advantages of the proposed variation, it might be thought that any reasonable unborn grandchild would be prepared to take this risk.

Stamp J held that it is not permissible only to consider the position of the class as a whole. If any individual grandchild was born after the specified date, but before the life tenant's death, then under the proposed variation, he or she would lose his or her entire interest. That individual would clearly not consent, since he or she would have no conceivable benefit. Since it was therefore possible to envisage unborn persons who could not possibly benefit, this was fatal to the proposed variation, and Stamp J refused his consent. It was not enough that the proposed variation would benefit the class as a whole, if it were possible to envisage *a single individual* who could not possibly benefit.

The argument that any unborn individual would have a greater chance of being born before 30 June 1973, because (since the life tenant was unlikely to live that long) more time would probably be available in which to be born, was also rejected on the ground that the court would not ascribe chances to a disembodied spirit. Stamp J observed:

Now it is of course perfectly true that as a result of this variation there would be a greater chance of there being some person or persons now unborn becoming beneficially interested in the trust fund [by being born], but to say that some particular unborn person will, immediately on the variation taking effect, have a better chance of being born within the qualifying period or a better chance of satisfying the necessary conditions seems to me to involve an excursion into metaphysics, on which I am unwilling to embark. Such a proposition seems to me to involve the logical conclusion that the court must regard one whose body may come into the existence in the future as having nevertheless such a present imaginary existence as to enable the court to ascribe to him a present chance of coming into existence at some specific time or during some specified period. My mind recoils at the idea of the unborn having prior to his birth such an identity as to enable the court to ascribe to him any such chance, or to enable one to say that he can more or less easily satisfy a condition of coming into existence during some particular period.

Only once birth (albeit in the future) had occurred could chances of benefit be ascribed to any individual.

Re Cohen's ST was distinguished in *Re Holt's Settlement* [1969] 1 Ch 100. There, the settlement was in essence that Mrs Wilson gave up part of her income from the fund (so increasing the size of the fund), but vesting of the children's interest in possession would be postponed. If a child was born the year after the variation, and his mother died very soon afterwards, that child could not possibly benefit. The benefit from Mrs Wilson surrendering part of her income under the trust would be minimal if Mrs Wilson died soon after the birth, whereas the postponement would operate entirely to his or her disadvantage. *Re Cohen's ST* was distinguished, however, because here two chances had to occur: that of the unborn person being born next year, and secondly, that child having been born (and thus become a legal entity), his or her mother dying shortly afterwards. The first chance could be disregarded on *Cohen* principles, but not the second. Both were independently unlikely possibilities, so approval for the scheme was given. Even once the theoretical unborn child had been born, he or she would still have been well advised to agree to the variation, and accept the slight risk of his or her mother dying shortly afterwards.

It follows that the reasoning in *Cohen* applies only when the date of *vesting in interest* (or in other words the date on closing the class) is altered, and does not apply merely to alterations in *vesting in possession* (see further on this distinction, chapter 6).

It might be objected that two independent chances also had to occur in *Cohen* before an unborn beneficiary was certain to lose: first, the hypothetical beneficiary being born after 30 June 1973 and, second, the life tenant living beyond the date of his or her birth. However, no unborn beneficiary born after 30 June 1973 could possibly gain from the variation, and might lose, so there could be no advantage in the hypothetical beneficiary consenting to the variation. In this regard, the proposed variation in *Re Cohen's ST* differed from that in *Re Holt's Settlement*, where the hypothetical beneficiary had a good chance of benefiting from the variation.

17.3.4 **Variation or resettlement?**

According to Megarry J in *Re Ball's Settlement* [1968] 1 WLR 899, the courts will not approve a proposal for a total resettlement which alters completely the substratum of the trust. This is a question of substance not form.

17.3.5 **Juristic basis of variation**

In *Re Holmden's ST* [1968] AC 685, Lord Reid took the view that a variation under the 1958 Act must be regarded as one made by the beneficiaries themselves, rather than by the court, with the court acting merely on behalf of those beneficiaries who are unable to give their own consent and approval. His view did not form part of the *ratio* of the case, nor was it explicitly shared by his Brethren, but it was accepted as being good law by the Court of Appeal in *Goulding* v *James* [1997] 2 All ER 239, probably as part of the *ratio*, since it followed that the adult *sui iuris* beneficiaries could consent to the variation for themselves, and that any reservations the settlor might have had were irrelevant. Since, however, as we saw earlier, even where all beneficiaries are *sui iuris* and consenting they may not be able to vary the trusts in all circumstances, it must follow that the jurisdiction under the Act takes the form of a *Saunders* v *Vautier* revocation, followed by a re-settlement (this presumably requires the consent of the trustees, since the re-settlement cannot be forced on them against their will).

On this view of the matter, however, it arguably follows that the adult beneficiaries at least ought to give their consents in writing so as to comply with s. 53(1)(c) of the Law of Property Act 1925. In fact, however, variations are seldom in writing. In *Re Viscount Hambleden's WT* [1960] 1 WLR 82, it had been stated that the court's approval was effective for all purposes to vary the trusts, and this has been relied upon in countless subsequent instances. The problem was posed directly in *Re Holt's Settlement*, considered above, where Megarry J, aware that possibly thousands of variations had been acted upon without writing conforming with s. 53(1)(c), accepted, though without enthusiasm, two grounds put forward by counsel in favour of the view that no writing was necessary.

First, it might be said that in conferring express power upon the court to make an order, Parliament had impliedly created an exception to s. 53. Second, and alternatively, the arrangement might be regarded as one in which the beneficial interests passed to their respective purchasers upon the making of the agreement, that agreement itself being specifically enforceable. The original interests under the (unvaried) trusts would thus be held, from the moment of the agreement, upon constructive trusts identical to the new (varied) trusts and, as constructive trusts, would be exempt from writing under s. 53(2). Whether or not these reasons are regarded as adequate, the assumption that no writing is required has continued to prevail.

The point was also important in *Re Holt's Settlement* because the order of the court took effect after 15 July 1964, whereas the original trust had been set up in 1959, and Megarry J thought that the provisions of the Perpetuities and Accumulations Act 1964 (see chapter 6) could apply. If all the court had done had been to provide consent then the perpetuity period would have been that applicable to a 1959 instrument (i.e., the common law period).

 online resource centre

FURTHER READING

Riddall [1987] Conv 144.

18

Breach of trust

18.1 A question of liability: what is breach of trust?

This chapter follows consideration given to the nature of trusteeship in chapter 15, and the nature of duties which arise from this, examined in some detail in chapter 16. In terms of 'locating' breach of trust within this text's overall coverage of trustee-ship, generally speaking, any failure to comply with the duties laid upon the trustee will amount to breach of trust. This is so whether the duties arise from the trust instrument itself, where there is one, or whether they arise from obligations imposed by equity. Such failure may take the form of some positive action, such as investing in unauthorised securities, or an omission, such as neglecting to have the trust property placed in the name of the trustee. Even a merely technical act of maladministration may result in liability if in fact it causes a loss to the trust estate. This can be illustrated by reference to *Armitage v Nurse* [1998] Ch 241, in which according to Millett LJ (at 251):

> Breaches of trust are of many different kinds. A breach of trust may be deliberate or inadvertent; it may consist of an actual misappropriation or misapplication of the trust property or merely of an investment or other dealing which is outside the trustees' powers; it may consist of a fail-ure to carry out a positive obligation of the trustees or merely of a want of skill and care on their part in the management of the trust property; it may be injurious to the interests of the beneficiaries or be actually to their benefit.

In addition, at least in the case of an express trust, it does not matter how the trust was created (although the duties imposed on constructive trustees, as we have seen, may be less). Volunteer beneficiaries are entitled to have their interests protected to the same extent as those who have given consideration, and it is of no relevance either that the trust was created voluntarily by the same person who, in his capacity as trustee, is now charged with breach of trust. In other words, a settlor-trustee is liable to the same extent as any other trustee.

18.1.1 Basis of liability

The basis of a trustee's liability is compensation to the beneficiaries for whatever loss may have resulted from the breach, or, if an unauthorised profit has been made, the restoration to the beneficiaries of property rightfully belonging to the trust. The objective is not to punish the trustee, so his personal fault is immaterial once a breach is established. Of course, fault in an objective sense may be relevant to the question as to whether there has in fact been a breach, there being, as we have seen, a general standard of care based on normal business practice.

In many of the cases considered earlier, the trust had generally not suffered a large loss, and the remedy sought against the defendant was actually account of profits. In most of the cases considered in this chapter, the remedy sought is compensation for breach. In *Target Holdings Ltd* v *Redferns* [1995] 3 WLR 352, the House of Lords held that this is governed by principles similar to damages at common law. The claimants Target Holdings Ltd, were persuaded to advance approximately £1.5 million on a mortgage, on the assumption that the selling price of the property was to be £2 million. In fact the property was sold for £775,000. The defendant solicitors acted for both vendor and purchaser. They had taken the money advanced and paid it over to the purchaser and associated companies before the purchase and mortgage were executed, and in this respect (because they had paid the money away before being authorised to release it) were clearly in breach of trust with the claimants.

The purchasers later became insolvent, and the claimants sold the property, but for only £500,000 (so that they had lost around £1m), and sued the defendants for breach of trust. The defendants argued that the claimants had suffered no loss, because the defendants had obtained for the claimants exactly the mortgages to which they were entitled. The claimants would have suffered exactly the same loss, whether or not the defendants had paid out the money in breach of trust. The House of Lords held in principle in favour of the defendants, that a trustee who committed a breach of trust was not liable to compensate the beneficiary for losses which the beneficiary would, in any event, have suffered if there had been no such breach. The defendants would therefore not be liable on the assumed facts, that the transaction would have gone through anyway, even in the absence of Target's advance. If the assumed facts were wrong, and Target's advance was necessary for the transaction to go through at all, then Target would be entitled to be compensated for the entire loss that they had suffered, since in that event, but for the breach of trust, nothing would have been paid over.

There are no degrees of breach, however. Liability can attach to a trustee who has acted honestly in the beneficiaries' interests, just as it can to a trustee who has acted fraudulently for his own ends. Further, since the standard of care is objective (i.e., measured against the level of competence of a notional reasonable man, rather than that of the particular trustee), liability can attach to a trustee who lacks the knowledge or skills to avoid the breach and is doing his incompetent best, if that best is not up to the objective standard required. Protection of the beneficiaries, and not the nature of the wrongdoing, is the crucial element.

The court may, however, take into account degrees of culpability in exercising its discretion to grant relief from liability, or in fixing the amount of interest which the trustee may be liable to pay on the sum lost to the trust estate, both of which are considered shortly.

18.1.2 Personal nature of trustee's liability

A trustee is liable personally for his own breach of trust, and not vicariously for breaches committed by fellow trustees. In *Re Lucking's WT* [1968] 1 WLR 866, Lucking had committed a breach of trust in entrusting large sums of money to a manager, without adequately supervising him. His fellow trustee, Block, was not liable for Lucking's breach of trust, but was entitled to rely on what Lucking had told him about the company's affairs, unless he had a positive reason to disbelieve him.

However, a trustee who passively permits a breach to occur may thereby put himself in breach of his own duties because, though trustees are not required to police each other's conduct, they are expected, as we have seen, to be active in the administration of the trust. Thus, a trustee who leaves funds under the control of a fellow trustee without enquiry, or fails to take steps to obtain redress if he discovers a breach, will be in dereliction of his own duty to the beneficiaries.

The personal nature of trusteeship can be appreciated through examining case law under the 1925 Act. By virtue of s. 30:

A trustee . . . shall be answerable and accountable only for his own acts, receipts, neglects, or defaults, and not those of any other trustee . . . nor for any other loss, unless the same happens through his own wilful default.

In *Re Vickery* [1931] 1 Ch 572, Maugham J assumed that s. 30 had altered the law, at least in relation to liability for agents, for he interpreted the phrase 'wilful default' as meaning 'a consciousness of negligence or breach of duty, or recklessness in the performance of duty'. If this meaning is applied in relation to co-trustees, the section clearly confers extra protection.

Apart from *Re Vickery*, it is generally accepted that s. 30 did not alter the previous law: the section does not alter the principle that a trustee remains liable for his own acts, upon which the liability in the extract set out above is based. Under the previous law liability was incurred where a trustee handed over money without securing its proper application, or permitted a fellow trustee to recover money without enquiring what he did with it, or refrained from taking steps to obtain redress for a breach of which he was aware. It has yet to be decided whether, in these circumstances also, it will be necessary to prove that a passive trustee was guilty of 'wilful default' as defined in *Re Vickery*, but we would suggest that this is unlikely. This position must now be seen in light of the repeal of s. 30(1) by the 2000 Act. The current position appears to be that a trustee now labours under the requirement to establish that he acted properly.

A trustee will not, upon accepting office, become liable for breaches committed prior to his appointment. His first steps on taking office, however, should be to examine the documents and accounts of the trust, and if he discovers that a breach has occurred, he should take action against the former trustee to recover the loss. Failure to do so may itself amount to a breach for which he will be liable, save perhaps in the rare case where he can show that action would have been futile (because there would then be no causal relationship between the breach and the loss).

A trustee cannot escape liability for his own breach of trust by retiring from office, for even after his retirement he remains liable for breaches committed while he was in office, and his estate remains liable after his death. He will not be liable for breaches committed after the date of his retirement, unless it can be shown that he retired in order to facilitate a breach of trust (*Head* v *Gould* [1898] 2 Ch 250).

18.1.3 Liability as between trustees

The liability of trustees is said to be joint and several, which means that if two or more trustees are liable, a beneficiary may choose to sue some or all of them, or perhaps only one, and recoup the entire loss from those against whom he chooses to proceed. Similarly, he may levy execution against any one of them for the whole amount.

As between themselves, however, the trustees were until 1978 regarded by equity as being equally liable, so that a trustee who was compelled to pay more than his fair share of the loss could in turn enforce a contribution from the others. In enforcing equal contribution, equity disregarded any differing degrees of involvement in the breach. Thus, in *Bahin* v *Hughes* (1886) 31 Ch D 390, a passive trustee was liable to the same extent as an active one.

There were exceptions to the principle of equal contribution, which were unaffected by the 1978 legislation (considered below):

(a) Where there has been fraud. A fraudulent trustee is solely liable, and can claim no contribution from the honest trustees.

(b) Where a trustee has got money into his hands and made use of it, he will be liable to indemnify a co-trustee who is obliged to replace the funds.

(c) Where one trustee was a solicitor and the rest relied on his judgement (*Re Partington* (1887) 57 LT 654). The mere fact that a trustee happens also to be a solicitor will not make him liable to indemnify the other trustees, for it is necessary also that the others rely on his judgement. Thus, he will not be liable if it is shown that the other trustees were active participators in the breach, and did not participate merely in consequence of the advice and control of the solicitor (*Head* v *Gould* [1898] 2 Ch 250).

(d) Where a trustee is also a beneficiary he will be required to indemnify his co-trustees to the extent of his beneficial interest, and not merely to the extent that he has personally received some benefit from the breach (*Chillingworth* v *Chambers* [1896] 1 Ch 685). Only after that interest is exhausted will further liability be shared equally. The principle seems to be that a beneficiary may not claim any share of the trust estate until he has discharged his liabilities towards it.

Departing from the principle of equal responsibility
The equitable position has been affected by the Civil Liability (Contribution) Act 1978. Under this Act, any person liable in respect of damage suffered by another person, including damage arising from breach of trust, may recover a contribution from any other person in respect of the same damage. By s. 2(1) the amount of the contribution is:

such as may be found by the court to be just and equitable having regard to the extent of that person's responsibility for the damage in question

—and may by virtue of s. 2(2) amount to a total indemnity. The Act therefore gives the court a discretion (but not a mandatory duty) to depart from the rule of equal distribution and have regard to degrees of fault.

The Act does not apply to the limited number of exceptions to the general equitable principle described above, and may indeed not affect the equitable position at all, since it is left to the court to determine what is 'just and equitable'. One other situation is clearly unaffected by the 1978 Act. If all the trustees were involved in a fraud, equity would not allow those who paid the damages to claim any contribution from the rest, on the ground that a claimant could not base a claim upon his own wrongdoing. The 1978 Act makes no special provision for such a case, but though the court is theoretically free to exercise its discretion in allocating liability to contribute, it is inconceivable that a fraudulent trustee would be allowed to sue.

Where some but not all of the trustees are excused from liability under s. 61 of the Trustee Act 1925, it would seem to follow that those who are not excused can claim no contribution from them. Under the 1978 Act, the excused trustees would seem not to be persons who are liable in respect of any damage, so presumably the court cannot direct them to contribute.

18.1.4 Trustees and criminal liability

In the course of a breach of trust criminal offences may be committed, but breach of trust is not of itself a criminal offence. There used to be a difficulty about theft, because the trustee as legal owner of the trust property could not be guilty of stealing it, and a special offence of conversion by a trustee had to be created in order to make him punishable. However, by virtue of the provisions of the Theft Act 1968, a trustee may be guilty of ordinary theft. This is possible through the statutory definition of theft found in sections 1(1) and 5(2) of the 1968 Act. Section 1(1) provides that 'A person is guilty of theft if he dishonestly appropriates property belonging to another with the intention of permanently depriving the other of it'.

The significance of s. 5(2) rests on the 'problem' that the trustee is actually the legal owner of trust property. Section 5(2) contains provisions for the meaning of property 'belonging to another' for the purposes of the s. 1(1) definition. By virtue of s. 5(2), 'property belonging to another' includes property held on trust so that 'where property is subject to a trust, the person to whom it belongs shall be regarded as including any person having a right to enforce the trust, and an intention to defeat the trust shall be regarded accordingly as an intention to deprive of that property any person having that right'.

This chapter is primarily a consideration of how breach of trust arises and the key dimensions of how the personal remedies against a trustee who has committed a breach of trust will operate. Previous editions reflected this position and, accordingly, attention paid to trustees' criminal liability was brief and confined to the above references to sections 1(1) and 5(2) of the Theft Act 1968, to draw attention to the way in which a trustee who misappropriates trust funds can also be guilty of theft and thus incur criminal liability. Although it was always deemed necessary to point to the way in which, according to the criminal law, a legal owner of property can nevertheless be guilty of its theft, this was also deemed sufficient.

There was always scope for considering the way in which the criminal law dimension formed part of a 'bigger picture' of questions of trustee liability and accountability for the property which is entrusted to him for the beneficiaries. In this vein, it may well be the case that the threat of *criminal* liability serves important functions in deterring misappropriations of trust property, because of the *stigma* which is believed by many to attach to exposure to criminal culpability. However, at this point it is now necessary to give criminal liability arising from the office of trustee much fuller consideration on account of the Fraud Act 2006.

Notwithstanding, this chapter remains a consideration of the consequences in equity which attach to a trustee's breach of his duties: this progresses from looking at what amounts to a breach, and how this becomes a 'measure' of the liability which can be incurred upon being found in breach. To preserve this emphasis, at this point only very brief reference is made to indicate that trustees *can* incur criminal liability in addition to that arising in equity. The more extensive consideration of the criminal consequences of trusteeship which is necessary in light of this recent change to English criminal law will close this chapter on breach of trust.

18.1.5 **Bankruptcy of a defaulting trustee**

If a trustee who is liable for a breach becomes bankrupt, the claim in respect of the breach is provable in his bankruptcy. His duties towards the trust are not affected by his bankruptcy, so the odd situation arises whereby he has a duty (as trustee) to prove in his own bankruptcy (as debtor to the trust). If he fails to do this, he commits a further breach of trust which is not affected by any subsequent discharge from bankruptcy and he will be liable to the trust for the resulting loss (i.e., dividend that he would have received in the bankruptcy).

18.2 **Qualifications and defences to liability**

English law's position on trustee liability is that where there is a breach of a duty this gives rise to breach of trust. The numerous ways in which breach of trust can arise are explained above, with illustrative reference made to Millett LJ's judgment in *Armitage* v *Nurse*. In terms of what breach of trust means across the spectrum of its possible manifestations is that a trustee is liable to account, to the beneficiary, for losses experienced by the trust and its assets. This is the position in principle, and it is, like liability across legal regimes, liability which operates within certain limitations. In trusts law, these limits are defined in reference to defences which a trustee accused of breach of trust may be able to invoke.

18.2.1 **Consent or participation by beneficiaries**

A beneficiary who consents to or participates in a breach of trust will not usually be able to succeed in a claim against the trustees, even if he has obtained no personal benefit from the breach. The consent or participation of one beneficiary will not, of course, prevent those who did not consent from claiming, and if it is uncertain which beneficiaries have consented, the court may order an inquiry. No particular form of consent is required.

To be effective, consent must be that of an adult who is *sui iuris* and not acting under an undue influence which prevents him from making an independent judgement. In *Re Pauling's ST* [1964] Ch 303, trustees of a marriage settlement had made a series of advances in breach of trust because the trustees did not ensure that the moneys advanced were used for their proper purpose. A wide range of defences was argued, both before Wilberforce J and in the Court of Appeal, but on this issue several of the payments which went to benefit the parents were presumed to have been the result of undue influence over the children. Whether undue influence has been exercised is a question of fact, depending on circumstances. The trustees will not be liable if it cannot be shown that they knew, or ought to have known, that the beneficiary was acting under such influence.

In *Re Pauling's ST* itself, the Court of Appeal held that where a presumption of undue influence existed, as between a parent and child who was still subject to parental influence (albeit a child who had reached her majority), an advance to the child which was given to her parents, could not be retained by the parent unless it was clear that:

(a) the gift was the spontaneous act of the child; and

(b) the child knew what her rights were. It was also desirable that the child had obtained independent and, if possible, professional advice.

In this regard, the courts treat with suspicion gifts from children to their parents, whereas the reverse was true of gifts the other way round (see, e.g., the presumption of advancement in chapter 7).

Acquiescence and the requirement of 'consent'
Consent involves more than mere awareness of what the trustees are proposing to do. Otherwise, trustees could protect themselves by simply telling the beneficiaries, beforehand. In *Re Pauling's ST* [1962] 1 WLR 86, Wilberforce J (at p. 108) explained that:

[T]he court has to consider all the circumstances in which the concurrence of the *cestui que trust* was given with a view to seeing whether it is fair and equitable that, having given his concurrence, he should afterwards turn round and sue the trustees.

He went on to say that it is not necessary that the beneficiary should know that what he is concurring in is a breach of trust, provided that he fully understands what he is concurring in. Nor is it necessary that he should personally benefit from the breach. This statement of the law was neither approved nor disapproved by the Court of Appeal in *Re Pauling's ST* itself [1964] Ch 303, but was approved by the Court of Appeal in *Holder* v *Holder* [1968] Ch 353, in which a beneficiary was held unable to set aside a sale after affirming it and accepting part of the purchase money.

18.2.2 **Release or acquiescence by beneficiaries**

A beneficiary will also be unable to succeed in his claim if, on becoming aware of the breach, he acquiesced in the breach or released the trustee from liability arising therefrom. A partial defence succeeded on the basis of the acquiescence doctrine in *Re Pauling's ST* [1964] Ch 303.

Release suggests some active waiver by the beneficiary of his rights. A waiver requires a positive act which is intended to be irrevocable. It is like making a gift and, as with gifts, no consideration need move from the donee (in this case the trustee). As with consent, there need not be any particular formalities and release may even be inferred from conduct.

If a release cannot be shown, it may still be possible to show that the beneficiary acquiesced in the breach. It is usually accepted that the acquiescence doctrine is based on an implied contract, whereby the beneficiary is taken to have agreed not to rely on his rights. The evidence required for this intention to be inferred is less than in the case of release, and the doctrine is often applied where a beneficiary has done nothing to pursue his claim.

Delay in making the claim is not in itself evidence of acquiescence, but where the length of time between the breach and the claim is very great, slight additional evidence will suffice. As in the case of consent, the release or acquiescence must be that of an adult who is *sui iuris*.

Undue influence or lack of full knowledge will prevent the trustee from relying on these defences, the test being as in the consent doctrine, above.

18.2.3 Impounding beneficiary's interest

The court has an inherent power to impound the interest of a beneficiary, thus providing the trustee with an indemnity to the extent that the beneficiary's interest will suffice to replace the loss to the trust.

The power can arise where a beneficiary has merely consented to the breach, but only if some benefit to him can be proved, and then only to the extent of that benefit. If the beneficiary has gone further, and actually requested or instigated a breach, the power can be exercised whether or not he has received a personal benefit from the breach.

Needless to say, the trustee has to show that the beneficiary acted in full knowledge of the facts, but it is not necessary to show that he knew that the acts he was instigating or consenting to amounted to a breach.

There is also a statutory discretion to impound. Section 62(1) of the Trustee Act 1925 (replacing an earlier enactment) provides:

Where a trustee commits a breach of trust at the instigation or request or with the consent in writing of a beneficiary, the court may, if it thinks fit, make such order as to the court seems just, for impounding all or any part of the interest of the beneficiary in the trust estate by way of indemnity to the trustee or persons claiming through him.

The courts seem to have treated this largely as a consolidating section, rather than extending their powers, except that Wilberforce J in *Re Pauling's ST (No. 2)* [1963] Ch 576 thought that it gave an additional right, among other things, to deal with a married woman beneficiary. This additional right is no longer necessary, because of changes in legislation on family property, and that part of the section was repealed in 1949.

The effect of the court making an order impounding a beneficiary's interest is that the beneficiary is not only debarred from pursuing his own claim against the trustee, but also liable to replace the losses suffered by the other beneficiaries, to the extent ordered by the court, and perhaps up to the full value of his own interest. To this extent, the trustee is protected at the beneficiary's expense.

The discretion is a judicial discretion, and though the section appears to extend the inherent power of the court by giving a discretion to impound a beneficiary's interest regardless of whether he obtained a benefit, it has received a restrictive interpretation. It seems that the court will make an impounding order in any case where it would have done so before the Act; generally speaking, in any case where the beneficiary has actively induced the breach (for which it has never been necessary to show benefit).

Requirement of full awareness by beneficiary
It must, of course, be shown that the beneficiary was fully aware of what was being done. In *Re Somerset* [1894] 1 Ch 231, a beneficiary had urged the trustees to invest in a mortgage of a particular property, but had left them to decide how much money they were prepared to invest. Lindley MR said (at p. 265):

In order to bring a case within this section the *cestui que trust* must instigate, or request, or consent in writing to some act or omission which is itself a breach of trust, and not to some act or omission which only becomes a breach of trust by reason of want of care on the part of the trustees.

The words 'in writing' have been held to apply only to consent, and not to instigation or request (*Griffith* v *Hughes* [1892] 3 Ch 105). So a request or instigation need only be oral.

The power to impound will not be lost on an assignment of the beneficial interest. Nor is it lost when the court replaces the trustees in consequence of the breach. In *Re Pauling's ST* [1962] 1 WLR 86, the trustees resisted removal because they were claiming an indemnity out of the interests of the parents. Wilberforce J held that they were entitled to such indemnity and that this would be unaffected by their replacement. They were therefore unable to use this as a ground for continuing in office: see *Re Pauling's ST (No. 2)* [1963] Ch 576.

Apart from statute, it is the practice, where trustees have under an honest mistake overpaid a beneficiary, for the court to make allowance for the mistake in order to allow the trustee to recoup as far as possible (*Re Musgrave* [1916] 2 Ch 417). An overpaid beneficiary is not compelled to return the excess but further payment may be withheld until the accounts are adjusted.

If a payment is made by mistake to someone who is not entitled, the trustee may recover on an action for money had and received if the mistake was one of fact, but not if it was a mistake of law (*Re Diplock* [1947] Ch 716). It is also certain that the error must be corrected where trustee-beneficiaries overpay themselves.

18.2.4 Trustee liability and lapse of time

Lapse of time may protect a trustee in one of two ways. By the Limitation Act 1980, limits are set upon the time within which certain actions for recovery may be brought, while in cases not covered by statutory limitation, a defendant may rely on the doctrine of laches.

Limitation Act 1980
By s. 21(3) of the Limitation Act 1980, any action by a beneficiary to recover trust property or in respect of any breach of trust (other than situations covered by the self-dealing and fair dealing rules) must be brought within six years from the date on which the right of action accrued.

A right of action in respect of future interests is not treated as having accrued until the interest falls into possession: this was also part of the *ratio* in *Re Pauling's ST* [1964] Ch 303 (discussed in this chapter).

Under s. 21(1), no period of limitation applies where the action is in respect of any fraud to which the trustee was a party, or privy, or where (in summary) it is sought to recover from the trustee trust property still in his possession, or the proceeds of sale of such property. Protection is also lost where the trustee converts trust property to his own use. Conversion to the trustee's own use, however, implies application in his own favour, so that if the funds have been used to maintain an infant beneficiary, or dissipated by a fellow trustee, the protection of limitation remains available.

Where fraud is the issue, this must be fraud by the trustee himself. In *Thorne* v *Heard* [1894] 1 Ch 599 a trustee was protected by a section in similar terms of an earlier Act, where he had left trust funds with a solicitor who had embezzled them, the trustee himself being no more than negligent. Where the trustee is in possession of trust property or its proceeds, however, no dishonesty need be shown. Fraud for these purposes is wider than common law fraud or deceit, but nevertheless requires unconscionable conduct on the part of the trustee, something in the nature of a deliberate cover-up: in *Bartlett v Barclays Bank Trust Co. Ltd (No. 1)* [1980] Ch 515, the bank was held able to rely on what is now s. 21(1) of the 1980 Act, in respect of income lost outside the limitation period, since, being unaware that it was acting in breach of trust, it could not be guilty of fraud for these purposes.

Section 22 prescribes a limitation period of 12 years for actions in respect of any claim to the personal estate of a deceased person. It is often hard to determine at what point executors have completed the administration of an estate and become trustees, but it is thought that the 12-year period will apply although for all other purposes the executors would be regarded as trustees.

Claimants 'under disability' are permitted an extended period in which to bring an action by s. 28, and by s. 32; where fraud, concealment or mistake is alleged, time runs only from the point when the claimant discovers the fraud or mistake, or could with reasonable diligence have discovered it.

It should be noted that a person other than a *bona fide* purchaser for value without notice who receives property from a trustee also falls within these rules.

Equitable doctrine of laches

Where no statutory limitation period applies, the defendant may rely on the equitable doctrine of laches, that is, he may show that it would be unjust to allow the claimant to pursue his claim in view of the time that has elapsed since it accrued. The court has a discretion to allow or refuse the defence, and mere delay may suffice, but, where possible, the courts have preferred to regard delay as furnishing evidence of acquiescence by the claimant.

18.2.5 Trustee Act 1925, Section 61

This section gives the court a wide discretion to excuse honest and reasonable trustees from liability for breach of trust. It applies also to executors. The section provides:

If it appears to the court that a trustee . . . is or may be personally liable for any breach of trust, whether the transaction alleged to be a breach of trust occurred before or after the commencement of this Act, but has acted honestly and reasonably, and ought fairly to be excused for the breach of trust and for omitting to obtain the directions of the court in the matter in which he committed such breach, then the court may relieve him either wholly or partly from personal liability for the same.

Dishonesty will obviously disqualify a trustee from obtaining relief, but a trustee is also required to act 'reasonably'. The standard applied appears to be the same as that for breach of trust itself, that of the prudent man of business in relation to his own affairs, and the bank failed on this test in *Bartlett v Barclays Bank Trust Co. Ltd (No. 1)* [1980] Ch 515. Failure to obtain directions might be thought to fall below this standard, but the section implies that relief may nonetheless be granted.

Unauthorised investments appear to be the most common circumstances in which applications are made, and it may not be easy to show that this sort of risk-taking meets with the standard of the prudent business person. Reasonable conduct may be more easily shown where the breach consists in some error made in the course of a complex administration. Professional trustees may claim the protection of the section, but the courts have been less ready to excuse failure where a high standard of expertise is professed by the trustee. See again *Bartlett* v *Barclays Bank Trust Co. Ltd (No. 1)* [1980] Ch 515.

It may be that, even if the trustee is shown to have acted honestly and reasonably, the question of whether he ought fairly to be excused will be separately considered.

18.3 Trustee exemption clauses

The position traditionally taken in this text in relation to exemption clauses has always been that '[t]here is no reason why an appropriately drafted exemption clause in the trust instrument should not protect a trustee who would otherwise be liable for breach of trust'. However, beyond this (and identifying the authority provided by *Armitage* v *Nurse* [1998] Ch 241 for this position), this represented the extent of coverage of the topic.

The essence of the trustee exemption clause is much like it sounds. Like exemption clauses found in contract law, the trustee exemption clause is a mechanism to restrict or exclude liability which may otherwise be incurred in the course of trusteeship. The context for such clauses is the occurrence of breach of trust, which flows from the duties trustees are subject to in their administration of the trust, or from the trust instrument, or duties imposed by law: it is any failure to comply with these duties which will amount to a breach of trust. And, as was made clear earlier, there are no 'degrees' of breach of trust; a breach can be innocent as well as fraudulent, and the law does not even distinguish flagrant incompetence from incompetence arising from misfortune. It is even the case that liability for breach of trust is not confined to situations which have detrimentally affected the trust—liability will arise equally where the breach has actually brought beneficial consequences for the trust. In short, all incidences of breach of trust leave the trustee open to incur liability for it.

This scope of breach of trust should therefore explain trustees' attempts to limit or exclude the liability which it is possible for them to incur—even trustees who are competent and *bona fide* might with very good reason elect to try to protect themselves in such a manner. This also serves as a reminder of the very close relationship between performance of the trust and its breach; itself a further illustration of the very close interrelationship between all these chapters on trusteeship, and the way in which the essence of trusteeship is actually very difficult to 'parcel' into more discrete aspects for study. Indeed, just as exemption clauses can be seen as a mechanism to protect trustees against breach of trust, they can also be seen as a measure of trustees' duties: this latter analysis emphasises them as devices to 'manage' expectations of trustees in the performance of their duties. In light of this 'dual perspective', this consideration of exemption clauses would therefore be equally at home in chapter 16 as it is in the present one.

18.3.1 Context for current discussion

A very narrow technical reading of exemption clauses would explain them as one of the 'guards' which can be used by trustees to exclude or to restrict their liability to beneficiaries arising from breach of trust. It will become clear in due course that there are a number of such mechanisms that have this effect, and so there is need to explain the significance of anchoring attempts of trustees to limit the liabilities which can flow from the performance of their duties to exemption clauses specifically. This is attributable to the current 'policy direction' for considering the liabilities arising from trusteeship, whereby the Law Commission has been asked specifically to consider the position of exemption clauses.

In 2002 the Law Commission published Consultation Paper No. 171 entitled *Trustee Exemption Clauses*. This was an extremely interesting and highly readable document, which provided an excellent point of reference for much of the coverage on trusteeship in this text in earlier chapters. In this more general sense, it provides an excellent opportunity to review understanding of many of the core issues, as well as an opportunity to examine them more critically. In July 2006 the Law Commission published its *Report on Trustee Exemption Clauses* No. 301 (Cm. 6874) following this Consultation. Before looking at the recommendations for reform which have been made, there will be a more general discussion about the issues arising in relation to exemption clauses, which will be pursued through an examination of leading case law and its historical development. Thereafter, reference is made to the lengthy attention given in the Consultation Paper to the 'economic dimensions' at stake, before moving on to considering whether the recommendations of the *Report* published in July 2006 point to an appropriate future direction to be taken in this area.

Meaning and significance of 'exemption clause'
In 2002 the Law Commission introduced its involvement in the consideration of trustee liability by identifying the 'unrestricted nature' of liability for breach of trust as explanation for the appearance in trust instruments of various mechanisms employed to try to provide some limitation on this, and some concomitant protection for trustees. There were a number of other mechanisms which the Law Commission identified as achieving this outcome by alternative means. First, reference was made to the **duty modification** clause as a potential means to limit or exclude exposure of trustees to legal accountability. This operates by restricting the scope of a trustee's duties at the outset (rather than restricting his liability *after* a breach has occurred) and has the effect of making a breach of duty harder to establish. Also identified was the **'extended powers'** or **'authorisation'** clause, capable of conferring wider powers on trustees expressly through the trust instrument, and even vesting them with authority in respect of acts which would otherwise be prohibited. A further mechanism which could achieve the protection of trustees against liability was the use of an **indemnity** clause. This would operate by attacking the traditional entitlement of beneficiaries in respect of 'any losses' to the trust arising from a trustee's failure to carry out his duties. Here, an indemnity could add to the way in which a trustee is currently entitled to be reimbursed for expenses legitimately incurred in his administration of the trust, extending this to any liability which he incurred for breach of trust (except perhaps that which was attributable to his own individual fraud).

The exclusion or **exemption** clause became the axis for the Law Commission's Consultation on account that it is the most widely used mechanism for limiting exposure to legal accountability, both within trust instruments themselves, and within a broader cultural setting of trusteeship in English law. And, it is this current state of affairs which thus provided the key point of reference for a broader consideration of the extent to which trustees should be able to protect themselves from legal accountability. On one level, the Law Commission appreciated that this would involve confronting the essence of the trust, as an institution in private law which derives its direction from the settlor of trust property. It is also the case that the exemption clause raises important issues of compatibility flowing from the way in which liability for breach of trust is actually intended to protect the beneficiaries under a trust, who are not owners of the trust property at law. Such difficulties were recognised by the Law Commission at many points in the Consultation. There is, for example, the insistence that any conclusion that the exemption clause can be accommodated alongside the need to protect beneficiaries' interests would have to involve extensive consideration of questions of scope: scope of the operation of such clauses, and the extent to which trustees should be able to limit their legal accountability in this manner.

An exclusion clause compatible with the institution of the private trust
In respect of the first consideration, arising from the need to confront the exemption clause in light of the institution of the trust, the Law Commission accepted that exemption clauses had arrived, and that they are here to stay. No small part of this assessment was attributable to the changing culture of trusteeship and the ever-growing professionalisation in the provision of trust services which has been occurring. However, the Law Commission's 2002 publication also noted in the document's early stages that the use of clauses either to limit or exclude liability flowing from breach of trust on account of the 'unrestricted' nature of this liability is not itself new, and trustees have long appreciated the need to try to protect themselves through such provisions. In providing a useful reminder of how modern trusteeship grew up, in the nineteenth century, strongly in the context of family-type settlement trusts, the Law Commission made a number of useful points relating to the historical formulation of the exemption clause and also the nature of its interpretation.

18.3.2 Exemption clauses commonplace within modern trusts

The Law Commission made note of the way in which earliest attempts at exemption clauses were drafted 'narrowly', denoting greater 'containment' of the notion of trusteeship than is the case today. Here, it pointed to the authority of *Seton v Dawson* (1841) 4 D 310, relating to the timelessness of the idea of limiting trustees' legal exposure for breach of trust, and its traditional application through early ideas on interpreting such attempts. Such early explorations into restricting and excluding liability were construed strictly against trustees, which is of course consistent with traditional ideas on the onerous nature of trusteeship and its location within a broader fiduciary context. What has brought the exemption clause so sharply into focus, can, according to the Law Commission, be explained on account of the changing conditions in which trusteeship now operates. The rise of the professional trustee is itself a reflection of the way in which the nature of trust assets has considerably changed; and the way in which the trust is now being used extensively for novel purposes has provided the context for extended powers being given to trustees in their management of trust assets and trust estates more broadly.

Professionalisation, the changing nature of trusteeship and approaches to exemption
Attention has been drawn to the changing nature of trusteeship throughout these chapters. Particularly prominent illustration of this can be found by reference to the powers trustees now have in relation to making investments, and the way in which they are able to make appointments which result in certain delegation of their duties in recognition of their growing need to enlist 'expert' services in the successful management of trust assets and estates. Greater powers and increasing dimensions to management of trusts does of course give rise to increasing expectations in 'delivery' and satisfaction, which is recognised in the Consultation as a potential source of increasing litigiousness among beneficiaries. It is to these reasons that the Law Commission attributed the common presence in trust instruments of clauses which purport to protect trustees from incurring liability in respect of acts and omissions which would normally be regarded as breach of trust. It noted also that, on reasoning outlined above '[a]s the powers of trustees have increased as a result both of express provisions in trust instruments and by legislation, so has the breadth of trustee exemption clauses'.

By the Law Commission's own admission in the 2002 Consultation Paper, while the Trustee Act 2000 (which was itself underpinned by extensive Law Commission consideration) had done much to liberalise trusteeship, and to better equip it for an entirely new context (provided by huge changes in the nature of trust assets, and even in the use made of the trust arrangement itself), this legislation which was responsible for the 'expansion of trustee powers' did not make any attempt to regulate the use made in trust instruments of exemption clauses. The Law Commission also emphasised that in many respects this was deliberate, and operated to maintain a crucial tenet of trusts law to provide a 'fall-back' position for situations where specific instructions are absent. This is a position which gives primacy of place to the trust instrument, and to the settlor as the right and proper source of directions on the trust's operations. The Law Commission cited as authority for this the pronouncement from Sch. 1, para. 7 that the statutory duty of care under the Trustee Act 2000 does not apply 'if or in so far as it appears from the trust instrument that the duty is not meant to apply'.

18.3.3 The key problem of exemption clauses in modern trusts

It is within this setting that in 2002 the Law Commission identified the nature of the problem at the heart of its remit in relation to the position of trustees and liability for breach of trust. Given that the way in which the rise of the professional trustee combined with the changing nature of trust assets and even trust usage has already been explained, these considerations can now be combined with the approach which it appears is being taken by the courts in relation to exclusion clauses. This is explained below in some detail, but for present purposes, it is sufficient to introduce what the Law Commission identified in 2002 as the central problem for its inquiries. The Law Commission explained (at para. 1.5) that:

English law does not at present provide a readily available means for beneficiaries to claim that a trustee exemption clause should not be invoked by a trustee and, as a result, trustees have considerable scope to protect themselves from liability for breach of trust. The question arises whether reliance on trustee exemption clauses is seriously endangering the interests of those whom the trust relationship is directed to promote.

Managing expectations, and the interpretation of exemption clauses in English Law
Affirmation of the exemption clause How and why this position is believed to have arisen in English Law then becomes apparent within the Law Commission's own narrative. This adds to the discussion of the ever-changing scope of attempted restrictions on liability, and the influence brought to bear on this by managing beneficiary expectations, by setting out a typical clause now to be found in trust instruments:

No Trustee shall be liable for any loss or damage which may happen to the Trust fund ... at any time or from any cause whatsoever unless such loss or damage shall be caused by his own actual fraud.

This illustration of a typical exemption clause is followed by the identification of, within recent judicial approaches, a particular pattern to interpretation. The courts are now clearly adopting an approach to exemption clauses which is 'less restrictive' (than older formulations, for which a number of other authorities are cited and considered). Explanation for this is then illustrated by reference to the decision in *Armitage* v *Nurse* [1998]. The Law Commission explained that from *Armitage*, there could be no doubt that such clauses are valid, and that they will be interpreted in a way by which liability for losses caused to the trust arising from negligence, and even gross negligence, can validly be excluded. And the position of the law in England and Wales is that trustees are currently able validly to protect themselves across the sphere of breach of trust through use of exemption clauses, except for losses which are caused by fraud. *Armitage* v *Nurse* expressed this through reference to the ability of a trustee to protect himself 'no matter how indolent, imprudent, lacking in diligence, negligent or wilful he might have been, so long as he has not acted dishonestly'.

Striking the best balance This endorsement of the authenticity of the exemption clause by the courts, and the limits of its application—apparently only stopping at actual fraud—and the way in which this in turn provides affirmation that exemption clauses are very strongly entrenched in trustee law and culture in English law, led the Law Commission to the not terribly startling conclusion that 'the protection offered to beneficiaries ... is weaker than in the past'. And, it conceded that within this setting, the task of the law was thus to strive to achieve the best possible protection for beneficiaries. This meant that for the Law Commission there was no possibility of absolute protection of beneficiaries, and for the purposes of the study made of trusteeship throughout *this* text (both direct and also less direct) this position has to be squared with the way in which beneficiary protection is the *raison d'être* of the way in which trusts are accommodated within the law. This is clearly a point of tension, which the Law Commission itself appreciated through its reference to the protection of beneficiaries as 'one of the prime concerns of trust law'. How the best balance in the law can be struck given these limitations thereafter provides the guiding framework through which discussions on the shape of future policy could take place. The discussion pursued throughout the first parts of the Consultation Paper makes very interesting reading, in terms of setting out the parameters for consideration, through an examination of leading case law and historical development.

18.3.4 Managing inevitability: empirical study of the economic dimensions to greater regulation of exemption clauses

The discussion gathers particular momentum after this initial 'setting the scene' which identified the problem, and also raised the question of whether the case could be made for some formal regulation of exemption clauses (which are currently considered only in the courts, case-by-case as a matter of construction and an assessment of merits). At this point, the Law Commission acknowledged that in considering the introduction of any legal regulation of exemption clauses, the economic impact that this might have was a central consideration. And in order to make an assessment of this, independent research had been commissioned from Trusts scholar Dr Alison Dunn. The Consultation reported that the empirical research confirmed wide usage of exemption clauses in trust instruments, and in a broader cultural sense this was particularly so in relation to professional trustees, where reliance upon them 'as a means of protection from liability for breach of trust' was particularly prevalent. Unsurprisingly, among professional trustees there was also strong feeling that such clauses are a necessary component in modern trust practice, that regulation would lead to a decline of the availability of trust services, increases in their cost, and even that it would result in a relocation of the industry as a whole to a different jurisdiction which did not seek to restrict such practices. It was suggested in the previous edition of this text that this formed part of a larger 'regulatory balance' argument which is ever more pertinent in an increasingly globalised society, in which both financial capital and also social capital (human beings) are highly mobile.

In 2002 the Law Commission clearly regarded these considerations very seriously, and accordingly identified its major concerns (at para. 1.13) as:

- the way in which increased regulation might lead to significant increases in charges made for providing trust services;
- that lay trustees may be deterred from undertaking trustee responsibilities on account that they might feel unable to protect themselves; and
- the risk that professional trustees may move their operations to less regulatory burdensome jurisdictions.

Equally, the Law Commission was also able to point to a lack of universality of opinion about the necessity of exemption clauses. This was because the commissioned research had revealed, even among professional trustees, credence that those who charge for their services should be properly accountable to the beneficiaries under a trust in the event of a breach of that trust.

Law Commission's initial position: limits of exemption within its broader acceptance
In the penultimate section of the 2002 publication which set out the case for the direction of future policy and the manner in which this might be pursued, the Law Commission set out the parameters of possibility. This placed outright prohibition of the use of exemption clauses at one end of the spectrum and allowed completely unrestricted use of them at the other, with a number of positions lying within these

extremes. The Law Commission at this point revealed its initial feeling that an absolute prohibition was not at this point in time justifiable. What is particularly interesting about its views in favour of allowing (rather than dis-allowing) exemption clauses in English law is the way in which this was explained. This position of favour 'in principle' was expressed with reference to the way in which it would not be in the interests of the parties concerned to prohibit such restrictions: this would undermine the settlor's capacity to determine appropriate administration of the trust, and to direct trustees accordingly. It was even proposed that there were persuasive arguments that a complete ban on exemption clauses might actually impact negatively on the nature of the trust arrangement itself, by interfering with its flexibility.

Striking a balance and moving forward: Law Commission's provisional proposals
The Law Commission's qualification of this lay in the way in which it believed that some regulation of trustee exemption clauses must be achieved, itself founded in its view that the present law does not strike the best balance between the points of interest and tension operating within the trust. The current law under *Armitage* v *Nurse* did, in the Law Commission's view, allow too much accommodation of trustees at the expense of other interested parties. The main body of the document's text explains how *Armitage* v *Nurse* allows trustees validly to exempt themselves from liability for breach of trust, except that attributable to fraud. And within this, on the construction of the clause in *Armitage* itself, this extended beyond 'equitable' notions of fraud (as explained and considered in chapter 11 of this text), and that establishing 'actual fraud' required dishonesty to be shown ([1998] Ch 241, 251): in this regard, the Law Commission made reference to the decision in *Walker* v *Stones* [2001] QB 902, where the test for dishonesty was where 'no reasonable trustee' would have considered the action in the interests of the beneficiaries. The scope of protection which *Armitage* affords to trustees seeking to resist liability for breach of trust was a matter of considerable concern to the Law Commission. Its view was firmly that the balance had swung too far away from the interest of beneficiaries, and that the law had become 'too deferential to trustees'.

Law Commission's initial proposals: a blueprint for reform, and a store of problems to resolve?
To complement this, in its initial outline of reform, on which responses were invited for consultation, the Law Commission recommended a number of proposals which would improve the current position of exemption clauses in English law. There were a number of proposals which would require legislation. In addition, the Law Commission suggested that, as a matter of good practice, at the outset of any trust arrangement, those responsible for drafting the instrument should bring to the settlor's attention the presence of any such clause. This should be accompanied by clear explanation of its implications and a discussion of the alternatives which might be available as protection for those acting as trustees thereunder.

The Law Commission summarised the directions requiring legislation as:

- All trustees should be given power to make payments out of the trust fund to purchase indemnity insurance to cover liability for breach of trust.
- Professional trustees should not be able to rely on clauses which exclude their liability for breach of trust arising from negligence.
- In so far as professional trustees may not exclude liability for breach of trust, they should not be permitted to claim indemnity from the trust fund.

- In determining negligence in the professional trustee, the court should have the power to disapply duty modification clauses or extended power clauses, where reliance on these mechanisms would be inconsistent with the overall purposes of the trust, and it would be unreasonable in the circumstances for the trustee to escape liability.

- Any regulation of trustee exemption clauses should be made applicable not only to trusts governed by English law but also to persons carrying on a trust business in England and Wales.

- Any legislation should apply to any breaches of trust which occur on or after the date when the legislation comes into force, but it should not act retrospectively.

The Law Commission also invited views on other possible directions for reform, including:

- Possible introduction of a 'reasonableness' requirement for exemption clauses: the question for discussion asked whether a requirement of reasonableness should be applied where a trustee seeks to rely on an exemption clause to exclude or restrict his liability for breach of trust.

- Possible role for reasonableness within the context of the professional trustee: the question for discussion asked whether professional trustees should (or should not) be able to rely upon a trustee exemption clause where it is not reasonable to do so by reference to all the circumstances (including the nature and extent of the breach of trust itself).

18.3.5 **After the Consultation: the Law Commission's** *Report on Trustee Exemption Clauses*

In the previous edition of this text, and in response to the 2002 Consultation Paper, it was suggested that the Law Commission's initial recommendations indicated a very strong orientation towards reform, emphasising 'reasonable' use of exemption clauses, and the desirability of distinguishing between trustees who are professionals who charge for their services and others who do not. It was noted that such a reasoning was entirely consistent with the approach taken by the law to expectations of professional trustees as enumerated in *Bartlett* v *Barclays Bank* [1980] Ch 515, and reflected also more recent ways in which the 'professional trustee' had informed legislative changes arising in the Trustee Act 2000. However, it was also suggested that the Law Commission's initial findings needed in several respects to be squared with many 'fundamentals' of the trust.

In the Consultation, the Law Commission suggested that in respect of trustees, and especially professional trustees, other interests in the trust have become much more obscured than they ought to be through the use of exemption clauses. At this time, this concern appeared to provide the rationale for reform, and the Law Commission stressed that it certainly was not an exercise designed to place obstacles in the way of efficient and cost-effective administration of trusts. It appeared that the exercise in reform would aim to restore some much needed balance in the overall calculus of interests. The analysis which was offered in this text at the time was that, in principle, this approach had strong justifications: as long as it really were the case that the hypothesis of 'imbalance' is the most appropriate basis for analysing the current state of trustees' liability for breach of trust, and the role of exemption clauses in limiting this. It was thus proposed by this text that *if* this were the case, this was a sensible and measured approach to take to reconsidering the position of exemption clauses, distinguishing the professional and the lay trustee, and emphasising that there are interests other than those of the trustee to be considered.

It was suggested that this was particularly important for the beneficiary who lies at the absolute heart of trust law's interests. The settlor may be the person who actually settles trust property, but he does this for the benefit of another, and through use of a mechanism which removes from that party all burden and responsibility arising from the trust property. To do otherwise could be achieved through an out-and-out gift: in the trust scenario the settlor intends the beneficiary's enjoyment of the property to be unburdened with responsibility, and to achieve this, responsibility is placed upon the trustee (and in the case of the professional trustee, charges will be made for such an undertaking). Thus, it was suggested that the interests which are currently balanced must be reconsidered, but that alongside this there must be a critical appraisal of whether following a rebalancing of interests a beneficiary will once again receive sufficient protection in respect of trustee-caused losses to the trust estate and its assets. This was so on account of the Law Commission's own admission that beneficiary protection is 'much weaker' than it once was, and that it was the law's responsibility to ensure that any recommended accommodation of exemption clauses will confer *sufficient* protection. It was in respect of this latter observation that this text's analysis asked whether the Law Commission was right to accept so readily the presence of such mechanisms as 'inevitable', and whether greater consideration should actually be given as to whether, fundamentally, exclusion clauses are actually compatible with a trust and its purposes.

This text's previous edition suggested that the Law Commission's proposals did try to address the 'economic implications' of regulation, and welcomed its appreciation that these considerations had to be balanced alongside the centrality of beneficiary protection. In this vein the text concurred with the Law Commission's concern that the actual provision of trust services would not be compromised as a result of regulation, either in decline in availability or through steep increases in costs. As part of its response to the Law Commission's consideration of the possible 'migration' of trusts services—if recommendations made encountered resistance from the providers of professional trusts services—this text suggested that too much accommodation of the providers of such services might have the effect of empowering these well-resourced businesses to an extent that regulatory 'reach' into their activities would be ever harder to achieve.

18.3.6 **The Law Commission's *Report on Trustee Exemption Clauses***

In 2006 the Law Commission reported on the responses it received following publication of the 2002 Consultation Paper. It reported that the responses clustered a number of key points which could be summarised as follows:

- There was strong concern about the way in which exemption clauses are used widely and even indiscriminately in trust instruments, and especially the way in which settlors are often unaware of their import, or even their existence. Accordingly, there was support for some degree of regulation, but there were

also concerns about the impact of any regulatory regime upon settlor autonomy and the protection of trustees in the performance of their duties.

- Although there was support for the Law Commission's proposals for legislation,
there was concern about the recommendations made in respect of duty
modification clauses on grounds that this could lead to uncertainty as to
whether trustees could actually rely on the 'apparent terms of the trust'.

- The proposed distinction between professional and lay trustees was considered
difficult to apply and capable of causing unfairness (especially in the case of professional trustees who acted in a *pro bono* capacity on behalf of certain trusts).

- Questions were raised about the practicality and financial implications of the
proposal that all trustees should have the power to purchase indemnity insurance using trust funds.

- Although there was support for the Law Commission's proposals, concerns
were also expressed about a number of adverse implications which could flow
from legislation that sought to restrict reliance which can be placed on exemption clauses. These clustered:

  — the increasing costs of indemnity insurance and the possibility that this
  might become prohibitive for trustees, and could even lead to insurance
  becoming unavailable if high levels of claims result in insurers no longer
  being prepared to insure the 'risk' of potential liability.

  — the operation of 'defensive trusteeship' which can lead to increased
  expense incurred by the trust: this is especially a consideration in respect
  of exercising *discretionary* powers, where trustees might be especially vigi-
  lant in seeking legal advice ahead of their proposed actions.

  — 'defensive trusteeship' also has the capacity to undermine a trustee's
  effective administration of the trust; and again that especial caution in
  respect of discretionary powers may result in dis-benefits both for the trust
  estate itself and its beneficiaries.

  — an increase in speculative litigation for breach of trust might well result
  from law which either reduces the protection of trustees, or makes their
  level of protection unclear and uncertain.

  — a decline in willingness to accept trusteeship on account of either perceived insufficient protection or uncertainty as to its extent (which might
  well occur in concert with increasingly costly indemnity insurance or even
  its unavailability).

At one level this summary of responses is clear and concise, and the Law
Commission was able to glean from the exercise a range of views and concerns on a
number of key issues. In this respect the Law Commission was able to ascertain that
there was 'instinctive support for reform of some sort'. However, in other respects,
it is clear that the Law Commission found the responses difficult to process, and it
accepted that the Consultation had not translated into 'unambiguous support for
any particular regulatory regime'.

Following Consultation: 'obstacles' to proposals for legislation
In light of this, the Law Commission has accepted that there are a 'number of
obstacles' to the statutory intervention which was initially proposed in opening the
Consultation. It accepted that attention needed to be paid to the following.

The impact on the operation of the trusts system as a whole The Law Commission accepted that exemption clauses operate to control risks which arise from trusteeship, and to keep costs incurred down, which encourages a 'sufficient number of trustees to operate in the market'. In proposing that there was no clear alternative protection available to trustees, the Law Commission accepted that the Consultation had revealed that indemnity insurance would not be capable of providing an alternative model for achieving protection for trustees.

The possibility of adverse consequences and the position of beneficiaries Although the Law Commission suggested it was impossible to assess what the precise impact of regulating the reliance placed upon exclusion clauses in this manner would be, it had concluded from the Consultation exercise that there was a 'significant risk that any such legislation could lead to adverse consequences', and these might be 'more damaging' than originally envisaged in the Consultation. Especially worryingly, given the impetus for the original Consultation, the Law Commission was concerned that any adverse consequences arising—such as trustees' reluctance to administer the estate if any part of this is deemed 'too risky'—would be felt most keenly by beneficiaries.

The impact of original proposals for legislation on the trust mechanism itself Attempts to restrict reliance on exclusion clauses in this manner would restrict the autonomy of settlors to determine the terms on which they settle assets. The Law Commission suggested that in turn, this would limit the flexibility of the trust 'and in doing so detract from one of its greatest attractions'.

After the Consultation: considerations on clauses restricting the liability of trustees which remain unresolved
In the 2006 *Report*, the Law Commission reiterated that serious concerns continue to pertain to the use of exemption clauses: this is because they are able—at their most extreme—to actually exclude liability, and this also renders them capable of undermining attempts which may be made to regulate them. But it sought to balance this with its assertion that '[s]uch clauses are often included in trust instruments for perfectly good and practical reasons not motivated by an intention to avoid liability for breach of trust'. In so doing, the Law Commission conceded that it had been 'unable to frame legislative regulation in a way which would effectively distinguish between these two types of use, other than by creating a complicated system with even greater potential adverse impact'. Thus, in the *Report* the Law Commission shifted its focus to an alternative strategy which reflected a core set of issues on which it did remain convinced following the Consultation, but which would pursue them through a system of 'rule of practice' rather than legislation.

A reiteration of core concerns In making its alternative proposals for regulation, the Law Commission indicated that it shared very strongly concerns held by 'reputable trustees' that trustee exemption clauses should not be included in a trust instrument 'without the full knowledge and consent of the settlor' (see *Report*, para. 3.40). This was so in light of an apparently common situation currently pertaining, in which many settlors 'appear to be unaware of the existence or the effect of' such provisions. The Law Commission stated this was completely unacceptable because it undermines settlor autonomy in determining the protection which they wish to give to trustees, and because it challenges the view that exemption clauses operate in a properly functioning market in which protection given to trustees is appreciated by settlors.

Accordingly, the Law Commission stated that its view was that trustees should be required to ensure settlors are aware of any exemption clauses within their trust deeds. In doing so it made two key points on the inculcation of this into the practice of those who provided trusts services. The *first* was the belief that many providers of trusts services would share this view and support its inculcation; and the *second* concerned whether this should be achieved through legislation 'or some other means'.

In this respect, the Law Commission reiterated that it had already considered the possibility of introducing a statutory requirement that trustees must disclose to the settlor 'any exemption clause on which they wish to be able to rely', but had rejected this during the Consultation on two grounds. *First*, because it would be likely to cause delay and additional cost when setting up a trust, and could create uncertainty as to the validity of the clause thereafter. *Second*, the Law Commission suggested it was unclear how such a statutory requirement could adequately frame the regulation of duty modification clauses at all (see *Report*, paras 6.16–6.21, and 6.28–6.32, and especially 6.34–6.40).

Beyond proposals for legislation: a new approach
In light of its continuing concerns about introducing legislation to regulate the use and operation of trustee exemption clauses, the Law Commission concluded that a better means for achieving reform is for a 'rule of practice' to be adopted by 'regulated persons'. The Law Commission suggested that such a 'rule of practice' would be the most 'appropriate and effective means of influencing and informing trustees so as to secure the proper disclosure of exemption clauses' because '[r]egulated persons would be required to adhere to defined good practice'. The Law Commission believes that such a scheme would not suffer the same defects which could undermine one based in statute because '[c]ompliance with the rule would be a matter of professional conduct for the trustee'. Being in breach of good practice in this manner will not invalidate the clause or affect a trustee's reliance upon it but it will '... render the trustee open to professional disciplinary measures' (*Report*, para. 6.43). In turn, this amounted to a 'proportionate response' to any failure by a trustee to ensure adequate settlor awareness of any exemption provisions within the trust instrument.

The *Report* thus recommended the following 'rule of practice':

> Any paid trustee who causes a settlor to include a clause in a trust instrument which has the effect of excluding or limiting liability for negligence must before the creation of the trust take such steps as are reasonable to ensure that the settlor is aware of the meaning and effect of the clause.

Reporting on its communication with regulatory and professional bodies on the matter, the Law Commission stated that a number, including the Law Society and the Institute of Chartered Accountants in England and Wales, are currently in the process of developing regulation to this effect which is appropriate to their disciplinary structures (*Report*, paras 6.58–6.60). Accordingly, the Law Commission recommended that Government should 'promote the recommended rule of practice as widely as possible across the trust industry'. The Law Commission added that:

> [w]e encourage relevant regulatory authorities to adopt a version of the rule appropriate to the particular circumstances of their membership, and to enforce such regulation in accordance with their existing codes of conduct.

18.3.7 **The Law Commission's** *Report on Trustee Exemption Clauses*: **a postscript**

As we await to see how the Government might promote the application of the rule across the trust industry, and the trust industry's response in adopting the rule and enforcing it in accordance with existing disciplinary structures, the Law Commission appears very optimistic that the 'rule of practice' route will 'overcome the technical difficulties presented by the use of duty modification provisions' where legislation would not be able to (*Report*, paras 6.45–6.50). Indeed, the Law Commission's confidence is evident in its statement that:

We anticipate that the successful adoption of the rule across the trust industry will significantly ameliorate the problems associated with trustee exemption clauses. It will ensure that such provisions represent a proper and fully informed expression of the terms on which settlors are willing to dispose of their property on trust.

In terms of the intended scope of the rule of practice, the Law Commission explains that such a rule should apply to most commonly created trusts, except where the settlor has been independently advised, and in which case 'it is reasonable for a prospective trustee to assume that the adviser will draw the settlor's attention to any exemption provisions' and it is not necessary for the trustee to do so (*Report*, para. 6.79).

Other circumstances where the Law Commission deems that no action is necessary on the part of the trustee to ensure that the settlor is aware of the existence and effect of exemption clauses are:

- In the case of *Commercial trusts* on the basis that 'the settlors of such trusts tend to be market equals of the trustee and so are in less need of protection' (*Report*, para. 6.80), and in any case it is 'already standard practice in many commercial trust situations for information to be provided to settlors about exemption and similar provisions' (para. 6.81).

In respect of 'commercial trusts' the Law Commission also wished to confirm that the rule would have no application in circumstances where *the trustee is subject to statutory regulation of exemption provisions*, such as in the case of unit trust schemes and trustees of debentures where 'an exemption clause can be rendered void by statute'; and where *the settlor acts in the course of a business* (which would cover the majority of corporate settlors and some individuals) unless it ought to be 'reasonably apparent to the trustee that the transaction is an unusual one for the settlor to enter into' (*Report*, para. 6.82).

- In the case of *Pension trusts* because '[p]ensions are to a great extent a law unto themselves'. Such trusts are 'conceptually different from other types of trusts and operate in a distinct manner' and they are already subject to the pensions regulator, created by the Pensions Act 2004 (*Report*, para. 6.83).
- In the case of *Charitable trusts* the draft rule will be largely inapplicable because such instruments do not include exemption clauses and/or have trustees who are remunerated. However, in charitable trusts where there is such a clause, and a paid trustee, making the rule applicable is complicated by the proposition that 'every donor to charity should be viewed as a settlor' for its purposes, and being

required to provide explanation to all donors would be 'wholly impractical' (*Report*, para. 6.87). In these circumstances, the Law Commission recommended that the rule should only be engaged in relation to the original settlor who is involved in establishing the terms of the trust (para. 6.88), and reported (in para. 6.89) that the Charity Commission has indicated that it will be considering an appropriate response to the Report's recommendations.

Ensuring settlor awareness in everyday trusts
These 'everyday' situations are ones in which 'asymmetries' between the person settling property on trust and those who are to be responsible for its administration will be most pronounced. In this vein, and through its ubiquitous and direct references to 'asymmetries', the Law Commission's *Report* does appear to attach considerable significance to the importance of 'settlor awareness', and is concerned that currently settlors frequently fail to 'understand a key component of the bargain negotiated with paid trustees for their professional services'; namely limitations or exclusions on the liability which can be incurred in relation to these professional services (*Report*, para. 6.3). The Law Commission believes that settlor autonomy is actually a powerful justification for upholding exemption clauses, to encourage effective and competitively priced trusts services. However, it insisted equally that while in these circumstances steps should be taken to ensure that the inclusion of such clauses is a manifestation of settlor autonomy 'and not something which has happened by accident rather than design', this does not require the settlor to be furnished with 'a detailed understanding of all the trust's terms'. Accordingly, the rule of practice is seeking to strike a balance between a settlor's entitlement to appreciate the basis on which trusts services are provided, and what is reasonable and practicable for a trustee to communicate.

As the Law Commission itself accepts (see *Report*, para. 3.20), it is perhaps easy to 'overplay' a settlor's capacity to influence the terms on which he engages trusts services, because of the conditions which *actually* operate in the market: this is so on account of 'take-it-or-leave-it' packages commonly on offer, and because such provisions can be buried in 'boilerplate' administrative provisions which the settlor is unlikely to read. However, the Law Commission is right at least to emphasise the *rhetoric* of settlor autonomy and choice because, although it is the beneficiary who will ultimately enforce the trust, settlors are at the heart of trusts created. Thus, settlors' intentions and wishes must remain at the rhetorical centre of trusts, and be paramount in the professional administration of trusts as far as this can be reflected in market provision and practice.

Balancing settlor awareness with the need to give trustees sufficient
protection in performance of their duties
It was noted above that in the *Report*, the Law Commission accepted that provisions which seek to 'manage' the risks which arise from trusteeship serve important functions in controlling the cost of trust services, and ensuring a 'sufficient number of trustees to operate in the market'; and furthermore that there was no clear alternative protection available to trustees, because the Consultation had revealed that indemnity insurance would not be capable of providing an alternative model for achieving protection for trustees. This is an important acknowledgement of the 'trustee dimension' in seeking to justify the continuing operation of clauses seeking to restrict a trustee's exposure to liability because '[s]uch clauses are often included

in trust instruments for perfectly good and practical reasons not motivated by an intention to avoid liability for breach of trust' (*Executive Summary*, para. 1.11). In seeking to confer appropriate protection, the Law Commission's view was that 'any regulation should focus on trustees who receive payment in respect of their services as trustees'. Drawing distinction on the basis of payment has occurred in response to concerns about situations in which an otherwise professional trustee acts in a *pro bono* capacity in respect of a particular trust, but 'payment' is intended to be interpreted flexibly to accommodate indirect financial benefits (*Report*, para. 6.67). Although it is argued by some that trusteeship is 'structurally duplicitous' and an 'asymmetrical' office which is open to easy abuse (see Shapiro (1990) 55, *American Sociological Review*), it is also the case that the office is a highly burdensome one. In its proposals the Law Commission is seeking to reflect this by drawing a distinction between those who are paid for undertaking this onerous office and those who are not.

Compliance with the rule of practice and the interests of beneficiaries

The Law Commission appears to be very convinced that the rule of practice route will provide a flexible and workable route to informing settlors, which is also 'proportionate' in the onus it places upon trustees to draw attention to clauses which affect their exposure to liability. And in drawing attention to 'reputable trustees' who support settlor awareness, the Law Commission must be hopeful that the providers of trusts services will be more open to a route which allows a rule to be accommodated within their own regulatory framework rather than being imposed by statute. And in terms of how compliance can be evidenced, the Law Commission envisions that because (as a result of the consequences of non-compliance) the rule does not require onerous formalities, making disclosure of a clause will not be unduly difficult, and accordingly establishing observance will be relatively straightforward and un-burdensome (*Report*, para. 6.101).

There is good cause for this optimism at one level from the responses it has received from organisations such as the Law Society and the Institute of Chartered Accountants, but the Law Commission does accept that decisions 'whether to invoke disciplinary sanctions would be in the hands of the relevant regulatory body' (*Report*, para. 6.44). In so doing it appreciates that '[t]he regulator's concern would be to promote compliance with the spirit of the rule and the wider aims of regulation'. This, according to the Law Commission, was an entirely different situation from that in which a court 'is asked to rule on whether or not a trustee could rely on a particular protection to escape liability' and in this vein that a regulator is thus 'unlikely to be concerned with unintentional, minor or technical breaches, provided the trustee had acted with reasonable care and in good faith'.

Fundamentally, it remains to be seen whether the Law Commission is correct in its prediction that '[w]e do not believe that the introduction of a rule of practice is likely to provoke great efforts at avoidance' (*Report*, para. 6.96), and to assume with confidence that in the enforcement of the rule, it will be 'applied sensitively with a view to ensuring compliance with the aims of regulation' (para. 6.101). In circumstances where the 'most severe remedies would be likely to be applied only where there was sharp practice or repeated breach' (para. 6.44) it remains to be seen how settlor awareness interacts with a trustee's incentive to take care in the performance of his duties, and whether sufficient protection will be afforded to beneficiaries accordingly.

In this vein the Law Commission also notes that regulatory bodies have a number of mechanisms for policing compliance with their rules, and that it would be open to 'interested parties', which included the settlor and also beneficiaries, to bring breaches to the attention of the relevant governing body. It added that although the consequences of a regulated person's non-compliance would depend on the penalties available to that body, and it accepts that few will have the power to order compensation to beneficiaries, it attached utmost significance to the way in which failure to comply can expose trustees to 'public censure fines and even expulsion from membership and removal of authorisation to act' (*Report*, para. 6.55).

It is in this light that the issue of beneficiary protection requires further thought because while many trustees *do*, according to the Law Commission, belong to such industry associations (in order to take advantages of 'restricted access' opportunities for marketing, networking and education) there are varying degrees of regulation operating between such bodies: while some have rules of conduct, others operate under the 'general principle that membership can be refused or withdrawn where appropriate'. The Law Commission suggested that these latter organisations 'should also promote the proposed rule of practice' (*Report*, para. 6.56), while expressing confidence that its discussions with several professional and regulatory bodies suggest that 'a number would be willing and able to introduce regulation on the basis of the recommendations in the *Report'*.

The 'rule of practice' and the implications of (self)-regulation of exemption clauses by trusts service providers
In many respects, this *Report* represents a balanced appraisal of current use and operation of exclusion clauses, and it is difficult not to be convinced that the Law Commission believes it has found a workable way forward in its recommendations for a rule of practice. This is premised on its belief that there are good reasons for upholding the use of such clauses, beyond providing protection for trustees. These pertain to the way in which 'interfering' with their use could impact considerably upon the cost of trusts services, and even their availability. In addition to the attention which has been paid to promoting 'settlor awareness', the Law Commission has continued to emphasise that upholding exclusion clauses also remains a delicate 'balancing act' of the interests of trustees and beneficiaries which are, it accepts, in many respects actually 'wholly opposed' (*Report*, para. 3.22). Thus, it is suggested that the Law Commission has made a convincing case in favour of the rule of practice to redress the widespread and indiscriminate use of exclusion clauses which is currently also too often undisclosed to settlors.

It is also the case that while enhancing good practice among trustees in respect of disclosing the limits of their liability will help to redress some imbalances between trustees and other interested parties, fundamentally fiduciary office remains one which in the opinion of some is intrinsically and structurally unequal. Those who take this view also propose that asymmetries which are stacked in favour of its occupants can be deployed at the expense of (if not actually against) those whose interests a trust scenario is intended to safeguard. What the rule of practice is in danger of adding to this are the possibilities for cushioning against liability which are commonly associated with the self-regulation of professional practice.

Mary Seneviratne's study of the legal profession (1999, Sweet and Maxwell) has a number of useful applications in this discussion of trustees' liability and compliance with disclosure of limitations which are placed on this. This work points to the powerful positions enjoyed by professional sectors in society, and the way in which this is connected with deeply-rooted perceptions of professionals and professional activity. Seneviratne points to the way in which, in contrast to the concept of a 'trade' or a 'business' (alongside and against which the idea of a 'profession' is often compared) that is a 'commercial enterprise designed for profit', a profession is commonly regarded as being based on 'complex and sometimes arcane learning, and a discipline capable of study which has to be mastered before professional membership becomes available'.

Seneviratne's work also uses theories of professionalism drawn from the work of Durkheim and Weber to make a critical assessment of whether professions really are embodiments of 'selflessness, service of the community and the common good' and 'making necessary sacrifices to obtain the relevant qualifications'. And in the context of this immediate discussion, it is the case that the 'professional' or at least *aspirational* professional dimension of trusts services provision was noted in the 2006 *Report* by the Law Commission's reference to the attractions of belonging to 'regulated bodies', attaching to networking and marketing opportunities, and 'access' to educational opportunities.

What is especially significant for this discussion is the emphasis Seneviratne gives to the close associations of professions with 'ascription to training, ethics, disciplinary action and self-regulation', because these occupational sectors perceive that they place clients' interests before their own, have the highest standards of training and integrity, and accept (as far as is reasonably possible) responsibility for members' failures. In this respect, the rule of practice shows a number of key features of Seneviratne's assessment of self-regulation, and in which relevant occupational bodies will 'lay down quality standards for practice'. However, although the proposed self-regulation of the rule of practice for trusts services providers is envisioned as being encouraged through 'government backing', the Law Commission's tenor in the 2006 *Report* is very much that of 'encouragement' and 'recommendations' of adoption. This is of utmost significance given that a number of discourses within 'regulation literatures' point to the way in which 'self-regulation can be seen to amount to 'self-interest'.

In this light, Seneviratne's observations on self-regulation as a means for achieving consumer protection are highly relevant for this discussion of the proposed rule of practice and the *consumers* of *trusts services*. Illustrating her contentions with the legal profession, she has suggested that self-regulation can be criticised because rules of conduct can be 'drafted in vague and ambiguous terms', and significantly that they can appear to reflect aspects of 'market control' or even the need to 'present an image of geniality', rather than consumer or even societal protection. And in the case of solicitors, her work points to the way in which increasing self-regulation does not necessarily translate into 'a tougher regime for professional discipline and conduct', and she also expresses concerns about lack of 'independence' on account that rules of conduct, along with any required licence to practice, will be controlled by bodies 'drawn exclusively or predominantly from the profession'.

Following on from this, Seneviratne suggests that 'conflicts' in regulation can arise from the way in which a 'governing body' seeks to *promote* as well as *regulate* its members. This means there are 'doubts as to whether one body can effectively both protect the public and serve [its members], as well as carrying out the necessary disciplinary functions'. Thus, it remains to be seen whether the rule of practice and its envisioned regulation will empower this already powerful office still further; an office which even the Law Commission readily admits can harbour 'asymmetries', and one which more extreme views propose is fundamentally 'structurally duplicitous', and one perhaps which needs more regulation rather than less.

18.4 Personal remedies against trustees

All the usual equitable remedies (detailed later in chapter 19) are available to guard against breach of trust, so it is possible, for example, to prevent such a breach by injunction. This section deals with the problems where a financial remedy, for example, an account of profits, is sought once a breach has been committed.

18.4.1 Measure of liability

This is the actual loss to the trust estate which arises, directly or indirectly, from the breach, usually with interest. Where an unauthorised profit has been made, the trustees must account for this profit, but this will be the limit of their liability. It should also be noted that the trustees are liable only for losses which arise causally from a breach of trust. They are not required to act as insurers for the beneficiaries, and any losses which arise despite the exercise of due diligence on the part of the trustees must be borne by the trust estate.

Subject to the above limitations, assuming the claimant can establish a causal connection between the breach and the loss, there are no rules governing remoteness of damage such as apply in tort or contract. Inquiries as to what a reasonable trustee ought to have foreseen or contemplated are not relevant in this context. This may not matter as much as in, for example, a tort action, because the spectre of virtually unlimited liability, such as could occur in a negligence action, for example, if a cigarette end negligently thrown away causes a large ship to explode, is unlikely to arise. The value of the trust property, and profits from its use, provide a natural limit to liability without the need for additional remoteness rules, but trustees could find themselves in difficulties where, for example, the property unexpectedly increases in value. Nor, incidentally, can a trustee set off against the amount which he is obliged to restore to the trust funds the tax which would have been payable on that amount, had he not lost it through his breach (*Re Bell's Indenture* [1980] 1 WLR 1217).

Further, a trustee cannot set off a profit made in one transaction against a loss made in another. The reason is that any profits made out of the trust property belong to the beneficiaries, so the trustees have no claim against those profits to lessen their own liability for loss caused by a breach. A frequently quoted authority is the old case of *Dimes* v *Scott* (1828) 4 Russ 195.

If the profit and loss can be seen to be part of the same transaction, however, the principle of *Dimes* v *Scott* will not apply. In *Bartlett* v *Barclays Bank Trust Co. Ltd (No. 1)* [1980] Ch 515, loss had resulted from a disastrous development, but another development had produced a profit. Although acknowledging the general rule, Brightman J allowed that gain to be set off against the loss, remarking that it would be unjust to deprive the bank of an element of salvage in the disaster. The explanation was that the loss and gain arose from the same policy of speculation in the *Bartlett* case, and that, where gains and losses arise in a single dealing or course of dealing, the trustees will be liable only to the extent that a net loss results.

18.4.2 Investments

Many of the cases concern losses arising from improper use by the trustees of their powers of investment, and some specific points should be noted:

(1) If trustees make an unauthorised investment, they will be liable for any loss which is incurred when that investment is realised. There are, however, qualifications to this principle.

   (i) If the beneficiaries are all *sui iuris* and collectively entitled to the entire trust property, they may adopt the unauthorised investment as part of the trust property. It is not clear whether, if they do this, they may nonetheless call upon the trustees to make good any loss which arises from that investment: *Re Lake* [1903] 1 KB 439 seems to suggest that they may, but this result appears contrary to principle. If the beneficiaries do not unanimously agree to adopt the investment, the trustee's duty is to sell it and to make good any loss.

   (ii) The trustee is alternatively entitled to take over the investment for himself, subject to refunding the trust estate, the beneficiaries having a lien on the investment until the refund is made.

   If an unauthorised investment brings in a greater income than an authorised one would have done, and this income has already been paid over to a beneficiary, the trustees cannot, it seems, require him to repay the excess above what he should have received, or set off this excess against future income.

   (iii) In *Nestlé* v *National Westminster Bank plc* [1993] 1 WLR 1260, Staughton LJ observed that trustees will not be liable if, although they applied the wrong criteria in their choice of investments, their decision is nonetheless justifiable on objective grounds, since then there will be no loss to the trust.

(2) Where unauthorised investments are improperly retained, the measure of liability is the difference between the present value of the investment and the price it would have raised if sold at the proper time; e.g., in *Fry* v *Fry* (1859) 28 LJ Ch 591, the trustees were liable for the difference between the offer of £900 and the sum eventually obtained.

(3) If the trustees are directed by the trust instrument to make a specific investment, and either they make no investment at all, or else they invest the fund in something else, their liability is to supply the same amount of the specific investment as they could have acquired with the trust funds had they purchased it at the proper time. Account will, however, be taken of any payments which the trustees would have had to make regarding the investment if they had acquired it at the correct time.

Where the trustees are given a choice of investments but make no investment at all, they will only be liable to replace any deficit in the trust fund, with interest. This is simply because it cannot be assumed that any particular investment would have been chosen by the trustees if they had acted properly, and it is therefore impossible to base their liability on the value of any particular investment.

(4) A trustee who uses trust money in his own business will be liable to hold any profit which he makes as a constructive trustee for the beneficiaries, or to account for the money with interest, whichever happens to be the greater. If he mixes trust money with his own, the beneficiaries may demand the return of the trust money with interest, or else claim a share in the profits proportionate to the amount of the trust money employed in the venture. Any loss must, of course, be borne by the trustee, and where he has become insolvent, the beneficiaries may have a proprietary claim for the return of the trust fund, in preference to his creditors (see chapter 19).

18.4.3 Interest

Normally, a trustee will be required to replace a loss with interest. Traditionally, the rate of interest was four per cent, which was in line with the rate produced on old-style trustee securities, but this is now recognised as unrealistic, and the proper rate at present appears to be that allowed from time to time on the court's short-term investment account established under s. 6(1) of the Administration of Justice Act 1965 (*Bartlett* v *Barclays Bank Trust Co. Ltd (No. 1)* [1980] Ch 515).

A trustee may be liable for a higher rate, at the discretion of the court. If he has actually received more than the standard rate, he will be liable for what he has actually received. Similarly, if it can be shown that he ought to have received more than he did, he will be liable for what he should have received, for example, where proper investment producing a higher rate has been wrongfully terminated. Traditionally, if the trustee was guilty of fraud or other active misconduct, the rate was raised from four per cent to five per cent, on the presumption that this represented what he had actually received. On the same presumption, compound interest may nowdays be charged, and it seems that this will be a matter of course if the trustee was under a duty to accumulate. Despite the frequent reiteration that higher rates are charged merely as reflecting the actual gain made by the defaulting trustee and not by way of penalty, the extent of the trustee's misconduct may be a relevant factor in the court's exercise of its discretion (see *Wallersteiner* v *Moir (No. 2)* [1975] QB 373).

18.5 Trustees and criminal liability: examining the implications of the Fraud Act 2006

18.5.1 The significance of the criminal law and its limitations

It was noted above (in 18.1.4) that the criminal law may be a very important mechanism for protecting trust property and promoting compliance with lawful behaviour on the part of trustees. However, this notwithstanding, it is also the case that the function of criminal law is different from civil wrongs such as breach of trust (along with commission of a tort or breach of contract), because in today's society it represents the state's concern to protect citizens from harm by making some harms liable to criminal punishment. Thus for a beneficiary, the criminalisation of misappropriations of trust property might have a deterrent effect, and could help to assuage anger against a trustee who has misappropriated property, but unlike remedies found in the civil law, the criminal law does not engage in financial recompense to victims. This is highly significant because in the context of misappropriation of trust funds, a beneficiary is most likely to be concerned with restoration of the trust property.

Fiduciary conduct and the limitations of the Theft Act provisions
Another factor which can severely limit the use of criminal law in the context of trustees' conduct is that it is clear from the commencement of this chapter that not all breaches will involve misappropriations of property by a trustee. This is very important because the legal definition of theft hinges on 'appropriation' of property belonging to another. So while some trustees might simply misappropriate trust property, chapter 15 pointed to numerous examples of trustees' behaviour which, in different ways, illustrated trustees profiting from their fiduciary positions which did not involve this. There was reference, for example, to trustees' 'interested' transactions with the trust's business or its property, and of course unauthorised profit-making. All these examples pointed to equity adopting a very strict approach to making trustees accountable where they have in any way compromised their fiduciary responsibilities, and under newly enacted provisions of the Fraud Act 2006, these activities have the potential to become criminal offences alongside actual misappropriation of trust property.

Although this might appear radical, there is some authority that secret profits were capable of incurring criminal liability for theft under the Theft Act 1968. However, secret profits did cause difficulty for the definition of theft's central concept of 'property belonging to another', and also that the authorities in this area make the criminal position of such behaviour uncertain. Even in situations where there is clarity—such as misappropriation of trust property amounting to 'appropriation of property belonging to another—establishment of criminal liability for theft is always dependant upon establishing that the *actus reus* of appropriating property belonging to another with intention of permanent deprivation is accompanied by the *mens rea* of acting dishonestly. The test for dishonesty in the criminal law is laid down in *R v Ghosh* [1982] QB 1053, which provides that conduct is dishonest if it is found that ordinary people would regard it as such, and also that the defendant knew that ordinary people would so regard it. *Ghosh* is a mechanism for what the Law Commission described in 1999 as 'ordinary standards of reasonable and honest people' to inform what is regarded as criminal conduct. Whether a defendant has acted dishonestly in a given situation is thus a question of *fact* to be determined by juries, and the operation of *Ghosh* is noted as leading to variations in outcomes even in cases which might otherwise appear very similar (see Wilson (2006) 70(1) *Journal of Criminal Law*, 75–92). It may well be the case that ordinary and decent people will consider conduct such as interested transactions or profiting from the trust which are not disclosed to beneficiaries to be dishonest alongside more straightforward misappropriations of trust property. Even if this appears to be the case, traditionally it has been very difficult to accommodate such conduct within the Theft Act's *actus reus* of theft, because of its reference to 'property belonging to another'.

18.5.2 The limitations of the Theft Act, fiduciary conduct, and wider policy movements

The technical difficulties traditionally pertaining to bringing some aspects of fiduciary breach within the scope of criminal liability were considered by the Law Commission in 1999 in the context of its general enquiry into the law relating to fraud. This exploration of the reliance which was being placed upon legislation relating to **theft** to address behaviour arguably more appropriately regarded as **fraud** commenced with publication of a Consultation Paper No. 155 *Legislating the Criminal Code, Fraud and Deception*, and culminated in a Bill first introduced in Parliament in May 2005. The Bill followed recommendations made in the Law Commission's *Report on Fraud*, published in 2002 (No. 276 (Cm. 5560), and government consultation (pursued in *Fraud Law Reform: Consultation on Proposals for Legislation*, launched in May 2004, and *Fraud Law Reform: Government Response to Consultations*, published in October 2004). In November 2006 the Fraud Act 2006 received Royal Assent.

The Consultation Paper was of course framed in reference to concerns about activities which are, in a number of discourses, commonly associated with the language of fraud, because they involve the application of some form of deceit in order to secure economic advantage or cause economic loss. It is important to stress this because although perpetrated across social and economic interests, these activities are not easy to attach criminal liability to. This is in turn because prior to 2006 there was no actual crime of fraud in English law, and so considerable and increasing reliance was being placed on Theft Act provisions relating to theft (which hinge on the appropriation of property belonging to another) and deception which in many cases were inappropriate as well as outdated.

Fiduciary conduct as part of the 'bigger picture' of fraud in wider criminal policy movements
As part of this, in 1999 the Law Commission (para. 4.28) nodded to the difficulties presented by secret profits for criminal liability and how the criminal law had creatively sought to respond to the conduct of wayward trustees which falls short of actual misappropriation of trust property. Reference was made to the decision in *Clowes (No. 2)* [1994] 2 All ER 316, which illustrates that under the current law, *criminal* liability for theft for a secret profit is determined by the *civil* question of whether the secret profit is held on trust for the beneficiary. But the Law Commission also stressed that this was a highly uncertain route to criminal liability. Pointing to the case of the Attorney General for *Hong Kong* v *Reid* [1994] 1 AC 324, the Law Commission noted that a constructive trust was found in respect of a bribe which amounted to a secret profit, and that in doing so the Privy Council declined to follow English authorities of *Lister & Co.* v *Stubbs* and the *Attorney-General's Reference (No. 1 of 1985)* [1986] QB 491. The Law Commission used these cases to highlight the limitations of criminal law premised on proprietary interest in the property in question, proposing (in para. 4.29) that were a general dishonesty offence to be introduced, it would be 'sufficient that the defendant had dishonestly made a gain which otherwise might have gone to another'.

In 2002 the Law Commission concluded that while the current criminal law relating to fraud required reform, this should not be pursued on the basis of a general dishonesty offence. A general dishonesty offence would reflect the argument that all dishonest conduct should in principle be criminal, and this model was rejected because of the dangers of extending criminal law too widely. The Law Commission concluded that a general offence of fraud would greatly improve the position of a number of activities which stretched the Theft Act's capabilities. Many of the resulting Fraud Act's provisions are beyond the scope of this discussion on fiduciaries and criminal liability, but the fraud offence within it does have some important dimensions for the position of trustees in respect of the criminal law.

18.5.3 New approaches in the criminal law: the significance of the Fraud Act 2006 for the conduct of fiduciaries

Within the new Fraud Act is a new offence of fraud. This is located in section's 1–5, and accordingly a person is guilty of fraud if he *dishonestly* makes a false representation; fails to disclose information while under a legal duty to do so; or abuses a position in which he is expected to safeguard or at least not to prejudice the financial interests of another, and in the commission of any of these matters intends to make a gain or expose another to loss.

What follows is a brief consideration of the provisions relating to fraud by virtue of abuse of position and also failure to disclose information, which have important implications for fiduciary conduct which is not easily caught by the offence of theft because of the requirement that property belonging to another is appropriated. How new law might respond to activities which fall short of this is now considered by reference to Law Commission's work, the Fraud Act itself, and the Explanatory Notes published by the Home Office in March 2006 which accompanied the Bill.

On a general level, the Act continues to reflect the current position whereby all potentially criminal conduct must be accompanied by proof that the defendant acted dishonestly: this also remains a question of fact, to be determined by *Ghosh*. It must also be shown that in the commission of any of these matters the defendant intends to make a gain or expose another to loss. For the purposes of the fraud offence, 'gain' and 'loss' extend only to that of money or other property, but include gain or loss which is temporary or permanent. It explains that 'gain' includes a gain achieved by keeping what one has as well as gaining that which one does not; and 'loss' includes a loss by not getting what one might get as well as loss by parting with what one has.

The discussion which follows concerns the two sections within the Act which have very strong resonances with trustees and fiduciary office. In addition, it is also the case that certain aspects of trustees' conduct can be caught by the provisions of s. 2 which relate to fraud by false representation. Indeed, in her exploration of fiduciary office, American scholar Susan Shapiro ((1990) above) contends that because of 'information asymmetries' virtually all such relationships are vulnerable to 'misrepresentation ... exaggeration ... distortion, fabrication of information by persons in positions of trust'. These exploitations of the 'physical and social barriers' to information and property held by trustees, created by their office and their accompanying access to expert information, would potentially fit well and easily into the fraud offence's definition of a false representation as one which is 'untrue or misleading and the person making it knows it is, or might be, untrue or misleading'.

Subject to the requirement of dishonesty, a false representation can pertain to a matter of fact, or law, or a person's state of mind, and as the Explanatory Notes clarify, it can arise impliedly by conduct. For those which are actually expressed, '[t]here is no limitation on the way in which the representation must be expressed' and accordingly it can be 'written, spoken or posted on a website'.

From this, it is apparent that this manifestation of fraud is intended to be widely applicable. Further illumination of this is evident in the examples given in the Explanatory Notes, which make reference to misuse of a credit card (even in the absence of a human operative, such as in the case of 'Chip and Pin' transactions) and 'phishing' activities which encourage recipients to divulge personal information through 'representation' that the request has come from a legitimate financial institution. Despite its clear potential applications for fiduciary activity, it is in the other two manifestations of fraud that *direct* reference is made to conduct arising from fiduciary relationships. Here, fraud arising from abuse of position and failure to disclose information will resonate strongly with previous discussions on appropriate conduct for fiduciaries.

Fiduciaries and fraud arising from failure to disclose information while under a legal duty to do so

In the provisions of s. 3, which makes it an offence to commit fraud by dishonestly failing to disclose information where there is a legal duty to do so, the Act has taken on board the Law Commission's articulation of a 'legal duty' (defined in its *Report on Fraud*, para. 7.28) as one which arises from a number of statutory and contractual relationships and also from the 'existence of a fiduciary relationship between the parties'.

According to the Explanatory Notes, there is a legal duty to disclose information 'not only if the defendant's failure to disclose it gives the victim a cause of action for damages, but also if the law gives the victim a right to set aside any change in his or her legal position to which he or she may consent as a result of the non-disclosure'. This proposition is illustrated in the Explanatory Notes by reference to 'a person in a fiduciary position has a duty to disclose material information when entering into a contract with his or her beneficiary, in the sense that a failure to make such disclosure will entitle the beneficiary to rescind the contract and to reclaim any property transferred under it'. This provision is clearly intended to create criminal liability in situations akin to those currently analysed as self-dealing cases, and ones in which a trustee acts in competition with the trust.

Fiduciaries and fraud arising from abuse of position

Section 4 of the Fraud Act provides that the crime of fraud can be committed by dishonest abuse of position. The Explanatory Notes explain that this applies where the defendant occupies a 'privileged position' and that by virtue of this position he or she is expected to safeguard the financial interests of another or not act against those interests. This is based on the Law Commission's recommendations (*Report on Fraud*, para. 7.38) that establishing requisite 'position' 'will be present between trustee and beneficiary' and across established fiduciary relationships, and extend beyond these as appropriate where there is, on the facts of a particular case, evidence that the relationship between the parties is not one 'at arm's length'. The Law Commission proposed that in nearly all cases where such a position arises, it will be in respect of situations recognised by the civil law as importing fiduciary duties, and the relationship between trustee and beneficiary clearly fits this model.

The Explanatory Notes make it clear that there is deliberately no definition which limits the meaning of the term 'abuse' because it is 'intended to cover a wide range of conduct', and the offence can be committed by omission as well as by positive action. In the language of abuse by act or omission, the Explanatory Notes explain that an employee who, at the expense of his employer, fails to take up a crucial contract because he intends the opportunity to pass to an associate of his commits an offence, and that a *positive* abuse arises when an employee uses his employment to develop products which he intends to sell for his personal benefit. There is no direct reference in the Explanatory Notes to the cases which are currently analysed as ones of conflict of interest and duty, but such conduct (e.g., that involving application of trust property to personal use, and unauthorised profits arising from use of opportunities and information rightfully belonging to the trust) could clearly potentially amount to fraud committed through abuse of position.

Where should the limits of criminal liability for fiduciary conduct lie?

In considering these provisions which have implications for trustees' conduct, it must not be forgotten to see these potentially considerable and wide-ranging new provisions in the context of their development and refinement. It is true enough that the Law Commission did imply that the Theft Act provisions do have limitations in so far as trustees' conduct is concerned, in its implied reference to the way in which wrongdoing will not always be straightforward situations where trustees misappropriate trust property, notwithstanding that this does on occasions happen. There was recognition by the Law Commission that wayward trustees would also engage in activities which were less direct than this, and at least some of these more marginal activities should be brought within the realms of criminal liability.

It is also the case that the Law Commission's remit arose from perceived inadequacy of the then current criminal law—especially the Theft Acts—which was much wider than this, and was particularly concerned with the position of fraud viz. the criminal law. This was at one level because fraud actually had no certain meaning, let alone any standing, within English criminal law; it is also because at the same time, activities which are deemed to be 'fraudulent' are hugely damaging and costly, but were not easily 'caught' by *criminal* provisions. This had led to the position whereby, in absence of any crime of fraud, considerable (and ever increasing) reliance was being placed on provisions relating to theft. It is also the case that while the Law Commission and more recently the Government and Parliament have consistently expressed concern that too many perpetrators of fraud (in the words of former Lord Chancellor, Lord Irvine) 'escape justice' on account of inadequate law and complex criminal proceedings, it is also the case that consideration of the new Fraud Act has entailed much discussion of the way in which any new law put in place must be restricted to 'matters which should properly be classed as criminal' (*Government Response*, 2004, para. 4).

There is little controversy involved in adopting the position that actual misappropriations of trust funds by trustees should incur criminal liability, and this was provided for by provisions of the Theft Act 1968, and there is no indication from the more general fraud enquiries of particular difficulties arising from this position. There is also some support that unauthorised profits were also capable of falling within the Theft Act 1968, through the constructive trust/proprietary interest reasoning. However, the secret profit cases point to wider questions for the new fraud offence which will potentially increase the scope of trustees' criminal liability considerably.

18.5.4 Trustees, personal interest, and criminal liability

It is clear from the very descriptive accounts above, relating to abuse of position and failure to disclose information, how easy it might be for a range of fiduciary conduct which has been encountered up to now potentially to be 'caught' by the provisions of the Fraud Act. This will make criminal liability for trustees in 'grey' areas outside actual misappropriations of property much easier to establish than has been the case. There will no longer be the need to 'find' that a beneficiary has a proprietary interest via the constructive trust route, and the very wide scope which can be applied to 'abuse of position', for example, will ensure that the offence is potentially very adaptable and flexible, and lacking the 'holes' associated with the Theft Act 1968. However, the core ideas of 'grey areas' and 'holes' which make the new fraud offence so attractive also point to a rather different dimension.

Even allowing for the 'safeguard' which is associated with jury determination of whether a defendant has acted dishonestly, it must be considered whether it is appropriate that all the 'fiduciary activities' which potentially *could* fall within the ambit of 'criminal fraud' actually *should* do so. Fraud under the fraud offence is a criminal offence which incurs criminal liability, which can mean a sentence of up to 10 years' imprisonment for those convicted on indictment. It is also the case that apart from any criminal punishment which might arise, there is a large body of literature relating to the criminal law and its 'functions' within society pointing to the unique nature of the criminal conviction.

This rests on the proposition that because of the unique character of the criminal law, in which the state enforces behaviour considered socially injurious, exposure to criminal conviction has consequences which simply do not attach to liability arising from civil wrongs. According to the famous criminologist Edwin Sutherland (in (1945) 10 *American Sociological Review*, 132–9, at 137), the stigma of crime 'places the defendant in the category of criminals and he becomes a criminal according to the popular stereotype of "the criminal" '. It is not simply a question of stereotypings, and being within 'the category of criminals' and incurring a criminal record accordingly is a matter of interest across societal participation. The impact which a criminal conviction can have upon participating in employment, and seeking new employment etc., simply does not attach to incurring liability for a civil wrong.

Fiduciary integrity, liability to account and the basis for criminal liability
The discussion in chapter 15 pointed to a number of activities which infringed the principle of fiduciary integrity: this included situations which resulted in transactions involving trust property being voidable at the election of the beneficiary, and that similar consequences attached to competing with the trust. It also considered how contentious it could be for unauthorised profits to give rise to liability to account. This was framed around the leading and controversial authority of *Boardman* v *Phipps* [1967] 2 AC 46 HL, and offered different perspectives on whether unauthorised profits occurring in absence of *mala fides*, and even conflict of interest and duty, should give rise to liability to account. The contention arising does so because in such situations liability to account (a) represents a 'windfall' for the

trust, and (b) often arises from initiatives taken by trustees which are beyond the call of duty, and in respect of which the trust can also benefit, and without which the trust will not benefit at all. And in this light the decision in *Boardman* itself is highly significant. It will be recalled that this majority decision was one with strong dissent from two judges who did not think that 'causation' between profit and position was sufficient to establish liability to account, in absence of clear conflict of interest and duty. It is also the case that the *ratio* of the case was very unclear on account of three quite different majority judgments.

The discussion of *Boardman*'s 'wider perspectives' in chapter 15 included a presentation of reasons in favour of allowing trustees to profit in circumstances where there is no apparent conflict of interest, and proposed that the trust can lose out from a trustee having no incentive to act entrepreneurially. This was pitched against the counter one based on fiduciary integrity which argues it is essential that an agent performs his duties in a disinterested manner to ensure he acts unequivocally in the interests of his principal. If questions of liability to account for profit-making are capable of dividing the House of Lords as they did in *Boardman*, then how appropriate is it that underling conduct is deemed to amount to breach of position or a failure to disclose information for the purposes of establishing *criminal* liability, which will confer a criminal conviction and the possibility of a sentence of imprisonment of up to 10 years?

This discussion returns to the work of Susan Shapiro considered in chapter 15 in support of maintaining a strict and rigid stand against profit-making by fiduciaries. This present consideration flows from Shapiro's contention (in (1990) above) that beneficiaries can be extremely vulnerable within the trust relationship because of its inherent 'asymmetries': these are ones in information, expertise, and legal ownership of the property, and they operate to empower the trustee. Note has already been made of Shapiro's contention that this position creates opportunities for fiduciaries to *lie* to beneficiaries, and she suggests in addition that the office of fiduciary also creates numerous opportunities for trustees to *steal*.

Shapiro suggests that there is considerable scope for fiduciaries to steal beyond more 'straightforward attainment of personal advantage' such as actual misappropriation of trust property. She proposes that the fiduciary office itself harbours numerous opportunities for other more 'safe and lucrative forms of fiduciary theft'. In this manner, she points to self-dealing, such as investing in companies where there is personal interest; use of trust assets for personal speculation and shoring up own businesses; and insider dealing by way of illustration. She also suggests that even those who are not prepared to use 'inside' opportunities for their own benefit might be tempted to pass them on to another who is an 'outsider' without access but who is prepared to pay for it. She also hints at secret profiting in her discussion of role conflict, whereby a trustee who is valued for his expertise and experience might be tempted to use this for his own purposes.

18.5.5 Fiduciary conduct and the proper limits of criminal liability

Shapiro's examples of 'fiduciary stealing' appear to be very close matches for activities which are envisioned by the provisions of the fraud offence. And if Shapiro is right to contend that trust relationships are '. . . structurally duplicitous', then perhaps it is right that such situations should be criminalised to encourage fiduciaries to act in a manner which keeps their personal interests completely separate from the performance of their duties. This does of course tie into the reference made earlier (in 18.1) that potential exposure to criminal charges may well act as a deterrent to 'wayward' trustees, and it might even be that possible criminal liability helps to promote good practice and diligence as well as honesty. But even in this case, how easy will it be to determine the limits of criminal liability, and to ensure only 'matters which should properly be classed as criminal' are so?

Given the potential reach of the fraud offence for trustees, even if there are good reasons in principle for conduct falling short of misappropriation of trust property to be criminalised, some consideration should be given to the potential difficulties which might arise in bringing within the *criminal* law framework of abuse of position or failure to disclose information situations currently analysed for liability in *equity* as use of opportunities and information rightly belonging to the trust.

For example, how extensively will the example provided by the Law Commission (*Report on Fraud*, para. 7.39), of 'where an employee omits to take up a chance of a crucial contract, intending to enable an associate to pick up the contract instead' at the expense of his employer, be applied, and how clear will its limits be in order to provide the 'fair warning' and 'legal certainty' which lies at the heart of the criminal law? How easy will it be to distinguish this type of situation from that arising in *IDC* v *Cooley* [1972] 2 All ER 162, where there was no prospect of the company principal benefiting from the lucrative contract Cooley ultimately took up, and in hypothetical circumstances where—unlike in *Cooley*—the defendant does not feign illness in order to be released from his existing contract? And in this vein, how will 'abuse of position' work if a fiduciary uses 'trust time' to further personal projects? This is perhaps especially significant because of new approaches to conflicts of interest arising in the corporate context (where a number of these cases can be found located): here provisions of the Companies Act 2006 require most dealings by directors merely to be declared. But given it is not obvious what significance liability to account *in equity* will have in relation to criminal liability envisioned by the Fraud Bill, will this new 'company law' position have any bearing on criminal liability at all? Considerations of fair warning and legal certainty might have particularly strong significance in respect of using very abstract and intangible ideas such as use of trust 'opportunities' or 'information' to establish 'abuse of position', because the conflict of interest cases show difficulties in their application in determining liability in equity.

Fiduciary activity as criminal activity: some concluding thoughts in contemplation of the fraud offence

It remains to be seen how extensively the fraud offence might be used as a mechanism to regulate fiduciary activity, but there is considerable emphasis of fiduciary relationships within both sections 3 and 4 which relate to fraud by abuse of position and fraud by non-disclosure of information required by a legal duty. However, there ought to be considerable care applied to activity which falls into the 'grey' areas 'short of' actual misappropriation of entrusted property. That is not to say that more subtle abuses of fiduciary office should not attract criminal liability, because this office is a very powerful one, and one that is very persuasively argued to be one which is asymmetrical, with inequalities which can make beneficiaries vulnerable. Equally, care must be taken in pursuing criminal liability. This is because although one reading of *Boardman* is that liability to account will arise in any situation where interest and duty *can* conflict, even if the possibility of conflict is a technical one, this is a controversial decision which divided the House of Lords. In circumstances which require a jury to find that a defendant has acted dishonestly, thought must be given to how much significance should be attached to standards which are applied in equity, and whether it is even relevant to inform a jury that behaviour capable of incurring a sentence of imprisonment of up to ten years and a criminal conviction might or might not attract liability in equity.

Aside from this, there is also Bob Sullivan's consideration (in (1989) 53 *Journal of Criminal Law*) that 'civil law questions such as whether a fiduciary duty has been broken ... do not fit easily into trial by jury'. This suggests that even questions of fiduciary breaches which are less controversial *in themselves*, such as self-dealing and unauthorised profit-making in the presence of conflict of interest, may not necessarily transpose well into criminal conduct. Perhaps the words of Lord Steyn in *R. v Hinks* [2001] 2 AC 241 (at 252) might cast light on the need for caution, in his observation that:

> the interaction between criminal and civil law can cause problems ... The purposes of the civil law and the criminal law are somewhat different. In theory the two systems should be in perfect harmony. In a practical world there sometimes will be some disharmony between the two systems. In any event, it would be wrong to assume on a priori grounds that the criminal law rather than the civil law is defective.

Indeed, even for the purposes of establishing liability in equity, the position adopted in respect of some aspects of trustees' conduct—such as profiting from position in absence of bad faith, and even conflict of interest—is not without criticism. This suggests attempts which are made to criminalise such conduct must proceed with due regard to the significance and gravity attaching to criminal liability.

Other issues pertaining to the criminalisation of fiduciary activity flow from the proposition that the criminal law might be a mechanism which helps to deter abuse of fiduciary office. The counter point to this might be that although many trustees today are paid professionals and are resourced and advised as such, not all trustees are in this position, and the office itself remains a highly burdensome one. In these circumstances particularly, there might well be scope for what Bob Sullivan (in (1989) above) has described as 'undermining the security of transaction' as non-professional trustees may be reluctant to contract business on behalf of the trust, and which could be dis-beneficial to the trust and the interests of the beneficiaries.

It is precisely because of the much vaunted 'gravity' of criminal responses that the criminal law could be a highly effective way to discourage abuse of fiduciary office. In this vein, there are very strong moral justifications for pursuing this route because the structural nature of the fiduciary relationship does mean it is easily abused, through asymmetries which empower the trustee. Further weight is added by Shapiro's contention (above (1990) at 355) that the 'social organisation of trust', built on inequalities of information and expertise, not only makes its abuse easy, but also ensures that it is easy to conceal misconduct from victims. In this respect, the fraud offence could be a highly effective tool in controlling the structural difficulties arising from the trust relationship. However, if this is to be the case, then it is vital that it does not occur at the expense of fair warning and legal certainty, which will undermine the integrity of the criminal law, and also its effectiveness.

online
resource
centre

FURTHER READING

Dal Pont [2001] 65 Conv 376–86.

Giddens (2000) *The Third Way and its Critics* (Polity, Cambridge).

Hayton (1990) 106 *LQR* 87.

Jones (1969) 84 *LQR* 472.

Seneviratne (1999) *The Legal Profession; Regulation and the Consumer* (Sweet & Maxwell, London).

Shapiro (1987) 93 *American Journal of Sociology* 623.

Shapiro (1990) 55 *American Sociological Review* 346–65.

Sullivan (1989) 53 *Journal of Criminal Law* 92–104.

Sutherland (1945) 10 *American Sociological Review* 132–9.

Wilson (2006) 70(1) *Journal of Criminal Law* 75–92.

Wilson and Wilson (2007) 71(1) *Journal of Criminal Law* (forthcoming).

19

Remedies

19.1 Structure of this chapter

The general principles applicable to equitable remedies have already been covered in chapter 1. Here personal remedies are now examined in greater detail. There is no point, however, in re-inventing the wheel, and so we assume now a familiarity with the main equitable remedies (as explained, e.g., in Terence Ingman's excellent *The English Legal Process*).

The second part of this chapter pays considerably more attention to proprietary remedies, with which (unlike personal equitable remedies) students are far less likely to be acquainted. The essential difference between the two (personal and proprietary) rests on the way in which a personal remedy is exercised against a 'wrong doer'. This may be for example a trustee who has acted in breach of trust, where a proprietary remedy amounts to an assertion to a right over trust property. The action will not necessarily be brought against the person responsible for the original wrong (in this example, the trustee), but against a third party who has come into possession of the property. The remedy is proprietary in the sense that it goes with the property, and the liability of the third party depends on his possession of that property.

We then move towards a consideration of the liabilities of third parties who may no longer be in possession of (for example) trust property, or where that property is no longer identifiable. The remedies here are again personal remedies, with the third party being liable in his own right for breach of trust as a constructive trustee.

Throughout there will be considerable emphasis placed on the huge complexities and uncertainties which characterise this difficult and at present highly dynamic area of law, within which a number of very different principles are very influential.

Finally, the latest developments will be set out so that some understanding of them can be achieved at a basic level. This is meant to ensure that, at the very least students will be able to appreciate the nature of the complexities which are characteristic of the remedies which are potentially available, their requirements and their relationships with others.

19.1.1 Tracing, constructive trusteeship, and 'conceptual purity'

In a review of the first edition of this book, C.E.F. Rickett objected (in [1992] *CLJ* 172) to Paul Todd's linking remedies and constructive trusteeship in the same chapter. We continue the same approach here because the fact situations which can give rise to a claim in tracing can also often give rise to claims for knowing receipt or knowing assistance, which have traditionally been very strongly associated with the constructive trust. Although this is a view which must be considered in light of the House of Lords' decision in *Foskett* v *McKeown* [2000] WLR 1299, it is also the case that this authority although questioning the constructive trust analysis of knowing receipt actually appears to align it more directly with the process of tracing. Thus the justification for considering tracing and constructive trusteeship alongside one another at the very least remains, and may even have been strengthened by this enormously important decision, which although noted was not given any significant treatment in the last edition of this book.

What this text has been working towards in the previous two editions is achieving a movement towards greater conceptual treatment of constructive (and indeed resulting) trusts and their analysis. An important part of this was setting up an introductory consideration of constructive trusts, which now occurs in the earlier chapter which introduces them along with resulting trusts. This has altered the overall text of the book in such a way that a number of detailed 'case study' chapters now follow on from this introduction to constructive and resulting trusts. In respect of constructive trusts, these are 'case studies' of the co-ownership of property, secret trusts and equitable fraud. Apart from this introduction, the decision was taken to continue treating these 'case studies' as distinct areas of study, and the same treatment can be seen in this chapter on remedies. This is because it deals with concepts which are possibly quite diverse, at least in the minds of conceptual purists. Decisions on structure are not helped by the way in which, despite movements which are suggesting particular directions in approaches to remedies (such as the cases which are pointing to proprietary considerations rather than those based in restitution), there remains a lack of clarity in many points throughout this chapter, and thus plenty of scope for confusion in understanding. Thus, for this edition at least, and most likely in the foreseeable future, the structure which has served this textbook so well over so many years has been maintained.

19.2 Personal remedies

19.2.1 The range of equitable remedies

The primary remedy at common law is damages, which are available as of right, whereas equity developed its own range of remedies, which were discretionary. The most important equitable remedies are specific performance and the injunction, but we have also seen examples of other equitable remedies, for example, account of profits and rescission (see the misrepresentation section of any textbook on the law of contract).

19.2.2 Types of injunction

The following discussion is intended to be an outline treatment only: detailed examination of the various types of injunction is beyond the scope of this book.

19.2.2.1 *Prohibitory and mandatory injunctions*

A *prohibitory* injunction, the commonest type, simply orders the defendant to refrain or desist from doing something. A *mandatory* injunction orders the defendant to do some positive act, such as demolishing a building. A mandatory injunction is very like specific performance, but whereas specific performance usually arises out of contract, a mandatory injunction usually arises out of tort. However, it could be used to force the defendant to undo something which he has done in breach of contract.

Mandatory injunctions are uncommon, and will not be issued when damages would be an adequate remedy, or when the court would be required to exercise constant supervision. Mandatory injunctions will be issued only when it is possible to frame the order very precisely.

19.2.2.2 Quia timet injunctions

'*Quia timet*' means 'because he fears', and this type of injunction may be granted if the claimant can show that there is a very real danger of substantial damage being done to his interests. The aim is to forestall the defendant from committing a wrong, and since by definition the defendant has not yet done anything unlawful, the claimant must make out a strong case, described in *Attorney-General* v *Nottingham Corporation* [1904] 1 Ch 673 as 'a strong probability almost amounting to moral certainty' of the threatened or apprehended infringement of the claimant's rights. This type of injunction is rare, and its refusal will not debar the claimant from obtaining an injunction if the defendant actually goes ahead and commits the wrong.

19.2.2.3 Interlocutory injunctions

High Court cases can take many months to come to court, so courts can, through a swift procedure, grant interlocutory injunctions pending trial. These have the same effect as any other injunction, except that they last only until the full hearing.

Obviously, if an injunction is not eventually granted at the final trial the defendant may have been restrained from doing something he was perfectly entitled to do. Before 1975 it was thought that an applicant for an interlocutory injunction therefore had to prove not only that there was a serious question to be tried, but also that he had a strong *prima facie* case and that the balance of convenience was in favour of the grant of the remedy. The last point was likely to be satisfied if, for example, the claimant was likely to suffer irreparable damage, which could not be adequately compensated by an award of damages, were the defendant's actions allowed to continue until the full hearing. For example, any action which seriously affected a claimant's ability to trade would qualify on balance of convenience.

In *American Cyanamid Co.* v *Ethicon Ltd* [1975] AC 396, however, the matter was reviewed by the House of Lords and the requirements were relaxed. Lord Diplock noted (at pp. 407–8) that the whole point of the procedure was to allow a remedy to be granted *before* the full trial of the main issues:

It is no part of the court's function at this stage of the litigation to try to resolve conflicts of evidence on affidavit as to facts on which the claims of either party may ultimately depend nor to decide difficult questions of law which call for detailed argument and mature considerations. These are matters to be dealt with at the trial. One of the reasons for the introduction of the practice of requiring an undertaking as to damages on the grant of an interlocutory injunction was that 'it aided the court in doing that which was its great object, *viz.* abstaining from expressing any opinion on the merits of the case until the hearing' (*Wakefield* v *Duke of Buccleuch* (1865) 12 LT 628, 629).

Requirement of strong prima facie case

Yet the necessity to show a strong *prima facie* case meant that many of the main issues had to be decided at the interlocutory stage. He also noted that if an interlocutory injunction is wrongly granted the defendant may have a remedy at the full trial, because the claimant will normally be required to give an undertaking as to damages to cover that eventuality. Except in exceptional circumstances, therefore (which remain undefined), there is no longer any requirement that the claimant shows a strong *prima facie* case. He only has to show that there is a serious question to be tried, although the balance of convenience test remains as before. In general, therefore, the merits of the case are not examined at the interlocutory stage.

Sometimes, however, the interlocutory stage is decisive, because the reality of the situation is that by the time of the full trial there will be nothing left to decide. Thus, for example, where an employer seeks to restrain strike action on the ground that it is tortious, it is unlikely that the industrial dispute will remain live until the full trial, so that success at the interlocutory stage is usually decisive. Yet it became clear as early as the decision of the Court of Appeal in *Hubbard* v *Pitt* [1976] 1 QB 142 that industrial disputes would not be treated as among the exceptional cases envisaged by Lord Diplock in *American Cyanamid*. However, in order to make the trade dispute immunities effective (which were in the 1980s and early 1990s rather more extensive then than they are now), legislation (now contained in the Trade Union and Labour Relations (Consolidation) Act 1992, s. 221(2)), provided that where a defendant claimed a trade dispute immunity the court was obliged, in deciding whether or not to grant the interlocutory remedy, to consider the likelihood of a defence based on that immunity succeeding at the full trial.

Since that legislation, which originated in the Employment Protection Act 1975, the House of Lords has held that, in cases where the interlocutory stage will in reality be decisive, the merits of the case may become a factor to be weighed up in assessing the balance of convenience. In *NWL Ltd* v *Woods* [1979] 1 WLR 1294, an interlocutory injunction was sought restraining industrial action. Lord Diplock noted (at p. 625) that *American Cyanamid*:

was not dealing with a case in which the grant or refusal of an injunction at that stage would, in effect, dispose of the action finally in favour of whichever party was successful in the application, because there would be nothing left on which it was in the unsuccessful party's interest to proceed to trial.

Cases of this kind are exceptional, but when they do occur, they bring into the balance of convenience an important additional element: the degree of likelihood that the 'claimant' would have succeeded in establishing his right to an injunction if the action had gone to trial. This is then a factor to be brought into the balance (of convenience) by the judge in weighing the risks that injustice may result from deciding the application one way rather than the other.

The Court of Appeal applied these remarks in *Lansing Linde Ltd* v *Kerr* [1991] 1 WLR 251, upholding a judge's refusal to grant an interlocutory injunction to restrain a former employee from working for a competitor in alleged contravention of a restraint of trade clause in his contract of employment. The trial was unlikely to take place until the period of restraint would have expired or almost expired, and the Court of Appeal held that the judge had been correct in these circumstances, in assessing the balance of convenience, to take account of the strength of the claimant's claim. The case should be contrasted with *Lawrence (David) Ltd* v *Ashton* [1991] 1 All ER 385, where the action was appropriate for a speedy trial, so that the (two-year) period of restraint would still have a significant time left to run, even after the full trial. In such cases, the Court of Appeal held that it is not open for the judge to consider the merits at the interlocutory stage, but that *American Cyanamid* should be directly applied. However, it should not be assumed that *Lansing Linde Ltd v Kerr* is limited to the case where there will be nothing at all left to decide at trial, and a similar approach was adopted by Nolan LJ in *Hanover Insurance Brokers Ltd v Schapiro* [1994] IRLR 82, where about a third of the 12-month period of restraint would have run prior to the trial of the action. Although the earlier case was not explicitly mentioned by Dillon LJ, he was also prepared to consider the merits of the case at the interlocutory stage. Probably little more can be said than that it is a matter of degree, but clearly in restraint clause cases of this type, the length of time prior to trial is relevant to the balance of convenience issue.

19.2.2.4 *Civil Procedure Rules 1999*

Under the very general head of interlocutory injunctions, previous editions of this book will have considered what were known as *Mareva* injunctions and *Anton Piller* orders, and this is the direction in which we shall now proceed, but not before considering why instead we shall be looking at 'freezing' injunctions and 'search' orders. *Marevas* and *Anton Pillers* were renamed respectively 'freezing injunctions' and 'search orders' in April 1999 by the Civil Procedure Rules as part of the Lord Chancellor's Department's drive to make the law and its language, and indeed the whole legal process, more simple, more user friendly and more generally accessible. This direction has its origins in the famous Woolf Report undertaken by Lord Woolf, which identified three central tenets in the (civil) law's failure to meet the needs of 'ordinary' people. The reader will find that a wealth of plain English changes were made to traditional legal terms, including replacement of terms like plaintiff (now 'claimant') and *ex parte* (now 'without notice'). In this context the reader must be aware that *Mareva* injunctions will cease to be named after that case (see below), and are now instead known as freezing injunctions; and *Anton Piller* orders have been renamed search orders.

19.2.2.5 *Freezing injunctions*

The freezing injunction is also a form of interlocutory relief, but whose object is to prevent the defendant from removing his assets out of the jurisdiction, or otherwise dealing with them, until the action pending against him has been tried by a court. Although the original basis for the (then) *Mareva* injunctions was obscure, like the search order (hitherto *Anton Piller* order) considered below, the courts' jurisdiction now has a clear statutory footing, under the Supreme Court Act 1981, s. 37(1) and (2) (powers of the High Court with respect to injunctions and receivers), which reads as follows:

(1) The High Court may by order (whether interlocutory or final) grant an injunction or appoint a receiver in all cases in which it appears just and convenient to do so.

(2) Any such order may be made either unconditionally or on such terms and conditions as the Court thinks just.

The original name *Mareva* comes from the case of *Mareva Compañia Naviera SA v International Bulk Carriers SA* [1975] 2 Lloyd's Rep 509 (although this is not in fact the first reported case in which the order appears). In *Mareva* itself, the claimants were shipowners who time-chartered their ship, *The Mareva*, to the defendants. The hire was to be paid in instalments, but after the third instalment the defendants defaulted and claimed to repudiate the contract. The claimants were afraid that the defendants would remove their assets from the jurisdiction before the claimants' claim could be heard.

Since the *Mareva* injunction is a form of interlocutory relief, the courts are reluctant to allow themselves to be drawn into attempting to make a lengthy and detailed assessment of the strengths and weaknesses of the applicant's case at trial. In *Derby & Co. Ltd* v *Weldon (No. 1)* [1990] Ch 48, Parker LJ said (at p. 58):

It is to be hoped that in future the observations of Lord Diplock and Lord Templeman [in *American Cyanamid*] will be borne in mind in applications for a *Mareva* injunction, that they will take hours not days and that appeals will be rare. I do not mean by the foregoing to indicate that argument as to the principles applying to the grant of a *Mareva* injunction should not be fully argued. With a developing jurisdiction it is inevitable and desirable that they should be. What, however, should not be allowed is (1) any attempt to persuade a court to resolve disputed questions of fact whether relating to the merits of the underlying claim in respect of which a *Mareva* is sought or relating to the elements of the *Mareva* jurisdiction such as that of dissipation or (2) detailed arguments on difficult points of law on which the claim of either party may ultimately depend.

Nonetheless, before a freezing injunction can be granted, the claimant must satisfy tests which are far more stringent than the *American Cyanamid* tests considered above, the requirements being summarised by Rattee J (whose views on the grant of the injunction were upheld in the Court of Appeal) in *Re BCCI (No. 9)* [1994] 3 All ER 764 as follows:

As has been said again recently by the Court of Appeal, there are three issues on which the court has to be satisfied before granting a *Mareva* injunction: (i) has the applicant a good arguable case; (ii) has the applicant satisfied the court that there are assets within and, where an extra-territorial order is sought, without the jurisdiction; and (iii) is there a real risk of dissipation or secretion of assets so as to render any judgment which the applicant may obtain nugatory?

Thus, the applicant must show a good arguable case, not merely (as in *American Cyanamid*) that there is a serious issue to be tried. The second requirement, that the applicant must show that there are assets within the jurisdiction, are relaxed where a worldwide injunction is sought (see further below).

Any kind of property belonging to the defendant may be the subject of a freezing injunction, and has included cars, jewels, and even aeroplanes. But the court will not order delivery of the defendant's clothes, bedding, household goods or tools of his trade, livestock, farm implements, or the like. The court should take care not to put the defendant out of business or prevent him earning his living. The remedy is also personal against the defendant, and is not intended to give the claimant security so as to place him in a preferential position in the event of the defendant's bankruptcy.

The last ten or so years have seen a number of frauds on a truly international scale, but until recently it was thought that freezing injunctions were available only to prevent removal of assets from within the jurisdiction. Since the jurisdiction is personal, however, as we saw in chapter 1, it should not in principle matter where the assets are situated, and it is now clear (in particular from *Babanaft International Co. SA* v *Basantine* [1990] Ch 13 and *Derby & Co. Ltd* v *Weldon (Nos 3 & 4)* [1990] Ch 65) that freezing injunctions can be granted on a worldwide basis. However, since in reality anybody with notice of the injunction can be affected by it, it is granted only in exceptional circumstances, and the courts are careful to frame the order so as to protect the position of third parties. In *Derby* v *Weldon (No. 1)* [1990] Ch 48, Parker LJ said (at p. 57):

In [exceptional] circumstances it appears to me that there is every justification for a worldwide *Mareva*, so long as, by undertaking or *proviso* or a combination of both, (a) oppression of the defendants by way of exposure to a multiplicity of proceedings is avoided, (b) the defendants are protected against the misuse of information gained from the ordinary order for disclosure in aid of the *Mareva*, (c) the position of third parties is protected. Whether, ultimately, the order *in personam* will be converted into an order attaching some or all of the assets disclosed will of course depend on (i) the court here giving the [claimants] leave to proceed in a jurisdiction in which assets have been found and (ii) the decision of the court in such jurisdiction whether to make an order.

19.2.2.6 *Search orders*

These are a type of interlocutory mandatory injunction which (like the freezing injunction) now derives its jurisdiction from the general power of the High Court, contained in the Supreme Court Act 1981, s. 37, to grant an injunction when it appears 'just and convenient' to do so. Before the renaming exercise in 1999, the order was named after the case which gave it judicial recognition by the Court of Appeal, *Anton Piller KG* v *Manufacturing Processes Ltd* [1976] 2 WLR 162. The order received House of Lords approval in *Rank Film Distributors Ltd* v *Video Information Centre* [1982] AC 380.

A search order is obtained what used to be known as *ex parte* (renamed 'without notice') which means in the defendant's absence, so as to catch him off his guard, and is used in cases where the court believes there is a danger that he will remove or destroy evidence in the form of documents or moveable property, such as money, papers or illegal copies of films. The evidence need not be the actual subject matter of the dispute. In addition to ordering the defendant not to move or destroy the evidence, the court may require her to allow the claimant to inspect the relevant evidence or property at the defendant's premises. It is not, however, a search warrant, and the defendant is merely required to allow the claimant to carry out an inspection of the property.

The order is very powerful and the courts are concerned to protect the interests of defendants. As Lord Wilberforce observed in the *Rank Film* case:

Because they operate drastically and because they are made, necessarily, *ex parte*—i.e., before the persons affected have been heard, they are closely controlled by the court: see the judgment of Lord Denning MR in *Anton Piller* [1976] Ch 55, 61. They are only granted upon clear and compelling evidence, and a number of safeguards in the interest of preserving essential rights are introduced. They are an illustration of the adaptability of equitable remedies to new situations.

Among the safeguards are that the applicant shows a strong *prima facie* case, that the damage (potential or actual) must be very serious for the applicant, that there is a real possibility that the evidence will be destroyed, and that the injunction would do no real harm to the defendant or the defendant's case.

19.2.2.7 *Name and function, form and substance and questions of conflicting interests*

At the heart of the Civil Procedure Rules 1999 lies simplicity and accessibility, but the purpose of this section is to ask whether the purported simplicity justifications have come without significant costs. However, this is not intended to be a full-frontal assault upon the recent changes and their underlying rationale. It will instead focus solely upon the freezing injunction and the search order as a means for exploring not only whether the alternatives really are that much better, but more importantly to look at the difficulties arising from their function and application, and the issues they raise which remain after their renaming. Leaving aside questions of whether or not they should have been renamed, it is easy to see why a *Mareva* might appropriately be called a 'freezing' injunction. This, of course, is a reflection of its function and intended effect of rendering the defendant unable to deal with his assets freely and in an unfettered manner. However, will changes in name always be so easy to equate with improvement when regard is had to identification and explanation of function? Here, it is suggested that renaming the *Anton Piller* order a 'search order' can actually illustrate how such advantages can be less obvious, or even more marginal. Whilst search can be an element of what was an *Anton Piller* order, its principal thrust is directed towards preventing the destruction of evidence. Indeed, the court *may, in addition* to compelling the defendant not to move or destroy evidence, order that the defendant be required to allow the claimant to carry out an inspection of evidence or property at the defendant's premises. At the time of these changes it was suggested in this text that renaming these instruments might actually give rise to confusion. But it was also suggested that aside from this, the renaming exercise was one of form rather than substance, so that the injunctions and orders themselves remain powerful instruments of intrusion and pre-trial condemnation—whatever their names.

It appears that we are still striving to strike the correct balance between potentially safeguarding claimants' abilities to bring actions on the one hand; and pre-judging defendants and their activities at a time before trial through discussions of the criteria which must be met before such an order can be granted, on the other. The potential for abuse is still there. However, the need to continually assess interests and consequences which are at best competing (and more often actively in conflict) is perhaps all that can be realistically expected (let alone hoped for) in an age characterised by international frauds and other frightening and less than *bona fide* operations. Indeed, in the following chapter, some of the lengths to which fraudsters will go to to hinder tracing (i.e., the identification of stolen property) and conceal assets more generally will become apparent. There, the display of deliberate self-interested behaviour indicates why powerful arguments of policy emerge to dictate that such activities must not be profitable.

19.2.3 Specific performance and contracts

For breaches of most contracts the only available remedies are at common law, but sometimes injunctions can be granted to restrain breaches of contract, and some contracts are enforceable by decree of specific performance.

Where the remedy of specific performance is granted, the court orders the party in breach to carry out his obligations under the contract. If he fails to do so, he will be guilty of contempt of court. Traditionally, the remedy has been granted only very sparingly in breach of contract cases, but that seems to be changing, and to some extent today the rigid requirements for specific performance have been abandoned in favour of the simpler requirement that specific performance must be the most appropriate remedy. So first we consider some of the more rigid requirements, and then look at whether they have indeed been relaxed.

19.2.3.1 *Damages not adequate remedy*

The traditional position is that if damages are an adequate remedy then an equitable remedy will not be available. Damages will generally be adequate in sale of goods contracts, because the buyer ought to be able to buy equivalent goods elsewhere, and indeed should do so in order to mitigate her loss (if specific performance were generally available then that would significantly weaken the contractual mitigation doctrine). However, it has long been recognised that contracts for estates and in land are enforceable in equity: e.g., *Walsh* v *Lonsdale* (1882) 20 Ch D 9. Even contractual licences are specifically enforceable, as in *Verrall* v *Great Yarmouth Borough Council* [1981] QB 202. The Great Yarmouth council had agreed to hire out the Wellington Pier pavilion to the National Front, but there were elections before the date agreed for the hire. The Labour Party took control from the Conservatives and purported to repudiate the contract. The Court of Appeal held this contract to be specifically enforceable, and though it came as no surprise that contractual licences were specifically enforceable, this was the first case where that was actually part of the *ratio*.

Although specific performance is not usually available to enforce contracts for the sale of goods, it may be if the goods are unique (e.g., a Van Gogh painting), or in other cases where the claimant could not reasonably be expected to find a substitute. Indeed, the courts are expressly empowered by the Sale of Goods Act 1979, s. 52 (re-enacting a similar provision in the Sale of Goods Act 1893), to grant specific performance of certain contracts for the sale of goods. The courts are, in general, reluctant to conclude that the goods in question are sufficiently unique. For example, in *Cohen* v *Roche* [1927] 1 KB 169, McCardie J refused to decree specific performance of a contract for the sale of a set of eight Hepplewhite chairs, on the ground that such chairs were merely ordinary items of commerce. Ordinary damages for breach of contract were awarded instead.

The relaxation of 'uniqueness': a new test emerges
Arguably, there have been relaxations in recent years, where uniqueness of the goods has been held to be not the only criterion in establishing whether the claimant could reasonably be expected to find a substitute. For example, in *Sky Petroleum Ltd* v *VIP Petroleum Ltd* [1974] 1 WLR 576, Goulding J granted an injunction restraining the defendant from withholding supplies of petrol, in breach of his contract with the claimant. Although the actual remedy was an injunction, it was accepted that it amounted to a decree of specific performance. Although petrol is hardly unique, the case arose during a worldwide petrol shortage, when the claimant could not easily obtain supplies elsewhere. Were the remedy not granted, the claimant might have been forced out of business, so that it could not be said that damages were an adequate remedy. Goulding J observed:

Now I come to the most serious hurdle in the way of the plaintiff company which is the well-known doctrine that the court refuses specific performance of a contract to sell and purchase chattels not specific or ascertained. That is a well-established and salutary rule and I am entirely unconvinced by counsel for the plaintiff company when he tells me that an injunction in the form sought by him would not be specific enforcement at all. The matter is one of substance and not of form and it is, in my judgment, quite plain that I am for the time being specifically enforcing the contract if I grant an injunction. However the *ratio* behind the rule is, as I believe, that under the ordinary contract for the sale of non-specific goods, damages are a sufficient remedy. That, to my mind, is lacking in the circumstances of the present case. The evidence suggests, and indeed it is common knowledge, that the petroleum market is in an unusual state in which a would-be buyer cannot go out into the market and contract with another seller, possibly at some sacrifice as to price. Here, the defendant company appears for practical purposes to be the plaintiff company's sole means of keeping its business going, and I am prepared so far to depart from the general rule as to try to preserve the position under the contract until a later date. I therefore propose to grant an injunction.

Beswick v *Beswick* [1968] AC 58 is another case where damages were considered inadequate, and specific performance granted to the estate, even though the obligation was only to pay money (an annuity). The problem was that the annuity was to be paid to a third party, and damages to the contracting party would therefore have been nominal only (because he personally had suffered no loss). There are, however, other justifications for the remedy in *Beswick* v *Beswick*. Lord Pearce thought that damages would not have been an adequate remedy even had it been an ordinary two-party contract, because a single award of lump sum damages is not appropriate where the contractual obligation had been to provide a continuing annuity. Further, the contract satisfied the mutuality requirement, since the obligation of the innocent party (whose personal representative was suing) was to transfer the goodwill of a business, and if he had failed to do so specific performance could have been awarded against him.

If, however, the courts regard the fact that a contract is intended to benefit a third party *per se* as a strong ground for the grant of the equitable remedy, then that provides support for the view that the requirements for specific performance have been relaxed.

19.2.3.2 *Remedy discretionary*
Specific performance will not be awarded where it is not the most appropriate remedy, and this may follow from the discretionary nature of the remedy. The remedy of specific performance is, in principle, available to enforce a contract for the sale of land, but it will not be granted, for example, where due to some special circumstance to grant specific performance would be grossly unfair to the defendant. *Wroth* v *Tyler* [1974] Ch 30 concerned a contract to sell a bungalow, for which specific performance would normally be available. As far as both parties to the contract knew, the only encumbrance on the title was the vendor's mortgage, which would ordinarily not matter as the vendor would use the purchase price to pay it off. Unfortunately, the vendor's wife objected to moving, and subsequently tried to stop the sale by entering a notice of her right of occupation under the Matrimonial Homes Act 1967. This put the vendor into an impossible position, since in order to fulfil his contract he would have had to sue his own wife in order to get the notice removed, and he withdrew from the sale. Megarry J refused to grant specific performance, and awarded the purchaser damages instead, which were based on the difference between the market value of the bungalow at the date of the contract and its value at the date of the judgment (and since house prices had risen considerably in the meantime, the award was substantial).

19.2.3.3 *Not granted where constant supervision required*
A one-off sale is one thing, but an order requiring the defendant to perform a series of acts over a period of time is quite another. The courts have no machinery for

exercising continuous supervision to make sure that the defendant carries out an order, and rather than risk the law being flouted, they will refuse to grant an order in such circumstances.

In *Ryan v Mutual Tontine Westminster Chambers Association* [1893] 1 Ch 116, the lessor of a flat agreed in the lease that he would appoint a porter who would be constantly in attendance to clean the passages, deliver mail, etc. In fact, he appointed a porter who also worked as a chef in a nearby club, and who was constantly absent. The claimant sought specific performance, but the Court of Appeal held that his only remedy was damages for breach of contract: the court would not attempt to supervise the daily goings-on in a block of flats.

Specific performance and contracts for building and repair

Contracts to build or repair will not normally be specifically enforced. This is partly because the courts will not supervise, but also because the wronged party can normally find another builder to do the work (in other words, damages are an adequate remedy, on the principles discussed in the previous section). Nevertheless, there are exceptional cases where specific performance has been awarded. One such case was the Court of Appeal decision in *Wolverhampton Corporation v Emmons* [1901] 1 KB 515, where the claimant corporation had actually sold the land to the defendant, who had contracted to erect a number of buildings on the land, in pursuance of a scheme of street improvement. The defendant had defaulted on his obligations regarding the buildings, but as purchaser had gone into possession of the land, so that the corporation could not have sent in a different firm of builders without committing a trespass. In this case, the court held that the corporation could not be adequately compensated by damages, and ordered the defendant actually to carry out the work. Another material factor was that the building obligations had been defined in detail in the contract, so the court could see the exact nature of the work required.

There are also a number of old cases involving railway companies. If the company had built a railway through a farmer's land, having undertaken to build a bridge to allow the farmer to go from one part of his farm to another, the courts used to regard damages as an inadequate remedy, and decree specific performance. The most important single factor in these cases is that the defendant is in possession of the land, so that it is impossible for the injured party to provide for the work to be done by other means.

19.2.3.4 *Mutuality requirement*

In any case involving land the contract is specifically enforceable by *both* parties (vendor as well as purchaser), and generally speaking any contract which is specifically enforceable by one party is also specifically enforceable by the other. This is termed the 'mutuality requirement', and though there are exceptions, a common ground for specific performance of a contract being refused is that the contract could not be similarly enforced by the other party.

In *Flight v Bolland* (1828) 4 Russ 298, for example, a minor failed to obtain a decree of specific performance, since specific performance will not normally be ordered *against* a minor. A contract is specifically enforceable, however, as long as there is mutuality at the date of trial—it does not matter if mutuality did not exist at the time the contract was made. In *Price v Strange* [1978] Ch 337, the defendant had agreed to grant to the claimant a lease, which contained a provision that the claimant should carry out internal and external repairs. The courts will not normally enforce a contract to repair, so there was no mutuality at the time the contract was made. However, by the time of the trial, the claimant had carried out the internal repairs and although the external repairs had been carried out by the defendant, the claimant had expressed willingness to pay for them. By the time of the trial, therefore, repairs were no longer an issue, and the only question was whether the agreement to grant the lease should be enforced. The Court of Appeal held that mutuality was now satisfied, and that specific performance could be granted.

An exception to the mutuality requirement is that a victim of misrepresentation may enforce a contract, even though the contract could not be enforced against him because the misrepresentation would entitle him to avoid the contract.

19.2.4 Damages in lieu of injunctions and specific performance

19.2.4.1 *Damages in lieu of specific performance*

Before the Chancery Amendment Act 1858, the Court of Chancery had no power to grant damages in lieu of specific performance, and a disappointed claimant was obliged to start his action all over again in the common law courts to recover damages. The 1858 Act gave the Chancery courts power to award damages in lieu, or even in addition to, specific performance. Additional damages are only awarded if there has been some special damage to the claimant.

The 1858 Act was repealed in 1883, but the power to award damages was preserved through a series of later enactments, and is now to be found in the Supreme Court Act 1981, s. 50.

Like specific performance itself, damages granted in lieu of specific performance are discretionary, and the claimant will only be able to obtain equitable damages where the court could have granted him specific performance at the date when the action was begun.

19.2.4.2 *Damages in lieu of injunction*

As with specific performance, a court can award equitable damages in lieu of an injunction, by virtue of the same section of the Supreme Court Act 1981. Since in this event, the defendant is able to carry on as before, subject only to a payment of damages to the plaintiff, the court must take pains to ensure that the defendant cannot use damages in lieu simply as a licence to continue committing a wrong.

In *Shelfer* v *City of London Lighting Co.* [1895] 1 Ch 287, A.L. Smith LJ took the view that damages should be awarded in lieu only where the injury to the claimant was small, was capable of being estimated in money terms, and would be adequately compensated by a small payment, and where it would be oppressive to grant an injunction. The Court of Appeal there granted an injunction restraining excessive vibration, despite the fact that this might interfere with electricity supplies.

The *Shelfer* principles are obviously open to interpretation (e.g., what is meant by 'small'?), but the courts are generally very reluctant to grant damages in lieu, especially where a continuing trespass, or a continuing nuisance is complained of. For example, in *Kennaway* v *Thompson* [1980] 3 WLR 361, the Court of Appeal set aside the trial judge's refusal to grant an injunction against power-boat racing, where damages of £16,000 were awarded in lieu, and substituted an order restricting the racing to certain times and limited noise-levels.

19.3 **Remedies and third parties: tracing, receipt of trust property, and breach of trust**

What follows is a consideration of the range of the different remedies which are potentially available to a beneficiary, and which do not depend on the retention of the property (i.e., that which was taken in breach of trust) by the original wrong-doer (in this case the trustee). These will vary according to the circumstances, and particularly according to what has happened to the property since it was taken in breach of trust. Moreover, they comprise a mixture of proprietary remedies and ones which are personal actions arising from receipt of trust property or assistance in the wrongdoing which has occurred.

Consider persons other than the original wrongdoer
The necessity for mechanisms to be available for the pursuit of persons other than the original wrongdoer lies in the reality that property which is stolen (and this will of course include property applied in breach of trust) is likely to change hands many times; because stolen property is 'hot property'. This may be the same property changing hands several times, and even ending up in the hands of someone unaware of its dubious origins. Equally, it may well be the case that what ends up in the hands of someone entirely unconnected with the original wrongdoing is actually not the original property itself but either the (monetary) proceeds of it or a completely different article. This latter position of the appearance of different property is another reality of stolen property being 'hot property', but whether the property is the original subject of the theft or replacement property, its original 'thief' is likely to want to off-load it at the earliest possible opportunity.

Remedies: range and application
The remedies which are potentially available in the circumstances can be fairly clearly set out. However, the way in which they have been set out here does not in any way capture the complexity of their operation in practice (and even at a theor-etical or conceptual level). This is a very complex area, and it is so because of its dynamism and the incredible pace at which the law is developing—to such an extent that any clear statement about the law as it stands in this area is virtually impossible; the current position of many of these remedies and their relationship and interactions with others is the subject of much complexity and even confusion. In a climate where the principles of restitution and proprietary entitlement are both very influential, students will need to have a grasp of the requirements of the applic-able remedies, and the factors which operate to distinguish them.

19.4 **Tracing**

In this section, distinction is drawn between common law and equitable tracing, and also between personal and proprietary claims. A proprietary tracing claim involves the claimant in identifying his property in the hands of the defendant. It is necessary for the defendant not only to have received but also to retain the claimant's property. Hence, if the defendant no longer has the property, a proprietary tracing claim will not be available. However, a proprietary claim is essential if the defendant is bankrupt, and is also useful if the property has increased in value, since the claimant by identifying the property can benefit from its increase in value.

At common law, there is also the restitutionary action for money had and received. This is a personal claim, which requires the claimant to show only (subject to the complete and partial defences described below) that the defendant received the claimant's property, and not necessarily that he still retains it. Though it is conceptually entirely different from a proprietary tracing action, it is nevertheless usually described as a form of common law tracing, and is considered in this section. There is also a personal form of equitable tracing, which is more conveniently dealt with subsequently, along with the other personal claims in equity.

A personal claim arises from the receipt by the defendant of the claimant's property, and the defendant remains liable even if she later divests herself of it, or indeed if the property is destroyed or is no longer identifiable. It is no use if the defendant is bankrupt, and unlike a proprietary claim, a personal claim will not allow the claimant to recover increases in the value of the property.

Knowing receipt, which is considered later, requires that the defendant has received property to which the claimant has equitable title. In order to establish this, it may be necessary to trace it into the defendant's hands using a proprietary equitable claim (as in *El Ajou* v *Dollar Land Holdings plc (No. 2)* [1995] 2 All ER 213).

19.4.1 Tracing at common law

19.4.1.1 *Proprietary tracing*

As we observed in chapter 1, legal title is, in principle, enforceable against anybody in the world, and it might therefore be thought that if the claimant can establish that the defendant has his property, he should be able to recover it. However, whereas the common law developed an action for the recovery of a specific piece of land, it never extended this 'real' remedy to allow a claimant to recover a specific chattel. Although the common law acknowledged the claimant's ownership of the chattel, his action was a personal action in detinue, the remedy for which was damages. The defendant could therefore choose whether to return the claimant's chattel or pay him its full value as damages.

The Common Law Procedure Act 1854, s. 78, gave the court a discretion to order specific delivery of the chattel, and this power is retained by s. 3 of the Torts (Interference with Goods) Act 1977. But there is no absolute right to the return of the chattel. The importance of the proprietary claim lies rather in the fact that it entitles the claimant to the full value of the chattel, in preference to the claims of the defendant's other creditors.

The common law also concluded that the claimant's right should continue even if the defendant had exchanged the claimant's property for some other property, or sold it and purchased other property with the proceeds. So long as it was possible to 'trace' his original property—i.e., to show that what the defendant now holds can be regarded as simply a substitute—his claim was unaffected. In *Re Diplock's Estate* [1948] Ch 465, Lord Greene MR explained the doctrine in terms of the claimant ratifying the wrongful sale of purchase, to enable the legal owner to claim the substitute.

In *Taylor* v *Plumer* (1815) 3 M & S 562, Sir Thomas Plumer had handed over money to a stockbroker with instructions to purchase exchequer bonds, but the stockbroker instead purchased American investments and bullion, and attempted to abscond with these. He was caught before he could leave England, and the investments and bullion were seized by Plumer. The assignees of the stockbroker then brought an action to recover them from Sir Thomas, but failed. The investments and bullion were held to be Sir Thomas's own property. In effect, Plumer's money was traced into the investments and bullion for, according to Lord Ellenborough, at p. 575, 'the product of or substitute for the original thing still follows the nature of the thing itself, as long as it can be ascertained as such'.

As Millett LJ observed in *Trustees of the Property of F.C. Jones & Sons* v *Anne Jones* [1996] 3 WLR 703, *Taylor* v *Plumer* was actually decided on equitable principles (see also Lionel Smith [1995] LMCLQ 240), but claims to substitute assets were upheld in *Banque Belge* v *Hambrouck* [1921] 1 KB 321 and *Lipkin Gorman* v *Karpnale Ltd* [1991] 2 AC 548 (below), and indeed, in *Trustee of the Property of F.C. Jones & Sons* v *Anne Jones* itself. So it is clear that a substitution doctrine is recognised by the common law.

Two other points need to be made about the substitution doctrine. First, if it depends on ratification, the claimant is equally entitled not to ratify the transaction and instead to claim the original property. Second, where (for example) money is paid into a bank account, at any rate where it is unmixed with other money, it is exchanged for a cause of action against the bank. In *Diplock*, Lord Greene MR thought that there was no reason why the common law would not allow the substitution of the money into the cause of action, and *vice versa*:

If it is possible to identify a principal's money with an asset purchased exclusively by means of it, we see no reason for drawing a distinction between a chose in action such as a banker's debt to his customer and any other asset. If the principal can ratify the acquisition of the one, we see no reason for supposing that he cannot ratify the acquisition of the other.

This passage was approved by Millett J in *Agip (Africa) Ltd* v *Jackson* [1990] 1 Ch 265, but he thought that it was limited to following an asset into a changed form in the same hands, rather than following the same asset from one recipient to another. Millett J did not think that it necessarily followed that the common law allowed free tracing of causes of action from one person to another.

19.4.1.2 *Money 'had and received'*

The proprietary tracing claim considered above depends on the claimant being able to trace his actual property, or as in *Taylor* v *Plumer* its product or substitute, into the defendant's hands. In the case of currency, title will pass to the recipient, but the law imposes on the recipient of (say) money stolen from the claimant an obligation to reimburse the claimant with an equivalent sum. From the recent House of Lords decision in *Lipkin Gorman* v *Karpnale Ltd* [1991] 2 AC 548, and in particular the speech of Lord Goff, the basis of the action appears to be that the defendant has been unjustly enriched at the expense of the claimant. The claim is established merely by showing that the defendant has received the claimant's property. The defendant's knowledge (or lack of it) is irrelevant. Nor is the action defeated by the recipient later disposing of the money, or mixing it with his own money, since the claim is a personal and not a proprietary one. It is defeated, however, if the recipient has not been unjustly enriched. Innocently to receive stolen money in return for full consideration is not to be unjustly enriched at all, so that for example, a shop which has innocently taken stolen money to pay for its goods is not liable to the victim of the theft.

Consideration recognised by the common law must be provided, however. In *Lipkin Gorman* v *Karpnale Ltd* [1991] 2 AC 548, Cass, a partner in the appellant firm of solicitors, by cashing cheques of which he was an authorised signatory, stole a large sum of money from the firm's clients' account. He took the cash to the Playboy Club, which was owned by the respondents, whereupon he gambled it away. The appellants successfully claimed the club's winnings from Cass, although property in the money had undoubtedly passed to the respondents and they no longer had the money. The owners of the club were unable to claim that they had provided consideration for the money, since contracts by way of gaming and wagering were rendered null and void by the Gaming Act 1845, s. 18. Gambling contracts were therefore not contracts for consideration.

Lipkin Gorman: two further points

Two further points arise from *Lipkin Gorman*. First, the claimants (the firm of solicitors) never had legal title to the money in the clients' account, only a debt (i.e., a cause of action) against the bank. The House of Lords held that they were entitled to trace the cause of action, however, since that was a species of legal property (but see the criticism of this by Margaret Halliwell [1992] Conv 124). On the tracing of causes of action see further below. There is, we would suggest, another possible explanation of the cause of action in *Lipkin Gorman*. There was nothing apparently wrong with the cheques that Cass presented to the bank, and the bank was entitled to pay him the money, as it did. But there is no reason to suppose that title to the money, which had, after all, been obtained by virtue of his position in the claimants' firm, passed to Cass. The correct analysis must surely be that he drew out the claimants' money, which he used to gamble at the Playboy Club.

Second, the case establishes a change of position defence to the restitutionary common law claim, where the defendant has altered his position in good faith, so that it would be inequitable to require him to make restitution or restitution in full. This defence was used in *Lipkin Gorman* to limit the claimants' right to recover to the net winnings taken by the casino, rather than all the money gambled by the thief. Paying out money as winnings constituted a change of position by the club.

Subsequent adoption of the change of position defence The change of position defence was applied by Tuckey J in *Bank Tejarat* v *Hong Kong and Shanghai Banking Corporation (Ci) Ltd and Hong Kong and Shanghai Bank Trustee (Jersey) Ltd* [1995] 1 Lloyd's Rep 239. Bank Tejarat had been induced, by a fraudulent transaction, to advance money (under a bankers' documentary credit) to the account of the fraudsters (CAK) at Hong Kong and Shanghai Banking Corporation (Ci) Ltd. Hong Kong later paid the money, in pursuance of an apparently legitimate instruction, to one Madame Parvin Farzaneh, a lady in Paris. When the fraud was discovered, Bank Tejarat sued Hong Kong for money had and received. They failed because they were unable to establish that Hong Kong had ever received any of their money, but also because Hong Kong had a change of position defence, having paid the money away, in good faith, before receiving any notice of Tejarat's claim.

It is not yet clear whether the change of position defence applies only to money had and received, or to any of the restitutionary claims considered in this and the following section.

It is also not clear what happens when money is paid to a second recipient, but Millett argues (convincingly, we would suggest) in (1991) 107 LQR 71, at p. 79, that since the action is personal and not proprietary, what happens to the money after it has been received by the first recipient is irrelevant. It becomes the property of the first recipient, and any subsequent recipient will be receiving the first recipient's money, rather than that of the claimant. It ought also to follow that the first recipient will be liable to reimburse only the value of what was received, and if he makes a favourable investment with it, he should be able to keep the benefit of that. Authority to the contrary can be found in Nourse LJ's judgment in *Trustee of the Property of F.C. Jones and Sons (a firm)* v *Anne Jones* [1996] 3 WLR 703, [1996] 4 All ER 721, but this looks incorrect in principle, and it is in any case weak authority as Millett and Beldam LJJ reasoned on the basis of a proprietary tracing claim.

19.4.1.3 *Identification of property at common law*

The main constraint on common law tracing is establishing that what the defendant has, or in the case of the money had and received claim, what he received, was in fact the claimant's property. While *Taylor* v *Plumer* shows that tracing is available where a straightforward exchange of the property has occurred, the position is more complicated where the property or its proceeds have been placed into a bank account, and it is in this area where equitable rules appear to be more generous. However, in *Re Diplock's Estate*, Lord Greene MR saw no reason in principle why money should not be substituted for a chose in action, or *vice versa*, at any rate where the entirety of the money was substituted for a chose in action, for example where it was used to open a bank account in which there was no other money.

The leading case

The leading authority is *Banque Belge pour L'Etranger* v *Hambrouck* [1921] 1 KB 321. Hambrouck, who was a cashier, stole cheques from his employer, altered them so as to make it appear that they were drawn by his employer on the claimant bank to Hambrouck's order, and used them to pay money into a new account (at Farrow's Bank) which he opened specifically for the purpose. Farrow's Bank collected the proceeds from the claimant bank and credited them to Hambrouck's account. Hambrouck then paid various sums, by cheque, from this account to Mlle Spanoghe, with whom he was living, either for no consideration, or in consideration for her future cohabitation, a consideration which would not be recognised at common law. She paid the cheques (and no other money) into a deposit account of her own at a different bank (London Joint City and Midland Bank). Mlle Spanoghe later spent most of the money in this account, but £315 remained, and the Court of Appeal held that the claimant bank was entitled to trace this money.

It is difficult precisely to ascertain the *ratio* of *Banque Belge* since the three judgments differ considerably. Scrutton LJ apparently took the view that the money could not be traced at common law, since it changed its identity when paid into the account at Farrow's Bank, but could be traced in equity (as is undoubtedly the case). Bankes LJ felt that tracing at common law was permissible, but only because the proceeds of Hambrouck's fraud had never been mixed with any other money, either at Farrow's or Mlle Spanoghe's bank. Atkin LJ appeared to take the view that the question of the property's identification was the same in common law and equity, in which case common law tracing would be possible even into mixed funds.

The orthodox view (but see Goode (1979) 95 LQR 360), is probably that of Bankes LJ, and it is impossible to support Atkin LJ's view in the light of the Court of Appeal decision in *Agip (Africa) Ltd* v *Jackson* [1991] Ch 547, considered further below. Bankes LJ appeared to treat the claim as a proprietary claim at common law. Clearly, the claimant bank started with legal title to the money, and since Bankes LJ rejected the proposition that the money passed between the banks as currency, the money would have remained the property of the claimants when it was transferred to Hambrouck's account at Farrow. It is not clear that any cash was transferred from Farrow to London Joint City and Midland Bank (Mlle Spanoghe's bank), so presumably the claimants could not continue to follow the money itself. However, since there was no other money in Hambrouck's account, they could presumably convert the money into the causes of action represented by the cheques, and convert back again into the money in Mlle Spanoghe's account (where again, there were no other funds). Bankes LJ did not accept that title ever passed to Mlle Spanoghe, so this must have been a proprietary common law tracing claim (since title passes with a money had and received claim—in any case, there would have been no reason to limit a personal claim to the £315 remaining in the account).

Identification, orthodoxy and restrictions in analysis
There are, however, serious restrictions on this analysis, which limit the value of common law tracing of money. We have observed the requirement in *Re Diplock* that the money must be exclusively converted into the cause of action, and *vice versa*. This implies (as Bankes LJ accepted) that if, at any stage, the claimant's money had become mixed with other funds belonging to Hambrouck or the defendant, it would have been impossible to trace it at common law. The common law will not trace into mixed bank accounts. Since mixing will often occur where funds are misappropriated, this severely curtails the usefulness of tracing at common law.

An unusual recent case, where a proprietary tracing claim succeeded at common law, is *Trustee of the Property of F.C. Jones and Sons (a Firm)* v *Anne Jones* [1996] 3 WLR 703. Mrs Anne Jones opened an account with a firm of commodity brokers in order to deal on the London Potato Futures Market, and paid into it three cheques totalling £11,700, drawn on the firm's partners' account, the money in which (it was held) belonged to the claimant. Mrs Jones's dealings in potato futures proved to be highly profitable. She received two cheques totalling £50,760 from the commodity brokers and paid them into a call deposit account (at Raphaels), in which there was remaining a balance of £49,860. This money was claimed by the claimant, on the grounds that the legal title was vested in him, and the Court of Appeal held that he was entitled to the entirety of the £49,860 remaining in the call deposit account, and hence the profit element. In Millett LJ's view, this was a proprietary claim, none of the money having been mixed with other money, and no property having passed to Mrs Jones. He thought that, in contrast, a money had and received action would have been limited to the amount of the money received, or £11,700, but that the trustee had made a proprietary rather than a personal claim. Indeed, a money had and received claim was not available here because title to the money had not passed to Mrs Jones. Nourse LJ agreed with Millett LJ, but also (apparently) took the view that the same result could be reached on the basis of a money had and received claim.

Receipt of money and the reasoning in F.C. Jones
Note that the reasoning in *F.C. Jones* can apply only where the money is not mixed. If Anne Jones had mixed the money with her own before investing it, legal title would have passed to her, in which case the only action at common law would have been for money had and received (for £11,700). Only if she had the requisite knowledge for a knowing receipt claim (see 19.3.2) would the claimant then have been able to claim the profit element, in equity rather than at common law. It might be thought that since Mrs Jones was a volunteer the claimant would also have been able to trace in equity, whatever the state of her knowledge, on the principles in *Re Diplock*, considered below, but this is not correct because the claimant originally had only legal but not equitable title to the money.

Apart from the problem that the common law cannot follow money once it has become mixed, another limitation was suggested by Millett J in *Agip (Africa) Ltd v Jackson* [1990] 1 Ch 265, that whereas the common law will substitute causes of action for tangible property, and *vice versa*, as long as the property remains in the same hands, it can only follow a physical asset, such as a cheque or its proceeds, from one person to another. Without the cheque, in other words, it would have been impossible to follow the chose in action it represented into Mlle Spanoghe's account. The inability to trace money into and out of mixed bank accounts, and to follow causes of action except where they are represented by a physical asset, such as a cheque, was fatal to the common law tracing claim (for money had and received) in *Agip (Africa)* itself.

Misappropriation and mixing: Agip (Africa) v Jackson
In *Agip (Africa)*, the claimant company's chief accountant fraudulently altered payment orders which had been signed by an authorised signatory of the claimant, altering the name of the payee to that of a company (Baker Oil) of which the defendants were directors and shareholders. The forged payment order (for over US$ half a million) was taken to the Banque du Sud in Tunis, which debited the claimant's account and sent telexed instructions to a London bank (Lloyds) to credit the account which Baker Oil had there. The Banque du Sud also instructed its correspondent bank (Citibank) in New York to reimburse Lloyds with an equivalent sum. Lloyds duly credited Baker Oil with US$518,000, of which about US$45,000 remained in the account. The claimants sued Baker Oil at common law for the full amount received by them. Had the claim succeeded it would have been irrelevant that Baker Oil had subsequently disposed of all but about US$45,000 of the money, but the claimants failed to show that the money received by Baker Oil was the same money that had left the Banque du Sud. Both Millett J and Fox LJ in the Court of Appeal (which upheld Millett J's decision) held that the money could not be traced through the New York clearing bank system, since there it clearly became mixed with other money.

Since Lloyds must surely have had a contractual claim against the Banque du Sud at the latest when they had received and acted on the telexed payment order, and Baker Oil a cause of action against Lloyds, the alternative would have been to trace the causes of action from Agip to Baker Oil, but at first instance Millett J distinguished between a payment order and a cheque, commenting that the payment order never moved from Tunisia, and that nothing passed between Tunisia and London but a stream of electrons. The common law can only follow a physical asset, such as a cheque.

Fox LJ did not adopt Millett J's distinction, relying instead on the fact that Lloyds had credited the money to Baker Oil before it was reimbursed with the claimant's money. They thereby took a delivery risk, Fox LJ commenting that whereas the Banque du Sud could be regarded as having paid with the claimant's money, Lloyds must be regarded as having paid Baker Oil with its own (Lloyds') money, since at the time of payment it had no other money with which to pay. The money in Baker Oil's account could not therefore be identified as the claimant's money. This, however, would seem to be merely an additional reason why the *money* could not be traced through the New York banks. It does not explain why Agip could not follow the causes of action, and it is necessary to adopt Millett J's distinction to do that.

Millett J's reasoning was applied by Tuckey J in *Bank Tejarat* v *Hong Kong and Shanghai Banking Corporation (Ci) Ltd and Hong Kong and Shanghai Bank Trustee (Jersey) Ltd* [1995] 1 Lloyd's Rep 239, the facts of which have been set out above. As in *Agip (Africa)*, the money was paid by telegraphic transfer, through clearing banks, and for the same reason a common law tracing claim failed. Bank Tejarat also failed successfully to argue that since (as is common in documentary credit transactions) they had paid against presentation of a draft (i.e., a bill of exchange) that operated similarly to a cheque. The draft was not being used, as a cheque would be, as the method of making the payment. Its presentation to the claimant bank was merely the trigger for payment, so the analogy with the cheque failed. Tuckey J observed that:

The simple answer to this submission is that the drafts were not the means by which Tejarat paid their money to CAK. The payment out of Tejarat's account ... was probably made by telex instructions ... (a stream of electrons). It was certainly not made by the drafts, so there is nothing from which Tejarat can trace.

Note incidentally that, since the common law does not recognise equitable interests in property, a beneficiary under a trust cannot follow trust property in the hands of a trustee, although he can in equity compel the trustee to trace the property at common law, where it has fallen into the hands of a third party.

19.4.2 Proprietary tracing in equity

Unlike the common law action for money had and received, tracing in equity is a proprietary claim. The claimant is claiming an equitable title to property in the hands of the defendant, so the remedy extends only to property in the hands of the defendant. If the defendant has parted with the property an equitable tracing action will fail (but see the other possibilities for continuing liability explored later).

Because the claim is proprietary, it will not be available if the property has ceased to be identifiable, for example where it has dissipated, or where its identity has been lost by being mixed in a manufacturing process. An equitable tracing claim can also be defeated by transfers to third parties who give value and do not have the requisite knowledge to be bound (see further below), whereas of course the common law recognises no such limitation. This is an application of the notice doctrine. In *Agip (Africa) Ltd* v *Jackson* [1990] 1 Ch 265, Millett J held that the claimant's funds could be traced in equity into the hands of anyone still in possession of the funds, except for a *bona fide* purchaser for value without notice of the trust (this was not an issue when the case went to the Court of Appeal [1991] Ch 547). Note that it follows that an equitable claim will persist against a volunteer for as long as he retains the property, even if he has come by it innocently (i.e., without notice of the claimant's interest): see the discussion of *Re Diplock's Estate* below.

Both common law and equitable rights can in some circumstances exist simultaneously, of course, and claimants often sue in the alternative (as in *Agip (Africa)* itself).

19.4.2.1 *Identification of property in equity*

When tracing in equity it is easier to establish that what the defendant has is the claimant's property. Thus, the equitable right is available not only in the common law situations where the claimant can identify his property *in specie*, or point to a fund representing its proceeds, but also where the defendant has created a mixed fund, and even when this fund has itself been converted into other property. The reason given in *Re Diplock* was that whereas common law ratification works only where it is possible to identify precisely which property is substituted for which other property, and therefore has no application where property is inextricably mixed, as in a mixed fund, equitable tracing works by the declaration of a charge on the property, which is not defeated by mixing.

In *Agip (Africa) Ltd* v *Jackson* the claimants were able to trace the money in equity (through the New York banking system, where it had certainly become mixed with other money), although the common law did not recognise that the money received by Baker Oil was the same money that had been stolen by the fraudster. The claim, being a proprietary claim, however, was only for the US$45,000 remaining in the account, not the entirety of the US$518,000 originally received, unlike the common law claim, which was personal, and was therefore for the entire amount.

Because tracing in equity works by the declaration of a charge on the property, in *Re Diplock* [1948] Ch 465 it was held that the remedy will not be granted where a charge on the property would be inequitable, as where an innocent volunteer has spent the money on alterations or improvements on his land, or indeed in paying off mortgages or other loans on the property. In such cases, the imposition of a charge enforceable by sale would be unreasonable (not to mention practical difficulties arising where the land is, e.g., a hospital). Of course, if the common law change of position defence also applied to equitable tracing claims, it would provide an alternative way of achieving the same result.

The reasoning in the last paragraph depends on the sale being unreasonable. It would not be if the innocent volunteer had mixed trust money with his own in order to make a purchase, since the sale would simply put him back into the position that he was in before receiving the trust money.

It has been noted that equity acts *in personam*. In *El Ajou* v *Dollar Land Holdings plc* [1993] 3 All ER 717, Millett J, whose decision on this point was upheld by the Court of Appeal ([1994] 2 All ER 685), held that it was possible to trace property through civil jurisdictions, such as Panama, which did not recognise equitable tracing, as long as the defendant was within the jurisdiction. It does not matter where the property actually is, therefore.

19.4.2.2 *Requirements for fiduciary relationship*

Unlike tracing at common law, tracing in equity requires that at some stage there must have existed a fiduciary relationship of some sort which was sufficient to give rise to an equitable proprietary right in the claimant. The clearest case is that of the relationship of trustee and beneficiary, so that in breach of trust cases there is no problem. Indeed, agents and bailees (and others) may also occupy a fiduciary position.

The requirement of a fiduciary relationship for tracing in equity is not easy to justify in principle, because it means that a mere equitable owner may have a better action than someone who is both legal and equitable owner of property (since there will always be a fiduciary relationship in the former case, with the trustee). Thus a beneficiary can always trace in equity—but someone who is both legal and equitable owner can do so only if he can find an additional fiduciary relationship.

Fundamental principle, or no more than historical accident?
The requirement appears to have arisen by historical accident. The original authority for tracing into mixed funds was *Re Hallett's Estate* (1880) 13 Ch D 696, on which see further below, which involved mixing by a trustee. The principle was extended in *Sinclair* v *Brougham* [1914] AC 398, from which (because the speeches of their Lordships differ substantially) it has always been difficult to extract a clear *ratio*, and indeed the case has recently been overruled in *Westdeutsche Landesbank Girozentrale* v *Islington London Borough Council* [1996] AC 669. However, as the case was interpreted in *Re Diplock's Estate*, the mixing was done by a fiduciary, and the case was interpreted as authority for the requirement of an initial fiduciary relationship. In *Re Diplock's Estate*, the claimants also succeeded on a personal claim, so it might be thought arguable that remarks on the proprietary tracing claim were *obiter*, except that the proprietary remedy was necessary for the interest claim. *Re Diplock* was accepted by Millett J in *Agip (Africa)* as Court of Appeal authority for the requirement, and it has in any case been reiterated by the Privy Council in *Re Goldcorp Exchange* [1995] 1 AC 74, by the Court of Appeal in *Trustee of the Property of F.C. Jones and Sons (a Firm)* v *Jones* [1996] 3 WLR 703, and by the House of Lords in *Westdeutsche* v *Islington LBC* [1996] AC 669. However, this now needs to be considered in light of *Foskett* v *McKeown* [2000], discussed below.

Initial fiduciary relationships and the affirmation in Westdeutsche
In *Westdeutsche*, Lord Browne-Wilkinson doubted the very concept of someone being both legal and equitable owner, on the ground that the equitable ownership would have no existence in the absence of separation of legal and equitable titles (e.g., on the creation of a trust). Since he also appears to take the view that if there is a trust there will inevitably be a fiduciary relationship, this may also justify the *Diplock* conclusion in principle, since it will be difficult to conceive of an equitable title existing in the absence of a fiduciary relationship. (Note that where legal title is transferred to someone who is not a *bona fide* purchaser for value without notice, and where there is therefore separation of legal and equitable title but not necessarily a trust, this proposition is not negated, since it depends on the initial creation of a trust, albeit that it is not between the parties to the action. There is no need for the fiduciary relationship to exist between the parties to the action, as long as it originally existed; this follows from *Re Diplock* [1948] Ch 465, above, where an action was successful against a volunteer.)

In *Chase Manhattan Bank NA* v *Israel-British Bank (London) Ltd* [1981] Ch 105, the claimant mistakenly paid a sum of money twice to the defendant, and on the defendant's liquidation was able to trace the money mistakenly paid into the hands of the liquidators. There was no fiduciary relationship initially between claimant and defendant, but Goulding J held it sufficient that a fiduciary relationship arose as a result of the mistaken payment. Goulding J's reasoning was heavily criticised in *Westdeutsche* (see further the 1998 or 2000 editions of this text), but the proposition that the fiduciary relationship need not have arisen initially appears to be good law. In *Agip (Africa)*, Millett J observed that:

> In [*Chase Manhattan*] however, equity's assistance was not needed in order to trace the plaintiff's money into the hands of the defendant; it was needed in order to ascertain whether it had any of the plaintiff's money left. The case cannot, therefore, be used to circumvent the requirement that there should be an initial fiduciary relationship in order to start the tracing process in equity.

The general proposition, then, is that it is necessary for the fiduciary relationship to exist before the tracing process starts. In *Agip* itself, therefore, it was necessary to show a fiduciary relationship before the money got into the New York clearing system.

Unfortunately, before Goulding J's reasoning in *Chase Manhattan* was criticised into oblivion in *Westdeutsche*, it led Tuckey J into error in *Bank Tejarat v Hong Kong and Shanghai Banking Corporation (Ci) Ltd and Hong Kong and Shanghai Bank Trustee (Jersey) Ltd* [1995] 1 Lloyd's Rep 239. He observed that Millett J's analysis of *Chase Manhattan* was wrong, since the money became mixed (in another bank account) before it reached the defendant. Tuckey J therefore concluded that where a payment is made under a mistake of fact (in *Bank Tejarat* itself the bank had been deceived into thinking that the shipping documents tendered to it represented goods that had been shipped, whereas in fact they were simply forgeries), a fiduciary relationship arises as soon as the money has been paid out; it is not delayed until it has been actually received by the recipient. In the light of *Westdeutsche*, this must now clearly be regarded as wrong; in any case, in *Westdeutsche*, Lord Browne-Wilkinson observed that Goulding J had been asked to assume that the money was traceable into the hands of the defendant, the only issue being whether the claimants had a proprietary claim.

A fiduciary relationship: more problematic in principle than in practice?
Millett has argued in (1991) 107 LQR 71, at pp. 75–6, that the fiduciary requirement is not particularly problematic in fraud cases, 'since the embezzlement of a company's funds almost inevitably involves a breach of fiduciary on the part of one of the company's employees or agents', as indeed was the situation in *Agip (Africa)* itself. Fraud by a stranger, such as that which occurred in *Bank Tejarat*, and such as would be typical in maritime frauds, presents greater difficulties in this regard, but if it can be established that the fraudster has induced the victim to convey property to him, then the fraudster may become a constructive trustee on the principles in *Bannister* v *Bannister* (see chapter 11). That would establish the fiduciary relationship for subsequent tracing purposes, but it would not help if, for example, it was necessary to trace through a mixed bank account to establish that the fraudster had received the victim's money in the first place. Victims of theft by a stranger will not normally be able to trace in equity, since the thief will not acquire legal title and therefore cannot become a trustee, whether constructive or otherwise. That is the main limitation of proprietary tracing in equity.

Establishing a fiduciary relationship may also be required for knowing receipt, where it is necessary to establish that the recipient received the claimant's equitable property: e.g., *El Ajou* v *Dollar Land Holdings plc* [1994] 2 All ER 685, and *El Ajou* v *Dollar Land Holdings plc (No. 2)* [1995] 2 All ER 213. A fiduciary relationship is also necessary for knowing assistance; this is why it was necessary to establish one in *Bank Tejarat* itself.

19.4.2.3 *Quantifying shares in mixed funds: the rule in Clayton's case, pari passu and the case for the North American Rolling Charge (NARC)*

Once it is accepted that equity can trace into mixed funds, it is necessary to consider the basis on which the fund is apportioned between rival claimants. Usually, the problem is that payments have been made out of the fund, leaving insufficient to satisfy all the claimants. But another possibility is that the payments out have been wisely invested, in which case claimants may prefer to claim a share of the payments out, rather than what remains in the fund.

The leading authority is probably again the Court of Appeal decision in *Re Diplock* [1948] Ch 465. The testator, Caleb Diplock, gave the residue of his property 'to such charitable institutions or other charitable or benevolent object or objects in England' as his executors should, in their absolute discretion, select. In the belief that this created a valid charitable trust, the executors distributed some £203,000 among 139 different charities. Then the next-of-kin successfully challenged its validity in *Chichester Diocesan Fund and Board of Finance* v *Simpson* [1994] AC 341. The next-of-kin, having exhausted their remedy against the executors, successfully recovered money from the various charities. The personal claim is considered later, but a proprietary claim also succeeded against some of the charities. The advantage of the proprietary claim was that it allowed the next-of-kin to claim interest.

On the proprietary claim, the Court of Appeal, extending the principles derived from *Re Hallett's Estate* and *Sinclair v Brougham*, held that the right to trace into a mixed fund is not limited to cases where the defendant is the person who has mixed the funds. Nor does there need to be a fiduciary relationship as between the parties to the action. The right to trace is available against an innocent volunteer. This is an application of the *bona fide* purchaser rule in chapter 1; a volunteer is not a purchaser, and provides no value. Here, the volunteer charities had mixed Diplock money with their own, and hence the question of apportionment arose.

Mixing of funds by a fiduciary: the rule in Re Hallett's Estate

Where a trustee wrongly mixes trust money with his own, the principles in *Hallett's Estate*, apply, essentially to the disadvantage of the trustee, but the volunteers in *Diplock* were innocent and the Court of Appeal did not apply the same harsh principles to them. They were treated just like any other innocent claimant to a share in a mixed fund and, in particular, as being no less deserving than the next-of-kin. The volunteer's duty of conscience is regarded as akin to that of a person having an equitable interest in a mixed fund towards the other equitable owners, and so, for example, where Diplock money was used to purchase stocks, where the charity already had similar stocks, the charity ranked *pari passu* with the next-of-kin (i.e., in proportion to the amount each has contributed to the amalgam). This is clearly the fairest method of apportionment in such a case.

The rule in Clayton's case

Mixing and current bank accounts For current bank accounts, however, the Court of Appeal in Diplock applied the rule developed in *Clayton's case* (1816) 1 Mer 572, which enshrines the principle of 'first in, first out': the first payment in is appropriated to satisfy the earliest debt. The basis of the rule is said to be the presumed intention of the person operating the account. A preferable solution, in the opinion of the authors of the Report of the Review Committee on Insolvency Law and Practice (Cork Report 1982, Cmnd 8558), paras 1076–80, would be to divide the mixed fund rateably (i.e., in *pari passu*). However, in *Barlow Clowes International Ltd* v *Vaughan* [1992] 4 All ER 22, noted [1993] Conv 370, the Court of Appeal held that *Clayton's case* normally applied, the court being bound by the *ratio* of *Diplock*. Actually, in *Barlow Clowes* itself, the presumption in *Clayton's case* was rebutted, but it would normally be very difficult to operate *pari passu* distribution with a running bank account, because *pari passu* distribution assumes a starting date for the fund (otherwise how can you determine how much each has contributed to the amalgam?).

Dissatisfaction and an entreaty to the House of Lords However, notwithstanding, it is clear from at least two judgments in *Barlow Clowes* that judicial support for the rule in *Clayton's case* is not altogether unequivocal. While Clayton's presumed authority was not being denied, Leggatt LJ offered that 'During the 175 years since the rule in *Clayton's case* was devised, neither its acclaim nor its application has been universal'. Even Woolf LJ's insistence that the rule was 'settled law' was unenthusiastic, claiming that this was so 'short of [intervention from] the House of Lords'. In the *Denning Law Journal* (1997, pp. 43–62), Lowrie and Todd argued that rather than being a restatement of the supremacy of the rule in *Clayton's case*, *Barlow Clowes* instead amounted to a strong entreaty to the House of Lords to consider the rule and its continuing application in the law. Here we have considered the operation both of the rule in *Clayton's case* and *pari passu* methods of distribution in some depth, and did so at least in part of our larger articulation of the appropriateness of the adoption by the English courts of the North American rolling charge considered below.

19.4.2.4 *Mixing by trustee or fiduciary*

The above principles assume that all claimants are equally innocent, or at any rate are treated as such, but as against a trustee who is in breach of trust, who has mixed trust money with his own, the beneficiary is entitled to a first charge over a mixed fund or property purchased with it. This will generally operate against the interests of the trustee.

In *Re Hallett's Estate* (1880) 13 Ch D 696, Hallett, a solicitor, was a trustee of his own marriage settlement. He had paid some of the money from that trust into his own bank account, into which he also paid money which had been entrusted to him for investment by a client. He made various payments into and out of the account, which at his death contained sufficient funds to meet the claims of the trust and his client, but not those of his personal creditors as well. Hallett attempted to rely on *Clayton's case* to show that the payments out had been of the trust money, and that what was left was his own, but the Court of Appeal held (Thesiger LJ dissenting) that both the trust and the client were entitled to a charge in priority to Hallett's general creditors, and that the various payments out of the account must be treated as payments of Hallett's own money. The principle is that *where an act can be done rightly, the trustee is not allowed to say that he did it wrongfully*. Hallett had the right to spend his own money, but not that of the trust or the client, and was therefore unable to claim that he had done so. Therefore, he must have spent his own money, leaving that of the trust and the client in the account.

Re Hallett's Estate
Application in Re Oatway A different application of the same principle can be seen
operating in *Re Oatway* [1903] 2 Ch 356. The trustee had withdrawn money from
the mixed account and invested it in shares, leaving a balance which at that time
was ample to meet the claims of the beneficiaries. Subsequently, however, he dissipated the balance further. The argument (based on *Hallett*) that he must be treated
as withdrawing his own money first (so that his shares would be treated as his own
property) was rejected. The beneficiaries' claim must be satisfied out of any
identifiable part of the fund before the trustee could set up his own claim. They were
entitled to the shares in priority to the general creditors. The principle is the same as
before. The trustee was entitled to dissipate his own but not the trust money, so
could not claim that what had been left in the account, and subsequently dissipated,
was trust money, rather than his own.

Limits of beneficiaries' choice However, there are limits to the rights of beneficiaries.
Once it is clear that all money belonging to the trustee has been withdrawn, so that
any further withdrawals must have been from trust money, they cannot claim that
any subsequent payments in must be taken as intended to replace the trust money,
unless the trustee shows an intention to make such repayment. In such a case, the
right to trace will apply up to the lowest balance of the account in the period
between the trust fund being paid into the account and the time when the remedy
is sought. For example, if the trustee mixes £1,000 of his own money with £3,000 of
trust money and later withdraws £2,000, the right to trace will not extend beyond the
£2,000 which is thereby left in the account, even if the trustee later pays in further
sums of his own.

   In such a case, of course, the beneficiaries will have a personal claim against the
trustee for any outstanding sum.

   Another limit on the beneficiaries' right to trace is that there may not be any principle of proportionate entitlement. Suppose, for example, that the trustee has used
the mixed fund to purchase property which has increased in value. Can the
beneficiary claim any part of the increase? It appears not on the basis of *Re Hallett's
Estate* and *Sinclair* v *Brougham*, where it was assumed that the beneficiary's remedy
was limited to a charge on the property for the amount of trust money expended in
its purchase. This is a surprising result given the strict rule against profits by
trustees, and some doubt has recently been cast on it (though only *obiter* in a first
instance decision).

Re Tilley's WT That *obiter* discussion took place in *Re Tilley's WT* [1967] Ch 1179,
where a sole trustee who was also the life tenant had mixed a small amount of trust
money in her own bank account before embarking on a series of property specula-
tions which were so successful that on her death her estate was worth £94,000. The
beneficiaries entitled in remainder claimed a share of this wealth in the proportion
which the trust money in the account bore to the balance of the account at that
time. Ungoed-Thomas J held them entitled only to the return of the trust money
with interest.

   His decision was based on a finding of fact, however, that Ms Tilley had not
invested the trust money in property but merely used it to reduce her overdraft. If a
trustee has in fact laid out trust money towards a purchase, Ungoed-Thomas J

thought that the beneficiaries would then be entitled to the property and any profit to the extent that it had been paid for with trust money.

The reasoning is that if the trustee draws on a mixed fund to purchase property but leaves enough in the account to cover the trust funds, the rule in *Re Hallett's Estate* requires that the purchase be treated as made entirely with his own money, in which case, should no further dissipations to the mixed fund occur, the property, and any profit, belong to him. But should he then go further and dissipate the remaining balance, the beneficiaries will have a charge on the property (*Re Oatway*), and this, according to Ungoed-Thomas J, may be for the proportionate part of the increased value and not merely for the original amount of the trust fund.

The solution is consistent with the rule applicable to unauthorised investment, where as we saw earlier in the context of trusteeship itself, the beneficiaries may elect to adopt the investment (see *Foskett* v *McKowen* below). Its effect would be to allow the beneficiaries the choice of a charge for an amount of the trust money, which will be to their advantage where the funds are depleted, or a share in the property where its value has risen.

Foskett v *McKeown: an important tracing landmark?*
In *Foskett* v *McKeown* [1998] Ch 265 trust funds collected in respect of holiday properties in the Algarve were used by the trustee to pay some of the premiums on a life policy which had been executed in favour of his wife and children. When the trustee committed suicide, the beneficiaries (also referred to as the purchasers) of the trust fund claimed that they were entitled to a proportionate share of the proceeds of the policy which were paid at the time of the suicide. In 1998, this case reached the Court of Appeal, and in a majority decision the beneficiaries were held only to be entitled to a charge on the proceeds to secure their restitutionary claim for the value of their money that went to pay the premiums. However, in May 2000 in the House of Lords it was held that the beneficiaries under the trust were entitled to trace in equity into the policy proceeds, and to do so in proportion to their contributions to the premium payments ([2000] 2 WLR 1299). Indeed, it was held that the beneficiaries' claim was simply an assertion of an equitable proprietary interest arising from the mixing of the value of the premiums with the value of the policy, which was analogous with the mixing of moneys in a bank account. It followed thus that the beneficiaries were entitled to a *pro rata* share of the policy moneys.

Whilst the majority view was that this was a vindication of the beneficiaries' proprietary interest in the fund, and their entitlement to a *pro rata* share, Lord Hope of Craighill and Lord Steyn dissented. The minority concurred with the Court of Appeal majority view which was founded on the basis of opinion that such a misapplication of trust moneys (to pay for insurance policy premiums) did not entitle the purchaser beneficiaries (not to be confused with the named beneficiaries under the deceased man's life policy) to a *pro rata* share in the property, and was thus more akin to use by a trustee of moneys held on trust for maintenance of his own property (thus invoking the principle that a trustee cannot profit from his own breach of trust) rather than mixing money in bank accounts. This was discussed at length in the Court of Appeal by Sir Richard Scott V-C, and the essence of his reasoning was that it followed that unless it could be demonstrated that he obtained a profit as a result of the expenditure, a trustee's liability to repay extended only to the money misapplied, thus invoking *Re Tilley's WT* principles. Here, the purchasers would be entitled to no more than the return of their contributions plus interest.

Mixed funds, competing claims and volunteers

As it has been observed, the Court of Appeal in *Re Diplock* did not apply the principles of this section to mixing by innocent volunteers, and there are other respects in which volunteers are treated differently. It seems that the volunteer is not liable to the full extent if any property purchased with the mixed fund has decreased in value, because otherwise he would be compelled to pay out of his own pocket for the mistake of the trustee who transferred the property to him in breach of trust. Nor is it obvious, if he purchases property with the mixed fund which increases in value, that justice requires him to share any increase, unless some allowance is made for his effort (see Hodkinson [1983] Conv 135).

19.4.2.5 *Clayton's case rebutted: pari passu distribution and the NARC*

Sir Kenneth Cork's Committee Report on the operation of insolvency law in the UK (considered earlier) discussed some of the difficulties pertaining to the operation of *Clayton's case*, and it is fair to say that at the very least in its application everything turns on the timing of particular investments and no more.

However, as Dillon LJ observed in *Barlow Clowes International Ltd* v *Vaughan* [1992] 4 All ER 22 itself, just as *Clayton's case* operated to the detriment of early investors, unless the fund had been invested profitably, it was equally the case that *pari passu* distribution can produce some interesting results:

A *pari passu* distribution will normally be disadvantageous to those who had 'come in' late, unless a profitable investment rather than a dissipated bank account ensues, in which case, later contributors will receive a proportion of a fund to which they have made no meaningful contribution.

It was against this backdrop that the *Denning Law Journal* study of the North American rolling charge (hereafter NARC) was made, and the key argument advanced that this mechanism could resolve many of the problems of the *pari passu* method without leading to the unfairness associated with *Clayton*. Even in *Barlow Clowes* itself Leggatt LJ could not resist commenting upon its attractiveness in terms of fairness. Basically, the NARC works not by looking at the time at which contributions were made, but instead at the relationship which contributions bear to one another at the moment before a withdrawal takes place. In the words of Woolf LJ again in *Barlow Clowes* the NARC:

... involves treating credits to a bank account made at different times and from different sources as a blend or cocktail with the result that when a withdrawal is made from the account it is treated as a withdrawal in the same proportions as the different interests in the account (here the investors) bear to each other at the moment before the withdrawal is made.

Distribution, Clayton and pari passu: strengths and weaknesses

The 1997 *Denning Law Journal* article considered the relative strengths and weaknesses of *pari passu* and *Clayton* alike through use of examples, which illustrated both dissipations and investments. This was done alongside detailed accounts of how and in what ways adoption by the English Courts of the NARC might transcend current difficulties, offering a brief description of the charge, its judicial basis and its justifications in principle. The article contends the NARC has a number of advantages, and will normally amount to the fairest method of distribution. Perhaps its greatest virtue, and one which arises from its consideration of the relationship existing between all contributions immediately prior to all withdrawals, is that it ensures that pre-existing property rights are never disturbed by subsequent transactions: here later payments do not diminish existing interests in the remaining fund, nor will they obtain the advantage of earlier investments, and there is no distortion of existing beneficial interests in property purchased using proceeds from the fund.

Making the case for the NARC
Moreover, the view was taken in the Canadian case, *Re Ontario Securities Commission v Greymac Credit Corporation* (1986) 55 OR (2d) 673 that once moneys have lost their identity by being mixed into an account, and that on the basis of the claimant's equitable lien, the proportions attributable to each contributor can be calculated, and should not change if the account is later diminished or divided into more than one account. *Re Ontario Securities* is the most important authority for the NARC, which was adopted by the Court of Appeal in this case involving competing interests in a fund. Indeed, on a more general level it is important to remember that although these cases can arise in disputed ownership of profitable investments, their context is often competing claims for a dissipated (and seldom adequate) fund.

The article suggested that the case in principle for the English courts' adoption of the NARC rests on the way it does not interfere with prior property interests and that, despite the Court of Appeal's misgivings in *Barlow Clowes*, there is no authority against its adoption. Indeed, despite the concern of Dillon LJ that the Court was constrained by authority provided by *Re Diplock* [1948] Ch 465 that decisively rejected the NARC, there is no evidence that it was decisively rejected in that case. Indeed, given its modern context, it would be surprising if the NARC would even have been conceived let alone considered, especially in light of the context provided by its technological underpinnings.

The NARC and the adoption of a middle way
Further on a practical level, the article identified a number of scenarios where the NARC will adopt a middle approach (between that arising from use of *Clayton* and *pari passu* distribution) and outcome, while suggesting why in practice it will seldom be any party's preferred option. In addition it identified reasons why the NARC will never be the cheapest method of distribution. However, although concerns about its cost were raised in *Barlow Clowes*, in *Re Ontario*, Mr Justice Parker submitted that there is no reason to suppose that in cases where its application is appropriate in principle (e.g., a situation other than that in *Barlow Clowes* itself: see above, where there is no intention that the fund should be owned communally, and also where money is never truly mixed, as was found to be the case in *El Ajou v Dollar Land Holdings* [1993] 3 All ER 717)—that in the silicon age of computerised banking it would always be the most expensive. Indeed, the article suggested that concerns over cost in the case of the NARC are conceptually no different from other types of litigation, and should be treated as such. How convincing do you believe this case made in favour of the NARC is?

There is no need to apportion where the defendant is solvent and the claim is based on knowing receipt of the claimant's money, since it is necessary only to trace the money into the hands of the defendant and not to apportion. The case of *El Ajou* [1993] 3 All ER 717 stands as authority for this proposition.

The 1997 article looked at the *El Ajou* cases in some depth, and in light of those thoughts and findings, it suggested that some discussion of the litigation and the difficulties it raises is timely.

El Ajou, fraud distribution and litigation risks
In *El Ajou* v *Dollar Land Holdings* [1993] 3 All ER 717, we see El Ajou, a victim of an extremely elaborate fraud. The litigation itself provides a number of important illustrations of the study of equitable tracing, and students will find that it raises questions of identification of property; and the requirement of a fiduciary relationship, for example. However, for immediate purposes, it ties in directly into the discussion above on quantification and apportionment, as it is here that the heart of its more narrow significance lies, and also the source we believe of some quite considerable difficulties. More broadly, it also serves as a salutary reminder of the complex nature of frauds perpetrated in modern times, and the concomitant determination of their perpetrators to ensure that their activities remain obscured, at least in legal terms. It is for all these reasons that a brief resume of *El Ajou No. 1* is worthy of inclusion. The extent of this saga can be seen in the appearance of *El Ajou* v *Dollar Land Holdings plc (No. 2)* [1995] 2 All ER 213 back in the Chancery Division in 1995, which also originated from the fraud which totalled about US$18.6 million, and in which the claimant lost about US$10.6 million.

Rather than seeking to uncover the precise nature of the fraud, this precis seeks to illustrate its many layers and intrinsic complexity. Indeed, at one point Millett J himself lamented the complex multi-layering through which money belonging to the claimant had to be followed, and was at one notable point forced to concede that the trail had gone cold, and was actually lost. See if you can follow what is going on by looking at this in conjunction with your own study of the case.

Essentially, the fraud involved a complex structure of several tiers of companies throughout the world, and started off in two companies (Tower and United Dutch) run by three Canadian fraudsters (Levinson, Caplan and Roth). Tower and United were boiler rooms which were subsequently closed down and declared bankrupt. Thereafter, most of the proceeds from the boiler rooms were redirected towards several Panamanian companies. The plot thickened with the imposition of further tiers of companies (including more Panamanian ones) and a considerable number of transfers of assets. Eventually, the Canadian fraudsters were themselves defrauded, but not before the claimant had lost US$10 million, and a number of others had been duped. El Ajou brought his claim as part of the activities of a Mr Von Apeldoorn who was trustee in bankruptcy for the original companies Tower and United Dutch.

The case raises questions of how quantification was achieved in respect of the way in which Millett J arrived at the figure of US$6.6 million which he deduced belonged to the claimant. Whilst this is not entirely clear, it is also the case that Millett J's assessment did entail correspondence of the dates with amounts involved, as a means for achieving a match between debits and credits. In *El Ajou (No. 2)*, Walker J thought that Millett was not applying *Clayton* to this fund, and instead that he was matching large cheques out from the claimant with receipts by Panamanian companies, and that the remainder was due to smaller investors (the origin of the 70:30 split in favour of the claimant which was reached). However, Von Apeldoorn thought the split was achieved by adopting *pari passu*. We have suggested that this might well have had implications for the timing and location of the loss of the trail and that matching cheques in this manner assumes that the claimant's money was never in reality mixed, and could be traced directly to first-tier companies.

The 1997 article also asked whether there were not serious problems with the arrangement which allowed the claimant to recover losses in a 70:30 split, and that at the very least, a question as to how certain it could possibly be that there would be no further claims from other victims? It may well have been that on the facts of the case, the trustee in bankruptcy was certain that there were no potential further claims, and that further victims of the fraud were unlikely to come forward, but even this assumes a great deal. However, more importantly: how wide an application can much of this case possibly have? Indeed, while mixing the money meant that it was not possible to trace at common law, this is actually crucial in taking this problem of potential litigants further. Indeed, the effect of mixing is presumably to transfer legal title to the fraudster (or the mixer whomever he was). Where the mixer had requisite knowledge, then on *Westdeutsche* principles (see below), a constructive trust ought to arise, in which case there is a fiduciary relationship.

19.4.2.6 *Some recent developments: Foskett v McKeown*

Tracing, trustees and mixed funds
We have already considered *Foskett* v *McKeown*, but the case does also provide an epilogue for how difficult this area of law is to grasp even on a level of basic understanding. Traditionally, the crucial distinction between tracing at common law and tracing in equity has been that through equity it was possible to trace money into mixed accounts (as illustrated by the authority provided by *Re Hallett's Estate* (1890)). The principle in *Re Hallett's Estate* works on the premise that when money from mixed accounts is withdrawn, equity regards the trustee as having withdrawn his money first, leaving the beneficiary to trace against any balance remaining. It has already been noted in the operation of *Re Oatway* that this principle did not prevent the beneficiary from enjoying a charge over any property purchased with monies from a mixed account. However, in commenting on the implication by Sir George Jessel in *Re Hallett's Estate* that in the case of a *mixed* fund the beneficiary could not choose to assert beneficial ownership over the asset in proportion to the amount of trust monies (mis)applied to its purchase, Lord Millett insisted that this view was inconsistent with the rule against (unauthorised) profit. Indeed:

> In my view the time has come to state unequivocally that English law has no such rule. It conflicts with the rule that a trustee must not benefit from his trust. I agree ... that the beneficiary's right to elect to have a proportionate share of a mixed substitution necessarily follows once one accepts, as English law does, (i) that a claimant can trace in equity into a mixed fund and (ii) that he can trace unmixed money into its proceeds and assert ownership of the proceeds. Accordingly, I would state the basic rule as follows. *Where a trustee wrongfully uses trust money to provide part of the cost of acquiring an asset, the beneficiary is entitled at his* option *either to claim a proportionate share of the asset or to enforce a lien upon it to secure his personal claim against the trustee for the amount of the misapplied money* [our emphasis]. It does not matter whether the trustee mixed the trust money with his own in a single fund before using it to acquire the asset, or made separate payments (whether simultaneously or sequentially) out of the differently owned funds to acquire a single asset.

The fiduciary relationship question
Although criticised in cases such as *El Ajou* v *Dollar Land Holdings plc* (1993) the requirement of a fiduciary relationship which is initial was reaffirmed in 1996 in the very important case of *Westdeutsche*. Notwithstanding the significance that *Westdeutche* is acknowledged to have had, it cannot be seen as the end of the matter.

It will be clear from the section which dealt with fiduciary relationships that the requirement of an initial fiduciary relationship has attracted considerable controversy throughout its history with some suggestion that it only arose in the first instance as a result of the historical accident in the earliest cases concerning mixing of funds by trustees. The questioned need for such arose once again in *Foskett* v *McKeown*, as did its dubious basis in principle, in Lord Millett's suggestion that:

There is certainly no logical justification for allowing any distinction between them to produce capricious results in cases of mixed substitutions by insisting on the existence of a fiduciary relationship as a precondition for applying equity's tracing rules. The existence of such a relationship may be relevant to the nature of the claim which the plaintiff can maintain, whether personal or proprietary, but that is a different matter.

Although Lord Millett was extremely critical of the requirement, he insisted that the present case ('a straightforward case of a trustee who wrongfully misappropriated trust money, mixed it with his own … Even on the traditional approach, the equitable tracing rules are available to the plaintiffs') was not the occasion for its consideration. Thus, the continuing operation of the initial fiduciary relationship requirement remains unclear.

A 'new' type of tracing?

Tracing has traditionally been regarded as a proprietary remedy, which works on allowing the pursuer (and in equitable tracing the beneficiary) to proceed against a particular asset which is in the hands of the defendant. However, as part of the huge reconsideration of the whole remedies question, there is a body of opinion gaining considerable strength which is linking tracing most appropriately to an exercise in identification. The central case law here is *Boscawen* v *Bajwa* [1996] 1 WLR 328, and particularly *Foskett* v *McKeown*. The latter case is a very important pointer to direction which is most likely in the area of remedies, and of particular relevance here is Lord Millett's consideration of the nature of tracing. Lord Millett talks about the appropriateness of tracing's alignment with the identification of property, and insists that:

The claimant claims the new asset because it was acquired in whole or in part with the original asset. What he traces is therefore not the physical asset itself but the value inherent in it. Tracing is thus neither a claim nor a remedy. It is merely the process by which a claimant demonstrates what has happened to his property, identifies its proceeds in the persons who handled or received them and justifies his claim that the proceeds can properly be regarded as representing his property. Tracing is also distinct from claiming. It identifies the traceable proceeds of the claimant's property. It enables the claimant to substitute the traceable proceeds for the original asset as the subject matter of his claim but it does not affect or establish his claim. That will depend on a number of factors including the nature of his interest in the original asset. He will normally be able to maintain the same claim to the substantial asset as he could have maintained to the original asset.

Once this idea of tracing as a process of identification rather than constituting a claim or even a remedy is accepted, then the traditional distinction between equitable and common law tracing is nonsensical. The sentiment explained in Lord Millett's judgment in *Foskett* v *McKeown* points to the lack of necessity for two distinctive regimes of tracing, and also the injustice which can be caused by current pursuers of tracing in equity:

There is no sense in maintaining different rules for tracing at law and in equity. One set of tracing rules is enough … There is certainly no logical justification for allowing any distinction between them to produce capricious results in cases of mixed substitutions by insisting on the existence of a fiduciary relationship as a pre-condition for applying equity's tracing rule.

Although earlier introductions to tracing explained it as a mechanism for 'following', and while Lord Millett in *Foskett* v *McKeown* noted that both are 'exercises in locating assets which are, or may be taken to represent, an asset belonging to the plaintiffs and to which they assert ownership', his judgment added yet further weight to his insistence that tracing is best considered as a process in the identification of property through its advancement that there were actually important distinctions to be recognised between tracing and following (with emphasis added):

The processes of tracing and following are, however, distinct. *Following* is a process of *following the same asset as it moves* from hand to hand. Tracing is a *process of identifying* a new asset as a substitute for the old. Where one asset is exchanged for another, a claimant can elect whether to follow the original asset into the hands of the new owner or to trace its value into the new asset in the hands of the same owner.

19.4.2.7 *Current movements: tracing and its relationship with restitution*

In light of the huge movements and upheaval in the whole area of remedies, it is vital for students to be aware of the significance of the common law action of 'money had and received'. It has been considered already above under the head of 'common law tracing', and has its best known application in *Lipkin Gorman* v *Karpanale* [1991] whereby although the plaintiffs failed to win their case on principles of equity, they succeed in their argument on principles of restitution.

The common law action of money had and received is a restitutionary claim founded on the principle of unjust enrichment, and it has a number of qualities which contribute to making it a particularly effective remedy. It is liability which is recipient-based; i.e., it arises and is 'complete' as soon as money comes into the hands of the recipient, and is not dependent on its retention. This operates subject to the defence of *bona fide* change in position, but makes it an effective remedy against innocent volunteers. Recent developments have seen the scope of restitutionary actions extended, and in *Kleinwort Benson Ltd* v *Lincoln City Council* [1998] 3 WLR 1095 the distinction whereby resitutionary claims were thought not to apply in cases where money had been paid over under mistake of law (as distinct from mistake of fact) was removed.

In light of this, it is not surprising that there have been calls for the facility for such personal liability to be provided by equity, based on the same principles. This is very clearly Jill Martin's message in her article 'Recipient liability after *Westdeutsche*' [1998] Conv 13, in which she proposes that this could be achieved through case law with intervention from the House of Lords, or if necessary through legislation. She cites reasons of justice, coherence and the prevention of unjust enrichment in support of the establishment of such liability which she claims would: eradicate unjustifiable distinctions between the rights of legal owners and beneficial owners; achieve coherence in equity's treatment of the rights of beneficiaries of trusts and the beneficiaries of estates; and prevent the unjust enrichment of volunteers who although innocent cannot establish the defence of change of position.

However, it should be noted that there are important limitations to the common law action of money had and received. It is first a remedy of common law, and as the common law does not recognise rights and interests other than ones subsisting at law, it is an action which is available only to those who own the legal title to the property which has been misappropriated. Furthermore, restitutionary claims also appear to suffer from the way in which their facility for recovery is limited to the amount of money which is misappropriated plus interest. This is evident from the House of Lords' decision in *Foskett* v *McKeown*.

19.5 Personal equitable remedies

For an equitable tracing action to operate the trust property must still be identifiable in some form, albeit that at least in equity it need not be *physically* identifiable, so that if, for example, the trust property has been sold, it may still be possible to trace the *proceeds* of sale. There are also rules in equity for the tracing of trust money which has become mixed with other money.

Suppose, however, that the property no longer exists in any identifiable form. Trust money may have been spent, for example, with nothing identifiable to show for it. If the trust property no longer exists, then clearly it is not traceable. Alternatively, it may be that it has been mixed with other funds in such a way as no longer to be traceable on the principles elaborated earlier. We also saw that the common law money had and received action depends only on receipt of the money by the defendant and that liability is unaffected by anything that later happens to the property, but that is not the case with proprietary equitable tracing.

The next section is about the personal equitable actions, which do not depend on the defendant's continued retention of, or indeed in the case of accessory liability even receipt of, the claimant's property. Here, recipient liability and the personal action in *Re Diplock* can thus be considered the equitable equivalents of the common law money had and received claim.

19.5.1 Knowing receipt and knowing assistance: 'recipient' and 'accessory' liability compared

It is possible for a stranger to become liable as constructive trustee if he either assists a trustee (or other fiduciary) in breach of trust (or other fiduciary duty) regarding property under his control, or receives trust property with knowledge of breach of trust (or other fiduciary duty). The first type of case has traditionally been termed 'knowing assistance' and the second 'knowing receipt'. A knowing receiver becomes constructive trustee of the property received. Since knowing assisters need never receive trust property, it is probably not correct to describe them as constructive trustees, but they are liable as if they were. You will of course remember from chapter 7 that these species of third-party liability in equity have recently been 're-badged' as 'recipient liability' and 'accessory liability', and greater explanation of both will follow shortly. Immediately attention is given to traditional approaches taken to third-party liability following a breach of trust which were pursued as liability arising from 'knowing receipt' of trust property, or 'knowing assistance' of a trustee's breach of trust. It is important to consider this initially because this will help us to appreciate why new approaches have emerged, and to consider how different these re-badged remedies might be from their traditional counterparts, and indeed why renaming these remedies has happened at all. For example, it will become clear that for both traditional approaches and newer ones alike, key issues arising have clustered around the degree of knowledge which is required for a third party to a trust to incur liability as a recipient of trust property or through assistance of a breach of trust.

The usual starting point for questions of degree of knowledge required for liability to be incurred is *Baden, Delvaux and Lecuit* v *Société Générale pour Favoriser le Devéloppement du Commerce et de l'Industrie en France SA* [1983] BCLC 325. In this case, Peter Gibson J suggested five possible categories of knowledge sufficient to found constructive trusteeship:

(i) actual knowledge;

(ii) wilfully shutting one's eyes to the obvious;

(iii) wilfully and recklessly failing to make such inquiries as an honest and reasonable man would make;

(iv) knowledge of circumstances which would indicate the facts to an honest and reasonable man; and

(v) knowledge of circumstances which would put an honest and reasonable man on inquiry.

It is clear that categories (ii)–(v) all represent varieties of constructive notice. Categories (i)–(iii) would normally suggest dishonesty, requiring either intention or something akin to criminal law recklessness. The test in categories (iv) and (v) is objective (i.e., akin to negligence), as opposed to the subjective test in (i) to (iii). Nevertheless, it is possible for someone to be dishonest even within (iv) and (v).

Yet although many of the cases take as their starting point these five categories, the courts have recently recoiled from using them as the only basis either for establishing liability, or for distinguishing between the two types of liability. It now seems that liability for both knowing receipt and knowing assistance can be founded on the basis of any of the five categories. In the case of knowing assistance, however, there is an additional requirement for dishonesty (or lack of probity). In the case of knowing receipt there is no dishonesty requirement, but constructive knowledge is required, which may be narrower than notice satisfying categories (iv) and (v).

It has long been clear that the test for knowing assistance is more stringent than that for knowing receipt. Indeed, in *Belmont Finance Corporation* v *Williams Furniture Ltd (No. 1)* [1979] Ch 250, and *(No. 2)* [1980] 1 All ER 393, a knowing assistance claim failed, whereas a claim for knowing receipt succeeded, on essentially the same facts. The first case was heard on the pleadings only, the full hearing being on the second case.

In the first hearing, the case was pleaded as a knowing assistance case; and on the pleadings, fraud or dishonesty on the part of the defendants could not be established. The Court of Appeal took the view that the defendants were not liable (on the pleadings) for knowingly assisting in a fraudulent design. In particular, the Court felt that constructive knowledge was not a sufficient basis for liability under that heading, Buckley LJ commenting (at p. 267):

The knowledge of that design on the part of the parties sought to be made liable may be actual knowledge. If he wilfully shuts his eyes to dishonesty, or wilfully or recklessly fails to make such inquiries as an honest and reasonable man would make, he may be found to have involved himself in the fraudulent character of the design, or at any rate to be disentitled to rely on lack of actual knowledge of the design as a defence. But otherwise, as it seems to me, he should not be affected by constructive notice.

The views of Goff LJ were similar (at p. 275):

Whilst wilfully shutting one's eyes to the obvious, or wilfully refraining from inquiry because it may be embarrassing is, I have no doubt, sufficient to make a person who participates in a fraudulent breach of trust without actually receiving the trust moneys, or moneys representing the same, liable as a constructive trustee, there remains the question whether constructive notice ... will suffice.

Lord Goff continued to explain that in his opinion, it would not. The case clearly suggests, therefore, that at any rate in a knowing assistance case, constructive knowledge without dishonesty will not suffice.

The case then went back to the Court of Appeal on the second hearing, when the pleadings were amended, to include a knowing receipt claim which was successful. As in the first case, dishonesty could not be shown on the pleadings. Buckley LJ (quoting *Barnes* v *Addy* (1874) 9 Ch App 244) said (at p. 405b):

If a stranger to a trust (a) receives and becomes chargeable with some part of the trust fund or (b) assists the trustees of a trust with knowledge of the facts in a dishonest design on the part of the trustees to misapply some part of a trust fund, he is liable as a constructive trustee.

Whereas dishonesty appears to be a requirement under part (b), there is nothing in this quote suggesting a need to show fraud or dishonesty under part (a). Since the facts of the two cases, and the knowledge of the defendants, were (to all intents and purposes) identical, the case strongly suggests that the knowledge requirements for knowing assistance and knowing receipt are not the same. It appears, then, that whereas in the case of knowing assistance knowledge dishonesty is required, it is not for knowing receipt.

19.5.2 Knowing receipt or 'recipient liability'

Belmont (No. 2) (above) clearly suggests that dishonesty is not required for a knowing receipt claim. It has often been assumed that something akin to constructive notice in land law (see chapter 1) is sufficient, but doubt was cast on this by *dicta* in *Re Montagu's ST* [1987] Ch 264, where chattels were transferred to the defendant in breach of a trust created by a family settlement, and the defendant sold the chattels. The defendant certainly had constructive notice in the strict land law sense, since his solicitor was aware of the terms of the trust and therefore the defendant had imputed notice. However, Megarry V-C thought that while constructive notice might be appropriate for a tracing claim, where the actual money or property can still be identified, something more should be required before constructive trusteeship is imposed. He seemed inclined to the view that even for a knowing receipt claim, and against a volunteer at that, only the first three heads of *Baden* knowledge would suffice.

Megarry V-C's view was unnecessary to the actual decision in the case, since he did not think that the Duke had the requisite knowledge under any of the five *Baden* heads. At p. 286B, he said that 'even if, contrary to my opinion, all of the five *Baden* types of knowledge are in point, instead of only the first three, I do not think that he had any such knowledge'. The distinction between constructive notice and the requisite knowledge for knowing receipt has also been criticised as being wrong in principle, for example by Harpum (1987) 50 MLR 217. It might also be argued that if, as Fox LJ thought in *Agip (Africa)* (19.3.3), all five *Baden* heads suffice for knowing assistance, it would be odd to require a *higher* standard of knowledge for knowing receipt. However, there is an additional dishonesty requirement for knowing assistance, which may deal with this criticism.

In (1991) 107 LQR 71, Millett, at pp. 80*ff*, argued that *Montagu* is wrong in principle, because once property is traced in equity into the defendant's hands, he becomes trustee of it for the claimant (a necessary consequence of legal title being vested in the defendant, when equitable title remains in the claimant). Disposing of the property is therefore a breach of trust, and while it might deprive a claimant of her proprietary remedy, there ought to be a continuing liability for breach of trust. That argues that the knowledge requirement for each should be the same, but the argument breaks down for volunteers, since tracing liability for volunteers is strict, whereas even for volunteers, some knowledge is required for knowing receipt. In any case, the assumption that separation of legal and equitable title necessarily implies the existence of a trust is no longer tenable in the light of *Westdeutsche Landesbank Girozentrale* v *Islington London Borough Council* [1996] AC 669.

Millett also argues for liability to be receipt-based, as at common law, rather than fault-based, subject to a change of position defence, but although the courts have shown some wariness of *Montagu*, they show no signs of following this route. Indeed, Millett J himself recognised that he was bound by authority in *El Ajou* v *Dollar Land Holdings plc* [1993] 3 All ER 717, and that the defendant did not have the requisite knowledge for knowing receipt (he was reversed on the facts in the Court of Appeal [1994] 2 All ER 685). Furthermore, the courts appear to be adopting a higher knowledge requirement than the land law notice doctrine, but for different reasons. The notice doctrine developed in land transactions on the assumption that there would be a full and careful investigation of title, and the courts appear unwilling to impose constructive trusteeship in commercial transactions without something more akin to constructive knowledge, as opposed to notice. In *Eagle Trust plc* v *SBC Securities Ltd* [1992] 4 All ER 488 and *Cowan de Groot Properties Ltd* v *Eagle Trust plc* [1992] 4 All ER 700 this was treated as being similar to the first three *Baden* heads, but it may be an oversimplification to assume that that will always be so.

Liability for knowing receipt probably requires more than mere possession of the trust property. In *Agip (Africa) Ltd* v *Jackson* [1990] 1 Ch 265, Millett J said of liability for knowing receipt that 'the recipient must have received the property for his own use and benefit'. It followed that a bank was not liable as a knowing receiver merely because money had been deposited in a customer's account.

Millett J's decision in *Agip (Africa)* was upheld by the Court of Appeal ([1991] Ch 547), but there was no appeal on the issue of knowing receipt and there is discussion only of knowing assistance. However, the same view was adopted in *Bank Tejarat*, where the fraudsters' bankers were held not liable as knowing receivers although Tejarat's money could be traced to them in equity and they had sufficient knowledge for knowing receipt, although not for knowing assistance.

Finally, in *Twinsectra* v *Yardley* [2002] 2 All ER 377 (which is primarily a case on the liability which can be incurred by third parties who are 'accessories' to a trustee's breach of trust) observations were also made in respect of recipient liability. Thus, the decision has been made to hold over Twinsectra's observations on recipient liability until after discussion of its primary significance.

19.5.3 **Knowing assistance or 'accessory liability'**

Unlike knowing receipt which is based on the receipt of trust property, assistance is based, much as it sounds, on assisting a trustee's breach of trust.

It has been clear since at least *Belmont (No. 1)* that dishonesty, or lack of probity, is required for a knowing assistance claim. In *Lipkin Gorman* v *Karpnale Ltd* [1989] 1 WLR 1340 in the Court of Appeal, the bank was unsuccessfully sued for knowing assistance, May LJ taking the view, after approving statements from *Belmont (No. 1)*, (at p. 1355D) that:

In our opinion, therefore, there is at least strong persuasive authority for the proposition that nothing less than knowledge, as defined in one of the first three categories stated by Peter Gibson J in *Baden, Delvaux and Lecuit* v *Société Générale pour Favoriser le Développement du Commerce et de l'Industrie en France SA* [1983] BCLC 325, of an underlying dishonest design is sufficient to make a stranger a constructive trustee of the consequences of that design.

A different position was taken by Fox LJ in *Agip (Africa) Ltd* v *Jackson*, however. He appeared to accept that dishonesty was a requirement for knowing assistance, but that, subject to this requirement, any of the five *Baden* heads of knowledge would suffice. A similar view had been taken by Millett J at first instance, who suggested caution regarding the five *Baden* categories:

I gratefully adopt the [*Baden*] classification but would warn against over refinement or a too ready assumption that categories (iv) or (v) are necessarily cases of constructive notice only. The true distinction is between honesty and dishonesty. It is essentially a jury question.

It seems fairly clear, therefore, that whereas any of the five *Baden* heads will probably suffice for liability, dishonesty or 'lack of probity' (a term used by May LJ in *Lipkin Gorman* v *Karpnale Ltd*, which requires more than mere negligence) is also required to found a constructive trusteeship claim based on knowing assistance. This has been reiterated by Vinelott J in *Eagle Trust plc* v *SBC Securities Ltd* [1992] 4 All ER 488 and by the Court of Appeal in *Polly Peck International* v *Nadir (No. 2)* [1992] 4 All ER 769. In *Eagle Trust* Vinelott J thought that knowledge of the fraudulent design had to be able to be imputed to the defendant, and that constructive notice of the fraudulent design would not be enough, although knowledge may be inferred in the absence of evidence if such knowledge would have been imputed to an honest and reasonable man.

Assuming that want of probity can be established, however, it does not appear to be necessary for the defendant to be aware of the precise details of the fraud. In *Agip (Africa)* the action succeeded against the money launderers' accountants, who may have believed only that they were participating in an illegal currency transaction, contrary to the exchange control laws of Tunisia. However, in *Bank Tejarat*, it was not enough simply for the defendants to be aware that CAK (who committed the fraud) was an offshore company of the type often used for fraudulent purposes, since anonymity is also a reason for operating through an offshore company.

In *Royal Brunei Airlines Sdn Bhd* v *Tan* [1995] 2 AC 378, the Privy Council held that the liability which can be incurred by a third party in relation to breach of trust depended on the dishonesty of that party. This meant that for liability as an accessory to a breach of trust by a trustee to arise for a third party, this breach by the trustee did not itself have to be dishonest and fraudulent. On the facts of the case, however, both the trustee and the third party had acted dishonestly, the latter by causing or permitting the trustee to apply money in a way he knew was not author-ised by the trust.

In its more general application *Royal Brunei Airlines* v *Tan* did, as it was suggested earlier, represent a very important development in respect of the liability of strangers to a trust for its breach: the decision has cast aside the position whereby, for liability as an accessory to a breach of trust to arise, the breach of trust commit-ted by the trustee must have been fraudulent or dishonest. This must be a welcome development because a different position would allow a very fraudulent accessory to be able to escape liability simply because the trustee himself was innocent, and the decision is noted both for seeking to locate accessory liability within more appropriate notions of dishonesty rather than knowledge, and for providing clarity in the highly complex occurrence of secondary breaches of trust. However, in 2002 the very important House of Lords decision in *Twinsectra* v *Yardley* [2002] 2 All ER 377 came to light. Reference has already been made to *Twinsectra*, and some exten-sive consideration given to it in respect of *Quistclose* trusts. At this point, a detailed consideration is now required of how it appeared to affect the position of accessory liability in the wake of the acknowledged high watermark provided by *Royal Brunei Airlines*.

Twinsectra and the context for considering accessorial liability
The case involved two solicitors and a loan transaction, and raised questions as to the status of the loan transaction concerning whether it was subject to a (*Quistclose*) trust or otherwise. The existence or otherwise of a *Quistclose* trust hinged on whether or not the (second) solicitor, Sims, held the loan subject to a trust (arising from its mandated application towards a purpose specified by the lender, through his instructions), and the question of accessorial liability involved the other (first) solici-tor, Leach. This followed the way in which the loan was in the event not applied in accordance with the lender's instructions, and then was not repaid. Twinsectra sued three parties: the two solicitors and the client Yardley. Sims was sued on account that his release of the money to the client amounted to breach of trust. The money was released to the client through Leach, and it was alleged that Leach's failure to take any steps to ensure the correct application of the money amounted to dishonest assistance of a breach of trust: this occurred when Leach paid out the money in contravention of the lender's instructions, acting on Yardley's behalf.

In respect of liability as an accessory, it was found at first instance that the first solicitor had not been dishonest although he had deliberately shut his eyes to the implications of the undertaking. The Court of Appeal reversed this finding and gave judgment against Leach for the proportion of the loan which had not been applied in the acquisition of property. The House of Lords' consideration arose following an appeal by Leach, and whether or not he had assisted in the breach of trust which had been committed by Sims (the Court of Appeal finding that the loan was subject to a trust was upheld on *Quistclose* principles), and could incur personal liability on account of doing so.

After Royal Brunei Airlines v *Tan, the direction of Twinsectra* v *Yardley*
Following the decision in *Royal Brunei Airlines* v *Tan*, the liability of a stranger to a trust who assists its breach (as distinct from being a recipient of trust property) is now referred to as 'accessory liability' rather than 'knowing assistance'. This revision

of terminology appears to be very welcome to commentators (e.g., Thompson [2002] Conv 387), and it does appear to address a number of difficulties evident in the law prior to *Royal Brunei Airlines* v *Tan*. Given that *Royal Brunei Airlines* v *Tan* had swept away the requirement of an initial fraudulent breach of trust, *Twinsectra* provided the opportunity to consider what new accessory-focused basis might be applied in order for personal liability as an accessory to a breach of trust to be incurred. The House of Lords focused this new vein of enquiry on the presence or otherwise of dishonesty in the assistant's actions, and the imposition of liability accordingly. However, actually finding a meaning to be given to dishonesty which would be appropriate for this species of liability was a complex and divisive exercise for their Lordships.

Accessory liability and three approaches to dishonesty
In considering what meaning might appropriately be given to the term 'dishonesty' in this context, greatest issue was taken with whether the test should be objective or a combination of objective and subjective elements. As Lord Hutton's judgment makes clear, a completely subjective approach to dishonesty—the 'Robin Hood' test (whereby a person is only regarded as dishonest if he transgresses his own standard of honesty, even if that standard is contrary to that of reasonable and honest people)—is not accepted in the courts. The difference between an objective test and one which combines objective/subjective criteria can be explained as follows. The former will involve the court determining that the defendant's conduct is dishonest as judged against the 'ordinary standards of reasonable and honest people, even if he does not realise this', while the latter makes reference to the defendant *himself* within a broad setting of objectivity. This latter combination test rests on whether the defendant's conduct was dishonest by the ordinary standards of reasonable and honest people, and that he *himself* realised that by those standards his conduct was dishonest. The majority of the Lords preferred the combination test with Lord Millett dissenting in favour of an objective test.

What is extremely interesting about this refocusing of accessorial liability on the honesty (or lack of honesty) of the potential accessory is the way in which, by extensive reference to Lord Nicholls' judgment in *Royal Brunei Airlines* v *Tan*, Lord Hutton concluded that the test for accessory liability was substantially the same as the test in criminal law for dishonesty, as laid down in *R* v *Ghosh* [1982] QB 1053. Indeed, in *Royal Brunei Airlines* itself, Lord Nicholls explained how the law determines dishonesty with reference to standards which are objective, but will assess the defendant's position in light of this by reference to what he actually knew, and not what a reasonable person would have known, having regard to his experiences and intelligence and reasons for acting in the way he did:

Whatever may be the position in some criminal or other contexts ... in the context of the accessory liability principle acting dishonestly, or with lack of probity, which is synonymous, means simply not acting as an honest person would in the circumstances. This is an objective standard.

But, notwithstanding this, Lord Nicholls continued that:

Ultimately, in most cases, an honest person should have little difficulty in knowing whether a proposed transaction, or his participation in it, would offend the normally accepted standards of honest conduct. Likewise, when called upon to decide whether a person was acting honestly, a court will look at all the circumstances known to the third party at the time. The court will also have regard to personal attributes of the third party, such as his experience and intelligence, and the reason why he acted as he did.

From the application of this proposition by the majority of the House of Lords, the outcome of *Twinsectra* appeared to be that incurring liability as an accessory to a breach of trust required the defendant to have acted dishonestly by the ordinary standards of reasonable and honest people, and have been himself aware that by those standards he was acting dishonestly. In this vein, the judgment of Lord Hutton explained that:

There is, in my opinion, a further consideration which supports the view that for liability as an accessory to arise the defendant must himself appreciate that what he was doing was dishonest by the standards of honest and reasonable men. A finding by a judge that a defendant has been dishonest is a grave finding, and it is particularly grave against a professional man, such as a solicitor. Notwithstanding that the issue arises in equity law and not in a criminal context, I think that it would be less than just for the law to permit a finding that a defendant had been 'dishonest' in assisting in a breach of trust where he knew of the facts which created the trust and its breach but had not been aware that what he was doing would be regarded by honest men as being dishonest.

   It would be open to your Lordships to depart from the principle stated by Lord Nicholls that dishonesty is a necessary ingredient of accessory liability and to hold that knowledge is a sufficient ingredient. But the statement of that principle by Lord Nicholls has been widely regarded as clarifying this area of the law and, as he observed, the tide of authority in England has flowed strongly in favour of the test of dishonesty. Therefore I consider that the courts should continue to apply that test and that your Lordships should state that dishonesty requires knowledge by the defendant that what he was doing would be regarded as dishonest by honest people.

This was of course a direct reference to Lord Hutton's understanding that *Royal Brunei Airlines* is widely considered the leading case on accessory liability, and one which is regarded as providing the law in this area with important (and much-needed) clarity. In making these observations, Lord Hutton attached much import to the defendant's awareness that his conduct would be regarded as dishonest by ordinary standards. However, his *Twinsectra* judgment also shows—rather incongruously—Lord Hutton being concerned that the *Royal Brunei Airlines* position should not allow a defendant to escape 'a finding of dishonesty because he sets his own standards of honesty and does not regard as dishonest what he knows would offend the normally accepted standards of honest conduct'. This reasoning was one of the concerns which is evident in Lord Millett's dissenting judgments.

Accessory liability flowing from Twinsectra, and Lord Millett's dissent
Lord Hoffmann's concurrence with Lord Hutton was manifested in his view that dishonesty requires a dishonest state of mind which amounts to 'consciousness that one is transgressing ordinary standards of honest behaviour', and that wrongful conduct of this species requires more than mere 'knowledge of the facts'.

   Lord Millett disagreed with this assessment. In his view, the appropriate approach to accessory liability should be formulated around the defendant's awareness that he was doing something he should not have been doing (rather than his perception of whether this was 'honest' or otherwise). He did not approve of the use of a criminal standard in the context of liability arising under the civil law. Lord Millett argued that the civil law was not concerned with whether the defendant has a 'guilty mind' (the *mens rea* in criminal law), and the issue was instead one of whether the conduct should be regarded as dishonest because the defendant knew (or ought to have been aware) that it was something he was not supposed to be doing. According to Lord Millett, the combination test found in criminal law:

[i]s not generally an appropriate condition of civil liability, which does not ordinarily require a guilty mind. Civil liability is usually predicated on the defendant's conduct rather than his state of mind; it results from his negligent or unreasonable behaviour or, where this is not sufficient, from intentional wrongdoing.

And furthermore that, (in Lord Millett's view) the law itself (in the form of *Royal Brunei Airlines* v *Tan*) appeared actually to reject this highly inappropriate position:

A dishonest state of mind might logically have been required when it was thought that the accessory was liable only if the principal was guilty of a fraudulent breach of trust, for then the claim could have been regarded as the equitable counterpart of the common law conspiracy to defraud. But this requirement was discarded in *Royal Brunei Airlines Sdn Bhd* v *Tan* [1995] 2 AC 378.

Lord Millett's view was that liability as an accessory to a breach of trust does not depend upon dishonesty in the normal sense of that expression. It is sufficient that the defendant knew all the facts which made it wrongful for him to participate in the way in which he did. Indeed, His Lordship contended that the only subjective elements allowed by *Royal Brunei Airlines* were the defendant's experience, his intelligence, and actual state of knowledge, and there was no requirement that he must have realised he was acting dishonestly.

Lord Millett's preferred test was an objective one, in which liability was not dependent upon the defendant's appreciation that he was acting dishonestly, or even his detailed knowledge about the details of the trust and its breach:

The question here is whether it is sufficient that the accessory should have actual knowledge of the facts which created the trust, or must he also have appreciated that they did so? It is obviously not necessary that he should know the details of the trust or the identity of the beneficiary. It is sufficient that he knows that the money is not at the free disposal of the principal. In some circumstances it may not even be necessary that his knowledge should extend this far. It may be sufficient that he knows that he is assisting in a dishonest scheme.

Lord Hoffmann's view of Lord Millett's judgment was that it was not open for the House to concur with a view other than that 'consciousness that one is transgressing ordinary standards of honest behaviour' was required for conduct to be wrongful and capable of incurring liability. In this vein, the previous edition of this text concluded that majority support for a combination objective/subjective test— which requires that conduct is dishonest by ordinary standards and the defendant realised that by those standards his conduct was dishonest in order to incur liability—must be considered authoritative. This was so notwithstanding that it was in many respects difficult to square with the spirit and intendment of *Royal Brunei Airlines* v *Tan*, which sought to liberalise accessory liability by transferring focus away from the trustee (and whether his initial breach of trust was dishonest or not) and placing it firmly upon the accessory himself. In this vein it was asked whether the very welcome decision in *Royal Brunei Airlines* would be able to achieve its full potential in the sphere of accessory liability in the wake of *Twinsectra*. Predictably, following *Twinsectra*, suggestions have been made in some quarters that the position it appeared to adopt—in what had to be present for accessory liability to be incurred—was too 'pro defendant' (see Ryan (2006) 70 Conv, 188).

However, *Twinsectra* itself must now be considered in light of the recent decision of the Privy Council in *Barlow Clowes International Ltd (in liquidation)* v *Eurotrust International Ltd* [2006] 1 All ER 333.

After Twinsectra v Yardley: accessory liability in the wake of Barlow Clowes International Ltd (in liquidation) v Eurotrust International

This case has very important implications for the discussion which has just taken place, which suggested that the majority in *Twinsectra Ltd* v *Yardley* appeared to attach '*Royal Brunei species*' of dishonesty to an individual's awareness that what he was doing would be regarded as dishonest by ordinary standards, to determine whether liability for assisting a breach of trust can be incurred.

The background to the decision in *Barlow Clowes* can be gleaned from earlier references to it in this chapter (and also to its discussion in Lowrie and Todd [1997] *Denning Law Journal*), which explain how during the 1980s a fraudulent scheme which purported to offer high returns on UK gilt-edged securities was run by Clowes, and operated through a company called Barlow Clowes International. Thereafter, it was into Isle of Man-based bank accounts maintained by Eurotrust International that investors funds were paid during 1987. The three defendants in this action were Eurotrust International itself and also two principal directors, and in the High Court of the Isle of Man, Barlow Clowes International claimed that the two defendants and, through them, Eurotrust International had dishonestly assisted Clowes and an associate in misappropriating investors' funds.

The High Court found all three defendants liable for dishonest assistance, and all three appealed, whenupon the appeals of the first and third defendant (the company and one principal director respectively) were dismissed. However, the appeal of the second defendant—Henwood—was allowed, on account that it was not supported by evidence. It was at this point that Barlow Clowes International appealed to the Privy Council.

Originally, in the High Court of the Isle of Man, it had been found that Henwood could incur liability for dishonestly assisting the misappropriation of sums paid into bank accounts during 1987. This was on the basis that the Court had found that the defendant had strongly suspected that the funds passing through his hands were funds received by Barlow Clowes International from members of the public believing they were making gilt-edged securities investments. With these suspicions it was found that no honest person could have assisted the subsequent disposal of the assets for the personal use of Clowes and his associate. In respect of this defendant, it was found that his decision not to make enquiries amounted to a conscious strategy to avoid running the risk that he would encounter the truth.

On appeal to the Privy Council, counsel for Henwood argued that on *Twinsectra* principles, the defendant's state of mind was not dishonest unless he was aware that by ordinary standards it would be regarded as dishonest: it was only in such circumstances that he could be said to be 'consciously dishonest' (as emphasised by Lord Hoffmann). Counsel argued that in the original ruling, finding was made only to the way in which by normal standards he had been dishonest, and that his own standard was different. It was thus agued that because there had been no finding about Henwood's understandings of normal standards of honesty, the High Court's findings in respect of Henwood did not satisfy the *Royal Brunei Airlines* test for dishonesty as this appeared in light of *Twinsectra*.

The Privy Council and reappraisal of Twinsectra

The Privy Council was unanimous in its rejection of the defendant's argument, and upheld the original findings in respect of Henwood. What is significant is the way in which the Judicial Committee reflected on the majority approach in *Twinsectra*, which had been relied upon by the defendant's counsel. Especially significantly in light of the nature of these reflections, this Judicial Committee included Lords Nicholls and Hoffmann.

The Privy Council's judgment was delivered by Lord Hoffmann, who sought to clarify the position of dishonesty under *Royal Brunei Airlines* in light of the apparent effect of *Twinsectra*. Especially, His Lordship sought to clarify that in *Twinsectra* in 2002 the House of Lords did not seek to alter or refine the *Royal Brunei Airlines* test, and their Lordships accepted that:

> There is an element of ambiguity in these remarks which may have encouraged a belief, expressed in academic writing, that *Twinsectra* had departed from the law as previously understood and invited inquiry not merely into the defendant's mental state about the nature of the transaction in which he was participating but also into his views about generally acceptable standards of honesty.

Indicating that this was not the intended import of Lord Hutton's judgment, Lord Hoffmann continued by explaining that:

> The reference to 'what he knows would offend normally acceptable standards of honest conduct' meant only that his knowledge of the transaction had to be such as to render his participation contrary to normally acceptable standards of honest conduct. It did not require that he should have had reflections about what those normally acceptable standards were.

In the course of proposing that the Privy Council has 'restored what appears to be the better interpretation of the *Royal Brunei* test' and has thus also 'clarified' *Twinsectra*, Desmond Ryan (in (2006) above) suggests that Lord Hoffmann's allusion to 'an element of ambiguity' which might have been created by *Twinsectra* is rather an understatement. It is difficult not to agree with this, or with his observation that *Barlow Clowes'* reading of *Twinsectra* is not 'a particularly obvious interpretation' of the implication that the defendant should know his actions 'would offend normally accepted standards of honest conduct'. In this vein, it is this text's view that it certainly is not the most obvious reading of it. Indeed, Ryan also points to the Court of Appeal decision in *Harrison v Teton Valley Trading Company* [2004] 1 WLR to propose that interpretations of *Twinsectra*, which Lord Hoffmann suggests were not intended, are not even confined to academic opinion, and have been adopted by judges.

The way in which this appears more as a retreat from the House of Lords' 2002 direction becomes difficult to avoid from examining Lord Hoffmann's reflections in *Barlow Clowes* of his own judgment in *Twinsectra*, in which he proposed that a dishonest state of mind required 'consciousness that one is transgressing ordinary standards of honest behaviour'. In *Barlow Clowes*, his Lordship explained that this was to denote the significance of 'consciousness of those elements of the transaction which make participation transgress ordinary standards of honest behaviour. It does not also require him to have thought about what those standards were.'

In this decision the Privy Council clarified that it is 'consciousness of the elements of transaction' which make participation in it transgressory, and this does not require the defendant to be aware at the material time that a trust was being breached, or even that it actually existed, and that suspicion that this might be the case was sufficient.

The outcome of this case is that for accessory liability to arise, a dishonest state of mind is required. However, it has also clarified that although this is a subjective mental state (based on factors such as knowledge, or in absence of knowledge suspicion which leads to deliberate failure to make enquiries which might reveal the truth; along with intelligence and reasons for the defendant's conduct), the standards by which the law determines *whether* a state of mind is actually dishonest is that of 'ordinary standards of honesty'. It is at this point that it is not relevant that a defendant ascribed to a different moral code, or that he was unaware that by ordinary standards his conduct would be considered dishonest.

To these ends, the position of *Royal Brunei Airlines* dishonesty has now been clarified, which has to be welcomed, along with its reappraisal of the very severe limitations for accessory liability potentially flowing from adopting the position that the defendant must know his actions 'would offend normally accepted standards of honest conduct'. However, as Desmond Ryan (in (2006) above) suggests, while there is a very attractive simplicity in Lord Nicholls' *Royal Brunei Airlines* proposition that '[i]n most situations there is little difficulty in identifying how an honest person would behave', a consideration of both *Twinsectra* and *Barlow Clowes* provides a salutary reminder of the 'formidable difficulties' confronting judges who must *apply* the test.

19.5.4 *Twinsectra* and 'recipient liability'

Notwithstanding that it might appear out of place within a substantive discussion of accessory liability, and sometime after similar consideration was made of third-party 'recipient' liability, the discussion of *Twinsectra*'s contribution to the legal position of recipient liability does actually follow on far better from its significance for accessorial liability, rather than going before it. This is because in framing the claim as one of assistance, Lord Millett explained why knowing receipt was not the appropriate basis for recovering sums from payments made to him in costs.

> Mr Leach received sums totalling £22,000 in payment of his costs for his own use and benefit ... But he did not receive the rest of the money for his own benefit at all. He never regarded himself as beneficially entitled to the money. He held it to Mr Yardley's order and paid it out to Mr Yardley or his companies. Twinsectra cannot and does not base its claim in respect of these moneys in knowing receipt, not for want of knowledge, but for want of the necessary receipt. It sues in respect of knowing (or dishonest) assistance.

The majority view insisted that for liability as constructive trustee in respect of trust property to arise, there must be fault on the part of the recipient. Indeed, this position of a requirement of fault is consistent with the authority provided by Lord Browne-Wilkinson in the House of Lords' landmark judgment in *Westdeutsche* that 'unless [the recipient of the trust property in question] has the requisite degree of knowledge he is not personally liable to account as trustee'. And, cases such as *Re Montagu's Estate*, and *Baden* as well as *Westdeutsche* stand as authority that what has occupied the courts' time is not discussion over the presence or absence of fault, but instead compositions of appropriate degrees of fault.

However, in his dissenting judgment in *Twinsectra*, Lord Millett took a very different approach, and his submission was based on making the case for 'no-fault strict liability' constructive trusteeship. This was because, in his Lordship's view:

Liability for 'knowing receipt' is receipt-based. It does not depend on fault. The cause of action is restitutionary and is available only where the defendant received or applied the money in breach of trust for his own use and benefit. There is no basis for requiring actual knowledge of the breach of trust, let alone dishonesty, as a condition of liability. Constructive notice is sufficient, and may not even be necessary. There is powerful academic support for the proposition that the liability of the recipient is the same as in other cases of restitution, that is to say strict but subject to a change of position defence.

A continuing role for the requirement of dishonesty: the majority view
Notwithstanding the considerable academic support which Lord Millett claims exists in respect of his position, the decision of his Brethren in *Twinsectra* illustrates that English law does not at present regard strict liability for stranger recipients of trust property, and fault-based liability (in equity) founded in the principles of constructive trusteeship remains central to the area of stranger liability. The way in which there remains contention as to the degree of knowledge which is required before a stranger to a trust can incur liability for the receipt of trust property is also evident in the approach taken by Nourse LJ in *Bank of Credit and Commerce International (Overseas) Ltd v Akindele* [2001] Ch 437. Nourse LJ proposed that a recipient's state of knowledge being such as to make it 'unconscionable for him to retain the benefit of the receipt', is powerful argument against the greater utilisation of no-fault restitutionary claims. Doubting whether strict liability coupled with a change of position defence would serve needs in this area adequately, and particularly the needs of commerce, Nourse LJ explained that it was doubtful whether the latter '... would be preferable to fault-based liability in many commercial transactions'.

19.5.5 **The personal action in** *Diplock*

In *Re Diplock's Estate* [1948] Ch 465, which was affirmed by the House of Lords on this issue in *Ministry of Health v Simpson* [1951] AC 251, the next-of-kin also succeeded in a personal action against the charities which, like the other personal actions considered in this section, was complete on receipt. Unlike knowing receipt, however, liability was strict, the defendants were innocent volunteers who took in good faith with no notice of the next-of-kin's title. The action appears to apply only to volunteers, but clearly cannot apply to all volunteers if *Re Montagu's ST* [1987] Ch 264 is correct, so we need to consider its limits.

In *Diplock*, the executors had made the payments to the charities under a mistake of law. The charities unsuccessfully argued that the personal action was limited to payments made under a mistake of fact (on analogy with the common law money had and received action) and where the administration of the estate had been made by the direction of the court. It is arguable that the action applies only to the administration of estates, but it seems more probable that it applies generally against volunteers. There is a requirement, however, that remedies against the wrongdoers (in this case the executors) should be exhausted first, which is presumably why no Diplock-based personal action was brought in *Montagu*. It is also possible (but not certain) that the change of position defence in *Lipkin Gorman* v *Karpnale Ltd* [1991] 2 AC 548 applies to this equitable action also.

19.6 Tracing, recipient and accessory liability: legal developments and the current state of play

As was suggested at the beginning of this chapter, a range of remedies are available following the commission of a breach of trust. It was also noted that this is a very complex area, because of its dynamism and the incredible pace at which the law is developing. This is why the discussion of the remedies potentially available to a beneficiary, and in respect of a number of potential defendants has stopped (considerably) short of making any clear statement about the law as it stands—because at the moment this is virtually impossible. However, in an area which is highly complex at best (and often confused), the developments have simply been set out in a matter-of-fact manner. This is designed to aid understanding, at the very least, of the difficulties which pervade current thought on the remedies available, the requirements which attach to them, and the factors which operate to distinguish them.

19.6.1 The high watermark case of *Westdeutsche*

The 1998 edition of this textbook contained an entirely new chapter which was dedicated to the then very recent case of *Westdeutsche Landesbank Girozentrale* v *Islington London Borough Council* [1996] AC 669. That chapter was written on account of the fact that the decision did not fit 'happily into any other chapters' in the book, yet it was a case which was 'of considerable importance to the law of trusts' saying much on the 'fundamental principles of the law of trusts'. We have come across *Westdeutsche* already in this edition in the consideration of resulting trusts, and there is much which was important about the decision in terms of the relationships operating between trusts, conscience and restitution; and indeed the dedicated chapter was called 'Trusts, conscience and restitution'. In light of the continuing dynamism of the area of law which we are now dealing with, the decision was made in this edition to drop the dedicated chapter on trusts, conscience and restitution on account of its primary focus on *Westdeutsche*. This was made with great regret on account of the way in which it sought to try to explore the relations between different types of remedies, but it was made because of considerations of space, and in particular as a reflection of the way in which things have moved on from *Westdeutsche* in a number of respects. It may well be the case that as things become clearer (instead of simply 'moving on') it might be possible and indeed necessary to reintroduce *Westdeutsche* as a central point of reference. But for present purposes, we deal only with the fundamentals of the case, and also the ways in which new authorities can be seen to have developed it.

The trust and a number of fundamental propositions

(a) The basis of all trusts is conscience.

(b) The notion of equitable title has no meaning unless there is a separation of legal and equitable titles. Where one person is absolutely entitled to the property, equitable rights are encompassed within the legal title. It follows that where a resulting trust is set up, it is not correct to see the settlor as starting with legal and equitable title, parting with legal title and retaining equitable title. The equitable title is instead created on transfer of legal title, because the conscience of the recipient is affected.

(c) It is possible to have a separation of legal and equitable titles without there being a trust. The most important circumstance (for the purposes of this book) is where an innocent volunteer takes trust property. The volunteer takes subject to a trust, but is not a trustee. By contrast, a knowing receiver is a trustee because equity imposes on her conscience (but note *Foskett* v *McKeown* [2000] above).

(d) An initial fiduciary relationship is required to trace in equity, with *Re Diplock* [1948] Ch 465 being approved (but note the subsequent development in *Foskett* v *McKeown* above).

The significance of *Westdeutsche* for the purposes of this chapter can be summarised as follows:

(a) Equity operates on the conscience of the owner of the legal interest. In the case of a trust, the conscience of the legal owner requires him to carry out the purposes for which the property was vested in him (express or implied trust), or which the law imposes on him by reason of his unconscionable conduct (via constructive trust).

(b) Since the equitable jurisdiction to enforce trusts depends on the conscience of the holder of the legal interest being affected, he cannot be a trustee of the property if and so long as he is ignorant of the facts alleged to affect his conscience, i.e., until he is aware that he is intended to hold the property for the benefit of others in the case of an express or implied trust, or in the case of the trust being constructive, of the factors which are alleged to affect his conscience.

(c) In order to establish a trust there must be identifiable trust property. The only apparent exception to this rule is a constructive trust imposed on a person who dishonestly assists in a breach of trust who may come under fiduciary duties even if he does not receive identifiable trust property (although, note *Foskett* v *McKeown* above).

(d) Once a trust is established, as from the date of its establishment, the beneficiary has in equity a proprietary interest in the trust property. This proprietary interest is enforceable in equity against any subsequent holder of the property (whether this is the original property or substituted property into which it can be traced) other than a purchaser for value of the legal interest for value without notice.

Since *Westdeutsche*, there have been considerable developments notably in fiduciary relationship and in its articulations of constructive trusteeship and third party liability. The two key House of Lords' decisions in *Foskett* v *McKeown* and more recently still in *Twinsectra* v *Yardley* also testify to the rapidity of the development of the law in this sphere as does Twinsectra's own swift re-visitation in *Barlow Clowes International Ltd (in liquidation)* v *Eurotrust International Ltd* [2006] 1 All ER 333.

FURTHER READING

Andrews [2003] 67 Conv 399.

Stevens [2001] 65 Conv 94.

Lowrie and Todd (1997) *Denning Law Journal* 43.

Martin [1998] Conv 13.

Millett (1991) 107 LQR 77.

Millett (1995) *Trust Law International* 35.

Ryan (2006) 70 Conv 188–97.

Thompson [2002] 66 Conv 387–99.

INDEX